Health Psychology

Challenging the Biomedical Model

Health Psychology
Challenging the Biomedical Model

Charles L. Sheridan
University of Missouri—Kansas City

Sally A. Radmacher
Missouri Western State College

WILEY

JOHN WILEY & SONS, INC.
New York • Chichester • Brisbane • Toronto • Singapore

ACQUISITIONS EDITOR / Deborah Moore
COPY EDITOR / Elizabeth Swain
PRODUCTION MANAGER / Joe Ford
SENIOR PRODUCTION SUPERVISOR / Savoula Amanatidis
DESIGNER / Laura Nicholls
PHOTO RESEARCH MANAGER / Stella Kupferberg
PHOTO RESEARCHER / Jennifer Atkins
ILLUSTRATION COORDINATOR / Sigmund Malinowski
MANUFACTURING MANAGER / Lorraine Fumoso
COVER PHOTO: David Woods/The Stock Market
INSET PHOTO: Mug Shots/The Stock Market

Recognizing the importance of preserving what has been written, it
is a policy of John Wiley & Sons, Inc. to have books of enduring
value published in the United States printed on acid-free paper, and
we exert our best efforts to that end.

Library of Congress Cataloging in Publication Data:

Sheridan, Charles L., 1937–
    Health psychology : challenging the biomedical
model / Charles L. Sheridan, Sally A. Radmacher.
        p.   cm.
    Includes bibliographical references and indexes.
    ISBN 0-471-50852-7 (cloth)   alk. paper)
    1. Clinical health psychology—Philosophy.   2. Medicine and
psychology.   I. Radmacher, Sally A.   II. Title.
    [DNLM: 1. Disease—psychology.   2. Health Behavior.   3.
Models, Psychological.   4. Psychology, Medical.   5.
Psychophysiologic Disorders.   WM 90 S552h]
R726.7S47   1992
610'.1'9—dc20
DLC
for Library of Congress   91-10347
                                                                  CIP

Printed in the United States of America

10 9 8 7 6 5 4 3 2 1

In Memory of Jimmy

Preface

The year 2055 is a kind of Armageddon for modern medicine. It is the year when, given present growth rates, health care costs in the United States are expected to reach 100% of the gross national product! If that happened, it would mean that every hour, every minute, every second of human production would be devoured by medical costs. Of course, this is an impossible scenario. But it tells us one thing very clearly: sometime between now and 2055 there is going to be a revolution in the health care system.

Thomas Kuhn in his pivotal work, *The Structure of Scientific Revolutions*, told us how such changes occur. They happen very slowly. Time after time the established system fails to deal adequately with the problems at hand. Alternatives arise, and they create controversy. Eventually, one of the alternatives or some combination of them becomes the new norm, or "paradigm." This new paradigm inevitably assimilates the old one and includes major facets of it within its own corpus.

Just this kind of thing is happening with the dominant paradigm of health care—the biomedical model. The main features of present-day biomedicine could be seen by the turn of the century. The biomedical model took the art of medicine and founded it squarely in the biological sciences. This laid the foundation for many great accomplishments; many of the early 20th century's most deadly biological killers have now been subdued. But the easy medical conquests are now but glorious memories, and biomedicine, along with its practitioners, is challenged and subjected to skeptical inquiry at every turn.

One of the most important challenges comes from those, like the present authors, who advocate a biopsychosocial model. We maintain that social and psychological factors are far too important to be ignored by medicine. Many have argued that lifestyle and one's psychological make-up are at least as important to one's health as availability of medical care. And nostalgia for the kind, wise doctors of yore has been transformed by many into serious proposals that medical effectiveness depends on good human relationships, and even that human contact can heal. The biomedical model must grow to include psychosocial factors.

We should expect that, in the early stages of this revolution, a wild variety of challenges to the old model will be put forth. Some of these alternatives will prove to be solid and will take their place as part of the structure of the new paradigm. Others will fall away and be forgotten, or be exiled to the realm of kooky or even quackish views.

Eventually, there comes a time when the wheat must be separated from the chaff, when someone has to take on the task of presenting a coherent view of the current status of the new model. This is what we have tried to do in the present work. We have done this in the form of a highly readable text because we want to include in our audience the young people who will go on to mold the new model into its mature form. So we have designed this text to be suitable for lower-level undergraduates as well as more advanced students.

SETTING THE BOUNDARIES

The rapid growth and diversity of our field makes it impossible for anyone to have a full grasp of all the traditions that have influenced health psychology. People of many contending persuasions have contributed to the development of health psychology. They range from strict behaviorists at one pole to those interested in holistic medicine at the other. Each of them, to one degree or another, has contributed to the development of a new perspective on health. It was a major task to decide which of the contributions should be part of the corpus of health psychology. We had to be selective, but we tried to do so without unduly narrowing the scope of our topic. Our own backgrounds and interests are diverse (ranging from clinical psychology and neuroscience to public health and community psychology), and we value the contributions made to health psychology from these and many other disciplines.

A glance at the detailed Table of Contents should make it clear that the familiar and favorite topics and references are covered; a look at our extensive and current bibliography is equally revealing. It includes both the latest and the "classic" references of health psychology.

Many "leading-edge" topics that have received little or no attention in other texts are included in this book. For example, we describe research on cognitive processes of physicians while they are formulating and validating diagnoses. We also discuss the role of psychologists in dealing with patients undergoing cosmetic surgery. We not only disclose the present state of health psychology, but also provide a glimpse of its potential and, perhaps, its future.

Our primary goal is to present a well-documented, comprehensive overview of health psychology to the undergraduate student while keeping the excitement that is so much a part of health psychology.

FEATURES OF THE BOOK

The book is theme oriented. We repeatedly contrast the biomedical model with the biopsychosocial model. These contrasting views of health, disease, and health care are clearly drawn, and powerful evidence is presented to indicate the pressing need for a change of models.

Throughout the book, we emphasize a hands-on, applied approach. We focus on the *practice* of health psychology without sacrificing the significance of experimental or theoretical work. The practical information on the training required for health psychologists will give students some idea of how they might pursue their interests in the field.

We have included a number of devices to make learning easier for the student. Key terms are printed in **bold type** and are clearly defined when they are first introduced; each is again defined at length in the Glossary at the end of the book. A summary and discussion questions are provided at the end of each chapter.

Finally, as our primary pedagogical device, we have used "stories" and examples selected to make the material more interesting and meaningful for the students. All of the stories are based on actual events that are either from the literature or that we know of personally. We have changed only the names and circumstances to make the narratives more readable, and to protect the privacy of those who were willing to share their stories.

ORGANIZATION OF THE BOOK

The first three chapters of the book provide a foundation for the study of health psychology. The first chapter acquaints students with the biomedical model, the dominant paradigm of the health care system, and introduces the challenging paradigm, the biopsychosocial model. This chapter also describes the health care crisis and its antecedents. One of the primary goals of this chapter is to impress upon students that they are beginning their study of health psychology during a period of crisis and revolution in the health care system. The second chapter defines health psychology, describes its breadth, and discusses the training and career opportunities for health psychologists.

Chapter Three provides students with guidelines for evaluating health-related information. We emphasize the distinction between well-controlled research and findings and claims that hold promise but have not yet been thoroughly tested. Students are taught to think critically about media reports of research findings and to develop healthy skepticism even for studies from the most prestigious journals.

Chapter Four uses the familiar issue of "mind over body" as a vehicle for delineating how the nervous system can control health. It explains the relationship between the central nervous system, the autonomic nervous system, and the immune system. A concise account of psychoneuroimmunology is included in this chapter.

The fifth chapter presents an overview of the therapies that are of use to health psychologists.

Cognitive behavioral therapy is featured, but the older psychodynamic approaches are also explained. Specific application of psychological treatments is further described throughout the book. For example, biofeedback and autogenic training are mentioned here, but we present them in more detail in later chapters.

Chapter Six is a cognitive-social perspective on physicians and patients. This chapter covers human information processing and its effect on medical decision making and compliance with medical procedures. It also looks at coping with illness from the perspective of patients and health care providers.

The seventh chapter is a comprehensive review of stress and synthesizes the most important, if not always the most publicized, theories and research in the field. Special emphasis is placed on social support, appraisal, and coping. Stress management is covered in this chapter and in Chapters Eight and Nine.

Chapters Eight and Nine feature the lifestyle factors that are important to health, including nutrition, weight control, exercise, addiction, cigarette smoking, and alcoholism. In both chapters, we have emphasized prevention and the importance of changing environments to promote healthy lifestyles and discourage unhealthy habits.

Chapter Ten provides an overview of the nature and treatment of pain. Since headache is highly prevalent, and often treated behaviorally, special attention is given to headaches and their treatment. This chapter applies autogenic training and biofeedback to the treatment of pain.

Chapters Eleven and Twelve cover the modern epidemics: coronary heart disease, hypertension, cancer, and AIDS. Prevention as well as treatment are discussed. Finally, Chapter Thirteen deals with the widening scope of health psychology. We present several areas of research and treatment in health psychology that are not commonly covered in health psychology texts, including temporomandibular joint syndrome, asthma, and skin disorders.

Acknowledgements

We set very high standards for this book and acknowledge the assistance of all of the people who helped us meet them. We begin by recognizing the contributions of the many talented people at John Wiley & Sons.

The constructive criticism and encouraging praise of the following professors also contributed greatly to the quality of our book:

Tony Albiniak, Coastal Carolina College; Stanley Ballard, Cedarville College; Barbara Fleischer, Loyola University; Jeff Holm, University of North Dakota; Paul Jose, Loyola University, Chicago; Charles Kaiser, College of Charleston; Wolfgang Linden, University of British Columbia; Kenneth Thompson, Central Missouri State University; Susan Todd, Bridgewater State University; Abraham Wandersman, University of South Carolina; Josephine Wilson, Wittenberg University; and Ray Zurawski, St. Norbert College.

Finally, we want to acknowledge the encouragement and support we received from our families, friends, and colleagues. A special thanks to Wm. J. Nunez, III, Missouri Western State College, for reviewing the section on the immune system, and to Betty Keller, also from Missouri Western, for all her help in acquiring interlibrary loan materials. A number of colleagues also provided us with important references for our text, and we thank all of them. We especially want to thank Lisa Terre of the University of Missouri–Kansas City, who was particularly helpful in this area.

Charles L. Sheridan
Sally A. Radmacher

Contents

13 The Widening Scope of Health Psychology   296

Changing Paradigms in Health and Health Care

M ary's 76-year-old father, Bill, was terminally ill suffering from cancer, diabetes, and heart disease. He was bedfast and unable to speak as a result of an earlier stroke. He was obviously in great pain and despair. Mary and her mother were told that he would be unlikely to live another week. Three days later, it was discovered that he had developed gangrene in his right leg. (Gangrene is a decay of the flesh that releases fatal gases as it progresses.) His physicians said that the only choices were to amputate his leg or let him die from gangrene. Mary asked them if her father could survive major surgery in his condition. They told her that his chances of survival were very poor. She then asked if the surgery would relieve his obvious suffering. They said that the pain he would suffer from the amputation could be quite severe. The physicians concluded their remarks by recommending the surgery. Mary and her mother were stunned. Bill was in the last week of his life with no hope for recovery, the surgery would not relieve his pain or prolong his life, and it was unlikely that he would survive it. And, finally, the surgery would cost several thousand dollars. Mary asked why they would recommend amputation under these circumstances. After a painful silence, one of them finally answered: "Because that is the way we have been trained to think. We fix the parts that are broken or remove them."

When the physician said "that is the way we have been trained to think," he was describing the dominant paradigm of his profession—the biomedical model. When Mary questioned the physicians' recommendation to amputate her dying father's leg, she was challenging that paradigm. The biomedical model is facing many challenges as we close the twentieth century. We are beginning our book with a discussion of these challenges and the events leading to them because health psychology has an important role in this revolution.

Our intention in this book is not to deny the great accomplishments of biomedicine or to advocate an exclusive "mind over body" approach as some kind of substitute for traditional medicine. Often biomedicine works very well. For example, recently a fellow professor with cataracts had the lenses of his eyes replaced surgically. He was back to work in a day or two with attained 20/20 vision.

We assume that our readers are well acquainted with the successes of contemporary biomedicine from their own experience and from that of family and friends. Indeed, most of us are constantly inundated with media accounts of medical "miracles." Most of us are not only aware of biomedical successes but we also tend to exaggerate them. Most people see psychological and social factors as having little or no importance to physical health. The evidence is against that view, as we will show. Our intention is not to malign biological-medical approaches but to help augment and strengthen them through the inclusion of powerful psychosocial factors.

PARADIGMS: THE MENTAL FRAMEWORKS OF SCIENCE

The human mind is always captivated by mental frameworks that help to determine how we see things. These frameworks are called schemata. Information processing theory states that we cannot process all the information that bombards us daily. To make sense of the world, information has to be filtered through mental frameworks. Many years ago, Walter Lippmann (1922/1965), American journalist, provided an eloquent description of this process:

For the most part we do not first see, and then define, we define first and then see. In the great blooming, buzzing confusion of the outer world, we pick out what our culture has defined for us, and we tend to perceive that which we have picked out in form stereotyped for us by our culture (pp. 54–55).

These mental frameworks influence the way we seek, organize, and interpret information. The zeitgeist plays an important part in shaping these mental frameworks. The **zeitgeist** is the general economic, political, and cultural climate of an era, the "spirit of the times."

Scientists call their mental frameworks paradigms. A **paradigm** is a model or framework of how science is to be conducted (Kuhn, 1962). It identifies the questions that can be studied, and it determines the research methods that may be used. Those problems that do not fit into the scientist's paradigm tend to be seen as silly or unworthy of study. Although paradigms may limit our ability to see certain things, they offer a coherent plan around which scientists can coordinate their efforts to understand the world.

Physicians, like scientists, are greatly influenced by paradigms or models, although they are often unaware of it. They learn, and take for granted, the paradigms of their profession which are part of "the cultural background against which they learn to become physicians" (Engel, 1980, p. 535). The old saying goes that "a fish will be the last to recognize water." Because we tend to become completely immersed in our paradigm, it is not easy to notice its influence on us. For example, the young physician described earlier had to do some real soul searching before he could tell Mary why he and his colleague recommended amputation for her father.

THE BIOMEDICAL MODEL VERSUS THE BIOPSYCHOSOCIAL MODEL

In the following section we describe the biomedical and biopsychosocial models and give a brief history of each model. The challenge to the biomedical model and the resistance that challenge is facing are also discussed.

The Biomedical Model

The dominant paradigm of medical science in the twentieth century is called the **biomedical model**. This paradigm has been strongly influenced by cartesian dualism. **Cartesian dualism** defines mind and body as separate substances. In the seventeenth century, René Descartes (1596–1650) was impressed with life-sized mechanical dolls that had been constructed to make human-like movements. Of course, they could not duplicate higher human operations, but these merely mechanical inventions seemed to execute certain human functions. This observation led Descartes to think that our bodies were like machines but that our minds were a very different kind of spiritual entity. Thus, functions of the mind and the body were radically split apart.

David McClelland, one of the leading researchers in health psychology, describes the biomedical model as a mechanistic model: "The body is treated like a machine that is fixed by removing or replacing the ailing part or destroying the foreign body that is causing the problem" (1985, p. 452). You can see that is just what happened with Mary's father. They were going to "fix" Bill by removing the "ailing part" without considering the psychological impact it would have on him and his family.

The role of psychological factors in determining health and illness was considered very important before cartesian dualism became accepted. Premodern physicians believed that images and emotions were major influences on the disease process. In contrast, the biomedical model sees images and emotions as belonging to the mind and therefore not capable of affecting the body.

The discovery of external agents of disease such as bacteria, viruses, chemicals, and vitamin deficiencies increased the strength of this model in modern medicine. Within the framework of the biomedical model, only the biochemical factors of illness are considered. Social, psychological, and behavioral dimensions fall outside its narrow framework and are therefore ignored (Engel, 1980).

Psychosomatic Medicine

The challenge to expand the biomedical model originally came from psychosomatic medicine

(Engel, 1977). In spite of the dominance of the biomedical model, psychosomatic medicine has been an organized science and treatment approach for over 50 years (Lipowski, 1986). **Psychosomatic medicine** is the study of the interaction of psychosocial and biological factors in health and disease.

We should note that psychosomatic does not mean "fake" or "imaginary." Psychosomatic means that both mind (psyche) and body (soma) are involved. This approach developed as it became more obvious that not everyone became ill after being exposed to a pathogen (Ader, 1980). It also became clear that the biological factors that influence risks for disease account for only a small number of the cases of illness (Syme, 1984).

Ader (1980) suggests that all disorders might be called psychosomatic because the brain receives and interprets all sensory input. It must still be shown, however, that biological, psychological, and social factors interact to influence health and illness. Psychosomatic medicine has gone a long way toward that end, producing a large body of data that support the mind/body connection. Researchers are now discovering the mechanisms that are involved (Borysenko, 1984; Pert, 1986). We will discuss these mechanisms further in Chapter 4.

A Paradigm Shift

The time seems right for expanding the biomedical model to the **biopsychosocial model**. The social and psychological influences on today's health problems do not fit the narrow framework of the biomedical model. Its mechanistic approach has stirred up discontentment with the health care system. The biomedical model tends to promote specialization and reliance on treatments that are costly and often harmful. Moreover, it does not promote prevention, health enhancement, or individual responsibility for health (Gordon & Fadiman, 1984).

There is great resistance to expanding the biomedical model to include psychological and social factors. Engel (1977, 1980) states that the biomedical model has gone beyond the limits of

a scientific model. He suggests that it has acquired the authority and tradition of dogma. A scientific model is revised or discarded when data are discovered that do not fit it. A dogma, however, distorts the conflicting data to fit the model or ignores their existence. You will be given research examples of these practices in Chapter 3.

In spite of resistance, the biomedical model is facing a serious challenge. The assumption that only the biological factors of health and disease are worthy of study and practice is being questioned. The model may have conditioned us to believe that disease is caused by a single type of influence, but there is a growing awareness that health and illness have many dimensions. Psychological and social factors influence biological functioning and play a role in health and illness. This role will become increasingly clear as you read this book.

The Biopsychosocial Model

The **biopsychosocial model** does not suggest that we disregard biomedical influences. Remember, the "bio" is still there in "biopsychosocial." The idea is to expand our model to include those important factors that now fall outside its narrow framework (Engel, 1980; Jasnoski & Schwartz, 1985). George Engel stated the problem at hand most eloquently in his 1977 landmark paper calling for an expansion of the biomedical model:

> We are now faced with the necessity and the challenge to broaden the approach to disease to include the psychosocial without sacrificing the enormous advantages of the biomedical approach. (p. 130)

Including psychosocial factors in the model provides for a treatment approach that takes into account the human qualities of both patient and physician. It is a more realistic model in light of the important role lifestyles play in twentieth-century diseases. It has been thoroughly documented that behavioral factors are implicated in seven of the ten leading causes of death in the United States (Raub, 1989).

The biopsychosocial model is based on

general systems theory. One of the basic assumptions of this theory is that systems exist within systems. In other words, nothing exists in isolation. This approach forces researchers and practitioners to develop a global view of their work. For example, it compels physicians to consider the effects of their treatment on the "whole" patient, not just the part they are trying to "fix." The systems approach is discussed in more detail in Chapter 2.

The biomedical model neglects the whole because it excludes everything but biological factors. Thus, it is preoccupied with the body and disease at the expense of the patient as a person (Engel, 1980). Again, however, we want to stress that biological factors are still important.

DEFINING HEALTH AND RELATED TERMS

Health is one of those words that we think is easy to define until we realize that it has many different meanings to different people. (See Box 1.1 for the historical roots of the word.) Stone (1979) has noted that until we can agree on the meaning of health and how it can be measured, we are going to be unable to answer questions about how we can protect, enhance, and restore health.

Changing Concepts of Health

Whether we are considered to be sick or healthy does not depend just on the way we feel or the state of our bodies. It may depend even more on the economic, political, and cultural climate of the times in which we live. There are many examples of how the zeitgeist has determined the "health" status of many conditions or behaviors. For instance, during this century attitudes toward homosexuality have undergone many transformations. It has gone from a "sin" to a "disease" to an "alternative lifestyle." Recently, the AIDS virus has turned many behaviors associated with male homosexuality into "risk factors."

Heavy alcohol consumption is now classified as a disease, but not so long ago, it was seen as a legal and moral problem. At about this same time, cigarette smoking was viewed as a desirable, glamorous behavior. Full-page ads featured physicians extolling the virtues of smoking.

Cigarette smoking became a health risk and a bad habit after the Surgeon General warned us in 1964 that it may be harmful to our health. With the increasing evidence that second-hand smoke is harmful to nonsmokers, it is becoming a socially undesirable behavior (Glantz & Parmley, in press; USDHHS, 1986).

Box **1.1**   **The Meaning of the Root Word of Health**

The meaning of the root word of health is wholeness. The word comes from the same Anglo-Saxon root that gives us whole, hale, and holy. It is intriguing to find that "holy" and "healthy" share the same root word. Health and religion have a long association and still do in many cultures. For instance, the medicine man has a religious as well as a healing role (Weil, 1983).

The link between health and religion is also strong in the Judeo-Christian tradition. Religion and psychology were removed from health when medicine became a science. Neither fit within the biomedical model. However, as we have said, there is a crisis, if not a revolution, in health care. Some prominent physicians are suggesting that both psychology and faith may have a place in healing after all (Benson, 1984; Siegel, 1986; 1989).

What is considered a disorder or a blessing varies between cultures. For instance, the Navajo are not pleased with twin births because twins are believed to be the result of promiscuity as well as chance. In contrast, until recently, hermaphroditism[1] was a highly valued condition. The Navajo also accept children who are born with extra fingers and with hip defects. On the other hand, they tend to have a negative reaction to cleft palates (Kunitz & Levy, 1981).

Childbirth offers another example of how cultures differ in their view of the same process. In some tribes, childbirth is not seen as a medical event. In these tribes, the women seem to experience little pain during birth. They may focus attention more on the creation of new life or the benefits and status of adding a new member to the family or tribe. However, most women giving birth in the high tech medical centers do associate childbirth with pain.

We are *not* suggesting that American women "imagine" their discomfort. We are suggesting rather that people tend to focus on whatever their culture has "picked out" for them. Women in our culture may focus on pain because childbirth is considered a medical event. Traditional hospital delivery rooms with their gleaming tools of technology make it difficult for mothers to consider birth a "natural" happening. Hospitals are increasingly offering mothers the option of "birthing" rooms. These pleasant settings together with efforts to make birth a celebration rather than an illness are examples of recent changes in health care that take psychosocial factors into account.

The Impact of Health Definitions

The way health and sickness are defined can have social, legal, and economic consequences. The label given to a particular behavior decides whether we will be punished or treated for it. This, in turn, decides who will pay for it and how it is treated. For example, now that alcoholism is considered a medical problem, alcoholics are sent to treatment centers or outpatient clinics.

[1] Hermaphroditism is the presence of both ovarian and testicular tissues in the same individual.

The treatment of alcohol abuse has become a major profit-making venture for the medical industry. When it was considered a legal and moral problem, alcoholics were often sent to the "drunk tank."

The way alcoholism is classified may be in the process of changing yet again. The United States Supreme Court recently upheld the right of the Veterans Administration (VA) to classify primary alcoholism as "willful misconduct" (*Traynor v. Turnage & McKelvey v. Turnage*, 108 S. Ct., 1988). The majority opinion was based, in part, on a large body of medical literature that "contests the proposition that alcoholism is a disease" (p. 1383). This decision permits the VA to deny the extension of educational benefits beyond the ten-year period to veterans who claim alcoholism as a disability. The disease model of alcoholism is discussed in Chapter 9.

The *Diagnostic and Statistical Manual of Mental Disorders* (3rd edition, revised) (DSM–III–R) provides a clear example of the economic and political impact of health-related definitions. The DSM III–R is essentially a catalogue of all the accepted psychological disorders with descriptions of their major symptoms. The disorders and their symptoms are classified by a panel of psychiatrists and psychologists chosen by the American Psychiatric Association (APA).

The manual is important because the courts, hospitals, and insurance companies generally recognize it. For example, it is very difficult to get insurance payments for treatment of symptoms that do not appear in the DSM–III–R. In 1980 the DSM–III recognized tobacco dependence as a disorder. Leo (1985) suggests that this disorder may have been created so that insurance companies would pick up the expense of therapy for smokers trying to quit.

The way that health and its related terms are defined has a profound impact on society and on us, as individuals. In 1946 the World Health Organization (WHO) defined health as "a state of complete physical, mental, and social well-being and . . . not merely the absence of disease or infirmity." The WHO definition resembles the notions of humanistic psychologists

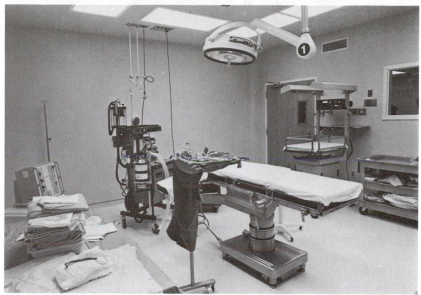

In order for childbirth to be seen as a natural event rather than a medical procedure, many hospitals are offering their expectant mothers the option of birthing rooms over traditional high tech delivery rooms.

such as Maslow (1971). They see the goal of human beings as striving to fulfill their highest potential.

In effect, defining health this way says that people cannot be healthy in the absence of ideal social, political, or economic conditions. Nor can a person be considered healthy until he or she has been able to love, to work, and to create. This kind of definition holds a lot of appeal for anyone who is enthusiastic about helping people to become "fully functioning" human beings.

Unfortunately, accepting such a definition

carries certain risks. This kind of definition allows anyone who is considered unfulfilled to be labeled "sick." Historically, corrupt governments have misused such definitions. They control dissent by placing those who do not conform to governmental ideals in institutions for the mentally ill.

Attempts to measure states of health have often focused on issues of impaired function. We need to be careful when we make decisions about how and by whom a person's "functions" should be evaluated. There is always the danger of viewing people solely as instruments rather than as ends in themselves. For example, Fanshel (1972) devised a measure based on assessing the extent to which people can carry out their usual daily activities. He proposed that decisions about the desired range of activities be made by "those responsible for health delivery services, the secretaries of state, and their administrators." Fanshel seems to view people as instruments of the state. This is one of the problems involved in defining disease as functional limitation.

The Wellness Continuum

Apparently, there is no one way to define health clearly. This is always the case when we try to define social constructs. As we mentioned earlier, certain genetic traits that one culture considers disorders may be seen as desired states in other cultures. Even within the same culture, some harmful behaviors are labeled disease and other, equally harmful, behaviors are not. Some behaviors are bad habits in one decade and become diseases in the next. However, there are some areas of agreement about what health is and what it is not.

There seems to be a consensus among health psychologists that health is *not* just the absence of disease (Stone, 1987; Weiner, 1982). In our everyday thinking we have been conditioned to hold a two-category view of health and disease. Just as one is either pregnant or not pregnant, one is either sick or not sick. Thus, we are labeled in one of two ways: we are either sick or healthy. To date health care has focused on

moving people from the sick to the healthy category.

The two-category concept of disease and health has been widely criticized. For one thing, it does not take into account the range of points in between sickness and health. A person who is not really sick, but at high risk, is very different from someone who is in robust good health. A person who has just a minor disease is not at all like someone who has several serious diseases.

A really accurate description of disease and health would place them on a continuum. The state in which a person is at high risk for premature death anchors one end of the continuum (see Figure 1.1). The other end is anchored by a state of optimal health in which the person is quite resistant to disease. Generally, the wellness end of the continuum also takes into account the degree to which the joy and fullness of life are experienced. The position we occupy on this continuum is not static. Even the most well occasionally have a bad day.

The dichotomous view of disease and health fails to make the finer distinctions that exist in the "real" world. It may also tend to set us up for the traditional idea that there are no health issues until we get sick. The conventional view of how to take care of our health has been to forget about it until we reach some form of breakdown. Only after the breakdown takes place do we seek out remedies. In contrast, placing disease and health on a continuum leads us to take actions that will move us further toward optimal wellness (Antonovsky, 1979).

THE CRISIS IN HEALTH CARE

Just as Mary questioned physicians about their recommended treatment of her father, we are all beginning to ask hard questions about the state of health care in the United States. Hardly a day goes by that some news broadcast, newspaper, or magazine does not feature an article about the crisis in the health care system. In the following section we will describe some of the problems that have contributed to this turning

Figure 1.1   The wellness continuum. Thinking of health and disease as an either/or concept is not realistic. It is more accurate to place them on a continuum.

point in the history of health care in the United States.

The Health Care System

We should begin our discussion of the health care crisis by again acknowledging the advances scientific medicine has made over the century. For example, earlier we mentioned a colleague who just underwent cataract surgery that restored his vision to 20/20, and it was done in an outpatient center. Miraculous! The contributions of medical science have been significant, and we owe a great deal to its development. At one time or another, we all have had reason to be grateful for the advances of technological medicine.

Yet, instead of widespread gratitude, the health care system is receiving growing complaints from the public and its own members. Weil (1983), a Harvard-trained physician and researcher, has charged:

> *The common complaints that medicine today is too expensive, too dangerous, and not effective at treating the diseases that really matter are all valid. The expense and risks of the system are direct consequences of its increasing reliance on invasive procedures, technological gadgetry, and dangerous drugs.* (p. 83)

Economic Factors

It is estimated that 37 million Americans do not have health insurance (Zinn, 1989). What happens to these people when they need medical care? Until recent years, most Americans believed that the government would take care of them, at least if they were desperate. That is, until they read in a national news magazine about Coby, a seven-year old, who died just $10,000 short of the $90,000 needed for his liver transplant. There was no help from the state because Oregon stopped funding organ transplants in 1987 so that it could fund prenatal care

instead ("Not Enough," 1990). Oregon is rationing health care because the demand for health care is *unlimited* and the resources to pay for them are *limited*.

Economic factors are always an important catalyst for change, and that is particularly true in our society. There is general agreement that the costs of the American health care system are out of control (Davies & Felder, 1990). The advances in technology and the post–World War II expansion of the health insurance system interacted to create skyrocketing medical care costs. Health insurance made expensive procedures and technology very profitable for the medical industry (Weisbrod, 1988).

As shown in Figure 1.2, the percentage of the gross national product (GNP) being spent on medical care in the United States rose sharply from 5.2 percent in 1960 to 11.1 percent in 1987 (NCHS, 1989; USBC, 1990). It is predicted that by the year 2000, health care will consume 17 percent of the GNP (Davies & Felder, 1990). These statistics may not have much meaning for many of us, but the fact that employee health insurance benefits already add $700 to the price of a car may make them more real (Zinn, 1990).

The United States has the most expensive health care system in the world, but it is clearly not the best. Compared to Americans, Japanese have a longer life expectancy, a lower infant mortality rate, and a lower mortality rate due to heart disease. Yet health care costs in Japan are significantly lower than they are in the United States (Macrae, 1984, NCHS, 1989). See Table 1.1 for an international comparison of health care costs and life expectancies at birth.

Some of the rise in medical care costs in the United States may be attributable to the increases in physicians' incomes. The medical profession is the highest paid occupation in our society (Starr, 1982). The median net earnings of

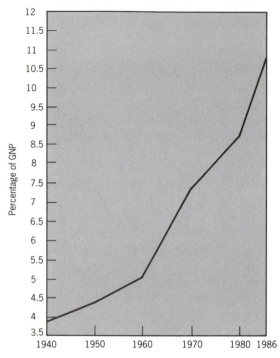

Figure 1.2   Percentage of the gross national product (GNP) spent on medical care in the United States: 1940–1986. *Source*: National Center for Health Statistics: *Health, United States*, 1988. DHSS Pub No. (PHS) 89–1232. Public Health Service. Washington, D.C.: U.S. Government Printing Office, March 1989.

Table 1.1   Comparison of Health Care Costs and Life Expectancies at Birth for Selected Countries

Country	Life Expectancy in Years (1980–1985)	Percentage of Gross Domestic Product (1986)
Japan	77.4	6.7
Sweden	76.9	9.1
Netherlands	76.3	8.3
Switzerland	76.2	8.0
Norway	76.1	6.8
Australia	75.6	6.8
Canada	75.5	8.5
United States	74.7	11.1
New Zealand	74.5	6.9
Denmark	74.5	6.1
Greece	74.1	3.9

Note: Gross domestic product differs slightly from gross national product.

Source: National Center for Health Statistics. (1989). *Health, United States, 1988*. DHHS Pub No. (PHS) 89–1232. Public Health Service. Washington, D.C.: U.S. Government Printing Office.

American physicians (after expenses and before taxes) rose from $58,400 in1975 to over $116,000 in 1987 (USBC, 1990).[2] Medicare is implementing cost control tactics because payments for physician services have increased 77 percent since 1985, while the number of beneficiaries has only risen 8 percent (Schiffman, 1990).

Physicians from other countries do not necessarily enjoy the same high economic status as those in the United States. Physician wages in the Soviet Union, for example, are reported to be less than the average wage paid to its industrial workers. The fact that the majority of Russian physicians are women may account for the dif-

ference in economic status between Russian and American physicians (Starr, 1982). See Box 1.2 for some interesting facts about the changing demographics of physicians in the United States.

The Technological Imperative

Davies and Felder (1990) charge that health care costs are out of control because of technology's domination of American health care. The excessive use of expensive medical technology without regard to its appropriateness or cost can be explained by the technological imperative (Fuchs, 1974). The **technological imperative** is the desire of physicians to do everything they have been trained to do and to use all the modern technologies that are available whether or not they are appropriate.

Physicians aren't the only ones who adhere to the technological imperative. Hospital administrators also want the latest technologies.

---

[2] Estimates of physicians' incomes may be lower than actual incomes. Their salaries do not reflect their actual financial status because many physicians are incorporated.

Box 1.2 The Changing Face of American Physicians

Not long ago, over 90 percent of American medical students and physicians were white males. Beginning in the 1970s, however, the number of female students increased while the number of male students began to decline. Only 48 percent of the 1989–1990 freshman class were white males. Although fewer white and black males are applying to medical school, the number of Asian-American male applicants has increased. If this trend continues, the majority of physicians will consist of men from racial minorities and women. The changes in the demographics of physicians should be reflected in the health care system. Women physicians tend to choose primary care specialties and have more moderate economic expectations. It is predicted that this changing young profession will be better able to meet the health care needs of the twenty-first century (Relman, 1989).

If present trends continue, it is predicted that the majority of physicians will consist of women and minority males.

One reason why hospital costs have risen so sharply is that each hospital insists on having all the latest technologies. It would, of course, be more cost effective to share such equipment within a community. For example, in 1988 a total of 141 hospitals in the United States offered heart transplants, but only 1,647 transplants were performed owing to an "organ shortage." In the same year, 37 percent of the hospitals offering kidney transplants did fewer than 15 transplants (Winslow, 1989). It would obviously be more cost-effective and the transplant teams would become more skilled if the limited number of transplants were divided among fewer centers. After all, the organ shortage is not likely to be solved. As Easterbrook (1987) notes, "Unless someone plans to start a crusade *in favor* of drunk driving, it is difficult to imagine what social trend would increase the availability of young human hearts for transplant" (p. 70).

Medical Imperialism

When technological medicine overextends itself, it falls into what Illich (1976) calls medical imperialism. **Medical imperialism** is the insistence that anything that is remotely connected with health belongs under the supervision of the medical profession. Illich claims that "The disabling impact of professional control over medicine has reached the proportions of an epidemic" (p. 3).

Physicians are well trained to deal with biological problems that can be solved by technological medicine. However, this is a very limited, though important, sphere. Physicians may have no better idea than a layperson of how to handle stress, raise troublesome children, cope with a difficult marriage, or even solve nutritional problems. Experienced mothers of several children can probably give better advice on getting youngsters in bed than physicians, unless, of course, the physicians also have the same kind of experience.

Some years ago, Jean Mayer (1968) reported a study that compared the nutritional knowledge of housewives to that of Harvard medical students. It found that housewives knew just as much about nutrition as the medical students and that housewives with a history of dieting knew more than either of the other two groups! The point is that both the general public and physicians themselves often have an exaggerated notion of what physicians learn in medical school. A good example was shown on a local news show recently:

A newscaster presented a week-long series on compulsive shopping. She interviewed compulsive shoppers and discussed the serious problems resulting from their behavior. On the last night of the series, she provided a list of compulsive shopping symptoms. She then recommended that viewers who recognized any of these symptoms in themselves or others should seek advice from their family physicians.

As Engel (1986) has suggested, few medical doctors have a sufficient knowledge base to treat psychological disorders effectively. He further states that, "It is this lack of knowledge that accounts for the excessive use of minor tranquilizers by non-psychiatrist physicians to treat vaguely defined 'behavioral problems' " (p. 467).

Limitations of Technological Medicine

Medical imperialism began in the twentieth century, in part, because of the impressive accomplishments of medical science. There is considerable evidence, however, that the positive impact of medicine is not nearly as great as its "image" would suggest. Several investigators have noted that much of the decline in disease that we commonly attribute to advances in technological medicine has been due to other influences (Dubos, 1959; Illich, 1976; McKeown, 1979).

For example, the decline of tuberculosis is often offered as confirmation of the effectiveness of medical science. Whelan (1988) cites the following statistics: "In 1900, 194 out of every 100,000 people died from tuberculosis; fewer than three died from this disease in 1970" (p. 7). But she presents only part of the statistical picture (see Figure 1.3). The mortality (death) rate of tuberculosis had already declined from approximately 500 per 100,000 in 1845 to less than 200 in 1900. There was a further decline to 50 deaths per 100,000 by 1945. During that 100-year period, no drug therapy was available and vaccination was not practiced (Dubos, 1959). Moreover, there has been an increase in the incidence of tuberculosis in the 1990s in some populations, due largely to its occurrence in people infected with the AIDS virus (Goldsmith, 1990). The accomplishments, then, of medical science are not as spectacular as the first set of statistics might suggest.

Dubos (1959) acknowledges the "startling achievements" of modern science in the health care field. However, he suggests that much of the war against disease was won by the humanitarians and social reformers of the nineteenth century. Dubos gives the following explanation for our tendency to give medical science the credit for these accomplishments:

When the tide is receding from the beach it is easy to have the illusion that one can empty the ocean by removing water with a pail. The tide of infectious and nutritional diseases was rapidly receding when the laboratory scien-

tist moved into action at the end of the past century. (p. 20)

Life Expectancy

The dramatic increases in **life expectancy** which we have experienced in the United States during this century are often offered as statistical proof of the effectiveness of modern medicine. In defense of modern medicine, Whelan (1988) cites the fact that life expectancy at birth increased from 47 years in 1900 to 74.6 years in 1982. For more recent life expectancy data, see Table 1.1.

There is a difference between life expectancy and life span. **Life expectancy** is the *average* number of years a person of a certain age can expect to live. Life expectancy has increased because of the decrease in infant and childhood mortality rates. In other words, more infants and children are surviving. **Life span** is the *maximum* age that can be obtained, and it has not increased. More people are surviving birth and childhood, but few years have been added to the life span of those who do reach old age.

Whelan (1988) acknowledges that life span has not increased significantly, but she points to the 13 percent increase in life expectancy at age 45 that occurred between 1950 and 1980. This statistic is given as evidence for the effectiveness of medical science. This increase is largely due to the drop in the mortality rate attributable to cardiovascular disease. However, a government study concluded that this decline in mortality rates may be due more to lifestyle changes than to medical technology (Bender, 1988).

Questioning Technology's Effectiveness

It may be surprising to learn that the advanced cardiac technology has not been a major factor in the decline of heart disease. Thousands of patients have received coronary artery bypass surgery to treat coronary vessel blockage. Yet, the evaluation of this procedure has not shown it to be as effective as we might think. It has been demonstrated to be effective in reducing chest pain, but there is some suspicion that this could be due to the placebo effect (Weisbrod, 1988).

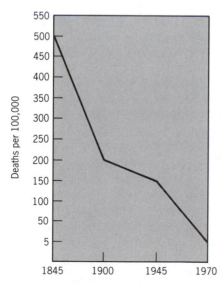

Figure 1.3 Tuberculosis mortality rates per 100,000 people: 1845–1970.

Coronary bypass surgery is discussed in more detail in Chapter 11.

Nor has medical science achieved great success in its fight against cancer. A report by the U.S. General Accounting Office (1987) concluded that, despite massive investments in cancer research, little progress has been made in finding a cure for most cancers. In a similar vein, a former Assistant Director of Public Affairs at the Memorial Sloan-Kettering Cancer Center has argued that the surgical and chemical interventions given to cancer patients are not effective in most cases (Moss, 1982).

Heroic Medicine

Not only are many of the expensive technological medical interventions of questionable effectiveness, but they are also often invasive, painful, and harmful. Illich (1976) has charged that "The medical establishment has become a major threat to health" (p. 3). Weil (1983) has suggested that we are now in a new age of heroic medicine.

The first age of **heroic medicine** occurred between 1780 and 1850 when medicine was characterized as heroic because of the reckless vigor of its methods. In other words, the patient had to be heroic to submit to the medical treatments of that day, which included bleeding, purging, induced vomiting, and "blistering." The following is a summary of an account of George Washington's death which Weil (1983) offers as an example of heroic medicine:

> George Washington was suffering from a very sore throat which was treated by removing four pints of blood, applying a blister to his throat, and a dose of calomel (a purgative). His treatment began on the morning of December 14, 1799 and he was dead by late evening on the same day.

Although medical treatment is more sophisticated today, many critics suggest that technological medicine "may be harmful to your health." Many of the tests, treatments, and procedures are extremely invasive or toxic. Moreover, they can sometimes be fatal. For example, one study reported mortality rates for

coronary artery bypass surgery on Medicare patients ranged up to 22.81 percent. At one hospital, 34 out of 152 bypass patients died in 1987 (Schiffman, 1990).

As early as 1968, researchers were finding that medical technologies were often overused at great costs of lives and money (Evans, 1968). The problem has apparently not gotten better. The Rand Corporation estimates that unnecessary tests add more than $50 billion yearly to the nation's health costs. These unnecessary procedures cost more than money. Rand found that two-thirds of a group of patients receiving carotid endarterectomies (removal of plaque inside vessel walls) were done for questionable reasons. Almost 10 percent of the patients suffered stroke or died as a result of the surgery (Winslow, 1990).

There are several reasons why potentially harmful medical technologies are overused. Part of the responsibility belongs to the patients themselves who expect to be "cured" through the use of the newest wonder drugs and machines that medical science has to offer. Another part belongs to the physicians who are paid much more for invasive procedures than they are for counseling patients to develop healthy lifestyles (Easterbrook, 1987). Furthermore, our traditional methods of health care payment do not encourage hospitals, physicians, or patients to control costs. Physicians and hospitals profit greatly from expensive interventions and the latest technologies. Patients tend not to be concerned about costs because a "third party" (insurance companies or Medicare) is paying them. This is the kind of medical care we have come to expect but can no longer afford (Zinn, 1989).

Too often modern medicine seems to ignore Hippocrates' admonition that "For the sick, the least is best." But then Hippocrates didn't have to contend with malpractice suits. It is estimated that the cost of defensive medicine accounts for almost 15 percent of the costs of physician services (Reynolds, Rizzo, & Gonzalez, 1987). Illich (1976) suggests that "attempts to avoid litigation and prosecution may now do more damage than any other iatrogenic stimulus" (p. 33). **Iatrogenic** is the term used to describe damage or deaths caused by physicians or their treatments.

The Diseases of Civilization

The nature of disease has changed dramatically in the twentieth century. At the beginning of the century, all three leading causes of death were infectious—influenza and pneumonia, tuberculosis, and gastroenteritis. As we approach the end of the century, the leading causes of death are heart disease, cancer, accidents, and cerebrovascular disease (stroke) (see Table 1.2). Heart disease, cancer, and stroke are often called the "diseases of civilization" and are recognized as having strong behavioral components.

A consistent finding in contemporary studies is that a major influence on health is lifestyle. Joseph Califano (1979), former Secretary of Health, Education, and Welfare, reports that Americans are killing themselves through "our own careless habits." He further states that we can do more to enhance our own health and well-being than "any doctor, any hospital, any drug, any exotic medical device." More recently,

former U.S. Surgeon General, Everett Koop, stated that lifestyle is the single most important factor in health promotion and disease prevention (cited in Melamed, 1984). Lifestyle factors are described in Chapters 8 and 9.

The well-known Alameda County study (Belloc & Breslow, 1972) identified seven health habits that significantly reduced the risk of experiencing illness. It estimated that a 45-year-old male adopting six or seven of these habits would increase his longevity 11 years. The seven health practices identified were: (1) never smoking cigarettes, (2) exercising regularly, (3) maintaining a normal weight, (4) not eating between meals, (5) eating breakfast daily, (6) sleeping seven to eight hours nightly, and (7) using alcohol moderately.

The increasing awareness that individual behavior is a significant influence on health is an important factor in the present health care crisis. The notion that we are accountable for our state of health conflicts with our traditional concept of the health care system. We tend to ignore our own health until we get sick, and then assume it is the physician's responsibility to "fix" us with some technological "miracle." Weil

Table 1.2 **Comparison of Ten Leading Causes of Death 1900–1986**

1900	1986
1. Influenza and pneumonia	1. Heart disease
2. Tuberculosis, all forms	2. Cancer
3. Gastroenteritis	3. Accidents
4. Heart disease	4. Stroke
5. Stroke	5. Chronic lung diseases
6. Kidney disease	6. Influenza and pneumonia
7. Accidents	7. Suicide
8. Cancer	8. Diabetes mellitus
9. Diseases of infancy	9. Liver diseases
10. Diphtheria	10. Homicides and legal interventions

Sources: U.S. Bureau of the Census. (1953). *Statistical Abstract of the United States*. Washington, D.C.: U.S. Government Printing Office. National Center for Health Statistics. (1989). *Health, United States, 1988*. DHHS Pub No. (PHS) 89–1232. Public Health Service. Washington, D.C.: U.S. Government Printing Office.

(1983) fears that these medical technological cures encourage "dangerous ways of thinking about health." One of our colleagues had the following experience that illustrates Weil's concern:

---

*A*s part of my doctoral training, I assisted in a wellness program for a group of businessmen. My tasks were to give presentations on environmental stress and nutrition. To illustrate the hidden fat in the American diet, I gave the percentage of fat calories contained in hot dogs and T-bone steaks. One of the participants angrily interrupted me saying, "You don't think much of your country, do you, lady?" Somewhat shocked at his reaction, I asked what I had said to give him the impression that I was anti-American. He replied that I was always saying our culture was stressful, and now I was suggesting that hot dogs and steaks were not "good" food. (I was certainly glad that I had not said anything about mothers or apple pie!) He concluded his scolding by saying he would continue to enjoy the "good things in life" and let *his doctor* worry about his cholesterol level.

ALTERNATIVE HEALTH CARE DELIVERY SYSTEMS

Imagine that your employer has switched to a different kind of health care plan to control costs. Under the new plan, you will have to pay much more if you stay with your family physician because he or she is not a "preferred provider." How would you feel about that? It is happening to people all over the country. Before the health care crisis, physicians and hospitals charged on a fee-for-service basis and much of the cost was covered by traditional insurance. Things are no longer that simple. The health care crisis is changing the way we receive and pay for health care. Many of these changes are being made to contain the spiraling costs of health care.

The Impact of Cost Containment

Changing the way we receive and pay for health care is proving to be a real challenge. Employers are adopting **managed-care health care plans** or forcing employees to bear the cost of traditional plans. Managed-care plans limit the employee's choice of physicians, hospitals, and treatments. Second opinions are being required to reduce the number of unnecessary surgeries. These attempts to reduce health care costs are meeting stiff resistance from employees. An increasing number of employer/union disputes involve health benefit issues (Ellwood, 1987; Garland, 1989).

Preferred Provider Organizations

A **preferred provider organization (PPO)** is the kind of plan we described at the beginning of this section. It is the fastest growing alternative to traditional insurance (Garland, 1989). Employers or unions enter a contract with a group of hospitals and physicians to provide services to their members at a reduced rate, usually 20 to 30 percent. In turn, physicians and hospitals are ensured an increased patient load and cash flow. Preferred provider organizations usually require pretreatment review, and members are forced to use the "preferred providers." If they go outside the PPO for services, they have to pay higher deductibles and coinsurance (Trauner, 1987).

The quality of care is an area of concern with all managed-care plans. It has been noted that PPO physicians are "preferred," not because they are good, but because they give a discount (Garland, 1989). Of course, determining the skill of a physician is always a problem. A recent editorial suggests that management needs to convince its employees that it is as concerned about the quality of medical care as it is about the cost. Only then will managed-care health care plans work ("Treating Our Ailing," 1989).

Health Maintenance Organizations

Health maintenance organizations (HMOs) are prepaid health care plans that provide stated services for a flat fee (Ermann, 1987). There are no extra charges regardless of the services rendered. A "staff" HMO employs physicians on a salary basis and provides them with a central office and administrative support.

"Group" HMOs contract with one or more physician groups that include a variety of specialists. An individual practice association is a network of physician offices and hospitals that provides services to enrollees in a large geographical area. Individual practice associations are more suitable for rural areas than the other types of HMOs (Savitz & Roberts, 1987).

There is evidence that the financial incentives offered by HMOs do influence physician decisions (Hillman, Pauly, & Kerstein, 1989). Salary-based and fee-per-enrollee payments were associated with reduced hospital use when compared to fee-for-service payment. The reduced rate of hospitalization may also reflect the greater degree of peer review found in staff and group HMOs. Of course, there is the concern that HMOs underserve patients to control costs. However, there is little evidence to suggest that HMOs lower costs by skimping on quality of care (Ermann, 1987).

Certain problems are associated with HMOs. Patients resent not being able to choose their own physicians and hospitals. It also appears that middle-class people are likely to fare better in this system than the urban poor. Middle-class people are more health conscious, better informed, and more likely to insist on adequate care from a program (Dougherty, 1988). Ironically, HMOs have not been the surefire cost-saving strategies it was hoped they would be. Their failure to live up to their expectations has been blamed on poor management (Norman, 1989).

Diagnostic-Related Groups

In an attempt to control spiraling Medicare costs, a law was enacted in 1983 that resulted in diagnosis-related groups (DRGs) reimbursement. Diagnosis-related groups are price controls based on the average cost of treating patients with a specific diagnosis. This average cost is the amount that hospitals are reimbursed for Medicare patients, rather than the actual amount involved in their treatment (Dougherty, 1988).

Diagnosis-related groups were designed to provide an incentive to hospitals and physicians to be cost-conscious. They have resulted in reduced length of hospital stays and lowered rates of hospital occupancy (Shaughnessy & Kramer, 1990). If patients stay longer than the DRG allows, the hospitals lose money. If patients can be treated for less than the DRG reimbursement, hospitals can keep the difference and make money (Dougherty, 1988). This system raises the concern that patients are being dismissed "quicker and sicker."

Alternative Health Care Settings

Diagnosis-related groups have resulted in an increased demand for home health agencies, nursing homes, and hospice programs. However, the need for these kinds of services is not due entirely to cost containment. For too long, the health care system has failed to adjust to the fact that the prevalent forms of illness are now chronic rather than acute (Strauss & Corbin, 1988). **Chronic illnesses** progress slowly and persist over long periods of time. **Acute illnesses** have a sudden onset and last a relatively short period of time or become chronic.

Chronic illnesses have social, economic, and behavioral consequences that are not addressed by the dominant biomedical model that emphasizes treatment of acute illnesses. Chronic illness may require long periods of care and greatly affect the lives of patients and their families. Visits to hospitals and physicians' offices are necessary for treating acute illnesses and for stabilizing chronic illnesses. However, during most phases of chronic illnesses, patients and their families manage the illnesses outside the hospital (Strauss & Corbin, 1988). Medical services are now being offered that reflect that reality.

Home Health Care

Hospital utilization has declined while the home health industry has enjoyed dramatic growth. Physicians are responding to this trend by returning to the traditional house call which had been steadily decreasing since the 1940s and was practically extinct by the 1980s. Surveys of physicians in family practice, general medicine, and internal medicine show that up to 82 percent of them make house calls. Undergraduate medical school programs are beginning to add home care rotations (Council on Scientific Affairs, 1990).

Home-based psychosocial interventions are often required because the burden of the patient's care falls on family members. Such interventions include family therapy, behavioral modification, education and counseling to enhance compliance. Home-based diagnoses are often more revealing than those made in the hospital or office. Psychobehavioral and safety hazard problems are more likely to be detected during a home diagnosis where patients are seen in their own environment. Mobile medical van services are being developed that allow physicians to make sophisticated medical diagnoses at home (Council on Scientific Affairs, 1990).

Nursing Home Facilities

It is estimated that 25 percent of people over the age of 65 will spend some time in nursing home facilities. Most patients are admitted to nursing homes because of functional disabilities, dementia, incontinence, or reduced levels of self-sufficiency. In addition, many long-term care facilities are assuming responsibility for the care of patients with acquired immunodeficiency syndrome (AIDS) (Libow & Starer, 1989). Traditional nursing homes provide for patients who have less need for medical and skilled nursing care. Skilled-nursing facilities serve patients with greater clinical needs (Shaughnessy & Kramer, 1990).

Some of the medical complications experienced by nursing home patients are over-medication, bed sores, and infections. However, patients commonly have psychological problems as well, including sleep disorders, depression, confusion, dementia, anxiety, hallucinations, and delusions. When patients are placed in a nursing home, they often feel rejected and abandoned. Their families may react with sadness, anxiety, conflict, guilt, or shame.

The concern that families "dump" patients in nursing homes may be unwarranted in the majority of cases. It is estimated that the families of about 70 percent of nursing home patients continue to visit them and remain actively involved in their care. The nursing home need not be a deadend street. It can be an effective place for restoring self-sufficiency even to very old patients, and sometimes a return home occurs (Libow & Starer, 1989).

Hospice Programs

Hospice is a program or facility that provides for the psychological, social, and physical needs of terminally ill patients and their families. Hospice care recognizes that the patient's lifestyle and preferences must be considered in all decision making. It also takes into account the needs and interests of family members and other caregivers. Hospice can be provided at home (home-care hospice) or in a hospital (hospital-based hospice). Although home care is the center of hospice, patients can move back and forth between the two settings (Mor, Greer, & Kastenbaum, 1988b).

Guidelines for full-service hospice programs are presented in Table 1.3. These guidelines are quite revolutionary for patient care that has been dominated by the biomedical model. The development of hospice was a reaction against a system that placed its convenience ahead of the values and preferences of terminally ill patients and their families. Hospice patients are not subjected to invasive, unnecessary treatments, nor are they abandoned. Proponents of hospice care believe that it provides better pain management and quality of life to patients and their families. In addition, it is more cost-effective than conventional care (Kidder, 1988).

There is a common misconception that hospice care means the patient must be cared for and die at home. Hospice is an alternative for terminally ill patients who do want to die at home and who have people to take care of them at home. It should be recognized, however, that home-care hospice places a great strain on the primary caregiver. Currently, there is a genuine

Table 1.3   Guidelines for Full-Service Hospice Programs

1. The patient and the people essential to the patient's life are considered the "unit of care."
2. Inpatient and home care are closely coordinated to provide continuity of care.
3. Care is available seven days a week, 24 hours a day.
4. Care is planned and provided by a medically supervised multidisciplinary team to secure the physical, emotional, and spiritual welfare of patients and their families.
5. The purpose of palliative and supportive care is to reduce the physical and emotional discomfort associated with terminal illnesses. **Palliative care** is a treatment that provides temporary relief for a patient but does not effect a cure.
6. Bereavement services are available to the family members and may include followup visits after the patient's death.
7. An educational program with two components is provided: (a) the patient, the family, and the multidisciplinary team are taught about death and dying, and (b) the family is trained to care for the patient at home.
8. Volunteers have an important role in the provision of care.

Source: Based on V. Mor, D. S. Greer, and R. Kastenbaum (1988). The hospice experiment: An alternative in terminal care. In V. Mor, D. S. Greer, and R. Kastenbaum (eds.), *The hospice experiment* (pp. 1–15). Baltimore, Md.: Johns Hopkins University Press.

concern that families may be getting the message that dying at home is the "right" thing to do. A hospice director related an instance involving a family that had received that message:

> The middle-aged children who were visiting had read Kubler-Ross and wanted Dad to die at home where he belonged. The elderly wife who had remained very quiet finally shouted into my face "Don't you understand I can't live here and remember him dead in the living room?" (Mor, Greer, & Kastenbaum, 1988a, p. xi)

Conclusions

Within the limited framework of the biomedical model, psychology has had only a small role to play in health care. Within this framework, the key to improved health is to make technological medicine more available to more people. But, as we are beginning to realize, we simply cannot afford this approach any longer. Moreover, many of today's diseases can be prevented through changes in lifestyle, and the delivery of technological medicine can be improved by taking psychological and social factors into account.

The perspective we gain through the biopsychosocial model indicates that psychology has significant contributions to make to the health care system. Modern medicine is important, but its domain has been extended well beyond its actual capacities. The bottom line seems to be that psychology has no reason to be humble about its importance to health. In the next chapter we will introduce the discipline of health psychology and describe the important role it has to play in the challenge to the biomedical model.

Summary

1. Information is filtered through schemata, or mental frameworks, so that we can make sense of the "confusion of our outer world." Paradigms are a kind of mental framework used by scientists, including physicians. Although paradigms provide a coherent plan for study, they can also exclude important factors worthy of study.

2. The biomedical model is the dominant paradigm of medical science. It is a mechanistic model that emphasizes biochemical factors to the exclusion of psychological and social factors. This model is now facing a challenge from proponents of the biopsychosocial model. The biopsychosocial model expands the dominant model to include the obviously important factors that now fall outside its narrow framework.

3. Whether we are considered sick or healthy depends not only on our physical condition, but also on the zeitgeist. The ways in which health and disease are defined are important because they have social, legal, and economic consequences. Health psychology rejects the two-category (sick or healthy) concept of disease and health in favor of the wellness continuum. Placing disease and health on a continuum encourages us to take actions that will move us toward optimal wellness. The two-category concept tends to promote the idea that there are no health issues until we get sick.

4. Although scientific medicine has made some significant advances during the twentieth century, American health care finds itself in crisis. The United States has the most expensive health care system in the world, but it is clearly not the best.

5. Economic factors have contributed greatly to the health care crisis. The percent of the gross national product being spent on health care costs has increased dramatically. One reason for the increase is the excessive use of expensive medical technology without regard to its appropriateness or cost. Traditional methods of health care payment do not encourage physicians, hospitals, or patients to control costs.

6. Contributing to the health care crisis is a growing awareness that (a) technological treatments are costly, often painful, and sometimes life threatening, and (b) these treatments are not always as effective as we once believed. For example, the tuberculosis rate had declined dramatically before drug therapy was available and vaccinations were given.

7. The health care crisis is also due to the changing nature of disease during the twentieth century. At the turn of the century, the leading causes of death were infectious. As we end the century, the leading causes of death are recognized as having strong behavioral components. The notion that we are accountable for our own health conflicts with the notion that physicians are responsible for our health.

8. The health care crisis is changing the way we receive and pay for health care. Many employers are adopting managed-care health care plans. These plans limit the employee's choice of physicians, hospitals, and treatments. Under a preferred provider organization (PPO), employers enter a contract between a group of hospitals and physicians to provide services at a reduced rate. If members go outside the PPO, they pay higher deductibles and co-insurance. Health maintenance organizations are prepaid health care plans that provide stated services for a flat fee.

9. Diagnosis-related groups (DRGs) are price controls based on the average costs of treating patients with a specific diagnosis. This system was initiated to provide an incentive to reduce Medicare costs by

encouraging hospitals and physicians to be cost-conscious. Concerns have been raised that patients are being dismissed "quicker and sicker."

10. The fact that the prevalent forms of illness are now chronic rather than acute has added to the health care crisis. Chronic illnesses have social, economic, and behavioral consequences that are not addressed by the dominant biomedical model. Hospitals and physician offices are necessary to handle acute illnesses, but chronic illnesses require management outside those settings.

11. Diagnostic-related groups have resulted in an increased demand for alternative health care settings. Home health care, nursing home facilities, and hospice programs have experienced a dramatic growth in recent years. Hospice is a program or facility that provides for the comprehensive needs of terminally ill patients and their families.

Key Terms

Acute illness

Biomedical model

Biopsychosocial model

Cartesian dualism

Chronic illness

Diagnostic-related groups (DRGs)

General systems theory

Health maintenance organizations (HMOs)

Heroic medicine

Hospice

Iatrogenic

Life expectancy

Life span

Managed-care health care plans

Medical imperialism

Palliative care

Paradigm

Preferred provider organization (PPO)

Psychosomatic medicine

Technological imperative

Zeitgeist

Discussion Questions

1. How are mental frameworks related to paradigms and how does the zeitgeist influence them?

2. What are the advantages of expanding the biomedical model to include psychosocial factors?

3. We gave several examples of behaviors and conditions whose health status has been influenced by the zeitgeist. How do you think the zeitgeist has affected the health status of body weight or size?

4. Why are the labels we give to behaviors and conditions important?

5. What are the criticisms of the two-category concept of disease?

6. Briefly describe the factors that have led to the health care crisis.

7. How do other countries manage to have higher longevity and lower infant mortality rates than the United States while spending much less on health care?

8. Give your own examples of medical imperialism and the technological imperative.

9. How has the nature of disease changed during the twentieth century? What do you predict for the next century?

10. How has the health care crisis affected the ways in which health care is delivered today?

Chapter 2

Introduction to Health Psychology

A diabetic telephone lineman suffered from depression and refused to maintain his insulin treatments. As a result, he was frequently rushed to the emergency room in a diabetic coma. What was his problem? He hated his job because he really wanted to be a journalist. After eight weeks of focused psychotherapy, he compromised by quitting his telephone job and becoming a proofreader for a publishing company. He resumed his insulin therapy, his depression vanished, and so did his soaring medical bills. Focused psychotherapy treats specific problems over a limited number of weeks.

This story was published in *The Wall Street Journal* (Winslow, 1990). Why would a financial journal publish an article related to health psychology? Because there is a growing awareness that psychology has the potential to reduce our country's runaway health care costs. The telephone lineman's story suggests that short-term psychotherapy may be an effective, relatively inexpensive intervention for some chronic health problems. The article went on to describe a four-year study that compared the medical costs of more than 44,000 patients receiving either focused therapy, traditional psychotherapy, or no mental health care. The study found that annual medical costs fell about 35 percent among patients who received focused psychotherapy. Changes in medical care costs ranged from slight declines to 25 percent *increases* for the other two groups. Nicholas Cummings, a psychologist, heads a multimillion dollar corporation that provides mental health services based on this study in several states.

A United States Senate committee has also recognized the importance of the issues that are addressed by health psychology. In its report on the fiscal year 1990 budget for the Department of Health and Human Services, the Senate Committee on Appropriations stated (cited in Raub, 1990, p. 3):

> *The Institute of Medicine, the Surgeon General, the NIH, and others have reported at length of the relationship between health and behavior in disease diagnosis, treatment, and prevention. These reports continue to doc-*

> *ument that . . . . 7 of the 10 leading causes of death in this Nation are in large part behaviorally determined and can be significantly reduced through changes in behavior.*

HEALTH PSYCHOLOGY: AN EMERGING DISCIPLINE

Health psychology has become a major field of inquiry that is expanding rapidly, and there is every indication that its strong growth will accelerate (Seeman, 1989). Soaring health costs and the realization that behavioral factors play an important role in modern epidemics are just two of many reasons for the phenomenal growth of health psychology. The challenge to the biomedical model opened the door for psychologists to apply their knowledge and research and clinical skills to health-related areas.

The health-related research from the behavioral and social sciences has greatly increased the challenge to the biomedical model. For example, studies have consistently found that lifestyle factors and emotional strain are important predictors of longevity. The indication that behaviors, attitudes, and life events can influence health has further weakened the dominance of the biomedical model. The success of psychological interventions, in cases like that of the telephone lineman you just read, pushes beyond the narrow limitations of the biomedical model.

Mind/body dualism, the basis of the biomedical model, has been challenged by the scientific verification that people can voluntarily control "involuntary" bodily processes. These processes include controlling the heart rate, blood pressure, brain wave activity, and blood flow to the extremities. The credibility of mind/body dualism has further been weakened by the discovery of the links between the immune and central nervous systems. The newly recognized field of psychoneuroimmunology is even suggesting that some of our immune responses may be "learned."

Defining Health Psychology

Health psychology was formally recognized in 1979 when the American Psychological Association (APA) approved the formation of the Division of Health Psychology (Division 38). It is one of the fastest growing fields in psychology today. Because it is a relatively new field, its nature and purposes can be defined in many ways. We define it in the broadest sense as the systematic application of psychology to the relevant areas of health, disease, and the health care system. Division 38 defines health psychology in greater detail as follows:

> Health psychology is the aggregate of the specific educational, scientific, and professional contributions of the discipline of psychology to the promotion and maintenance of health, the prevention and treatment of illness, the identification of etiological and diagnostic correlates of health, illness, and related dysfunction, and to the analysis and improvement of the health care system and health policy formation (Matarazzo, 1982, p. 4).

The Scope of Health Psychology

The scope of health psychology is very broad. As you read this book, you will learn that some health psychologists help patients cope with pain, others do basic research on psychological factors that influence the immune system, and still others search for the best ways to help people develop healthier lifestyles. These are only a few examples of the diverse activities of health psychologists.

Most of the theories and methods of psychology can be applied to health-related topics. Learning theorists apply their concepts and findings to such problems as the treatment of pain and the control of immune response. Clinical psychologists test and evaluate patients to see which of them is likely to benefit from elective surgery. Such evaluations can also provide a sense of how well a patient is likely to fare in the recovery process. Research and theory on human information processing are being applied to such topics as the quirks of the mind that lead physicians to make diagnostic errors or that cause patients to misunderstand medical instructions.

Health psychology is open to basic and applied research as well as practical application in the clinic or workplace. Some people are doing very basic work with animals to find out, among other things, how our bodies respond to stress and which kinds of stress are most lethal. Others are working in treatment programs to teach people to control their own migraine headaches or better manage their diabetes.

Psychoneuroimmunology has now been recognized by the Peanuts gang. Reprinted by permission of UFS, Inc.

Health psychology can be applied at any stage of the wellness continuum. Health psychologists can provide primary treatment, for example, biofeedback training to treat high blood pressure. In addition, they can augment the treatment provided by physicians by performing such tasks as delivering stress-management programs for recovering heart patients.

Health psychology can be used to prevent illness by helping people control behaviors and attitudes that pose risks to their health. For example, behavioral and cognitive therapy can be used to help people quit smoking or to control weight. Theoretical concepts like Antonovsky's (1979) sense of coherence and Bandura's (1977) self-efficacy are being applied to help us understand more about optimal health. These concepts are discussed in several chapters throughout the book.

Health psychology also has important contributions to make to the wellness movement. We are used to thinking of health in the narrow framework of a "disease model." Both the disease and prevention models focus on the breakdown of health. In contrast, the wellness model does not limit itself to the prevention or treatment of disease. Furthermore, it is in direct conflict with the view that humans should be treated like machines that break down.

Seeman (1989) notes that the wellness movement is closely related to the emergence of health psychology. Both, for example, demand that increased emphasis be placed on health enhancement. Health psychology has been instrumental in providing a theoretical basis to enhance the wellness literature. An excellent example of health psychology's contribution in this area was the publication of *Behavioral Health: A Handbook of Health Enhancement and Disease Prevention* (Matarazzo, Weiss, Herd, Miller, & Weiss, 1984).

Health Psychology and Mind-Over-Body

My 90-year-old great-aunt was very excited to hear that we were writing a book about health psychology. When I (SAR) seemed surprised that she knew about health psychology, she was more than a little offended. She informed me that she watched Phil Donahue regularly, and she knew all about the power of the mind over the body. In fact, she had seen many wonderful examples of "mind-over-body" among her friends at her retirement home.

Of course, health psychology is *not* limited to the mind-over-body approach. This approach states that our minds have far more control over our bodies than the biomedical model allows us to believe. Later chapters will argue that this notion is true and that mind-over-body is an important part of health psychology. However, the field would be alive and well even if such notions were not true. Many other health-related areas can benefit from the application of psychology.

For example, many health psychologists are focusing on learning more about health care providers and patients. Just two of the topics under study are the improvement of physician/patient communications and the development of techniques to help health care providers cope with the stresses of their jobs. Decision-making and other cognitive theories are being applied to improve medical diagnoses. Knowledge gained from these studies can be used to improve health care delivery and make it more effective.

MAJOR APPROACHES TO HEALTH PSYCHOLOGY

Health psychology has benefited greatly from the concepts, methods, and discoveries of other disciplines and areas of psychology. Specifically, it has borrowed from public health, epidemiology, physiology, medical anthropology, and sociology. In addition to these disciplines, health psychology has been greatly influenced by the major approaches described below.

The Behavioral Approach

The **behavioral approach** grew from the transformation of psychology in the 1920s from the study of "mind" to the science of behavior. Behaviorism allowed only for the study of variables that could be directly observed. This shift from the study of mind to behavior had a great impact on the character of modern psychology. Classical and operant conditioning became the dominant areas of study for psychologists.

Because learning theories are so important in health psychology, we have included a "mini" refresher on the basics of classical and operant conditioning below. These principles are widely applied to health psychology, and they will be discussed throughout the book. For more information on conditioning, consult an introductory psychology or learning text.

Classical Conditioning

We learned about **classical conditioning** from the work of Ivan Pavlov (1849–1936). He showed that the central nervous system forms new connections between "neutral" stimuli and stimuli that cause unlearned responses. While studying digestion in dogs, he noticed that they began to salivate at the mere sight of their food. He hypothesized that any stimulus preceding the food could elicit salivation from the dogs. Pavlov's research supported his hypothesis. Later research found that many of the "gut" responses that are important to health have been learned. A brief description of classical conditioning principles follows:

---

*T*he "classical" example of classical conditioning is training a dog to salivate when a bell is rung. But we are going to give an example related to health psychology that actually happened to a little boy we know. Michael developed an allergic rash to a powerful antibiotic that was in the form of a strawberry-flavored liquid. He was immediately taken off the antibiotic and the rash went away. A few days later, after eating strawberry ice cream, Michael developed another rash. He had never been allergic to strawberries before.

This is what we think happened to Michael: Strawberry flavoring was a neutral stimulus (NS) because Michael had never had an unconditioned response (UR) to it before. An unconditioned response is an involuntary

reaction like salivation or a rash. The antibiotic was an unconditioned stimulus (US) because people often have an unconditioned response to antibiotics. After pairing the strawberry flavoring with the antibiotic, Michael became conditioned to break out in a rash without the antibiotic being present. The strawberry flavoring became a conditioned stimulus (CS), and Michael's rash was a conditioned response (CR). A model of Michael's classical conditioning experience follows:

Strawberry flavoring (NS) ————> No rash
Antibiotic (US) ————————> Rash (UR)
Flavoring + US ————————> Rash
Strawberry flavoring (CS) ————> Rash (CR)

Operant Conditioning

B. F. Skinner (1904–1990) is the researcher most closely associated with operant conditioning. **Operant conditioning** occurs when voluntary behavior is influenced by its consequences. At first, students of operant conditioning studied the basic laws of this learning using rats pressing bars or pigeons pecking keys. Soon, however, they began to apply these laws to human actions that had previously been considered to be uncontrollable responses. One early example was the control of the behaviors of severely autistic children and psychotic adults through operant conditioning.

After a time, the behaviorists began to see that operant conditioning could be applied to health-related behaviors. For example, programs have been developed to help people reduce risk factors such as obesity and smoking. Other programs are designed to control symptoms like pain, vomiting, poor circulation, or the impaired breathing found in asthma. Thus, behavioral techniques are very important in health psychology. Here is a brief description of operant learning principles.

---

*O*perant conditioning involves voluntary behavior that is emitted to bring about some desired change in the environment. In classical conditioning, the organism's response is passive. Such stimuli as bells and food are paired without regard to the response of the organism. Operant conditioning, on the other hand, requires an active response from the organism. The organism is not reinforced unless it gives the desired response. For example, the rat gets food only if it presses a bar.

Skinner studied operant behavior by observing rats in a cage or a "Skinner Box." The box contains a lever or bar and a food cup. When the rat accidentally pushes the bar, a food pellet drops into the cup. After a few of these events, the rat has learned to press the bar through "reinforcement."

Reinforcement can be positive or negative. In operant conditioning, these terms have nothing to do with "good" or "bad." A "positive" event means that a stimulus is *added* to the organism's environment, and a "negative" event means that a stimulus is *removed* from the organism's environment. Negative reinforcement is *not* punishment. Both positive and negative reinforcement are events that follow a response and *increase* the likelihood that it will be repeated. For example, positive reinforcement occurs when people drink to feel relaxed because relaxation is "added" to their environment. It is negative reinforcement if they drink to forget their problems because they are "removing" their problems, temporarily anyway.

Operant conditioning is also used to decrease behavior. That is accomplished through punishment or omission. Punishment is an event that *follows* a response and decreases the likelihood that it will be repeated, for example, a spanking. Punishment is always a "positive" event because the stimulus is added to the environment. Omission involves removing something rewarding to the organism to decrease a target behavior. An example of omission is the classic "time out" that is used so often with toddlers. Say, little Susie really likes to play with Timmy from next door, but she has been biting him lately. To decrease her biting behavior, we will send her to her room for five minutes every time she bites him. Operant learning procedures are shown in Figure 2.1.

The Cognitive-Behavioral Approach

One limitation of the behavioral approach is that it is either difficult or impossible to observe

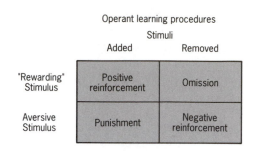

Figure 2.1 Operant learning procedures.

central human activities such as imagery, thought, and the silent "self-talk" we carry on constantly. This means that a lot of what most people consider to be part of psychology is either left out or handled very crudely.

A psychology that has a hard time including thoughts and images is surely incomplete. But the problem is even worse than it sounds. Pavlov and his followers had discovered very early that inner speech, besides being of psychological import in its own right, also regulates other behaviors—the very ones studied by orthodox behaviorists. Inner speech *directs* observable behavior. No real understanding of behavior, whether private or public, seems possible without an understanding of this inner speech.

Although many nonbehaviorists long ago put cognition at the center of psychology, it took a while for those in the behavioral tradition to acknowledge its importance. Today, the **cognitive-behavioral approach** plays a featured role in behavioral psychology. Its role in health psychology is at least as great as that of traditional behavioral methods. As Seeman (1989) states, "if there is one dominant subsystem in its impact on health, it is the cognitive subsystem" (p. 1108).

If a patient is treated by a health psychologist, much emphasis is likely to be placed on assessing the role of thoughts and images in acquiring, maintaining, or eliminating health-related behaviors. For example, a person with headaches will be asked to keep records of subjective feelings of pain and of what he or she was thinking and imagining before, during, and after headache episodes. Changing the thoughts and images is likely to be a central aspect of the treatment.

The following case is a good example of the use of cognition and imagery in helping a patient:

---

*D*oug was a very youthful 41-year-old who watched his diet very carefully and exercised regularly. As a result of an old sports injury, he developed severe low back pain. While being treated for the back problem, he had a couple of high blood pressure readings in the doctor's office. He was told he would have to go on medication for the blood pressure, but he resisted, hoping the readings would drop back if he watched his salt intake and coped better with stress. (An obvious possibility seems to have escaped both him and his doctor—that the high readings were *due* to the pain.) To Doug, being on medication meant the end of his healthy, youthful existence and was the beginning of a downward trend toward old age and death.

One day Doug's wife noticed that he had yellow streaks radiating from his spine. He went into a panic over the possibility that he had developed an infection in his spine. He rushed to have the doctor examine him. He was terrified as he drove to the doctor's office, imagining that he had a crippling or fatal disease. His mind was filled with images of the physician giving him the bad news and with thoughts of how catastrophic the results might be. On top of it all, he kept thinking that, even if the outcome was not so bad, he would certainly have a very high blood pressure reading and end up on medication. His anxiety mounted to a dizzying level.

Fortunately, Doug had previously received training in thought and image management in a stress-management class. One of the things he had learned was to view feelings of distress as a *cue* to redirect his cognitions. Before the training, he had tended, like most people, to react to signs of distress with thoughts like "Oh lord, I am falling apart; I'm going out of control!" Such thoughts make the situation worse. Now the mounting distress reminded him that it was time to bring his thoughts and images into control. He said to himself, "I can probably get this under control if I just direct my thoughts and images in a more supportive, healthy way—at least I can make a dent in it." He began telling himself that, of all the things he had worried and gotten upset about in the past, very few had ever really turned out to be as bad as expected. He pictured the physician telling him that it was not serious and that he would be okay. He then told himself that he was at least as likely to hear his physician tell him that he was okay as to give him really bad news. As he continued his soothing thoughts, he began to calm down.

When he got to the doctor's office, he told the nurse he was upset and his blood pressure might reflect that. As she took the readings, he continued to soothe himself. He also redirected his attention, keeping it off upsetting aspects of the situation. For example, he focused on relaxing thoughts instead of dwelling on fretful ideas about the outcome of his blood pressure reading. The result was excellent. His pressure was not high at all. Moreover, it turned out that the streaks were just due to small blood vessels being broken due to the spasming muscles. This was painful, but not at all dangerous. Not only had his soothing, supportive thoughts made him feel better and lessened his agitation physiologically, but they were a more accurate reflection of reality.

The Psychophysiological Approach

Psychophysiology is the subfield of psychology that studies the relationships between physiological and psychological processes. For example, a psychophysiologist might measure how the heart responds during performance of a mentally demanding task. Psychophysiology has a place in health psychology because it reveals health-related physical reactions to psychological events and vice versa.

An excellent example of the **psychophysiological approach** is work by Rosanski et al. (1988) showing that mental stress produces serious abnormalities of heart function in patients with known heart disease. These abnormalities were comparable in magnitude and clinical significance to those produced by demanding physical exercise. The mental stresses included those that are common in daily life. For example, one involved talking to two people about personal problems, and others were just mentally demanding. Also important was the finding that patients were not able to tell when the mental stress was causing potentially lethal abnormalities of heart function. Thus, the dangers of physical stress are probably much more controllable than the dangers of mental stress. A person can usually avoid strenuous exercise, and a rapid heart rate makes it obvious when the exercise is placing heavy demands on the heart. But mental stressors can come up any time. Furthermore, they do not produce a high heart rate even when they are making the heart pump inefficiently.

Biofeedback is an example of applied psychophysiology. Biofeedback instruments are designed to monitor, amplify, and "feed back" a variety of bodily reactions such as muscle tension, blood flow to the extremities, heart rate, and brain activity. In other words, the machines provide trainees information about their biological processes. This information allows trainees to become aware of the psychological and physiological states that produce the desired changes. Once they become conscious of those states, they can modify or control bodily reactions that are normally thought to be beyond voluntary control. For example, people who are tense and have trouble sleeping may be connected to a device that measures brain wave activity and gives them feedback about which mental states are relaxing and compatible with sleep. Gradually, the person may learn to create the desired state at will.

Simple physical reactions often go hand in hand with risk factors or diseases. Learning to control these reactions results in learning to control the risk factors and diseases. To illustrate, control of blood flow to the skin of the hands is related to control of the sympathetic nervous system (SNS). The SNS is the part of the nervous system that produces the "fight or flight" response (see Chapter 4). It is worthwhile to learn control of this response because it allows us to deal more effectively with various kinds of stress. There is also fairly good evidence

that controlling blood flow to the skin may be useful in treating disorders such as migraine and essential hypertension. We will say more about biofeedback in later chapters.

The Clinical Psychology Approach

Clinical psychologists are trained to evaluate and treat psychological problems. These skills are also very useful when applied to health care problems. The **clinical psychology approach** is probably more common than any other.

Clinical psychologists can evaluate whether a particular patient is a good candidate for a certain medical treatment. For example, Buffone (1989) described the use of clinical skills to assess whether patients are suited for major elective orofacial surgery. (This is a kind of plastic surgery that involves such things as making the jaw longer or shorter.) Although many people can undergo this kind of surgery without problems, others may need help to cope with it. Still others are not psychologically able to handle such surgery at all (see Chapter 13). Failure to evaluate patients psychologically can lead to harm and may encourage malpractice suits against surgeons.

Clinical psychologists can also apply their skills to other areas of health. They design and implement preventive programs, help people deal with the trauma of illness, and provide support for medical personnel. **Clinical neuropsychology** is perhaps the most established use of clinical psychology in the health care system. For some time now, clinical neuropsychologists have been providing a major service in testing patients with head injuries. They have also devised various methods for helping patients cope with the physical, mental, and emotional aftermath of their injuries.

The General Systems Theory Approach

As we mentioned in Chapter 1, the biopsychosocial model is based on systems theory; therefore, it is one of the most important theories of health psychology. Systems theories have been widely applied in biological and social sciences. A basic assumption of systems theories is that systems exist within systems. For example, an organism is composed of tissues, and tissues are composed of cells, and cells are composed of molecules, and molecules are composed of atoms, and so forth. In other words, nothing exists in isolation.

The **general systems theory approach** is important because it forces researchers and practitioners to develop a global view of their research question or treatment. This global view emphasizes the fact that intervention at one level of a system can often have unexpected effects at other levels. For instance, most medications have some sort of side effect. Aspirin can relieve a headache, but it can also cause excessive bleeding.

Even biofeedback training can have quite unexpected side effects. A woman took biofeedback training because her husband's verbal abuse caused her to be extremely nervous and agitated. When his verbal attacks no longer caused her to cry and shake uncontrollably, he began to abuse her physically.

The Community Psychology Approach

Community psychology also takes a systems approach. It traces its formal beginnings back to 1965. The founders of the **community psychology approach** believed that many psychological problems were caused by social systems. Therefore, the system, rather than the individual, should be "fixed" (Rappaport, 1977). Community psychology is a value-oriented discipline that places great emphasis on systems theory, field research, prevention, and community interventions.

Community psychologists have moved from the laboratory to the field to conduct research. It is their belief that social systems cannot be studied in controlled laboratory settings with rats or first-year college students. Instead, they advocate that interventions take place in settings where people spend most of their time, including schools, work sites, and community centers.

The founders of this approach rejected the medical model for psychology because it placed too much emphasis on "cure" rather than prevention. A major goal of community psychology is the prevention of psychological dysfunction. According to this model, prevention should occur at the systems level and become embedded in the social structure. You will find this theme being echoed in several chapters in this text. Enhancement of well-being and competency are also major goals of community psychology.

Typical of this approach is the work of Roosa, Gensheimer, Ayers, and Short (1990) on prevention of alcohol abuse. Instead of the familiar method of trying to treat people who are already alcoholic, they dealt with elementary school children who were at risk of developing alcohol problems because they lived with an untreated alcoholic parent.

Roosa et al. identified factors that place children of alcoholics at risk of developing mental health problems, and factors that influence the children's ability to cope with stress. They developed a brief program to help the children reduce their risk. It involved such aids as teaching them to relax when stressed, to consider their options and choose the best one, and to seek help. They also used a cognitive approach to enhance the children's self-esteem. For example, the children were taught to say such things to themselves as "When I do something that's good, I tell myself: I knew I could do it!"

The impact of this intervention is still being assessed, but preliminary results seem promising. For example, teachers were asked to rate the children's "negative behavior." As the children's ability to cope with stress increased, teacher ratings indicated they engaged in less negative behavior. Obviously, long-term research on many children is needed to fully evaluate the impact of this program.

If the program continues to show promise, community psychologists will have to find ways to spread the word about its usefulness and get it implemented in more schools. This last step is an important facet of the community psychology orientation—to turn the program over to the people who most need it rather than have a program that requires the efforts of specialized professionals.

Community psychology has clearly had an influence on health psychology. The impact it has had is most obvious in public health psychology, which is discussed later in this chapter. Many of the leaders in health psychology have ties with community psychology, for example, Bernard Bloom, Barbara and Bruce Dohrenwend, Ira Iscoe, and Rudolf Moos. The two disciplines share an emphasis on systems theory, prevention, and field research. The disciplines also overlap greatly in stress and social support research.

The Family Systems Approach

General systems theory states that we cannot always understand a system simply by knowing the actions of the people within the system. Nor can we comprehend these actions without knowing the system in which they occur. The **family systems approach,** though it has many forms, concurs with the views of systems theory. There is a general assumption that the pathological behaviors of family members reflect an attempt to adapt to the family system. Such individual pathology may be *needed* to keep the family system in balance.

For the most part, family systems theorists have focused on problems of mental rather than physical illnesses. However, very important work has been done relating to issues of physical illness. Minuchin and his colleagues showed that the failure of insulin to maintain diabetic children could be due to family pathology. In these cases, insulin failed to control diabetes even when given in doses many times higher than those that are normally effective (Minuchin, Rosman, & Baker, 1978). Similar results have been found in studies of serious asthmatic attacks in children. It has even been suggested that for certain children the most effective cure for asthma would be "parentectomy" or removal of the parents (Alexander, 1977).

Seltzer (1985) took a family systems approach by comparing families of children with nervous system illnesses to those with psycho-logical problems that mimic these illnesses. The latter are called *conversion reactions*. The differences between the two types of families were clear. For example, families that produced conversion reactions in their children tended to have a father from a much lower social class than the mother. The father had usually accomplished far more than his original social standing would lead us to expect. The family was typically dedicated to denying any differences between family members. Seltzer found that sometimes medical misdiagnoses could be identified simply because a child thought to have no neurological disorder came from a family that did not fit the pattern typical of "conversion reaction families."

The Existential-Phenomenological Approach

Behaviorism has prevailed in the English-speaking world, but the **existential-phenomenological approach** has been of central importance in Europe. This approach is based in phenomenology, which is a very complex technique for describing the essential features of human experience.[1] Phenomenological analyses of humanness show that we have certain basic potentials that cannot be ignored and that we all try to fulfill. If we are thwarted in developing these potentials, they constantly press for expression.

According to this approach, things happen to us in life that frustrate our means of expression and fulfillment of our essential humanness. This frustration sometimes leads us to express these basic themes in the form of pathology. We develop a wide range of methods for expressing these inescapable aspects of ourselves. Because the human body is one of the media for such expression, we sometimes express ourselves through symptoms. We use not only psychological symptoms, but also full-blown diseases to serve our self-expression. This self-expression is considered a major facet of disease. Therefore,

---

[1] Phenomenology is *not* a form of introspection, though English-speaking writers commonly confuse it with that. It is actually a very specialized form of empiricism.

treatment should include an attempt to understand which expressions of humanness have been thwarted and are being expressed through the sickness. The therapist then attempts to help the patient express the blocked potentials in a free and healthy way. The expressive type of treatment is described more thoroughly in Chapter 5.

This approach seems to have had limited impact on American health psychology, though some important works have been published in English. They provide some rather striking examples of this approach to healing illnesses that have failed to respond to routine medical approaches (see Boss, 1979).

The Holistic Approach

The **holistic approach** differs from most other approaches to health psychology: it places much greater emphasis on spirituality. As a result, it tends to use methods that are outside the scientific framework. Holistic approaches are quite varied, but they generally view humans as existing at several levels, for example, the physical, mental, and spiritual. Like the biopsychosocial model, many holistic approaches accept the biomedical approach, but only as *part* of the treatment process. Also like the biopsychosocial model, the holistic approach takes the impact of psychological and social influences on health seriously. The holistic view is likely to differ from the biopsychosocial in the inclusion of the spiritual.

Thus, physical illnesses are seen as having mental and spiritual causes as well as those stressed by traditional medicine. In the words of Dossey (1984), a renowned holistic physician:

> There are some thoughts that physicians early on learn to keep to themselves. They have mainly to do with concepts that have not survived the unforgiving scrutiny of science and which have therefore faded from our list of respectable concerns in the profession. They have to do with spirit.
>
> The mention of the word immediately causes the deepest furrowing of the scientific brow. Eyes are averted in the direction of the measurable and the precise when spirit announces itself, and choruses of objection warn of the dangers inherent in any flirtation with "mysticism."

> Yet for all the problems in addressing such a murky concept, all of us in medicine know privately it is a notion that has never died and never will die. For, oddly, "spirit" has seemingly thrived on being officially ignored in medicine in the scientific era by peskily asserting its presence in every doctor's encounter with a patient and in every patient's encounter with illness. (p. vi)

With this approach, remedies for physical ailments often focus on nonphysical treatments. For instance, patients might be urged to change their attitudes toward other people. Another suggested remedy might be to develop a more spiritual outlook, such as handing one's problems over to a higher being or freely loving oneself and others.

It is a very long way from the behavioral approach to the holistic approach. Academic psychology places great emphasis on the scientific method. Consequently, holistic approaches have been ignored in the past and to a great extent still are. Yet at times scientists have confirmed the claims of holistic healers (see, e.g., Benson, 1984 or Green & Green, 1977). Holistic healing should not be dismissed before it is investigated—if for no other reason that it has been the source of ideas later verified by the scientific method. (See the discussion of the process of discovery versus the process of verification in Chapter 3.)

HEALTH PSYCHOLOGY AND RELATED DISCIPLINES

Health psychology has developed some close and rather unique relationships with other disciplines. With the exception of medicine, the lines between health psychology and these other disciplines often become blurred. The following paragraphs describe these other disciplines.

The Relationship to Medicine

Health psychology and medicine have many common interests, but they differ greatly in their approaches. At the present time, the primary focus of medicine is on the diagnosis and cure of illness. It also has a biological orientation toward the causes and treatment of illness. The focus of health psychology goes beyond that of medicine to stress the prevention and enhancement of health. It expands the biological framework of medicine to include psychological and social factors as well. Thus, health psychology tends to have a broader focus than traditional medicine.

The great strength of medicine is its ability to deal with the physically ill. We are not suggesting that health psychology, in any way, replace medicine. However, there is ample evidence that medicine could profit by including psychological insights and practices into its system. We will discuss this evidence throughout the book.

Behavioral Medicine and Behavioral Health

Behavioral medicine is an interdisciplinary field that developed within the behaviorist tradition. In addition to health psychologists, social workers, nurses, epidemiologists, and physicians have contributed to the field of behavioral medicine (Belar, Deardorff, & Kelly, 1987). It began as the application of behavioral analysis and therapy to medicine, though a reading of its literature shows that its scope has been extended beyond that of strict behaviorism. As the name *behavioral medicine* implies, its primary focus is on the diagnosis and treatment of illness. Matarazzo (1982) defines **behavioral health** as a subarea of behavioral medicine that is concerned with illness prevention and health enhancement.

Behavioral medicine deals with such problems as obesity, smoking, pain, and hypertension. More recently, it has been concerned with the treatment of arthritis, diabetes, and cancer. A special issue of the *Journal of Consulting and Clinical Psychology* (1982) reviews 15 specific areas in behavioral medicine. This issue also includes general discussion articles from pioneers in the field. Some of the areas covered are obesity, chronic pain, adherence to long-term medical regimens, diabetes, cancer, type A behavior, and asthma. All these topics are covered in later chapters of this book.

Medical Psychotherapy

Medical psychotherapy is a newly defined field that applies psychology to medical treatment. Medical psychotherapists are likely to work in a medical setting as part of a collaborative health care team. They tend to use more varied methods than those who practice behavioral medicine. Medical psychotherapists come closest to the clinical psychology approach described above. Although they might be involved with prevention and wellness, their focus is on treatment.

Medical psychotherapists generally work with medical personnel in treating medical problems. These treatments might include helping patients cope with plastic surgery (Pruzinsky, 1988) or with the psychological problems of artificial insemination (Zolbrod, 1988). Patients who have diseases that respond poorly to presently known medical treatments may benefit from psychotherapy (Jones, 1989). We will discuss various treatments in later chapters.

THE PRACTICE OF HEALTH PSYCHOLOGY

As you read this chapter, we hope you begin to see that health psychology is a far-reaching discipline. It provides many points of contact between psychologists and the health care system. These points range from one-on-one therapy to political action.[2] The following descriptions should give some idea of the diverse nature of the practice of health psychology.

Therapy

Clinical and counseling psychologists are highly qualified to provide many kinds of therapy to medical patients. The most obvious treatment would be that for depression and anxiety which often result from health problems. In addition, they also provide direct treatment for such problems as essential hypertension, cholesteremia

---

[2] These points are loosely based on the social stress model developed by Dohrenwend (1978).

(high blood cholesterol), stress disorders, smoking, and eating disorders (Matarazzo, 1980).

Belar and her colleagues (1987) note that clinical health psychologists often find themselves in the role of patient advocate. They give the following example from their own experience:

We remember well the case of a 45-year-old former alcoholic who complained of back pain and was considered a hypochondriac, but who was actually suffering from a recurrence of bowel cancer. Through documentation of the nature of the complaints, the lack of evidence for psychological mechanisms to explain the symptoms and several phone calls to the attending physician persuaded him to do a more extensive workup. As a result, the patient felt more "authenticated" and, through therapy, worked out her anger at care givers as she became increasingly dependent upon them until her death. (p. 25)

Crisis Therapy

Crises are disruptive events that exceed a person's ability to cope with them. Brief therapies offered at the time of crisis may avert later problems that could be more serious. Crises, of course, are quite common in medical settings. Health psychologists can provide services to help patients and their families cope with medical procedures such as surgery, chemotherapy, organ transplants, and invasive or frightening tests. Other crisis therapies involve pain management, group therapy for chronic diseases,

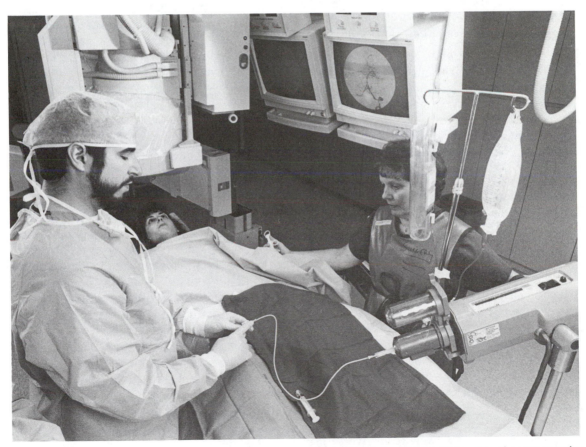

An angiogram is an example of an invasive and sometimes frightening test for which crisis therapy may be appropriate.

and increasing medical compliance (Tulkin, 1987).

Lifestyle Training

Lifestyle is a highly important factor in preventing disease and enhancing health. However, changing lifestyles is not an easy task. Psychologists can provide training that builds the personal skills that the individual needs to develop a healthy lifestyle. Such training includes stress management, biofeedback training, and time management. This training can be given in a counseling setting, but more often it is offered to groups through work, school, or community programs. The prevention program for children of alcoholics described earlier is an example of a lifestyle training program.

Community and Organizational Programs

A good way to prevent illness and promote health is through community and organizational programs. These kinds of programs allow a great number of people to be reached at a low cost. Moreover, these programs can become part of the setting and have long-term effects for its members. A good example of this practice can be seen in the rapid growth of employee wellness programs. School health programs are another example. Health psychologists can serve at this level as educators, administrators, researchers, and program evaluators (Altman & Cahn, 1987).

Public Education

We often have to change our attitudes before we can change our way of life. Attempts to change attitudes work best when they are directed at the general public. For example, this country is changing its attitude toward cigarette smoking. That change required a massive public campaign. Presently, there is a special need to target the undereducated, unemployed, and semiskilled. These people have the highest health risks and are the least likely to receive or use health information (Iscoe, 1982). Psychologists with a background in public health, commu-

nication, or organization are well qualified to intervene at this level.

Political Action

The kinds of changes mentioned above often require political action. For example, political action was used to remove cigarette advertising from television. Political action is often necessary to improve the health of the poor. Compared to other economic groups, poor people are less healthy. They do not live as long, and their infant death rate is higher. Moreover, they are more likely to eat poorly and have an increased risk for mental disorders and substance abuse (Weiner, 1982).

Psychologists can intervene at this level by conducting quality, meaningful research, but their work should not end there. To make it count, they must get the results of their research to the public and government agencies. They also act as amicus curiae (friend of the court) in cases involving public health. For example, the American Psychological Association has been very active in pushing a bill through Congress to prevent AIDS in intravenous drug users by dispensing bleach to them to clean their needles (Landers, 1990).

Research

Research is the basis for the practice of health psychology at every level. As Stone (1979) so aptly stated, "One should know before one practices or teaches" (p. 53). The professional practice of health psychology requires a "scientist-practitioner" model (Belar et al., 1987). The research methods used by psychology are very well suited to the topics of health and illness. Psychologists are well trained in research methods and statistics throughout their education. Indeed, undergraduate students are often dismayed to find that their time is spent learning statistical analysis rather than psychoanalysis.

It is obvious that knowing how to conduct quality research is a valuable skill. Although we may not be as aware of them, other related skills are also very useful. For example, literature reviews are an important part of research. It is now generally accepted that this country has left the industrial age and has entered the information age. This change has made the ability to gather, condense, and communicate information even more valuable. The ability to evaluate research results and conclusions is also a critical skill in the information age. In Chapter 3 we discuss the importance of thinking critically about health-related research.

The official recognition that seven of the ten leading causes of death are linked to behavioral factors has led to an increased demand for research in this area. The National Institutes of Health has supported studies dealing with three types of processes linking behavior and illness: (1) health-impairing habits and lifestyles, for example, smoking and lack of exercise; (2) reactions to illness by both health care providers and patients; and (3) direct alterations in tissue function through the brain's influence on hormone production or through physiological responses to psychosocial stimuli, particularly stress (Raub, 1990, p. 5). See Table 2.1 for other research topics in health psychology.

Career Opportunities

It is hard to predict what the job market will be in any profession because so many factors are involved. However, if present trends continue, there should be ample career opportunities for health psychologists in many settings, for exam-

ple, health maintenance organizations (HMOs), wellness programs, government agencies, educational institutions, hospitals/clinics, and private practice. It is predicted that the number of corporate wellness programs will continue to increase. Employers are highly motivated to reduce health care costs and costs related to absenteeism and lost productivity (Follick, Abrams, Pinto, & Fowler, 1987).

Psychologists have a lot of competition for positions in the health care system. In addition to fellow psychologists, other professional groups compete in these areas, including social workers, public health administrators, physicians, and nurses. Psychologists should be strong contenders because of their unique training. In seeking positions, public health psychologists should stress their research, administrative, and statistical skills. Those psychologists who want to provide direct services should underscore their clinical background with its strong emphasis on evaluation and treatment of patients. All psychologists should have highly developed writing, analytical, quantitative, and interpersonal skills. Today these skills are very much in demand for almost any field.

Although there may be a great many openings for health psychologists, the greatest potential may lie in the creation of new positions. These positions will be created to meet needs that have not yet been recognized or defined by employers. Sometimes the health psy-

Table 2.1 Research Topics in Health Psychology

1. Finding the psychosocial factors that impact on health and illness (Lipowski, 1986).
2. Learning about the relationship between coping styles, pain, and other health-related problems (Stone, 1987).
3. Learning the interactions between stress, cognition, and the immune system (Stone, 1987).
4. Exploring the relationship between self-treatment efforts and health risk behaviors, for example, drug abuse and overeating (Hirsch, 1988).
5. Identifying the traits of those people who overcome great problems without adverse effects to their health (Antonovsky, 1987; Kobasa, 1979).
6. Searching for effective methods to change self-destructive behaviors (Henderson, Hall, & Lipton, 1979).

chologist may develop a new area of employment rather than fill an already established position. This is certain to happen in a growing new field. See Table 2.2 for possible career areas for health psychologists.

TRAINING OF HEALTH PSYCHOLOGISTS

For health psychologists entering the field today, the issue of entry-level credentials is still being discussed. Taylor (1987) argues that a predoctoral background is enough for students who have received adequate training in their programs. However, the guidelines from the Arden House National Working Conference on Education and Training in Health Psychology in 1983 are much more demanding. Their recommendations include a required two-year postdoctoral training program for service providers in health psychology (Belar et al., 1987).

Taylor (1987) suggests that there is a certain irony in insisting on lengthy programs for future students. Because health psychology is relatively new, many health psychologists are "converts" from other areas of psychology. As Taylor notes, "We educated ourselves through whatever haphazard and piecemeal methods were available to us and if our track record to date is any indication, we have done a fine job of it" (p. 82).

Course Work

Although total agreement regarding the training of health psychologists does not exist, there is a general consensus that they must first have a solid foundation in psychology. In addition, they must understand the roles, values, and terminology of the other health-related disciplines (Altman & Cahn, 1987; Miller, 1987). Still others recommend that health psychologists have a background in epidemiology in order to understand the research. They suggest that if psychologists are going to design programs to change habits, they need to know which habits need changing and in whom (Miller, Fowler, & Bridgers, 1982). For more complete details about health psychology programs, see Stone et al. (1987).

Public Health Psychology

A growing number of programs are available in **public health psychology** for those who want to work in community or organizational settings. The public health psychology program at the University of Hawaii is a good example. It includes courses in psychology, public health, and business administration (DeLeon & Pallack, 1982). Psychologists can acquire the training needed for public health psychology through course work in graduate public health programs. For example, a Ph.D. in psychology can be combined with a master's in public health (MPH) (Matthews & Avis, 1982).

Public health psychologists focus on communities rather than individuals and on prevention rather than cure. Their knowledge of public health gives them a broad outlook on health issues and an awareness of important health problems (Matthews and Avis, 1982). Their research, evaluation, management, and organizational skills can be utilized in either the

Table 2.2   Career Areas in Health Psychology

Rehabilitation psychology
Biofeedback training
Corporate consulting
Community programs
Grant programs
Private practice
Medical school faculty
Health maintenance organizations
Employee assistance programs
Research programs
Wellness programs
Higher education
Hospital patient assistance programs

public or private sector (Altman & Cahn, 1987). Community psychologists and public health psychologists have similar training.

The Bottom Line

Training programs for health psychologists are as diverse as the career opportunities in this fast growing field. There is general agreement that education in health psychology requires a solid basis in psychology and knowledge of the health care system. In addition, Miller (1987) presents a convincing case for preparing health psychologists for a "lifetime of continuous, autonomous learning" (p. 9). An important part of this preparation is learning to judge the quality of research. (We address this issue in Chapter 3.) Because the body of knowledge is growing so rapidly, we must be prepared to learn throughout our careers.

Conclusions

By now it should be clear that health psychology is important and that it has a great deal to offer to the health care system. This is true not only for treatment of disease, but for disease prevention and health promotion as well. The causes of illness and death have changed during this century. The great epidemics of infectious diseases of the past have been replaced by diseases in which lifestyles or behaviors play an important role.

There is a growing consensus that changing health-related behaviors will have an even greater effect on the general health of the American public than medical technology (DeLeon & Pallack, 1982). Because these behaviors are so important to present-day health problems, we need to know as much as we can about how to make positive changes in these behaviors. No other discipline is better able than psychology to provide that knowledge. As Matarazzo (1982) notes, "Psychology is a discipline

with 100 years of experience in the study of individual behavior, including behavior change" (p. 1).

We believe that health psychology has great potential. Changes in the health care system and the growing acceptance of the roles of psychological and social factors in health have opened many doors for health psychology. Psychologists are finding that they are being accepted as members of the health care team (Millon, 1982). It is also expected that appointments of psychologists to medical school faculties will increase as health psychology gains acceptance (Miller, Fowler, & Bridgers, 1982).

Clinical health psychology will likely be the most common specialization in our field. However, public health psychology has the potential to be especially strong in health promotion. Changing behaviors to prevent illness and improve public health is commonly more cost-effective than technological cures (Miller, Fowler, & Bridgers, 1982). The best solutions to the practical problems of medicine and public health will come from the team efforts of related disciplines. The psychologist is an important member of that team (Hamburg, Elliott, & Parron, 1982).

Although the outlook for health psychology is bright, it cannot reach its full potential until the medical community accepts the importance of psychology to its field. Many still resist efforts to link biological and psychosocial phenomena. For example, it is very difficult for health psychologists to have their papers published in medical journals (Engel, 1977; Taylor, 1987). This problem is reflected in the following statement made by David McClelland (1985):

> I have found it very difficult to get scientific papers containing motivational variables published in medical journals because the reviewers have never heard of the variables, do not believe they could be objectively measured, or simply find it impossible to believe that they could be objectively measured, or simply find it impossible to believe that they could affect physiological processes. (p. 466)

Summary

1. The challenge to the biomedical model has created opportunities for psychologists to apply their considerable knowledge and skills to health-related topics.

2. Health psychology is defined as the systematic application of psychology to the relevant areas of health, disease, and the health care system. It is one of the fastest growing fields in psychology today.

3. The scope of health psychology is very broad because many of the theories and methods of psychology can be applied to health-related topics. Health psychology can be applied at any stage of the wellness continuum. The wellness movement is closely related to the emergence of health psychology.

4. Health psychology is not limited to the mind-over-body approach. Many other health-related areas can benefit from the application of psychology, for example, improving physician/patient communications and helping health care providers cope with the stresses of their careers.

5. Health psychology has been greatly influenced by the behavioral and cognitive-behavioral approaches. Classical and operant conditioning have played an important role in understanding various health-related behaviors, ranging from immune system functioning to such risk factors as smoking and overeating. Changing thoughts and images is often a central part of treating disorders, such as obesity and headaches.

6. Psychophysiology is important to health psychology because it reveals the relationship between health-related physical reactions and psychological events. Biofeedback is an example of applied psychophysiology. Biofeedback equipment provides trainees information about their biological processes, which allows them to become aware of the physical and psychological states that allow them to make desired changes.

7. Clinical psychologists are trained to evaluate and treat psychological problems; their skills find important application in the health care field. Clinical neuropsychology is perhaps the most established use of clinical psychology in the health care system.

8. Health psychology has been greatly influenced by general systems theory, community psychology, and the family systems approach. General systems theory emphasizes the fact that an intervention at one level of a system can often have unexpected effects at other levels. Community psychology shares with health psychology an emphasis on systems theory, prevention, and enhancement of well-being and competency. The family systems approach has influenced health psychology through its focus on understanding the relationship between family systems and pathology.

9. The existential-phenomenological and holistic approaches are influential at the farther reaches of health psychology. The existential-phenomenological approach is more popular in Europe than in the United States and sees physical symptoms as a medium for expressing our frustrated humanness. The holistic approach is also concerned with our frustrated expression and fulfillment of our essential humanness. It takes a serious attitude toward the impact of psychosocial factors on health. The holistic approach is unique among the various approaches because it includes spirituality.

10. Health psychology has a broader focus than traditional medicine. The great strength of medicine is in dealing with the physically ill. Medicine could profit

by including psychological insights and practices into the system. Behavioral medicine deals with maladaptive behaviors, pain, and health enhancement. Behavioral health is concerned with illness prevention and various diseases. Medical psychotherapy applies psychology to medical treatment. Medical psychologists tend to come closest to the clinical psychology approach described earlier.

11. There are many points of contact between psychology and the health care system. These points range from one-on-one therapy to political action, and include crisis intervention, lifestyle training, community and organizational program development, public education, and research. If the present trend continues, there should be ample career opportunities for health psychologists in health-related settings.

12. The issue of entry-level credentials is still under discussion. There is a general con-

sensus, however, that health psychologists must have a solid foundation in psychology and understand the roles, values, and vocabulary of other health-related disciplines. There are a growing number of programs in public health psychology for those who want to work in community or organizational settings. These programs include courses in psychology, public health, and business administration.

13. Health psychology is an important discipline that has a great deal to offer to the health care system. There is a growing consensus that changing health-related behaviors will have greater impact on health than medical technology. No other discipline has a greater knowledge base than psychology in the study of human behavior. The best solutions to the crisis in the health care system will come from the combined efforts of related disciplines. The psychologist is an important member of that team.

Key Terms

Behavioral approach
Behavioral health
Behavioral medicine
Biofeedback
Classical conditioning
Clinical neuropsychology
Clinical psychology approach
Cognitive-behavioral approach
Community psychology approach
Existential-phenomenological approach
Family systems approach
General systems theory approach
Health psychology
Holistic approach
Medical psychotherapy

Operant conditioning
Psychophysiological approach
Psychophysiology
Public health psychology

Discussion Questions

1. Define health psychology and describe the breadth of its scope.
2. What is the place of the concept of "mind-over-body" in health psychology?
3. List and briefly describe the major approaches to health psychology.
4. What is the relationship of health psychology to medicine?
5. Briefly explain the relationship of health psychology to behavioral medicine and behavioral health, and medical psychotherapy.

6. Explain the role of psychotherapy and behavioral therapy in health psychology.
7. What is the role of psychologists in efforts to change lifestyles?
8. Explain how community-oriented psychologists play a role in health-related organizational change, public education, and political action.
9. What is the role of research in health psychology?
10. What kind of career opportunities are available for health psychologists? What application of health psychology interests you?
11. Describe the basic education that is necessary for health psychologists.
12. What do you think the future of health psychology will be and what is the basis for your opinion? What obstacles do you think health psychology faces?

Chapter 3

Thinking Critically About Health-Related Research

*J*ane was an attractive woman in her late twenties who was interested in "New Age" concepts. She knew a lot about astrology and did Tarot readings. She also was fascinated by spiritual methods of healing. While getting her B.A. in psychology, she took courses in health psychology. She thought it was too rigid, especially about research methodology. However, it was the closest thing at the university she could find to her real interests.

One day Jane noticed a very small lump in her right breast. She was surprised at how frightened she felt. But she knew that many women have lumps in their breasts that are not malignant, so she put it out of her mind. Later, at a scheduled appointment with her physician, she mentioned the lump. What happened after that seemed like a blur; she was soon diagnosed as having breast cancer.

Surgical removal of the cancer was recommended, with a followup course of chemotherapy. At first Jane agreed to the surgery, but she soon began to doubt her decision. She sought out an alternative treatment program that focused on use of imagery and changing attitudes. Her physician became increasingly upset as she began to drift in this direction. One day, he burst into an angry attack on her. Jane was furious. How could he be so vicious to her at a time like this? She decided to stop seeing him, and, after much soul-searching, she decided to forgo the surgery and limit herself to spiritual and psychological treatment methods.

Many students of health psychology are drawn to the field because of their interest in alternative methods of treatment. So there may be some readers who feel that Jane made the right decision. Be sure to notice that her decision was not to *support* her medical treatment with spiritual and psychological methods, but to *forgo* medical treatment and use the alternative methods instead. That is a much riskier thing to do. We surely all agree that a decision this important should have been based on realistic evidence. If the evidence on which she based her decision was flawed, it could cost Jane her very life.

THE COSTS OF FAULTY RESEARCH

Since health-related decisions are very important, an ability to tell the difference between good and bad information is critical. Sometimes claims about what influences health are based on evidence that is so informal that it cannot be dignified with the name "research." At other times health claims are based on work that has all the trappings of scientific research but is defective in some crucial way. People often make the mistake of viewing any report done within a scientific framework as if it were valid. In fact, even a single serious flaw can ruin an otherwise elegant "scientific" finding. Failure to evaluate health claims can be very costly in both personal and monetary terms.

Economic Costs of Faulty Research

Entire industries can be based on claims about what makes us healthy or ill. For example, concerns about obesity have given rise to the multi-million dollar weight loss industry. It is estimated that in 1989 Americans spent more than $30 billion on diet-related products and commercial weight-loss programs. The safety of these programs has been questioned, and their success rate for long-range loss maintenance is dismal (Johnson, 1990). We discuss some of these programs, including the popular "liquid diets" in Chapter 8. The point is that these programs and weight-loss gimmicks are often based on unsound research. The people who market these programs may either be unaware of, or ignore, valid research. The result is that people often risk their health and waste their money on ineffective, and sometimes dangerous, programs.

The "Cry Wolf" Effect

Faulty research also creates a "boy who cried wolf" effect. In other words, it keeps people from taking action to preserve their health. Many of us feel overwhelmed by the warnings we get about the foods we eat and the various pollutant chemicals in foods, cosmetics, or the air. Too often, the advice we get one day is contradicted a short time later. Many people end up taking

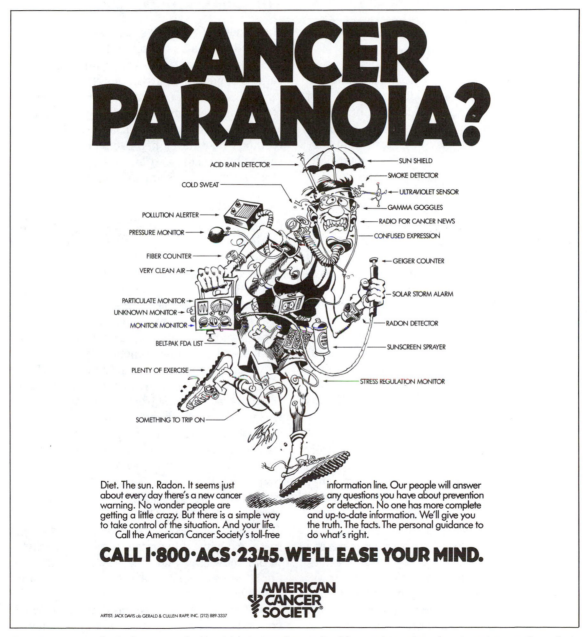

Sometimes people feel so overwhelmed by contradictory health warnings that they just ignore the advice altogether.

the attitude that it is best just to ignore the advice. Such people say things like "everything makes you sick" or "everything seems to cause cancer so you might as well enjoy life." But buried in the warnings are crucial facts that need to be taken seriously, and consumers must learn to evaluate the quality of the research that affects their lives.

THE DIFFICULTY OF EVALUATING RESEARCH

Unfortunately, most people do not know how to judge the "goodness" of evidence. It takes a lot of training and skill to do a good job of judging research. Even people who have training in scientific methodology may not apply what they have learned. Once they answer the questions on their examinations and pass the courses, they may not apply those skills.

Part of the problem is the tedious nature of extracting solid evidence from nature. Since we are human, we want the answers *now* and *painlessly*, but it takes a great deal of hard work and self-discipline to obtain reliable and valid information. It is much easier to follow the advice of a dynamic speaker, a persuasive writer, or even just a group of friends with strong opinions. But can we afford to go along with our heartfelt or our common-sense reaction to such sources? Can our spontaneous strategies for getting the truth be trusted?

Psychologists have studied many of the natural strategies people use in making judgments. For example, psychology has learned a lot about the rules people follow when they subjectively judge the likelihood of something. These rules are handy and work much of the time, but they also lead us astray because they fail to take important factors into account.

For example, we judge the likelihood of something on the basis of how readily we can imagine it. Since we can easily imagine things we have often experienced, this approach will work for us much of the time. On the other hand, we can also readily imagine things that are especially *vivid* or that we have often seen portrayed on television. When a handsome actor like Rock

Hudson is shown on television looking emaciated and ravaged by AIDS, we tend to think that *we* are more likely to get AIDS. Prior to seeing that image, we might have judged the likelihood to be much lower.

THE SCIENTIFIC METHOD

These natural strategies can lead us to make very bad estimates of probabilities. We discuss these flaws in human reasoning and their implications at greater length in Chapter 6. The point for now is that our natural ways of making judgments can lead us astray unless they are used within the discipline of special methods. These methods were developed over centuries of history as humankind became aware of the defects in its ways of processing information.

In the Beginning

It took hundreds of years to develop a firm method for gaining objective knowledge of the world. When scientists talk about "objective knowledge," they mean the kind to which any competent person can agree. It is also knowledge that can be clearly demonstrated by repeating the procedures. Scientific data must be capable of being reproduced, both by the original researchers and by others.

In order to reach the firm level of knowledge that is typical of science, factors must be identified that actually control whether or not something happens. Such factors are called the **controlling variables**. For example, if physicists want to know how much one physical body attracts another, they measure the mass of the bodies and their distance apart. These variables control the strength of attraction. Isaac Newton identified them long ago.

It was not easy for humankind to discover methods that would permit this kind of accuracy in our knowledge and they are often difficult to apply. We appear to have a strong resistance against really using them, and we repeatedly slip away from them. We assume that we know the controlling variables without actually using the methods needed to identify them.

The Marriage of Reason and Observation

The ancient Greeks took a key step toward devising an adequate methodology when they saw the importance of reason. They recognized the value of reason, and they also knew that it must be systematized. They developed clear definitions, identified basic assumptions, and polished the processes of correct inference from those basic assumptions. Euclid's (c. 300 B.C.) closely reasoned system of geometry is a good example of the high levels the Greeks attained in systematizing reasoning.

The ancient Greeks also recognized a great difference between *seeming* and *being*. They were very aware of perceptual illusions. For example, a stick partially immersed in water appears to bend at the water's surface. They knew that to get to the truth we cannot rely on the way things seem. We would do well to keep this principle in mind when we make judgments about factors that affect health. Too often we treat a mere impression that something improves our health as an established fact.

To some degree the Greeks joined their systematic reasoning with direct observation. For example, Archimedes (287?–212 B.C.) developed a science of mechanics and designed useful machinery based on that science. But the Greeks did not emphasize this marriage of reasoning and observing nearly enough; this emphasis came much later.

During the Renaissance, Galileo (1564–1642) came very close to embracing the full method. He combined mathematical reasoning with measured observations of the physical world. For example, to learn about the laws of acceleration, he dropped balls off the leaning tower of Pisa and measured their rate of falling. Yet Galileo sometimes slighted observation when he felt that his rational demonstrations were compelling.

Another significant step toward the marriage of reasoning and observation was taken by Francis Bacon (1561–1626). Observation was extremely important to Bacon. For example, when asked where his books were, he pointed to some animals in a cage and said, "These are my books." Yet even he did not fully appreciate the importance of observation and measurement. He tended to mix careful observation with mere hearsay.

It was Isaac Newton (1642–1727) who fully combined systematic reasoning and meticulous observation. He made his discoveries in the eighteenth century, over 2000 years after the Greeks started the long process of learning how to understand the world. With Newton the scientific method reached its full development. According to Newton, the scientist reasons carefully and systematically and, if possible, mathematically. But this is not enough: careful reasoning must always be tested through observation and measurement.

All of us share the tendency to become impatient and to skip necessary steps. Although we believe that casual or intuitive knowledge can give us a realistic assessment of the world, a great deal of evidence shows that such an approach will leave us to stagnate in flawed knowledge.

DISCOVERY VERSUS VERIFICATION

Our purpose in tracing the history of scientific method is to show that: (1) it is a basic way to gain real knowledge about the world, and (2) we all tend to slip into thinking we can know about the world without conducting a rigorous check of findings. By these statements we do not want to imply that the more speculative facets of health psychology have no valid place. On the contrary, we believe that it is wise to use the best method available to solve a given problem.

At times we must, at least temporarily, settle for less than full scientific rigor. For example, if you are in the midst of a heart attack and have to decide whether to try an experimental drug your doctors recommend, you have to go with the evidence you have and decide *now*.

There are even times when we can be downright wild in our speculations—as long as we see the limitations of our knowledge at any given stage. Creative ideas often come from an unruly part of our being. However, it is a big mistake to think we have verified something when we have not. We have to discriminate between intuitions and wild ideas versus verified parts of our knowledge.

Differences Between Discovery and Verification

The **process of discovery** and the **process of verification** differ. The scientific method, which emphasizes verification, is an elaborate procedure for checking our ideas about the world. Necessarily, it emphasizes ferreting out errors. The discovery mode is quite different. In that mode, we are searching for a subtle answer, something that has escaped notice, or a new angle on a problem. When using this method, we have to emphasize sensitivity to the subtle and creative openness to the unfamiliar. Since we want to detect something that has previously been missed, we brainstorm and lay aside criticism. If we focus strongly on avoidance of errors at this stage, we may set our standards of evidence so high that the needed clue escapes us.

There is nothing wrong with operating in the discovery mode. Many of science's most valued discoveries were made in this uncritical manner. This mode is especially important in a new field like health psychology where we have to be especially open to unexpected facts and unfamiliar theories. Health psychology is, after all, challenging the dominant paradigm. It is unwise to hastily reject all data that have not been completely verified. The attitude we should take is, "That's interesting. Let's see if we can verify it."

Sources of Discovery

Much of the drive for developing the new field of health psychology comes from ideas that are still much closer to the discovery mode than to the stage of full verification. For example, Bernie Siegel, the well-known surgeon and cancer specialist has given us many promising research leads. Among these leads are his notion that certain attitudes create "exceptional patients" who are sometimes able to rid themselves of cancer. His ideas are interesting hunches and invitations to experiment, not established facts. For instance, it is not a *fact* that he can identify exceptional patients by merely asking, "Who would like to live to be 100 years old?" and noting members of the audience who put up their hand *immediately*.

Similarly, it is not a "fact" that Norman Cousins, author of *An Anatomy of an Illness*, cured himself of an "incurable" collagen disease through laughter. Even a little investigation reveals that the story, as often told, is not quite accurate. The disease was not as incurable as most accounts of this case suggested. In fact, spontaneous remissions from this disease are not unusual. Nor did Cousins rely simply on humor to cure it. For example, he also used megavitamin therapy. It would be a serious mistake to decide on the basis of Cousins' story that we can cure otherwise incurable diseases by laughing a lot. But there are many promising leads here, and we can pursue them systematically. (Indeed, there *is* some pretty good evidence that humor is healthy; see, e.g., Vaillant, 1977).

Discoveries can come from almost any source, including those that are intuitive and unscientific. In fact, quite a bit of evidence exists that great discoveries in science and mathematics tend to come from intuitive sources. Descartes is regarded as a key figure in the development of the scientific-mechanistic world view, yet his method was "given" to him by a character who came to him in a dream. Similarly, the discovery of the ring molecule played a key role in the development of organic chemistry and came to Kekulé (1829–1896) in a dreamlike state, not simply through systematic reasoning (Selye, 1964).

Some of the impetus for health psychology has come from scientists who decided to test some of the claims of Eastern mystics. For example, Benson (1975) took physiological measures of changes that occur during meditation and discovered the importance of what has come to be called the relaxation response. Benson (1984) went on to study the claim that Tibetan practitioners of *tumo* (the yoga of the psychic heat) can voluntarily raise their body temperature. He was able to verify that claim with careful measurements.

Elmer Green and his associates at the Menninger Foundation developed the Voluntary Controls Project to study the ability of these unusual people to exert mental control over their physiological functions. They found that a yogi called Swami Rama could indeed stop his heart from pumping and change the temperature of specific spots on his skin (Boyd, 1976; Green & Green, 1977).

Many more such examples could be given. It seems clear that, at the stage of discovery, we should be very permissive about our sources of information. Findings from tests of mystical claims can sometimes be applied to clinical problems. For example, voluntary control of temperature seems to be useful in dealing with a range of problems, including circulatory disturbances, high blood pressure, and headaches.

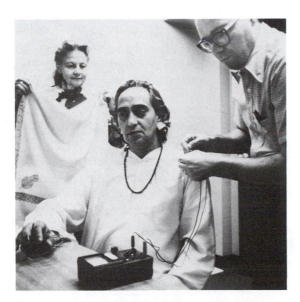

Researchers from the Voluntary Control Program at the Menninger Foundation found that yogi Swami Rama could exert mental control over his physiological functions.

Details of these applications are presented later in this volume (e.g., see Chapters 10 and 11).

Confusing Discovery with Verification

A major problem develops when we *confuse* findings obtained in the discovery mode with findings established in the verification mode. The scientists mentioned above would be no more than wild-eyed visionaries if they had not gone on to verify their ideas through careful measurement and controlled research. Even Bernie Siegel (1989) and Norman Cousins (1989) have tried to compile systematic evidence to support their views, thus implicitly acknowledging the need for verification. In the excitement of the discovery process, it is easy to forget the importance of verification. Yet we have historical evidence that thorough verification is essential if we are not to be misled and even do harm.

Bloodletting is a good example. The use of bloodletting as a cure was generally accepted for perhaps 2000 years. Physicians used this method as a treatment during the great bubonic plague that swept Europe in the sixteenth century. They were actually bleeding people to death because they had an exaggerated notion of the amount of blood in the human body. We should consider the possibility that we *might* be doing something similar when we come up with psychologically oriented "alternative cures" for diseases such as cancer.

The physicians who used bloodletting were no less astute than we are today. Yet they used a harmful treatment without noticing its negative effects. (Let's remember the account of George Washington's death from Chapter 1.) Controlled experiments on bloodletting had to be conducted before it could be seen that it did more harm than good.

We cannot rely on ordinary observation. Remember, a crucial step in developing an adequate methodology occurred when the Greeks saw that ordinary levels of observation can be illusory and that common sense is inadequate. It would be foolish to forget the great methodological discoveries of the past as we develop the new discipline of health psychology.

THE EXPERIMENTAL METHOD

Verification requires the full use of scientific methodology, which means we have to do experiments. Experiments allow us to isolate the influence of one variable, called the **independent variable** (IV), on a second variable, called the **dependent variable** (DV). With the **experimental method**, we manipulate the IV while holding the effects of other variables constant. That way we can tell that the independent variable really produced the outcome (see Figure 3.1).

Experiments allow us to show that the controlled variables are not responsible for the outcome. Every control group or control condition is designed to help us gain confidence that other variables did not produce the observed changes in the dependent variable (see Figure 3.2).

When issues of health are at stake, we seldom have the power to manipulate and control variables. For example, suppose we want to manipulate the IV, "presence or absence of Type A behavior." We cannot select a random group of people and get them to be Type A. Or suppose we want to study the IV "smokes versus does not

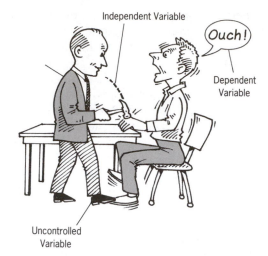

Figure 3.2   Relationship of independent, dependent, and uncontrolled variables. The experimenter deliberately manipulates the independent variable and indirectly produces a change in the subject's behavior. If an uncontrolled variable is inadvertently introduced, there is no way to tell whether the independent variable or the uncontrolled variable produced the behavioral change. *Source*: Figure 1.3 from *Methods in Experimental Psychology* by Charles L. Sheridan, copyright © 1979 by Holt, Rinehart and Winston, Inc., reprinted by permission of the publisher.

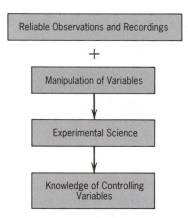

Figure 3.1   Experimental science combines reliable observation with manipulation of variables. It yields knowledge of controlling variables. *Source*: Figure 1.2 from *Methods in Experimental Psychology* by Charles L. Sheridan, copyright © 1979 by Holt, Rinehart and Winston, Inc., reprinted by permission of the publisher.

smoke." We cannot randomly select people to smoke three packs of cigarettes a day. Nor can we randomly select people to live a highly stressed lifestyle if we want to study "degree of stress" as an IV. Practical and ethical considerations force us to settle for a level of evidence that falls short of the ideal.

One fundamental principle that we must follow, however, is to *avoid acting as if we have verified our hypotheses, data, and theories more than we actually have*. If true experiments have not been done, we can be assured that uncontrolled variables might be responsible for the results. To verify our hypotheses, we must be able to reject other interpretations of the data. For example, when we think that a given independent variable, such as Type A behavior, is related to coronary disease (dependent variable), we must show that the relationship exists. But we must also show that other explanations for their relationship are implausible. We have to show that the results are not due to chance or to such factors as habits, like smoking, drinking, or eating unhealthy foods, that might accompany Type A behavior.

The Null Hypothesis

Whenever we conduct a study, we always have to consider the possibility that our results happened by chance. Just as people sometimes win a lottery or get four aces in a poker game, a researcher might just happen to get an exciting result by dumb luck. We have well-established ways to become confident that this did not happen in a given study.

We call this possibility that results happened by chance the **null hypothesis**. Statistical analysis can tell us whether or not our results can reasonably be interpreted as due to mere chance. If the analysis says this is highly unlikely, we can *reject the null hypothesis*. That is what tests of statistical significance are all about. When you hear it said that a research finding is significant at the ".05 level," it means that there are just 5 chances out of 100 (or 1 in 20) that the finding would happen by mere coincidence. If it was due to coincidence, it would imply that the independent variable we thought produced the effects only *appeared* to do so. Chance factors really produced them. Until we reject the null hypothesis, we cannot correctly say that the variable we are testing really works.

But the possibility that our results occurred by chance is only one of the explanations we have to refute. When we talk about "chance," we generally mean lots of small independent factors that just happen to act in concert to produce an effect. But bigger, more noticeable variables might also coincide with our independent variable. By calling on our experience and brainstorming, we can think of other variables that require controls. For example, could it be that the real cause of the relationship between Type A behavior and coronary disease is that Type A people also smoke, drink, or eat more? Or perhaps they alienate people, and social supports might be the key to a healthy heart. All these possibilities must be investigated before we can conclude that Type A behavior influences heart disease. Not all of them can be checked in a single experiment, but over many studies, they must be checked. (Type A behavior is discussed in detail in Chapter 11).

Treating Speculations as Verified Principles

People often treat mere hypotheses or speculations as if they were verified principles. We might think that only a very naive person would make such a basic error, yet even sophisticated investigators can fall into this trap. For example, Kobasa (1982) developed the hypothesis that a characteristic she calls "hardiness" acts as a protective buffer against stressful life experiences. She arranged an experiment to test this hypothesis and was able to provide substantial verification for it. The subjects in her study were army officers. Later, she attempted to repeat the study using a different group of subjects, who happened to be lawyers. Hardiness did not prove to have a significant effect in this new group.

Kobasa speculated that there was a difference in reaction to hardiness between army officers and lawyers. This is a perfectly legitimate speculation, but keep in mind that it is *merely* an hypothesis. It cannot be regarded as verified until it is shown in a substantial and representative sample of army officers and lawyers. Although this has not yet been done, in the literature it is sometimes treated as an established fact (see, e.g., McClelland, 1985, p. 456).

Even if we had clearly shown differences in the effects of hardiness on army officers versus lawyers, we *still* would not know which differences between them were the controlling influences. We would have to consider the many differences between these two groups and speculate about the controlling factors. We would then have to submit our speculations to systematic testing. In so doing, we would make the transition from the discovery mode to the verification mode. We would also learn a lot about what determines health.

The above discussion makes clear the importance of scientific method as well as the importance of the discovery mode. It is most crucial, however, to recognize the difference between the discovery stage and the verification stage. We must not substitute the excitement of discovery for the painstaking process of verification. In addition, we have to be able to recognize adequate verification and distinguish it from verification that falls short of acceptable standards.

COMMON PITFALLS IN HEALTH RESEARCH

Presumably some of you have already taken a course in research methodology, but others have not. We cannot really teach you methodology in a short chapter if you are unfamiliar with it. But we can point to some of the common pitfalls to watch for as you read research in health psychology and in other fields. Even people who know a lot about research often fall into one of these pits. (We've fallen into some of them ourselves.) We will give examples from some of the most prestigious edited journals. So whether you are learning about these pitfalls for the first time or are merely being reminded of them, the warnings should help you become a more critical reader of health literature.

Conclusions Based on Testimonials, Opinion, or Authority

Testimonials are statements given by individuals about how a certain treatment or variable influenced them. It is very tempting to accept them especially if they come from someone we love or respect. You should regard testimonials with a grain of salt, however, because they can be wrong even when the person giving them is sincere (see Box 3.1). This caution applies even if the person doing the testifying has strong scientific or medical credentials.

Early in their search for the best way to "know" things, researchers learned that statements based on the testimonials and opinions of other people, including authorities, must not

be accepted without investigation. Reliable methods demand that statements of "fact" *must* be testable by others and cannot be based merely on another person's authority. Next, we will discuss some of the main problems associated with testimonials.

Those who offer testimonials may select the best cases for presentation, ignoring the failures. In addition, testimonials are *verbal reports*. What people say is often markedly different from what actually happened. Direct measures are needed of what happened rather than of what people *said* took place. Testimonials, like other verbal reports, "are often poor reflectors of nonverbal reality" (Sheridan, 1979, p. 90).

Testimonials usually lack control procedures that could tell us whether some other variable might have produced the effect. For example, many disorders go away spontaneously. If the treatment is given at the right time, the patient may show immediate relief, even though the treatment had no effect.

To illustrate a contemporary case of the use of opinion and authority to back up a health claim, let us take an example from a book by Cousins (1989). He has been an eloquent spokesperson for the view that psychosocial factors are an important influence on health. When his point of view came, predictably, under severe attack from biomedicine, one of his responses was to send out a "national survey of cancer specialists."

He asked them to report their *opinions* on the importance of various psychosocial factors that might influence cancer. Cousins states that "Those views were based on their treatment of more than 100,000 cancer patients." The 649 responding doctors came out very strongly in support of the idea that psychosocial factors are important. For example, 79 percent felt that a strong will to live was important, 75 percent agreed that family support was important, and 68 percent affirmed the value of the patient's hopefulness.

This is interesting information for health psychologists because it indicates that medical doctors might take their work seriously (al-

---

Box 3.1   Darwin's Case of Faulty Testimony

Darwin provides a quaint illustration of the unreliability of testimony (1898; reprinted in Sheridan, 1976). Darwin begins by pointing out how his "first-formed" hypothesis nearly always had to be changed once he made direct observations and that this led him to be quite skeptical of reasoning that had not been checked by observation.

He then tells of "the oddest case which I have known" of faulty testimonial. A botanist wrote him saying that the common field bean in eastern England had "this year everywhere grown on the wrong side of the pod." Since Darwin had no idea what the "right" side of the pod might be, he wrote back for more information. But before he got an answer, he noticed that two different newspapers had pointed out the remarkable fact that "the beans this year had all grown on the wrong side."

Darwin then went to his gardener, who came from eastern England, and asked him whether he had heard anything about it. The gardener replied "Oh, no, sir, it must be a mistake, for the beans grow on the wrong side only on leap-year, and this is not a leap-year." Darwin asked how they grow in common years and in leap years, respectively, only to find that the gardener "knew absolutely nothing of how they grew at any time, but he stuck to his belief."

Eventually the botanist wrote back full of apologies, since his original statement had been based on the testimony of several farmers, who, when pressed, had no idea what "growing on the wrong side" meant. Darwin concludes: "here a belief—if indeed a statement with no definite idea attached to it can be called a belief—had spread over almost the whole of England without any vestige of evidence."

This tells us a lot about the reliability of testimonials. Many of you may feel that in modern times we would not make such a silly error, but there is no reason to believe we humans have changed that much in the last 90-odd years. Many people are making judgments about factors that influence health on the basis of evidence no better than that of the botanist.

---

though one wonders about the representativeness of the sample of physicians). Unfortunately, these results tell us about the opinions of the physicians, not about the causes of cancer. The influence of psychosocial factors on cancer can be determined only by measurement and experiment. Authoritative opinion will not permit firm conclusions to be drawn about it. But it is the basis for hypotheses that can be tested systematically.

Studies Concluding That Variables Have No Effect

We said earlier that researchers have to reject the null hypothesis. They have to give convincing evidence that their results did not occur by mere chance. Standard methodology is well equipped to show us how to reject the null hypothesis. But it is not at all well equipped to let us *accept* the null hypothesis. The best we can say is that we *failed to reject* the null. You should be cautious about studies that say a given variable did not have an effect, and you should view them with skepticism.

Most studies in health psychology will show that a given independent variable (IV) had an effect on a specified dependent variable (DV). For example, a study might show that people high in Type A behavior are more prone to heart attacks than people low in Type A behavior. This indicates that the IV "degree of Type A behavior" predicts the DV "frequency of heart attacks."

Similarly, a study demonstrating that people who felt distant from their parents as they were growing up tend to be less healthy later in life would be showing a relationship between the IV "degree of avowed closeness to the parents" and the DV "level of health later in life." Both types of study provide evidence that the variables are related. This is quite normal in research.

But it is different when a study purports to show that one variable does *not* have an effect on another. It is easy to see why these studies are questionable. Those of you who have taken a chemistry course know how often students fail to verify the basic laws because they did not perform the standard experiments correctly. We certainly do not want to change the laws of chemistry on that basis! There are limitless ways to muddle results and fail to detect an influence that is actually there.

Failure to detect the effects of a potent IV are not necessarily due to carelessness. This can happen to even the most skilled and careful researcher. A good example comes from the history of electromagnetics. For a long time physicists were sure that electricity and magnetism were not related. They missed this relationship because they assumed that the magnetic field would be parallel to the electric current. In fact, it is at right angles to the current. The relationship was finally discovered when someone accidentally rearranged the apparatus. Some of the greatest physicists of all time overlooked the simple variation of method that would one day bring to light the entire field of electromag-

netism. Present-day health researchers are no more adept than were these physicists.

When we fail to detect a relationship between variables, it may mean there is no relationship. Or it may mean that we are not looking at the right facet of the variables of interest. It may also indicate that we have inadvertently introduced confusion into the measurements in some other way. Thus, we must be cautious in evaluating studies that say there is *no* relationship between two sets of variables.

A good example of a health-related study that did not find the influence of one variable on another was published in a leading medical journal (Cassileth, Lusk, Miller, Brown, & Miller, 1985). These researchers found no relationship between a number of psychosocial factors and survival of cancer. They asked 359 patients diagnosed as having advanced cancers to fill out a self-report questionnaire measuring their status on seven variables identified by previous research as important to cancer outcome. The variables were: (1) social ties and marital history, (2) job satisfaction, (3) use of psychotropic drugs, (4) general satisfaction with life, (5) general health before getting cancer, (6) hopelessness-helplessness, and (7) adjustment to diagnosis. No relationship was found between any of these variables, or the total score, and survival of the cancer.

This kind of finding should not be given as much weight as one that showed a relationship between psychosocial factors and cancer. It should be carefully examined for factors that might influence the results. For example, the measures of psychosocial factors in this study were based on self-reports of past events. These tend to be inaccurate (Sheridan, 1976).

Another problem was that the sample of patients is, of course, not representative of people in general or even of cancer patients in general. They were *advanced* cancer patients. Cassileth et al. (1985) were aware of this limitation and curtailed their conclusions accordingly. The limited conclusion was well put in a later statement made jointly by Cassileth and Cousins (quoted in Cousins, 1989): "in advanced cancer, biology overwhelms psychology." Even this conclusion is too strong for a study that failed to detect a relationship between variables. In general, studies of this kind should lead you to *hold your judgment and be cautious*. It should not be concluded that the independent variables had no effect.

Another relevant study (Swain et al., 1990) created quite a stir in the media because it concluded that eating oat bran did *not* lower serum cholesterol levels. A major marketing effort involving oat bran products had been launched based on previous research. The earlier work had indicated that oat bran in the diet lowered cholesterol levels.

In the study by Swain and colleagues (1990), measures of serum cholesterol were taken on 20 people during a one-week baseline in which they continued their usual diet. After a two-week break, roughly half were given oat bran supplements, while the remainder of participants got a low-fiber wheat product. An attempt was made to keep participants from being able to tell which supplement had the oats. However, this did not work, since almost all subjects accurately guessed when they were getting oat bran.

In a second phase of the study, those who had gotten oat bran were shifted to the wheat product and those who had originally been given the wheat product were shifted to the oat bran. So by the end of the study each subject had been through the "treatment" condition (oat bran) as well as through the control condition (low-fiber wheat). Thus, each person served as his or her own control. When control subjects are shifted to the treatment and treated subjects are shifted to the control condition, the experimental design is called a crossover design.

When comparisons were made of serum cholesterol levels, there were no statistically significant differences between the oat bran and control conditions. So the oat bran variable seemed to have no effect. The investigators concluded that "oat bran has little inherent cholesterol-lowering action in persons with normal serum cholesterol levels" (Swain et al., 1990, p. 152). This obviously is too strong a conclusion to

draw from such a study. The only clear conclusion from this study could be that their data did not support a relationship between oat bran and lowered cholesterol levels.

When we use such data to infer that there is no relationship between the variables, we must consider other facets of the study. An extremely well-done study might incline us to take the "lack of relationship" hypothesis more seriously. So we examine various strengths and weaknesses of the study. Later in this chapter we will use this "oat bran study" to illustrate many of the pitfalls that we can fall into.

Studies That Confuse Correlation with Causation

The fact that two things are *associated* with one another does not mean that the one caused the other. This is true even if one follows the other in time. A **correlation** means that two things are associated with each other or vary together. Often the invalid inference that one thing causes another is made from evidence of mere correlation.

A classic example is the correlation between women's average skirt lengths and the Dow Jones stock average. This is a much cited relationship that held over a period of many years. The existence of such a correlation does not mean that changes in the Dow Jones average can be caused by changing the average skirt length.

A correlation between two things could mean that changes in one of them causes changes in the other. But there are other equally plausible hypotheses. It could be that both are under the influence of a third factor. For example, short hair is probably correlated with criminal behavior. Women commit fewer crimes than men and generally have longer hair. Hair length presumably doesn't cause criminal behavior. Various factors lead men to wear shorter hair and commit more crimes.

Many studies in health psychology are correlational. For example, most studies relating chronic stress to disease are of this type. It is clear that the relationship between stress and disease exists, but this does not have to mean that stress causes disease. Attempts to change your health by lowering your stress imply that the relationship is causal. (There are other reasons to suspect that the stress–health relationship is not a mere "nonsensical" correlation like that between the Dow Jones average and skirt length. Recent work showing the effects of stress on immune response is an example. The criticism here is directed only at the use of merely correlational evidence for the relationship between stress and disease.)

By looking at the examples of correlation given above, we can see why we want to show causality. For one thing, mere correlation does not let us know how to modify the outcome. Changing skirt or hair length is not likely to change the Dow Jones average or criminal behavior. Furthermore, the correlation, no matter how strong, may one day disappear. For instance, changes of customary hair style could eliminate the relationship between hair length and criminal behavior or even reverse its direction. Note that this could happen even if the correlation were very high or even perfect. If *every* criminal had short hair and *every* solid citizen had long hair, the relationship could still disappear in a trice if the styles changed. So don't assume that a mere correlation between two variables establishes that one of them *caused* changes in the other.

Studies with Defective Measures of Variables

Many studies look good on the surface, but when you look closely at how the variables were measured, serious problems are apparent. These measurement problems can happen in several ways; we will discuss some of the more striking ones below.

Redundant Measures

The independent and dependent variables are sometimes redundant, that is, they overlap each other. Both measure the same thing, at least to some extent. If the two variables are measuring the same thing, it is clearly not much of a discovery to show there is a relationship between

them. This point should be quite obvious, but often the two measures of the "same thing" are given names that make them sound as if they measure different things. Then the investigators mistakenly think they have discovered a relationship between two variables when they have not.

This very objection has been raised against certain stress measures. Often the things that are being called stress are actually symptoms of illness. For example, there is a tried and true inventory of stress called the Social Readjustment Rating Scale. Just about everyone has seen some variant of it in magazine articles about stress. It includes life events like getting a divorce, taking on a mortgage, and getting married.

Unfortunately, many of the stress items on that scale "could be symptoms of physical or mental illness, thus confounding the measure of stress with the measure of health outcomes" (Dohrenwend, Dohrenwend, Dodson, & Shrout, 1984). In fact, Hudgens (1974) argued that as many as 29 of the 43 items on this stress scale might be either symptoms or the consequences of illness.

We should always look closely at exactly *how* the IV and DV are measured and preferably be familiar enough with the measuring instruments to tell whether they are both measures of the *same thing*.

Unstandardized Nominal Scales

A second measurement problem that should make us wary has to do with "measurements" that are really just categorizations of the variables. The variables are merely identified and named, not quantified. The technical term for this categorization is **nominal scaling**. A nominal scale is simply a set of category names for variables. It is best explained with an example. Many studies are done on the effects of such methods as relaxation training and biofeedback on various symptoms. These are merely named variables. There is no quantitative scale of comparison between them. Researchers differ in how they use the terms "relaxation training" and "biofeedback." So we cannot properly generalize from one study of these variables to another. Probably the best we can do at present with respect to comparing biofeedback and relaxation training is to agree on standard procedures and then make comparisons, but this has not yet been done.

For example, the length of treatment can vary, the training methods can differ, the number of sessions can be greatly different, and so on. Thus, one study comparing these two might easily get a different result from another study making what is nominally the "same" comparison. This can give the impression that there are contradictions in the research literature when there are actually only variations in the procedures.

At least we must have precise descriptions of the factors defining the categories. As a reader, you should delve into the actual description of the procedures before making any comparisons between one study and another. It would be best if researchers would standardize their procedures so that everyone would do them the same way, but this rarely happens. Without such standardization or, at least, exact description, a study done with nominally scaled items may be of little use.

Unreliable Measures

A third problem is the use of unreliable measures. Imagine having a bathroom scale that varies greatly from weighing to weighing even when your actual weight stays the same. Such a measuring device is "unreliable." **Reliability** refers to the degree to which the measures are stable and repeatable. (We assume here that the thing being measured is itself stable; phenomena that occur fleetingly are another problem altogether.) A bathroom scale that weighs you at 120 pounds on one day and 140 the next is not a reliable instrument.

Given how obvious this point is, you may be surprised to learn that unreliable measures are not uncommon in health research. For example, identical blood samples sent to laboratories for measurements of cholesterol levels can give drastically different readings. A given blood sample might result in your being categorized as dangerously high in cholesterol or as within very safe limits, depending on when and where you sent it.

Similar variations have been pointed out in blood pressure readings. For example, Lynch (1985) has shown that talking when your blood pressure is being taken will dramatically increase the reading. Yet many health providers chat during these measurements. The result can be readings that differ from one measurement to another, depending on how talkative the parties happened to be.

When you are evaluating a paper in health psychology, you should expect some evidence for the reliability of the measures to be provided. There are standard procedures for evaluating the reliability of instruments. In general, they take the form of measuring the degree of relationship between the measure and other instances of that same measure. Look for some kind of statistic indicating how stable (reliable) the measures are.

Invalid Measures

Validity refers to the extent to which something measures what it is intended to measure. Invalid measures of the variables of interest are *not* like the "real thing." For example, three five-minute biofeedback sessions are not typical of clinical biofeedback training. Eight 30- to 50-minute sessions would be more representative. A study using measures that are not representative may yield results that cannot be generalized to the real world. The results of a study using three five-minute biofeedback sessions to treat headaches may conclude that biofeedback training is not effective. However, this finding has little meaning because it does not tell us about the effects of biofeedback training as it is practiced. The measure is an invalid one.

The problem with studies like this one is that their measures are not representative. To generalize correctly we need representative measures. Scrutinize research to see if measures are valid representatives of what the investigators wanted to study. It is hard to get good measures, so you will often find that studies fall short of the mark.

Often when we want to measure a psychological or health-related characteristic, it is hard to get a sample of the actual thing we want to know about. Then we have to use *indirect* measures. That is why we have so many psychological tests that provide indirect measures of psychological characteristics. When we have to use such indirect methods, we must ask if there is evidence that the measures are valid.

In other words, we have to show that our indirect measurements actually tell us something about the real world characteristics of the person with whom we are dealing. Specialists in testing have devised a number of ways to tell whether measures are valid.

Evidence for validity can be provided in several ways, including the following: (1) there is a substantial correlation between the authors' measure and other *well established* measures of the same variable; (2) the measure tends to be higher in groups known to have a lot of the quality being measured, for example, air traffic controllers end up having high scores on a stress scale; and (3) the measure predicts things that we are virtually certain it should predict, for example, a stress measure predicts the occurrence of diseases.

When evaluating research in health psychology in which indirect measures are used, we must consider whether evidence for validity is given. Sometimes measuring instruments are so familiar that authors may neglect to point out the evidence for the validity of the instrument, although they really should do so. It is important to recognize that, even though there *may* be unstated evidence for the validity of the measure, the reader must remain skeptical until he or she knows that evidence.

It is surprisingly common for investigators to construct an ad hoc measuring instrument for the study they happen to be doing, and either to fail to establish validity or to neglect mentioning the work they have done on it. Keep in mind that

you do not know the validity unless evidence for it is provided.

Studies with Small or Unrepresentative Samples

When the news broke that the prestigious *New England Journal of Medicine* had published an article that said oat bran did not lower cholesterol (Swain et al., 1990), even the reporters seemed dismayed to learn that the study included only 20 participants. Could such a well-established premise be torn down on the basis of this small sample? Most reporters failed to notice that the participants were mostly dietitians, and not likely to be representative of the general population. Findings from such a sample may well not generalize to the rest of us.

When you read a research study, ask "How representative was the sample of participants?" In the study by Swain et al. (1990), it was not very representative. There were only 20 subjects, and no effort was made to sample them randomly. All but a few of them were women, and they were mostly dietitians who were doing a good job of controlling their serum cholesterol before entering the study. This might well make it hard to show an effect of oat bran.

An ideal way to make it likely that our findings will generalize is to study a *representative* sample of subjects. There are two ways to determine whether a sample is representative. One is simply to make sure that the sample has characteristics we know exist in the broader population. Thus, if we were sampling human beings, we would want about half of them to be male and about half female. So, based on our knowledge of the population being studied, we try to be sure that our sample has the same balance of characteristics.

If we rely exclusively on such "rational" methods, however, we are likely to make errors because of our limited knowledge of the relevant characteristics of the population. There may even be properties of the population that we do not recognize as important but that would change the outcome of our study. The way we get around this problem, at least in theory, is to select a *random sample* of subjects from the population. A random sample is not the same as a haphazard sample. In a random sample each member of the population must have an equal and independent chance of being selected. This is very difficult to obtain if we are interested in very large populations. To deal with limitations on randomization, we use what we *know* about the population and supplement it by randomizing for features we may not know enough about.

When you read studies in health, keep in mind that your confidence in the generalizability of the results should depend on how close the sample approaches the ideal. When the sample falls far short of the ideal, be prepared for the likelihood that results will fail to generalize.

In psychology we tend to use "convenience" samples. This means we use whoever is handy and willing to participate—often students enrolled in psychology courses. This practice is not limited to psychology, by the way. We suspect that the Swain study also used a convenience sample. This kind of sample may give results that do not generalize to a wider population of people. We encounter another pitfall when we ask large numbers of people to participate but only a small percentage of them are willing to do so. This willingness to participate may mean that the subjects who opted to take part in the study differed in important ways from those who were not willing to participate. You should note the percentage of people who agreed to participate in a study and ask yourself how likely it is that those who refused might have responded differently.

Ideally, then, studies should contain a true random sample of subjects. If the investigation is not based on a random sample, we must consider whether there are other good reasons to think the sample is representative. Sometimes we will find studies in which they simply report something like "measures were taken on 158 subjects." There is no indication that either reason or randomization assured that the population was representative.

Researchers should make a serious effort, despite adversity, to get a representative sample. A good example of such effort is a study by Fleming et al. (1987). In a study on the effects of stress, they used a sampling procedure that provided some assurance of representativeness, even though they could not attain the textbook ideal. They used census data to identify demographically comparable blocks in a city and then randomly sampled individuals in those blocks. Over 70 percent of the people they approached agreed to participate in the study.

Note that those who participated may have differed from those who did not, or even that the city in question may have been somehow unrepresentative, but these risks are better controlled than those we find in many studies. Fleming et al. (1987) took the problem of sampling seriously and probably did the best one could do in a real world situation. As studies of this kind are replicated in different locales, we steadily increase our confidence in the findings. (The Fleming study found that chronic stress influences cardiovascular reactivity.)

Another factor to consider when deciding whether a sample is representative enough is our overall understanding of the consistency of what we are studying. We should be able to take any sample of matter to verify the principles of physics. We understand that these principles apply very consistently throughout the universe. On the other hand, such things as opinions about who should be president of the United States vary drastically from one place to the other or one type of person to the other. So you should be especially vigilant about representativeness if the phenomenon under study is not very consistent, as the laws of physics or physiology are.

It would be very silly to think that we could sample 20 people from a prestigious Boston hospital to predict who would win a presidential election. It is not as silly to think such a sample could tell us something about the relationship of diet and cholesterol. Here, again, we refer to the study by Swain et al. (1990). We can see at least some basis for their thinking that a small unrepresentative sample of people might tell them something general about oat bran and cholesterol. Physiological reactions tend to be more consistent than opinions about presidents.

In any case their sample was very small, and the problem was aggravated because the sample consisted almost entirely of dietitians with well-regulated cholesterol and blood pressure. So oat bran might affect them quite differently than it would the average person. Specifically, it might well be harder to create a positive change in people who are already in excellent health.

As is apparent, we do not have a pat formula that will help you recognize the right kind of sample of subjects. You will have to use your head and ponder the nature of the sample of subjects and the probable consistency of the thing being studied. Then you will have to decide on the ramifications of these factors for the outcome of the study.

Before leaving our discussion of the size and representativeness of samples, we have to deal with an aspect of the problem that is a little tricky to detect. If you merely look at the number of participants and make a mental note of whether they seem to be a fairly representative group, you may still be fooled into accepting a study with too few participants.

To make our point, let's look at an absurd extreme. What would you think if you saw a research paper comparing men's and women's stress and found that the researchers had compared one man and one woman? And suppose they said the man's score was much higher than the woman's, and they did a statistical test on the scores and found the man was significantly more stressed. Further imagine that they concluded from all this that men are generally more stressed than women. Hopefully, you would dismiss the study and wonder if the researchers had gone out of their minds.

Now, suppose you opened the pages of a journal and found a similar study with ten men and ten women as subjects. That would be a little better but still skimpy. But suppose that you found the researchers reporting that they had done ten different statistical comparisons and found one of them to indicate a statistically significant difference. Can you see how similar this would be to the study with only one man and one woman? In effect, when you do many statistical comparisons in one study, you are actually turning it into lots of studies and dividing the sample of subjects into smaller and smaller subsamples. Therefore, you have to take into account how many comparisons are being made on the sample of subjects before you can decide if there are "enough."

Conclusions

The purpose of this chapter was not to teach students "how to" do research in health psychology. We really had two goals. First, we wanted to help students appreciate the scientific method and the long history of its development. It is unlikely that any of us today can develop a method that will equal its power and accuracy. So we should think long and hard before abandoning its precepts. Second, in addition to gaining an appreciation of the scientific method, we wanted students to know that even the most rigorous researchers may fail to utilize it fully.

The chapter was also devoted to helping students understand and evaluate the massive amounts of health-related information that we are confronted with daily. This kind of knowledge and skill is essential for health psychologists. It is also important for all individuals who want to take responsibility for their own health. Moreover, the importance of this kind of knowledge and skill is not limited to health-related research. It is essential for all citizens who must cope with the "great blooming, buzzing confusion" of the information age.

Summary

1. Health claims are often based on informal evidence or faulty research. Failure to evaluate these claims can be costly in personal and economic terms. Faulty research creates a "cry wolf" effect that may lead people to ignore sound advice.

2. Evaluating research can be a tedious task, and even people with training in scientific methodology often fail to apply their skills. As humans, we want answers immediately without doing the hard work required to get reliable and valid information. We tend to rely on advice from persuasive others or "common sense."

3. The scientific method took hundreds of years to develop. It was not easy to discover methods that would allow us to gain "objective knowledge" of the world. The development of the scientific method was a major human accomplishment. Scientific methods are difficult to apply, and there is a strong resistance against using them fully.

4. The scientific method emphasizes verification. It is an elaborate procedure for checking out our ideas about the world. These ideas come originally from the process of discovery. In the discovery mode, we want to detect something that has previously been missed, so we brainstorm and temporarily lower our standards of evidence. Discoveries can come from sources that are intuitive and unscientific.

5. Some of the impetus for health psychology came from scientists who tested the claims of Eastern mystics. Some of these claims, for example that they can control their body temperature have been verified. A major problem develops, however, when we confuse findings obtained in the discovery mode with findings established in the verification mode.

6. Scientific experiments allow us to isolate the influence of the independent variable on the dependent variable by controlling the effects of other variables while we manipulate the independent variable. In health research, practical and ethical considerations force us to settle for a level of evidence that falls short of the ideal, and we must acknowledge that fact.

7. Statistical analysis is used to determine whether research results were due to mere chance. By "chance," we mean the many small independent factors that happen to act together to affect the dependent variable. Larger, more noticeable variables that might confound the results require experimental control.

8. Often people treat hypotheses or speculations as if they were verified principles. Even the most sophisticated investigators make that error. This error occurs when we fail to recognize the difference between the discovery stage and the verification stage. The excitement of discovery must not be substituted for the painstaking process of verification.

9. There are common pitfalls that even experienced investigators fall into as they conduct research. Research reports containing these flaws often go undetected and are published even in the most prestigious edited journals. The pitfalls that we need to watch for as we read and evaluate health-related research are summarized in Box 3.2.

10. An appreciation and knowledge of the scientific method and the ability to understand and evaluate health-related research are essential for health psychologists. It is also becoming increasingly important for today's citizens to have these skills to evaluate all kinds of information.

Box 3.2 Guidelines for Evaluating Research

1. Take testimonials with a grain of salt.

2. Be skeptical of studies that purport to show that a variable does *not* have an effect.

3. Avoid confusing mere correlation with causation.

4. Familiarize yourself with measures enough so that you can tell whether the measures of the IV and DV *overlap* each other.

5. Be careful about generalizing from one study to another if the variables are merely named and categorized without being quantified or at least standardized.

6. Require good evidence for the reliability of the measures.

7. Look over measures to be sure they are validly representative of what the authors wanted to study.

8. Be sure there are enough participants to justify our expectation that the results will be generalizable and stable.

9. If some people refused to participate, notice whether there were enough refusals to bias the results if those who refused were different from those who agreed.

10. Take into account how many statistical comparisons are being made before deciding if there were enough participants.

11. If evidence does not meet the above standards, view it with skepticism even if a person with fine credentials proposes it. This applies even if the evidence is presented in elegant scientific jargon.

12. If a claim is based on many studies that contain these kinds of flaws, do not be deceived by the number of studies. Multiplying faulty evidence may just be compounding errors. No matter how many times you multiply zeros, the result is still zero.

13. Sometimes people will claim that scientific principles do not apply to their claims because they are not scientists. You should ask them and yourself how their claims are kept safe from the errors to which human judgment has always been subject.

Key Terms

Controlling variables

Correlation

Dependent variable

Experimental method

Independent variable

Nominal scaling

Null hypothesis

Process of discovery

Process of verification

Reliability

Validity

Discussion Questions

1. Why is it important to have a systematic methodology for finding out about health-related issues? Relate your answer to the gradual discovery of the scientific method.

2. Distinguish between the discovery mode and the verification mode. Show how the distinction influences our attitude toward research in health psychology.

3. What special advantages does the experimental method have over other methods?

4. What do we accomplish by controlling variables?

5. Explain why testimonials should be "taken with a grain of salt"?

6. Explain why you have to use more caution with regard to studies that claim a variable does not have an effect than with those studies that show a variable does have an effect. Give at least one real example of research that seemed to indicate no effect of a variable.

7. What is the difference between correlation and causation? Why should we not deduce causation from correlation?

8. Explain each of the following and tell why they can lead to errors: (a) redundancy of independent and dependent variables, (b) nominal scales, (c) failure to establish validity, and (d) failure to establish reliability.

9. Explain the purpose of representative sampling and tell why it is important.

10. What considerations are important in evaluating studies that do not have random samples of subjects?

11. Why is it important for health psychologists and research consumers to be able to understand and evaluate research?

Chapter 4

Psychobiological Mechanisms of Health and Disease

Recently, one of the major television networks ran a series on the mind and cancer. The series portrayed a woman in late middle age with cancer who was trying to use imagery to cure her disease. She was lying down with her eyes closed, intently imagining that her immune system was destroying her tumor. Afterward, in an interview, she seemed sure that she could kill her tumor in this way. Against this lone woman, who had no medical training, they placed high-ranking doctors from a major cancer center. These doctors saw her belief as naive. The case they presented against her view was very convincing. How could images destroy a tumor? Surely this was mere wishful thinking. No one mentioned all the evidence in favor of the idea that emotions and thoughts influence cancer. There was not so much as a whisper about the many cases in which cancers regress when people try this kind of "mind-over-body" approach. It was all too easy to forget this as we saw the contrast between a body of medical scientists and this seemingly deluded woman.

Years ago, I (CLS) heard Dr. Pat Norris of the Menninger Foundation describe the moving case of a nine-year old boy with an inoperable brain tumor that disappeared after he used similar methods (Norris & Porter, 1987). Later, I asked an oncologist (cancer specialist) what the chances were that this recovery was due to spontaneous remission. He said the chances that a remission would take place *and* that the patient would happen to be in this kind of therapy were too small to consider. Even knowing about this case, it was hard to watch the television report without thinking such claims are absurd.

But are they absurd? And what about the evidence that imagery controls various other bodily states (Barber, 1978)? Is that also absurd? Are there any known mechanisms that could provide a way for this kind of thing to happen? And if there are such mechanisms, why does biomedicine seem so resistant to acknowledging them? In part, this resistance stems from the historical development of the scientific paradigm in general, and of the biomedical framework in particular. The views of René Descartes moved Western science away from an integrated approach to mind and body.

THE MIND/BODY PROBLEM

René Descartes was a key figure in the development of the modern, scientific view of the world.

He saw the world as a huge clockwork. He thought we could best understand it by analyzing it into its parts and then seeing how they work together. But Descartes allowed for one important exception to the mechanistic view—the human soul. To him, animals were machines, and to a great extent, humans were also machines. But humans had an immaterial soul that could influence the machine. How could an immaterial being cause physical effects? This was the mind/body problem. This problem was a plague on Descartes' system, and it continues to vex us today.

Perhaps we should make it clear that we do not need to prove that psychological factors influence the body directly for health psychology to be important. There are many indirect ways in which mind could influence body. For example, changes in lifestyle could result in changes in health. Psychological influences could lead us to eat or drink too much or to smoke. These, in turn, would influence health. There would still be a role for health psychology. It would help us to change the behavior and thereby improve health.

But psychological influences on health often seem to be direct. In fact, researchers usually control for the obvious indirect factors when they study psychological influences on health. For example, Rozanski et al. (1988) showed that mental stress made the heart pump less efficiently. The impairments were as great as those produced by physical exertion. Here the mental influence seems direct. It is not like cases where a person is under chronic stress and gets sick. In those cases, it is much harder to exclude the possibility that the stress produced changes of behavior or lifestyle first.

As we've already mentioned, investigators commonly control for the obvious mediating factors. Still, there is disagreement on the extent to which psychological factors have a direct effect on health. One problem has been that, until recently, we did not know about the clear anatomical and physiological mechanisms that might allow the direct influence. Even though many studies show a relationship between psychology and health, we cannot integrate them into the larger scientific framework until underlying mechanisms are understood. We know some of those mechanisms; this chapter describes the most important ones.

THE AUTONOMIC NERVOUS SYSTEM

How does the brain create bodily reactions? The answer to this question would go a long way toward solving our problem. The brain is but a part of the nervous system. Brain and spinal cord constitute the **central nervous system (CNS).** There is also a **peripheral nervous system**. The peripheral nervous system consists of the sensory and motor nerves, which provide input to and output from the CNS. A third part of the peripheral nervous system of special interest here is called the **autonomic nervous system (ANS).** The term *autonomic* means "self-governing." It is a system that has been believed to operate pretty independently of the parts of the CNS that give rise to voluntary behavior.

Functions of the Sympathetic Nervous System

The ANS has two main parts, the sympathetic and the parasympathetic nervous systems (see Figure 4.1). The **sympathetic nervous system** was known even by the ancient Greeks. But the modern view of its functions was presented only several decades ago by the great physiologist, Walter Cannon (1871–1945). Cannon saw that the functions of the sympathetic system were linked with the part of the adrenal glands that secretes **epinephrine** (also called adrenalin) and the related hormone, **norepinephrine** (also called noradrenalin). The core, or medulla, of the adrenal gland secretes these hormones. (*Hormone* is the name given to glandular secretions that travel through our bloodstream to stimulate or retard the activities of bodily organs.)

Most people know what adrenalin does. We talk about having an "adrenalin high." Epinephrine (adrenalin) arouses us. Norepinephrine (noradrenalin) has effects similar to those of epinephrine. The sympathetic nervous system and the **adrenal medulla** taken together constitute a **sympathoadrenal system** that prepares the body for fight or flight. It creates a beautifully adaptive pattern of responses that are well suited for fighting for one's life.

The pupils dilate to let in more light. The air pathways dilate, easing the passage of air into the lungs. The flow of watery saliva is replaced by a kind of sticky saliva that will not flow into the lungs. The blood vessels of the skin constrict, and the tendency of the blood to coagulate is increased. Both of these latter effects minimize the loss of blood if the body is cut. The flow of blood is shunted away from the intestines and into the skeletal muscles. This, along with changes that increase the availability of energy stores and of blood cells, readies the muscles for action.

The heart is stimulated to pump harder and faster, so that its output is increased. During fight or flight the voluntary nervous system is likely to induce tensing of the muscles. Paired with the constriction of blood vessels in the skin, this produces more resistance to blood flow. Blood pressure tends to go up when blood flow is restricted. It is the body's way of being sure its parts are not starved of needed oxygen. It also insures the flow of blood in the tensed muscles.

These are only some of the reactions of this system that prepare us for a life-or-death struggle. Most of us know them well. But we usually have had them in settings where there was no

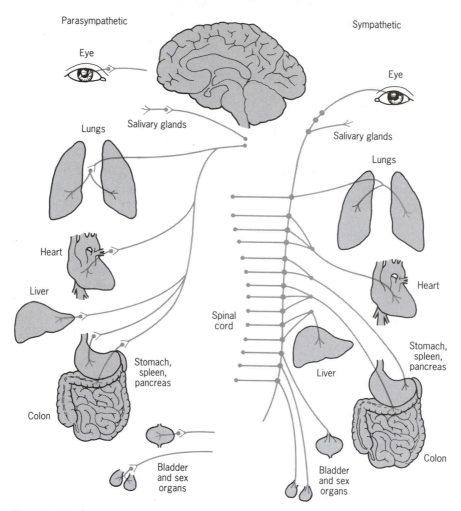

Figure 4.1   Schematic layout of the autonomic nervous system. *Source:* Figure 8.3 from *Understanding Human Behavior*, 6th ed., by James V. McConnell, copyright © 1989 by Holt, Rinehart and Winston, Inc., reprinted by permission of the publisher.

threat to our lives. When we are getting ready to make a speech or are going for a job interview or asking someone if they will go out with us, these reactions are usually unwelcome. The dilated pupils may make us more attractive, but the dry mouth, pounding heart, and cold hands are not helpful.

Some of the changes, such as increases in clotting of blood and rises in blood pressure, can be quite unhealthy, especially if we have stiff, clogged, blood vessels. Worst of all is that,

repeated often enough, these reactions tend to become permanent. They lead to chronic unhealthy states, such as stable high blood pressure.

So a pattern of responses that would help us in a primitive, violent environment is a health hazard in a civilized environment. It is easy to see how the concept of "diseases of civilization" (Dubos, 1965, pp. 237–241) makes sense. There are lots of "civilized" situations that can stimulate a person's fight or flight system. Frankenhaueser (1980) has shown that people under stress have high levels of epinephrine and norepinephrine. Under mild stress, epinephrine levels go up, and as stress increases, norepinephrine levels also rise. These levels normally drop toward evening, but when stress is severe and chronic, they stay high beyond the end of the workday.

Functions of the Parasympathetic Nervous System

The second major part of the ANS is the **parasympathetic nervous system** (see Figure 4.1). Usually, the sympathetic and parasympathetic nervous systems have opposing effects. The sympathetic nervous system increases the heart rate, and the parasympathetic system decreases it. The sympathetic system dilates the pupils, and the parasympathetic system constricts them. The sympathetic system shunts blood to the skeletal muscles, and the parasympathetic shunts blood to the intestines.

The sympathetic system is arousing, whereas the parasympathetic is best described as relaxing. The two systems are antagonistic to each other. However, there are exceptions to this antagonism. For example, in the control of salivary flow, the two systems do not just turn on and shut off flow. They produce two different kinds of saliva. The parasympathetic system stimulates flow of watery saliva, and the sympathetic system results in sticky, "mucinous" saliva. Another exception is the control of blood flow in the skin. There is little or no parasympathetic influence on the small blood vessels of the skin, but the sympathetic nervous system constricts these vessels. Thus, we get cold hands and feet when we are frightened or stressed in some way. When blood flow increases to our extremities they become warmer. Warming hands or feet, then, is a fairly good index of relaxation.

Another example is that of control of the male sexual response. It is a case in which the two systems cooperate. Penile erection is under parasympathetic control, but ejaculation is under sympathetic control. It is for this reason that

a male who is highly stressed may not be able to get an erection. Then, if he finally gets an erection, he may ejaculate too soon. Both reactions indicate that the person's sympathetic nervous system is highly activated.

Whereas the functions of the sympathetic nervous system may pertain to "fight or flight," the parasympathetic system's actions are those involved in restoring the individual or species. Thus, when one is eating, resting, or throwing off bodily waste, the parasympathetic nervous system tends to dominate. At least a substantial part of sexual response also involves parasympathetic dominance.

Given these basic rules about how these two parts of the ANS work, we can predict which of them controls a given type of bodily reaction. You could predict which system dominates when a person is working on a highly stressful job, arguing with a spouse, or having a medical examination while worried about a serious illness. Similarly, you could predict which system dominates when one is sitting peacefully in the woods or getting drowsy after a big meal. You could also predict which system makes the output of the heart go up or which causes movements in the intestines.

THE LINK BETWEEN THE AUTONOMIC AND CENTRAL NERVOUS SYSTEMS

The ANS relates closely with the central nervous system (CNS) despite the "self-governing" property of the ANS. The autonomic fibers start in the central nervous system. Why, then, is the ANS considered to be self-governing? Primarily because we do not normally control its output consciously and voluntarily. There seem to be some important limitations in the linkup between the ANS and those parts of the nervous system that start willed acts.

But this does not mean that the CNS does not influence autonomic output. This should be clear from our examples of factors that create reactions of the ANS. Stressful events commonly

It is likely that this corporate executive's sympathetic nervous system is dominant as she works on a highly stressful project.

produce sympathetic reactions, and these events are recognized and analyzed by the CNS. Similarly, stimuli, like quiet scenes, that induce parasympathetic response must be analyzed by the CNS.

The Hypothalamus

Long ago the great neurophysiologist, Charles Scott Sherrington (1861–1952), called a part of the brain, the **hypothalamus**, the "head ganglion of the ANS." The phrase "head ganglion of the ANS" implies that the hypothalamus is the system that governs the ANS. The hypothalamus is a part of the brain that lies just above the roof of the mouth and is closely connected to the pituitary gland.

The hypothalamus has long been known to control basic biological functions. There are regions in it that control eating, sleep, sexual behavior, temperature, strong emotions, and even immune reactions. The hypothalamus is also part of a system that controls the endocrine glands. Endocrine glands secrete a wide range of

chemicals into the bloodstream that enhance or retard the functioning of other bodily organs (see Table 4.1). The hypothalamus influences the output of the **pituitary gland**. The pituitary is the "master gland" that regulates the other endocrines.

The Limbic System

The CNS control of autonomic activity is much more complex and elegant than that of merely being controlled by the hypothalamus. The hypothalamus is at the base of a much larger system in the brain known as the **limbic system.** Many years ago a neuroanatomist named J. W. Papez (1937) published a classic paper on the brain structures that produce emotion. Before he wrote that paper, it was already known that the hypothalamus controlled rage.

When the brain is cut away above the level of the hypothalamus, we can see the reactions of an organism that are not controlled by any of the higher brain centers. It will show "sham rage." The animal seems fiercely angry when stimu-

Table 4.1   **Locations and Major Functions of Endocrine Glands**

Endocrine Gland	Location	Regulates
Pituitary (anterior)	Cranial cavity	Other endocrines, bodily growth, production of milk
Pituitary (posterior)	Cranial cavity	Resorption of water in kidneys, contraction of uterus, milk release
Pineal gland	Brain	Ovaries, menstrual cycle
Hypothalamus	Brain	Other endocrines
Thyroid	Throat	Cell's release of energy from foods, ratio of calcium in bone versus blood
Parathyroid	Throat	Effect of thyroid on ratio of calcium in bone versus blood (indirectly influencing the function of brain and heart)
Adrenals (Medulla)	Top of kidney	"Fight or flight" reactions
Adrenals (Cortex)		Blood glucose, blood pressure, inflammation of tissue, immunity and allergy, level of blood minerals, body's water level, sexual characteristics
Islands of Langerhans (in pancreas)	Abdomen	Blood glucose
Ovaries	Pelvic cavity	"Feminization," reproduction
Testes	Scrotum	"Masculinization," reproduction
Thymus	Chest	Development and function of immune system

Source: Modified from Thibodeau and Anthony (1988).

lated, but its emotion is not under normal control. Its rage tends to start and stop very quickly when we start and stop a stimulus. The animal is like a "rage machine."

This differs from the normal rage of an intact organism. Normally, our anger varies in intensity from mild irritation to full blown rage. It is also under control of subtle sensory stimulation, and we often stay angry long after the event that triggered it has passed. Moreover, we may be in a certain "mood" that makes us more or less prone to anger. Sometimes it takes very little to "set us off," and at other times we feel so good that we can just laugh off things that might otherwise irritate us. All of these more refined properties are influenced by parts of the brain above the level of the hypothalamus.

Papez (1937) made a major contribution to identifying the brain regions above the hypothalamus that modify its output. He described some of the major parts of the limbic system that regulate emotion (see Figure 4.2). We know now that this system regulates not only emotion, but also various aspects of the body's physiology. It is probably the major system of the brain we would point toward in trying to account

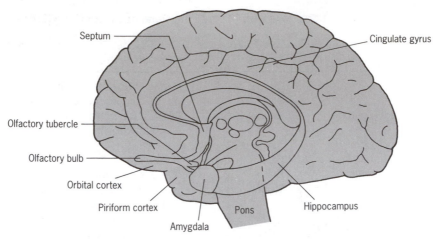

Figure 4.2   The limbic system. Reproduced with permission from *Body and Self* by George Bloch, copyright © 1985 by William Kaufmann, Inc., all rights reserved.

for findings that indicate a direct effect of psychological factors on bodily functions relevant to health.

The Interconnections

If the CNS regulates the hypothalamus, which in turn controls the ANS, why do we say that the ANS is self-governing? Because the system that controls "willing" and "choosing" is poorly linked to it. Papez (1937) pointed this out. He saw that the brain is divided into major systems that are strongly connected within themselves but that have weak connections with each other. The limbic system is most centrally involved in emotions and related physiological reactions, but it is not strongly connected to the system that controls thought and language. Our inability to do what we think we should do or to feel what we prefer to feel is based on this relative skimpiness of linkages between these systems. The relative isolation of the limbic system makes it hard, though not impossible, for us to voluntarily regulate the physiology of our body.

THE HYPOTHALAMIC-PITUITARY-ADRENAL CORTICAL SYSTEM

The **hypothalamic-pituitary-adrenal cortical system** is another system for regulating the body that is at least as important as the sym-

pathoadrenal and parasympathetic systems. The outer layer of the adrenal glands, which is called the **adrenal cortex,** secretes hormones that maintain a balanced physiological state. The adrenal cortex is controlled by the hypothalamus, which secretes various releasing factors that determine its activity. The pituitary gland, which is considered the master gland, is intimately linked to the hypothalamus and also regulates the activity of the adrenal cortex.

The Hormones of the Adrenal Cortex

The adrenal cortex secretes two major classes of hormones, the **mineralocorticoids** and the **glucocorticoids.** It also secretes small quantities of anabolic steroids, the sex-related muscle-building hormones that have come to public attention because athletes use them to improve performance.

Mineralocorticoids regulate the balance of materials dissolved in the fluids that surround the cells of the body. Thus, such things as the concentration of sodium and potassium in bodily fluids are regulated by mineralocorticoids. Aldosterone is a good example of a mineralocorticoid. By regulating the concentration of sodium in bodily fluids, it also regulates blood pressure.

The major roles of the glucocorticoids are to (1) regulate blood glucose levels, (2) control blood pressure, (3) control inflammation, and (4) regulate immune, including allergic, reactions. **Cortisol** is a major glucocorticoid. It is considered one of the "stress hormones" of the adrenal cortex.

The General Adaptation Syndrome

Long ago, Selye (1956) discovered a pattern of stress response that he called the **General Adaptation Syndrome** (GAS). It involved the activities of the adrenal cortex. The GAS is the body's front-line reaction to potentially damaging influences. Selye observed that it took place in the early stages of disease, even before the illness had become a specific, diagnosable disease entity. Selye went on to show that this GAS occurred when the body confronted just about any kind of stressor. At first, he limited himself to physical stressors, but later it became clear that the GAS also occurred when the stress was psychological.

An important part of the GAS is the secretion of **Adrenocorticotrophic Hormone (ACTH)** from the pituitary. This hormone causes the adrenal cortex to swell and increases the secretion of the hormones of the adrenal cortex that we mentioned above.

Selye divided the GAS into three stages (see Figure 4.3). The first, and the one that has been most studied, he termed the **stage of alarm.** In it, the body reacts strongly to a foreign entity. During the next stage, the **stage of resistance,** the body's reactions may appear to have returned almost to normal. However, its resources have been taxed, and the body may not be able to react as effectively to a new stressor. In the final stage, the **stage of exhaustion,** endocrine activity is heightened. Increased levels of cortisol produce effects on the immune, digestive, circulatory, and other systems of the body, which may lead to death.

A facet of the GAS that has been studied a great deal is the secretion of cortisol, which we described earlier as one of the major stress hormones of the adrenal cortex. Cortisol is secreted under stress. The degree of its secretion depends not only on the amount of stress, but also on how well the organism can predict or control the noxious events (see, e.g., Frankenhaeuser, 1980, 1986). Unpredictable and uncontrollable events tend to raise cortisol levels. We will have more to say about this hormone below.

The CNS and the GAS

The GAS is partly under control of the CNS, since it involves regulation via the hypothalamus. Remember also that it responds to rather subtle, cognitive aspects of stimuli such as their predictability. So far as we know, only the brain could process this level of information.

In addition, there is a neural feedback loop from the adrenals to the hypothalamus. This loop was first shown when investigators found that damage to one adrenal gland produced changes in the hypothalamus only on the side opposite the damaged adrenal. This could not be due to diffuse secretion of hormones in the blood. Further research has confirmed that

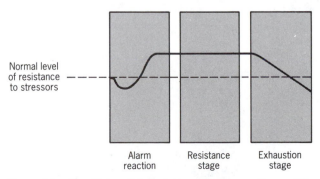

Figure 4.3 The General Adaptation Syndrome. *Source: The Stress of Life,* Hans Selye, copyright © 1978 by McGraw-Hill, Inc., New York, p. 163. Reprinted by permission.

it is neurally mediated (Vernikos-Danellis & Heybach, 1980). Thus, there is a neural system that allows the brain to send commands to the hormonal system of the adrenal cortex, and there is also a system that permits the adrenals to tell the brain their response to the command.

CNS Control of Other Hormones

We have emphasized the fight or flight system and the system underlying the GAS because they were the first known to respond to stress. In fact, however, the hypothalamus controls almost all pituitary output (see Table 4.1). Specialized neurons in the hypothalamus secrete releasing factors that control the pituitary output, which in turn controls the other endocrine glands. Thus, the hypothalamus seems to be the "command central" for a very wide range of the body's functions. For example, a hypothalamic substance known as **corticotrophin-releasing factor (CRF)** controls the release of cortisol from the adrenal cortex. Cortisol has many important influences on the body, including suppression of the immune system.

Besides their physical effects, many hormones produce psychological changes. For example, people with abnormal thyroid glands are often intensely anxious. Many psychological effects of anabolic steroids are known. Undue aggressiveness is one of them. Anabolic steroids are the hormones that many top athletes take illicitly to increase their strength and to give them a competitive edge.

Space does not permit full coverage of these many influences; the interested reader is referred to the summary provided by Asterita (1985).

We now know that hormones also act as transmitters in the nervous system and as modulators of nervous activity. Pituitary hormones not only are poured out into the bodily system, but also are carried to the brain. They are called **neuropeptides** when they participate in brain activity. They are among the most important regulators of brain functioning. Some thinkers even consider the brain to be a kind of gland (Bergland, 1985).

THE IMMUNE SYSTEM

The odds are that a multitude of skirmishes, and maybe even a full-fledged war, are taking place in your body right now. Your **immune system** is constantly vigilant on your behalf. It engages in life-or-death battles with unseen enemies, some so small that 10,000 could fit on the period at the end of this sentence. It orchestrates a complex team effort to detect and destroy (or at least control) viruses, bacteria, protozoa, and even inanimate materials such as pieces of asbestos that menace your body. It also watches for and attacks the crazed cells that, if allowed to flourish, will violate the integrity of your body in the form of cancerous tumors. The two main subdivisions of the immune system are the innate and the acquired systems of immunity.

The Innate System of Immunity

The **innate system of immunity** does not actually recognize **antigens** (the name for potentially destructive materials in the body; if they are destructive, they are called **pathogens**). It consists of a variety of systems that rather blindly keep foreign materials out of the body. For example, the mucus lining of your nose and throat keeps pathogens at bay. So, to some extent, does hair in the nose.

Sometimes the innate system ejects foreign substances after they have already made their way into the body. There are hairlike structures in the lungs, called *cilia*, that perform this function. Coughing also works to get rid of foreign materials.

Another stratagem used by our bodies to get rid of harmful agents is to make the bodily environment in some way unsuitable to the harmful substances. For example, when certain germs begin to flourish in our bodies, our temperature goes up. Germs often require a narrow range of temperatures to survive. The elevated temperature diminishes their chances of survival.

Some think this is the reason babies run exceptionally high temperatures when they are ill. Their acquired system of immunity is not yet fully functioning, so they rely heavily on this facet of innate immunity. Changes in the acidity of the body can also work to destroy invading organisms. So our innate system of immunity is important to us. But we also have two systems of acquired immunity.

The Acquired System of Immunity

Acquired immunity is present only in vertebrates. Whereas the innate system takes a kind of "shotgun" approach to attacking enemies, the acquired system identifies the enemy and then uses complex, coordinated strategies to neutralize them. With the acquired system our bodies *recognize* specific pathogens and take action to destroy them.

The Cellular System

The system of acquired immunity has two major subdivisions. The cellular system is the more primitive of the two. It involves special cells that recognize pathogens and set in motion mechanisms that destroy them. These days, many people have heard about immune cells because part of the cellular system of immunity is impaired by AIDS, and much has been written about this disease in the popular press. We discuss AIDS from the point of view of health psychology in Chapter 12.

The acquired system of immunity recognizes enemies and distinguishes between them and one's own body. Our bodies contain cells that can recognize just about any known substance and take appropriate action, depending on whether or not the substance belongs there. The cellular system is especially good at dealing with viruses, parasites, and fungi. In dealing with bacteria, the more recently developed **humoral system of immunity** (see below) is more capable than the cellular system.

The cellular system of immunity has two major classes of cells, the **phagocytes** and the **lymphocytes** (see Figure 4.4). Phagocytes are "feeding cells" that actually devour and destroy antigens. We will deal with them below. The two main types of lymphocytes are known as **T-cells**

and **B-cells.** T-cells originate in the bone marrow, but they migrate from it while still immature and go to the **thymus,** which is a gland that lies right on top of the heart. Hence, the "T" in T-cells comes from the "T" in thymus.

In the thymus, T-cells differentiate into subtypes, and they are "taught" to recognize tissues from one's own body. This "schooling" of the T-cells is essential to our survival because the immune system can attack and destroy our own tissues if it mistakes them for enemy substances. Although various devices prevent these attacks on self, they do sometimes occur. They underlie the **autoimmune diseases** such as *lupus erythematosus.*

Normally, T-cells do not attack one's own tissues because they have learned to recognize markers that indicate "self." These markers are called histocompatibility antigens. A histocompatibility antigen is like a password shared only by friends. If a cell does not have the "password," it will be attacked.

Even if the cell has the password alongside other signs of being the enemy, the immune system will be attacked. This is much like the well-known procedure in which soldiers question someone who may or may not be a foreign enemy by asking such questions as "Who won the World Series in what year?" or "Who is Oprah?" Even if the person answers correctly some of the time, signs of not really being "one of us" may reveal that he or she is probably a foreign agent. T-cells go on the attack when they detect that a "self" cell (histocompatible cell) also contains a foreign antigen. So if there is a virus in your cell and they detect that, the war is on.

The presence of histocompatibility antigens is responsible for the difficulties surgeons have in getting the body to accept organ transplants. The histocompatibility antigens of donor and recipient are not likely to match, so the immune system attacks the donated organ.

There are three main subclasses of T-cells. They are the helper T-cells, the killer T-cells, and the suppressor T-cells. Helper T-cells guide the immune system to enter the battle or to rest.

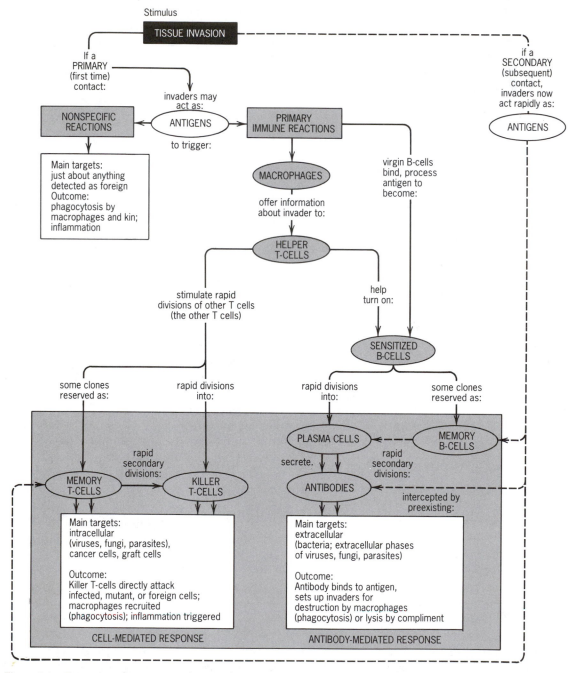

Figure 4.4   Summary of primary and secondary immune pathways: the key events, key participants, and their interactions. Solid lines show primary routes; dashed lines show secondary routes. *Source:* From *Biology: The Unity and Diversity of Life*, 4th ed., by C. Starr and R. Taggart, copyright © 1987 by Wadsworth, Inc., reprinted by permission of the publisher.

They use chemical signals to tell other immune cells to attack antigens. Killer T-cells attack and destroy cells that contain antigens. Suppressor T-cells turn off the defensive activity of the T-cell system.

You may wonder why the immune system has cells that make it stop working. Remember, the body is always in danger of experiencing too much or too little reaction of the immune system. The activity of destructive immune cells must be kept within strict limits, lest the body itself be destroyed. Thus, such things as suppressor T-cells are essential to survival. The regulation of the immune system is actually a complex one involving the cooperation of many types of cells and chemicals.

Helper T-cells use chemicals to tell other cells what to do. They use chemical messengers called **lymphokines** to regulate many types of immune cells, including killer T-cells. Two often cited kinds of lymphokines are the interleukins and interferons. The lymphokines also regulate B-cells, which are central to the humoral immune system, and mast cells, which play a key role in allergic reactions.

We have said that macrophages are a type of feeding cell or "phagocyte." The name "macrophage" means a "big feeding cell." These cells are big, white cells with a big appetite. They eat an estimated 300 billion dead red blood cells every day. At the same time they devour germs and pollutants from our airways. In half an hour, a macrophage can devour an amount of material half its own size (Dunlop, 1987).

Prior to engagement in battle, the body contains cells known as **monocytes;** these become macrophages once they leave the bloodstream and enter connective tissue to engage in battle (Borysenko, 1987). Macrophages engulf and destroy foreign invaders. They also cooperate with helper T-cells in sounding the original alarm that an invader is present. When they devour an intruder, they snip off pieces of protein that identify the enemy, and they display it on their membrane to be recognized by T-cells. They also secrete interleukin-1, which tells T-cells to start fighting.

Killer Cells (K) and **Natural Killer (NK) cells** look like lymphocytes but are believed to come from a different source. They cannot be categorized as either T- or B-cells. These are *not* the same as killer T-cells. Unlike killer T-cells, K-cells can only attack an antigen after it has first been coated with antibodies. They are probably part of a system for destroying cancer cells. We often produce antibodies for cancer cells, but the antibodies fail to destroy the cancer. The K-cells come in to finish the job.

NK-cells are able to destroy antigens without help from the rest of the immune system. But they do even better when they receive chemical signals from T-cells. T-cells release interferon, which has some virus- and tumor-killing properties. But interferon also activates NK-cells to kill virus-infected and tumor cells.

Humoral Immunity

Humoral immunity is accomplished by large, Y-shaped molecules known as **antibodies, immunoglobulins,** or gamma globulins. The double-pronged side of the Y, which is called the FAB (fragment antigen binding) fragment, contains a molecular code that matches similar patterns on a given foreign substance or pathogen, just as a key matches a given lock. Remarkably, the body already contains immunoglobulin cells that match any antigen that might enter the body. By latching onto the antigens, the antibodies create a wide range of effects that neutralize and destroy the antigens.

For example, in some cases they link the foreign invaders together in such a way as to force them to clump into helpless bundles. (This is called agglutination.) The stem of the antibody molecule, which is called the Fc fragment (fragment crystallizable) does not bind to antigen. Its role is to start the antibody's attack on the antigen by activating a system of destructive biochemicals known as "complement." This happens after the FAB fragment has recognized the antibody and latched onto it.

Once the antibody recognizes the antigen, it stimulates other antibody molecules of its kind to join it in the battle against the antigen. Antibodies are produced in specialized cells known as **B-cells.** As the number of antibodies specific to the invading antigen increase, more and more of the invading agent is neutralized.

This neutralization may be accomplished in several ways. Sometimes the antibodies cause agglutination of the antigens. The antibodies may also immobilize the antigens or make them no longer soluble in bodily fluids so that they form ineffective solids that are easily removed from the tissues. This last method of destroying antigens is called precipitation.

Cancer and Immune Surveillance

Even though you may be clinically healthy, it is very likely that you have had cancer many times in your life. This is not to say you have had clinically diagnosable cancer, but you probably had cancer cells that could have grown into a tumor but were quickly detected and destroyed by your immune system. So the immune system is essential to your avoidance of developed cancer. This notion is supported by observations that people with compromised immune systems tend to develop tumors (Antoni, 1987; Greenberg, 1987).

The concept of **immunologic surveillance** states that we develop cancer cells frequently but that the immune system surveys the body and destroys the malignant cells. It is not an easy idea to put to the test. The tiny, isolated malignant cells and the immune reaction to them might well be hard to detect. Furthermore, the surveillance concept may not apply to all kinds of tumors because only certain select kinds of tumor tend to develop in response to suppression of the immune system (Greenberg, 1987).

We really do not know how general such surveillance might be, but it would seem to be wise to keep our immune systems as healthy and competent as possible. We will present evidence below that psychological well-being plays a significant role in enhancing the immune system.

One way we may set ourselves up for getting cancer is by tolerating chronic stressors,

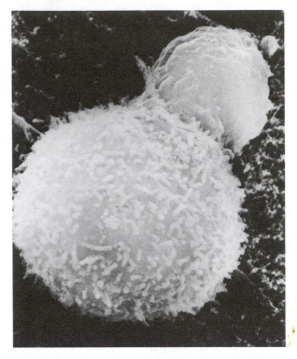

Antigens on the surface of this large cancer cell have identified it as nonself, making it a target for attack by a killer T-cell.

causing changes in our endocrine response that in turn suppress immune activity. We said earlier that the hormones of the adrenal cortex are controlled by the CNS. These same hormones inhibit the activity of macrophages, T-lymphocytes, and NK-cells, all of which are needed to combat cancer (Antoni, 1987).

Chronic toleration of stress can produce something called *hyperadaptosis*, an excessive reaction of the adaptation system of the body. It is related to chronic stress, mental depression, and normal aging (Dilman & Ostroumova, 1984). In hyperadaptosis, CRF released from the hypothalamus tells the adrenal cortex to secrete cortisol; this goes on for so long that the hypothalamus changes its set point to tolerate higher levels of cortisol.

Normally, high levels of cortisol cause the hypothalamus to shut off its output of CRF, just as high temperatures cause the thermostat to shut off a furnace. People who keep their thermostats up very high tend to get used to the higher temperatures and feel cold unless they are kept high. The same kind of thing happens with chronically high levels of bodily chemicals. They can result in the establishment of a new set point. The brain comes to treat the higher level as "normal." Thus, the brain learns to accept high levels of cortisol.

Measures of this kind of resetting have been devised, and they predict both onset and survival of cancer (Antoni, 1987). Interestingly, this resetting tends to be related to passive coping and depression. It may well be that behavior, mood, and physical health status are different facets of a common phenomenon. But we must be cautious here. It has long been believed that depression tends to precede cancer, and there is some systematic evidence to support this idea (e.g., Shekelle et al., 1981). But there is controversy about it, and we must await fuller evidence (see Chapter 12).

Dilman and co-workers (1984) have pointed out that hyperadaptosis alone may not be enough to permit cancers to develop. They argue that another condition interacts with hyperadaptosis in the development of cancer. It is characterized by high levels of *lipids* (e.g., triglycerides and free fatty acids) in the body. These elevated levels are correlated with reductions in the number of T-cells and with diminished functioning of macrophages.

A combination of hyperadaptosis and high levels of these lipids leads to *cancrophilia*—a tendency to develop cancers. All of this is consistent with observations that prolonged periods of stress and depression tend to precede diagnoses of cancer and that clinical observations indicate a better prognosis for "optimistic, well-balanced" patients as opposed to those who are passive and depressed (Antoni, 1987).

This account of immunologic surveillance and the conditions for development of cancer rests only partly on data. We cannot be certain that this is the way cancer develops. But it is a plausible interpretation founded on good physiology and confirmed to a degree by research.

Within any framework, biomedical or biopsychosocial, there is much that we do not understand about the onset of cancer and the process of surviving it.

Psychoneuroimmunology: Does Mind Matter?

There can be no doubt about it: our hormones tell our immune system what to do. Yet, books on immunology give the impression that the full range of immune activity can take place outside the body as readily as inside it. These texts put little emphasis on the influence of other systems, even of the hormones. It is hard for an immunologist to imagine that the *brain* also controls the immune response. If that is true, immunologists will have to make drastic changes in their way of looking at things. Immune reactions seem to be a matter of chemistry. How could the brain influence the immune system?

But somehow your immune system learns to turn itself on and off in appropriate contexts. Many sophisticated studies have shown that the brain influences immune function. We will discuss a number of them. Sometimes, however, a very simple demonstration brings an idea home to us better even than a solid body of evidence. A fascinating study done on skin grafts in guinea pigs strikes us as one of those pithy demonstrations.

It is common knowledge that the Russian physiologist, Pavlov, found that the nervous system could change its reactions to once "neutral" stimuli. When Pavlov sounded a buzzer in the presence of his laboratory dogs and followed the sound immediately with food, the dogs soon salivated to the sound even when there was no food. This came to be called classical conditioning.

A very similar thing was done with skin grafts onto guinea pigs in the place of food. The grafts were of rabbit skin, and T-cells recognized them as foreign tissue and attacked forcefully. In place of Pavlov's buzzer, the skin graft was done with music playing in the room and lights flashing on and off. Furthermore, a local anesthetic was injected and a big bandage wrapped on the guinea pigs after the transplant. So music, lights, anesthetic, and bandage were paired with the rabbit skin graft.

In the words of Dwyer (1988): "If you do this three times, but on the third time you do not place any rabbit skin on the side of the animal, what happens? There is no skin to reject, of course, but if you biopsy the skin a week or so later, where the graft *would* have been you find the skin full of angry-looking T-cells searching everywhere for a foreign graft that is expected to be present but is not" (p. 235).

Either the immune system learned to react to the "neutral" stimuli, or something that controls the immune system, presumably the CNS, did. So if this little study holds up, we must conclude that the immune system is governed by learning and very likely is under the control of the nervous system. But we will want a good deal more evidence before accepting this conclusion. That kind of evidence is what we are about to discuss.

Conditioned Suppression of the Immune System

Robert Ader has done some of the most systematic and best controlled work on Pavlovian conditioning of the immune response. (For a summary of Ader's work, see Ader & Cohen, 1984.) Because of this work, Ader is considered a founder of the new field of **psychoneuroimmunology**. This field attempts to understand the ways in which psychological, neural, endocrine, and immune systems interact.

Ader is one of many contemporary scientists who continue to mine the rich lode first discovered by Pavlov. We continue to learn more and more about classical conditioning even today. This is one of the marks of a great discovery; it leads to more questions than it answers.

Ader's research originally centered on conditioned taste aversion in rats. Earlier, a researcher named John Garcia had made the intriguing discovery that the rules of classical conditioning were quite different when stimuli such as smells and tastes were paired with intense gut responses like nausea and vomiting (Garcia & Ervin, 1968). Ader was trying to learn

more about these new rules of conditioning when he and his co-workers happened on evidence that the immune responses could be conditioned.

With rats as experimental subjects, Ader linked the taste of a saccharin solution with the effects of a substance, called cyclophosphamide, that produces nausea. This approach was typical for investigators doing research stimulated by Garcia's work. But things were not going well. Ader's rats kept dying. Why?

It so happens that cyclophosphamide suppresses immune response. Could it be that the immune suppression was being conditioned? Anyone sophisticated in immunology would have *known* this could not be. But Ader was a psychologist, naive to the doctrines of immunology. Ader called on Cohen, an obviously open-minded immunologist, to investigate this implausible hypothesis. They tested to see if immune suppression was taking place, and found that indeed it was (Ader & Cohen, 1975).

They and other investigators have gone on to verify that immune suppression can be conditioned. The studies have been widely replicated, and many subtle controls have been run. Research has strongly confirmed the original supposition that classical conditioning of the immune response was taking place.

Ader has verified the basic finding and has pinpointed many of the variables that control it. The following are some of the basic conclusions we can draw from his work:

1. It is a highly reliable finding; Ader and other researchers have no trouble repeating it.

2. The size of the effect is small.

3. It seems to be true conditioning, and not just some kind of response to aversive stimulation. For example, the effect does not happen with a substance (lithium chloride) that produces the gut responses but does not suppress immunity. Many controls have now been run to assure that it is true conditioning.

4. The effect does not seem to be secondary to a hormonal stress reaction. Since cortisol

suppresses immune response, conditioned changes in cortisol might have produced the suppression of immunity. None of the evidence supports this hypothesis. This kind of conditioning takes place even after removal of the adrenal glands, which are the source of the cortisol. This indicates that conditioned immunosuppression may be of great biological importance, since more than one bodily system can produce it. This is called *redundancy* and tends to be found in organic systems that are of great significance to survival.

Ader and his co-workers have even found that conditioned suppression of the immune system has a beneficial effect on rats with *lupus erythematosus*, which is commonly known as lupus (Ader, 1989). Lupus is an autoimmune disease, and neither its causes nor its cure are known. However, it can be controlled with drugs that suppress immune activity, including the cyclophosphamide Ader used in his work. When the suppressant was paired with the taste of saccharin, it was then possible to control the lupus at least partially with the conditioned stimulus. In other words, a dosage of cyclophosphamide that was normally ineffective would work if paired with the taste of saccharin. This leads to the possibility of immediate clinical applications of conditioned immunosuppression. Maybe we can reduce side effects by administering lower dosages of chemical suppressants, while getting the full benefit by adding conditioned suppression to the treatment.

Communication Between Brain and Immune System

What evidence do we have that the brain controls immune responses? The evidence given so far shows that *learning* controls it, but there is an outside chance that this is not mediated by the brain. However, there is good evidence of a central role of the brain in the regulation of the immune system.

For example, Bulloch (1981) did anatomical studies of the relationship between brain and thymus, and found not only that specific brain areas are connected to the thymus, but also that certain types of innervation were there prenatally. She suggested that these nerve fibers might play a key role in the differentiation of the gland.

Numerous studies have shown that damage to various brain areas, especially those of the hypothalamus and limbic system, result in changes in immune activity. Many of these changes have been summarized by Locke and Hornig-Rohan (1983). In particular, damage to the hypothalamus causes changes in cellular immune activity. For example, injury to the front part (anterior) of the hypothalamus results in suppression of measures of cellular immunity (Brooks, Cross, Roszman, & Markesbery, 1982). Damage to the back part of the hypothalamus or to a part of the limbic system known as the hippocampus seems to enhance at least certain aspects of cellular immune activity.

The control system from hypothalamus to immune system seems to be a two-way street. Besodovsky and his co-workers (1977) have recorded the electrical activity of individual nerve cells in the hypothalamus when antigens were introduced into rats. There were marked increases in the firing of cells in specific parts of the hypothalamus. This is similar to what happens in the brain's visual region when we show something to the animal. So it seems that the brain registers immune activity just as it registers what is going on in the outside world.

There is even evidence from more than one study that the familiar difference between the right and left brain halves applies to control of the immune system. Geschwind and Behan (1982) found that autoimmune diseases tend to occur selectively in left-handed people. Handedness is related to cerebral dominance. Furthermore, NK-cells react less after damage to the left brain of mice, but not after damage to the right brain (Bardos et al., 1981).

The brain also exerts control over humoral immunity, as can be shown by examining the effect of brain injury on the development of anaphylactic reactions. Anaphylaxis is a severe, sometimes fatal response to a foreign protein for which the body has previously developed antibodies. Insect stings and medications such as penicillin tend to produce these kinds of reactions. Symptoms include odd sensations such as numbness, tingling, and burning; hives; gut disturbances, including stomach cramps and loss of bowel or bladder control; and difficulty in breathing. These symptoms may go on to include loss of consciousness, convulsions, and even death. Anaphylaxis occurs when the previously developed antibodies stimulate an overreaction the next time they encounter the antigen. Anaphylaxis is easily produced in experimental animals by injecting them with a foreign protein such as egg albumin, letting the antibodies form, and then presenting the antigen once again.

Damage to the front part of the hypothalamus keeps the anaphylaxis from occurring. Apparently there is some reduction in the formation of the antibodies, since the brain damage has to occur during the stage in which they would normally be forming. This has been shown in carefully controlled studies (Keller, Shapiro, Schliefer, and Stein, 1982). Keller et al. damaged the anterior hypothalamus in guinea pigs either before or after sensitizing them with egg albumin. As controls, they had guinea pigs that went through the surgical procedure but did not receive the brain damage. They also had an unoperated control group. Prevention of anaphylaxis occurred only in the animals whose brains were damaged before the albumin was introduced.

Stress and the Immune Response

Common lore tells us that people who are under stress are more likely to get sick, and a lot of research evidence confirms this idea (see Chapter 7). Is this effect due to changes in immune response? Keep in mind that changes in health following stress might be due to other processes such as failure to eat or sleep well or perhaps a tendency to use unhealthy chemicals, like alcohol, in coping with stress. No doubt these "behavioral mediators" play an important role in

making it more likely for people to get sick. But we also have good evidence that changes in immune activity that are not secondary to changes of lifestyle occur in response to stress. It is likely that these mediate between stress and illness.

Many investigators working with animal subjects in carefully controlled experiments have shown that stress depresses immune response. This occurs with a variety of measures of immune competence and with a range of different types of stressor. Crowding, handling, electric shock, forced swimming, and spinning are common stressors imposed on rats and mice, which are the typical subjects of these studies. Monjan (1981) and Solomon and Amkraut (1981) have reviewed these studies. They generally indicate that stress impairs immune function, but some studies yield a different result. At times, stress even seems to enhance immune response.

Stress seems clearly to influence the immune response, but why would the effects be variable, even sometimes reversing direction? We really cannot say exactly why this happens, but Shavit and Martin (1987) have produced an elegant body of research that clarifies some of the underlying factors. They have shown that two physiologically distinct mechanisms underlie response to stress. One of the mechanisms is mediated by **opioids** (opium-like substances), and the other is not.

Opiates have long been used to produce euphoria or relieve pain, but it was very surprising to find that the nervous system actually has receptors that are attuned to opium-like substances, or "opioids." It made little sense for these receptors to be in the brain unless the brain produced opioid transmitters. Researchers tried to find these transmitters and soon succeeded. (For an interesting account of this work, see Goldberg, 1988.)

Scientists immediately became very excited over the potential applications of the brain's natural opioids, which came to be called **endorphins.** They were so-called because they were naturally found within the nervous system ("endogenous''), and they resembled a major opiate, morphine. Morphine is an excellent pain killer, but it has major side effects and is addictive. The brain's natural "morphine" might do a better job. Perhaps even a form less addictive than morphine could be found.

Furthermore, the presence of endorphins provided a framework to account for a variety of otherwise puzzling facts, like the increased resistance to pain following mild stressors, such as jogging or the effectiveness of acupuncture as a surgical anesthetic. We can verify that such effects are produced by endorphins, since there are drugs (e.g., naloxone or naltrexone) that block opioids. If, say, jogging produces pain resistance because it causes secretion of opioids, then opiate antagonists should eliminate the pain resistance. Haier et al. (1980) have shown that this is actually the case.

Before long, it became clear that endorphins were far more complex than we originally thought and that they had effects well beyond the control of pain. Indeed, these major effects have probably contributed to the failure, so far, to develop a synthetic form of endorphin for use as a pain reliever. There are many different kinds of endogenous opioids (Bloom, 1987), and they serve functions in the brain, hormonal systems, and immune system. With respect to the immune system, researchers have found that many of the types of immune system cells have receptors for opioids.

Opioids typically suppress immune response. Opiate addicts are prone to get infections, and several studies have shown they have immunological deficits. Since many factors, such as lifestyle, might produce this effect, studies have been done on animals to pin down the source of the problem. These studies show that opioids suppress immune response and that opiate antagonists, such as naloxone, block that suppression.

The influence of opioids on tumors has also been shown. For example, the spread of lung tumors to other sites is increased if opiate-producing brain areas are stimulated (Plotnikoff, Faith, Murgo, & Good, 1986).

Let's now return to the work of Shavit and Martin (1987). As noted above, they found that two distinct systems mediated stress response. One of them was mediated by opioids, and the other was not. Seemingly minor details about the delivery of the stressor determined whether the opiate-mediated system was activated. Most important, however, was the finding that the opiate-mediated system suppressed NK activity, but the other system did not. The magnitude of this immune suppression was comparable to that produced by a large dose of morphine.

They went on to show that the stress-induced immune suppression probably took place via the brain. Morphine put directly into the brain produced a powerful suppression of the immune system, and this could be blocked by naltrexone. On the other hand, a morphine-like drug that failed to cross over into the brain, but circulated in the body, did not produce suppression of NK activity. They also found that the adrenal cortex was necessary for the NK suppression to occur.

Later, Shavit and Martin directly tested the effects of this immune suppression on artificially implanted malignant tumors. Rats given the opiate-mediated kind of stress before the tumor implants were more likely to die than were unstressed controls. This tumor-enhancing effect was blocked by naltrexone.

The work described by Shavit and Martin (1987) is a good step in the direction of understanding some of the variability in immune effects produced by stress. Next, we look at related work done on human subjects.

Humans also commonly show suppressed immune reactions when submitted to stress. For example, medical students showed suppression of T-cell and NK-cell activity during highly stressful examination periods, and these findings have been replicated (Kiecolt-Glaser, Glaser, & Strain, 1986; Kiecolt-Glaser & Glaser, 1987; see Figure 4.5). In a similar vein, several measures of immune competence have been taken in people who live near the Three Mile Island nuclear facility. They have been submitted to the long-term stresses of dangers

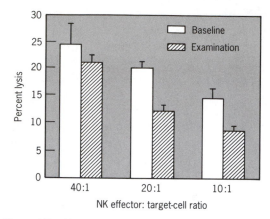

Figure 4.5   Means (± SE) for the three NK-cell effector- to target-cell ratios at baseline and during examinations. *Source*: From "Modulation of Cellular Immunity," by Kiecolt-Glaser et al., *Journal of Behavioral Medicine*, 4, Figure 2, p 16, copyright © 1986 by Plenum Corporation, New York. Reprinted by permission.

stemming from a nuclear accident that took place in that plant. Several of the immune measures were significantly suppressed in these people, as compared to controls who lived farther away (McKinnon et al., 1989).

Naturalistic studies are useful in finding out what happens to the immune system under stress. Their realism gives them a certain edge of credibility. However, we cannot fully control various factors that might influence the outcomes. Factors other than stress might co-vary with medical school exams (e.g., seasons of the year, holidays) or with living near an infamous nuclear plant (e.g., exposure to radiation, selection of people who stay near the plant despite the accident).

It is important to augment such studies with experimental studies in which we have control over delivery of the independent variable. Animal studies are helpful in this area, but some work can be done with humans. For example, the medical students were given training in deep relaxation to see if they could thereby prevent the immune suppression. By conscientious practice of relaxation training, they were indeed able to avoid having suppressed immune reac-

tions. Similarly, relaxation training improved measures of immune competence in a geriatric population (Kiecolt-Glaser, Glaser et al., 1985).

Physiological Mechanisms

Peppered throughout this discussion of how mind-brain influences immunity and health are references to physiological mechanisms that act as the underlying medium for these influences. We summarize the main mechanisms here. First, we know that hormones produce changes in the immune system. For example, ACTH lowers the production of antibodies. Glucocorticoids influence immune activity. They reduce activity of immune cells, decrease the number of lymphocytes, and shrink the tissues that contain lymphocytes. Furthermore, epinephrine influences lymphocyte metabolism (Asterita, 1985, pp. 136–146).

Second, the CNS can influence factors that are involved in innate immunity. For example, the CNS can influence the pattern of blood flow in the body. This causes things like temperature changes that have an effect on pathogens. Tumors may be influenced by thermal changes. Many other aspects of innate immunity are at least partially controlled by the CNS. Another example would be secretion of mucus, which tends to block out pathogens.

Third, there seems to be an as yet poorly understood way in which immune cells and the nervous system influence each other. Receptors for certain hormones and neurotransmitters have been found on several types of immune system cell. There is growing evidence that the brain, endocrine, and immune systems are a single network or system (see, for example, Pert, 1986).

Ader and Cohen (1984) have summarized the reasons for supposing that the immune system interacts with the CNS. They point out that the lymphoid tissue, which is the cradle of immune cells, is innervated by the CNS and that changes in the hypothalamus result in changes in immune response. They also point out that changes in immune response result in changes in hormonal and neurotransmitter levels and that many studies show that stress influences health. Finally, they point to their own seminal research indicating that immune activity can be learned through conditioning.

Conclusions

Before ending this chapter, let's take one last look at the example with which we began—that of a cancer patient who was trying to remove her tumor with imagery. At first, her idea seemed absurd, but much of the information in this chapter suggests that it is not absurd after all. In fact, we can give a fairly plausible account of how the imagination might influence the body.

We know that when a person sees something, the primary visual cortex at the back of the brain is activated. From there, activity goes to the visual "association cortex." When we imagine something that is not really there, the activity is in the visual association cortex, but not in the primary visual region (see, e.g., Schatzman, 1982; for more detail along with distinctions between types of imagery, see Kosslyn, 1987).

From the visual association areas, information goes to the lower part of the temporal lobe, and from there it enters the limbic system, probably by way of the amygdala (Geschwind, 1965). From the limbic system, information can be sent to the hypothalamus, which is known to influence the activity of the pituitary gland and therefore the rest of the endocrine system, as well as to influence both the innate and the acquired immune systems.

We know that the effect of imagery is focal enough to produce changes in specific places in the body. For example, imagery of poison-ivy like substances causes appropriate skin reactions in the spot where the leaves were imagined to be (see Barber, 1984). Adam (1967) has shown that the brain contains detailed information about the intestines. We are not aware of this information, but our brains are reacting. Thus, even highly pinpointed healing influences could be exerted on the body through the use of imagination.

Since this discussion centers on the problem of cancer, you might be misled into thinking that it applies only to that disease. Actually, changes in immune functioning are bound to have an effect on a wide range of disorders. Furthermore, some of the influences on health are not by way of the immune system. For example, early in this chapter we mentioned the finding that mental stress has an effect on heart function that is comparable to the effect of physical stress. Later in this book, you will see many examples of psychological control of health and disease. These include cases in which imagery has a powerful effect on functions such as bleeding and blistering, which are not likely to be mediated by the immune system.

Although we are forced to speculate at several steps in our account of how imagination can influence disease, we have shown that there is nothing implausible about claims of such an influence. Furthermore, the specific psychobiological influences over health functions we have dealt with here are firmly based in scientific evidence and have been shown to be very general across functions relevant to health. When we affirm that the brain-mind has a powerful influence on the health of the body, the scientific "ice" on which we tread is not at all thin. Indeed, it seems thick enough for some pretty vigorous stomping.

Summary

1. The purpose of this chapter was to identify mechanisms that interrelate psychological processes to bodily reactions relevant to health.

2. The autonomic nervous system is a well-known system that regulates bodily reactions. It has two parts, the sympathetic and parasympathetic nervous systems. The

sympathetic nervous system is closely related to the part of the adrenal gland that secretes adrenalin, and the combined sympathoadrenal system mediates "fight or flight" reactions, which can cause major health problems. Examples include increased blood clotting and higher heart rate and blood pressure.

3. The parasympathetic nervous system creates reactions that are almost always the opposite of those stemming from the sympathoadrenal system. In general, the parasympathetic system results in "relaxation" responses.

4. A part of the brain called the hypothalamus controls the autonomic nervous system and regulates bodily systems directly. It is linked to the pituitary gland, which, in turn, controls the output of the endocrine glands and thereby regulates a wide range of the body's organs.

5. The hypothalamus is regulated by brain centers above it that are collectively called the limbic system. These are relatively, but not absolutely, isolated from the brain regions most central to thought and imagery. Thus, it is difficult but not impossible to control our bodily responses voluntarily.

6. The hypothalamus and pituitary regulate the output of the outer part of the adrenal gland, called the adrenal cortex, which secretes hormones that regulate a wide range of bodily processes, including such things as blood pressure, inflammation, and the immune system.

7. Hans Selye described a pattern of bodily responses that occurs under stress and that involves activity of the hypothalamic-pituitary system and the adrenal cortex. It is called the General Adaptation Syndrome. It has three stages: (a) the stage of alarm, in which the adrenal cortex swells in response to output from the pituitary; (b) the stage of resistance, in which the body seems to return to a fairly normal state but cannot react well to further stress; and (c) the stage of exhaustion, in which increased levels of cortisol produce effects on the immune, digestive, circulatory, and other systems, which may lead to death.

8. Specialized neurons in the hypothalamus secrete releasing factors that control pituitary output, which in turn controls the other endocrine glands.

9. Cortisol secretion is regulated by the hypothalamus, and it suppresses immune activity. However, neural control of immune activity is apparently much more extensive than that.

10. There are two main systems of immunity, the innate and the acquired systems. The innate system consists of various mechanisms that eject harmful substances, create barriers to them, or cause the bodily environment to be inhospitable to them. Coughing, sneezing, and getting a fever are examples of innate immunity. In the acquired system various mechanisms are capable of recognizing and neutralizing substances, such as bacteria and viruses, that are harmful.

11. The acquired system of immunity is further divided into a cellular and a humoral system. The cellular system involves special cells that recognize pathogens and set in motion mechanisms that destroy them. Within the cellular system of immunity, there are two major classes of cells, the phagocytes, which devour and destroy harmful substances (called antigens) and the lymphocytes. There are two main types of lymphocytes: T-cells and B-cells.

12. There are three main subclasses of T-cells: helper, killer, and suppressor. Helper T-cells use chemical signals (e.g., interleukins and interferons) to tell other immune cells to attack antigens. Killer T-cells attack and destroy cells that contain antigens. Suppressor T-cells turn off the defensive

activity of the T-cell system when appropriate.

13. The main function of the B-cells is to regulate the humoral immune system, which works by stimulating the production of antibodies. Antibodies are complex chemicals that recognize invaders and neutralize them.

14. A major type of phagocyte is the macrophage. Macrophages engulf and destroy foreign invaders. They also cooperate with helper T-cells in sounding the original alarm that an invader is present.

15. Killer cells (K) and natural killer (NK) cells look like lymphocytes but are not. They work in a cooperative way with the T-cells and humoral systems. They are probably part of a system for destroying cancer cells.

16. Natural killer cells can destroy antigens without help from the rest of the immune system. But they do even better when they receive chemical signals from T-cells. Interferon from T-cells activates NK-cells to kill virus-infected and tumor cells.

17. The humoral system is based on molecules known as antibodies that are produced by B-cells. These antibodies attach to the invading antigens and neutralize them by such devices as hooking them together (agglutination), immobilizing them (immobilization), or keeping them from being soluble in bodily fluids (precipitation).

18. The immune surveillance theory of cancer states that we all get cancer cells from time to time but that the immune system detects and destroys them. The theory was stimulated by observations that people who have to undergo immune suppression tend to develop cancers. Since chronic stress can suppress the immune system, it may play a role in the development of cancer.

19. Chronic toleration of stress leads to hyperadaptosis, which means that the hypothal-amus tells the adrenal cortex to secrete cortisol. This goes on for so long that the hypothalamus changes its set point to tolerate higher levels of cortisol, and thus immune suppression.

20. Measures of hyperadaptosis have been devised, and they predict both onset and survival of cancer. Interestingly, this resetting is related to passive styles of coping and depression.

21. The effects of hyperadaptosis are increased when people have high lipid levels, which are correlated with reductions in the number of T-cells and with diminished functioning of macrophages. The term *cancrophilia* has been coined to describe the resulting tendency to develop cancer.

22. Ader and his co-workers showed that suppression of immune response can be classically conditioned. This finding has been repeated by other investigators. It is not merely due to conditioning of cortisol activity, since it occurs after removal of the adrenal glands. In addition to its value in showing that the immune system is subject to classical conditioning, there may be a clinical value in applying such conditioning to people with autoimmune diseases.

23. Evidence from many sources indicates that the brain can influence immune activity. For example, (a) the nervous system innervates the thymus; (b) damage to specific brain areas can result in suppression or enhancement of both cellular and humoral immune activity; (c) the hypothalamus monitors immune activity; (d) receptors for certain hormones and neurotransmitters have been found on several types of immune system cell; (e) the left and right hemispheres of the brain influence immune activity in different ways; and (f) stress influences immune activity.

24. There are two systems that mediate stress response: one uses the brain's natural opiate-like substances and a second does

not. Opiates in general suppress immune response, and stimulation of the opiate-mediated stress system suppresses NK-cell activity. Animals undergoing tumor implants are more likely to die if they are under opiate-mediated stress.

25. Many studies done with humans under natural stress have shown that they have suppressed immune systems. Some work indicates that this suppression can be prevented through conscientious use of relaxation training.

Key Terms

Acquired immunity

Adrenal cortex

Adrenal medulla

Adrenocorticotrophic hormone (ACTH)

Antibodies

Antigens

Autoimmune diseases

Autonomic nervous system (ANS)

B-cells

Central nervous system (CNS)

Corticotrophin-releasing factor (CRF)

Cortisol

Endorphins

Epinephrine

General Adaptation Syndrome (GAS)

Glucocorticoids

Humoral system of immunity

Hypothalamic-pituitary-adrenal cortical system

Hypothalamus

Immune system

Immunoglobulins

Innate system of immunity

Killer cells

Limbic system

Lymphocytes

Lymphokines

Mineralocorticoids

Monocytes

Natural killer cells

Neuropeptides

Norepinephrine

Opioids

Parasympathetic nervous system

Pathogens

Peripheral nervous system

Phagocytes

Pituitary gland

Psychoneuroimmunology

Stage of alarm

Stage of exhaustion

Stage of resistance

Sympathetic nervous system

Sympathoadrenal system

T-cells

Thymus

Discussion Questions

1. What do the sympathetic nervous system and the adrenal medulla have in common?

2. How do the functions of the sympathetic and parasympathetic nervous systems differ?

3. Describe the role of the limbic system and hypothalamus in regulating health.

4. What functions does the hypothalamic-pituitary-adrenal cortical system have in relation to health?

5. What is the General Adaptation Syndrome and what are its stages?

6. List and explain the main subsystems that compose the immune system.

7. Briefly describe the body's system of humoral immunity.

8. Briefly describe the body's system of cellular immunity.

9. Describe the main evidence that the immune system is under psychological or central nervous system control.

10. Explain the immune surveillance theory of cancer and tell why it suggests an important role of psychological factors in cancer.

11. List and briefly explain the major research evidence indicating that stress influences immune responses.

Chapter 5

Psychological and Behavioral Therapies in Health Psychology

*K*arl was a very intense, aggressive, and even coarse 54-year-old man who, despite his age, was still built like a middleweight boxer. He described himself as a Type A, and he suffered from dangerously high blood pressure. On one occasion he went to an emergency room with blood pressure of 210/140. His wife had left him to move in with another man, his business was not doing well, and he was in trouble with the IRS. His doctor found it very difficult to control his blood pressure with medicines. Furthermore, after 20 years on various medications, he complained increasingly of sexual impotence as a side effect. Eventually his doctor sent him to a university clinic headed by Dr. James Lynch. Dr. Lynch deals with hypertension by showing people how their blood pressure is influenced by emotions they would prefer to deny.

During the treatment in Dr. Lynch's clinic, Karl was shown that his blood pressure tended to increase when he discussed topics that might reasonably be expected to be upsetting, *especially* if he did not notice he felt upset by them. He also learned to bring his blood pressure down by relaxing and breathing deeply. His blood pressure dropped steadily through several sessions. Then, during one session he mentioned having talked to his doctor about reducing his diuretic[1] dosage. He was annoyed by the frequent need to urinate that accompanied this medication.

The doctor categorically refused to lower the dosage. But Karl had a "little secret." To put it in his own words, "Only problem is I cut those damn pills out a week before I called him!" As he went on describing his discussion with the doctor, his blood pressure shot up from 145/90 to 195/140. A nurse colleague of Lynch's, Dr. Sue Ann Thomas, was working with Karl and calmly said to him, "Look at what your little secret did to your blood pressure! Do you think your little secret is worth such a big price?" Karl was shocked to see what had happened to his blood pressure. He said, "Christ, I've never seen my blood pressure change like that. And you know, I didn't feel anything. I didn't feel a damn thing . . . I must be totally disconnected from my body and my feelings. I didn't feel a damn thing!" (Lynch, 1985, p. 248 ff.)

There is reason to believe that the central factor that is keeping Karl from controlling his blood pressure through medication is his failure to recognize his own feelings, which he calls being "disconnected from my body." Clearly, psychological treatment is needed to get at this aspect of his illness. Medication alone might only distance him still more from his feelings.

IMPACT OF BIOMEDICAL VERSUS BIOPSYCHOSOCIAL MODELS

Throughout this book, we give examples of the many facets of health care that are strongly af-

fected by psychological factors. All these uses of psychology become apparent when we adopt a biopsychosocial model. Even the present biomedical model reserves a place for psychological treatment. When patients seek treatment for physical illnesses but medical tests fail to find a basis for them, their physicians usually refer them to psychiatrists or psychologists.

People often think that psychological intervention can help treat a disease only if the disease originated from psychological factors. This notion leads many patients to feel that psychological referral implies that the disorder is "all in the patient's head." This is a serious misconception that deprives people of valuable treatments based in psychology. Actually, we often find that even illnesses that originated from nonpsychological causes can be controlled psychologically.

[1] Diuretics are often given as one of the first medications in attempts to control blood pressure. A diuretic causes the body to throw off fluid, reduces the body's fluid volume, and thereby lowers blood pressure.

A good example is the case of epileptic seizures, which typically originate in brain abnormalities, but nevertheless seem at least somewhat subject to psychological control (Richard & Reiter, 1990).

PERSPECTIVES ON PSYCHOSOCIAL PROCESSES IN HEALTH

But how do psychological factors control health and disease? Although there are many perspectives on this problem, two very basic views seem most important. One view is that various illnesses are *behaviors* that are controlled according to psychological principles. Clearly, actions that create health risk, such as smoking and eating a high-fat diet, are behaviors.

Less obvious is the possibility that many "medical" problems such as being in pain, having high blood pressure, or developing an ulcer may be behaviors. If they are behaviors, the implication is that they can be controlled through the same principles as those that govern learning. If so, treatment can take the form of behavioral therapy or its more recent variant, cognitive behavioral therapy. We will explain these therapies below, but first let us discuss a second view of how psychological factors influence health.

The second view is a *psychodynamic* one. Sometimes it is called the psychosomatic view, since it played a key role in creating the field of psychosomatic medicine. Regardless of what we call it, the underlying idea is that sicknesses can be, at least in part, ways of expressing tensions and conflicts of which we are not consciously aware. This includes real physical illnesses, not just problems that are "all in one's head." For example, an ulcer is physically real, but psychological distresses can contribute to its development and continuation.

The psychodynamic idea that we express unconscious conflicts in the form of symptoms is strongly identified with Freudian theory. But we do not have to accept Freudian theory to believe that symptoms express unconscious problems. This should become apparent later in the chapter.

Therapy within the psychodynamic framework tends to emphasize helping the patient find healthier ways of expressing the unconscious contents. For this reason such therapies are often called **expressive therapies**. This term is more theoretically neutral than the terms "psychodynamic" and "psychosomatic", which are strongly linked to Freudian theory.

THE BEHAVIORAL MODEL OF THERAPY

The learning or behavioral model is probably more influential in modern health psychology than any other model. In this view, many aspects of health are either learned behaviors or are influenced by them. For example, chronic pain patients may be viewed as engaging in "pain behaviors" such as getting what they need by expressing pain, staying in bed most of the time, not doing work and narrowing their interests, or complaining about pain a lot.

The person who smokes, overeats, drinks too much, and works too hard may be seen as having learned many high risk habits. In all such cases, people have ways of behaving that fall under the laws of learning. Seeing symptoms, lifestyles, and risk factors as learned behaviors can help us discover the influences that are maintaining them. For example, we can observe how family members, friends, or health care providers reward them, often unwittingly.

The Cognitive-Behavioral Model of Therapy

A very important variant of the behavioral model is the cognitive-behavioral model. This model emphasizes the role played by what we say to ourselves and by what we imagine, rather than focusing on behaviors that can be observed directly.

Since behaviorists place exclusive emphasis on measurable behaviors, they originally resisted seeing self-talk and imagery as factors that control behavior. But the successes of the cognitive approach have been great enough that most behavioral psychologists seem to have put that kind of theoretical problem aside and have embraced cognitive interventions as a means of augmenting behavioral interventions.

Certain features of behavior therapy and cognitive-behavioral therapy make them especially useful to health psychologists. Their basic principles are relatively easy to learn. Therefore, brief training in them can be put to good use. Furthermore, psychologists often get to work with a patient for only a few sessions. Simple behavioral treatments tend to fit in well with the sharp time limits that are placed on the psychologist's work.

Another advantage of behavioral and cognitive behavioral analysis is that it clarifies the factors that keep a person symptomatic. For example, in the study of pain, this kind of analysis has enriched our grasp of what we are dealing with when we try to treat "pain." It also reveals the many ways family and health care professionals can unwittingly reward the behavior of being sick (see Chapter 10).

Another positive feature of behavior therapy is the fact that therapeutic practice and scientific verification tend to go hand in hand. Behavior therapists measure behaviors rather exactly and gather careful data not only during treatment, but also before and after treatment. In that way they have control conditions which they can use as comparisons with what takes place during treatment. This practice has resulted in much scientific data attesting to the effectiveness of behavior therapies.

CHARACTERISTICS OF BEHAVIOR THERAPY

Behavior therapy is based on our understanding of conditioning and learning. Behaviors can be learned and perpetuated through conditioning. Sometimes, however, we can treat a behavior with conditioning methods even if it originated with some other process. How behaviors got started is not as relevant as it might seem in determining whether they can be modified. For example, it is likely that reacting painfully to needle pricks is an inborn reaction, but conditioning can change it. We see this when needle pricks get linked to narcotics.

On the other hand, conditioning can make mild, harmless stimuli produce very strong negative reactions. The sights, sounds, and smells and even thoughts and images of a doctor's office can produce nausea and vomiting in patients who link them with chemotherapy. Laszlo (1987) has described this phenomenon very vividly:

> We have seen patients drive into the hospital parking lot and promptly begin to vomit, or vomit when they smell the alcohol sponge used to clean off the arm prior to chemotherapy or even vomit when they see the nurse who administers the chemotherapy—even if that person is encountered out of uniform in a supermarket or elsewhere away from the hospital. (p. 52)

Classical Conditioning

The two basic types of conditioning are classical conditioning and operant conditioning. (Refer to Chapter 2 if you need a refresher on classical and operant conditioning.) Since Pavlov's day, classical conditioning has been shown to work in a very wide range of species, including humans, and with a remarkable array of responses, including those of organ systems that have significance to our health.

To illustrate, in Raynaud's disease, the blood vessels of the skin constrict abnormally, and painfully, usually in response to cold or to stimuli that create strong emotions. Jobe, Sampson, Roberts, and Kelly (1986) showed that classical conditioning allows patients with this disease to dilate their small blood vessels instead of constricting them. This finding is parallel to Pavlov's dogs learning to salivate to the sound of a buzzer, but in this case it controls the symptoms of the disease.

Operant Conditioning

With classical conditioning, the stimuli are paired by experimental plan, not according to whether or not the organism responds a certain way. With operant conditioning, reinforcement is given only when the organism emits the desired behavior. In practice, we usually reinforce approximations to the behavior and then become successively more stringent in our requirements until only the full behavior is reinforced.

For example, an operant approach to changing pain behavior would not require the person to be pain free before getting reinforced. We would break the task down into very small units, each of which would be as easy as possible for the patient. In fact, if we could do it, we would break the task down into units so easy that the patient would always get it right and get reinforced.

Health-Related Behaviors as Conditioned Responses

The following case of a woman named Marie illustrates how operant conditioning can reward headaches.

Marie was a "supermom." She had four children, a high-powered physician husband, and was enrolled in a doctoral program in social work. She was doing very well in her doctoral work, and, although her husband gave her virtually no help, she managed the household efficiently. Unfortunately, she suffered from crippling, classical migraine headaches. With these headaches, the patient gets a configuration of warning symptoms, called a prodrome, just before the headache starts. When asked what happened during her prodrome, she said, "People appear to be far away." When asked what she did as a consequence of the migraine, she said she had to go upstairs, dim the lights, and go to bed. Exploration of her relationship with her husband revealed that she saw him as a very important doctor who could not be bothered with such things as child care. She felt she had no right to ask him to take over this care so she could have some time for herself, and he agreed. The migraines seemed to serve as a means for her to insist on his help without putting it into words. A review of the history of her migraines revealed that they were sometimes absent for years and that their occurrence was inevitably related to situations (e.g., with her mother when she lived with her parents) in which she did not feel she could assert her right to say "No." She was unable verbally to get people to be "far away," but her

migraines could do that job for her—at a great price.

When Marie reported having migraines, it was important to find out *what happens after the migraine*—the reinforcing consequence. It was also important to know in what contexts the migraines tend to begin, the antecedent stimuli. This is how psychologists find out what they must change to bring the headaches under control.

Behaviors, including symptoms of illness such as headaches, are controlled by the reinforcers that follow them. To control health-related behaviors—for example, headaches, smoking, overeating, sedentariness—we have to be aware of the patterns of reinforcement that keep the behavior going. We call these **contingencies of reinforcement.**

We also have to be alert for cues that set off the behaviors or make them more likely. For example, it is more likely that we will eat fattening foods if we bring them home from the store and have them around the house in plain sight. We may be able to regulate the eating by controlling the cues. This regulation of behaviors by cues is technically called **stimulus control.** When the likelihood of a response varies systematically with the presence or absence of a cue, the response is said to be "under stimulus control." When a response is under such control, we can regulate the response by manipulating the stimuli.

Precision and Measurement

An important feature of the behavioral approach is its emphasis on pinpointing the variables of interest. What exactly is a headache, and what would constitute a treatment success? What exactly is Type A behavior, and how would we know if we succeeded in getting a person to change it? Regardless of the health behavior we want to deal with, we must first identify what it is.

The required precision is gained by careful measurement. Recordkeeping is very important in this kind of work. Records may be kept in various ways and by various people, including the patient, significant others, or health care workers. As a first step, it is important to be very precise about the nature of the target behavior.

Often we feel that we clearly "know" the nature of the behavior we want to control. When we try to stipulate measurements of it, however, we find that our idea is not at all clear. Thus, apparently simple concepts such as "pain" (Fordyce, 1976), "relaxation" (Poppen, 1988), or "fear" (Rachman, 1990) prove quite interesting when submitted to behavioral analysis.

To illustrate with the example of "fear," it turns out that this familiar and seemingly simple concept can be usefully broken down into three major components: (1) the subjective experience,[2] (2) the set of physiological reactions characteristic of fear, and (3) fearful behavior. Rachman (1990) notes that results of studies and clinical interventions vary depending on which of these meanings of "fear" is examined. Such analyses commonly show that what appeared clear and unitary can actually be reduced to several different factors.

Knowledge of this factor may help improve the treatment by breaking it down into steps that focus on each of the different components of the problem. Such analyses also let us know exactly what it is we should be reinforcing. For example, we can selectively reinforce "nonpain talk" or normal behavioral patterns and ways of dealing with others ("nonpain behavior").

Clear definitions and measurements also help us share information with others, including patients, families, and co-workers, who are part of the treatment team. With clear measurements, we can be confident that the whole team is working in a consistent, coordinated way.

Interviews or asking the patient to vividly imagine the circumstances surrounding an episode of the disorder may help us see what leads to symptoms. Open-ended diary keeping may also help. However, counting and recording precisely defined behaviors and the stimuli that precede and follow them is much more informative.

Behavior can be measured in many ways, each of which has its special applications. For example, we can (1) count how often a behavior occurs ("frequencies"), (2) count how often it occurs per unit of time ("rates"), (3) observe if it occurs during specified time periods ("time samples"), and (4) rate some facet of the behavior, such as intensity, on a scale ("rating scales"). Counting the frequency or rate may be best for a clearly definable behavior with a definite beginning and end. On the other hand, it is sometimes hard to tell when an episode of certain behaviors begins and ends. In such cases it may be better to observe every X minutes to see if it is occurring.

Several measures can be used to converge on the same target behavior. We may want to measure in more than one way ("multimethod assessment"), to gather data from more than one source, such as self versus other ("multisource assessment"), and to take measures in several different settings, such as in the clinic, at home, and at work ("multisetting assessment"). These methods strengthen our conviction that we are getting at the problem behavior in a stable, meaningful way.

After we have clearly identified the target behavior in an appropriately precise way, we record it. Often the patient is asked to record it, and this can work very well. We can also ask someone else, such as a family member who can observe the behavior, to do the recording.

People often get confused about what is being recorded, so it helps to do *reliability checks*. That is, someone other than the main person who is recording keeps an independent record of the behavior during at least some of the measurements. We have to make sure they do not cue each other in any way that would give a false impression of reliability. The two records are then compared to be sure the two independent observers are in agreement.

Various devices may be used to help with recordkeeping. These may be as simple as note pads or index cards on which tallies are made when the behavior occurs. Often, more details are also noted. For example, when we get mea-

[2] This must, of course, be measured as a verbal report, since we cannot directly measure a subjective experience.

sures of headaches, we commonly ask for a rating of the intensity on a scale ranging from "no headache" to the "severest kind of headache." This is usually a scale ranging from 0 to 4. We might also ask for a record of medication intake.

Recording more than one facet of the behavior gives us a stronger form of measurement than recording only one. However, we must be careful not to overload the person with obligations to measure. Asking for too many measurements can lead people to stop keeping the records altogether or to keep them carelessly.

More complicated measuring devices can also be used. One handy device is the "golf counter," which can be worn on the wrist. It enables a person to record the occurrence of a behavior with little effort and often without its being noticed by others. In addition, special recording devices may be attached to the person to record such variables as heart rate and blood pressure without any effort on the part of the patient. Biofeedback machines are an example of this kind of recording, and they can break down the information as well.

We usually ask patients to make notes about anything that happened before or after the target behavior. What was happening in the social and physical environment? What were they thinking and imagining? What foods or chemicals did they consume? This helps both them and us to notice factors that act as cues or reinforcers.

Once we have the recordings, we have to convert them into a format, such as a graph, that makes what happened obvious. The patient should usually be the one who does this conversion. The important point is that the patient, the health psychologist, and anyone else who is collaborating in the treatment effort should see the patterns of occurrence of the behavior and how these patterns relate to the physical, social, and internal environments.

Behavioral Management

After measuring the behavior, we are in a position to intervene and modify it. Ideally, we first gather baseline data without intervening. This step is essential for research and should be performed in clinical settings if possible. Obtaining a baseline makes it possible for us to know if our interventions are effective and to convince skeptical patients that changes have occurred.

The main tools at the disposal of the behavior therapists are **selective reinforcement, extinction** and **punishment,** and development of **stimulus control**.

Selective Reinforcement

With **selective reinforcement,** we reinforce desirable responses and withhold reinforcement for undesirable responses. In effect, we encourage the person's strengths instead of weaknesses. In the case of a pain patient, we reinforce nonpain talk instead of pain talk. We encourage return to normal activities rather than inactivity and the patient's independence instead of dependence on others. Pain medication is given on schedule instead of as a consequence of pain.

Extinction and Punishment

Extinction means that reinforcement is withheld for a response that was previously reinforced. When this tool is used, the rate of that response will eventually decline. Take the example of a person who eats while watching television. Various physiological responses (e.g., salivation, stomach activity), which are experienced as "urges to eat," "images of getting favored foods," and so on, have been reinforced in the presence of the TV. The urges will be felt for some time when the person stops eating in front of the TV. Eventually, however, the urges and images related to eating will disappear if no further food reinforcers are given.

This is true provided no other reinforcers for the response are present. We must be alert to that possibility, since it can lead to an apparent failure of the extinction procedure. It may also take a very long time to extinguish a behavior. A valuable supplement to the extinction procedure is simultaneous reinforcement of a desired alternative behavior. For example, people working with a pain patient might avoid giving attention for "pain behaviors" and at the same time

The person who usually eats while watching television has urges to eat reinforced by its presence. The urges will be felt for some time even if she quits eating in front of the television.

give lots of attention and praise for positive accomplishments.

Behaviors can be suppressed at least temporarily by presenting a noxious stimulus after the behavior. This is called **punishment**. Unless the punishment is very severe, the suppression of the behavior will likely be short-lived. But temporary suppression can provide an opening for new, more adaptive behaviors to get reinforced, so therapists sometimes use punishment.

Patients can also be trained to give mild punishments to themselves. One method is for the person to wear a rubber band around his or her wrist and snap it each time the undesirable behavior, for example, an urge to smoke or eat a fatty food, occurs.

Stimulus Control

We bring a behavior under **stimulus control** when we want it to occur only under specific conditions. Take the case of weight control. Overweight people tend to eat in the presence of

just about every cue in the house. Each of these cues signals the availability of food reinforcers. This will be experienced as constant food-related thoughts, images, and urges. When the person walks in the door, a mouth-watering image of a delicious sandwich is seen. When the television is turned on, the idea of having some ice cream comes to mind.

Obviously, we cannot extinguish all eating behavior. One way to reduce it is to eat only in the presence of specific cues. Programs to modify eating often require that the person only eat at a table setting while fully dressed, and without engaging in other behaviors such as reading and watching television. If a behavior is reinforced only in the presence of a certain set of stimuli, the behavior will eventually come under the control of these stimuli. Other cues will cease to encourage the behavior.

Limitations of Behavioral Management

The main strengths of the behavioral approach are: (1) it is relatively easy to learn, (2) it clarifies aspects of what we are studying that would otherwise remain cloudy, (3) it is often very effective and helpful, and (4) its results are usually clear cut and more verifiable than those obtained with other techniques. Not surprisingly, health psychologists widely use this approach.

At times, however, the therapist should help the patients express feelings, deepen their understanding of themselves, or come to grips with matters that are of ultimate concern. It is all too easy to jump in and control people who are more in need of being understood and of widening their self-understanding.

An example of the application of behavioral control techniques that might bring home what we are saying here is a study by Redd (1982) entitled "Treatment of Excessive Crying in a Terminal Cancer Patient: A Time-series Analysis." The patient was a man who cried during "48 percent of waking time." The behavior was brought under control by taking away "social stimulation" when the patient cried, and reinforcing behavior that was not compatible with crying.

One can imagine that reducing the crying was more convenient for personnel charged with the care of this patient. But it is clear that important value judgments underlie the decision to minimize this patient's crying. These are not questions of technology or science, but questions of whose comfort is going to be given priority and what is best for people to do in the last days of their life. For example, it might well have been better for this patient to be allowed to go through the depths of grief in order to come to grips with the reality of what was happening to him.

Notice that there is no essential reason why a behavioral approach could not help a person express things that are difficult to express. So this is not a criticism that strikes at the core of behavioral therapies. It is more in the nature of a cautionary note. Too much emphasis on controlling behavior through manipulation of variables can readily slide over into imposing one's own values (or those of one's employers) on patients.

Cognitive Behavioral Therapy

Cognitive therapies emphasize the importance of thoughts and images in producing problematic mental and physical conditions. Our thoughts and images regulate whether we are depressed, anxious, or angry. These cognitions also influence whether our stomach juices flow, our blood pressure surges, or our heart pounds. Table 5.1 illustrates some common patterns of distorted thinking which are of significance in health settings.

There are various cognitive therapies. Cognitive *behavioral* therapy has it roots in behaviorism, but nevertheless emphasizes the controlling function of thoughts and images. It uses the methods described above for behavior therapy, but it highlights the power of thoughts and images in controlling behaviors. Because it is widely used in health psychology, we will give a basic description of it.

A key feature of cognitive behavioral therapy is the transformation of the patient's symptoms into identified, potentially solvable problems instead of vague, overwhelming ones (Turk, Meichenbaum, & Genest, 1983). The essence of this transformation lies in getting patients to rethink issues that have them trapped in maladaptive binds. If we are to get the needed changes in thoughts and images, it will not do merely to lecture to the person. Let's say a client named Sam has come to an emergency room fearing that he is having a heart attack. After establishing rapport with one of the nurses, he says:

---

*T*he girl I've been dating, Holly, stood me up for our date; I know it's because I am stupid, unlovable, fat, and ugly. No one will ever love me and I'm going to have to live my life alone. I don't want to go on this way; there's no use living.

Table 5.1 Common Patterns of Distorted Thinking in Medical Settings

Catastrophizing	Magnifying the potential importance or consequences of one small problem or mistake. This style is often evidenced by the use of the words "what if." For example, if your x-ray results are late, you think, "What if I have cancer, a fracture, or other negative possibilities?"
Mind reading	Making assumptions and arbitrary conclusions about how someone else feels or thinks without checking the data. Your nurse doesn't answer the call light. You think, "She doesn't care about me." "She is angry because I call too often." In fact, she is busy with a cardiac arrest down the hall.
Overgeneralization	Making broad negative generalizations based on one experience or fact. The words "always" and "never" are common with this pattern. "I will never feel happy again." "I will never be able to read a book again." "I will never be free of pain."
Personalization	Blaming yourself for events that you did not have complete control over and using this bit of data to reinforce your lack of self-esteem. For example, your family doesn't visit you. You blame yourself for being bad company when in fact their car broke down.
Should fallacies	Based on a personal set of inflexible rules for how people should behave and how life should be. "I shouldn't make mistakes." "I must be a good nurse." "I should never feel depressed." "I should never feel angry at patients."

Source: From "Cognitive-behavioral interventions," by J. K. Dreyfus, *Medical Psychotherapy: An International Journal*, 3, Table 1, p. 159, copyright © 1990 by Hogrefe & Huber, Toronto, Ontario. Reprinted by permission.

It won't do for the nurse just to tell Sam that he is overgeneralizing from Holly to everybody, catastrophizing about the implications of one date, exaggerating his bad points, and so on. Friends often use this approach, and it may help a little. However, more often Sam will resist changing his point of view, responding with "Yes, but . . ." Or he may pretend to agree while inwardly holding on to his view of things.

A key step in cognitive therapy would be to form a collaborative team with Sam. We might say something like the following:

This isn't going to be a matter of my telling you how to think. Instead we are going to work as a team to explore how your thoughts and images influence your reactions, including your symptoms. We are also going to look closely at what kinds of things happen before and after your symptoms that may play a role in keeping them going. Really, only you can do this; you're in charge here and I can only help.

The bottom line here is that any real changes in patients' cognitions are going to come from testing and validating the new ways of thinking in their own life situations. The therapist can help patients see that certain thoughts and images tend to be related to symptoms and recognize that there are other ways to think and imagine. Then mutually agreeable homework assignments have to be worked out so that patients can try the new ways of managing problems and see what impact they have. Validating the new ways of thinking in real life is the key to gaining their acceptance. Later, under "thought stopping" and "thought countering" we will have more to say about methods of changing thoughts.

The Importance of Teamwork

In this kind of therapy it is important to draw solutions out of the patient, much as an obstetrician draws a baby out of the mother. It is the *mother's* baby, not the obstetrician's. We also may have to ask family members and health care providers to collaborate in changing the way the symptoms are to be treated. Those responsible for the purely medical side of the treatment, as well as significant others, must be fully aware of the nature of behavioral treatment. Otherwise, they might unintentionally work against each other, making adherence to the program far less likely. In other words, we strive for a real team effort, with the patient at the center.

Cognitive Behavioral Therapy Tools

Problem Definition. The first phase of cognitive behavioral therapy involves defining the problem and placing it within a framework that renders it solvable. Methods used in this stage include interviews, image-based reconstructions, self-monitoring, and direct observation of the patient's behavior. We discuss each of these methods below. The goal of these procedures is to note: (1) situations that influence the symptoms (e.g., act as cues that trigger symptoms or as buffers that minimize them), (2) the actions the patient has taken to cope with the problem and the effects of those actions, and (3) the consequences of the symptomatic behavior.

Interviews include the client and significant others, and the focus is on finding the specific factors that trigger the symptoms (including external factors as well as internal thoughts and images) or that make them worse or better. It is also important to find out what the patient *believes* is useful in dealing with the problem. If the patient is to remain cooperative, the therapist has to work from the patient's own view of things.

With image-based reconstructions, the patient is asked to relax with eyes closed and to picture in detail a recent episode of the disorder. This exercise often helps to retrieve specific details that could not be accessed in the interview. In particular, the patient is encouraged to retrieve information about images and self-statements that may be pertinent.

Self-Monitoring. Both the interview and the image-based reconstruction rely on faded memories, so it is also helpful to use self-monitoring. With this method, the patient keeps

an ongoing record of specified behavior or symptoms. For example, a headache patient may receive forms that are to be filled out four times per day indicating the occurrence of headaches and their intensity. The patient may also be asked to note aspects of the physical and social environment that preceded the headache, as well as any potentially relevant thoughts and images. Recall Marie for whom the pressures of being a "supermom" were relevant to her headaches.

Self-monitoring can be done with easily carried forms or index cards, with wrist counters, or even by keeping a focused diary. A typical self-monitoring form is shown in Figure 5.1. By reducing the reliance on memory, this method can give more accurate information than methods that rely primarily on recall. However, patients may fail to comply with these procedures and fill in the forms at the end of the week, just before their scheduled therapy session. So recordkeeping is not foolproof. In some instances it is worthwhile to arrange for direct observation of their responses.

The therapist can arrange to be present during an actual episode of the behavior. For example, a patient whose blood pressure shoots up when medical personnel record it can be observed, and the therapist can gather information about external and internal factors that are relevant.

Skills Training. The first phase of cognitive therapy focuses on assessing the problem and the conditions under which it occurs, but this assessment phase may also produce therapeutic results. During the process of "re-framing" the problem and carefully monitoring the symptoms as well as the conditions that increase or decrease them, the patient may already show signs of better coping. There is also a specific stage of teaching the patient to deal better with what are now more clearly specified problems. Having defined the problem, the person may need help in developing strategies and skills for dealing with it.

Many different methods can be used at this stage. For example, the person may learn to use

Thought Record				
SITUATION What were you doing or thinking about when you started to feel bad?	FEELINGS What symptoms did you notice (e. g. anger, apathy)? How bad did you feel? (On a scale from 0-100 with zero as "terrible" and 100 as "fine.")	AUTOMATIC THOUGHT(S) What was going through your mind immediately before you started to feel bad?	REALISTIC ANSWER(S) How can you answer the negative thoughts realistically and constructively? Is there anything you can do to test out the thoughts or handle the situation differently in the future?	OUTCOME How do you feel now that you have tried to answer the thoughts? (on a scale from 0-100 with 100 as "fine.")
Had to wait two hours for my X-ray on a hard stretcher in pain.	Anger	How can they do this to me? Nobody cares I'm in pain. I'm powerless.	Have I told anyone I'm in pain? People can't read my mind.	
MD told me my Leukemia is no longer in remission. I willl need chemotherapy again.	Scared Depressed	It's not fair. I won't be able to stand the nausea again. I'll never see my daughter get married.	What data do I have that says I won't have another remission. I handled the nausea last time.	

Table 3– Weekly Activity Schedule							
	Monday	Tuesday	Wednesday	Thursday	Friday	Saturday	Sunday
9–10	Watch TV P = 2						
10–11							
11–12							
12–1	Walk in hall M = 3						
1–2							
2–3	Write a letter M = 4						
3–4							
4–5							
5–6	Eat supper P = 2						
6–7	Talk on phone P = 2						
7–8							
8–12	Sleep						

Note: On a 1-5 scale grade yourself for M = Mastery; P = Pleasure; for each activity.

Figure 5.1 A typical self-monitoring form that reduces reliance on memory. *Source*: From "Cognitive-behavioral interventions," by J. K. Dreyfus, *Medical Psychotherapy: An International Journal*, 3, Tables 2 and 3, p. 161, copyright © 1990 by Hogrefe & Huber, Toronto, Ontario. Reprinted by permission.

operant conditioning to bring his or her own behavior or that of significant others under control. (The therapeutic change does not always have to be primarily a change in the *patient's* behavior.) The patient may have to learn the skill of postponing judgment and action long enough to brainstorm and sensibly pick the course of action that is most likely to work. It may also be necessary to teach the patient assertiveness or other communications skills.

A good deal of the focus in this stage of the therapy is on changing thoughts and images in order to test out whether better results can be produced after such cognitive changes. Self-statements and images are called into question, and alternative possibilities are placed on the agenda. Sometimes the behaviors are punished or more supportive alternatives are reinforced. Keep in mind that the spirit here is one of teamwork. The therapist and patient jointly have to consider which changes are worth testing for their impact. Specific examples of techniques used at this stage are thought stopping and thought countering.

Thought Stopping. One of the psychologist's goals is to control thoughts that are disturbing or that undermine the person's mood or behavior. The need to control obsessive thoughts is a good example. Obsessive thoughts recur over and over and torture the patient.

Thought stopping is essentially a method of self-punishment for undesirable thoughts. The patient learns to inwardly shout "STOP!" when the thoughts occur. Training in thought stopping usually starts with the therapist shouting "STOP!" each time the thought occurs. The therapist first arranges for the patient to signal occurrences of the thought. Alternatively, the patient may be told to do the shouting after each episode of the thought. Eventually the shouting is diminished until it becomes purely mental, with no outward shout.

Thought Countering. We have said that cognitive therapists emphasize getting rid of or modifying thoughts that produce symptoms or undesirable behaviors. To do so they have to challenge, dispute, logically analyze, or test the validity of the thoughts. There are many ways to perform this **thought countering**. For example, an obese person may say to himself or herself: "I'm starving to death! I can't help eating this pastry!" These thoughts can strongly influence eating behavior, so it is important to teach the person to challenge and modify them.

Two main approaches to thought countering are **rational disputation** and **experiential testing**. With rational disputation the therapist examines the meaning, premises, and logical coherence of the thoughts in an attempt to demonstrate fallacies. The therapist might ask such questions as: "What is 'starving', and does it really apply here? What would happen if you didn't eat this pastry; would you really die? You are assuming that something awful will happen if you don't eat the pastry, and that you can't stand it, but you would probably just feel some tolerable discomfort." Eventually the patient may be persuaded to substitute appropriate self-statements for the injurious ones.

With experiential testing the person also challenges the thoughts, but emphasis is on examining situations in which the "catastrophic" event has happened. What was the actual result? We try to arrange for the person to go through the experience and see what really results. So obese persons can arrange to be hungry and look at the experience objectively. That way they soon find out that they neither starve nor die. Then they can say things to themselves based on the trial experience. "When I tried it I felt uncomfortable for a while, but once I got interested in something else it wasn't so bad" might be the kind of cognition they carry away with them.

Learning New Skills. Patients learn the new skills through several approaches, including modeling, behavioral rehearsal, imaginary rehearsal, role playing, and actually testing them in real life situations.

As an example of **modeling**, say the person is unable to be assertive in a given setting. The therapist can volunteer to role play the patient, while the patient plays the role of the "opponent" and barrages the therapist with provocations. A well-trained therapist can show options that have never occurred to the patient, who may well have a limited repertoire of assertive behaviors.

To illustrate **behavioral rehearsal**, take the case of a highly stressed police officer who carries out the task of writing a speeding ticket for an offender. The offender may be angry and very provocative. Police officers have to control their own angry reactions to these situations. It may be useful to have someone play the role of the person getting the ticket, while the police officer practices her skills at controlling her anger. If the officer does this in her imagination, we have **imaginary rehearsal**.

It is essential that patients be given homework assignments to try out the new skills in the actual situations where they are needed. This is *experimenting* with the new skills. Therapist and patient can decide on relatively easy applications of the methods so that the patient can proceed through a graded series of homework assignments. This continues until the patient's skills are adequate to deal with the full-fledged problematic situation.

Later Stages of Therapy

The cognitive behavioral approach to therapy is flexible about how problems are to be solved. The focus is on what works in practical situations. When using these methods, we do not have fixed notions about what will work and what will not. We develop what seem to be the best options, and then we try them out. If they work, that is all to the good; if they do not, we go back to the drawing board and modify them. The patient should be made aware of this attitude and be prepared for failures of the technique as a normal part of learning new ways of coping.

Specific skills in dealing with such failures must also be developed. It is all too easy for the patient, having experienced such a routine failure, to start saying, "This doesn't work for me," or "I'm a hopeless case." The therapist should anticipate this outcome and teach the patient to say things such as "The only way I'm going to find out how to do this is to try things, and the only way to avoid mistakes is to quit trying." Or, "I can work this out in my next therapy session and find out how to get a better result."

If patients learn to anticipate failure as a normal part of learning and to see it as a cue for further problem solving, the chances of permanent relapses are reduced. In order to make it more likely that patients will maintain the changes and generalize them to the full range of problem situations, they need to attribute the changes to their own efforts. The therapist must encourage this sense of "self-efficacy" by emphasizing the importance of the patient's role as the central member of the skill-learning team. The therapist is a consultant and coach, but the patient is a full participant who takes much of the responsibility and carries out the real life experiments. Sometimes patients may not notice what they did to create change or even that change has occurred. The therapist can help with this situation by asking the patient to note the relevant data indicating change and what he or she did that seemed to produce the change.

A CENTRAL TECHNIQUE: RELAXATION TRAINING

Therapeutic methods such as recording, monitoring, and various kinds of role playing and rehearsal represent only a small percentage of the available techniques. More detail on these methods may be found in Foreyt and Rathjen (1978), McMullin (1986), Meichenbaum (1985), and Turk, Meichenbaum, and Genest (1983). Full coverage of the range of techniques would be far beyond the scope of this book. However, **relaxation training** is one method that deserves to be singled out because it is so widely used. There are several types of relaxation training. Two widely used variants are **progressive relaxation training** and **autogenic training**. We discuss progressive relaxation training in this chapter and autogenic training in Chapter 10.

Progressive Relaxation

The major form of relaxation training was first developed by Edmund Jacobson (1929). Jacobson's view was that all forms of tension, including mental tension, were based in contraction of the muscles. If people could be taught to relax their muscles, they would be completely relaxed. Those cases in which people think their muscles are relaxed, while mental or emotional tension persists, are those in which unnoticed muscular tension is present.

This idea of unnoticed muscular tension is a key one. Jacobson believed that few people accurately sensed muscular tension. The correctness of his view is easily demonstrated. If we ask a group of people to place the inside of their forearm on a table and to point their fingers up toward the ceiling, and then ask them to relax and tell where the tension was, many of them will locate it incorrectly. Some will say the tension was in the inside of the forearm; but that is stretch and pressure, not tension. Others will say that it was in the wrist; but that is stretch on one side and compression on the other. Actually, the locus of tension is in the muscles at the top of the forearm.

This simple demonstration exercise was actually the first step of Jacobson's method, which he called **progressive relaxation training** (PRT). It involved developing a very clear sense of the nature of tension and of the difference between tension and relaxation. Patients were asked to tense small groups of muscles very gently and then to relax them abruptly, noting the difference between the feelings of tension and relaxation. Note that very small groups of muscles, such as those of the forearm, were used. This method is different from many modern methods of relaxation in which large groups of muscles are alternately tensed and relaxed.

Jacobson used small groups of muscles because he wanted people to learn to discriminate between tension and relaxation. To use larger groups of muscles is to spread the attention too much. Furthermore, Jacobson took complete sessions working with a single small group of muscles. He did not have people work their way through the entire body, alternately tensing and relaxing muscles as is so common today. This approach, too, was consistent with his concept of learning to discriminate muscular tension from other sensations. The goal was to have the rise of a sense of muscular tension be as noticeable as the honk of a car horn.

Jacobson, being knowledgeable of basic physiology, was aware that skeletal muscles tense only in response to signals from the brain. This is basic physiology. He drew the obvious conclusion that the way to stop tension was to learn what it was and then to learn not to send the signals from the brain to the muscles. He stated this conclusion in the phrase "Relaxation is *not* doing." Many people get more tense when they try to relax because they do not recognize that relaxation is "not doing."

Jacobson also knew that relaxation can go much deeper than we think. Many of us believe we have relaxed completely when actually a lot of tension remains. An outside observer can detect this tension by such signs as the mouth remaining closed instead of dropping open, as it must when relaxation is complete. Today we can show a patient the residual tension by using a biofeedback machine that feeds back audible or visible signals when muscles are active. A person new to such training may be quite puzzled that the machine keeps indicating the presence of tension when he or she feels relaxed. Relaxing

A patient is shown the residual tension in her muscles through the use of a biofeedback machine that feeds back audible or visible signals of active muscles.

beyond the point where one *feels* completely relaxed is called relaxation beyond the zero point.

Jacobson and others (see, e.g., Haugen, Dixon, & Dickel, 1958) used and evaluated PRT over a period of many years, and presented convincing evidence of its great effectiveness with a range of disorders related to anxiety and tension. However, their method of training required several months, as well as considerable commitment on the part of the patient. Soon the method was modified into a quicker and easier, though perhaps not a better, form. It, too, is commonly called progressive relaxation. With this method, *large* muscular groups are tensed and relaxed. Therefore, less emphasis is placed on training to discriminate muscular tension. In fact, in some ways this method resembles isometric exercise more than discrimination training. With isometric exercise, muscles are also tensed in a fixed position.

The muscles are alternately tensed and relaxed, progressing from one part of the body to another. The person being taught to relax is periodically reminded to notice the difference between tension and relaxation and that relaxation is not doing. The trainer also gives periodic reminders that relaxation can go "beyond the zero point."

It is also common to include suggestions, imagery, and such techniques as a hypnotic "countdown" as part of the progressive relaxation procedure. A hypnotic countdown involves giving instructions similar to the following:

I am going to count from 10 to zero, and with each count you will find yourself becoming more and more deeply relaxed . . . deeper and deeper relaxed. With each count, deeper and deeper relaxed until, when I reach zero you will be very deeply, very pleasantly, completely relaxed . . . 10 . . . very deeply, very pleasantly relaxed . . . 9 . . . deeper and deeper and deeper relaxed . . . 8 . . . (and so on).

Jacobson himself held firm to the idea that relaxation training should be a purely physiological matter of learning to relax muscles. The current method is a kind of "no holds barred" approach that includes just about anything that will contribute to quick, deep relaxation.

PRT and its variants have many different applications. For example: (1) Pain patients may be taught to reduce painful muscle contractions that worsen their pain; (2) the impact of stressful situations can be minimized; and (3) the side effects of chemotherapy in cancer patients may be reduced. Lichstein (1988) describes other useful relaxation techniques.

Systematic Desensitization

One particular variant of PRT, **systematic desensitization,** deserves special mention because of its many uses and known effectiveness. In systematic desensitization, deep relaxation is combined with imagining stressful or anxiety-producing situations.

Early in the history of behavioral psychology, a researcher named Mary Cover Jones did a demonstration experiment in which a little boy who greatly feared white, furry objects such as white rats and rabbits was treated with a method known as **counterconditioning** (Jones, 1924). In counterconditioning, a disturbing response to a given stimulus is replaced by a more positive one. The boy's fear reaction involved the "fight or flight response" that we explained in Chapter 4.

Because the relaxation responses are incompatible with the fight or flight response, a relaxation response was induced to oppose the fight or flight response. Jones induced relaxation by giving the boy treats such as ice cream. Slowly, and at a distance, she introduced a white rat. The relaxation response predominated because the aversive stimulus was weak due to the safe distance. Gradually, she brought the white rat closer, being careful that the boy would not get scared. Eventually she was able to supplant the fear response with a relaxation response to the previously noxious stimulus.

During desensitization we do essentially the same thing, generally by using the imagination rather than by introducing real stimuli. Patient and therapist develop a hierarchy of aversive stimuli, ranging from the least to the most disturbing. Then the patient, while deeply relaxed, is encouraged to imagine the least disturbing event while remaining relaxed.

The therapist usually arranges a relatively unobtrusive signal (e.g., lifting of a finger) to indicate loss of the relaxed state. If it is lost, the procedure is halted until relaxation can be renewed. Eventually, the patient can imagine the full range of disturbing events while remaining relaxed. After that, the patient is commonly asked to enter the real situation, if possible in small steps, while remaining relaxed.

Systematic desensitization in health psychology can be used to help a patient cope with asthma (Alexander, 1977). The first step is to take the patient through relaxation training. Next, the therapist helps the patient construct a hierarchy of asthma symptoms ranging from the least to the most disturbing. A typical hierarchy might include: (1) merely thinking about the possibility of starting to wheeze, (2) feeling tightness in the chest, (3) just a little wheezing, (4) increased wheezing along with fearful thoughts of its getting worse, (5) having the medication fail to give quick relief, (6) rushing to the emergency room with an attack, (7) struggling to breathe while waiting for the treatment to work, and (8) having to take intravenous medication during an attack.

While relaxed, the patient visualizes each of these situations for about 30 seconds, starting with the least disturbing one. If the patient gets anxious, he or she stops visualizing immediately and signals the therapist. Relaxation has to be reestablished before the patient goes to the next step. When the patient is able to visualize a given step of the hierarchy while feeling no anxiety, he or she goes on to the next imaginary stimulus.

Sometimes the asthma patient goes through systematic desensitization while having real, not just imaginary, symptoms. The following is such a case:

> . . . one child at the National Asthma Center was experiencing anxiety whenever he wheezed, even mildly, but not when just talking or thinking about asthma. By withholding regular oral bronchodilators for successively longer periods preceding relaxation training sessions, this child was taught to relax while actually experiencing progressively more wheezing. (Alexander, 1977, pp. 19–20)

EXPRESSIVE THERAPY AND HEALTH PSYCHOLOGY

An alternative approach to therapy, mentioned at the beginning of this chapter, is one that attributes symptoms to distortions in the expression of hidden impulses and feelings. It is referred to as psychodynamic, psychosomatic, or expressive therapy.

Expressive Versus Behavioral Therapy

Some health psychologists believe that rejection of psychodynamic ideas was a major liberating step in the history of the field (e.g., Weiss, 1989). Others still work within some variant of this tradition. In a Divisional Presidential Address at the 1989 annual meeting of the American Psychological Association, Copeland (1989) argued that a psychodynamic framework was ideal even for those therapists who take a behavioral approach to therapy. She held that the timing of interventions, including behavioral ones, should be influenced by psychodynamic considerations, at least in many patients. Furthermore, Woody (1988) has pointed out that in cases of legal action, the courts tend to view the psychodynamic approach as the "standard of medical care." So therapists in general should know about it.

Apparently, cognitive and psychodynamic therapies are reaching the point of rapprochment. Cognitive therapists recognize the importance of what is beneath the surface and of the therapist-patient relationship. For example, Beck, Rush, Shaw, and Emery (1979) list slighting the therapeutic relationship first among "common pitfalls in learning cognitive therapy." They point out that the cognitive therapist "must never lose sight of the fact that he is engaged with another human being in a very complicated task."

The Psychodynamic Model of Therapy

The **psychodynamic model** holds that hidden feelings and impulses underlie symptoms. The impulse or feeling is hidden because we feel conflict about its expression. It might be an impulse to be angry, or aggressive, or sexual, or dependent, and so on. Since the impulse is in some way dangerous (at least to our minds), it causes anxiety. To avoid the anxiety, we erect a defense. So the overall pattern is that a hidden feeling or impulse results in anxiety, which then results in a defense.

Sickness can act as a defense or as a means of expressing hidden desires, as the case of Marie illustrates. She feared telling people to leave her alone, so she got a migraine that required her to be alone. "The migraine" told her husband and children that they must leave her alone (cf. Sanders, 1988). It fulfilled her wish to distance herself temporarily from her family while defending her against the anxiety she would feel if she did so openly.

Uncovering Versus Covering Therapies

Getting people to express something that has been hidden is not always the goal of this kind of therapy. Sometimes it is best not to express what is hidden in too open a way. In these instances, the therapy may direct itself toward giving the patient better defenses. A person with defenses that are symptomatic may discover defenses that are healthier. Fenichel (1954) called the form of therapy that leads to expression of hidden things "uncovering" therapy and the kind that strengthens defenses, "covering" therapy.

The classic case of "Anna O." published by Breuer and Freud (1895) exemplifies the relationship between uncovering and covering therapies. She presented a dreadful array of symptoms, some of which seemed physical and others of which were clearly psychological.

Breuer worked with Anna O. just prior to the full-fledged development of psychoanalysis. He treated her through hypnosis regressing her back to the time when the symptoms first appeared. As a result, she remembered the triggering event and, at the same time, discharged the pent-up emotions associated with it. This is a clear prototype of expressive, uncovering therapy. Insight into the basis of symptoms with new access to hidden feelings leads to relief from symptoms.

One symptom Anna O. developed was an inability to drink. She could relieve her thirst only by eating fruits. When regressed back, she remembered an incident in which she was a guest at someone's house and observed that the hostess allowed her dog to eat out of the dishes. Though disgusted, Anna O. was unable to express her feelings about it. Once she remembered the event, saw its meaning, and discharged her feelings, the symptoms went away.

Anna O. did not complete her therapy because she developed a passion for Breuer, which led him to terminate the therapy. Neither Breuer nor any of the physicians who followed him was able to cure her. She improved only when she became a leader in a social movement. Her contribution to the Austrian social work movement (her real name was Bertha Pappenheim) was recognized by a commemorative postage stamp West Germany issued in 1954. From a psychodynamic point of view, she discovered a way to sublimate her unconscious wishes and express them in socially useful form. She was using the ego defense mechanism of "altruism" (caring for others and placing a high value on their needs), and it worked for her.

So Anna O. fell on her own method of "covering" hidden feelings and impulses. A therapist can help a patient do so by acting as a supportive and guiding role model. The therapist serves as something of a new parent whose goal is to improve on the work done by the original parents. The emphasis, then, is on learning new ways of coping rather than on helping the patient express what has been thwarted in its expression. Such "covering" therapy has a strong resemblance to cognitive behavior therapy.

Methods of Expressive Therapies

It is difficult to summarize the methods used in expressive therapies. Before a therapist can use them competently, they often require not only years of training, but also, as in the case of psychoanalysis, lengthy personal therapy. Here we will merely attempt a brief description of some of these approaches. Within the psychoanalytic tradition, there are two main approaches: the **unconscious conflict model** and the **object relations model**.

The Unconscious Conflict Model

The unconscious **conflict model** posits that symptoms stem from conflicts of which we are not aware. "Aware" in this context really means "fully aware," and that implies both cognitive and emotional awareness. Some people can "intellectualize" and show an awareness at the "head" level without the accompanying affect. This kind of awareness would not be expected to relieve the symptoms.

Pennebaker (1990) gives a nice example of what seems to be a case of conflict producing symptoms. He describes how he had suffered from asthma attacks since childhood and had attributed them to allergies. When he moved away from home to college, he stopped having asthma attacks, which he naturally explained as being due to the change in allergens. But when his parents paid him a visit, he quickly had an attack of asthma. He then recognized that asthma can have as much to do with conflicted feelings as with allergens.

Within this model, cure comes from "making the unconscious, conscious." Why should bringing unconscious materials to awareness help get rid of symptoms? Freud (1959) observed that when impulses are *not* discharged into the brain centers that control consciousness, they tend to be discharged via other systems, such as the motor system. This leads to what therapists call "acting out," that is, doing something that fulfills a hidden impulse without consciously acknowledging it. If we are consciously aware of it, we do not have to act it out.

With our modern grasp of brain function, it is easy to see that another alternative path of discharge might be the limbic-hypothalamic system that controls emotions, motivations, endocrine output, and even the immune system (see Chapter 4). We can discharge feelings and

impulses we are not aware of by activating this system. This is likely to produce physiological illnesses. Thus, a person who cannot express a feeling may get high blood pressure or headaches instead.

In research dealing with hypertension, Lynch (1985) showed that elevations of blood pressure correspond to the triggering of strong feelings of which the hypertensive patients are unaware. When they come to recognize that the rises in pressure are expressions of denied feelings, they can learn to control their hypertension. Lynch shows that learning how to direct these impulses through the system of consciousness will relieve symptoms in a rather stable way.

Paradoxically, the patient in need of expressive therapy is already abundantly expressive. The problem is that the expression is in the form of symptoms rather than awareness and verbal articulation. The therapy consists of careful, very specialized listening (Langs, 1978). It takes advantage of the fact that people who are preoccupied with given themes will tend to be attracted to various instances of those themes. For example, a child who is powerless may be fascinated with cartoon characters who wield great power. An adult who has lost a lover may readily become engrossed in a movie that centers on lost love.

The underlying theme that preoccupies a person will also show itself in the person's chosen topics of conversation. For example, a patient who was consciously pleased that her therapist had asked to borrow a book found herself talking about her dentist who had hurt her (Casement, 1985). The hard to express theme of "You, the therapist hurt me" came out in the form of "My dentist bungled and hurt me." The theme found expression, but it was transplanted or *displaced* to a similar person.

The task of the expressive therapist is to know how to decode such encoded communications. Therapists must realize the importance of what appear to be topics brought up casually. They must also know how to be alert to encoded communications without jumping to conclusions. They have to note the themes that are brought up and to generate silent hypotheses until evidence mounts that a certain message is being conveyed. The psychotherapist would not immediately interpret complaints about a dentist as a reference to the therapist. For such an interpretation to be appropriate, the patient would have to make repeated references to the theme of poor professional performance, to being hurt by caretakers, and the like.

Even when the therapist has become fairly confident of the meaning of an encoded message, it is essential that he or she reveal this meaning to the patient in a well-timed way. It will do no good to give patients interpretations that they may not be ready to handle. The goal is to help patients express these hidden messages through consciousness. If this material is revealed too early, they may pay mere lip service to the message rather than becoming fully aware of their *ownership* of it. As we said earlier, a full understanding of this process of decoding and interpreting requires extensive study. We cannot hope to cover it fully here.

The Object Relations Model

We mentioned earlier that Copeland (1989) recommended a version of psychodynamic therapy as a framework for health-related interventions. The specific form she advocated is known as an object relations point of view.[3] It emphasizes the role of very early parental modeling from which we learned how to regard ourselves and how to treat ourselves. In other words, our view of self stems from identifications with parents who viewed us in a certain way. And the way we treat ourselves—for example, whether, when under stress, we soothe, ignore, or berate ourselves—also stems from this identification with parental images.

Of particular interest are those people whose parents failed to provide them with a good model of how to see themselves and how to treat themselves. The way caregivers handle children during the stage of development known

---

[3] Actually, she included a related psychodynamic point of view known as self-psychology. An account of the distinction may be found in St. Clair (1986).

as the "terrible twos" is seen as especially crucial. This is regarded as the stage of separation-individuation, during which the child should learn to be a reasonably trusting, self-confident, autonomous person.

Many psychologists believe that children who fail to receive appropriate support during this phase may have severe problems centering on the sense of their own value, on their ability to get close to others without feeling engulfed, and on their ability to venture out into the world and create a life of their own.

Patients with such problems are quite resistant to treatment through verbal interpretations directed at bringing unconscious conflicts to awareness (Balint, 1968; Masterson, 1981, 1988). Therapy for this kind of disorder focuses instead on improving how patients perceive and relate to self and others. Before going into a fuller discussion of therapy based on object relations, we must examine the background of object relations theory.

Object Relations Background. Years ago, one's beloved was commonly described as "the object of my affections." Today, we shun the term "object" in that context because it has come to mean a mere object, a thing to satisfy one's needs. The term "object" in object relations theory is meant in both senses, but most often it refers to other human beings, originally the mother, who is our first "object." Object relations theory places the growth of our ability to relate to human "objects" at the center of personality development.

Advocates of an object relations model would not deny the importance of unconscious conflict, but their emphasis is different from that of conflict theorists. Object relations theory focuses on failures during early childhood to develop a clear, mature sense of others and of self. So object relations theorists stress the role of *developmental arrest* without denying the role of unconscious conflict.

The child, they argue, does not have a clear sense of self versus other at birth. This sense must be developed through interactions with caregivers, especially the mother. Having gone through the struggle of biological birth, the child must next accomplish a "psychological birth" (Mahler, Pine, & Bergman, 1975). This psychological birth, if successful, involves a transition from a state of undifferentiated fusion with the mother to one of mature autonomy and ability to relate to others.

The concept of "object" stemmed from Freud himself, but it was fully developed by various of his followers who worked with children rather than adults. They found that children use rather **primitive defenses**. For example, children seem unable to see people and things in their world as having a mixture of good and bad features. Rather, they tend to isolate the good and bad parts of significant "objects" as if they were totally separate entities. Thus, at one moment they might be totally bathed in the glory of "good" mother and at another moment completely immersed in hatred of "bad" mother. This mechanism is called **splitting**. It permits some measure of coping with the good and the bad that life brings. On the other hand, it creates extreme and often distorted views of people.

To give another example of children's primitive defenses, they seem to deal with the "bad" parts of themselves through fantasies of "putting these parts in other objects." For example, a child, having been thwarted by a parent, may say that "Dolly doesn't like you," attributing their feelings to the doll. One can carry on a therapy session with a child in which the discussion centers around their doll or pet. Often the child will slip up and interchange reference to self and the "stand in." The defense of "putting bad parts of ourselves" in a proxy with whom we identify is called **projective identification**.

These, together with other primitive defense mechanisms such as fantasy and denial, are the central mechanisms used by children and by very disturbed adults. Object relations theorists believe that the continuation of primitive defenses into adulthood indicates a failure in the process of child development. Adults who persist in the use of such mechanisms commonly have more than average problems of living, in-

A therapist can deal with the primitive defense of projective identification by centering therapy sessions around the child's doll or pet.

cluding trouble relating to others and both psychological and physical health problems (Vaillant, 1977).

Difficulties in object relations and resulting deficits in perceiving and relating to others and self are seen as central factors in the development of severe psychological disturbances. These include psychosis and those disorders, such as borderline and narcissistic disorders, that are regarded as more severe than neurosis but are not really psychotic.

The Importance of Understanding Object Relations. Some understanding of the special vulnerabilities of patients with disturbed object relations is very important to any helping professional, including the health psychologist. We have said that such disturbances go hand in hand with poor physical and mental health. In addition, the patients' problems in relating will influence how they deal with the health care provider.

These patients can be very troublesome. Think of what it is like to relate to a patient who regularly uses the defense mechanism of splitting. The patient may tend to idealize you, the professional caregiver, but may also regard you with profound contempt and rage. Worse, the patient may make rapid, disconcerting shifts from one stance to another.

If patients use projective identification and "place their bad parts in you," you may be the recipient of powerful rage and desire for vengeance. If they were abused as children, they may try to abuse you in a similar way. The consequences for the treatment process and for both patient and health care provider can, of course, be very bad. Such patients may feel very upset with your work and do unpleasant things like file malpractice suits against you. A recent survey of health care professionals revealed that such patients are seen as "difficult and dreaded" (Bongar, Forcier, & Peterson, in press). They are particularly difficult and especially anathema to the health care provider who does not understand their special vulnerabilities and predilections. They are far more manageable by a professional who understands them.

Such patients do, indeed, have special vulnerabilities, and they may be badly hurt by the unwitting health care provider. The case of Patty, who would probably have been diagnosed as having a borderline personality disorder if dealt with properly, illustrates one aspect of this problem:

Patty was a very tense person, highly reactive to stress, who regularly went to doctors seeking help for a variety of illnesses. She suffered from severe headaches that appeared in some ways to be migrainous and in other ways to be tension headaches. She also suffered from panic attacks that forced her to spend most of her time isolated at home.

Patty had a neighbor, Ted, who was a general practitioner with an interest in stress-related disorders. He used biofeedback and relaxation training and emphasized treatment of stress problems to the point where it constituted the bulk of his practice. His education in the use of these methods had been minimal, but he felt that his medical background made it appropriate for him to use them. In the context of these treatments he also did "low-level" psychotherapy, for which he had essentially no training. His strategy was to refer patients he

couldn't handle to a psychologist friend in whom he had confidence.

One night when Ted was visiting Patty and her husband, he suggested she come to his office for "biofeedback treatment." Patty decided to try it, and made rapid progress. Her headaches largely went away, and she was soon able to go out, although with difficulty. She and Ted became close friends, and often went to lunch together. She worshipped him. It became obvious to people that she had quite a crush on Ted and many began to wonder if they were having an affair.

Patty called Ted regularly at the office and at home—sometimes just to make contact and at other times to get his advice on how to deal with symptoms. Her demands began to wear on him, and his wife became annoyed. Her relationship with Ted gradually began to create a strain in Patty's own marriage as well. The relationship between her husband, Mike, and Ted became quite tense. Finally, Ted made an abrupt decision to terminate her treatment and refer her to the psychologist. About the same time, her husband asked her for a divorce because of all he had been through with her, and his suspicion of her relationship with Ted.

Patty was completely overwhelmed by the sudden loss of these two people on whom she had depended. She fell into a state of severe anxiety punctuated by panic attacks. She was also severely depressed. One day she took a massive overdose of an array of medicines from the large collection she had accumulated from her various treatments. Her life was saved only because her son discovered her in time.

What Ted failed to realize is that patients like Patty tend to latch onto powerful figures like him and idealize them. He had, in effect, become "good mother." Such patients can often appear to undergo amazing cures when they feel united with a substitute "good mother."

By mixing personal and professional roles as he did with her, Ted set up a situation in which she would be likely to develop unrealistic fantasies about their relationship. It takes training and skill to handle this kind of relationship and to guide it toward a resolution in which the patient grows toward maturity. Ted utterly lacked such training. He simply did not know what was hitting him. He was hurt by the experience, but Patty was much more seriously injured.

In cases like Patty's, the therapeutic emphasis is on providing **corrective emotional experiences** to enable the person to mature in ways that the original parenting did not permit. For example, some parents respond to the child's signs of becoming independent either by attacking the independence or by abruptly withdrawing from the child, who is ready for a only a safe, small amount of autonomy. These painful and frightening consequences of independent behavior can lead to serious immaturity and fear of separateness in later adulthood, with major problems at each of the transitions normal to adult maturation (e.g., graduating, moving out, being successful in a job, or marrying and having children). These people often try to satisfy their needs inappropriately in medical settings and to express themselves symbolically through symptoms. Health care providers need to be aware of the extreme sensitivity of such patients even to such simple things as canceled or delayed appointments.

Such "developmentally arrested" patients usually need one form or another of supportive psychotherapy, in which the therapist provides a reliable base for developing mature adult responses and temporarily compensates for the patients' limitations. Wallerstein (1986) has reported the results of a long-term study indicating that such therapy is highly effective. In practice, most therapists of this persuasion agree that people with such developmental deficits were, while growing up, also quite likely to develop unconscious conflicts. Therefore, interpretation of unconscious conflicts is combined with a supportive approach as needed.

Much of this information is familiar to cognitive behavior therapists, although they would say it in a different way. Cognitive therapists generally recognize that there are deep lying assumptional systems or "schemata" that must be dealt with for optimal change to occur. Simi-

larly, the psychodynamic therapist operating in the supportive mode is providing an opportunity for skills learning on the part of the patient, with help in applying the new skills in the outside world. Turk, Meichenbaum, and Genest (1983) have seen the similarity between psychodynamic and cognitive behavioral approaches. They cite the following statement by Bieber (1974) to illustrate the point:

> Outside the analysis, patients become involved in various testing maneuvers related to reinforcing or relinquishing an irrational belief. In steps one and two, irrational beliefs are delineated and patients, hopefully, become convinced that their beliefs are irrational. I view these steps as the "working out" phase of therapy. These steps proceed concurrently, though they may be sequential. Step three is the "working through" phase. The patient comes to identify the operations of his beliefs in his life situation and in his interpersonal transactions. If the analysis proceeds well, this phase will see the extinction of symptoms and an alteration from neurotic or maladaptive to appropriate behavior. (p. 98)

The major contrast between the two approaches probably lies in the systematic way in which the cognitive therapists arrange the kinds of experiences described in that paragraph. Furthermore, psychodynamic therapists seem to place greater emphasis on the intensity of the relationship to the therapist (the "transference") and on the particular view of psychological development put forth by object relations theorists. Of course, the classical psychodynamic therapists also focus on drawing out the expression of hidden feelings and impulses. All these differences seem more a matter of emphasis than of categorical disagreement.

Conclusions

There is more order and continuity than there is conflict about how psychological therapies may be of use to patients with physical health problems. It is useful to retain some of the insights that come from traditional, psychodynamically based therapies, while affirming the usefulness of behavioral and cognitive behavioral approaches. From the point of view presented in this chapter, these approaches fit into a coherent framework, and they provide useful tools for the health psychologist.

Most health psychologists in the United States use the behavioral and cognitive behavioral approaches because these methods have been successful and are both brief and cost-effective. Furthermore, psychodynamic approaches are less amenable to experimental evaluation, and thus they cannot claim the same degree of scientific verification as the more behavioral methods. They are also relatively long term and expensive to apply. Both therapists and patients have to make a very large investment in order to use them. Yet some of the insights given by these therapies are very important in revealing the larger context in which the patient is operating and can help us to time and manage our interventions more effectively. In more difficult cases, these longer term therapies may be the best thing for the patient.

Summary

1. The role of psychology in the biomedical model is too restricted; for the most part it is used when medical tests fail to explain symptoms. But even disorders, such as epilepsy, that start physically may sometimes be controlled psychologically.

2. From a behavioral view, health status can be seen as controlled by prior behaviors (e.g., "lifestyle"), and many "medical" problems, such as pain, high blood pressure, or ulcers can be interpreted as behaviors that follow familiar psychological laws. The psychodynamic view is that sicknesses, including physical ones such as ulcers, can be ways of expressing tensions and conflicts of which we are not consciously aware.

3. The behavioral approach emphasizes pinpointing the variables of interest, which is done through measurement and record-keeping. Pinpointing is important for the following reasons: (a) it clarifies what we are trying to control; (b) communication is improved among the different members of the treatment "team"; (c) problem behaviors can be broken down into more manageable, smaller units; (d) it identifies exactly what it is we should be reinforcing; and (e) it permits us to see successes and failures clearly.

4. We assess behaviors with methods that vary in precision. They include: (a) interviews; (b) asking the patient to vividly imagine the circumstances surrounding an episode of the disorder; (c) open-ended diary keeping; and (d) counting and recording precisely defined behaviors and the stimuli that precede and follow them. Each of the many ways of measuring behavior has its special applications.

5. The patient is often asked to record the measured behavior, but sometimes a health professional, family member, or friend of the patient may also keep such records. Because people often get confused about what is being recorded, it helps to do *reliability checks*. Thus, someone other than the main person who is recording keeps an independent record of the behavior, and we see if the two *independent* observers are in agreement.

6. Use of more than one measure at a time gives a fuller picture of what is happening but can lead to overburdening the person doing the recording, with consequent noncompliance.

7. After recordings have been obtained, they must be summarized so that trends and patterns can be seen. This summarizing may best be done by the patient.

8. We should keep records of the target behavior prior to any intervention so that we can compare it to the effect of the intervention. Then we intervene, mainly through the following: (a) selective reinforcement of desired responses; (b) punishment and

extinction of undesired responses; and (c) bringing the target behavior under stimulus control. Punishment refers to delivering a noxious stimulus after a behavior, whereas in extinction a person ceases to reinforce a previously reinforced behavior.

9. Cognitive *behavioral* therapy uses the methods of behavior therapy, but highlights the power of thoughts and images in controlling behaviors. Furthermore, the patient's symptoms are transformed into identified, potentially solvable instead of vague, overwhelming problems. It is important that this work be done as part of a collaborative team effort with the patient at the center of the team. Patients test and validate new ways of thinking in their own life situations.

10. The first phase of cognitive behavioral therapy involves defining the problem and placing it in a framework that renders it solvable. The goal is to note the following: (a) situations that influence the symptoms, (b) the actions the patient has taken to cope with the problem and the effects of those actions, and (c) the consequences of the symptomatic behavior.

11. The second phase involves skills training. The patient may learn to use operant conditioning or changes in images and self-statements in order to change symptomatic reactions. An attempt is made to decrease harmful self-statements through (a) disputing them, (b) punishing or teaching the patient to punish them (e.g., thought stopping), (c) arranging real world experiences to disconfirm them, or (d) reinforcing more supportive self-statements.

12. Patients learn new skills through such procedures as the following: (a) modeling of the desired behavior by the therapist; (b) rehearsing the behavior while under the tutelage of the therapist; (c) rehearsing in the imagination; (d) role playing; and (e) doing small, relatively safe experiments at trying the new behaviors in actual life situations.

13. The therapist should prepare the patient for failures of the technique as a normal part of learning new ways of coping. If patients learn to prepare for failure as a normal part of learning and to see it as a cue for further problem solving, the chances of permanent relapses are reduced.

14. Progressive relaxation training is a method in which the patient alternately tenses and relaxes muscles while observing and becoming more familiar with the resulting sensations. In addition, the patient is trained (a) in the skills of turning off the commands that create muscular tension and (b) in knowing what full relaxation feels like ("relaxing below the zero point").

15. An important variant of progressive relaxation training is systematic desensitization. With this method, a hierarchy of disturbing stimuli is prepared. The patient then relaxes deeply and imagines the stimuli from least to most disturbing. The goal is to proceed through the entire hierarchy without getting tense, and thus to break the linkage between distress responses and the stimuli. The method has been highly successful.

16. An "expressive" approach to therapy attributes symptoms to distortions in the expression of hidden impulses and feelings. Some health psychologists feel that rejecting of this approach was a major liberating step. Others continue to affirm it, at least as one part of their therapeutic approach. Within the legal system, it is also still considered the "standard of medical care," so it is important at least to know about it.

17. In this view, a feeling or impulse that was once dangerous and is now hidden results in anxiety, which then results in a defense to neutralize the anxiety. Sickness can act as a defense or as a means of expressing the hidden impulse. This type of therapy usually tries to help the patient express the hidden impulse in a safe, socially ac-

ceptable way, or to help the patient become more effective in covering that impulse with a defense.

18. A second major approach to expressive therapy is the object relations model, which focuses on failures during early childhood to develop a clear, mature sense of others and of self. Emphasis is on the role of *developmental arrest* instead of unconscious conflict.

19. Like very young children, patients with such developmental problems use primitive defenses such as (a) splitting (mentally separating people into "good" and "bad" parts with nothing in between); (b) projective identification (in fantasy, placing dangerous parts of the self in others); (c) denial; and (d) fantasy.

20. The problems of developmentally arrested patients originate before they have mastered language, and they are quite resistant to treatment through verbal interpretations directed at bringing unconscious conflicts to awareness. Instead, they require the therapist to provide a corrective emotional experience that enables the person to mature in ways that the original parenting did not permit.

21. There are many points of convergence between expressive and cognitive behavioral therapy. Cognitive therapists generally recognize that deep-lying "schemata" must be dealt with for optimal change to occur. Similarly, the psychodynamic therapist operating in the supportive mode is providing the patient with an opportunity for skills learning, with help in applying the new skills in the outside world.

Key Terms

Autogenic training
Behavioral rehearsal
Contingencies of reinforcement
Corrective emotional experiences
Counterconditioning
Experiential testing
Expressive therapies
Extinction
Imaginary rehearsal
Modeling
Object relations model
Primitive defenses
Progressive relaxation training
Projective identification
Psychodynamic model
Punishment
Rational disputation
Relaxation training
Selective reinforcement
Splitting
Stimulus control
Systematic desensitization
Thought countering
Thought stopping
Unconscious conflict model

Discussion Questions

1. How do behavioral and cognitive behavioral therapies differ?
2. What are the advantages of behavioral and cognitive behavioral therapies for the health psychologist?
3. What is systematic desensitization? Give a specific health-related example, preferably based on your own experience.
4. How do cognitive therapists help patients change harmful thoughts? Include specific techniques.
5. What is meant by expressive therapies?
6. Briefly explain how expressive therapy is conducted. Give a health-related example of how it might be used.

7. Explain how to do relaxation training and why it is useful to the health psychologist.

8. What is the relationship between behaviorally based and expressive therapies?

9. According to the unconscious conflict model, how does bringing unconscious material to awareness help get rid of physical symptoms?

10. Describe the primitive defenses of splitting and projective identification.

11. Why is it important for those in the helping professions to have an understanding of the special vulnerabilities of patients with disturbed object relations?

12. Why do American health psychologists most often use behavioral and cognitive therapies as opposed to expressive therapies?

Chapter 6

A Cognitive-Social Look at Physicians and Patients

George was a noted psychologist, well known for his high energy and strong will. The day he was scheduled to lecture at a university in a neighboring state, he felt unusually tired and even briefly considered canceling the lecture. But since it was not his style to back out of a commitment, he made himself get behind the wheel of his car, and he drove the several hundred miles to give the lecture. Allowing himself a somewhat dramatic lapse from his usually disciplined, unemotional approach to things, he mumbled melodramatically, "The show must go on."

While he drove, he felt a little better, but during the lecture he grew increasingly anxious and broke out in a profuse sweat. He gave the appearance of having "stage fright." He was short of breath and a little dizzy, and he felt as if there was a great pressure on his chest. It was in fact somewhat painful, and, as he walked out of the lecture hall, the pressure grew into a substantial pain.

He thought, "Maybe I'm having a heart attack!," and his anxiety mounted. His hosts invited him to join them for a drink, but he said, "I'm not feeling well, and had better head back home." He hurried to his car, alternating between thinking he might be having a heart attack and reassuring himself that he was just exhausted and needed a vacation.

As he arrived in his home town, he decided to drive to an emergency room. He pulled into a parking space in the emergency room lot, walked into the hospital, and collapsed in front of the receptionist's desk. Swift action on the part of emergency room personnel kept him alive, but the damage created by the exertion and long delay in getting treatment created complications that could not be overcome by medical intervention. His brain suffered massive damage, and he was never to recover.

George may well have been destroyed almost as much by psychological failures as by the failure of his heart. He failed to evaluate the signals from his body correctly, and accurately to estimate the likelihood that they meant he was having a heart attack. His case points toward a problem that is quite common in dealing with disease but is not given enough acknowledgment. Under pressure and flooded with information, both patients and medical personnel reach limits of their ability to process significant information, and they therefore fail to take the right action. Psychological influences prevent them from taking effective action to cope with disease.

In reality, all medical encounters involve two or more human beings relating to each other. Each of them, whether patient or professional, has personal needs and psychological limitations that influence the encounter. In fact, at every step in the process of dealing with disease, whether on the part of the physician or on the part of the patient, the impact of cognitive, emotional, and motivational factors is felt.

Psychological factors influence virtually every facet of health care. Remarkably enough, patients may give more importance to the personal qualities of their physicians than to their technical competence. Cousins (1985) describes a survey done on 1500 people in which they were asked about their thoughts and experiences concerning changing from one physician to another, and their reasons for either actually doing so or considering it. Seventy percent of the people responded, and 85 percent had either changed physicians in the past five years or were thinking about it.

People tended to change because they were unhappy with the doctor's style or office manner. They took their physician's medical competency for granted, so that was not generally a reason for leaving a practice. These patients were most bothered by insensitivity to their needs, poor communication, lack of respect for their views, and overemphasis on technology. It seems that not knowing how to deal with patients as people is costly to physicians as well as to patients.

HUMAN INFORMATION PROCESSING AND MEDICAL REASONING

Interpersonal skill is not the only psychological influence on encounters between physicians and patients. Technical skill rests on the ability to process information efficiently and correctly. Physicians, despite great pressure, must succeed in asking the right questions, giving the right tests, and utilizing the resulting information efficiently to arrive at a correct diagnosis. They are often under great strain and are flooded with information. They have to stretch their capacity to handle information close to it's limits.

Patients, too, must deal with high demands to process information under duress. They have to monitor what is going on in their bodies and judge correctly whether they should seek medical help. They must then take in information and instructions, often presented in an unfamiliar language, and find ways to implement the needed treatment plan. At the same time they may be dealing with intense emotional reactions to the losses and limitations imposed by the disease.

Our Limited Channel Capacity

One of the most striking limitations of our ability to process information is our limited **channel capacity**. It has to do with the amount of information we can process at one time. Psychologists have borrowed units for measuring information from engineers. The basic unit is called a bit, which is the amount of information needed to decide between two equally likely alternatives. So if it is equally likely that something is or is not "bigger than a breadbasket," and you ask someone "Is it bigger than a breadbasket," you are asking for one bit of information. If I tell you "I am thinking of a number between 1 and 7, can you guess what it is?" If you say "Is it four or above," you are asking for one bit of information.

Physicians are often under great strain and flooded with information and must, therefore, make maximum use of their limited human information processing capacity.

Despite the vastness of the body of information we can retrieve from the world and from our memory, all of it has to be processed at a relatively slow rate and through a very "narrow" channel of information-handling capacity. Evidence summarized in a classic paper by George Miller (1956) indicated that our channel capacity is about 2.5 bits. That is the amount of information required to decide between seven alternatives. For example, take a psychological test in which you can respond like this:

1. Very much like me.
2. Much like me.
3. Like me.
4. Neither like nor not like me.
5. Not like me.
6. Much unlike me.
7. Very much unlike me.

This test has seven alternatives, and it requires you to process 2.5 bits of information to give your answer.

For most of us, it seems odd that this is our channel capacity. If we give people more alternatives, they will tend to "chunk" alternatives together so they can shave the problem down to 2.5 bits. That implies that they have to lose some information. All our lives we work our way around this limited 2.5-bit channel capacity.

Probabilities, Heuristics, and Cognitive Errors

We simply cannot do things that require more than our brains can handle. We lose information constantly, and we make errors because of these limitations. Our channel capacity, though a central problem, is not the only limitation on our ability to handle information. For example, we are notoriously poor at making intuitive judgments of probabilities. If you estimate how likely it is you will die of AIDS, unless you know the real statistics you will probably guess incorrectly. If you estimate how likely it is you are having a heart attack when you feel a pain in your chest, you are also likely to be far off the

mark. These **subjective probabilities** are central in dealing with disease, since both physicians and patients have to note symptoms and select actions that they deem most likely to help.

Another thing we do poorly is to make judgments based on a large amount of information. We are good at telling what kind of information is important, but we do poorly when we try combining several items of information to make a judgment or decision. We are not good at combining probabilities. For example, a doctor who conducts a physical examination and orders various test results can be expected to have trouble using the gathered information efficiently.

Any human being faced with a task that makes excessive demands on his or her ability to process information will lose information and make errors. Medical professionals are no exception. "Physician bashing" is a popular sport in some circles these days, and certainly physicians make some costly errors. But how many of these errors are due to limitations anyone would have? And to what extent do the situations physicians find themselves in set up information processing demands that assure the occurrence of the errors?

One function of this chapter is to examine the impact of information processing limits on the performance of medical personnel. We will also look at the ways in which information processing influences patients.

The Gambler's Fallacy

We have said that a major shortcoming of human cognition lies in the way we judge probabilities. Some of us are well schooled in calculating probabilities, but our intuitive judgments of them may nevertheless be far off the mark. A good example of faulty estimation of probability is something known to mathematicians as the **gambler's fallacy.**

We commit this fallacy when we think that something that just happened is not likely to happen again. "Lightning never strikes twice in the same place" is a good example of it. For another example, many of us would think that someone who just won a lottery is much less likely to win it today. Actually, the probability of winning it yesterday is independent of the probability of winning it today (assuming, of course, that the winner keeps buying tickets the same way).

A person operating according to the gambler's fallacy is making a subjective judgment of probability. These judgments tend to be inaccurate because the implicit rules we use to estimate probabilities tend to bias the results. Psychologists have identified some of these rules. These rules for deriving subjective probabilities are technically called **heuristics**. Next, we will discuss some of the major heuristics people tend to use.

The Availability Heuristic

The **availability heuristic** is a common one. It involves judging the probability of something based on how readily we can imagine or recall that particular thing. This is not a totally useless way to estimate the chances of something happening. Obviously, familiar things tend to come readily to mind, and familiarity tends to be correlated with likelihood of occurrence. So we will be right a lot of the time when we use the availability heuristic.

Some images come readily to mind not because they occur often, but because they are emotionally intense or easily imagined. For example, if we see a bloody accident, vivid images of it may quickly come to us. Something may be easily imagined if it has gotten special media attention. For example, airplane crashes, which are extensively covered in the media, tend to seem more likely to occur than they are. Certain diseases that are often discussed on television will also seem to pose a greater risk than they do in reality.

One way in which availability influences health-related judgments is that we tend to overestimate the likelihood of serious diseases (Elstein & Bordage, 1979). Serious diseases come readily to mind because they are so frightening and press on our awareness. Therefore, we tend to overestimate their chances of occurring. Obviously, physicians, being human, use the

availability heuristic, too. If a physician has recently missed a diagnosis of a given disease, he or she may promptly think of this disease when doing diagnostic work and will have a tendency to overdiagnose it. Physicians who have a special interest in a given kind of disease may also tend to use that diagnosis too readily.

Similarly, Lichtenstein et al. (1978) asked people to judge death rates due to various factors. The judges were strongly influenced by the mental availability of the different causes of death. Events that were heavily covered in the media and brought forth vivid images were deemed more likely to happen. For example, judges thought it more likely that a person would die as a result of a tornado than of asthma. Actually we are 20 times more likely to die of asthma.

The threat of a given risk factor helps determine whether we take preventive action. Thus, we can see that the availability heuristic can diminish the effectiveness of our health-related decisions. Health professionals also make errors using the availability heuristic, such as incorrect diagnoses or erroneous judgments about whether a patient is following a medical regimen. (See below for a discussion of compliance with medical regimen.)

The Representativeness Heuristic

Another heuristic that can lead us astray is the **representativeness heuristic.** Stereotypes about what is most typical of a given category of object distort our probability estimates. Sometimes judgments about what is "typical" are not logical. For example, with respect to the class "fruit," Bourne, Dominowski, Loftus, and Healy (1986) point out that people usually regard "apple" as more representative of fruit than "grapefruit" is.

How does this heuristic influence judgments about probability? The point is well made in the following example from Kahneman and Tversky (1982, p. 126):

Linda is 31 years old, single, outspoken, and very bright. She majored in philosophy. As a student, she was deeply concerned with issues of discrimination and social justice, and also participated in antinuclear demonstrations.

The description of Linda is, in some sense, *representative* of feminists. But her description does not particularly fit our idea of a bank teller; she is relatively *unrepresentative* of a typical image of bank tellers. Based on the representative heuristic, we might estimate that it is unlikely that Linda is a bank teller but likely that she is a feminist bank teller. College students did just that. Over 80 percent judged it more likely she was a feminist bank teller than that she was a bank teller. This is a fallacy since the number of bank tellers obviously exceeds the number of feminist bank tellers. Their judgments were heavily influenced by the low degree of representativeness she displayed for being a bank teller and the high degree she had for being a feminist.

A nursing faculty colleague, who happens to be quite overweight, often complains that whenever she has a medical problem, she has to struggle with doctors to get them to attend to the actual medical evidence in her case, since they have a strong inclination to assume that her health problems *must* stem from her obesity. This is a good example of representativeness distorting medical judgment.

Base-Rate Errors

We make a **base-rate fallacy** when we judge probabilities and fail to take base rates into account. The base rate of a category or event is its overall frequency in the population we are judging. Bourne, Dominowski, Loftus, and Healy (1986) give an excellent illustration of the impact of failure to consider base rates:

> It is known that 5 percent of the population is afflicted with the disease "rubadubitis." A new diagnostic test has been developed which is rather good. If a person has rubadubitis, the test gives a positive result 85% of the time. If a person does not have the disease, there is only a 10 percent chance of getting a positive test result from the test. All in all, a pretty good test. Here's the situation: the test has just been given to John Doe and the test result is positive. What is the probability that John has rubadubitis? (p. 294)

People usually think the chances of John's having the disease is about 85 percent. Thus, the odds would be 85/15, or about 6 to 1 in favor of his having the disease. Actually, because the base rate is only 5 percent, the calculated probability of his having the disease after getting this positive test result is only 0.31, and the odds are 2 to 1 against his having it! This is calculated by a formula known as Bayes Theorem. If you feel skeptical of the result, you can look up the theorem and calculate it for yourself (for the formula see Eddy, 1982).[1]

In many instances, physicians are better able than the rest of us to consider base rates of diseases. Think of how often people go to a physician because they think they are sick with an ailment that has been much discussed on television, and the physician provides them with reassurance that it is too unlikely to worry about.

Physicians do know more about the base rates for diseases than laypeople. They use information from their clinical experience, whereas the rest of us have little more than media presentations and our own limited experience to judge the likelihood of diseases. We rely on the availability heuristic very heavily, whereas physicians can correct that with considerable information about the actual frequency of disease. Still, there is evidence that physicians could do better by using accurate base rates (Elstein & Bordage, 1979).

Medical Diagnosis and Information Processing

Elstein and Bordage (1979) have summarized a body of systematic investigations of how physicians process information during the process of making diagnoses. When diagnosing a disease, physicians quickly generate a handful of hypotheses about the underlying causes of the presenting symptoms. Then they gather new data to evaluate the hypotheses. The resulting evidence either confirms, disconfirms, or is noncontributory to the evidence for the hypothesis. One

---

[1] If you are not mathematically inclined, see Bourne, Dominowski, Loftus, & Healy (1986) for a simple arithmetical demonstration that these odds are the correct ones.

error they tend to make is to overemphasize confirmatory findings and to neglect or dismiss findings that disconfirm a hypothesis. Several studies have shown that even when a hypothesis is wrong, confirming evidence can be found for it. There is no way to correct this problem without attending to the evidence against our favored hypotheses.

Theory Perseverance

Physicians, like all of us, tend to be overconfident of their hypotheses. The tendency to hold onto an idea in spite of evidence to the contrary is called **theory perseverance**. The relationship between the accuracy of our judgments and our confidence in them is less than perfect. The difference between accuracy and confidence tends to be largest when confidence is high (Bourne, Dominowski, Loftus, & Healy, 1986). Furthermore, we tend to increase our confidence as we gather new data, even when the data are *irrelevant* (see, e.g., Oskamp, 1965).

A further problem arises when physicians gather new evidence and on the basis of the added data must change their notion of the likelihood of a certain disease. Evidence indicates they are likely to make gross errors in judging these new probabilities. One of the major problems is their tendency to ignore something called **false alarms.** A false alarm occurs when a test result is positive, yet the person does not have the disease in question. Many tests have notoriously high rates of false alarms. For example, one person in seven taking a cardiac stress test will be identified as having heart trouble and yet have a healthy heart. Even very good tests are likely to have significant numbers of false alarms.

Eddy (1982) examined the use of mammograms to assess the presence of breast cancer and found that physicians tended to act as if false alarms were insignificant. Physicians, even in published literature, tended to focus on a test's ability to detect cancer in those who actually had it. At the same time, they ignored the test's tendency to falsely indicate cancer in some people without it. If there is any false

alarm rate at all, the test will overestimate the chances of a patient having cancer.

Since this is not an easy idea to grasp in the abstract, we have an extreme example that may help. Imagine the following absurd case. Suppose the slightly mad, but brilliant, Dr. Levity modifies the mammogram in some way so that it gives a positive finding for 100 percent of women who actually have breast cancer. This would be called having a 100 percent *hit rate*. Does this mean Dr. Levity's new test is 100 percent accurate? This is pretty close to the way the medical literature reviewed by Eddy would interpret it. Now, suppose we now learn that the test also indicates the presence of cancer in 100 percent of women who do *not* have it. Would you still say it was 100 percent accurate? Of course not. It would be totally useless.

Now no one in his or her right mind would use a test with a 100 percent false alarm rate. But you can see that, whatever the false alarm rate may be, a correction has to be put in for its influence. Failure to do so can lead to remarkable inaccuracies. To illustrate, Eddy (1982, pp. 255–257) analyzed probability estimates made for positive mammographic findings. He found that estimates were generally inaccurate, and at least in one case they were off by a factor of about 150!

You can easily see how awareness of the false alarm rate is essential when you adjust a probability in the light of new test results. Imagine that a woman's gynecologist estimates the odds that she has breast cancer before the physical examination. The physician's best guess would be the frequency of that cancer in the overall population. That is the "base rate." The physician examines her breasts and finds certain kinds of lumps in a certain quadrant. This information will result in an adjustment of the base probability in light of the new evidence. Certain kinds of lumps are more likely to be cancer, and cancer more often occurs in certain parts of the breast.

Now suppose the physician arranges a mammogram, and the results are positive. First, consider the absurd case above in which mammographic findings in people who actually have cancer would indicate that they had it 100 percent of the time, but there was a 100 percent false alarm rate. What adjustment should be made in the estimated probability of cancer? The answer is that it should not be changed at all, since the test gives no useful information.

Take the opposite extreme—if the test indicated cancer in 100 percent of real cases and had no false alarms at all. Now it's a foolproof test, and the woman's physician would correctly adjust the probability to 100 percent. It is easy to see that for in-between cases we would have intermediate estimates. These intermediate values can be calculated from Bayes Theorem, which is given in Eddy (1982) and in many statistics books. Thanks to this formula, we know how to tell the real probability by calculation. Intuitively, however, we will not make this adjustment correctly. We tend to estimate it as nearer the hit rate than is correct. Predictably, then, physicians incorrectly adjust probabilities when evidence is added from test results.

Manipulating Large Amounts of Data

We pointed out earlier that people have difficulty in correctly pooling items of information. We may gather the right data and gather it well, but then put it all together poorly.

In general, mistaken medical diagnoses stem not from faulty but from excessive data gathering. Excessive data flood the physician with unusable information. Most of the time, physicians make errors because they incorrectly interpret the data. A major facet of this problem lies in the failure to manipulate large amounts of data correctly.

We humans are quite good at identifying which variables are relevant to making the judgments we want to make. With respect to medical tests, this procedure would consist in selecting which tests are of importance in reaching a correct diagnosis. But we are not likely to combine variables well. What typically happens is that we fail to use all the variables we think are important. For example, experts may say that ten different factors are important to a decision, but,

without realizing it, they will tend to use just a few of them in coming to their conclusions.

Since people are good at picking the important variables, this leads to a paradoxical result. Say we have experts pick out the variables they deem important in making a given judgment. If we then go on to make a judgment using even the crudest calculations that include *all* the identified variables, our results will be more accurate than those of the experts who identified the variables for us in the first place! For example, Fryback (1974) found that *calculations* based on radiologists' own selection of information led to more effective decisions than the uncalculated judgments of those radiologists.

Conclusions

This discussion leads to some fairly straightforward conclusions. Physicians can be helped to make better judgments about diseases and treatments. To improve, they need an accurate source of base rates of the diseases being considered. They also need to obtain calculated figures instead of subjective estimates indicating the strength of association between given symptoms and specified diseases.

Furthermore, they need to improve their estimation of changes in probabilities when new test results come in. These new figures must be based on the relevant factors including hit and false alarm rates of the tests. Intuitive judgments of the probabilities are likely to be inadequate.

Similarly, the combination of test results to make a diagnostic procedure should be based on at least some simple calculation that assures us that all the relevant variables are actually taken into account. Ideally, the doctor would use the best weightings of the variables, with some variables counting more than others. Even if they are given equal weighting, the result of a calculation is likely to be better than the result of an intuitive judgment.

It may seem out of the question that physicians would spend time in their offices calculating probabilities. Given the fast pace characteristic of most medical offices, this effort would be very expensive and would require physicians to reduce their patient load. But there is no reason why a simple computer could not provide storage of the base rates and of such factors as the probability that a given symptom means that a certain disease is present. The same computer could easily do the calculations that include all the relevant variables, and even provide optimal weightings of the variables. Programs to perform this sort of measurement were developed long ago (e.g., Vinsonhaler, Wagner, & Elstein, 1977).

Having analyzed these major cognitive influences on the performances of physicians, let us now shift our emphasis to the patient side of the physician-patient interaction.

COPING WITH ILLNESS

The case of George, with which this chapter began, illustrates one facet of the problem of coping with physical illness. He had symptoms indicating the onset of a life-threatening disease. It was essential to his survival that he evaluate the symptoms appropriately and initiate what is technically called **illness behavior.** Illness behavior includes the perception of symptoms as well as the initiation of action to find out their meaning and to get treatment for them.

Stages in the Formulation of Disease

We will use the case of George to distinguish between several stages in the formulation of health breakdown. First, he had subjective, bodily **sensations,** such as pain in the chest, which he attempted to interpret. He also had objective **signs** of distress, including profuse sweating. He went back and forth, thinking of these sensations and signs at times as "tiredness" and "needing a vacation," and at other times as "having a heart attack."

We do not always interpret signs and sensations as **symptoms** of disease. George had trouble making this interpretation, holding out for the possibility that they just indicated fatigue. At some point, however, he decided they were symptoms that required professional treat-

ment—even emergency medical treatment. At that point, he made the transition to what we call **illness behavior**, and he went to the emergency room. Illness behavior refers to the seeking of medical help. Once in the emergency room, George was diagnosed as having a heart attack. The professional diagnosis with all its ramifications provides a patient with a socially sanctioned **sick role.**

Achievement of the sick role is important, since it dramatically changes societal reactions to a person. Insurance companies pay various benefits, employers usually become more permissive about work absences, family and friends usually make great changes in their expectations of the sick person, and medical personnel may shift from regarding the patient as a "hypochondriac" to seeing him or her as a "real patient."

Dispositional Versus Process Analyses of Coping

George's case illustrates an important aspect of coping with illness. The actions needed to cope with a health problem depend on the stage of the problem. What is required in the early stages may be different from what is required later on. It is well known that patients with heart attacks tend to deny the significance of their symptoms. If this denial comes at the early stage of illness behavior, it may have dire consequences. The same kind of denial once the person is in intensive care could actually be helpful because it could reduce anxiety.

Much research has been done on how personality characteristics or dispositions influence the ability to cope with illness. The results have been disappointing. There *does* seem to be a broad statistical tendency for certain coping styles to be healthier than others. For example, Vaillant (1977) identified the characteristics of people who coped well with difficult life situations. They tended to use humor, to lay problems aside when necessary, to care about others and not just themselves, and to be farsighted about problems that might come along in the future. These dispositional influences are probably outweighed by the demands of specific situations encountered in the process of a given illness.

Lazarus has emphasized the importance of process as opposed to dispositional analyses (Lazarus & Folkman, 1984). **Dispositional analyses** emphasize the impact of the person's abiding traits on coping with illness. **Process analyses** emphasize the fit between various situational demands and coping responses. As in the case of George, it may be a mortal error to deny the significance of a disease process at one stage; yet denial may be adaptive when there is really nothing more to be done about it. The value of inaction and passivity may also vary in different contexts.

The best coping reaction may vary with the particular people the patient has to deal with. Certain family members or medical personnel may need passivity, denial, or some other coping mode from the patient. Patients will sometimes seem to have a "disposition" to use a particular mechanism with one person, only to have that style of coping vanish in the presence of another person.

When we accept the "process" view of coping with illness, we face a more complex challenge in trying to understand it. If we want to help patients cope with illness, we must have a fairly detailed knowledge of the specifics of that particular disease. Furthermore, we have to develop a sensitivity and openness that allow us to understand how patients operate in many contexts, including family, friends, work, and medical environments.

The Psychology of Physical Symptoms

Patients often feel alone and are frightened as things happen to them that they do not understand. It can mean a lot to the patient to be told what to expect and how to interpret it. Patients also need to be connected to someone who understands and cares. Lynch (1977) described a cardiac patient, a derelict in life, who was dying with no known connection to a relative or friend. His heart was beating irregularly until a nurse merely touched him. Then it began to beat in a regular pattern. The impact of contact with

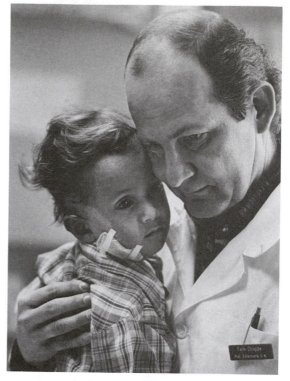

Patients need to have contact with someone who understands and cares. The impact of this connection can be quite dramatic and sometimes help a person recover.

someone who cares or of being helped to understand what is happening may be quite dramatic and can sometimes help a person recover.

Within the biomedical model we tend to oversimplify the relationship between physiological stimuli and their interpretations. As a result, we may underestimate the impact of providing clear interpretations to patients.

Two people given the same physiological stimulus may react quite differently. Weil (1980) pointed out that psychedelic mushrooms grow plentifully in the northwestern United States and that many young people take delight in the "high" they get from them. But from time to time a family may be out picking edible mushrooms for their evening meal and inadvertently get hold of one of the psychedelic ones. Often they end up in an emergency room. The same physiological stimulus can give rise to a pleasurable or to a distressing experience, depending on how people perceive the experience. We have an understanding of this phenomenon thanks to the work of Schachter and Singer (1962).

Schachter and Singer showed that the kind of experience a person has during a given physiological state depends on the interpretation it is given. They injected adrenalin into volunteers and manipulated their expectations of the symptoms. Some people were not told what to expect at all, others were told to expect physical symptoms, and still others were encouraged to experience either euphoria or anger. Their reactions to the adrenalin depended largely on their understanding of what "should" happen. The same kind of effect is illustrated by the following clinical case:

Susan, a woman in her late thirties, was raised in an extremely protective family with an invalid mother, who worried about the potential dangers of her slightest exertion. Susan decided to join an aerobics class, but went into a panic during her first lesson, because her heart rate increased to alarming levels. A lengthy series of physical examinations, including an exercise cardiac stress test, failed to reveal any flaw in her heart. Apparently, she had so little experience of physical exertion that she was terrified by the strange experience of having her heart speed up in response to exercise, and the panic made it speed to faster and faster rates. She had never been given a framework for interpreting such cardiac responses which are so familiar to most of us.

Health psychologists, then, must know the details of the physical and psychological effects of their patients' diseases. They must also know how these effects vary over time and in different contexts. If we want to understand the process of coping with illness, then, we will have to understand the impact of specific situations. This is what Lazarus and Folkman (1984) are emphasizing when they advocate a process view of coping.

Still, a number of useful attempts have been made to give a general account of the tasks that must be mastered in coping with illness. Most of this work focuses on adaptation after the person has received a diagnosis. Some earlier stages are also highly important. The case of George, with which we started this chapter, is a case in point. He failed to deal effectively with symptoms prior to any diagnosis.

Each stage in the formulation of illness may present its own problems. At first, we have subjective sensations or bodily signs that have not yet been identified as symptoms. We use the term "sensations" here to mean bodily feelings that are not observable by others. Signs, on the other hand, are objective indicators that others can observe. Such observation might be by naked eye or with the use of special measuring instruments, such as the devices used for measuring blood pressure.

Sensations and signs may go hand in hand, but sometimes they do not. Thus, a person may have a headache that fits the description of a tension headache, but direct measures made on the muscles, an objective sign, may show no high tension. In another patient, muscular tension may correlate quite well with the subjective experience of headache.

A disturbance that very commonly produces signs without sensations is essential hypertension. It is very common for a person to have elevations of blood pressure in the absence of any subjective awareness of a health problem.

Judgments about health are very complex. This is reflected in a study that identified over 100 variables that influence health-related decisions (Cummings, Becker, & Maile, 1980). People differ in how they make these difficult judgments. Men and women probably differ in this regard, with women being more likely to interpret something as a symptom and men more likely to ignore signs and sensations until they are forced to acknowledge them, often after hard physical damage. Within a given gender, wide variations also occur, with some people being what are commonly called "health care overusers," and others, such as those who have silent heart attacks, being "health care under-users."

Most of us feel that when we say we have a symptom we are giving an accurate description of our physiological state. People tend to get annoyed if you suggest that they are not accurate about what is going on in their bodies. Pennebaker (1982), after extensive research on the psychology of physical symptoms, suggested that reporting symptoms has only a loose relationship to physiological states. We are not especially good at identifying these states.

Many factors influence our judgments. For example, external stimuli can provide distractions that make us less aware of our bodies. If you compare the feel of riding an exercise bike in the house with that of riding a real bike in the countryside, you will get a sense of the impact of having an attention-getting context. You are much more likely to enjoy the ride in the country partly because you won't notice the bodily discomfort as much.

External stimuli can also create a context that leads us to focus on certain limited interpretations of bodily reactions. Pennebaker (1982) reported several studies in which merely directing people's attention to bodily states such as warming of the hands or nasal stuffiness led them to report more warming or stuffiness. Our frame of mind can lead us to focus on given bodily states and thus bias our decision about the kind of symptom we have. Furthermore, unlabeled emotions can be confused with physical symptoms. The same bodily states may, for example, be interpreted as bodily sickness or psychological depression.

Obviously, children have to learn to label their bodily states, and this learning takes place primarily in the family. Pennebaker (1982) describes a little girl holding her throat and saying "My tummy hurts." A child can be trained to label bodily states in many different ways. Family conflict, social insecurity, and reinforcement for having symptoms influence how many and what kind of symptoms we report.

Pennebaker's research indicates that the symptoms that correspond to a given physiological state, such as the level of blood pressure or of blood glucose, are specific to a given individual. One person may have shortness of breath, a racing heart, and cold hands when systolic pressure is up, while another might have sweaty hands and a tight stomach instead. The given pattern is quite reliable within individuals. If averaged across individuals, no strong correlations of symptoms and physiological states emerge.

So it is clear that the process of deciding that one has a given physiological condition is very complex and subject to a great deal of situational variation and to differences in individual processing of the raw data from the body. Yet the ability to cope with this stage of potential health breakdown is of vital importance. It determines whether we decide we have a symptom, whether we seek help in dealing with it, and what kind of help we seek. That, in turn, will influence whether we are assigned a "sick role" and what kind of diagnosis we get.

Coping with the Sick Role

Several investigators have identified adaptive tasks that a person must deal with once he or she has been assigned a sick role. Cohen and Lazarus (1979) and Moos (1977) have developed lists of the essential tasks. A composite of these lists would include:

1. Modifying harmful environmental conditions in such a way as to aid recovery. This includes such behavior as changing lifestyle in order to assist in the recovery process. The patient who must quit smoking after a heart attack is a case in point.

2. Dealing with the medical environment and special treatment procedures. Patients commonly have to deal with an alien environment in which the "foreign language" of medical talk is often spoken. They must tolerate very unusual role adjustments and often distressing procedures over which there is little personal control. Patients must also

overcome obstacles to carrying out pre-scribed treatments.

3. Adjusting to negative events and realities that result from the illness. These include physical pain, disfigurement, and losses of functional capacity.

4. Preserving a satisfactory self-image. Many aspects of the patient's self-image are un-dermined by disease. Such factors as changes in appearance, work and family roles, and ability to act in usual ways may have to be dealt with. Often several stages of grief over lost aspects of self-image must be handled, and the patient must find an ac-ceptable concept of self based in the new reality.

5. Preserving a reasonable emotional balance. The patient may be tempted to become anx-ious and even panicked, may become hope-less and depressed, and may grow irascible and hostile to medical personnel, family, and other associates. But a calm, hopeful attitude and maintenance of good relation-ships may be important to living with the sickness and to the process of recovery.

6. Preserving satisfying social relationships. Changing roles may require great changes in the usual ways of relating to significant oth-ers. The once independent patient may have to learn to live with the help of others; the patient who related on the basis of activity may have to curtail that activity, and so on.

7. Developing adequate relationships with professional staff. A major clash of role ex-pectations and of values may well occur in dealing with health care personnel. A power-ful personality may have to come to grips with being in an environment in which roles require submissiveness. A dependent per-son may find medical personnel, with their technological bent, cold and uncaring. Somehow a working relationship must be developed, and this relationship may be im-portant in coping with the disease and aid-ing in the process of recovery.

8. Preparing for an uncertain future. The pa-tient and loved ones must prepare for losses of function and possibly death. Sometimes they must cope with uncertainty about whether functional losses or death will oc-cur. In an age of technological innovation, a patient with a stroke or spinal cord injury may have to adjust to loss of speech or movement while still hoping for eventual recovery. A person with a clear loss, such as a woman after breast removal, may be un-certain about the kind of life she will lead after this traumatic bodily change.

The success with which people get through these tasks is quite varied. We all know of people who had a relatively minor health problem but who died anyway. On the other hand, there are people who manage to live their lives to the fullest in the face of terminal and debilitating diseases. What is the difference between those who succeed and those who fail? Richard Bloch (Bloch & Bloch, 1981), a survivor of lung cancer and founder of a nonprofit organization for help-ing patients deal with this disease, summarized, about as well as one could, a central problem in understanding the process of coping with dis-ease. He said:

> . . . *every case of cancer is different. Not only are there different types of cancers, but they are in different places, happening to people of different ages, of different back-grounds, and of different strengths and weaknesses. Each case of cancer is as unique as a fingerprint.* (p. 10)

A similar statement could be made for any dis-ease. This is why it is hard to come up with broad generalizations about how to cope. Variations are even greater from one disease to the other.

Attentional Versus Avoidant Strategies

Nevertheless, some insights have been gained through attempts to understand general prin-ciples of coping with disease. For example, many studies have been conducted on the relative effectiveness of *avoidant* versus *attentional* strate-gies. An **avoidant strategy** is one in which pa-tients turn their attention away from aspects of the disease. They might deliberately distract themselves or unconsciously deny painful aspects of the disorder. **Attentional strategies** are those in which the person focuses on the distress, for example, by seeking information or changing their appraisal of it.

Suls and Fletcher (1985) did a systematic analysis of research literature comparing avoidant and attentional strategies. They found little evidence of any *overall* superiority of avoidant versus attentional strategies. However, when the data were broken down into long-term versus short-term studies, avoidant strategies appeared to be better under short-term conditions. "Short term" meant that the outcomes were measured on the same day as the stressor occurred. Avoidant strategies tended to be better at the beginning in long-term studies, but their initial advantage was reversed as time went on. So attentional strategies tended to work better in the long run. Holmes and Stevenson (1990) affirmed in pain patients that short-term patients did better with avoidant strategies and long-term chronic patients did better with attentive strategies.

There are two broad categories of attentional strategy. In one class of this strategy, the person focuses on the disease in order to identify and express emotions brought on by that disease. In a second type, the patient focuses on sensory aspects of the disease, usually breaking them down into separate sensory elements. For example, a person experiencing pain could analyze the pain into its component sensations, such as sharpness or dullness, speed of onset, and muscular tension. Suls and Fletcher (1985) found that sensation-focused attentional strategies were better for both short- and long-term disease. Strategies centering on emotional expression did not fare well in this meta-analysis.

Cohen and Lazarus (1979) have suggested that coping strategy might vary with type of disease. More work needs to be done on this subject, since there is at least some evidence for the usefulness of emotional expression. For example, women with breast cancer who express more anger seem to have a better chance of recovering (Cox & MacKay, 1982). Levy et al. (1985) confirmed that women with breast cancer who were "well adjusted" to the disease had less natural killer cell activity. Natural killer cells play a role in destroying tumors. In contrast to the case of breast cancer, emotional expression in chronic obstructive pulmonary disease tends to make symptoms worse (Cohen & Lazarus, 1979).

Needed Coping Skills

Moos (1977) has compiled a list of coping skills necessary in dealing with illness. One of these skills is the ability to control emotions while carrying out actions necessary to deal with the disease. Each skill can be applied in the wrong situation or carried to an extreme. In such cases, it becomes ineffective coping. A useful listing, modified from Moos, is shown in Table 6.1.

THE ROLE OF THE HEALTH CARE PROFESSIONAL

The problem of coping with disease is clearly very complex, and our understanding of it is limited. Nonetheless, we can state certain rules of thumb that might be useful for the health care professional (see Moos, 1977). First, it is important to realize that disease is likely to create a "teachable moment." At these times, patients come to grips with aspects of their lives that are otherwise kept in the background, and they are unusually open to changes in lifestyle. The role of the health provider in supporting the patient's resolution of such issues is a particularly important one.

Dealing with Defense Mechanisms

The health care provider must have some understanding of the complexity of the psychological impact of disease for patient and family. Many important psychological and social implications of the disease are not obvious to the outsider. Among other coping methods, patients and families may have to utilize powerful psychological defenses in dealing with these implica-

Table 6.1 List of Illness Coping Skills

1. Being able to contain and control emotions in order to carry out needed actions.
2. When appropriate, avoiding, minimizing, and denying the meaning or impact of a crisis or redirecting one's reactions to make them safer.
3. Using intellectual resources, especially in seeking information.
4. Eliciting reassurance and social support from family, friends, and medical personnel.
5. Expressing meaningful feelings to others.
6. Learning specific procedures involved in managing the disease, thereby dealing with it and increasing one's sense of control.
7. Setting concrete, limited, and realistic goals for recovery.
8. Rehearsing alternative outcomes, such as results of medical procedures, and communicating these thoughts to significant others in order to prepare them, reassure them and oneself, or begin the mourning process.
9. Finding meaning and purpose in the course of events.

Source: Modified from Moos (1977).

tions, including "primitive" defenses such as denial, repression, and fantasy (Vaillant, 1977). It is essential to remember that these methods may vary over time and with context. To breach needed defenses is to expose the defended person to unbearable anxiety.

The person who is avoiding painful realities may appear silly or even "crazy," especially to someone dedicated to dealing with disease rationally and technologically. However, there is a higher wisdom in the defenses, and people tend to come to grips with realities when the time is right for them. There must be a continuing give and take between health care provider and patient, with the provider confronting the patient with realities when necessary, while understanding the need for sometimes keeping them at bay.

Keeping Patients Informed

In working with patients, health care providers should know about the experience of the disease and about its common psychosocial effects. This is different from knowing about its underlying physiology and technical treatment. An example pointed out by Moos and Tsu (1977) follows:

> Mastectomy patients, for example, should be told that they may have crying spells, trouble sleeping, and numbness in their arms after the surgery. Then, if these occur, they need not fear they are having an emotional breakdown, or, as one woman did, that a nerve was mistakenly cut. (p. 18)

In addition, the mastectomy patient has to deal with major cosmetic and interpersonal issues (e.g., sexuality) and needs psychological and social help with these.

Lynch (1977, 1985) has summarized a large body of evidence showing that being connected to another person, or even to a pet, has positive effects on health and recovery from illnesses. For example, touching or even being in the same room with a pet tends to lower blood pressure and heart rate.

It is not surprising, then, that patients are helped by getting a correct interpretation of their symptoms and by having a connection to another person. Health care providers can provide both to their patients. Register (1987) has pointed out that people are often relieved to get rather drastic diagnoses, such as lupus erythematosis or polycystic liver, since then at least they have a fairly clear interpretation of their symptoms. Patients may be unable to grasp this kind of information at first. It may well have to be repeated many times.

Health care providers should be alert to the situational factors that press on the patient. For example, hospital personnel are adapted to that environment and may not be sensitive to its impact on the patient. The patient's family and

There is evidence suggesting that having contact with pets has positive effects on health and recovery from illness.

larger social environment are also very central to coping with the disease. They may compete in importance with biomedical factors.

Health Care Provider Stress

Helping patients cope with their illnesses contributes to the patients' well-being, but it does add to the burden of the health personnel. They, too, have to deal with major emotional material. The well-known cancer surgeon, Bernie Siegel (1986) often talks about asking patients for a hug because *he* needs the hug. This is a very important concept. Health providers need to be supported in work and home environments if they are going to be nurturing to patients. Emotional "dumping" (Langs, 1982) can be very toxic to patients. This means that health care personnel who do not deal with their emotions may dump them on the patient, who is ill equipped to cope with them.

The health care "culture" fails to provide for the well-being of its members. This idea is well expressed in the following statement by Pfifferling (cited in Ferguson, 1980), an anthropologist who studied medical "culture":

Of all the physicians in the study, very few were what I would call healthy. Most were barely surviving. This was especially true of the medical students and hospital residents. There were a few physicians—very few—who had made superhuman efforts to maintain a high quality of life, but everything in the medical system—competitiveness, on-call schedules, peer pressures—worked against it. There is no clinical setting I've seen that really addresses the well-being of health workers as an important issue. (p. 6)

Pfifferling was studying physicians; the problems are probably as, or more, severe for nurses. It is no coincidence that half of all nurses end up leaving nursing (Kirby, 1980).

It is clear that changes in the norms of medical culture would be helpful to both patients and health personnel, but there is always great resistance to cultural change. It will be a long time coming. In the meanwhile, certain tactics can help. The approach advocated by Siegel (1986) is a case in point. Some researchers focus on changing the coping styles of health personnel. For example, physicians tend to be perfectionists, rigid in their thinking, compulsive, skeptical, dominant, and controlling, and to deny personal problems and weaknesses (Orman, 1989). Orman argues that changing these cognitive and behavioral tendencies can lead highly stressed physicians to cope much better with their lives.

More effective coping often leads to improvements in the internal management of stress. These cognitive and behavioral changes can also improve the external environment. Take the case of malpractice. In some surveys, over half of the participating physicians had been sued for malpractice, and they often deemed the experience the most stressful of their lives (Orman, 1989). Nevertheless, physicians can do certain things to make it less likely that they will be sued for malpractice.

Physicians who are arrogant, hostile, insensitive, or oblivious to their patients' needs are probably more likely to be sued (Orman, 1989). Those physicians who are empathic and caring, and who communicate well with patients are probably less likely to be sued. Courses designed to improve physicians' skills in relating to patients are now available, and some insurance companies reduce premiums for those who have completed such courses. Such changes in the physicians' social skills might well make the emotional quality of the work environment more pleasant, while at the same time improving its objective qualities.

ADHERENCE TO MEDICAL PROCEDURES

Several of the "tasks" faced by the patient in coping with disease involve adhering to preventive or treatment regimens. Medicine invests a great deal of energy and ingenuity in developing the biomedical aspects of treatment. Yet, social and psychological influences may create a "bottleneck" that is crucial to delivering the biomedical treatment. A very good example is in the creation of cardiac intensive care units.

Starting in the late 1940s, a system of resuscitating cardiac patients whose hearts stopped beating was devised, and it was quite effective. However, it required that someone trained in the technique (which is now called cardiopulmonary resuscitation or CPR) start work on the patient within minutes after the cardiac arrest. In some hospitals, this posed no great problem, since resident physicians were available round the clock. In other hospitals it would take far too long to bring a physician to the patient's side.

A cardiologist named Hughes Day devised a new way of handling this problem. He arranged for the heart patients to be kept in one section of the hospital to be hovered over by a nurse. This was the beginning of the intensive care unit, and the idea spread quickly. However, by the late 1960s it became apparent that it was saving almost no lives!

The problem was that nurses were not allowed to perform one of the procedures that was of greatest importance, that of applying electrical shock to the failed heart ("defibrillation"). The key factor in making CPR useful was to let the nurses defibrillate the patients. It was finally decided that nurses would be allowed to perform this procedure if a physician could not be brought on the scene within 60 minutes. As Moore (1989, p. 159) has pointed out:

> It was an object lesson that rigid organizational attitudes could be just as formidable an obstacle to saving lives as lack of scientific knowledge. And many cardiologists would remember later that the real problem in setting up coronary care units was not getting the money or equipment, but changing attitudes and giving nurses a much larger role in coronary care.

Importance of Correct Implementation

It is useless to have a fine technology for curing people if that technology fails to be applied. Moreover, both the providers and their patients must use the technology correctly. Massive studies are conducted to evaluate the effectiveness of such medical procedures as the use of drugs, but they all assume that the drugs are being taken and that they are being taken in a way that makes them effective. Based on such studies, we know, for example, that antibiotics are very useful in getting rid of many bacterial infections. However, they can be effective only if they are actually taken, and they can be harmful if not taken according to the prescribed regimen.

Failure to take *all* of the prescribed antibiotics can lead to much worse infections than the one that provoked the patient to come to the physician. The hardy bacteria survive the first onslaught of the antibiotic. Symptoms may go away after the mass of less resistant bacteria have been destroyed. The patient thinks the disease has been cured. If the antibiotic regimen is stopped at that point, the hardy germs may reproduce and then the patient ends up with a serious infection that cannot be treated with the customary antibiotic.

Completing the course of antibiotics is important, but many parents may fail to give the complete course to their children. For example, researchers checked urine samples to determine whether a prescribed antibiotic was being taken halfway through a ten-day treatment program. Over half the mothers had stopped giving the medicine by that time (Becker, Drachman, & Kirscht, 1972).

Physicians and other medical staff often feel that their job is done when they have diagnosed the patient and prescribed the correct treatment. They can take pride in the established record of the designated intervention. They may be living in a world of fantasy, for many patients fail to follow the correct procedure. Effectiveness of treatment is really a function of (1) the likelihood that the treatment will work if correctly applied, and (2) the likelihood that the treatment is correctly applied. Even the most reliable treatment can have an effectiveness of zero if the social-psychological side of treatment is neglected.

It can be argued that the responsibilities of scientific medicine end with prescription of the correct treatment and that the rest is up to the patient. This position is a pseudoscientific one, however. As the scientific method developed, it was quite common for people to limit its sphere unduly. Why should *behavior* be excluded from the scientific analysis underlying medical treatment, especially when it is so clearly a crucial factor?

To exclude the study of adherence to a correct treatment regimen from the science and practice of medicine is to revert to a marginally scientific attitude. The principles of patient and practitioner behavior should be taken as seriously as the principles of bacterial behavior. Physicians who neglect to look at this aspect of their role may be severely reducing their effectiveness.

Prevalence of Failures to Implement Biomedical Treatment

Both patients and physicians frequently fail to implement biomedical procedures. Many studies have been done on both topics, although the emphasis is usually on patient failure to "comply" with the medical regimen. Averaging results over many studies of self-administered medications, Sackett (1976) concluded that 50 per-

cent of patients do not take prescribed medications according to instructions. Twenty to 40 percent of recommended immunizations are not obtained. Scheduled appointments for treatment are missed 20 to 50 percent of the time. Where compliance requires dealing with well-established habits and going against strong motives (e.g., stopping smoking, reducing food intake), compliance is likely to be even worse.

Beneficial medical treatments provoke a strong tendency to noncompliance when they do not relieve symptoms or when they produce disturbing side effects. The treatment of essential hypertension is a case in point. Various studies indicate that patients with this deadly disorder are commonly not in treatment (perhaps about one-half of them), and of those who are in treatment about half of them have uncontrolled hypertension, owing largely to noncompliance with the regimen.

The treatment of hypertension tends to produce noncompliance because many patients have no clear symptoms prior to treatment, the medicines are expensive, treatment must go on for a lifetime in most cases, and the medicines are likely to produce side effects. Typical is the finding of McKenney et al. (1973), who observed compliance in 50 hypertensive patients for seven months. They found that about 65 percent of the pills were actually taken. Only 20 percent of the patients took as many as 90 percent of the prescribed pills.

Viewed from another angle, several studies show that, after detection of high blood pressure, only about 50 to 70 percent of hypertensives will seek treatment. About one-third of those will drop out of treatment, and roughly another third will remain uncontrolled. Thus, only about a third of hypertensives end up with their blood pressure controlled (Leventhal, Zimmerman, & Gutmann, 1984).

We can easily see why a patient would be reluctant to follow prescribed procedures with respect to hypertension. In some cases, however, the motives are less obvious. For example, Richardson et al. (1987) examined the blood serum levels of medication in 92 patients who were under treatment for various forms of cancer of the blood. The study was done on patients who had agreed to participate in such a study— presumably a group somewhat biased, if anything, toward greater adherence to the treatment regimen.

Blood serum levels of allopurinol were measured. This drug has few side effects but is critical to preserving the kidneys from toxicity due to the anticancer medication. Study results showed total noncompliance 77 percent of the time. Total noncompliance means that none of the medicine could be detected in the serum. In addition, nearly 8 percent of the patients were using the medication, but less than required. Thus, patients were at least partially failing to follow this important regimen 85 percent of the time. Similar results were obtained with the anticancer medication, prednisone. Around 69 percent of the time there was total noncompliance.

Wysocki, Green, and Huxtable (1988) observed compliance with a program in which insulin-dependent diabetic adolescents were to monitor their own blood glucose levels, using a meter that gives patients their blood glucose levels. The device also retained the readings in memory so that the investigators could find out whether the patient really used it. They noted that patients' use of the meter declined steadily over a 16-week period. The percentage of days (using four-week blocks) on which the patient completed the required measures dropped from 77.6 to 58.1 by the end of the study.

Similar results are abundant. Various findings in the same vein are described in such sources as Kirscht and Rosenstock (1979), Dunbar and Agras (1980), Leventhal, Zimmerman, and Gutmann (1984), and Meichenbaum and Turk (1987). The bottom line is that people fail to implement a wide variety of types of health regimen, including prevention and risk reduction (e.g., for exercise, see Belisle, Roskies, & Levesque, 1987; or for inoculation, as well as treatment, see Mortimer, 1978).

Awareness of Noncompliance

It would be natural to assume that physicians would be vividly and painfully aware of so important and prevalent a problem as patients'

failure to implement health prescriptions. Yet, they seem to be remarkably unaware of it. In one study, 89 percent of physicians believed that all, or virtually all, of their patients were carrying out the prescribed treatment. Actually, only about 50 percent were doing so (Davis, 1966).

In an even more striking study, physicians working on a gastrointestinal ward were asked to rank order their patients according to their degree of compliance with the treatment. When their rank orderings were correlated with actual compliance, the rank order correlation was 0.01. This is negligibly different from a total lack of correlation, which would be 0.0. Thus, the physicians did no better than chance in judging who was noncompliant. Further discussion of this study and related investigations may be found in DiMatteo and DiNicola (1982).

Although most investigators focus on the patients' adherence to correct medical procedures, medical professionals often do not follow procedures themselves. Most of us are familiar with the physician's reluctance to carry out such procedures as culture an infection to determine the nature of the pathogen. It is also quite common for physicians to prescribe inappropriate medications, such as antibiotics for sore throats which are almost certainly viral. (Antibiotics are totally ineffective in treating viral infections.)

A striking example of failure to follow known medical procedures was described by Albert and Condie (1981), who observed how often medical personnel washed their hands after touching patients and before going on to other patients. Albert and Condie made the observations under the pretense of studying traffic patterns in a hospital unit. They found that physicians washed their hands only 28 percent of the time, and nurses only 43 percent of the time. They commonly failed to wash even after procedures like dressing wounds.

Transmittal, Reception, and Retention of Information

A major reason why patients fail to implement medical procedures is that the physician fails to convey information. Pratt et al. (1957) found that, particularly if a person seemed initially ill informed, physicians tended not to take the time to translate medical information into terms the patient could understand. It is important to note here that generally physicians grossly underestimate the comprehension level of their patients (Segall & Roberts, 1980). This consideration is particularly important if this judgment then leads the physician to neglect telling them important information.

Waitzkin and Stoeckle (1976) directly recorded the proportion of time physicians spent informing patients about their illness or treatment. The average time spent with the patients was 20 minutes, of which an average of 1 minute was spent informing them. When asked to estimate how much time they had spent dispensing this kind of information, the same physicians estimated that it had been 10 to 15 minutes.

Svarstad (1976) recorded the instructions given to patients and compared those to the instructions attached to medication containers. She found that about 17 percent of the time physicians did not even discuss their intentions to prescribe medication. Ninety percent of the time no specific advice was given on how to use the medication.

Physicians often changed the dosage of a drug patients had at home without giving any written instructions. Written instructions on medication almost never included the length of time the medicine was to be taken. Written materials often left out important information, and in 20 percent of the cases the final written information on the medication was in error. In 29 percent of the cases the physician did not give the patient any information about the drug or its purpose.

Patients frequently lose information given during visits with the physician. Patients are often tense and anxious, and they are on "stimulus overload." Thus, more information is coming in than they can process, so a lot of it is lost. Remember, people have very limited channel capacity. Tension tends to overload our "channel." Although we are more aware of the information we get through sight and sound, the largest source of information is from the mus-

cles (Sheridan, 1986). So it makes sense that tense people will fail to comprehend and remember a good deal of what is being said to them.

Consider the typical scene in which a patient goes to the physician, possibly in great fear that a major illness will be diagnosed. The patient is tense and anxious, so the nervous system is already running on overload. The environment is unfamiliar to most patients. Often there are many patients as well as many medical personnel in the office.

Questions are fired at the patient rapidly, whether in person or by filling out forms: "What kind of insurance coverage do you have?" "What is your insurance group coverage number?" "What is your Social Security number?" Are you allergic to any medicines?" The patient often does not know the answers and fumbles around looking for information, or has to place phone calls while leaning over the receptionist's desk and being observed by various people.

Having passed through that barrier, the patient is guided into an even stranger environment where he or she hears various observations, and these are often confusing and anxiety provoking. "Hmm—you weigh 207 pounds. (*Oh my god, have I gained that much*!?) Hold out your arm *this* way so I can take your blood pressure. (*I've got to stay relaxed or it might be high*!)" Or the physician checks something and mutters a "Hmm" that has an ominous ring to it. (*She must have found something pretty bad*!) Physicians and nurses talk to the patient in a language that is only partially understood. According to information theory, things that are unfamiliar or not readily understood are high in information content, so there is more overload.

Throughout this procedure the patient may well be thinking thoughts like "Maybe they'll tell me I have cancer! I haven't put away enough money for Mary and the kids to get along if I have cancer." The distressed patient can be having some very alarming images of deadly diagnoses and their consequences.

Finally, the physician quickly runs over the conclusions of the visit and rattles off a quick description of the treatment plan and various details about how to implement it. The physician is also likely to be on information overload, since nearly always other patients are waiting in various examination rooms and in the waiting room. As a result, he or she might well forget to mention procedures that are fairly important in making it easy to use the medicine. For example, a medicine to be taken on an empty stomach may cause stomach problems. It may be okay to eat a few crackers with it, but the doctor may not mention that relatively minor consideration and the patient may eventually stop taking the medicine because it causes distress.

This all too familiar hypothetical scenario has radically important consequences. Joyce et al. (1969) interviewed patients either immediately after a visit or at home two weeks later. In both groups they had forgotten two-thirds of the diagnoses and treatment evaluations and half of the instructional statements. The greater the amount of information given, the more they forgot.

Other research indicates that the way the material is organized influences patients' recall. Systematic presentation is better. Visual aids help. Over a three-day period, patients retained 10 percent of orally transmitted information, 20 percent of visually transmitted information, and 65 percent of information transmitted in both ways (Boyd, Covington, Stenaszck, & Coussons, 1974).

Physicians generally make heavy use of medical jargon, as a number of studies have documented. These studies show that patients often seriously misunderstand physicians' language. For example, many patients in one study thought that "as needed for water retention" meant that they should take the pill at night so they would not have to wake up to urinate. Samora, Saunders, and Larson (1961) found that patients understood an average of 56 percent of technical terms physicians deemed appropriate to use with them.

Physicians are not entirely to blame for the failures in communication. For their part, patients tend to be very passive in discussions with their physicians. In one study, patients asked questions of their physicians only 7 percent of the time. They commonly expressed their confusion through facial expressions, body movements, and tone of voice.

Improving Compliance

A large body of literature is available on the topic of compliance with medical procedures, but the results are not always consistent and vary depending on the kind of health-related action being considered. For example, to get compliance for an alcohol abuse program, a good deal of focus may have to be placed on the problem of relapse. When alcohol abusers have a "slip," it is likely to set up conditions that lead them to go back to regular drinking.

Relapse prevention programs have been designed to prevent this pattern (Marlatt & Gordon, 1985). Whether a lapse turns into a relapse depends on how individuals view the lapse. If it is seen as a brief slip that happened at a specific time due to a specific situation, they are less likely to relapse. The slip is more likely to become a relapse if they attribute it to internal causes such as lack of "willpower." Relapse prevention deals with these cognitions and helps contain the lapse.

Marlatt and Gordon (1985) suggest that the principles underlying relapse might be general across all behaviors. However, when Kirkley and Fisher (1988) applied this model to patients who were trying to control diabetes through dietary restrictions, they found that there was little tendency in the first place for a lapse to turn into a relapse. In their own words, "Overall, the results suggest that most nonadherence to dietary treatment of diabetes may be best understood as intermittent lapses that typically do not develop into full-blown relapses" (p. 221).

Nevertheless, certain fairly consistent factors do emerge as widely applicable influences on compliance. When we look at this literature it is often difficult to see the forest for the trees. Fortunately, a number of investigators have attempted to summarize the main findings and to construct models that give a certain coherence to the data. Table 6.2 summarizes a large body of research on factors that have been examined as influences on compliance.

Notice that a number of factors seem to operate consistently. The patients' belief that the problem poses a real threat to their health is one of these, as is the belief that they can take actions that will reduce that threat. Knowledge of what they are to do and why is also important. The presence of support from other people in carrying out the regimen is a significant factor, as is stability of the group of supportive people.

The presence of symptoms generally encourages patients to stick to the regimen. So do

Table 6.2 Factors That Influence Adherence Behaviors

	Following Prescribed Regimen	Staying in Treatment	Prevention
Social characteristics			
Age	0	+	−
Sex	0	0	+(female)
Education	0	0	+
Income	0	0	+
Psychological dispositions			
Beliefs about threat to health	+	+	+
Beliefs about efficacy of action	+	+	+
Knowledge of recommendation and purpose	+	+	+
General attitudes toward medical care	0	0	0
General knowledge about health and illness	0	0	+?
Intelligence	0	0	0
Anxiety	−?	−	?
Internal control	0?	0	+
Psychic disturbance	−	−	?
Social context			
Social support	+	+	+
Social isolation	−	−	−
Primary group stability	+	+	+
Situational demands			
Symptoms	+	+	NA
Complexity of action	−	−	−
Duration of action	−	−	−
Interference with other actions	−	−	−
Interactions with health care system			
Convenience factors	−	−	−
Continuity of care	+	−	+
Personal source of care	+	+	+?
General satisfaction	0	0	0
Supportive interaction	+	+	?

Note: Many of the 0 entries represent inconsistent findings; in the case of education, for example, there are positive relationships to medication compliance in several studies but no relationships in many others.

Source: From "Patients' problems in following recommendations of health experts," by J. P. Kirscht & I. M. Rosenstock, In G. C. Stone, F. Cohen, N. E. Adler, & Associates (Eds.), *Health psychology—A handbook: theories, applications, and challenges of a psychological approach to health care,* Table 1, p. 215, copyright © 1979 by Jossey-Bass, Inc. Reprinted by permission.

various factors that have to do with having some kind of stable, personal, and supportive relationship with the health care provider.

Stanton (1987) has developed and evaluated a model of adherence behavior for essential hypertension. It is somewhat generalizable to other health-related behaviors. It provides a clear way of showing how factors influence these behaviors, and it is clearly consistent with the factors summarized in Table 6.2. The model is shown in Figure 6.1.

The patient–provider communication factor is consistent with the previously mentioned influence of rapport with health caretakers. It also encompasses the influence of knowledge of the medication regimen. Internal locus of control is directly related to our previous statement that patients must feel that they can take actions that will reduce the threat of illness. The perceived social support was also mentioned above.

Only the role of the treatment's disruption of the patient's lifestyle has been added here.

This factor is probably not always relevant to adherence (see Table 6.2 under "Situational demands"). It may be especially important in the case of hypertension where the treatment can important facets of the person's life, such as their sexual activities.

Here we will try to give a brief summary of rules of thumb that should make it more likely that health prescriptions will be followed. Many, if not all, of these rules are useful both to medical personnel and to the health psychologist who is trying to help people behave in ways that foster their health. Our list of principles will follow, to some degree, the recommendations made by Levy (1987) and by Dunbar and Agras (1980).

1. Behave in a warm, empathic manner with patients. Listen to them, and follow common courtesies such as introducing yourself and shaking hands. Interact actively with the patient. If possible, try to arrange for the

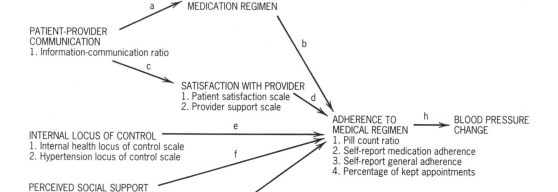

Figure 6.1 Hypothesized structural model for the determinants of adherence. The measures employed as indicators of each construct are listed under the construct heading. Source: From "Determinants of adherence to medical regimens by hypertensive patients," by A. L. Stanton, *Journal of Behavioral Medicine*, 10, p. 379, copyright © 1987 by Plenum Corporation, New York. Reprinted by permission.

patient to have the same treatment personnel consistently. Try to view the patient as a key member of the treatment team, without whose cooperation you can accomplish nothing.

2. Be sure you give specific details about what the patients are to do and why. Check with them to be sure they understood your instructions. Keep in mind that they may be distressed and that there are real limits to their ability to process information. Keep the quantity of information low, and if you have to give a lot of information, break it down into smaller chunks and keep it simple. Presenting the information both by word of mouth and with visual aids will increase retention. Present the material in a rational, organized way.

3. Give skill training when necessary. Sometimes the patient will not understand what to do or how to do it; a brief training session will remedy the problem. This training may include oral and written instructions as well as modeling on the part of the professional followed by practice on the part of the patient. For example, a patient may be trained to take his or her own blood pressure in this way.

4. Be sure the patient understands the rationale behind the treatment plan and the evidence that it will work. If you want the patient to follow the regimen, you have to create positive expectations about its efficacy and about his or her ability to carry it out.

5. If possible, arrange social support and reward for adherence. To some degree this may have to come from health care personnel. When rewarding a patient it is important to be sincere about it. Many patients will be turned off by insincerity. Patients can be taught to reward themselves for correct actions. If possible, solicit the support of family, or recommend support groups.

6. Provide at-home reminders that will help the patient carry out the task. For example,

pill containers that have each pill in a slot for a given day have been shown to increase compliance. Written reminders to be posted in a convenient place by the patient may also help.

7. Try to anticipate barriers to compliance, including any negative effects it may have. Compliance is likely to be enhanced if the patient is told ahead of time that there will be various kinds of inconvenience, discomfort, pain, and the like. In addition, the patient should get specific instruction, modeling, and rehearsal on how to cope with these problems. Essentially, provide a brief cognitive behavioral therapy (see Chapter 5) in how to cope with these difficulties.

8. Keep in mind the prevalence of noncompliance, and monitor it as well as you can. Even patient self-reports are better than nothing. Monitoring should not be carried to the point where it impairs your relationship with the patient. For example, having the patient's spouse monitor his or her behavior can corroborate self-reports. But insisting on it might produce reactions that eventually lead to noncompliance.

Conclusions

This chapter is an especially important one, since it reveals a facet of health psychology that is not very well known. When people hear about our field, they usually assume it is about alternative cures for disease. Perhaps they recognize a place for health psychology in helping people deal with risk factors. Few people are aware, however, that psychological principles are often highly applicable to medicine.

As our book was in the process of development and was reviewed by many an astute and helpful editorial consultant, a large number of interesting and exciting suggestions were made for additional materials that this chapter should cover. If we had followed all these suggestions, this already lengthy chapter might have turned into a book in its own right. This push toward expansion occurred, we think, because so many facets of psychology are of significance to medical care, and so many facets of medical care could profit from applications of psychology.

The work of psychologists is significant for any human enterprise. Here, with selected examples, we have shown that it is important and useful to health care providers in doing their job and to patients in actively fostering successful treatment.

Summary

1. Our brains have very limited channel capacity, which makes it hard to avoid certain errors of perception, reasoning, and judgment. Information overload leads to breakdown of communication between doctors and patients.

2. We are also limited by the rules, called heuristics, that we use to estimate probabilities. This can lead to errors of diagnosis, failures of patients to follow medical prescriptions, and so on.

3. Major heuristics lead us to err in our assessments of probability. For example, in the "availability heuristic" we judge the probability of something based on how readily we can imagine or recall that particular thing. Another is the "representativeness heuristic," in which stereotypes about what is most typical of a given class of object distort our probability estimates.

4. Another important source of error is failure to consider "base rates" (i.e., the frequency of, say, a disease in the general population). New information, for example, from medical tests, should lead us to adjust our assessment of probability upward or downward from the base rate. If we ignore the base rate, our estimates can be very far off.

5. Direct studies of medical diagnosis indicate some important sources of cognitive error. For example, doctors tend to overemphasize confirmatory findings, and to neglect or dismiss findings that disconfirm a hypothesis. This leads to "theory perseverance." Another major problem is that doctors tend to ignore the "false alarm rate" of tests. Many medical tests mistakenly flag healthy people as ill, and this distorts the probability that a positive test result really indicates they have the illness.

6. Doctors are not very good at combining data from several tests to make an accurate judgment of the likelihood of a disease. None of us is good at combining data in our heads, and doctors should use some form of calculation to improve their accuracy.

7. Limits of information handling also influence patients who are trying to cope with disease. The patient has to recognize objective signs and subjective sensations from the body and determine if they are symptoms and if professional help is needed ("illness behavior"). Ultimately, the person may or may not receive a diagnosis, whereupon he or she gets a "sick role," that is, a professionally sanctioned status as "sick."

8. Much research has been done to identify characteristics that are related to the tendency to fall ill. Such analyses are called "dispositional," and they have met with some success; for example, certain ego defense mechanisms seem to predict the likelihood that a person will fall ill. But good coping often varies with such factors as type and stage of disease. Thus we also need "process" analyses that take into account the variations in response needed for good coping.

9. We usually assume that a mentally healthy person can generally make accurate judgments about his or her bodily states to decide if they are symptoms. A good deal of research shows that the relationship be-

tween bodily states and symptoms is a complex one and is influenced by cognitive, emotional, and motivational factors. This is important, for example, in understanding why some people "overuse" and others "underuse" medical care.

10. When people have to cope with the sick role, in addition to their physical problems they have many psychological and social difficulties (e.g., dealing with a changed self-image, finding status in the family when the usual roles are suspended). These are among the most important facets of coping with disease.

11. Important research has been done on two broad ways of coping with disease— avoidant strategies, in which the patient tries not to attend to the disorder, and attentional strategies in which the patient monitors details of the disorder, perhaps in order to take action. Neither strategy has been shown to be superior overall, but it seems that avoidant strategies are more effective in the short run, with attentional strategies emerging as better after some time has passed.

12. To be maximally effective, the health care provider must understand a good deal about the patient's psychological reactions to a given disease. For example, patients may use primitive defenses at first and process the information more realistically later, when they are ready. It is important to respect this timing. There may be consistent patterns of reaction to a given disease; health care providers should be aware of them and, if possible, help the patient to understand them.

13. Patients' needs are boundless, and health care personnel have limited resources. Furthermore, the "culture" of health care is remarkably unsupportive. Health providers can do a great deal to improve their coping and thereby reduce distressing events, such as malpractice suits.

14. No matter how good a medical treatment is, it is useless if not implemented. Thus, it is essential to get patients and medical personnel to follow procedures. Evidence indicates that failures to comply with medical regimens are extensive and largely outside the awareness of physicians. One important study indicated that they had *no* ability to tell who was complying and who was not.

15. A major factor leading patients to fail to adhere to medical regimens is the failure of doctors to convey information or to recognize how overloaded the patient is when given instructions. Patients retain remarkably little of what they are told in the doctor's office.

16. Health care providers can improve adherence in several ways, including (a) being warm and empathic, (b) giving specific details of treatment, (c) teaching people how to carry out complicated procedures, (d) explaining the rationale behind the treatment, (e) arranging social support and a reward system, (f) providing at-home reminders to follow the procedures, and (g) monitoring the degree of compliance.

Key Terms

Attentional strategies

Availability heuristic

Avoidant strategy

Base-rate fallacy

Channel capacity

Dispositional analyses

False alarms

Gambler's fallacy

Heuristics

Illness behavior

Process analyses

Representativeness heuristic

Sensations

Sick role

Signs

Subjective probabilities

Symptoms

Theory perseverance

Discussion Questions

1. What is a heuristic and how do heuristics influence our judgments about reality?
2. Name and describe the major heuristics discussed in the text.
3. List several reasons why psychological knowledge and skill are important to health care providers.
4. What is human channel capacity and how does it influence our way of dealing with the world?
5. Explain the major features of medical reasoning during the process of diagnosis.
6. Discuss our limitations at adjusting probabilities based on new data and show how they influence medical reasoning.
7. Explain the importance of taking false alarm rates into account in evaluating the results of medical tests.
8. What are the main problems people have in dealing with large bodies of data?
9. Explain the stages in the formulation of disease from signs and sensations through the sick role.
10. Explain dispositional versus process analyses of coping with sickness and tell why process analyses have been advocated.
11. Describe the role of psychological factors in the formation of physical symptoms.
12. Briefly describe the major adaptive tasks that must be mastered in coping with the sick role and the role of attentional versus avoidant strategies in coping.
13. Outline what you would tell a health care provider who asked you, as a health psychologist, what he or she should do to help patients cope with a disease.
14. Construct an argument designed to persuade a health care provider to focus on the problem of patient adherence to medical procedures. Remember, these people want *evidence*.
15. Briefly summarize the most important things health care providers can do to improve their patients' adherence to medical procedures.

Stress and Health

Theresa taught in a suburban school in a nice middle-class neighborhood, but this particular year she felt like she was teaching in a war zone. She was assigned several students notorious for behavioral problems. One student had a history of abusing administrators, teachers, and his fellow classmates. Another child suffered from an emotional trauma and was not only aggressive, but self-destructive as well. In addition, several children in her class had severe family problems. The problems all these children brought to the classroom often interacted, creating a most difficult teaching environment. Although at times Theresa became discouraged, she managed to finish the school year without adverse effects. She reasoned that this was a temporary situation, and she saw it as a challenge to her teaching skills and coping resources. Nancy, the teacher who inherited Theresa's problem children the next year, did not fare as well. She developed several stress-related symptoms including irritable bowel syndrome, tension headaches, and a series of illnesses which suggested a lowered resistance to disease.

These two women were about the same age and came from the same socioeconomic background, yet they had very different reactions to similar situations. Perhaps Theresa was better at "handling stress" than the other teacher. The concept of stress and its relationship to health has played a major role in expanding the biomedical model to the biopsychosocial model. Rarely have people found a scientific concept so relevant to their lives. It would be hard to find many people who have not heard about stress and its effects. Certainly there has been a media blitz about the dangers of stress.

THE NATURE OF STRESS

Researchers are in general accord that we are in the midst of an epidemic of stress that is causing illness and even death, but few agree about how to define stress. Some psychologists tend to define it as a stimulus, whereas physicians tend to describe it as a response. Lately, research and treatment have focused on appraisals and coping. No wonder there is so much confusion about the meaning of the term. This confusion recalls the fable of the six blind men describing an elephant. The blind man who touched its tusk said it was clear that the elephant was like a spear. Another who touched its ear said it was like a fan, and so forth.

A STRESS MODEL

Stress is probably best approached as a "construct." By that we mean that it is a synthesis of several interacting elements. Each element of stress and its relationship to the other elements and the whole need to be considered. In other words, a systems approach is required. (This approach is described in Chapter 2.) To help students better understand the construct of stress, we have integrated several models (Antonovsky, 1979; Dohrenwend, 1978; Lazarus & Folkman, 1984).

We present this model in Figure 7.1. In this model, the term **stressor** refers to anything that makes a demand on us. **Cognitive appraisal** refers to the way we appraise the stressor and the resources we have to meet its demands. **Short-term reaction** is our temporary response to the demands of the stressor. **Stress resistance resources** are all the material, physical, social, and psychological resources we have to cope with the stressor and our short-term reaction to it. **Eustress, distress,** and **neutral effects** are the possible outcomes that can result from exposure to a stressor. We will explain each term in more detail below.

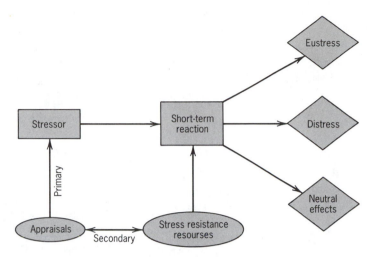

Figure 7.1   An interactive model of stress. Stress is better understood as a construct with several interacting elements.

Stressors

The term "stressor" was introduced by Selye (1978) to distinguish between the cause (stressor) and the effect (stress). A **stressor** can be anything from lost car keys to the death of a spouse. We are using the term "stressor" because it is so accepted. However, it is not the best term because it implies that every demand results in distress. As we will discuss in this chapter, that is not the always the case. Lazarus and Cohen (1977) identified the following categories of stressors.

Cataclysmic Stressors

Cataclysmic stressors refer to those events that happen to several people or whole communities at the same time. They are usually unpredictable, have a powerful impact, and require great coping efforts. Natural disasters, wars, massive layoffs, and technological disasters are all examples of cataclysmic stressors. People coping with these kinds of stressors often find that being in "the same boat" with so many others provides support and a source of comparison for feelings and behaviors. In addition, cataclysmic stressors often result in a good deal of community or government aid.

Personal Stressors

Personal stressors affect individuals and include events like failing an exam, becoming unemployed, or getting divorced. They may or may not be predictable, but they do have a powerful impact and require great coping efforts. Personal stressors can sometimes be more difficult to cope with than cataclysmic stressors because of the lack of support. In recognition of this fact, support groups have been formed to meet the needs of individuals undergoing personal stressors. For example, "Parents Without Partners" is a support group for single parents.

Researchers frequently use life event scales to measure personal stressors. The Social Readjustment Rating Scale (SRRS) is the "grandfather" of stressor scales (Holmes & Rahe, 1967). It is a 43-item checklist of potentially stressful events. The items include both positive and negative events, ranging from "death of a spouse" to "vacation." Most introductory psychology texts publish the SRRS. The scale has done much to further research into the relationship between stress and health. It is still widely used, although its limitations have been recognized by a growing number of researchers (Billings & Moos, 1982; Radmacher & Sheridan, 1989; Redfield &

Stone, 1979). The SRRS fails to take into account people's appraisals of the stressor, nor does it consider their stress resistance resources. As we will discuss later, these factors are very important in the experience of stress.

Background Stressors

Background stressors are the "daily hassles" of life. They are the small, but persistent, problems that irritate and distress people (Lazarus & Folkman, 1984). They include problems like a noisy workplace, poor lighting, or an unreasonable professor. If we fail to seek support or help in solving these stressors, they may cause more damage in the long run than cataclysmic or personal stressors.

The Hassles Scale is often used to measure background stressors (Kanner, Coyne, Schaefer, & Lazarus, 1981). It covers relatively minor events of daily life, for example, "inconsiderate smokers" and "too many responsibilities." Compared to life events scales, the Hassles Scale may be a better predictor of psychological symptoms and physical symptoms (Banks & Gannon, 1988; Kanner et al., 1981). However, researchers have noted that the scale is confounded because many of the stressors are also symptoms (Dohrenwend, Dohrenwend, Dodson, & Shrout, 1984).

Cognitive Appraisals

It has been assumed for centuries that the way we perceive or appraise our situations is important. Shakespeare once wrote: "There is nothing good or bad, but thinking makes it so." During the latter part of the twentieth century, this "folk wisdom" has received support from an extensive body of research data. The concept of **cognitive appraisal** has been very valuable in increasing our understanding of individual differences in stress, emotion, and health.

There is concern that the emphasis this concept has received has created an attitude that objective reality is not important (Antonovsky, 1987; Sheridan, 1983a). Richard Lazarus (1984), a pioneer in this area of research, is troubled by the trend in our society to "downplay the negative and accentuate the positive." He argues that

it leads to the trivialization of distress and "blaming the victim." For example, cancer patients may be blamed for being depressed because they did not try to have positive thoughts.

Primary Appraisals

Cognitive appraisal has two basic forms: primary and secondary. **Primary appraisal** refers to the evaluation of the stressor. When we are confronted with a stressor, we ask ourselves "What is this going to cost me?" Generally, we appraise events as either irrelevant, benign-positive, or stressful. We will evaluate a stressor as irrelevant if it appears that it will not have an impact on our well-being. If we believe that it will preserve or enhance our well-being, we evaluate it as benign-positive. A stressor that involves harm, loss, threat, or challenge will be appraised as stressful (Lazarus & Folkman, 1984).

For example, students who are auditing courses appraise final exams as irrelevant because they are not receiving a grade for the course. There may be a few professors who give an "A" for "attempt" on finals. (We realize that this example is a bit far-fetched, but maybe such a professor exists somewhere.) In this case, students would appraise the exam as benign-positive because they know that all they have to do is be there. A final that accounts for 50 percent of the total grade, would be evaluated as extremely stressful by most students.

Secondary Appraisal

Secondary appraisal refers to our evaluation of our ability to use our stress resistance resources to overcome our short-term reaction to the immediate stressor. During secondary appraisals, the question we ask ourselves is, "How can I handle this stressor?" Primary and secondary appraisals occur almost simultaneously. For example, when you are confronted with an exam, your primary appraisal of it will depend in part on your secondary appraisal of how well prepared you are for it. If it is an important exam and you have not been in class all semester, you will view the event as very stressful. Taking the exam will be a low-stress situation, if you feel confident that you have the necessary knowledge.

In a review of the social support literature, Cohen and Wills (1985) concluded that the appraisal of support is more important than the support that is actually available. Their conclusion was supported by the findings of a matched-control study of Israeli soldiers who suffered combat stress reaction during the Israeli–Lebanon War (Solomon, Mikulincer, & Hobfoll, 1987). These data showed that subjective indicators of stress and social support were stronger predictors of combat stress reaction than were objective indicators.

Stress Resistance Resources

A growing emphasis is being placed on the role that resources play in the experience of stress (see Box 7.1). Antonovsky (1979) has noted that most of us survive and even thrive in a world filled with physical, psychological, social, and cultural pathogens or, in other words, stressors. He suggests that we manage these stressors with **generalized resistance resources;** we use the term **stress resistance resources** (SRR). These are all the things we have at our disposal

---

Box 7.1 The Conservation of Resources Model

Stephan Hobfoll (1988, 1989) has presented a stress model based on the assumption that people try to keep, protect, and build resources. Stress is seen as a response to either the threat or the actual loss of resources. Perceived as well as actual loss of resources can produce stress. Stress also results when we fail to experience a net gain from investing our resources. This model has identified four kinds of resources.

Object Resources

Object resources have a physical nature and often serve as status symbols. For example, homes provide shelter, but they are also concrete symbols of our social status. These kinds of resources are not mentioned in the stress literature, but they are important. Dohrenwend (1978) has found a strong link between socioeconomic status and stress.

Conditions

Conditions are states of being that we value. Having a spouse, children, citizenship, and a job are examples of conditions. Hobfoll notes that there is a dual edge to conditions as resources. Conditions can be of great value, but they also require a great investment in time, energy, and other resources. If we fail to experience a gain from our investment, it can result in stress. For example, a person can invest a great deal in a marriage, only to have it fail.

Personal Characteristics

Personal characteristics refer to stable traits and skills possessed by individuals such as a sense of mastery, self-esteem, positive outlook, and work-study skills. Research has generally demonstrated that many personal traits and skills aid in stress resistance. Of course, some personal traits and skills are not assets. Whether or not a resource is helpful often depends on the situation.

Energies

Energies include such resources as time, money, and knowledge. These resources do not have great intrinsic value, but they are valuable in helping us to obtain the other kinds of resources.

that allow us to cope with most of life's stressors. Next we will briefly describe some of these resources. Others will be discussed in more detail in later sections of this chapter.

Material Resources

Material resources include money and all the things it can buy—food, clothing, shelter, health care, and so on. They are among the most useful resources we have, and yet they are paid scant attention in the literature. As an example of how material resources work, let's suppose an unemployed garment worker and a successful lawyer each received a large heating bill. The heating bills are stressors because they are demands. The short term reaction will quickly be managed by the lawyer who has money to pay the bill. The unemployed garment worker will have a harder time managing her reaction because there is no money to meet the demand.

Physical Resources

Physical resources are the positive physical attributes of a person. Attributes like strength, health, and attractiveness can be helpful in coping with stressors. For instance, it is generally assumed that being physically attractive is a good resource for building social support networks (Walster, Aronson, Abrahams, & Rottman, 1966). Research has found that, depending on the crime, being attractive is a decided benefit for defendants appearing before juries (Landy & Aronson, 1969).

Intrapersonal Resources

Intrapersonal resources are those "inner strengths" that help us cope with life's events. One of the most important resources of this type is self-esteem. For example, Bettelheim (1947) observed that concentration camp prisoners tried to keep their egos or sense of self intact by supporting their self-esteem. Some prisoners found support for self-esteem by reasoning that the Gestapo obviously thought them important enough to be a threat. The upper class prisoners segregated themselves and developed such a sense of superiority that nothing could touch them.

Self-esteem is strongly related to ego integrity. Erikson (1963) explains ego integrity as an acceptance of oneself and one's life. Antonovsky (1979) discusses a similar concept—ego identity. Ego identity refers to a stable and integrated sense of self that is still dynamic and flexible. Those with a strong ego identity maintain their independence while still being in touch with their social and cultural reality. Regardless of what it is called or how it is defined, a strong sense of self can be essential in coping with many stressors.

Informational and Educational Resources

Knowledge is a most valuable resource to possess. For example, if our unemployed garment worker knew that there were agencies to help her with her heating bill, she could overcome the short-term reaction associated with that stressor. Knowing about nutrition, exercise, risk factors, safety, and first aid procedures can be important resources in coping with stressors that affect our health. And, in this age of information, knowledge is a source of income.

Education may account, in part, for the lower morbidity and mortality rates of the higher socioeconomic classes (Antonovsky, 1979). Education also helps us obtain material resources. College graduates can expect to earn several hundreds of thousands of dollars more than high school graduates (Finn, 1988).

Cultural Resources

Antonovsky (1979) writes that our culture gives us a **sense of coherence.** This resource is the extent to which a person has an enduring sense of confidence that there is meaning to life, even though it is not always evident. Antonovsky (1987) believes that a sense of coherence plays a major role in our ability to manage tension. Sense of coherence will be discussed in more detail later in this chapter.

The traditions, customs, and rituals of a culture contribute to our sense of coherence. For example, the British monarchy serves that purpose for the Commonwealth nations. Prime ministers may come and go, but the royal family and the traditions surrounding it continue from

The traditions and rituals that surround the British monarchy contribute to the sense of coherence of the people of the commonwealth nations.

one generation to the next. A former student found that sense of continuity when she visited England a few years ago. The description of her experience follows:

> *I* attended an evensong at St. George's Chapel in Windsor Castle on a cold January evening. This particular service has been performed every night, in the same place and at the same time, since the year 1326 A.D. The history and tradition of the evensong were as pervasive as the fog that engulfed the great castle that night. As the choir sang and the prayers were read, I thought of all that the British people had endured during the centuries since the first night of this evensong. Although I was thinking of the past, I had never felt so centered in the present—in a moment of time. The experience left me with a different perspective of life and my place in it.

We should not leave the impression that we have to be British to have meaningful traditions and customs. They have been at it longer than Americans, but we have some of our own. For example, Independence Day is a uniquely American tradition and serves a similar purpose. Weddings, baptisms, graduations, funerals, and Sunday dinner at grandma's also provide a feeling that this is an orderly and stable world. Antonovsky suggests that this sense of order and continuity makes the meaning of life easier to grasp.

Short-term Reaction

Short-term reaction refers to our temporary response to the demands of a stressor. Another way to describe it might be arousal. If you lose your car keys, you become aroused enough to direct your attention and energy to finding them. Even if this reaction is uncomfortable or harmful, its effects are temporary. Dohrenwend (1978) refers to this step in the model as a transient stress reaction. She proposed that our immediate reaction to a stressful life event (stressor) is self-limiting. She has found that the symptoms people experience in disasters are almost always temporary. Stressors, then, do not always lead to distress or permanent damage. However, we are likely to experience distress if we do not have sufficient resources to cope with the stressor or our short-term reactions. For example, the heating bill probably resulted in distress for the unemployed garment worker we mentioned earlier.

The short-term reaction involves the responses of the Alarm Reaction of the General Adaptation Syndrome (GAS). This syndrome is discussed in detail in Chapter 4. Remember that the GAS has three stages: Alarm Reaction, Resistance, and Exhaustion. It is the Alarm Reaction stage that involves activation of the sympathetic nervous system. Some of the responses of this stage include the constriction of blood vessels in the skin and increases in heart rate, blood pressure, and glucose levels. These responses can be very mild or strong depending on the stressor. Obviously we respond more strongly to having our car stolen than we do to losing our car keys.

Eustress, Distress, and Neutral Effects

As we have worked our way through this model, we hope it is clear that not every stressor has to make us sick. Stressors, our resources, and our appraisals of both, all interact to determine the outcome of our experiences with life's stressors. Selye (1978) observed that to talk about being "under stress" is as pointless as talking about "running a temperature." What we are concerned about is an *excess* of stress or body temperature. After all, the only people who are not under some stress or running a temperature are dead.

Eustress

Undergoing the stress process can actually have positive effects that are commonly referred to as **eustress** or "good" stress. Antonovsky (1979, 1987) has urged for some time that researchers search for the variables that allow some people to thrive in spite of serious stressors. However, this is a difficult direction to follow because it falls outside the framework of the biomedical model. Remember that paradigm emphasizes the diagnosis and cure of "sickness."

There is growing evidence that even noxious stressors can have positive effects. Researchers

compared the tumor rejection rate of rats exposed to inescapable shock, escapable shock, and no shock (Visintainer, Volpicelli, & Seligman, 1982). As expected, the rats in the inescapable shock condition had the lowest rate of tumor rejection. However, the rats that got the *escapable shock* had the *highest* rate of tumor rejection even when compared to those that received no shock at all!

Other researchers also found that rats given an escapable shock showed improved immunological functioning over rats receiving inescapable shock, *and* two control groups that received *no* shock (Laudenslager et al., 1983). In both studies, the authors only mentioned in passing that the escapable shock group showed the highest level of immune functioning. Research is conducted by forming hypotheses, and hypotheses are formed within the dominant paradigm. The biomedical model directs questions about why organisms get sick, not what makes them healthy.

Although it may not always be obvious, exams, tests, and term papers are stressors that often result in positive effects. Writing term papers is a significant stressor for most students. However, there is no better way to develop your information-gathering and writing abilities, both of which are very marketable skills. Reading this book is a stressor, but if you have good reading skills and time to read it, then you should experience some positive effects from it. Another everyday example of positive effects from stressors is fitness training. Weight trainers have to stress their muscles if they are going to gain strength, and jogging is a stressor for the cardiovascular system that makes it stronger.

Distress

In this model, we are using the term **distress** to describe the negative effects that can result from exposure to a stressor. As distress is used here, it has the same meaning as the term "stress" does for many people. For example, Antonovsky (1979) defines stress as "the strain that remains when tension is not successfully overcome" (p. 3). "Strain" is a much better term to describe these negative effects. However, distress and stress are so widely used now, it would be difficult to change. Selye (1978) confessed that, had his English been better, he would have used the word "strain" instead of stress.

Although we have emphasized that not every stressor *has* to result in distress, we recognize that distress is very common in today's world. As we mentioned in Chapter 4, the stress response was very adaptive for our ancestors but not for us. It is often called the "fight or flight" response because it prepares the body for action. We are ready to fight our stressors or run away from them. We respond to today's stressors just as our ancestors responded to theirs. But the nature of stressors is very different today. Their stressors were saber-tooth tigers, and ours are tax audits or traffic jams.

Many students consider final exams a significant stressor and find themselves in a stress response. Their heart rate and blood pressure increase, their mouths are dry, and their hands are cold and sweaty. Their bodies are ready to fight or run! However, either of those responses will create more problems. They can't hit the professor or run from the classroom. Instead they have to sit quietly at their desks. This is somewhat like slamming one foot on the gas pedal and the other on the brake. No wonder distress is a major concern today.

Prolonged distress can lead to **psychophysiological disorders.** (These diseases were formerly known as psychosomatic disorders or diseases.) Psychophysiological diseases refer to physical symptoms that have psychological origins. Stress researchers define psychophysiological disorders as those that are either caused by or worsened by stress. These psychophysiological disorders are not "all in the mind"; they involve physical symptoms with real tissue damage. People with these kinds of disorders are not hypochondriacs or pretending to be ill.

Most psychophysiological disorders occur during the resistance and exhaustion phases of the GAS. During the resistance phase, resistance to the immediate stressor is increased, but general resistance to disease may be lowered. The exhaustion phase is the third phase of the GAS. According to Selye (1978), adaptation energy is finite (limited). When a system or organ be-

Many students find themselves in a "fight or flight" response during final exams; however, neither fighting nor running are adaptive to their situation.

comes exhausted, the organism returns to the alarm and resistance phase to get "help" from another system. However, if the stressor is prolonged and unabated, the organism will exhaust its energy and die.

Neutral Effects

Many of the stressors that we confront every day are managed without affecting us one way or the other. Dohrenwend (1978) suggests that many stressful events can be overcome without any notable effects. Either the demands made by the stressors are so small or our resources to meet them are so great that they are scarcely noticeable. For example, the heating bill probably resulted in **neutral effects** for the lawyer we mentioned earlier.

SOCIAL SUPPORT

Social support is one of the most thoroughly researched stress resistance resources. Because of the voluminous literature in this area, we are devoting an entire section to it. We define **social support** as the resources provided to us through our interactions with other people. It is not that simple, however. In the following paragraphs you will learn that there are two models of social support and several different types. You will learn about the links between social support and health. You may also be surprised to find that social support sometimes has negative effects.

Main Effect Versus Buffering Models

The two dominant models of social support are the **main effect model** and the **buffering model.** Because there are two models, it is difficult to agree on a more specific definition of social support. There does seem to be general agreement that these models represent two different aspects of social support (Cohen & Wills, 1985; Ganster & Victor, 1988; Hobfoll, 1988). The main effect model involves large social networks that have positive effects on well-being unrelated to stress. The buffering model focuses on aspects of social support that act as a "buffer" to protect us against the negative affects of stress.

The Main Effect Model

Being embedded in a large social network provides positive experiences and a sense that life is predictable and stable. The **main effect model** focuses on basic social relationships and networks. These aspects of social support are sometimes described as the structure of social support. Structure includes factors such as marital status, membership in organizations, social roles, and church attendance (Ganster & Victor, 1988). For example, being a member of a church is an example of structural support. According to the main effect model, membership will enhance well-being no matter what level of stress is experienced.

In a classic epidemiological study, Berkman and Syme (1979) found a relationship between social ties and mortality. Social ties were measured by marital status, contacts with close friends and relatives, church membership, and informal and formal group associations. Regardless of gender or age, people with many social contacts had the lowest mortality rates and those with the fewest contacts had the highest. Marriage and contact with friends and relatives were stronger negative predictors of mortality than church membership or group associations. Single people with many friends and relatives seemed as well off as married people with fewer contacts with friends or relatives.

The findings of this study are remarkable because the researchers did *not* control for the quality of the social ties. The beneficial effect of social support may well have been greater if only positive relationships had been considered. They did, however, control for important extraneous variables, including health status, socioeconomic status, and health behaviors. Health behaviors include smoking, alcohol use, physical inactivity, obesity, and low utilization of preventive health services.

The Buffering Model

The **buffering model** refers to interpersonal resources that protect against the negative effects of stress by meeting specific needs created by stressful events. This model focuses on functional rather than structural supports. However, structural supports can be the source of functional supports. Functional supports involve the qualities of social relationships that are related to stress responses. There are three broad categories of functional support: instrumental, informational, and esteem. These categories are not mutually exclusive and are often interrelated.

Instrumental support provides direct aid in the form of loans, gifts, or services. This kind of support may reduce stress by directly solving the problem or by increasing time for relaxation or entertainment (Cohen & Wills, 1985). The person who lends us money, types our term papers, or fluffs our pillow when we are sick has provided us instrumental support. An example of instrumental support in childbirth is provided in Box 7.2.

Box 7.2   A Research Investigation of Instrumental Support in Childbirth

The following is a summary of an *experimental* field study of the effects of social support on perinatal problems, length of labor, and mother-infant interactions (Sosa et al., 1980). The research setting was a maternity unit of a large hospital in Guatemala. Hospital policy did not permit family members, friends, or continuous caretakers to be present in the labor or delivery rooms.

Expectant mothers were randomly assigned to an experimental or control group when they were admitted to the hospital. Women were removed from the study if they experienced complications during labor. To obtain 20 women with uncomplicated deliveries for each group, it was necessary to admit 33 women to the experimental group and 103 women to the control group.

The experimental treatment involved the presence of an untrained laywoman (*doula*) who stayed with an expectant mother during labor. The doula provided social support for the mother through conversation and physical touch. She did not provide professional care. Because of the hospital policy described above, women in the control group received professional care only and not on a continuous basis.

The results of the study were striking. Mothers in the treatment group had much shorter labor (8.8 versus 19.3 hours). They were more awake after delivery, and they stroked, smiled, and talked to their babies more than the other mothers. Although these women were not actually included in the study, it is a noteworthy finding that 79 percent of the control group mothers developed complications, compared to only 37 percent in the treatment group.

The researchers reasoned that the social support provided by the doulas resulted in those expectant mothers being less anxious than the controls. Acute anxiety is associated with increased levels of epinephrine which have been shown to decrease contractions, lengthen labor, and cause fetal distress in animal studies. This explanation is a good example of research conducted within the biopsychosocial model.

Informational support involves giving information, advice, or feedback about how a person is doing. Information can help people recognize and cope with their problems more easily. We often get instrumental and informational support from our social companions. These are the people we can count on to do things and go places with us. By the way, knowing people who will relax and have fun with us is also a form of support.

Esteem support provides us with a sense that we are valued and held in esteem (Cobb, 1979). Self-esteem is an important part of successful stress management. Hobfoll and Leiberman (1987) found that high self-esteem was important in limiting postpartum depression. We get esteem and other kinds of support from close and confiding relationships. These relationships give us reassurance that we are cared for and loved.

It has been observed that a single relationship of this nature is enough for stress buffering. Women seem to benefit more from such confidant relationships than men (Cohen & Wills, 1985). However, one study found that male Israeli students with fewer social ties were negatively affected by war-related stressors, whereas those with more intimate ties remained relatively unaffected (Hobfoll, London, & Orr, 1988).

Negative Effects of Social Support

Social support does not always have positive effects on the people who receive it. Kulik and Mahler (1989) found that married patients whose spouses visited frequently recovered from coronary bypass surgery more quickly than married patients whose spouses did not visit as often and unmarried patients. Interestingly, unmarried patients recovered somewhat more quickly than the married patients whose spouses did not visit frequently. The authors suggest that the unmarried patients may have been more self-reliant than the married patients. Thus, the absence of the married patients' spouses made coping more difficult. In the following paragraphs, we present other factors that may contribute to the negative effect of social support.

Social Support Versus Social Demands

Lazarus and Folkman (1984) note that social network measures assume that having a relationship is the same as getting support from it. Researchers have found that women who have large, intimate social networks are likely to be exposed to the problems of others (Solomon, Mikulincer, & Hobfoll, 1987). That is, they react to other people's stressors in addition to their own. Imagine the woman who has grandchildren, children, a spouse, parents, siblings, coworkers, and close friends. This woman has a large, intimate social network. However, because of her closeness to all of these people, their stressors become her stressors.

Of course, people with large social networks have many sources of help when they need it. But remember the old saying, "There's no free lunch." One of the basic norms of our society is the principle of reciprocity. That is, when we receive something from another person, we are expected to return the favor. For those people who have few resources, accepting social support may be a luxury they cannot afford.

Indeed, social support seems to be one of those cases where the "rich get richer and the poor get poorer." Researchers have found that social support was associated with positive effects for women with strong personal resources. The positive effects were not found for women who lacked personal resources. Personal resources include education, income, and psychological traits (Riley & Eckenrode, 1986; Solomon, Mikulincer, & Hobfoll, 1987).

Two psychological traits that interact with social support are mastery and intimacy. Hobfoll and his colleagues have found a relationship between **mastery** and social support. Mastery is the sense that we are responsible for what happens to us and that our actions can lead to a favorable outcome. Hobfoll and Lerman (1988) found that women high in mastery experienced less psychological distress and benefited more from social support than did women low in mastery. They suggest that social support may intensify the latter group's feelings of being a burden to others.

The relationship between **intimacy** and social support is more complicated. Intimacy is a sense that we are appreciated and held in affection and that important thoughts and feelings can be shared. A study of Israeli mothers found that intimacy with a spouse was related to greater stress resistance; however, intimacy with family had the opposite effect (Hobfoll & Lerman, 1988).

The Bottom Line

Social support is not always a positive experience for people. In our society, we place great emphasis on independence. Accepting help from others can make some people feel dependent or inferior. There are also times when social support can be damaging because it does not allow the recipients to develop their own resources. For example, parents who protect their children from every stressor do not allow them to develop their own resources. In addition, as we mentioned earlier, accepting social support can result in feelings of obligation that cannot be met. In these cases, people often feel resentment toward the helper rather than gratitude.

The Link Between Social Support and Health

Although a wealth of research supports the link between social support and health, much work remains to be done in uncovering the mechanisms of that link. Of course, some explanations are obvious, especially those that involve direct aid. People recovering from illness are going to recover more quickly if they have family to help them. We receive information and advice from other people that can help us solve problems more effectively (Ganster & Victor, 1988). We could give hundreds of these kinds of examples.

Social support interacts at all levels of the stress model. The availability of support affects our appraisal of a stressor and our ability to cope with it. Ganster and Victor (1988) note that social support can enhance health by reducing the negative psychological consequences of stress. They also suggest that close relationships may result in positive affect and increased confidence in the availability of future support.

A number of work-related studies support the link between social support and physical health. Prospective data from the Framingham Heart Study showed that female clerical workers with unsupportive supervisors were more likely to develop coronary heart disease than those with supportive supervisors (Haynes & Feinleib, 1980). A more recent study found greater supervisory support was associated with lower blood pressure (Matthews et al., 1987).

COPING

Folkman and Lazarus (1988) define **coping** as the "cognitive and behavioral efforts to manage specific external and/or internal demands that are appraised as taxing or exceeding the resources of the person" (p. 310). In the stress model we are using, coping involves using our stress resistance resources to overcome the short term reaction created by the stressor.

Cognitive Components

Antonovsky (1979) proposes that every coping strategy has three major components: **rationality, flexibility,** and **farsightedness**. These components are interrelated, and effective coping requires that all three be used to a high degree.

Rationality

Rationality is defined as an accurate, objective assessment of the situation or stressor. The strong emphasis that has been placed on cognitive appraisal has led to a tendency to overlook the importance of objective reality (Antonovsky, 1979; Sheridan, 1983a). It may be the case that our belief that a stimulus is harmful will cause our bodies to respond in kind. However, it is not true that perceiving a harmful stressor as benign will protect us from its harmful effects. For example, rock concerts that reach 110 decibels may be appraised as beautiful music to many, but they still have the potential to cause hearing loss.

Flexibility

Flexibility refers to the availability of a variety of coping strategies to overcome a stressor *and* the willingness to consider all of them. Antonovsky (1987) is not suggesting that being flexible means that "anything goes." Flexibility involves choosing the most appropriate strategy within our cultural constraints. It is especially important in this rapidly changing world. Many times new problems cannot be solved with the same old solutions, and new solutions are being found to solve old problems all the time. People who lack flexibility do not manage stress well. Either they have a limited number of coping strategies available to them, or they are willing to consider only a limited few. Have you ever tried to help a friend solve a problem only to have every suggestion met with "Yes, but . . ."?

Farsightedness

Farsightedness is the ability to anticipate the consequences of our various coping strategies. People with farsightedness ask themselves, "If I do this or don't do this, then what will happen?" Farsightedness is related to the stage of cognitive development called formal operations. It requires that we form hypotheses and mentally test them. Unfortunately, those who lack farsightedness often find that their solutions are worse than the problems themselves. For example, people who drink to forget their problems may become alcoholics with all the attending problems. Farsightedness returns us to rationality. We begin with an accurate, objective assessment of the stressor and end with an accurate, objective assessment of the consequences of our coping strategy for that stressor.

Problem- and Emotion-Focused Coping

Lazarus and Folkman (1984) have classified coping as either problem-focused or emotion-focused. **Problem-focused coping** is directed at controlling the *stressor* to reduce or eliminate its stressfulness. **Emotion-focused coping** is directed at controlling the *emotional response* associated with the stressor. For example, students who study for a final exam (the stressor) are using problem-focused coping. Students who try to reduce tension about the exam by making jokes or downplaying its importance are using emotion-focused coping. Problem-focused and emotion-focused coping are often employed concurrently. Students can study for exams and joke about them at the same time.

There is great variability in individual coping patterns. The situation and how it is appraised have the greatest influence on coping strategies. If people think the stressor can be managed, they are more likely to choose problem-focused coping; otherwise, they tend to rely on emotion-focused coping. This tendency may explain why problem-focused coping is used more often with work-related stressors and emotion-focused coping is used more often with health-related stressors (Folkman & Lazarus, 1980).

Problem-Focused coping

Matheny et al. (1986) have identified several **problem-focused coping** tactics, including stress monitoring, structuring, and social skills. Stress monitoring involves being aware of increased tension and the things that might be causing it. Structuring includes gathering information about the stressor, taking inventory of available resources, and planning for their use. Social skills include assertiveness, intimacy, and self-disclosure. They can be used to manage stressors through increased social support, negotiation, or communication.

Successful problem-focused coping requires good use of the cognitive components we mentioned earlier—rationality, flexibility, and farsightedness. Effective coping requires realistic and accurate evaluations of the stressors *and* available resources. Problem-focused coping is not directed solely at the stressor. It often requires action directed at the individual as well. For example, a realistic evaluation might cause a student to seek tutoring or to develop better study habits.

Emotion-Focused coping

Any number of strategies can be used to reduce emotional distress. **Emotion-focused coping** often involves reappraisal. If a problem cannot be solved, one way to control tension is to reappraise it. We can compare our situations with others and decide ours is not so bad. For example, we know a re-entry student who has coped with a number of major personal stressors. She frequently makes statements like "It could be worse. I could be living in downtown Beirut."

We can also "look for the silver lining" to find something positive in the experience. For instance, people who lose their jobs might view unemployment as an opportunity to develop a more interesting or promising career. The objective situation has not been changed; only the way it is construed has been changed (Lazarus & Folkman, 1984).

Avoidance and denial are common emotion-focused coping strategies. Avoidance refers to physically removing oneself from the presence of the stressor. This is an "out of sight, out of mind" kind of situation. For example, a mother with a terminally ill child might spend long hours at the office to avoid painful hospital visits.

Denial involves mentally escaping a stressor by ignoring it or trying to explain it away. A person might ignore a cancer diagnosis or decide the doctors are wrong. Substance abuse of all kinds is often an attempt to avoid emotional distress. For example, some people overeat to avoid feeling anger, grief, or loneliness (Matheny et al., 1986).

Emotion-focused coping may seem unhealthy because it sometimes involves self-deception and reality distortion. However, as Lazarus (1983) notes, a little illusion is necessary for good mental health. There are also healthy tactics to cope with emotional distress such as work, hobbies, exercise, and relaxation techniques. Humor can be a very effective emotion-focused coping strategy. Mechanic (1985) found that humor is frequently used to help doctoral students defend against the stress of comprehensive exams.

Individual Coping Styles

The study of stress and coping is intriguing because of the great variation in responses to the identical stressor. As we have noted, differences in stress resistance resources and in cognitive appraisals explain much of that variation. Individual coping styles also contribute to the variation.

Personality Traits

The Hardy Personality.   For a long time philosophers and social scientists have observed that some people adapt better to life because of certain personality traits. Recently, researchers have made some progress in identifying those traits. Kobasa (1979, 1982) developed the concept of **hardiness.** Hardy personalities have a high degree of commitment, control, and challenge in their lives. She defines commitment as "the ability to believe in the truth, importance, and interest value of who one is and what one is doing" (Kobasa, 1982, p. 6). Control is the degree to which people believe and act as though they can influence the events in their lives. Challenge is the view that change is normal and is an opportunity rather than a threat.

Researchers have found a relationship between measures of hardiness and health. Their findings suggest that hardiness has a direct effect on illness and an indirect effect through health practices (Wiebe & McCallum, 1986). Another study found that hardy individuals tended to report fewer stressors and to perceive daily hassles as less stressful compared to those who are less hardy (Banks & Gannon, 1988).

Sense of Coherence.   Antonovsky (1979) studied the traits of healthy survivors of WWII concentration camps and found that they shared a **sense of coherence** (SOC). After years of research, he identified comprehensibility, manageability, and meaningfulness as the core components of SOC. Comprehensibility is the ability to make sense of the world. Manageability is the feeling that one has adequate resources to meet life's demands. Meaningfulness is the sense that life's "demands are challenges, worthy of investment and engagement" (Antonovsky, 1987, p. 19). Antonovsky (1987) has developed a measure of sense of coherence with excellent reliability and validity (Radmacher & Sheridan, 1989).

Antonovsky (1979) found that people with a strong SOC tend to make sense of even the worst situations. They also have confidence that they can either manage the stressor itself or their response to it. He is not suggesting that they always overcome stressors. Compared to those with a weaker SOC, however, they do manage stressors better. They are also better able to cope with distress from insoluble problems.

Similarities. In comparing his concept to others, Antonovsky (1987) concluded that "we are all talking about exactly the same thing" (p. 49). For example, "commitment" and "meaningfulness" seem to be descriptive of having a purpose in life. Both "manageability" and "control" refer to having the confidence to cope with life's problems. However, most regard a sense of control as "I am in control." Antonovsky sees it as "*things are in control.*" Manageability implies a "trust in legitimate others as well as in oneself" (p. 52). After some personal communication, Kobasa and Antonovsky agreed that her concept of "challenge" was parallel to his "comprehensibility."

The Physical Link Between Control and Health. There seems to be general agreement about the links between a sense of control, stress, and health. Frankenhauser (1986) discovered an interaction between effort, sense of control, and neuroendocrine functioning. Situations involving a high degree of effort *and* sense of control are associated with increased catecholamine release. However, situations that involve a high degree of effort with a low sense of control result in increased catecholamine and cortisol release.

Frankenhaueser (1986) notes that there are indications that damage to the myocardium (the thickest layer of the heart wall) involves this simultaneous release of catecholamines and cortisol. These findings suggest a neuroendocrine link basis for the well-established relationship between a sense of control and physical and mental well-being. As we discussed in Chapter 4, cortisol secretion is also associated with depressed immune functioning.

Approach and Avoidance

Roth and Cohen (1986) have proposed two basic modes of coping with stress—approach and avoidance. Approach refers to activity that is directed toward the stressor, and avoidance is activity directed away from the stressor. They use the approach–avoidance distinction to understand individual coping styles such as repression–sensitization and reduction–augmentation. For example, sensitizers actively seek out (approach) information and warnings

Data entry is often associated with a high degree of effort and a low sense of control that may result in increased catecholamine and cortisol release.

about stressful events. Repressors, however, often use selective inattention and forgetting to avoid warnings and information about stressors. Repressors report low anxiety while their physiological measures of arousal are high. Self-reported anxiety and physiological measures for sensitizers tend to be just the opposite. They report high anxiety accompanied by low physiological arousal (Roth & Cohen, 1986).

Roth and Cohen (1986) suggest that approach has greater benefits and fewer costs than avoidance. A study of hospital stress in children found that sensitizers were more likely than repressors to observe procedures, ask questions, and protest, but they required fewer hours of monitoring in intensive care (Field et al., 1988). However, costs and benefits are associated with both approach and avoidance, and their effectiveness is determined by the interaction of many variables.

Defensive Styles

A person's selection of **defense mechanisms** has an important impact on health and general well-being (Sheridan, 1983a). In Freudian terms, defense mechanisms are unconscious processes used to defend against anxiety by distorting or denying reality. Most defense mechanisms are considered maladaptive emotion-focused coping. However, Vaillant (1977) found that people who use the mechanisms of suppression, sublimation, anticipation, humor, and altruism tend to be healthier than those who use less mature defenses. See Box 7.3 for a summary of the most common defense mechanisms.

Suppression is a *conscious* effort to avoid thinking about stressful things. If there is no solution to a problem, it can be healthy to control tension by not thinking about it. Humor can be used as problem-focused as well as emotion-focused coping. Many difficult interpersonal conflicts have been resolved through a sense of humor. Humor is also being used as a treatment thanks to Norman Cousins (1979) who used laughter as a pain-control device. Altruism is "other-directedness." It involves directing atten-

tion away from one's own problems by helping or caring for others.

The classic case of Anna O., mentioned in Chapter 5, illustrates how unhealthy mechanisms can be replaced by healthier mechanisms. Remember, Anna was a profoundly disturbed hysteric who was treated by Breuer, an associate of Freud's. They may have found the cause of her hysteria, but they did not cure her. Anna was not impressed with their treatment, but in later years she unwittingly found a remedy of her own. It seemed she had an untapped potential for using altruism as a style of defense. She was able to function quite well once it was discovered (Freeman, 1972).

Costs of Coping

The costs of coping may contribute to distress as well as the direct effects of the stressor. Many coping behaviors are maladaptive, for example, smoking, overeating, and chemical abuse. Coping can also cause excessive physiological reactions that can become pathological. Prolonged coping, even if successful, can cause a drain on physical, psychological, and social resources. Successful coping can also result in overgeneralization. That is, there is a tendency to continue using a successful coping strategy even when it is inappropriate to the situation (Cohen, Evans, Stokols, & Krantz, 1986).

STRESS MANAGEMENT

As we discussed earlier, stress is a construct with many interacting parts. Therefore, effective stress management requires action at *every* level of the stress model. The biopsychosocial model and the system approach should be applied here. Successful stress management involves the interactions between the biology, psychology, and environment of the individual. This section will present a broad overview of stress management.

Managing Stressors

There is growing agreement that the first step in stress management should be removing as many unnecessary stressors as possible

Box 7.3 **A Summary of Common Defense Mechanisms**

Rationalization involves justifying, making excuses, or belittling a goal to limit feelings of responsibility, guilt, or disappointment. The fable of the "Fox and the Grapes" is the classic example of rationalization. The fox couldn't reach the grapes, so he said they were sour. In other words, he belittled the goal that he could not reach. Humans do that too.

Repression is an *unconscious* mechanism that keeps anxiety-provoking thoughts out of our conscious minds. People who repress thoughts, feelings, or events have no awareness of them or that they are repressing them. For example, a person who was molested as a child may repress that memory and have no conscious awareness that it ever happened.

Suppression is a *conscious* effort to avoid thinking about stressful things. This defense can be a healthy one if nothing can be done to solve the problem. For example, it may be healthy for patients waiting for medical test results to use suppression. After all, they cannot do anything until they receive the results. However, it would be unhealthy to use suppression after the results are received if action is required.

Displacement involves redirecting negative feelings and actions away from their cause to a safer or more available target. Employees may be afraid to express anger at their bosses, so they *displace* their anger onto family members.

Sublimation is redirecting energy away from an unacceptable goal to an acceptable goal. The classic example is the little boy who liked to cut up frogs and grows up to be a surgeon. Freud believed that the greatest contributions to our culture were the result of sublimation. Sublimation is considered a healthy defense mechanism.

Projection is an unconscious mechanism that involves attributing one's own unacceptable behaviors, traits, or feelings to other people. Some people call projection, "Painting someone with your own stick." For example, people who have problems with honesty may accuse clerks of shortchanging them.

Denial involves mentally escaping a stressor by ignoring it or trying to explain it away. The middle-aged man with coronary heart disease might deny his condition by insisting that his chest pain is due to indigestion.

Altruism involves directing attention away from one's own pain through unselfish devotion to the welfare of others. For example, we know a grandmother who coped with the death of a grandchild by becoming a volunteer at a children's hospital. Vaillant (1977) identified altruism as a healthy defense.

Anticipation is another healthy mechanism identified by Vaillant (1977). It involves anticipating problems and finding solutions for them before they happen. An example of healthy anticipation are students who begin writing term papers early because they have several due in the same week.

(Matheny et al., 1986; Sheridan, 1983a; Tache & Selye, 1986). Some stressors such as traffic jams and crime require community action, but many, particularly background stressors, can be attacked at the personal level. One of our re-entry students with four teenagers at home identified noise as a significant background stressor. As each child would get up in the morning, she would turn on her radio or the television. Of course, they were not always set on the same station. When the mother realized how the radios and television added to the morning confusion, she asked that the radios be tuned to the same station and that the television and radios not be played at the same time. With several reminders, her daughters complied with her request and her mornings were a little more peaceful.

Noise is an environmental stressor. Other environmental stressors such as temperature, air pollution, and lighting can have an impact on our health. We can change those stressors that are under our direct control. For example, we can purchase brighter light bulbs, open a window, and turn down the television. We can also change some things that are not under our direct control. For example, many companies now have "smoke-free" workplaces. These policies have come about because nonsmokers are no longer willing to "adapt" to smoke-filled air.

Perhaps some of our most potent stressors come from our interactions with other people. These social stressors can range from a destructive relationship to everyday irritations. Assertiveness training can be an effective method for reducing social stressors. Other people may not be aware that they are causing distress unless someone tells them. Many stressors can be removed just for the asking. However, the original request may have to be followed by an occasional reminder.

We are not suggesting that all stressors can be easily removed; some require drastic action. What we are saying is that good stress management begins with taking control of as many stressors as possible. Before that can happen,

however, we have to be aware of them. We tend to ignore stressors that occur gradually, but they can still affect our health. This is particularly true of background stressors. Scripture (1899) found that frogs would submit to being boiled if the water temperature was increased gradually. Adaptation Level Theory suggests that humans are not so different (Sheridan, 1983a).

We can gain awareness of background stressors in several ways. One method is to keep a stress diary, which involves recording stress reactions and the events that precede them. Keeping a diary will help identify the stressors that trigger the reactions. For example, a student discovered that she often got a headache after talking on the phone to a certain friend. With some soul searching, she found the problem was not with the caller. The problem was the length of the calls. She became tense when they ran on too long, which they often did. It was a small matter, then, to shorten the calls. (This method is discussed in more detail in Chapter 5.)

Modifying Appraisals

Our appraisals of stressors have a profound effect on stress outcomes. Taché and Selye (1986) suggest that some stress responses are like allergy attacks. When people have allergy attacks, the overmobilization of their immune system rather than the allergen itself, makes them sick. Similarly, some people are harmed by stressors, not from their direct effect, but because they have overreacted. For example, no student has ever died from taking an exam. Yet, we all know students who react to exams as though they were life-threatening events. To avoid excessive reactions, we may need to modify our appraisals of the stressors. Many times this effort involves a more realistic appraisal of the stressor.

Realistic appraisal of our stress resistance resources is equally important to good stress management. Under- or overestimating the resources that are available to cope with a problem can cause problems. We knew an honor student who would vomit before every exam because she was so anxious. She underestimated the many academic resources she possessed, for example, good study habits and intelligence. Another student overestimated his academic ability and was placed on academic suspension. He was bright enough, but his attendance was poor and he rarely studied.

Effective appraisal has a lot to do with setting priorities. In other words, we have to get in touch with what is really important to us. People generally tend to let trivial things become major stressors. Robert Eliot, a cardiologist, spelled out two rules for coping with stress: "Rule No. 1 is, don't sweat the small stuff. Rule No. 2 is, it's all small stuff" (cited in Wallis, 1983). Of course, it's not all "small stuff," but many people waste adaptive energy on things that are not so important.

Developing Stress Resistance Resources

Stress resistance resources are the tools we use to cope with stress. Remember the old saying, "You have to have the right tools to do the job right." This is true for stress management as well. We need the right kind of resources to cope with today's stressors. For instance, there seems to be no doubt that a healthy lifestyle is a crucial resource (Sheridan, 1983b; Taché & Selye, 1986). By healthy lifestyle, we mean regular hours, good nutrition, physical activity, recreation, and the like. (Lifestyle factors are discussed in detail in Chapters 8 and 9.)

In addition to developing resources, good stress management requires that we learn how to use them. In other words, we have to develop sound coping skills. The bright student whom we mentioned earlier failed to use his intelligence properly. He needed to use it *with* some good study habits. Developing an effective response to specific stressors usually takes some time to learn. It is worth the effort because effective coping skills have many benefits. A quick, effective response can prevent a short-term reaction from ever becoming distress. In addition, appraisals of stressors will be less threatening with the knowledge that an effective coping strategy is available (Taché & Selye, 1986).

Controlling Stress Reactions

Removing or reducing stressors, realistic appraisals, and developing and using resources are all important. However, no matter how effective our interventions are at these levels, there will always be some unpleasant sensations left to control. A number of different methods can be used to control these sensations, including autogenic training, progressive relaxation, biofeedback training, cognitive restructuring, and meditation. These methods are described in greater detail in Chapter 5 and other chapters throughout the book.

Stroebel (1982, 1983) has combined several of the methods mentioned above into a procedure he calls the quieting reflex. This six-second procedure is designed to condition the subject to respond to a stressor by means of relaxation rather than tensing. For example, we know an executive who was tensing every time her very busy phone rang, resulting in a large buildup of tension. By replacing tensing with the quieting reflex, after a time she relaxed instead of tensing when the phone rang.

Although it involves a lot of preliminary training, basically the quieting reflex requires the following steps in response to a stressor:

1. *Smile.* Smile inwardly and with your mouth and eyes while telling yourself "Alert mind, calm body."
2. *Inhale.* Inhale an easy, natural breath.
3. *Exhale.* As you exhale, let your jaw, tongue, and shoulders go loose and feel a wave of limpness and warmth flow all the way down to your toes.

Stress Management Programs

The workplace has become a common setting for stress management programs, but labor has not always accepted these programs. Though both share a limited view of stress management, employers and labor have a very different view of stress and stress management. Employer programs for employees emphasize personal responsibility and change, and focus on adapting to stressors and developing healthy styles. Corporations tend to favor in-house stress management programs or consultants. Control is discussed primarily in terms of teaching employees what they can and cannot control (Singer et al., 1986).

In contrast, labor prefers a head-on attack against work-related stressors. For example, union officials want to reduce stress from job insecurity with contract agreements rather than jogging programs (Singer et al., 1986). The union approach to stress management is reflected in the following statement from a United Auto Workers pamphlet:

We do not seek to help workers manage their stress better or to adjust to the conditions that are potentially dangerous to their health. Rather when we speak about stress reduction we are really talking about stress prevention—creating healthy work places. (p. 174)

Conclusions

The primary goal of this chapter was to give students a general overview of the many interacting facets of stress. This overview serves as a framework for organizing the massive amount of information generated on this subject. ''Stress'' is more than life events, and stress management is more than relaxation training. Stress is related to many other topics in health psychology and is discussed in more specific detail in chapters throughout this book.

Many other disciplines are investigating stress and related topics. Why are so many people interested in learning about stress? Selye (1978) believed that understanding the nature of stress would give physicians a new way to treat illness. But more than that, he believed that it would give us a new way of life. Folk wisdom has long held that life's demands and our responses to them have a powerful impact on health and well-being. The research efforts of many different disciplines are beginning to verify the existence of this relationship. These efforts are an important part of the challenge to the biomedical model.

Summary

1. Stress and its relationship to health have played a major role in the challenge to the biomedical model. Stress is actually a construct that involves a synthesis of several interacting parts.

2. Stressors are defined as anything that makes a demand on us. Three categories of stressors have been identified: cataclysmic, personal, and background stressors. Background stressors may cause more damage than the other types if we fail to seek support or help to solve them.

3. Appraisal is an important part of the stress construct. The two types of appraisal are primary and secondary. Primary appraisal is our evaluation of the impact the stressor will have on us. Secondary appraisal is our evaluation of our resources and abilities to cope with the stressor.

4. Stress resistance resources are all of the material, physical, social, and psychological resources we have to cope with a stressor and our reactions to it. An example of a material resource is money or shelter.

5. Short-term reaction refers to our response to the demands of stressors. The short-term reaction involves the responses of the Alarm Reaction phase of the General Adaptation Syndrome (GAS). Short-term reactions can be very mild or strong depending on the stressor.

6. The long-term impact of a stressor can result in eustress, distress, or neutral effects. Stressors, our resources, and our appraisals all interact to determine the outcome of the stressors to which we are exposed. Eustress is the positive impact that results from stressors. There is compelling evidence that exposure to even noxious

stressors can have positive responses. Distress is the negative effect that results from our exposure to stressors, and neutral effects are reserved for those times when we overcome stressors with no notable effect.

7. The two dominant models of social support are the main effect and buffering models. The main effect model refers to our involvement in large social networks that have positive effects on our well-being that are unrelated to stress. The buffering model focuses on aspects of social support that protect us against the negative effects of stress.

8. Research indicates that the effects of social support are not always positive. Being part of a large social network may provide support, but it also places demands on an individual. Social support can also erode people's feelings of independence, damage their self-esteem, and foster dependency. The links between social support and health have been established, but work remains to be done to uncover the mechanisms of those links.

9. Coping refers to all the various efforts we make to manage the demands we see as exceeding our resources. Rationality, flexibility, and farsightedness are the cognitive components of a coping strategy. Rationality is an accurate, objective assessment of a situation. Flexibility is a variety of strategies that are available to overcome a stressor and the willingness to consider all of them. Farsightedness is the ability to anticipate the consequences of the various coping strategies.

10. Problem-focused coping is directed at controlling the stressor to reduce its impact. Emotion-focused coping is directed at controlling the emotional response associated with the stressor. We are more likely to choose problem-focused coping if we think the stressor can be managed. Otherwise, we tend to rely on emotion-focused coping.

11. Several personality traits contribute to the great variations in stress coping. For example the "hardy" personality has a high degree of commitment, control, and challenge. People with a strong sense of coherence find life comprehensible, meaningful, and manageable. Research findings suggest that a sense of control has an impact on endocrine system functioning that may explain the link between control and health.

12. Removing or reducing stressors, employing realistic appraisals, and developing and using stress resistance resources are important to effective stress management. Unpleasant stress responses can be reduced through a number of self-regulation techniques.

13. The workplace has become a common setting for stress management programs. Employers and labor have different views of stress and stress management. Employers tend to emphasize personal responsibility and change, whereas unions want to focus on interventions to improve the work environment and reduce job insecurity.

Key Terms

Background stressors
Buffering model
Cataclysmic stressors

Cognitive appraisal
Coping
Defense mechanisms
Distress
Emotion-focused coping

Esteem support

Eustress

Farsightedness

Flexibility

Hardiness

Informational support

Instrumental support

Intimacy

Main effect model

Mastery

Neutral effects

Personal stressors

Primary appraisal

Problem-focused coping

Psychophysiological disorders

Rationality

Secondary appraisal

Sense of coherence

Short-term reaction

Social support

Stress resistance resources

Stressor

Discussion Questions

1. Briefly describe the various components of the stress model in Figure 7.1 and how they relate to each other and to the construct of stress.

2. Describe the three major categories of stressors and give an example of each.

3. What are the two types of appraisals and how do they interact to influence our experience of stress?

4. Describe and explain the major categories of stress resistance resources (SRRs). Make a list of your own SRRs.

5. What is the sense of coherence and what is its significance? How is it similar to the hardy personality?

6. Explain the conditions under which stressors can result in positive effects for us. Describe a stressor you have experienced which has resulted in positive effects.

7. Describe the main effect and buffering models of social support and explain how they relate to each other.

8. Name and explain the main categories of functional support.

9. Under what conditions does social support make it more difficult to deal with stress?

10. What are the specific mechanisms whereby social support is thought to influence stress reactions?

11. Explain the nature and functions of rationality, flexibility, and farsightedness. Give an example of a situation when you have used these cognitive strategies effectively or not so effectively.

12. Distinguish between problem-focused and emotion-focused coping and give examples of each.

13. Explain the physical link between control and health.

14. What should a health psychologist know about the attitudes of management and labor before designing a workplace stress management program?

Lifestyle Factors I: Health, Food, and Exercise

*B*ill loved to eat, drink, and "party." He described his lifestyle as fun-loving; his friends and family called it self-destructive. He ate too much of the wrong kinds of food, never exercised, drank to excess, and smoked two packs of cigarettes a day. Yet, Bill lived to be 76 years old! If lifestyle is so critical to health, how did he manage to live so long? For one thing, his death at age 76 may have been *premature*, given his family history. His parents lived well into their 80s, and some of his close relatives lived to be over 100. The more appropriate question should be, not how long Bill lived, but how well he lived. There we find a different story. His health began to fail in his 50s when he developed hypertension and borderline diabetes. He had coronary bypass surgery when he was 62. In his late 60s, he developed gout and was treated for chronic alcoholism. When he was 73, it was discovered that he had lung cancer that metastasized to his hip. A minor fall led to a fracture which required a hip replacement less than a year before his death. The quality of the last 25 years of Bill's life steadily declined, and the last two years were filled with pain for him and his family. (We described the circumstances of Bill's death at the beginning of the first chapter.)

Perhaps the greatest challenge to the biomedical model has come from the realization that **lifestyle** is one of the most significant factors affecting health. Lalonde (1975) defines lifestyle as the health-related decisions and behaviors that are, to an extent, controlled by individuals. Health officials agree that lifestyle plays a critical role in health promotion and the prevention and treatment of disease (Jeffery, 1989; Koop, 1983; USDHEW, 1979). Lifestyle involves many of the psychological and social factors that are excluded from the biomedical model.

PREVENTING LIFESTYLE DISEASES

Lifestyle diseases account for about 80 percent of the annual mortality rate in the United States. Lifestyle diseases are related to faulty living habits and include heart disease, hypertension, accidents, stroke, cirrhosis, osteoporosis, and suicide. The recognition of the importance of lifestyle and the economic crisis in the health care system have created a growing demand to make the focus on prevention a public policy (Hefferman & Albee, 1985). There are three kinds of prevention:

1. **Primary prevention** reduces the risks of illness for an entire population. A school program that encourages children not to smoke would be an example of primary prevention.

2. **Secondary prevention** involves reducing risk factors in high risk groups. In a later chapter, we mention some prevention programs to reduce AIDS in high risk populations.

3. **Tertiary prevention** seeks to reduce the duration of illness in those who are already afflicted. For instance, most recovering heart patients are placed on a low-fat, high-fiber diet and an exercise program.

Prevention makes good sense. It is usually much less expensive than trying to undo damage already done, and often we do not have the means of undoing the damage in any case. A good example is the case of sudden coronary death, which kills about a third of a million Americans each year, yet happens so swiftly that people die before they can get medical care. Unfortunately, prevention is often difficult to implement. There are many social and psychological barriers to carrying out preventive actions even when people know very well how important they are.

Furthermore, the results of prevention programs are hard to evaluate because it may take years for the results to be seen, and the effects of "cures" are immediate and often dramatic. For example, we mentioned in Chapter 1 that Oregon has shifted funding from organ transplants to prenatal care. Prenatal care should prevent a host of developmental problems for thousands of children over the years, but the effect will not be seen immediately. In the meantime, the public's attention is occupied by the death of Coby, the little boy who could not be saved because funds were not available.

In this chapter we discuss some of the lifestyle issues that have been identified as important determinants of health. They include nutrition, weight control, and exercise. We also present some general and specific interventions for changing health-related behaviors.

NUTRITION

Epidemiological studies indicate that nutrition plays a significant role in health (USDHHS, 1988b). However, the American public seems frustrated and confused about the foods they should eat and the foods they should avoid. Warnings against some foods and beneficial claims for other foods are surrounded by conflicting reports. We are not going to attempt to solve the controversies over nutrition and weight control in this chapter. We will discuss the areas of general agreement and try to clarify some of the issues.

The American Diet

There is general agreement that the American diet is too high in calories, fat, cholesterol, sugar, protein, and sodium. In addition, it is too low in complex carbohydrates and fibers. Although some segments of our society do not have enough to eat, the majority suffer from a different kind of malnutrition. Our problems are due primarily to the types and amounts of foods we consume. In other words, we need to eat more grains, fruits, and vegetables and less fat, meat, and processed food which are often loaded with sugar, fat, and salt. (See Table 8.1 for a listing of dietary guidelines.)

Table 8.1 Dietary Guidelines from the Surgeon General

1. Eat a variety of foods.
2. Maintain desirable weight.
3. Avoid too much fat, saturated fat, and cholesterol.
4. Eat foods with adequate starch and fiber.
5. Avoid too much sugar.
6. Avoid too much sodium.
7. If you drink alcoholic beverages, do so in moderation.

Source: Based on USDHHS. (1988b). *The Surgeon General's report on nutrition and health*. (DHHS [PHS] Pub. No. 88–50210). Washington, D.C.: U.S. Government Printing Office.

Our desire for high-fat, sweet foods can be traced to the hunting and gathering cultures of our ancestors. These cravings were very adaptive for them. For example, fat, in very small quantities, is essential for life. Yet it was hard to obtain in a "stone age" environment. Because of its limited availability, humans had little need to develop mechanisms for limiting its intake. Cravings for high calorie sweet or fatty foods motivated our ancestors to do the necessary hard work to get food that was not readily available.

For example, rainforest pygmies still live in a hunting and gathering culture. They climb trees over 100 feet tall to extract honey from hives. They also catch and eat flying termites because of their high-fat content. We, on the other hand, are surrounded by an abundance of food that requires little physical effort to obtain. Thus, the preference for high calorie foods, based on conditions that held thousands of years ago, may lead us to overeat in today's "land of plenty."

Food manufacturers are happy to take advantage of our biological urges regarding food. The mixed blessings of "Madison Avenue" are clearly seen in the area of nutrition. Although television commercials and print advertisements do feature healthy products, they more often promote highly processed foods of questionable nutritional value. Most of the money-saving coupons that bloat our Sunday papers are for these kinds of food.

Many consumers feel that advertisements for food or health products are misleading (Schutz & Diaz–Knauf, 1989). Good examples of misleading advertisements are those that promote themselves as "light" or low-fat foods (see Box 8.1). The old adage "Let the buyer beware" implies that responsibility for making critical judgments of products should lie with the consumer. This may apply to adults, but what about children? It is estimated that young children are exposed to an average of 10,000 commercials per year. Most of these commercials are for high-sugar, high-fat, low-nutrition products (Dawson, Jeffrey, & Walsh, 1988).

Diet and Health

The American diet has been implicated in three of the top four leading causes of death—heart disease, cancer, and cerebrovascular disease (stroke). There is general agreement that as much as 25 to 35 percent of deaths due to cancer could be related to dietary factors. Studies indicate that high-fat, low-fiber diets and inade-

quate vitamins and minerals are associated with higher rates of many common cancers (Greenwald & Sondik, 1986).

High-Fat Diets

High-fat diets are linked to cancers of the breast, colon, rectum, and prostate. Excessive fat intake is also implicated in heart disease and stroke. On average, Americans consume approximately 44 percent of their calories in fat (USBC, 1989). The American Cancer Society and the American Heart Association are now recommending that fat calories be limited to 30 percent (USDHHS, 1988b). Those who are at high risk for cancer or heart disease may want to limit their fat intake to 20 percent. Some have even advocated levels to 10 percent, which is probably closer to the levels our hunter-gatherer ancestors consumed.

There are three different kinds of fat: saturated, monounsaturated, and polyunsaturated. For some time nutritionists have recommended avoidance of saturated fats, which are high in cholesterol. Saturated fats can usually be recognized by their tendency to become solid at room temperature. Good examples are butter and lard.

Box 8.1 Buyer Beware: Watch the Hidden Fat!

Food producers use some very misleading advertisements to sell their products. For example, foods advertised as low fat may not necessarily be low fat. There are 4 calories per gram in carbohydrates and protein. There are 9 calories in a gram of fat. To find the percent of fat calories in a serving of food, multiply the number of fat grams by 9 and divide that number by the total number of calories. For example, a package of ground turkey boasts

that it contains only 9 percent fat. That statement is misleading because it is referring to the percentage of volume rather than calories. One serving of turkey contains 150 calories with 9 grams of fat. Using the formula above, we find that fat accounts for 54 percent of the calories in the "91 percent fat-free" turkey. Fat accounts for over 51 percent of the calories in a snack cracker advertised as "cholesterol free and low in saturated fat."

Cholesterol

Cholesterol is associated with high-fat diets, but the body produces around 80 percent of its own cholesterol. Cholesterol is not a fat; it is more like a wax. It is an essential chemical found and produced in every cell of the body. Diet, then, is far from being the sole source of blood cholesterol. In fact, several investigators have proposed that stress-induced failure to metabolize cholesterol in the liver may be at least as significant as the amount of cholesterol consumed in the diet (Friedman & Ulmer, 1984; Ornish et al., 1990).

Cholesterol becomes a concern when increased amounts of it are found in the blood. This condition is referred to as cholesteremia, and it is associated with hardening of the arteries. Cholesterol lodges in artery walls causing them to harden and narrow. Islands of this hard material in the inner layer of the arteries are called plaque. Arterial plaque consists of cholesterol, fat, collagen, and other substances. As plaque builds up and closes arteries, blood flow is blocked, and tissue being fed by that artery dies. If the tissue is in the heart, a myocardial infarction (heart attack) occurs. A stroke is caused when the starved tissue is in the brain (USDHHS, 1988b). See Chapter 11 for more information on the effects of cholesterol on the cardiovascular system.

Currently, there is great interest in high-density lipoprotein (HDL) cholesterol. There is just one kind of cholesterol, but it is wrapped with five different kinds of lipoprotein. Cholesterol is considered "good" or "bad" depending on its lipoprotein wrapping. High-density lipoprotein is considered good because it transports cholesterol away from the arteries and other tissues to the liver. Most cholesterol exists in the form of low-density lipoprotein (LDL). It is considered the "bad" lipoprotein because it contributes to formation of plaque in the arteries (Gordon & Rifkind, 1989).

Levels of HDL cholesterol are influenced by a number of biologic, environmental, and behavioral factors. If we exercise regularly, we are likely to have higher HDL levels. If we drink a little alcohol, these levels are also likely to be higher. On the other hand, if we let ourselves become overweight, or if we smoke, HDL levels will tend to be lowered. Cross-cultural studies suggest that low levels of HDL may be mainly a risk factor in combination with high-fat diets.

Cholesterol is one of the controversial topics that we mentioned earlier. There are questions about how low serum cholesterol levels should be and about the best methods for reducing them. A ten-year study found that colon cancer patients had significantly lower cholesterol levels compared to matched controls (Winawer et al., 1990). However, the authors suggested that a genetic factor may lead to both decreased cholesterol and colon cancer.

The expert panel of the National Cholesterol Education Program has not set specific therapeutic goals for HDL or LDL cholesterol levels. Instead it has recommended low risk hygienic measures to raise HDL levels, for example, exercise, smoking cessation, and weight reduction (Gordon & Rifkind, 1989).

Vitamins and Fibers

Vitamins C, E, B complex, and the carotenoids have been linked to cancer prevention. These vitamins can be found in a variety of fruits, grains, and vegetables. The effectiveness of these dietary factors in cancer prevention is still under study. However, the National Research Council recommends an increase in the daily diet of the foods rich in these vitamins (Committee on Diet, Nutrition, and Cancer, 1983).

High-fiber diets may protect against cancers of the colon and rectum. Soluble fibers dissolve in water and absorb fat and may prevent heart disease and some cancer. Recent evidence suggests that some fibers can even shrink polyps in the colon (Raub, 1989). Foods with moderate to high amounts of soluble fiber include oat bran, beans, peas, and apples. Insoluble fiber provides "roughage" and may prevent constipation and colon cancer. Soluble fiber appears to be more important in preventing heart disease. These fibers include such foods as oats, beans, peas and apples (Rinzler, 1987; USDHHS, 1988b).

Protein

Protein is an essential part of a healthy diet. However, it is estimated that the typical American diet contains two to three times the required amount of protein. Excessive protein intake results in urinary overexcretion of calcium and increases the likelihood of osteoporosis (Garrison & Somer, 1985; USDHHS, 1988b).

Protein places a heavy load on the kidneys. The body uses seven times as much water per calorie to metabolize protein compared to carbohydrates. The extra water is required to dilute the toxic byproducts formed by protein metabolism. Excessive amounts of protein combined with simple sugars can increase insulin blood levels, producing low blood sugar. High protein intake may also result in increased uric acid levels. Increased uric acid levels create a risk of gout (Pritikin, 1979). Gout involves painful inflammation of joints, especially of the big toes.

Sugar, Health, and Behavior

The American sweet tooth seems to be getting sweeter all the time. Although there has been a steady decline in the use of refined sugar in the United States, the overall use of sweeteners has increased. In 1970 each person was consuming about 121 pounds of refined sugar and corn sweeteners per year. By 1987 that number had risen to about 131 pounds per year, and the use of noncaloric sweeteners had more than tripled (USBC, 1990). Refined sweeteners are relatively new, and humans are not biologically adapted to cope with them. The only sugar our ancestors ate was contained in fruits, honey, and vegetables (Hamilton, Whitney, & Sizer, 1982).

Our consumption of sugar is not entirely voluntary. Sweeteners are often added to processed foods. Luncheon meats, peanut butter, cereals, and salad dressings are frequently high in sugar content. The ingredients on labels are listed in the order of their quantity in the food. Many cereals list sugar first and then name other types of sugars as additional ingredients. Many catsups have a higher percentage of sugar than does ice cream. See Table 8.2 for the percentage of sugar in popular cereals. Sugar is

Table 8.2   Refined Sugar in Breakfast Cereals

Cereal	Percent Sucrose
Super Orange Crisp	68.0
Sugar Smacks	61.3
King Vitamin	58.5
Cocoa Pebbles	53.5
Lucky Charms	50.4
Froot Loops	48.4
Trix	46.6
Cocoa Krispies	45.9
Frosted Flakes	44.0
Cocoa Puffs	43.0
Super Sugar Crisp	40.7
Alpha Bits	40.3
Frosted Mini Wheats	33.6
Bran Buds	30.2
Quaker 100% Natural/dates & raisins	25.0
All Bran	20.0
100% Bran	18.4
Granola, plain	16.6
Granola with dates	14.5
Raisin Bran, Kellogg	10.6
Rice Krispies, Kellogg	10.0
Total	8.1
Grape Nuts	6.6
Product 19	4.1
Cheerios	2.2
Shredded Wheat, large biscuit	1.0

Source: Based on E. M. N. Hamilton, E. N. Whitney, and F. S. Sizer. (1982). *Nutrition: Concepts and controversies* (3rd ed.). St. Paul, Minn.: West Publishing Co.

often listed as corn syrup, molasses, dextrose, fructose, glucose, and so on. Any word on a label that ends with "ose" is probably a form of sugar.

Refined sweeteners are sometimes referred to as "empty calories" because their nutritive value is limited to calories. One concern is that we will substitute the empty calories of sugar for nutritious calories. If our diets meet our nutritional requirements and we add our empty sugar calories on top of that, then we risk becoming overweight. Sugary foods that stick to the teeth and remain there for periods of time also contribute to dental caries (cavities).

Many parents have other concerns about sugar. Parents of children who "bounce off the walls" often blame sugar for their children's lack of attention and hyperactivity. Folk wisdom has accepted the relationship between sugar and inappropriate behavior in children, but research findings have been inconsistent. Correlational studies support parent observations, but experimental studies generally do not (Spring & Alexander, 1989). However, experimental studies in this area have tended to be designed in a way that makes them poor detectors of the claimed effects. Several studies used inadequate amounts of sugar (equivalent to one candy bar or less). Moreover, the sample sizes were relatively small ranging from 8 to 50 subjects (e.g., see Rosen et al., 1988).

Conclusions

Nutrition is obviously important to preventing illness and enhancing health. For thousands of years, humans devoted most of their time to finding enough to eat. With today's technology, it takes less than 3 percent of the population to feed the entire United States, and we have more food than ever. In addition, technology has resulted in highly processed food that is aggressively advertised. A descriptive study found a relationship between the foods children saw advertised on television, the foods they asked parents to buy, and the foods the parents bought (Taras et al., 1989). The children most commonly requested highly sweet, fat, or salty foods.

WEIGHT CONTROL

Weight control is a problem in many affluent, industrialized countries. In the United States, it is estimated that about 110 million adults and 10 million teenagers are overweight (Weltman, 1984). The large number of overweight people in the United States should not come as a surprise. We tend to eat too much of the wrong foods, and we exercise too little. This combination results in excess calories being stored as fat. For most of us, high calorie food is all too available. Ironically, the mania for thinness in this land of plenty has led to an obsession with dieting. A *Wall Street Journal* article (Zaslow, 1986) reported that more than half of 100 fourth grade girls said they were on a diet. One little girl was quoted as saying, "Boys expect girls to be perfect and beautiful . . . and skinny" (p. 1).

Unfortunately, the frantic attempts to lose weight may actually be causing people to gain weight. Polivy and Herman (1985) have concluded that "dieting is associated with and appears to precede **binge eating**. Binge eating is defined as episodic rapid eating of large amounts of food within periods of two hours or less. It is estimated that more than half of overweight people engage in binge eating. There is a high incidence of self-reported binge eating among college students. Polivy and Herman argue that dieting creates a state of chronic hunger, and binge eating is the body's attempt to restore weight. Some of the theories that support their argument follow.

The Glucostatic Theory

The **glucostatic theory** suggests that receptors monitor the glucose levels in our body. Glucose is the fuel of our bodies, as gasoline is for our cars. According to this theory, hunger and satiety (satisfaction) depend on the rate at which our bodies use glucose. We feel satiated when our cells have enough glucose. When we go for longer periods without food, our glucose levels become low, resulting in hunger. Hunger then motivates us to seek more food.

Insulin also plays an important part in the glucostatic theory. Insulin allows cells to absorb glucose. We experience hunger when our cells are not absorbing glucose. When we eat, our insulin levels go up to permit us to utilize the resulting glucose. Large amounts of glucose may trigger the secretion of too much insulin. This, in turn, can lower our blood glucose level to the point where we are hungry again.

The Set-point Theory

Many of us maintain our weight at a fairly constant level without giving it much thought. If we consume more calories than we need at one meal, we automatically eat less at our next meal. The **set-point theory** (Nisbett, 1972) attempts to explain our long-term eating control. According to this theory, our bodies are programmed to contain a certain amount of fat. When the fat in our cells exceeds that amount, we automatically reduce our food intake. When the fat falls below the set amount, we increase our food intake.

Unfortunately, some of us may have set points that are too high for our cultural standards, so we keep gravitating toward that unduly high weight. If we try to reduce our weight, we only lose and gain the same 10 or 20 pounds over and over again. The set-point principle is familiar to most of us, since the same principle applies to the thermostat on a furnace. Just as the thermostat signals the furnace to go on when the temperature falls, our fat cells trigger the brain to initiate eating behavior when their fat levels fall.

There is evidence that body-weight set points can be altered. Keesey (1986) suggests that high-fat diets can raise set points. His work with laboratory rats indicates that prolonged high-fat diets increase fat cell size and number. He also proposes that set points may be lowered by exercise. However, the set point apparently returns to the pre-exercise level when exercise is discontinued.

Restrained Eating Theory

The **restrained eating theory** (Herman & Mack, 1975) proposes that many obese people are actually "restrained" eaters. That is, they are in a constant fight to weigh less than their biological set point. Restrained eaters differ from normal eaters in many ways. For example, restrained eaters tend to respond to depression or anxiety by overeating, whereas normal eaters usually lose their appetites when they are depressed or anxious. The restrained eating theory suggests that emotions disinhibit the restraint. If normal eaters eat a heavy snack, they will eat less the rest of the day. This "pre-loading" tends to increase eating in restrained eaters.

Dieting and Metabolic Rates

When calories fall below a certain level, the basal metabolic rate (BMR) is decreased by 20 to 40 percent. The BMR is the minimum amount of energy required to maintain vital functions in a complete resting state. Thus, it indicates how many calories we are burning even when we are not exerting ourselves. Our total caloric consumption includes the basal rate plus whatever calories we use up through activities like exercise and keeping our bodies warm on a cold day. Since calories are burning at the basal rate for 24 hours a day, any changes in that rate will likely add up to large changes in body weight. When we drastically decrease our food intake, the reduced calories produce signals that the body is starving. The BMR is then reduced to conserve energy.

Low Calorie Food: Friend or Foe?

Ironically, the many low calorie foods that have been developed to meet the demands of a weight-conscious society may be contributing to obesity. If we have not received sufficient nutrients or calories from our food, hunger will motivate us to seek more food. It does so by stimulating our thoughts about food and eating. In humans, the sight and smell of food trigger increases in insulin levels. Insulin is involved in increased appetite and storage of nutrients as fat. The increases in insulin in response to food cues are greater in obese people than in lean people. Artificial sweeteners also provoke these insulin increases in rats and humans. Thus, the low calorie soft drink may actually be promoting overweight rather than reducing it (Blundell, Hill, & Lawton, 1989).

OBESITY

Obesity is an excessive accumulation of fat, most notably in the subcutaneous tissues located immediately beneath the skin (Dox, Melloni, & Eisner, 1985). **Morbid obesity** is obesity that threatens health or restricts activities. It is generally agreed that people are morbidly obese when their weight is 100 percent or more than their ideal weight (Bray, 1986). Although there is a tendency to consider obesity an eating disorder, the DSM–III–R classifies it as a physical disorder (American Psychiatric Association, 1987).

Measuring Obesity

A person is usually considered obese when his or her body weight exceeds the ideal weight by 20 percent. A height/weight chart devised by the Metropolitan Life Insurance Company is often used to find ideal weight. The chart is based on height and body frame and gives desirable weight ranges for men and women. The first table was published in 1959 and was revised again in 1979. The desirable weights are based on national norms for the United States, and, interestingly, the weights generally tend to be higher in the 1979 tables (Smith & Smith, 1990).

Researchers commonly use the body mass index (BMI) to determine obesity. BMI is the ratio of weight to height. (See Box 8.2 for more information on BMI.) This is a useful statistic for researchers, but it may not always reflect whether or not we have excessive accumulations of fat in our tissues. The methods that allow accurate estimations of body fat are either complicated, time consuming, expensive, or all three.

One simple way we can judge our fat accumulation is to take a good look at ourselves in a full-length mirror without any clothing. This method will reveal fat deposits that have not been recorded by the scales. Lean tissue weighs more than fat tissue, so our bathroom scales do not always accurately record fat accumulation (Shephard, 1989b). Of course, this method will not work for everyone because many people have a distorted body image.

Box 8.2 **Finding Ideal Weight Through the Body Mass Index (BMI)**

BMI is found by dividing your weight by the square of your height. It is a metric measure, so you will need to convert your weight to kilograms and your height to meters using the following steps:

1. Divide your weight in pounds by 2.2 to obtain kilograms.

2. Divide your height in inches by 39.4; then multiply the number you get by itself to obtain the square of your height in meters.

Now to get your BMI, multiply the number you obtained from Step 1 by the number you got from Step 2. For example, a student is 65 inches tall and weighs 125 pounds:

1. 125 pounds divided by 2.2 = 56.6 kilograms

2. 65 inches divided by 39.4 = 1.65 meters
   1.65 meters × 1.65 meters = 2.72 meters^2

To find the BMI for this student, we will divide her weight in kilograms by her height in squared meters:

$$\frac{56.8 \text{ kilograms divided by}}{2.72 \text{ meters}^2} = 20.9$$

Desirable BMI for women is between 21 to 23, with obesity beginning at 27.5 and serious obesity at 31.5. Desirable BMI for men is 22 to 24, with obesity beginning at 28.5 and serious obesity at 33.

Causes of Obesity

We have yet to gain a clear understanding of the causes of obesity. According to the Surgeon General, several factors should be considered in the causation of obesity: (1) heredity, (2) overeating, (3) inactivity, (4) defective or decreased thermogenesis (the process of converting calories into heat), and (5) altered metabolism of adipose tissue (USDHHS, 1988b). Psychological and behavioral factors may also play a role in causing obesity, such as unconscious personal conflicts, emotional responses, personality traits, environmental eating cues, and responses to dieting (Striegel–Moore & Rodin, 1986).

The tendency to be overweight may be hereditary. Stunkard et al. (1986) studied 540 middle-aged adults who had been adopted as children. There was little relationship between their BMIs and that of their adoptive parents. There was a strong relationship between the BMIs of the women and their biological parents, especially their mothers. However, there was no relationship between the BMIs of the men and their biological parents of either gender.

Earlier, Stunkard (1986) concluded that "Social factors must be considered as one of the most important influences on the prevalence of obesity in Western society" (p. 215). To back his statement, he points to the negative correlation between socioeconomic status (SES) and obesity. The highest percentage of obesity is found in populations of the lowest SES. The prevalence of obesity decreases as SES increases. The relationship between obesity and social class is quite complex. Cultural beliefs play a prominent role in the obesity of many ethnic groups who associate fatness with health and happiness (Laguerre, 1981; Harwood, 1981).

Being thin is not necessarily a desired state among inner-city women. Thinness is often associated with hunger, drug addiction, and AIDS in this population. Freeman (1991) reports that ghetto neighborhoods have created an environment that promotes obesity. "Junk food" is marketed aggressively in the inner city and many use it as an inexpensive means of coping with the high-stress environment. One young girl ex-plained, "Food and TV are a way of calming my nerves" (p. 44).

Effects of Obesity

Regardless of the causes of obesity, its effects can be painful. The following statement from an overweight man gives us a vivid impression of its impact:

> Just looking at myself in a store window makes me feel terrible. It's gotten so I am very careful not to look by accident. It's a feeling that people have the right to hate me and hate anyone who looks as fat as me. As soon as I see myself I feel an uncontrollable burst of hatred. I just look at myself and say "I hate you, you're loathsome!"

And an overweight woman had this to say:

> Nobody wants to go out with a tub, which was my nickname. By going to a dance all I did was stand against the wall listening to music. Nobody ever asked me to dance. I made believe I didn't care. But I just thought I was a big nothing. (p. 1297, Stunkard & Mendelson, 1967)

Studies have shown that obesity is a risk factor for hypertension, hyperlipidemia, diabetes, pulmonary and renal problems, osteoarthritis, complications in childbirth, and recovery from surgery. The increased risk has not been established for those who are 10 to 30 percent overweight. However, weight loss is associated with such health benefits as lowered blood pressure, reduced cholesterol, and increased physical activity (Wilson, 1984).

Distribution of fat appears to be an important risk factor for diabetes, stroke, and coronary heart disease. Fat in the abdominal area is more dangerous than fat in the hip and thigh area. Pear shapes are at less risk than apple shapes. Abdominal fat becomes a risk factor when the waist measurement begins to exceed hip measure. For males, the ratio between waist and hips should not exceed 1.0. For women, the ratio should probably not exceed 0.80 (Bjorntorp, 1986). Researchers have found that the waist-to-hip ratio is the most powerful predictor of HDL levels—the "good" cholesterol (Ostlund et al., 1990). Pear shapes, regardless of gender, have higher levels of the good cholesterol than apple shapes.

Treatment of Obesity

Not many years ago physicians would routinely hand their obese patients a printed "diet" sheet and tell them to go home and follow it. The prescribed diet plan was not adapted to patients' individual characteristics, nor to family or ethnic ways. It is no surprise that patients routinely failed to adhere to these diets. If they lost weight, they were quite likely to gain it back.

But people desperately wanted workable ways to lose weight, preferably, as advertisements often put it, "painlessly and without having to do strenuous exercise." Millions of people, many of whom were not obese, wanted to lose weight and no one had really found a good way to do it. The mania for weight loss was a breeding ground for weight loss plans that promised quick solutions. Publishers began grinding out books that claimed to offer a real solution that would "take off pounds fast."

Quick Weight-Loss Diets

Diet plans generally stipulate caloric reductions either directly or by drastic modification of the types of food consumed (see Box 8.3). The more spectacular plans often play on quirks of our physiology that will give at least the impression of very quick loss of large amounts of weight. A good example of a type of diet that has been recycled many times under many different names is a high protein diet which is also low in fats and carbohydrates. This kind of diet causes us to lose water (and perhaps important substances, like calcium, that are dissolved in it). Since we eat less fat and fewer calories, we lose body fat on such a diet. Since we lose water, our weight diminishes to give the impression of far more fat loss than is real. In the process, we may damage ourselves, especially our kidneys. Furthermore, the weight lost in excretion of water will be quickly regained when we go off the diet.

This kind of diet, like many of them, creates an illusion of success and is unhealthy. When people tell you they are on a "wonderful new diet" and have lost "15 pounds in two weeks,"

Oprah Winfrey lost 67 pounds in four months on a high-protein liquid diet; however, like most people, she regained the weight after a relatively short period of time.

you can be sure that they have not lost 15 pounds of fat. A pound of fat contains about 4200 calories. To lose 15 pounds of fat in two weeks, we would have to create more than a daily caloric deficit! Unless you are truly dedicated to eating, it is unlikely that you even consume 4200 calories a day. Most studies indicate that overweight people do not consume many more calories than do people of normal weight. So, that kind of quick weight loss is a tipoff that the diet plan is using "smoke and mirrors" through some quirk of bodily physiology to give a false impression of fat loss.

In general, diets fail, and there are good reasons why. We said earlier that dieting forces the body into a starvation pattern that makes it

Box 8.3 **Very-Low-Calorie Diets**

In 1988, 18 million viewers watched with fascination as Oprah Winfrey lost 67 pounds in four months before their very eyes. She revealed the secret of her spectacular weight loss on her show—Oprah had not eaten a bite of solid food for four months! She had been on a medically supervised very-low-calorie diet (VLCD). VLCDs are high protein liquid diets limited to 400 to 800 calories daily. They place patients in a fasting state that spares body protein and maximizes fat loss.

These diets are appealing to people because they can lose weight quickly and there are no complicated diets to follow that require measuring and calorie counting. Moreover, there are relatively few complications when they are used by select people and are supervised by physicians who are thoroughly trained in their use (Wadden, Van Itallie, & Blackburn, 1990). Weight loss is very rapid, averaging 45 pounds in 12 weeks. Unfortunately, most patients regain their weight almost as quickly as they lose it (Brownell & Wadden, 1986; Wadden, Van Itallie, & Blackburn, 1990). Even Oprah regained her weight, in spite of the public scrutiny she believed would motivate her to keep it off.

The tendency to regain weight is reduced somewhat when VLCD programs use multidisciplinary teams consisting of physicians, psychologists, and dietitians (Wadden, Van Itallie, & Blackburn, 1990). Qualified VLCD providers need thorough training in clinical nutrition and extensive knowledge of the causes, effects, and treatment of obesity. As Wadden and colleagues note, most physicians are not prepared to treat patients with VLCDs. Although there is a growing recognition that nutrition and obesity are important topics, most medical schools do not include them in their curricula.

VLCDs are not recommended for patients with the following conditions: cerebrovascular insufficiency (insufficient blood supply to the brain), recent myocardial infarction, severe liver or kidney complications, pregnancy, and juvenile-onset diabetes. In addition, VLCDs should not be used by patients who are on lithium or who may be psychologically unstable. Even patients without these conditions may experience some of the following side effects: temporary dizziness, constipation, and temporary cessation of menstruation. Patients might also experience dry skin, mild fatigue, hair loss, and cold intolerance.

VLCDs should not be used by people who are less than 30 percent overweight. The vast majority of the studies demonstrating the safety of VLCDs have examined their effects on people who were at least 50 percent overweight. Their findings may not generalize to those who are mildly obese. Mildly obese patients tend to experience larger losses of lean body mass compared to the more severely obese. Large losses of lean body mass may result in life-threatening damage to the heart and other organs. The loss of lean body tissue also lowers the metabolic rate, increasing the difficulty of maintaining desirable weight (Wadden, Van Itallie, & Blackburn, 1990).

harder to lose weight. Furthermore, diets focus on creating short-term caloric deficits without changing any of the factors that make people gain weight. There is little reason to expect that the losses will be maintained. Habits have to change if weight is not to be regained. Weight is gained within a social system that encourages, sometimes even demands, excesses of caloric intake and deficits of caloric output.

There are talented people who make their living trying to get us to buy the very foods we want to avoid. To change weight permanently we have to do something about how people cope with the seductions of advertising and with the temptations the grocery stores and restaurants have arranged. We also have to deal with pressures to stay with old behaviors that are, often unwittingly, created by family, ethnic groups, and friends. It is a formidable task and one that health psychologists certainly cannot claim to have mastered. We will discuss some of their efforts, but first we will say a few things about some more strictly medical approaches to weight loss.

Biomedical Approaches

The dream of a cure for overweight within a biomedical framework would be a medication for weight loss or, lacking that, a surgical procedure. Surgical approaches have focused on modification of the digestive system or direct removal of fat from under the skin. Intestinal bypasses have had to be modified and moderated because they can produce serious side effects, including death. They are generally reserved for extremely overweight people who have "tried everything" and failed.

Surgical removal of fat, called *liposuction*, is now in vogue. It is limited to "spot" removals and appears, for now, to be useful if done by someone with adequate training. However, there is nothing to prevent unskilled physicians from doing these operations, and people have been mutilated in that way. Keep in mind that we said "appears, for *now* to be useful." Many surgical procedures may look good for a while, only to have devastating side effects show up later.

Behavioral Modification

One promising alternative to dieting might be changing food-related behaviors through behavioral modification. Behaviorists have devised programs based on long-term change of behaviors rather than on short-term reduction of caloric intake. In recent years, behavioral modification has become an important part of weight control programs. Initially, it appeared to be a powerful method for attaining permanent weight control. The following statement illustrates prevalent attitudes after the first few years of research on modification of weight: "Where it has been systematically compared to other more conventional programs, behavior therapy can be demonstrated to outperform other popular approaches by an impressive margin" (Beller, 1977, p. 266).

Behavioral modification techniques include self-monitoring, reducing the number of food cues in the environment, and providing reinforcement for weight loss. Self-monitoring in weight control involves keeping food diaries and regularly charting weight. Food diaries often include charting situations that precede eating. This practice increases the dieter's awareness of the cues that trigger eating. Even behaviors that set up the conditions for overeating, such as buying junk food, are monitored and subjected to behavioral control (see Figure 8.1).

Unfortunately, longer term studies indicate that, even with behavioral modification, people tend to regain weight (Stuart, 1980). However, such programs remain one of the best alternatives for long-term weight loss, and much work is being done to improve them. Current programs are multifaceted and emphasize, along with behavioral control of eating, cognitive modifications and changes in activity or exercise patterns. Behavioral and cognitive-behavioral therapies are discussed in more detail in Chapter 5.

Multidimensional Approach to Weight Control

Brownell and Wadden (1986) propose a multidimensional approach to weight control. Their program has five components: behavior modification, exercise, cognitive change, social sup-

Figure 8.1 Behaviors that set up conditions for overeating. These kinds of behavior are identified through the use of food diaries and other self-monitoring techniques. *Source:* From *Nondrug Treatment for Essential Hypertension,* by E. Blanchard, J. Martin, and P. Dubbert, Figure 7.2, p. 183, copyright © 1988 by Pergamon Press, Inc., Elmsford, N.Y.

port, and nutrition. The five components are woven throughout the sessions so that in a given session, participants receive relevant information on each component. They also suggested that weight control programs be extended beyond the customary 10 to 12 weeks to at least 16 to 20 weeks. Longer programs allow patients to lose more weight and learn maintenance skills.

Group Approaches

A variety of community-based weight control programs are available. Take Off Pounds Sensibly (TOPS) is the largest nonprofit organization, with chapters in all parts of the country. Membership consists predominately of white, middle-class females who are moderately obese. Members set their own goals and use their own methods to lose weight. Meetings involve weight recordings, sharing diet tips, and social support. The effectiveness of TOPS has been difficult to evaluate because of the high attrition rate. Stunkard (1986) reports that long-

term members do lose weight but slowly regain it in spite of their continued membership.

Weight Watchers also involves weekly meetings and weigh-ins and attracts clientele similar to the TOPS memberships. Weight Watchers programs include behavior modification and nutritional programs. Weight Watchers also has a high dropout rate, making its effectiveness difficult to evaluate. However, the problems of the high attrition rates of both these group approaches are offset by their ready availability. Although Weight Watchers costs considerably more than TOPS, both groups are more cost-effective than individually based treatments (Stunkard, 1986).

To date, the most cost-effective group programs for weight control appear to be work-site competitions. Competitions *between* work sites are more effective than those *within* work sites. A competition between banks resulted in an average weight loss of 13 pounds during a 12-week period, with only a 5 percent attrition rate. Individual competitions are less effective than either between or within work-site competitions. A program in which individuals competed against each other had higher dropout rates and less weight loss than traditional programs. The increased motivation found in group competitions may be the result of an increased spirit of cooperation (Stunkard, 1986).

EATING DISORDERS

The fear of being obese and the desire to be thin may result in gross disturbances in eating behaviors. Anorexia nervosa and bulimia nervosa are most often found in young women of college age, although they are not limited to that group. As we will discuss below, the consequences of these eating disorders can be quite serious and can even lead to death. Help is available on most college campuses through counseling or health centers for students who may have developed these disorders.

Anorexia Nervosa

Anorexia nervosa (AN) is an eating disorder marked by (1) an insistence on below-normal body weight, (2) intense fear of gaining weight or becoming fat, (3) distorted body image, and (4) amenorrhea (absence of menstruation). AN is usually suspected when weight is 15 percent below the expected weight for a given age and height. Although the term "anorexia" implies loss of appetite, anorexics rarely lose their appetites. They literally starve themselves to become thin. When self-starvation is accompanied by self-induced vomiting, excessive exercise, and laxative abuse, bulimia nervosa may also be present. Anorexics tend to deny the existence or severity of their conditions and are very resistant to treatment (American Psychiatric Association, 1987).

The etiology of AN is still under study, and no clear consensus has developed as to its causes. However, there does seem to be agreement that AN involves the complex interaction of many factors. It has been suggested that young girls become anorexic to avoid their sexuality. Starvation stops or reverses the changes associated with puberty, including menstruation and breast development. Other proposed influences are society's mania for thinness, family interactions, need for control and perfection, abnormal cognitive styles, and endocrine malfunctioning (Szmukler, 1987).

AN has the potential to be fatal as it was in the case of the popular singer Karen Carpenter. AN commonly consists of a single episode with return to normal weight (American Psychiatric Association, 1987). Treatment of AN involves restoration and maintenance of a normal healthy weight. Hospitalization is often required during the weight restoration phase of treatment. In addition to skilled nursing care, the hospitalization phase includes gradual increase in caloric intake, behavioral therapy, and emotional support. The weight maintenance phase of treatment often involves a cognitive-behavioral approach, with emphasis on the patient's feelings and belief systems (Szmukler, 1989).

Bulimia Nervosa

A local television news show recently featured a spot on racing horses and their jockeys. A reporter was discussing the fact that jockeys were disqualified if they did not meet the weight requirements. She was broadcasting from the race track as the jockeys were checking their weight for the race the next day. She asked a jockey who just stepped off the scales how he managed to maintain his weight at such a low level. He replied with an edge in his voice: "It's easy—you gorge yourself, then get rid of it."

The reporter and the news anchors on that television show were visibly shocked by the jockey's admission. Yet a national survey found that 10.5 percent of female tenth graders who dieted used vomiting as a means of weight control (ASHA, 1989). When this behavior continues for three or more months, **bulimia nervosa** is suspected. Bulimia nervosa is an eating disorder marked by recurrent episodes of binge eating accompanied by a sense of loss of control. Bulimics are overly concerned about their weight and body shape. To avoid weight gain, binges are followed by self-induced vomiting, use of laxatives or diuretics, fasting, or vigorous exercise to avoid weight gain. Most bulimics are within a normal weight range; however, some may be overweight and others may be slightly underweight (American Psychiatric Association, 1987).

Bulimics have attitudes similar to those of anorexics. They are dissatisfied with their weight and shape and often present symptoms of depression. Bulimics may be any weight, but often they have been heavy or have a family history of obesity. Binging and purging can result in serious health problems including sore throats, hair loss, muscle spasms, kidney damage, dehydration, erosion of tooth enamel, menstrual irregularity, loss of sex drive, and myocardial infarction (Szmukler, 1989).

Surveys indicate that about 1 percent of adolescent and young women suffer from bulimia nervosa. However, this figure may underestimate the actual number of bulimics in this population. There is evidence that people with eating disorders do not cooperate with these surveys (Fairburn & Beglin, 1990). Bulimia nervosa is most common in white females between the ages of 14 and 40 years. Bulimic behavior has long been suspected in athletes like jockeys who must meet strict weight requirements.

Several different approaches are presently being used to treat bulimia nervosa. A small number of bulimics seem to be responsive to anticonvulsant drugs. Because bulimia nervosa is associated with depression, antidepressants are commonly given to bulimics. Their effectiveness has received inconsistent support. Psychological interventions tend to combine various approaches, including cognitive-behavioral, family, and group therapies. Although much evaluation research remains to be done, the cognitive-behavioral approach, applied either individually or in groups, seems to be the most promising. Cognitive-behavioral treatments include advice, self-monitoring, stimulus control, and a prescribed eating pattern (Palmer, 1987).

EXERCISE

The human body was designed for an active life. We become painfully aware of this fact when we sit in front of a computer terminal all day or spend long hours in a cramped airplane or car. There is ample scientific evidence that suggests physical activity contributes to good physical and mental health. Studies have shown that exercise decreases risks of coronary heart disease, colon cancer, osteoporosis, and stroke. A recent study found a strong relationship between physical fitness and mortality due to all causes, especially cardiovascular disease and cancer (Blair et al., 1989). Exercise also appears to help in the management of diabetes, obesity, and depression (Koplan, Caspersen, & Powell, 1989). In other words, "It's the right thing to do."

Aerobic Exercise

Kenneth Cooper, a cardiologist, really started something when he published *Aerobics* in 1968. Cooper (1970) developed the concept of aerobic exercise to "counteract the problems of lethargy and inactivity which are so widely prevalent in our American population" (p. 5). He has appar-

ently been successful. George Gallup reported that the resulting fitness movement was the biggest behavioral change that he had seen in his years as a pollster (Hank, 1979).

Aerobic literally means "with oxygen." **Aerobic exercise** is any exercise that stimulates heart and lung activity for a time period sufficiently long enough to produce beneficial changes in the body. Aerobic exercise involves using the large muscles of the body in rhythmic or dynamic movements. Typical aerobic exercises are brisk walking, jogging, cycling, swimming, running, and some active sports. Golf and bowling are not considered aerobic because there are frequent pauses in the activity.

The three components of exercise are frequency, duration, and intensity. **Frequency** refers to the number of exercise sessions per week. **Intensity** is expressed as the percentage of the individual's maximal capacity such as maximum heart rate. For example, running is a more intense exercise than walking. **Duration** is the length of the training time and is dependent on the intensity of the exercise. Lower intensity exercise should be conducted for longer periods.

For healthy adults, the American College of Sports Medicine (1978) recommends 15 to 60 minutes of continuous aerobic activity at 60 to 90 percent of maximum heart rate, three to five days a week. The length of the aerobic session depends on the intensity of the activity. Maximum heart rate can be obtained by subtracting an individual's age from 220 (220 − age = maximum heart rate). Lower intensity–longer duration programs appear to be as beneficial as higher intensity–shorter duration in developing and maintaining cardiorespiratory fitness and body composition.

Stretching and Weight Training

In addition to aerobics, stretching exercises and weight training are important to a total exercise program. However, they are more difficult to learn, and many of us need some instruction to do the exercises correctly and avoid injury. Stretching exercises increase flexibility, and weight training improves muscle strength and endurance. Flexibility is defined as the range of possible motion about a given joint or combination of joints. Poor flexibility and inadequate muscle strength contribute to musculoskeletal disorders. It is estimated that muscular deficiency is involved in 80 percent of people suffering from low-back pain. Flexibility exercises need to be practiced daily until the desired level of flexibility is reached. Three or four sessions a week are necessary for maintenance. Weight training programs usually involve three to five sessions per week (Moffatt, 1988).

Physiological Benefits of Exercise

DeVries (1977) has shown that many of the negative physical characteristics of aging can be reversed through exercise. He worked with a group of 70- and 80-year-old people in a progressive walking–jogging program. At the end of a six-week program, many were able to run a nonstop mile. In addition, they had gained many physiological benefits including lowering of systolic and diastolic blood pressure. DeVries also notes that the physiological characteristics of aging can be produced in young people by keeping them in bed for several weeks.

A more recent controlled study found that a four-month aerobics program was associated with a number of physiological and psychological gains in healthy adults ranging in age from 60 to 83 years. Among the physiological gains were improved cardiorespiratory fitness, lower cholesterol levels, diastolic blood pressure levels, and a trend toward an increase in bone mineral content among subjects at risk for bone fracture (Blumenthal et al., 1989).

Osteoporosis is a disfiguring, painful, and crippling disease that involves bone loss. It is a major public health problem and affects more than 20 million people in the United States. You have seen the effects of this disease in elderly women who have a hunched back. This is a preventable disease, but the time to start prevention is at a young age. Calcium-rich diets and weight-bearing exercise help build peak bone mass. The more bone mass we have at 35, the less likely we will have thin, brittle bones when we are 70, especially if we continue an active life. Inactivity is clearly associated with bone loss in people of all ages and both genders. Exercise slows or reverses bone loss in middle-aged and elderly people. Forty to 50 minutes of aerobic weight-bearing exercise, three to four days a week, is recommended to maintain bone mass (Smith, 1988).

Psychological Benefits of Exercise

Think about it: Do you feel in better spirits on days when you are active rather than inactive? Now, think about how you feel when you reach a goal that you set: Do you feel pride, confidence, a sense of control? When good spirits are combined with pride, confidence, and a sense of control, it results in a sense of well-being. A massive body of research indicates that is what happens when people successfully engage in

There is compelling evidence that regular exercise programs improves our sense of physical and mental well-being.

regular exercise programs. For example, the older adults in the four-month exercise program mentioned earlier also showed improvement on a number of psychological variables (Blumenthal et al., 1989). They reported improved self-esteem, body self-concept, family relations, memory, and concentration. In addition, they reported that they had more energy, slept better, and their sex lives had improved. The psychological gains were found in a yoga exercise program as well as the aerobics program.

Anxiety and Depression

DeVries and Adams (1972) found that a 15-minute walk produced more relaxation than a standard dose of a mild tranquilizer. Raglin and Morgan (1987) reported that both aerobic exercise and quiet rest reduced anxiety. However, the reduction of anxiety was sustained for longer periods following exercise when compared to quiet rest. The exercises included jogging, racquetball, basketball, swimming, or stationary cycling.

Although there is always a concern about methodological problems, fairly solid evidence suggests that depression can be prevented or treated with a program of exercise (Folkins & Sime, 1981). Depression is associated with low levels of norepinephrine, and exercise increases this neurotransmitter. Other researchers suggest that depression can be overcome through the sense of mastery and self-control gained through exercise. Enhanced body image and feelings of self-worth are also common side effects of exercise that might counteract depression (Sime, 1984).

Self-Esteem and Body Concept

Research consistently indicates that aerobic exercise can have important psychological benefits for all age groups. A study of preschool children found an increase in self-esteem, as well as fitness and agility, at the end of an eight-week aerobics program (Alpert, Field, Goldstein, & Perry, 1990). College students showed an increase in self-esteem and improved body concept after participation in a semester-long aerobics class (Johnson, Radmacher, & Terry,

1986). Similar results were obtained in a population of healthy, middle-aged adults (King, Taylor, Haskell, & DeBusk, 1989). This study found that a regular exercise program improved the participants' concept of their perceived fitness and satisfaction with their physical shapes and weights.

Stress Management

As a result of the positive physiological and psychological effects of physical activity, exercise is considered an essential part of comprehensive stress management (Sheridan, 1983b). Brown and Siegel (1988) investigated the ability of exercise to buffer the negative effects of stress on the health of 364 adolescent girls. They found that stressful life events were associated with illness primarily among those with low levels of exercise. Stress was not a strong predictor of illness in students with high activity levels. These findings support the notion that exercise buffers the effects of stress on illness. The subjects in this sample were mostly white females from a private school in California. The authors caution that their results may not generalize to other populations.

How Much Exercise Is Enough?

How much physical activity is enough? There is a growing consensus that we need not become marathon runners to enjoy the benefits of physical fitness. After all, the first marathon runner died at the end of his journey! A recent study has found that a major reduction in mortality rates is associated with a very modest level of physical fitness. The findings hold after controlling for age, serum cholesterol level, blood pressure, smoking, glucose level, family history of CHD, and length of followup. This level of fitness can be reached through a daily 30- to 60-minute brisk walk (Blair et al., 1989). A controlled study found that a low-intensity exercise program resulted in greater systolic blood pressure reductions in older adults with essential hypertension than did a moderate-intensity exercise program (Hagberg, Montain, Martin, & Ehsani, 1989).

There are many good arguments for moderate exercise programs. It is no doubt easier to motivate inactive people to start a walking program than a jogging or running program. Moderate exercise programs also avoid some of the injuries associated with strenuous programs. Some common problems are caused by overuse, such as shin splints or tennis elbow. Other injuries are caused by colliding with the ground, objects, or other people. Moderate exercise programs are particularly advised for patients with diabetes, asthma, and kidney failure (Haskell, 1984).

Getting Motivated to Exercise

Based on clinical observations, Brownell and his colleagues note that attitudes and personality factors affect people's participation in exercise programs (Brownell, Rubin & Smoller, 1989). They believe that the attitude that exercise must be vigorous and prolonged discourages many people from starting an exercise program. This attitude is often communicated to novice exercisers by "gung ho" professionals who are trained athletes.

Personality factors can affect adherence to exercise programs when there is a poor match between personality type and exercise. For example, "social types" generally prefer exercise with other people and join an aerobics class, a tennis club, a biking club, or the like. A "solo type" prefers walking, cycling, or jogging alone. Exercise programs that prescribe the same kind of exercise for all personality types can expect problems. This is an area that needs more research attention (Brownell, Rubin, & Smoller, 1988).

Although more people are exercising, it is estimated that only about 15 percent of adult Americans are physically active (Ivancevich & Matteson, 1989). As a result of increased automation, the amount of physical activity required at home and work has declined steadily. Getting people off the couch and out of their cars has proved to be a difficult task. It is going to take the combined efforts of the school systems, health professionals, and community and organizational development to get people moving (Koplan, Caspersen, & Powell, 1989). We will

discuss some of the theories and methods of motivating lifestyle changes later in this and following chapters.

DEVELOPING HEALTHY LIFESTYLE BEHAVIORS

It is one of life's ironies that good habits are so much harder to instill than bad habits. A lot has to do with the time that elapses between the behavior and the reinforcer. For example, it usually takes several weeks for the positive effects of an exercise program to be experienced. Staying in a warm bed on a cold morning provides instant reinforcement. Too often good habits provide short-term pain and long-term pleasure, while bad habits give us short-term pleasure and long-term pain. Unfortunately, it is a basic principle of operant conditioning that to be effective reinforcers must quickly follow the desired response. (See Chapter 2 for more information on operant conditioning.)

Theories of Lifestyle Change

Operant conditioning is just one factor in the development of healthy lifestyles. Several theories have been applied to the problem of understanding health-related behaviors. Three of the most commonly used theories are **self-efficacy theory** (Bandura, 1977), **health belief model** (Becker, 1974), and **reasoned action theory** (Ajzen & Fishbein, 1980). We will briefly describe each theory below.

Self-efficacy Theory

Self-efficacy is the degree to which we believe we are capable of meeting some particular challenge. According to Bandura (1982), our self-efficacy judgments determine our choice of activities and settings. Self-efficacy also influences how much effort we will expend when we are faced with obstacles. For example, dieters with a strong sense of self-efficacy will be even more determined to "stick to it" if they experience a temporary weight gain. Dieters with a weak sense of self-efficacy will be more likely to become discouraged and quit.

Self-efficacy is determined by (1) our previous successes or failures, (2) vicarious experiences, that is, observing the performances of other people, (3) feedback from others about our abilities, and (4) our physiological states. A person, then, who has repeatedly failed in attempts to diet is likely to have a weak sense of self-efficacy. It will be further weakened if his friends have not been successful either and if his wife constantly reminds him of his previous failures. The arousal he feels from the stress of dieting is likely to be interpreted as a sign of vulnerability (Bandura, 1982).

Health Belief Model

The **health belief model** was developed to apply specifically to health-related behaviors (Becker, 1974). According to this model, our health-related behaviors can be predicted by our assessments of (1) the perceived threat of illness or injury, and (2) the costs and benefits of the particular behavior (Becker & Rosenstock, 1984).

Whether we perceive something as a threat depends on a number of demographic and social variables, and our answers to the following questions:

1. How likely is it that we will develop the particular problem (perceived susceptibility)?
2. How serious are the consequences of the problem if we develop it or leave it untreated (perceived seriousness)?
3. How salient are the cues that remind us of the seriousness of the problem or that we need to take action (cues to action)?

According to the health belief model, we also take into account the costs and benefits of a particular health-related behavior. If we perceive the threat to be great and the benefits outweigh the costs, then we are likely to adopt that behavior (Becker & Rosenstock, 1984). For example, a friend of ours was told by his physician that his cholesterol level was very high and he was at high risk for a heart attack. His brother had recently died from heart disease, so Frank saw it as a real threat. However, he loved his bacon, eggs, and sausages of all kinds. It would cost him a great deal of pleasure to give up those foods. In the end Frank decided that the benefits of a low cholesterol diet were greater than the costs when he weighed his life against his eating pleasures.

Reasoned Action Theory

Reasoned action theory (Fishbein & Ajzen, 1975; Ajzen & Fishbein, 1980) states that "intention" is the best predictor of behavior. An intention toward a behavior is influenced by our attitude toward that behavior. This attitude is influenced by the strength of belief that the behavior will result in a certain outcome and the evaluation of the outcome. Say, you intend to start exercising to lose weight. You will have a strong intention to exercise, if you believe exercise (behavior) will result in losing weight (outcome) and losing weight is important to you (evaluation).

Intention is also determined by what we believe other people think about our ability to obtain a certain outcome and how they evaluate that outcome. This is called the subjective norm. For example, if your family and friends think it unlikely that you can stick with an exercise program or that weight loss for you is not desirable, your intention to exercise may be weakened. It depends, in part, on how much you care about what they think. Intention, then, is determined by the individual's attitude toward the behavior and subjective norms.

Goal Setting and Contracts

Goal setting can increase motivation to stick with lifestyle changes. The most effective goal-setting programs are those that are realistic, challenging, and self-set. Goals set by third parties are not as successful (Ivancevich & Matteson, 1989). Contracts similar to the one shown in Box 8.4 are often used to help people meet their goals. We are more likely to stick to a program if our goals have been clearly and specifically stated. Vaguely defined goals are easily forgotten. For example, individuals who begin

Box 8.4 **Behavioral Change Contract**

I, <u>Determined Dora</u>, have decided to walk <u>3 miles a day</u> by January 1, 2000. I will obtain this goal by reaching the following schedule of subgoals:

Dates	Subgoals
10–1	1/2 mile daily
11–1	1 mile daily
12–1	2 miles daily
1–1	3 miles daily

I will use the following methods to accomplish my goal:

1. I will get a pair of good walking shoes that fit.
2. I will ask my spouse to walk with me.

3. I will reserve the time from 6:00 to 7:00 in the morning for walking.
4. I will get up an hour earlier in order to have that time.

I will get feedback on my progress with the following methods:

1. I will stick a star on the calendar every day I walk.
2. My spouse will verify that I have gone the appropriate distance for each subgoal.
3. I will check and record my resting heart rate once a week.
4. I will weigh myself at the end of each month.

I will reward myself for reaching my subgoals and goal on the following schedule:

Dates	Subgoals	Rewards
10–1	1/2 mile daily	Book
11–1	1 mile daily	Concert Tickets
12–1	2 miles daily	Jogging Suit
1–1	3 miles daily	Weekend Trip

Signature _____

Witnessed _____

an exercise program because they want to be "more active" are not likely to stick to it.

The contract is useful because it clearly states the goals and the dates that are to be reached. More than that, it lists the methods by which the goal can be obtained. Bandura (1982) suggests that adopting reachable subgoals is the best way to obtain and maintain large future goals. Dividing a large goal into several subgoals that are rewarded can be an effective behavioral change tool. This is sometimes called shaping a

behavior. (Shaping behaviors is discussed in more detail in Chapter 5.)

Conclusions

People who are interested in public health generally agree that Americans need to develop healthier lifestyles. (Take the Healthstyle Self-Test on pp. 194–195 to see how you are doing.) Far too many people have unhealthy lifestyles that put them at high risk for the leading causes of death. We talked about the health behaviors of one man, Bill, at the beginning of the chapter. In his defense, we should mention that he developed many of his "bad" habits at a time when little was known about the relationship between lifestyle and health. Moreover, at the time, many of his bad eating habits were considered good nutrition. For instance, the thick rare steaks he loved were seen as good food. Cheese was considered a healthy high protein snack instead of a high fat/cholesterol snack loaded with calories.

Unfortunately for Bill and his family, his habits were firmly established by the time he realized that his behaviors were harmful to his health. He did manage to lose 50 pounds around his fiftieth birthday, but he increased his smoking and drinking habits as he lost the weight. Making lifestyle changes is just plain hard to do. The challenge for health psychologists is to apply their knowledge base and skills to help people make these difficult changes. We also need to know much more than we do about many things, for example, causation in obesity and the problem of relapse. More than that, we need to focus on primary prevention by creating environments that discourage health risk behaviors and encourage health-enhancing behaviors.

Summary

1. Lifestyle is defined as the health-related decisions and behaviors that are controlled by individuals. It plays a critical role in health promotion and the prevention and treatment of disease.

2. There are three kinds of prevention: (a) Primary prevention, which reduces health risks for an entire population; (b) secondary prevention, which involves reducing risk factors in high risk groups; and (c) tertiary prevention, which seeks to reduce the duration of illness in those who are already ill.

3. Nutrition plays a significant role in health. The American diet is too high in calories, fat, cholesterol, protein, sugar, and sodium and too low in grains, fruits, and vegetables. Our innate desire for high-fat, sweet foods is exploited by food manufacturers who constantly promote these foods in advertising media.

4. Health experts recommend that fat calories be limited to 30 percent. High-fat diets are associated with high serum cholesterol levels which are, in turn, associated with heart attacks and strokes.

5. Vitamins C, E, B complex, and the carotenoids have been linked to cancer prevention. High-fiber diets may protect against cancer of the colon and rectum. Insoluble fiber may prevent colon cancer, and soluble fiber appears more important in preventing heart disease.

6. Although protein is an essential part of a healthy diet, Americans typically consume two to three times the required amount. Excessive protein places a heavy load on the kidneys, which may lead to several disorders, including gout.

7. Americans consume about 131 pounds of refined sugar and corn sweeteners per year. Sweeteners are often added to processed foods. Sugar provides little nutritional benefit, except calories, and it contributes to dental caries. In addition, parents blame sugar for hyperactivity in their children. Correlation studies support parental observations, but experimental studies generally do not. However, the experimental studies typically lack statistical power.

8. Several theories suggest that dieting may actually cause people to gain weight. The glucostatic theory states that dieting results in lowered glucose levels and increased hunger. The set point theory holds that our bodies are programmed to contain a certain amount of fat. When the fat falls below the set point, fat cells trigger the brain to initiate eating. The restrained

eating theory states that restrained eaters are in a constant struggle to weigh less than their biological set point. Emotions disinhibit their restraint, causing them to overeat. Unacceptable snacks also disinhibit restrained eaters.

9. Basal metabolic rate is decreased by 20 to 40 percent when calories fall below a certain level. After prolonged calorie deprivation, dieters may gain weight when they return to normal eating. There is some evidence that low calorie foods may contribute to obesity. Artificial sweeteners provoke increases in insulin levels, and insulin is involved in increased appetite and storage of nutrients as fat.

10. Obesity is a physical disorder that involves an excessive accumulation of fat. Obesity appears to be caused by a number of interacting factors, for example, heredity, emotional responses, personality traits, overeating, and inactivity.

11. Obesity may result in social, occupational, and psychological problems. It is a risk factor for hypertension, hyperlipidemia, diabetes, pulmonary and renal problems, osteoarthritis, and complications in childbirth and surgery. Part of the risk appears to be related to body shape. Pear-shaped people tend to be at lower risk than apple-shaped people.

12. The quick results of some quick weight-loss diets may be due to water loss rather than fat loss. In the process, kidneys may be damaged and important minerals may also be lost. Weight loss is usually quickly regained. Surgical procedures such as intestinal bypasses are generally a last chance procedure reserved for the extremely obese.

13. Behavioral modification is an alternative to, or at least augments, dieting. Techniques include self-monitoring, reducing environmental food cues, and providing reinforcement for weight loss. Although behavioral modification has not lived up

to its promise for attaining permanent weight control, it is still an important part of multidimensional weight control programs.

14. Group weight control programs, whether nonprofit or for-profit, have high attrition rates, but they are more cost-effective than individually based treatments. Work-site competition programs appear to be the most cost-effective.

15. Anorexia nervosa and bulimia nervosa are serious eating disorders. Anorexia involves self-starvation and can be fatal. Bulimia is marked by binge eating, followed by self-induced vomiting and other means of purging to prevent weight gain. It can result in serious health problems ranging from hair loss to myocardial infarction. Anorexia often requires hospitalization until weight is restored. Treatment of both disorders often involves cognitive-behavioral, family, and group therapies.

16. Exercise has been shown to improve cardiovascular functioning and to slow or reverse bone loss in osteoporosis patients. Research also indicates that participation in exercise programs results in improvement on a number of psychological variables, including self-esteem, reduced anxiety and depression, and memory and concentration. Positive health results can be obtained with low-intensity exercise programs. Motivating people to exercise regularly remains a challenge for health psychologists.

17. Self-efficacy theory, the health belief model, and reasoned action theory are the most commonly used theories to understand health-related behaviors. All three theories emphasize the importance of our beliefs about our ability to perform a particular behavior. The health belief model and reasoned action theory also include our evaluation of the outcomes of the behavior. Reasoned action theory includes our beliefs about other people's attitudes toward the behavior and outcome.

healthstyle a self-test

All of us want good health. But many of us do not know how to be as healthy as possible. Health experts now describe *lifestyle* as one of the most important factors affecting health. In fact, it is estimated that as many as seven of the ten leading causes of death could be reduced through common-sense changes in lifestyle. That's what this brief test, developed by the Public Health Service, is all about. Its purpose is simply to tell you how well you are doing to stay healthy. The behaviors covered in the test are recommended for most Americans. Some of them may not apply to persons with certain chronic diseases or handicaps, or to pregnant women. Such persons may require special instructions from their physicians.

Cigarette Smoking

If you never smoke, enter a score of 10 for this section and go to the next section on *Alcohol and Drugs*.

	Almost Always	Sometimes	Almost Never
1. I avoid smoking cigarettes.	2	1	0
2. I smoke only low tar and nicotine cigarettes *or* I smoke a pipe or cigars.	2	1	0

Smoking Score:_____

Alcohol and Drugs

	Almost Always	Sometimes	Almost Never
1. I avoid drinking alcoholic beverages *or* I drink no more than 1 or 2 drinks a day.	4	1	0
2. I avoid using alcohol or other drugs (especially illegal drugs) as a way of handling stressful situations or the problems in my life.	2	1	0
3. I am careful not to drink alcohol when taking certain medicines (for example, medicine for sleeping, pain, colds, and allergies), or when pregnant.	2	1	0
4. I read and follow the label directions when using prescribed and over-the-counter drugs.	2	1	0

Alcohol and Drugs Score:_____

Eating Habits

	Almost Always	Sometimes	Almost Never
1. I eat a variety of foods each day, such as fruits and vegetables, whole grain breads and cereals, lean meats, dairy products, dry peas and beans, and nuts and seeds.	4	1	0
2. I limit the amount of fat, saturated fat, and cholesterol I eat (including fat on meats, eggs, butter, cream, shortenings, and organ meats such as liver).	2	1	0
3. I limit the amount of salt I eat by cooking with only small amounts, not adding salt at the table, and avoiding salty snacks.	2	1	0
4. I avoid eating too much sugar (especially frequent snacks of sticky candy or soft drinks).	2	1	0

Eating Habits Score:_____

Exercise/Fitness

	Almost Always	Sometimes	Almost Never
1. I maintain a desired weight, avoiding overweight and underweight.	3	1	0
2. I do vigorous exercises for 15-30 minutes at least 3 times a week (examples include running, swimming, brisk walking).	3	1	0
3. I do exercises that enhance my muscle tone for 15-30 minutes at least 3 times a week (examples include yoga and calisthenics).	2	1	0
4. I use part of my leisure time participating in individual, family, or team activities that increase my level of fitness (such as gardening, bowling, golf, and baseball).	2	1	0

Exercise/Fitness Score:_____

Stress Control

	Almost Always	Sometimes	Almost Never
1. I have a job or do other work that I enjoy.	2	1	0
2. I find it easy to relax and express my feelings freely.	2	1	0
3. I recognize early, and prepare for, events or situations likely to be stressful for me.	2	1	0
4. I have close friends, relatives, or others whom I can talk to about personal matters and call on for help when needed.	2	1	0
5. I participate in group activities (such as church and community organizations) or hobbies that I enjoy.	2	1	0

Stress Control Score:_____

Safety

	Almost Always	Sometimes	Almost Never
1. I wear a seat belt while riding in a car.	2	1	0
2. I avoid driving while under the influence of alcohol and other drugs.	2	1	0
3. I obey traffic rules and the speed limit when driving.	2	1	0
4. I am careful when using potentially harmful products or substances (such as household cleaners, poisons, and electrical devices).	2	1	0
5. I avoid smoking in bed.	2	1	0

Safety Score:_____

What Your Scores Mean to YOU

Scores of 9 and 10

Excellent! Your answers show that you are aware of the importance of this area to your health. More important, you are putting your knowledge to work for you by practicing good health habits. As long as you continue to do so, this area should not pose a serious health risk. It's likely that you are setting an example for your family and friends to follow. Since you got a very high test score on this part of the test, you may want to consider other areas where your scores indicate room for improvement.

Scores of 6 to 8

Your health practices in this area are good, but there is room for improvement. Look again at the items you answered with a "Sometimes" or "Almost Never." What changes can you make to improve your score? Even a small change can often help you achieve better health.

Scores of 3 to 5

Your health risks are showing! Would you like more information about the risks you are facing and about why it is important for you to change these behaviors. Perhaps you need help in deciding how to successfully make the changes you desire. In either case, help is available.

Scores of 0 to 2

Obviously, you were concerned enough about your health to take the test, but your answers show that you may be taking serious and unnecessary risks with your health. Perhaps you are not aware of the risks and what to do about them. You can easily get the information and help you need to improve, if you wish. The next step is up to you.

YOU Can Start Right Now!

In the test you just completed were numerous suggestions to help you reduce your risk of disease and premature death. Here are some of the most significant:

 Avoid cigarettes. Cigarette smoking is the single most important preventable cause of illness and early death. It is especially risky for pregnant women and their unborn babies. Persons who stop smoking reduce their risk of getting heart disease and cancer. So if you're a cigarette smoker, think twice about lighting that next cigarette. If you choose to continue smoking, try decreasing the number of cigarettes you smoke and switching to a low tar and nicotine brand.

 Follow sensible drinking habits. Alcohol produces changes in mood and behavior. Most people who drink are able to control their intake of alcohol and to avoid undesired, and often harmful, effects. Heavy, regular use of alcohol can lead to cirrhosis of the liver, a leading cause of death. Also, statistics clearly show that mixing drinking and driving is often the cause of fatal or crippling accidents. So if you drink, do it wisely and in moderation. *Use care in taking drugs.* Today's greater use of drugs—both legal and illegal—is one of our most serious health risks. Even some drugs prescribed by your doctor can be dangerous if taken when drinking alcohol or before driving. Excessive or continued use of tranquilizers (or

"pep pills") can cause physical and mental problems. Using or experimenting with illicit drugs such as marijuana, heroin, cocaine, and PCP may lead to a number of damaging effects or even death.

 Eat sensibly. Overweight individuals are at greater risk for diabetes, gall bladder disease, and high blood pressure. So it makes good sense to maintain proper weight. But good eating habits also mean holding down the amount of fat (especially saturated fat), cholesterol, sugar and salt in your diet. If you must snack, try nibbling on fresh fruits and vegetables. You'll feel better—and look better, too.

 Exercise regularly. Almost everyone can benefit from exercise—and there's some form of exercise almost everyone can do. (If you have any doubt, check first with your doctor.) Usually, as little as 15-30 minutes of vigorous exercise three times a week will help you have a healthier heart, eliminate excess weight, tone up sagging muscles, and sleep better. Think how much difference all these improvements could make in the way you feel!

 Learn to handle stress. Stress is a normal part of living; everyone faces it to some degree. The causes of stress can be good or bad, desirable or undesirable (such as a promotion on the job or the loss of a spouse). Properly handled, stress need not be a problem. But unhealthy responses to stress—such as driving too fast or erratically, drinking too much, or prolonged anger or grief—can cause a variety of physical and mental problems. Even on a very busy day, find a few minutes to slow down and relax. Talking over a problem with someone you trust can often help you find a satisfactory solution. Learn to distinguish between things that are "worth fighting about" and things that are less important.

 Be safety conscious. Think "safety first" at home, at work, at school, at play, and on the highway. Buckle seat belts and obey traffic rules. Keep poisons and weapons out of the reach of children, and keep emergency numbers by your telephone. When the unexpected happens, you'll be prepared.

Where Do You Go From Here:

Start by asking yourself a few frank questions: *Am I really doing all I can to be as healthy as possible? What steps can I take to feel better? Am I willing to begin now?* If you scored low in one or more *sections* of the test, decide what changes you want to make for improvement. You might pick that aspect of your lifestyle where you feel you have the best chance for success and tackle that one first. Once you have improved your score there, go on to other areas.

If you already have tried to change your health habits (to stop smoking or exercise regularly, for example),don't be discouraged if you haven't yet succeeded. The difficulty you have encountered may be due to influences you've never really thought about—such as advertising—or to a lack

of support and encouragement. Understanding these influences is an important step toward changing the way they affect you.

There's Help Available. In addition to personal actions you can take on your own, there are community programs and groups (such as the YMCA or the local chapter of the American Heart Association) that can assist you and your family to make the changes you want to make. If you want to know more about these groups or about health risks, contact your local health department or the National Health Information Clearinghouse. There's a lot you can do to stay healthy or to improve your health—and there are organizations that can help you. Start a new HEALTHSTYLE today!

For assistance in locating specific information on these and other health topics; write to the National Health Information Clearinghouse.

National Health Information Clearinghouse
P.O. Box 1133
Washington, D.C. 20013

Key Terms

Aerobic exercise

Anorexia nervosa

Binge eating

Bulimia nervosa

Duration

Frequency

Glucostatic theory

Health belief model

Intensity

Lifestyle

Morbid obesity

Obesity

Osteoporosis

Primary prevention

Reasoned action theory

Restrained eating theory

Secondary prevention

Self-efficacy theory

Set-point theory

Tertiary prevention

Discussion Questions

1. Describe the three stages of prevention and give your own examples of each.
2. In general terms, what is wrong with the average American diet?
3. Briefly summarize the current status of our understanding of weight control.
4. Why do diets usually fail?
5. How is obesity technically defined, what causes it, and what impact does it have on health?
6. What are the main characteristics of behavioral modification programs for weight loss and how successful have they been?
7. How have behavioral modification programs been modified in recent years to make them more effective?
8. Explain the nature of anorexia and bulimia and describe their current treatment.
9. What are the physical and mental benefits we gain from exercise?
10. How much exercise is enough?
11. Briefly describe self-efficacy theory, health belief model, and reasoned action theory. Think of a health-related behavior you would like to develop and predict your chances of success using each theory.

Chapter 9

Lifestyles II: The Invisible Drugs

Drug Addiction
- Physical Dependency and Tolerance
- Set and Settings
- Effects of Psychoactive Drugs

Nicotine
- The Effects of Smoking Tobacco
- Passive Smoking
- Why Smoking Is Hard to Quit
- How Smokers Become Ex-Smokers
- Preventing Cigarette Smoking
- Smokeless Tobacco

Alcohol
- Who Uses Alcohol
- Alcohol Dependence and Abuse
- What Causes Alcohol Dependence and Abuse
- The Biopsychosocial Effects of Alcohol
- Treatment of Alcohol Dependence and Abuse
- Prevention of Alcohol Dependence and Abuse

Conclusions

Summary

*J*ack was a respected business executive with a well-hidden drinking "problem." However, one night the police found him unconscious in his parked car. His daughter picked him up at the scene and drove him directly to a hospital. This was not Jack's first trip to the hospital under these conditions. Previously he had been admitted as a "heart patient," given tranquilizers, and was released in a few days. This time he was admitted to the Drug Rehabilitation Unit (DRU). When Jack regained consciousness, he was furious to find himself in a DRU with a "bunch of drug addicts."

It never occurred to Jack that he, too, might be an "addict." Actually, the rates of addiction and mortality associated with alcohol and tobacco are much higher than those for drugs like cocaine (USDHHS, 1988a). This is due in large part to the acceptability and availability of these invisible drugs.

We usually think of drug addicts as people who are using illegal drugs like cocaine or heroine. We have an image of street people sharing needles or of some jaded young professional "snorting" cocaine. We rarely stop to consider that we might be using addictive drugs ourselves. If you regularly use tobacco products or drink alcoholic beverages, coffee, tea, or other caffeinated beverages like Mountain Dew or Coke, you may be addicted to one of the "**invisible drugs**." These drugs are so much a part of our lifestyles that we have never thought of them as addictive psychoactive drugs, but they are nonetheless. The most commonly used invisible drugs are nicotine, alcohol, and caffeine. We are going to limit our discussion to nicotine and alcohol.

DRUG ADDICTION

Before we discuss invisible drugs, we should consider what is meant by **drug addiction**. We define drug addiction as the compulsive use of a psychoactive substance to produce pleasure or to avoid physical or emotional discomfort. According to a report of the Surgeon General (USDHHS, 1988a), the primary criteria for drug addiction are:

1. The drug controls the behavior of the user who is driven by a strong, overpowering urge to use the substance. The behavior may be described as abusive or compulsive, irresistible, or habitual.

2. The drug is a psychoactive or mind-altering substance. A psychoactive drug is one that reaches the central nervous system and modifies brain functions. These modifications may include changes in mood, feeling, thinking, perception, and behavior.

3. The drug acts as a reinforcer that strengthens the tendency for the individual to self-administer it. Addiction occurs through positive and negative reinforcement. Positive reinforcement brings pleasure, and negative reinforcement reduces distress or pain.

Physical Dependency and Tolerance

There is a general misconception that drug addiction always involves **physical dependence** and **tolerance**. Experts now seem to agree that these features do not necessarily have to be present in drug addiction (Glover et al, 1989; USDHHS, 1988a). Physical dependence is the alteration of bodily processes to the extent that continued use of the drug is necessary to prevent **withdrawal symptoms**. Withdrawal symptoms are the unpleasant effects caused by abstaining from a drug. Some common symptoms are tremors, nausea, headache, and hallucinations. However, there is great variation between specific drugs and the individuals using them. Tolerance occurs when a drug becomes less effective with repeated use. As tolerance increases, more frequent and larger doses are required to achieve the same effect.

Set and Settings

Drug addiction is a complex concept that cannot easily be diagnosed with any great precision. This is due in part to the fact that the effects of any psychoactive drug are determined by **set** and **setting**. Set refers to the individual's personality and expectations that are brought to the use of the drug. Setting is the physical and social environment in which the drug is taken. The importance of set and setting was clearly seen in studies of veterans who became addicted to heroin in Vietnam. Upon their return to the United States, 88 percent of these "addicts" were involved in just occasional use of heroin and only about 10 percent of them became readdicted (USDHHS, 1988a).

Many methodologically sound studies support the significant effects of set or expectancy (Cox & Klinger, 1988; Niaura et al., 1988). In these studies, subjects were randomly assigned to receive either an alcoholic or a nonalcoholic drink. The drinks were mixed so that it was not possible to tell by taste whether they contained alcohol. Half of the subjects in each group were told that the drink contained alcohol, and the other half were told that it did not. The belief that they were consuming alcohol resulted in stronger urges to drink and drinking rates among alcoholics. The alcohol itself had no significant effect on their urge to drink or drinking rates. The following incident gives a real life example of the findings of this study:

---

*f*our suburban housewives had gathered for one last afternoon bridge party before their children were out of school for the summer. It was a beautiful day in May, and the hostess decided to serve Bloody Marys on the patio before they began to play cards. A Bloody Mary contains several ingredients which the hostess carefully mixed in a lovely crystal pitcher. As her guests drank, they became very lighthearted and began to act somewhat silly—one might have suspected that they were "sloshed." They quickly consumed that pitcher and decided that they would postpone their bridge game for one more round of Bloody Marys. The hostess went

into the house to prepare another pitcher but returned red-faced. She had forgotten one of the ingredients in the first pitcher of Bloody Marys—the vodka! These four young women had become intoxicated because of their expectations (set) and the comfortable social environment (setting). Feeling rather foolish after their "sobering" experience, they decided to forego the "real" Bloody Marys and play bridge instead.

Effects of Psychoactive Drugs

The stimulation of various areas of the brain by psychoactive drugs acts as a powerful reinforcement for continued use of the substance. Wise (1988) contends that these areas of the brain exist to motivate us to respond to biologically significant stimuli, for example, food, fluid, and sexual partners. Unfortunately, the highly refined and concentrated drugs are more potent than the stimuli provided by nature. These drugs are so reinforcing that lab animals will starve to death rather than give up the opportunity to work for them. Wise describes the human consequences of these drugs:

> To the degree that drug reinforcers compete successfully with natural reinforcers, they constitute a serious risk to health and to social institutions as we know them. They have the potential to seduce us from what is good for us and they can do so without satisfying either a normal or an acquired physiological need. (p. 127)

We see the evidence of what humans will do for these drugs almost nightly on the evening news. Recently, a young mother in a Midwestern city tried to sell her baby to buy crack-cocaine.

NICOTINE

It may be difficult for many smokers to accept the Surgeon General's conclusion that "Cigarettes and other forms of tobacco are addicting" (USDHHS, 1988a, p. i). After all, tobacco is relatively inexpensive, legal, readily available, and, until recently, its use was perfectly acceptable. Yet, nicotine is classified as an addictive psychoactive drug. It leads to addiction in much the same way as other drugs such as cocaine and heroin. When tobacco is first used, it often produces dizziness, nausea, vomiting, headaches, and dysphoria. However, those symptoms disappear as tolerance for the toxic effects develop. The nicotine levels of smokeless tobacco users and pipe smokers who inhale are similar to those of cigarette smokers. That is particularly true of former cigarette smokers who have switched to pipes.

The Effects of Smoking Tobacco

It is estimated that cigarette smoking is responsible for more than 300,000 deaths each year in the United States. It is the chief avoidable cause of death in our society (USDHHS, 1989). Cigarette smoking, like the American diet, has been implicated in three of the four leading causes of death in the United States: cardiovascular disease, cancer, and stroke. Conclusive evidence has been provided that links the use of tobacco to an increased risk of developing cancer at a variety of sites. Cigarette smoking is the major single cause of cancer mortality in this country (USDHHS, 1982).

Coronary Heart Disease

The effects of cigarette smoking on the cardiovascular system are well known. Carbon monoxide decreases the oxygen supply to the heart, while nicotine increases the oxygen demands of the heart resulting in an oxygen imbalance. Nicotine also increases heart rate, cardiac output, and blood pressure while constricting capillary blood flow. This has an effect similar to turning on a garden hose full force and at the same time shutting off the nozzle. In addition, cigarette smokers tend to have elevated levels of LDL cholesterol and reduced levels of HDL cholesterol. (See Chapters 8 and 11 for a discussion of cholesterol.) Nicotine is also associated with arrhythmias and myocardial ischemia in susceptible people (USDHHS, 1988a). Myocardial ischemia is reduced blood flow to heart muscle.

Other Tobacco-Related Disorders

It is no small coincidence that the American Heart Association, the American Cancer Society,

and the American Lung Association are all waging a battle against cigarette smoking. In addition to coronary heart disease, cigarette smoking has been implicated in complications of hypertension, reproductive disorders, and gastrointestinal disorders (USDHHS, 1989). Cigarette smoking is the major cause of lung disease, including emphysema and chronic bronchitis (USDHHS, 1984). Cigarette smoking also affects wound healing because it reduces blood flow to the skin. Particles from cigarette smoke destroy phagoyctes, important defenders of the immune system (Jaret, 1986). Chapter 4 presents further information on the immune system.

Health Attitudes

A relationship between cigarette smoking and other lifestyle factors related to cardiovascular health has been shown (Castro, Newcomb, McCreary, & Baezconde–Garbanati, 1989). The Castro study concluded that smokers are less health conscious and that their lifestyles involve other cardiovascular risk factors in addition to smoking. There is a positive correlation between the number of cigarettes smoked, unhealthy lifestyles, and resistance to making healthy behavioral changes.

Body Weight

Although smokers may be less health conscious, weight control is one reason they often give for smoking. There is indeed evidence that a relationship exists between cigarette smoking and body weight. On average, smokers weigh about 7 pounds less than nonsmokers. Unfortunately, many people do gain weight when they quit smoking (USDHHS, 1988a). The evidence suggests that caloric intake increases and that resting metabolic rate decreases during smoking cessation. This rapid change in energy balance is quickly reversed when smoking is resumed (Perkins, Epstein, & Pastor, 1990). Nicotine gum seems to postpone this weight gain during smoking cessation, but it does not prevent it (Gross, Stitzer, & Maldonado, 1989).

Passive Smoking

Would you object if a person stopped at your table in a restaurant and spit into your plate of food? Of course you would! Yet, every day people are forced to breathe air that has been contaminated by tobacco smoke. We can choose not to eat the contaminated food, but we do not have a choice about breathing. Nonsmokers who are forced to breathe smoke-filled air are called **passive smokers**. There is growing evidence that passive smoking has serious long-term health effects. A very conservative estimate places adult mortality in the United States from passive smoking at 46,000 deaths per year (Wells, 1988).

There are two sources of tobacco smoke: **sidestream smoke** and **mainstream smoke.** Sidestream smoke comes from the burning end of the cigarette, cigar, or pipe. Cigarettes emit sidestream smoke the entire time they burn. Mainstream smoke is the smoke that is pulled through the mouthpiece into the smoker. Nonsmokers are exposed to mainstream smoke when it is exhaled by smokers. Sidestream smoke contains more noxious and irritating compounds than mainstream smoke (USDHHS, 1986a).

Ironically, low-tar and nicotine cigarettes may actually be producing more smoke than regular cigarettes. Smokers tend to puff longer and harder on these cigarettes and to smoke more of them. Passive smokers may also be exposed to more smoke in domestic settings because of the construction of air tight houses (Shepherd, 1989).

Passive smoking is the involuntary exposure of nonsmokers to the effects of tobacco smoke. Until recently, nonsmokers quietly endured smoke-filled rooms with little protest. However, many passive smokers are becoming increasingly assertive, if not aggressive, as the public becomes more aware of the dangers of second-hand smoke. Although some smokers may feel that nonsmokers are exaggerating the discomfort caused by second-hand smoke, there is strong evidence that the irritation is very real. For example, urinary analyses of nonsmoking commercial airline passengers found a relationship between eye and nasal irritation and levels of cotinine, a marker for nicotine exposure (Mattson et al., 1989).

In a background paper prepared for the Environmental Protection Agency, Glantz and Parmley (in press) concluded that passive smoking is the third leading preventable cause of death. They also estimated that environmental tobacco smoke increases risk of death from heart disease by 30 percent among nonsmokers living with smokers. It significantly reduces the exercise capabilities of healthy people as well as those with heart disease. Other researchers estimate that "approximately 17 percent of lung cancers among nonsmokers can be attributed to high levels of exposure to cigarette smoke during childhood and adolescence" (Janerich et al., 1990, p. 632).

Many other effects are associated with passive smoking: Coughing, wheezing, nausea, increased heart rate, and decreased mental performance. Passive smoking is also associated with increased respiratory infections, even after controlling for socioeconomic status (SES). It is necessary to control for SES because lower SES children are more likely to be exposed to increased urban air pollution. Asthmatic children are especially vulnerable to second-hand smoke (Shephard, 1989b).

Researchers from Great Britain and New Zealand have concluded that passive smoking is a major public health concern (Kawachi, Pearce, & Jackson, 1989; Strachan, Jarvis, & Feyerabend, 1989). Researchers from the United States have found significantly higher levels of carcinogens in the blood of nonsmokers who were heavily exposed to cigarette smoke (Maclure et al., 1989).

The pressure for a smoke-free environment is being backed by federal, state, and local laws. During the 1980s, more than 320 local communities restricted smoking in public places (USDHHS, 1988a). In 1990 federal law essentially banned all smoking on domestic flights (Dahl, 1990). Providing nonsmoking sections on aircraft has not been satisfactory because the ventilation systems distribute the smoke-filled air from the smoking zone throughout the cabin. The ultra-low air humidity, elevated levels of ozone, and the subnormal air pressure appear to worsen the effects of tobacco smoke (Ramstrom, 1985).

Among the most helpless victims of passive smoking are the unborn children of smoking expectant mothers. The fetus of a smoking expectant mother has increased risks of low birth weight, prematurity, perinatal complications, and possible retardation of the child's physical and mental development over the first ten years of its life. Although there is increasing protection for the nonsmoker from the ill effects of second-hand cigarette smoke, little has been done to protect the unborn. Many women continue to smoke during their pregnancies in spite of knowledge of possible damage to their unborn children (Shephard, 1989b).

Why Smoking Is Hard to Quit

Like most of our bad habits, cigarette smoking is a behavior that has been operantly conditioned. One way a behavior can be operantly conditioned is to have it reinforced. When a behavior is reinforced, it increases the likelihood that the behavior will be repeated. Both positive and negative reinforcements play a role in establishing smoking behavior. Positive reinforcement increases behaviors by adding something rewarding to the person's environment. Negative reinforcement increases behaviors by removing something unpleasant from the person's environment.

Many aspects of smoking reinforce the behavior. The aspects that are associated with positive reinforcement are improved concentration, memory, psychomotor performance, alertness, and pleasure enhancement. All these effects increase the likelihood that the behavior will be repeated.

When habitual smokers do not smoke, they are actually punished in the short term with withdrawal symptoms. The symptoms of nicotine withdrawal include craving, irritability, frustration, anger, anxiety, difficulty in concentrat-

ing, restlessness, decreased heart rate, and increased appetite or weight gain. (The withdrawal symptoms from smokeless tobacco are similar but not as intense.) In heavy cigarette smokers, symptoms may begin in as little as two hours (American Psychiatric Association, 1987). If smokers begin to smoke again, these aversive effects are reduced and smoking behavior is thus reinforced (Jarvik & Hatsukami, 1989).

Some withdrawal symptoms, including craving tobacco, may return a few days after an individual quits. Ex-smokers have reported that the urge to smoke occurs off and on for up to nine years after they have quit (USDHHS, 1988a). The recurrence of the urge to smoke may be explained by the phenomenon known as spontaneous recovery. **Spontaneous recovery** is defined as the reappearance of a conditioned response after it has been extinguished. Operantly conditioned responses are extinguished by withholding the reinforcement. For example, when a person has the urge to smoke but does not reinforce it by smoking, the urge will gradually be extinguished. People who are quitting some behavior should be aware that spontaneous recovery might happen, so they have a plan to cope with it. Spontaneous recovery might occur several times before a behavior is completely extinguished.

How Smokers Become Ex-Smokers

Although it may be not be easy, nearly 40 million people in the United States have quit smoking (USBC, 1989). About 90 percent of the ex-smokers report that they did it without the aid of formal treatment or smoking cessation devices (USDHHS, 1988a). At least one investigator even proposed that people who quit on their own are more successful than those who go into formal treatment programs. He conducted an informal study to support this idea (Schachter, 1982).

Schachter's findings were later challenged by a meta-analysis[1] of long-term prospective

---

[1] A meta-analysis is one in which a large number of studies done with a particular independent variable are pooled together systematically to see whether the overall data support the notion that the variable has a certain effect.

studies (Cohen et al., 1989). This overall analysis indicated that it makes *no* difference whether people choose to quit on their own or enter formal programs. Success rates between self-quitters and those attending formal programs do not differ. Obviously, these studies and the methods of smoke cessation, formal or informal, need to be scrutinized carefully. This is a very promising area of research for the health psychologist.

Nicotine Replacement Programs

One facet of the addiction to tobacco is physiological dependence on nicotine. Some treatments focus on helping people to quit smoking by minimizing the physiological withdrawal during smoking cessation. This can be done by nicotine replacement. Nicotine replacement requires a prescription from a physician and can take the form of chewing gum, nasal solution, or transdermal patch. Patient and physician alike should clearly understand that nicotine replacement only relieves nicotine withdrawal symptoms. It does nothing to reduce the patient's psychological dependency on smoking. The majority of people using nicotine gum report side effects including mouth sores, nausea, gastrointestinal distress, and headaches (Fortmann, Killen, Telch, & Newman, 1988).

A survey of internists suggests that many physicians give their patients incorrect advice on the use of nicotine gum (Cummings et al., 1988). It should *not* be prescribed to help patients "cut down" on smoking. Nicotine gum should only be used to reduce nicotine withdrawal symptoms in patients who have completely stopped smoking. Smoking and chewing nicotine gum at the same time may increase the adverse effects of nicotine. This same survey also found that one-fourth of the internists prescribed sedatives as a smoking cessation aid even though there is little evidence that sedatives are useful for that purpose (USDHHS, 1988a).

There is evidence that nicotine replacement does not improve long-term abstinence unless it is augmented by psychological interventions

(Killen, Fortmann, Newman, & Varady, 1990). Schneider et al. (1983) found very low success rates when nicotine or placebo gum was merely dispensed to subjects. The success rates were much higher in a followup study that added clinical support. The nicotine gum subjects, then, had a success rate of 30 percent compared to 20 percent for the placebo subjects. The differences between the groups were statistically significant. Clinical support involved careful monitoring of gum use, discussing problems, and developing coping skills. In addition, the experimenters provided reinforcement and encouragement.

Aversive Procedures

Aversive procedures attempt to extinguish smoking behavior by pairing it with aversive stimuli, for example, electric shock and negative images. The idea is that smokers will quit smoking because they associate it with the aversive stimulus. Rapid smoking is an aversive procedure that uses cigarette smoke as the stimulus. Smokers are "forced" to smoke continuously, inhaling every few seconds until they feel ill. Although rapid smoking appears to be relatively effective, it is only advised for healthy adults without medical conditions, such as cardiovascular disease, diabetes, pulmonary disease, and hypertension. These high-risk populations should be advised to seek alternate forms of treatment that appear to be about as effective (USDHHS, 1988a).

Cognitive-Behavioral Programs

Coping response training is a cognitive-behavioral intervention that teaches skills to cope with urges to smoke and stressors. It involves two basic components: (1) learning to recognize situations in which smoking is likely to be triggered, and (2) developing cognitive and behavioral coping responses for those high-risk situations (Leventhal, Baker, Brandon, & Fleming, 1989). An example of cognitive coping might be "thought stopping" when one is confronted with cravings. A common behavioral strategy is the use of chewing gum or cinnamon sticks. The American Cancer Society's FreshStart program furnishes rubber bands that people wear on their wrists and snap when they think about smoking. The slight pain experienced is suppose to decrease thinking about smoking. (See Chapter 5 for a more detailed account of thought stopping.)

General Education and Socialization

For many years, cigarette smoking was considered a normal part of our culture, but it is no longer a social norm in the United States (Burnham, 1989). College students were recently asked to rate the social image of a female college student after reading a brief story about her. Half the students were given a story that described the young woman as a smoker; the other half received the same story describing her as a nonsmoker. The "smoker" was rated more negatively than the "nonsmoker" on a variety of characteristics ranging from femininity to self-discipline (Cooper & Kohn, 1989). Statistics indicate that cigarette smoking is becoming a habit of the less educated. Only 16.1 percent of college graduates are still smokers; however,

32.9 percent of high school graduates smoke (USBC, 1990).

There has been both an official and public outcry as tobacco companies increasingly target lower socioeconomic groups, especially African-Americans and young, uneducated women. For example, plans to test market Uptown, a cigarette developed explicitly for African-American smokers, were canceled. The same company is also planning to introduce Dakota, a cigarette that critics claim is directed at young, blue-collar women. Company officials claim that the cigarette will appeal to both sexes, but it is meeting stiff resistance from antismoking groups, especially those from North and South Dakota. (McCarthy, 1990).

Cigarette advertisements no longer appear on television, and print ads must contain specific warnings about the health hazards of smoking. One study found that specific warnings may indeed reduce the influence of cigarette advertisement (Loken & Howard–Pitney, 1988). However, this study also found that the use of attractive, healthy models *increased* the persuasiveness of cigarette advertisements.

Tobacco company advertising is increasingly targeting African-Americans and young women of lower socioeconomic status as smoking declines among the middle and upper socioeconomic classes.

Current advertising codes are supposed to restrict advertisements that associate smoking with vigorous physical activity or sexual attractiveness (Warner, 1986). Although this sort of advertisement may not be as blatant as it once was, it still exists. For example, two cigarette advertisements in a recent issue of a weekly magazine show images of football, baseball, race cars, and bicycles. Another advertisement in the same magazine has a drawing of a woman in a black evening gown with one leg exposed to her upper thigh. It is pushing an "ultra thin cigarette that gives you more than a sleek shape." (See Box 9.1 for information about tobacco advertising.)

Preventing Cigarette Smoking

Tobacco companies spent $650 million in 1989 alone to promote cigarette advertising. Public health officials in California are fighting back with an antismoking advertisement campaign financed by a voter-initiated cigarette tax. This ambitious campaign is motivated by health concerns and economics. It is estimated that there are 30,000 smoking-related deaths among Californians each year. Kenneth Kizer, California's health director, states that "smoking costs the citizens of this state more than $7.1 billion in health care and lost productivity" (cited in Nazario, 1990, p. B1). The California campaign does not focus on the dangers of smoking. Instead, it

---

Box 9.1 Tobacco Companies Fight Back

Philip Morris publishes a magazine entitled *Philip Morris Magazine*. A 1988 issue contains a variety of articles not related to smoking. There are articles about tall ships, velcro, and pumpkins, and there are only a few cigarette advertisements. However, woven throughout the magazine are **peripheral route** messages about smoking. Peripheral route messages avoid careful or deliberate thinking about an issue. This type of communication is most effective with a weak argument. Peripheral route persuasion is the opposite of **central route** communication. Central route messages involve careful and thoughtful consideration of the issue. It is most effective when one has a strong argument. The Surgeon General's warnings on cigarette packages and advertisements are a good example of a central route message.

The peripheral route persuasions presented in *Philip Morris Magazine* are often recollections of the "good old days." One article described a sailor's fond memories of smoking on shipboard. He says, "I'm an ex-Navy man who longs for simpler times when we smoked in peace." There is another nostalgic piece about the role smoking has historically played in politics. For example, it is suggested that Gerald Ford's pipe smoking sent a message to the American public that he was a "calm and reflective" president. This same article expresses a longing for the good old days when "men were men."

In the early republic, voting—like tobacco—was a male prerogative. Tobacco was a natural concomitant of masculine political discourse in taverns and meeting halls, fostering an air of thoughtful conviviality that politicians were quick to exploit. (Ackerman, 1988, p. 19)

appeals to emotions by attacking the glamorous and refreshing images created by the tobacco company ads. For example, one ad has an African-American youth singing: "We used to pick it. Now they want us to smoke it."

Based on the **impersonal impact hypothesis**, the California approach is more effective than emphasizing the health risks of smoking (Tyler & Cook, 1984). This hypothesis states that mass media reports may have an impact on beliefs about the seriousness of a problem as it affects the larger community, but they do not influence beliefs about how a risk factor affects individuals personally. For example, media campaigns that focus on the dangers of smoking might influence smokers to believe it is a national health problem. However, smokers would not believe that smoking was a risk factor for them personally. Tyler and Cook suggest that judgments at the personal level can be affected by media reports when they are presented so that individuals can identify with the problem and see application to themselves.

General education and socialization are basic tools used in primary prevention interventions. Such interventions may motivate smokers to quit and may prevent people from ever starting. It is especially important to prevent tobacco use in young children. If children have not started smoking by the time they are 21 years old, it is unlikely they will ever start. When asked why they started to smoke, many people will say it was the "cool" thing to do at the time. If children can be convinced that smoking is not cool, a major incentive to start smoking will have been removed.

Schools are the ideal place to begin primary prevention programs. Such programs should emphasize the negative social aspects of cigarette smoking (Leventhal, Baker, Brandon, and Fleming, 1989). Some negative social factors might be bad breath, smelly clothes, and stained teeth. For example, one antismoking metaphor that creates a vivid image is: "Kissing someone who smokes is like licking a dirty ashtray." Young people are more likely to respond to that kind of message than to one focusing on health-related risks.

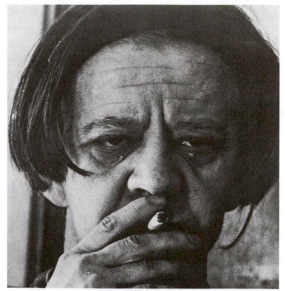

Young people are more likely to respond to smoking prevention programs that emphasize the negative social aspects of cigarette smoking rather than its health risks.

The Midwestern Prevention Project (Pentz et al., 1989) is a multicomponent community program for smoking and drug abuse prevention. The intervention is designed for young adolescents and involves the school, media, parents, community organization, and health policy programs. A primary goal of this program is to create supportive environments by encouraging nonsmoking and antidrug norms. Individuals are also provided resistance skills training. This training involves role play and other techniques to help children resist the pressure to begin smoking. Preliminary evaluations of the effectiveness of the program are encouraging.

Efforts to prevent smoking seem to be paying off. One review of the literature indicated a reduction of 10 to 25 percent in the number of new smokers (Leventhal, Baker, Brandon, &

Fleming, 1989). The prevalence of smoking among Canadian males has declined by about 30 percent. Researchers found that workplace smoking bans are associated with reduced rates of smoking (Borland, Chapman, Owen, & Hill, 1990). Leventhal et al. (1989) suggest that smoking cigarettes is now considered unhealthy, offensive, and even deviate. They predict that social pressure will discourage people from beginning the habit.

Smokeless Tobacco

If current trends continue, smoking cigarettes in public will become as unacceptable as chewing and spitting tobacco in public. Until about 100 years ago, however, the use of smokeless tobacco, such as snuff and chewing tobacco, was quite common. Its use began to decline when it was learned that "spitting" spread tuberculosis. In the interest of public health, laws were enacted to prevent public spitting (USDHHS, 1986a). Ashtrays began to replace the spittoon as smoking tobacco became more socially acceptable than chewing it. However, recent data suggest that use of smokeless tobacco is growing faster than any other form of use (Cullen, 1989).

Forms and Types of Smokeless Tobacco

Smokeless tobacco is commonly referred to as chewing tobacco; however, there are two forms and several types of smokeless tobacco. The use of these products is generally considered a disgusting habit because it generates large amounts of saliva, causing users to have to spit a great deal. Many people who say they are using chewing tobacco are actually using moist snuff. Its use is increasing because it supposedly generates less saliva. However, it also has the strongest association of any tobacco use with oral cancer (USDHHS, 1986b).

Who Uses Smokeless Tobacco and Why

The use of smokeless tobacco by young men increased greatly between 1970 and 1986. Surveys from various regions indicate that the rates of use are highest among young males who reside in nonmetropolitan areas. There has been a decrease in the use of smokeless tobacco by females, but their use has always been low (USDHHS, 1988b; Williams et al., 1989). American tobacco advertisements have targeted young men with "macho" images of smokeless tobacco users such as country western stars and sports heroes (Jacobs et al., 1988; Millar, 1989).

The group at highest risk appears to be teenage males from rural areas. A survey of 1539 seventh grade students from New York State found that 43 percent of the rural males reported using smokeless tobacco (Botvin et al., 1989). Smokeless tobacco may be more acceptable in rural areas where cigarette smoking could be a fire hazard in fields, barns, and grain bins. Millar (1989) reports that the use of smokeless tobacco in Canada is more common among miners, construction workers, and others with outdoor occupations.

A survey of seventh and eighth grade students revealed that the majority of students used smokeless tobacco when they participated in sports. Many of the students reported that its use increased their sports performance ability. The results of the survey also suggested that some students used smokeless tobacco because they were trying not to smoke cigarettes (Williams et al., 1989). Cigarette smoking, alcohol, and other substance use is often correlated with the use of smokeless tobacco. Its use may be yet another youthful risk-taking behavior with long-term consequences (Boyd & Glover, 1989).

Health Effects of Smokeless Tobacco

Habitual smokeless tobacco users and cigarette smokers have similar nicotine intake and nicotine levels (USDHHS, 1986b). In addition to nicotine, smokeless tobacco contains nitrosamines (potent carcinogens) in levels 100 times higher than the regulated levels found in bacon, beer, and other foods (Boyd & Glover, 1989). A report to the Surgeon General concluded:

Oral use of smokeless tobacco represents a significant health risk. It is not a safe substitute for smoking cigarettes. It can cause cancer and a number of noncancerous oral conditions and can lead to nicotine addiction and dependence. (USDHHS, 1986b, p. vii)

It has been established that smokeless tobacco increases the risk of cancer. The evidence is strongest for the association between oral cancer and chronic use of snuff. Smokeless tobacco also contributes to the development of oral leukoplakia, a disease of the mucous membranes. It results in white, irregular, thickened patches on the oral cavity and tongue which has the potential of becoming a carcinoma (malignant cellular tumor). The tissues that come into direct, prolonged contact with the tobacco are the most frequent site of oral cancers. One fellow developed a carcinoma in his ear after placing his snuff there for years. One can only imagine his reasoning for parking his snuff there (USDHHS, 1986b).

Tucker (1989) found that regular users of smokeless tobacco were 2.5 times more likely to have elevated cholesterol levels than nonusers of tobacco. This relationship existed even when the confounding effects of age, education, physical fitness, body fat, and other tobacco use were controlled. However, it could be that those with hypercholesteremia may be more likely to use smokeless tobacco or to have a high cholesterol diet. The data do suggest the possibility that smokeless tobacco may be a risk for coronary heart disease.

Interventions

Public health officials are becoming alarmed about the growing use of smokeless tobacco among young Americans. Smokeless tobacco packages are now required to carry health warnings regarding its use. The American Cancer Society has developed a self-help cessation manual that emphasizes the use of a buddy system. Two programs have been developed to target 4-H Club members and Little League baseball players. Both groups have members who are at high risk. It has also been suggested that PTAs distribute materials to parents to alert them to the dangers of smokeless tobacco. As with smoking cessation, media campaigns that create an image of a smelly, unattractive habit will be more powerful than campaigns featuring health risks. This is particularly true of campaigns that target young people (Boyd & Glover, 1989).

ALCOHOL

Alcohol is a colorless, flammable liquid made from fermented sugars and starches. It serves many purposes and comes in many forms, from solvents to fine wines. Intoxication is caused by the effects of alcohol on the central nervous system. Depending on several factors, alcohol consumption can be mildly relaxing or fatal. Humans have a long history of using alcohol. *The Symposium*, written by Plato around 385 B.C., gives a vivid description of early Greek drinking practices and serious hangovers. The Bible also contains many references to the use of alcohol. For example, the following words of advice come from the Old Testament:

> *Drunk at the right time and in the right amount, wine makes for a glad heart and a cheerful mind. Bitterness of soul comes of wine drunk to excess out of temper or bravado.* (Eccles. 31:28–39)

Who Uses Alcohol

Generally, Americans are not heavy drinkers, and the overall rate of alcohol consumption is declining. The amount of ethanol (alcohol) consumed by each person in the United States over the age of 14 during a ten-year period is shown in Figure 9.1. Notice that there has been a steady decline since 1980 in the per capita consumption of alcohol in the United States. Americans are switching to drinks that have less alcohol content like "light" beer and wine coolers. At the same time, there has been a gradual decline in the consumption of distilled spirits. Distilled spirits, or "hard" liquor, refers to beverages like whiskey, rye, scotch, vodka, or gin. They have a higher alcohol content than wine or beer.

Alcohol consumption varies by age and sex. Young people in the 21 to 34 year age range are the heaviest drinkers. At all ages, males are more likely than females to be heavy drinkers. Only a very small fraction of the population over 65 years of age are considered heavy drinkers (American Psychiatric Association, 1987). There

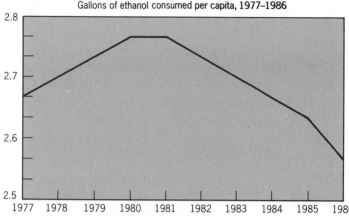

Figure 9.1 Apparent per capita alcohol consumption for beverages by number of gallons in the United States, 1977–1986. *Source:* Modified from the CDC (1990). Apparent per capita ethanol consumption—United States, 1977–1986. *Journal of the American Medical Association,* 263(3), 354–360.

are regional differences in drinking patterns as well. The area with the highest per capita ethanol consumption is our nation's capital—the District of Columbia. Utah and West Virginia have the lowest consumption rates (From the CDC, 1990).

Alcohol Dependence and Abuse

About half of the alcoholic beverages used in the United States is consumed by just 10 percent of those who drink (From the CDC, 1990). The American Psychiatric Association (1987) estimates that about 13 percent of the adult population has suffered from **alcohol dependence** or **alcohol abuse** at some time in their lives. Based on DSM–III–R, alcohol dependence may be defined as the impaired control of alcohol use that continues over a period of time in spite of its adverse consequences. Varying levels of severity are listed for alcohol dependence. The symptoms include, but are not limited to, tolerance and withdrawal. Alcohol abuse is a chronic pattern of maladaptive drinking that has never met the criteria for dependence but continues despite an awareness that it causes persistent or recurrent problems.

There may actually be two types of alco-

holism[2] (Goodwin, 1988). These are most often referred to as Type 1 and Type 2 alcoholism. Type 1 alcoholism is described as a mild form that tends to appear later in life and rarely requires treatment. It is found in both genders and appears to be related to environmental influences. Type 2 alcoholism is a severe form that is more likely to require treatment. It tends to occur at an earlier age and is usually found in males of alcoholic parents. Goodyear (1989) also states that the current evidence suggests two types of alcoholism. He suggests that biological factors do not play an important role in Type 1 but may be important in Type 2.

What Causes Alcohol Dependence and Abuse

Textbooks are expected to provide students with answers to their questions, but in many cases, and this is one of them, a clear-cut answer does

---

[2] The DSM–III–R does not define the term "alcoholism" or list it as a psychoactive substance use disorder; however, the term is frequently used throughout the manual. The absence of a scientific or professional definition of alcoholism has created serious problems for researchers and practitioners (Gordis, Tabakoff, Goldman, & Berg, 1990; Searles, 1988).

not exist. As Goodyear (1989) noted, that may be because the right questions have not yet been asked. Many factors appear to be involved in the etiology of alcoholism, and, as we mentioned above, there appear to be two types of alcoholism. Yet, the narrow framework of the dominant biomedical model forces an "either/or" kind of question: Is alcoholism a disease (inherited trait) or a learned behavior? The biopsychosocial model is leading us to a more realistic question: What are the relevant biological, psychological, and social factors involved in alcoholism and how do they interact?

Biological Factors

Donald Goodwin and colleagues conducted a well-known series of studies in the 1970s which are often referred to as the Danish adoption studies. Goodwin (1988) has summarized these and other adoption and twin studies that suggest a genetic transmission of alcoholism from alcoholic parents to their sons but not to their daughters. The adoption studies have found that adopted sons of alcoholics are at higher risk for alcoholism than other adoptees. They also found no significant differences between the adopted sons of alcoholics and those who had been raised by their alcoholic parents, indicating that environmental influences were not critical.

Some, but not all, twin studies have found the concordance rate for alcoholism higher for identical twins than for fraternal twins. A higher concordance for identical twins suggests genetic transmission because of their shared genetic makeup. (See Box 9.2 for the status of genetic research.) Concordance rates describe the percentage of twin pairs in which both twins exhibit the same trait. It is clear from Goodwin's reviews of the twin studies that the results have not been consistent. Searles (1988) has also noted the inconsistencies across the twin studies.

Questions have also arisen about the methodology of the adoption studies. Several researchers have noted that the vague criteria for diagnosing alcoholism create problems with all genetic studies (Gordis, Tabakoff, Goldman, &

Berg, 1990; Searles, 1988). For example, Searles has suggested that the genetic effects disappear in the first Danish study when the categories of "problem drinker" and "alcoholic" are combined (Goodwin et al., 1973).

The study of adopted sons of alcoholics and their nonadopted brothers had a combined total of only 50 subjects for both groups (Goodwin et al., 1974). The authors concluded that environment had little effect on alcoholism based on the acceptance of the null hypothesis. (There were no differences between groups.) You will recall from Chapter 3 that this is a risky practice, especially with a small sample.

Researchers have identified some biological factors that might account for the genetic transmission of alcoholism. There is some evidence that alcoholics may inherit a high tolerance for alcohol. Because they do not feel intoxicated, there is nothing to signal them to stop drinking. This high tolerance was identified in young males with a family history of alcoholism before they developed drinking problems (Schuckit, 1985). Several researchers have also reported that alcoholics and their sons have lower than normal levels of alpha brain wave activity. Alpha activity increases in these groups after they consume alcohol (Peniston & Kulkosky, 1989).

Psychosocial Factors

A number of studies involving different populations have found a relationship between drinking, high self-consciousness, and negative life experiences (Pervin, 1989). For example, researchers checked the relapse rates of participants three months after an alcohol treatment program (Hull, Young, & Jouriles, 1986). They found the subjects with the highest relapse rates had experienced stressful life events and were highly self-aware. The findings of these studies suggest that some people may drink to lower their awareness of negative or painful experiences.

Regardless of the biological factors involved in alcoholism, we know that drinking alcoholic beverages involves learning. Alcohol provides both positive and negative reinforcements for its

Box 9.2 The Gene for Alcoholism: Looking Beyond the Headlines

Blum and his colleagues (1990) made headlines when they reported a strong association between a gene of the dopamine D_2 receptor and alcoholism. Dopamine is a neurotransmitter that has been strongly linked with the rewarding effects of cocaine and, to a lesser degree, alcohol. The brain tissue was obtained from the cadavers of 35 alcoholics and 35 non-alcoholics. The diagnoses of alcoholism included alcohol dependence and abuse and were based on records and interviews. The A1 allele was present in 69 percent of the alcoholics and 20 percent of the nonalcoholics.

The news media announced that finally research had "proved" that alcoholism was genetically transmitted and therefore a disease. One resident television network physician flatly stated it was a "done deal." This is not what the researchers had concluded at all. Unfortunately, when the media report research findings, they often misrepresent them. The authors of the study urged that their findings be interpreted with caution. They noted that there had been many difficulties in using molecular genetic techniques to discover the genetic basis of behavioral disorders. They clearly stated the need for replication in other populations, and they called for more research on living alcoholics and their relatives.

The newswriters apparently did not read the editorial (Gordis, Tabakoff, Goldman, & Berg, 1990) that was published in the same issue of the journal with the Blum et al. article. The editorial noted that there are apparently multiple forms of alcoholism. Thus, it is unlikely that one kind of gene actually determines alcoholism as it does in disorders like muscular dystrophy. The authors of the editorial also expressed concern about the methodology of the study. The primary problems with the study seemed to be with the lack of precision in identifying alcoholics and nonalcoholics. This is a chronic problem in genetic studies. The editorial also cited the problems that even well-executed studies in behavioral genetics have encountered. The authors concluded with the following challenge to researchers:

Genetics accounts for only part of the vulnerability to alcoholism. Understanding how genes and environment interact to produce alcoholism in any individual is the larger challenge to both genetic and psychosocial research. (p. 2095)

---

use. For example, the increased alpha wave activity that some alcoholics and their sons experience after consuming alcohol may act as a positive reinforcement for further drinking (Niaura et al., 1988). The reduction of self-consciousness acts as a negative reinforcement for continued drinking because it removes something unpleasant. Alcohol can also become a conditioned stimulus. Many people associate alcohol with the positive feelings that go along with celebration, social occasions, or intimate moments. Those positive feelings then become an additional reinforcement for drinking through a combination of classical and operant conditioning.

Social learning also plays an important role in the development of our drinking habits. Many people begin to drink because of normative social (peer) pressure. They want to be liked and accepted by the group so they conform to the norms of that group. If drinking alcohol is one of those norms and group membership is important, they will drink alcohol too. People may also drink because the behavior is modeled for them by their peers, family, and the media. Weil (1983) has noted that alcohol abuse is uncommon in cultures that do not condone drunkenness and have traditions surrounding its use. Sports heroes and beautiful people drinking in advertisements may serve as role models for many Americans.

The social learning model suggests that alcoholics experience a decrease in self-efficacy which contributes to the likelihood of relapse in high risk situations. Self-efficacy is the belief we have that our efforts will be successful (Bandura, 1977). High risk situations occur when alcoholics are exposed to drinking cues for which they lack effective, adaptive coping responses. A lapse, or slip, is likely when the expectation that the individual cannot resist the drink interacts with the expectation that alcohol will result in positive outcomes, for example, improved mood and relieved withdrawal symptoms. After the lapse, a conflict is experienced between the drinking behavior and the person's self-perception as a nondrinker. Conflict results in an uncomfortable state which the person is motivated to reduce. That may lead to drinking more, or changing the self-perception from nondrinker to drinker (Niaura et al., 1988).

Conclusions

We began this discussion by stating that clear-cut answers to the etiology of alcoholism had not yet been found. It is unlikely that the answers will be found until we begin to ask the right questions. The narrow framework of the biomedical model is not adequate to formulate those questions. There are encouraging signs, however, that there is a growing recognition that alcoholism is best understood from the biopsychosocial model. For example, although Wallace (1989) views alcoholism as a disease, he has repeatedly urged the acceptance of a biopsychological model to account for the obvious heterogeneous nature of alcoholism.

The Biopsychosocial Effects of Alcohol

Brody (1982) aptly describes alcohol as presenting a Jekyll–Hyde personality. For example, alcohol has varied effects on sexual performance. As Shakespeare said "It provokes the desire, but it takes away the performance." Alcohol must have been one of the things Aristotle was referring to when he advised "Moderation in all things." Moderate use of alcohol is identified as one of the seven health practices associated with increased longevity in the well-known Alameda County study (Belloc & Breslow, 1972).

Heavy drinking can seriously damage the heart, but moderate use may protect the heart through increased levels of high-density lipoproteins (Mooney, 1982). Physicians are understandably reluctant to prescribe even moderate alcohol use to their patients because it can have the serious, and sometimes, deadly effects discussed below.

Central Nervous System Effects

There is no doubt that alcohol is a psychoactive drug because of the powerful effects it has on the central nervous system. The short-term effects of alcohol can range from impaired decision making to death (see Figure 9.2). Large amounts of alcohol consumed in short periods can paralyze the most primitive vital reflex centers. Alcohol at lower blood levels can impair the visual system and depress gross motor functions, which seriously affect the ability to drive (Mooney, 1982). The long-term effects of excessive alcohol use are associated with malnutrition and a variety of central nervous system disorders, including dementia, vision problems, inability to stand or walk, mental confusion, apathy, and memory problems (Charness, Simon, & Greenberg, 1989).

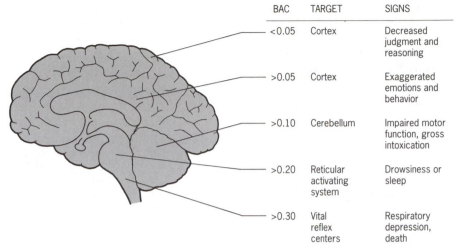

BAC	TARGET	SIGNS
<0.05	Cortex	Decreased judgment and reasoning
>0.05	Cortex	Exaggerated emotions and behavior
>0.10	Cerebellum	Impaired motor function, gross intoxication
>0.20	Reticular activating system	Drowsiness or sleep
>0.30	Vital reflex centers	Respiratory depression, death

Figure 9.2   Functional impairment at various blood alcohol concentrations (BAC). *Source:* From ''Alcohol Use,'' by A. J. Mooney III, in R. B. Taylor, J. W. Denham, and J. R. Ureda (eds.), *Health Promotion: Principles and Clinical Applications,* p. 251, copyright © 1982 by Appleton–Century–Crofts, Norwalk, CT. Reprinted by permission.

Long-Term Health Effects

People who drink heavily are at higher risk for cancers of the head and neck, large bowel, liver, and breast, all of which have been linked to excessive alcohol intake (Greenwald & Sondik, 1986). Chronic alcoholics often have difficulty walking because of damage to the skeletal muscles. Chronic alcohol use is also associated with hypertension, cardiac arrhythmias, heart failure, and cardiomyopathy which involves damage to heart muscles (Regan, 1990; Urbano–Marques et al., 1989). Alcoholic cirrhosis is another potentially fatal disease caused by fatty deposits in the liver from alcohol metabolism (Dox, Melloni, & Eisner, 1985).

Withdrawal Effects

For those who develop a physical dependency on alcohol, withdrawal from it can be tough. The symptoms of alcohol withdrawal may include nausea and vomiting, insomnia, nightmares, confusion, and agitation. Signs of autonomic hyperactivity may also be present, for example, rapid heart beat, extremely high fever, and profuse sweating. **Delirium tremens (DTs)** may also accompany withdrawal. DTs are marked by sweating, tremor, anxiety, and visual and auditory hallucinations. They often begin within four days after withdrawal and persist for one to three days (American Psychiatric Association, 1987).

Fetal Alcohol Syndrome

Fetal alcohol syndrome is a collection of symptoms found in about 6 percent of the offspring of alcoholic mothers. The symptoms include prenatal and postnatal growth retardation, a small head, an abnormally shaped face, and a variety of neurologic abnormalities. The full fetal alcohol syndrome is seen only with heavy alcohol abuse throughout pregnancy. Lesser amounts of alcohol during pregnancy are associated with a group of less severe abnormalities called fetal alcohol effects. It has been suggested that prenatal exposure to alcohol is the leading cause of mental retardation in the United States. More than three drinks a day triples the risk of having a child with a subnormal intelligence (Charness, Simon, & Greenberg, 1989).

The Cost to Society

When we consider the impact of alcohol on the central nervous system, it is not surprising that alcohol is associated with a large number of problems that affect society. One of the most deadly problems is drunk driving. It is estimated that 50 percent of fatal road accidents and 25 to 30 percent of injury road accidents involve alcohol (Donelson, 1988). Alcohol has also been implicated in a number of other fatal accidents, including drownings, fires, falls, and industrial accidents. Alcohol is frequently involved in cases of family violence and other crimes (Mooney, 1982). A large body of statistics shows that alcohol is associated with various crimes somewhere between 20 percent and 80 percent (Critchlow, 1986). The economic costs of alcoholism are also significant. The cost of lost productivity and health expenses related to alcoholism in the United States is estimated to be $117 billion annually (Charness, Simon, & Greenberg 1989).

Treatment of Alcohol Dependence and Abuse

The complex nature of alcoholism has led to the development of a wide variety of treatment programs that often take an eclectic approach. Programs tend to offer a variety of treatment methods including individual counseling, medical care, group therapy, relaxation training, and stress management (Chapman & Huygens, 1988; Wallace, 1989). Miller and Hester (1986a) found that controlled-outcome studies suggest that some methods are more effective than others. The effective methods included aversion therapies, self-control training, community reinforcement, family therapy, social skills training, and stress management. Peele (1988) notes that most of the supported methods focused on the alcoholic's dealings with his or her environment.

A Transtheoretical Model

Prochaska and DiClemente (1986) have developed a comprehensive model of change to synthesize the many diverse treatments. They have identified a cyclical pattern of four stages of change that people experience as they overcome an addictive behavior (see Figure 9.3). The four stages are contemplation, action, mainte-

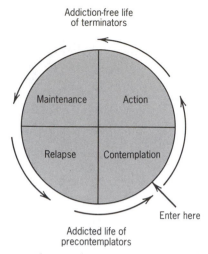

Figure 9.3 The revolving-door model of the transtheoretical model of the stages of changes. *Source:* From "Toward a Comprehensive Model of Change" by J. Prochaska & C. DiClemente, in W. Miller & N. Heather (eds.), *Treating Addictive Behaviors: Process of Change,* p. 6, Copyright © 1986 by Plenum Press, New York. Reprinted by permission.

nance, and relapse. Ideally, we would enter the contemplation stage and move through action and maintenance to live free of temptation happily ever after. However, most people relapse and try again several times before they exit the cycle. And, of course, some people get stuck in a particular stage and never become free from their addictive behaviors.

This model should be very useful in organizing the various methods into successful treatment programs. For example, education and feedback techniques might be used to increase client self-awareness during the contemplation stage. Methods to help clients develop their self-efficacy are important during the action stage. During maintenance, clients need to review the coping skills they have developed from the previous stages. Prochaska and DiClemente (1986) found that measures of self-efficacy increased with movement through the stages to maintenance and stabilized at about 18 months. The model has been applied to a variety of behaviors, including alcohol abuse, cigarette smoking, weight control, exercise, and AIDS (Rossi, Rossi, & Prochaska, 1990).

Inpatient versus Outpatient Treatment

Unfortunately, careful organization and carefully evaluated methods are not the hallmark of many treatment programs being offered today. Indeed, these programs have become the target of critics who charge that the providers benefit from their programs more than the patients (Goodwin, 1988; Peele, 1988). Alcoholism treatment programs are placing an additional drain on our overburdened health care resources. Furthermore, there is substantial evidence that expensive inpatient programs are no more effective than less expensive approaches.

Miller and Hester (1986) reviewed 26 controlled comparisons that consistently showed no particular advantage for inpatient programs over outpatient programs. Nor were there outcome differences based on length or cost of the programs. Researchers have also compared the effectiveness, cost, and safety of inpatient versus outpatient detoxification programs and have found no significant differences except that inpatient costs were much greater (Hayashida et al., 1989).

Alcoholics Anonymous

Alcoholics Anonymous (AA) is the most well-known treatment for alcoholism. It was founded in 1935 by two alcoholics and has become an international organization with thousands of members. AA members are encouraged to follow the "Twelve Steps" to cope with their alcoholism and their lives generally. The first step requires them to admit that they are "powerless over alcohol." This is the basis for two of AA's basic beliefs: (1) alcoholics are always alcoholics even if they never drink again, and (2) total abstinence is necessary because they are only one drink away from being where they were. AA is not a religion, but members are encouraged to recognize a "power Greater than themselves" that can restore them to sanity (Rudy, 1986).

Meetings are the backbone of the AA treatment program. The format for Speaker meetings involves members sharing their drinking experiences, the reasons why they sought help at AA, and the benefits of sobriety. Overcoming denial of being an alcoholic is critical to recovery, so testimonials begin with this admission: "My name is _____, and I am an alcoholic." Discussion meetings are based on one of the Twelve Steps or may focus on other topics or a problem that may be bothering a particular member.

Newcomers are encouraged to attend meetings often. Many members attend at least one meeting a day. Most AA members have sponsors who guide them through the program. The stated purpose of AA members is to stay sober and help other alcoholics achieve sobriety. To accomplish these objectives, many members believe that a total commitment to the organization is required. This commitment is sometimes described as a "total way of life" (Rudy, 1986).

AA has greatly influenced the treatment of alcoholism. Many treatment programs offer AA meetings to their patients. Many other group programs are based on the Twelve Steps, for example, Overeaters Anonymous and Narcotics Anonymous. How effective is this approach to treating alcoholism? Evaluation studies of the overall program have not been possible because the organization is committed to anonymity and it does not keep systematic records. The few controlled studies that have been conducted indicate that AA is somewhat less effective than other treatments (Peele, 1989). However, these studies involved subjects who had been referred by a court and were randomly assigned. Therefore, they are not typical of the alcoholic who voluntarily joins AA. Vaillant (1983) found that the AA membership consisted of a high number of dropouts and a hard core number of long-term abstainers.

Prevention of Alcohol Dependence and Abuse

The Prohibition Act of 1920 was the ultimate alcohol prevention program. According to Peele (1989), prohibiting the legal sale of liquor actually increased drinking among the middle class. During Prohibition distilled spirits were easier to obtain than beer and wine. In addition, the "flapper" era of the 1920s made drinking more acceptable than it had previously been. Prohibition may have failed because it did not really change public attitudes toward drinking.

Mass Media Interventions

More recently, prevention programs have been implemented through mass media campaigns and community organizations. As might be predicted by the impersonal impact hypothesis, these programs have increased public awareness but have shown no evidence of attitudinal or behavioral changes (Barber, Bradshaw, & Walsh, 1989). However, Barber and his colleagues found that television advertisements designed to moderate drinking were effective when preceded by a letter announcing the campaign. Heather (1986) has developed a self-help manual based on these principles that appears to be effective for low-dependence problem drinkers with a controlled drinking goal.

Public Health Prevention Model

Nathan (1985) advocates the Public Health Prevention Model (PHPM) because it recognizes the importance of a multifaceted attack on the complex problem of alcoholism. The PHPM extends prevention efforts to the host (population or group), agent (alcohol), and environment. Prevention programs within this model target specific populations, such as women and young people. Alcoholism is found less often in women, but women appear to suffer more serious consequences from its use.

Such prevention programs also attack the agent itself, in this case alcohol. There is modest evidence that increasing the legal drinking age and the price of liquor will reduce alcohol consumption and its consequences. Prevention programs that target the environment have focused on schools and, lately, the workplace. Primary prevention in the workplace has not been given a high priority. Secondary and tertiary preventions are seen in the growth of Employee Assistance Programs.

Inside are 48 little reasons not to drink and drive.

Help stop drunk driving. Support Mothers Against Drunk Driving.

The Mothers Against Drunk Driving (MADD) program is a public campaign designed to decrease the number of automobile accidents caused by people driving while intoxicated.

Conclusions

The recognition that lifestyle is an important factor in health requires a new approach to health care. Interventions that have focused solely on changing the individual have not been very successful. The rate of relapse is high in these programs, and they do little to prevent new people from beginning high risk behaviors (Brownell, Marlatt, Lichtenstein, & Wilson, 1986). Interventions that consider individuals in their environments are needed. Our lives take place in social and physical contexts that greatly influence our behaviors (Syme, 1989). For example, Brown (1988) offers the following description of the family environment of a recovering alcoholic: "Everybody in my family drank. That's who we were! . . . Uncles, aunts, everybody had such a good time drinking together" (p. 38). We can imagine that it would be hard to abstain from alcohol in that family environment.

Jeffery (1989) suggests that we need to develop individual and environmental interventions that provide mutual support for one another. Individual strategies tend to emphasize education. Environmental action involves economic incentives and sanctions, passive protection from environmental hazards, and control of promotional practices. For example, education about the health risks of tobacco is more convincing when tobacco advertising is limited and public smoking is regulated. Credit for the decline in alcohol-related diseases in Great Britain is generally given to the gradual increases in excise taxes. Individual change is hard to maintain unless the environmental factors contributing to the behavior are also modified. There is encouraging evidence that some of these environmental changes are now taking place and their effects are being seen. Remember the nearly 40 million people who have quit smoking and the steady decline in alcohol consumption in the United States.

Summary

1. Invisible drugs are substances like alcohol and nicotine that are so much a part of our lifestyles that we do not realize they are powerful psychoactive drugs. Drug addiction is the compulsive use of a psychoactive substance to produce pleasure or to avoid physical or emotional discomfort. It does not always involve physical dependence and tolerance. The effects of any psychoactive drug are determined in part by the user's expectations and the setting in which the drug is used.

2. Psychoactive drugs stimulate areas of the brain that motivate us to respond to biological stimuli that are necessary for survival, for example, food and sexual partners. Drugs are more potent than the stimuli provided by nature and are so reinforcing that users will ignore natural stimuli to obtain the artificial stimuli.

3. Nicotine is an addictive psychoactive drug. Cigarette smoking is implicated in cardiovascular disease, cancer, reproductive disorders, gastrointestinal disorders, lung disease, and stroke. Particles from cigarette smoke destroy phagocytes, a type of immune system cell. It is estimated that cigarette smoking is responsible for over 300,000 deaths a year.

4. Cigarette smokers tend to weigh less than nonsmokers, and many people do gain weight when they quit. Calorie intake tends to increase, and resting metabolic rate decreases during smoking cessation.

5. Sidestream smoke from the burning end of the cigarette contains more noxious and irritating compounds than mainstream smoke. Passive smoking is the involuntary exposure of nonsmokers to the effects of tobacco smoke. Passive smoking is the third leading preventable cause of death. It is implicated in cancer, and heart and lung disease. It is estimated that 46,000 deaths per year can be attributed to passive smoking. Passive smoking is especially harmful to the unborn children of smoking expectant mothers.

6. It is difficult to quit smoking because of the addictive qualities of nicotine and the presence of unpleasant withdrawal symptoms, which include craving, difficulty in concentrating, and increased weight gain.

7. Almost 40 million Americans have quit smoking and about 90 percent of them have quit on their own. Nicotine replacement programs provide relief from nico-

tine withdrawal symptoms, but they do nothing to reduce the psychological dependency. Nicotine replacement does not appear to improve long-term abstinence unless it is supported by psychological interventions.

8. Aversive procedures attempt to extinguish smoking by pairing it with a noxious stimulus. Cognitive-behavioral programs train participants to recognize high risk situations and develop coping responses for them. There has been an intense effort to discourage cigarette smoking through public education and changing cultural norms. Primary prevention programs are now being offered in schools. Emphasis is being placed on the negative social factors of smoking. These programs are beginning to see some success.

9. The use of smokeless tobacco by young men has greatly increased during the past several years. The highest risk group is teenage males from rural areas. Oral use of smokeless tobacco is implicated in oral cancer and can lead to nicotine addiction. There is also some evidence that it is a risk factor for coronary heart disease. Prevention programs are now being targeted at high risk groups like 4-H club members and Little League baseball players.

10. Generally, Americans are not heavy drinkers, and the overall rate of consumption is declining. It is estimated that about 13 percent of the adult population has experienced alcohol dependence or abuse at some time.

11. The causes of alcoholism have not yet been clearly identified. There is some thought that there are two types: Type 1 is a mild form that appears to be related to environmental factors; Type 2 is more severe, and biological factors may be more important in this form. Adoption and twin studies suggest that the genetic transmission of alcoholism is from alcoholic parents to sons rather than daughters. However, the methodological problems associated with these studies plague all behavioral genetic investigations. Psychosocial factors that influence alcoholism focus on operant and classical conditioning and social learning.

12. There may be some benefits from moderate alcohol consumption, but excessive consumption is implicated in heart disease, central nervous system disorders, musculoskeletal disorders, and cancers. Withdrawal symptoms can be severe for those who develop a physical dependency on alcohol. Alcohol consumption during pregnancy can result in fetal abnormalities ranging from mild to severe. Alcohol is associated with car accidents, drownings, fires, industrial accidents, family violence, and crime.

13. A wide variety of programs are available to treat alcoholism. Some of the more effective methods include community reinforcement, social skills training, and family therapy. A comprehensive model identifies a cyclical pattern of four stages of change that people experience as they overcome addictive behaviors. Appropriate interventions are targeted for the various stages. Evaluation research suggests that there is no particular advantage for inpatient programs over outpatient programs.

14. Alcoholics Anonymous (AA) is the most well-known treatment for alcoholism. AA advocates total abstinence based on the belief that alcoholics never overcome their addiction, no matter how long they have abstained. AA has greatly influenced alcoholism treatment, and it is often included in other kinds of programs. Evaluation of AA has not been possible because it is committed to anonymity and it does not keep systematic records.

15. Prevention of alcoholism has been implemented through mass media campaigns

and community organizations. The public health prevention model advocates a multifaceted attack on alcoholism. These programs identify and target high risk groups, encourage increasing the legal drinking age and the price of liquor, and focus on specific environments, for example, schools and work sites.

16. There is a high relapse rate in behavioral change programs that target the individual, and they do little to prevent high risk behaviors. Interventions that consider the individuals in their environment are needed. Individual change is hard to maintain unless the environmental factors contributing to the behavior are also changed.

Key Terms

Alcohol abuse

Alcohol dependence

Central route

Delirium tremens

Drug addiction

Fetal alcohol syndrome

Impersonal impact hypothesis

Invisible drugs

Mainstream smoke

Passive smokers

Passive smoking

Peripheral route

Physical dependence

Set

Setting

Sidestream smoke

Spontaneous recovery

Tolerance

Withdrawal symptoms

Discussion Questions

1. What is drug addiction, and how is it related to "set" and "setting"?

2. Is nicotine an addictive drug? Give reasons for your answer.

3. What are the health effects of smoking cigarettes?

4. What are the health effects of passive smoking?

5. Why is it hard to quit cigarette smoking?

6. How does the success of self-quitters of smoking compare to that of people who go through formal programs?

7. How should nicotine gum be used, and is it likely to help people quit smoking in the long term?

8. Describe a cognitive-behavioral approach to helping people stop smoking.

9. Briefly outline the best possible program to prevent people from starting to smoke.

10. Compare the health impact of cigarette smoking to that of smokeless tobacco.

11. Briefly describe current patterns and trends in American alcohol use.

12. Explain and critically evaluate the evidence that alcoholism is inherited.

13. What are the main health effects of moderate and heavy alcohol consumption?

14. Explain the four main stages in changing an addictive behavior.

15. Why is it difficult to evaluate the effects of Alcoholics Anonymous, and what do available studies indicate about its effectiveness?

16. Briefly discuss attempts to prevent the onset of alcoholism.

Chapter 10

Pain and Health Psychology

*E*lise was a talented dancer who had become a member of one of the world's leading ballet companies. She worked very hard and looked forward to an outstanding career. Then one day both her legs abruptly became paralyzed and completely numb. She felt terrified that she might never recover but soon convinced herself that her symptoms would go away in time, especially if she got excellent medical care. But after a lengthy series of medical tests, her doctors informed her that the condition was incurable. She had suffered permanent damage to the nervous system and would never dance or even walk again.

This was immeasurably difficult for Elise to accept, but with great courage she began to live within the boundaries of her new life. But one terrible day the feelings of numbness gave way to spasms of pain that seemed to come from her lifeless legs. She hoped and even prayed that the pain would soon go away, but instead it grew in intensity until it was unbearable. If her legs were touched even by a light breeze, she experienced an avalanche of pain that led her to cry out in anguish. Her doctors prescribed narcotics to relieve her pain, and she became addicted to the drugs. Despite very strong doses of these narcotics, her pain persisted.

Eventually, Elise's primary physician asked a neurosurgeon to remove her spinal cord below the level of its diseased parts. This procedure, it was thought, would get rid of any neural pathway the pain might use to reach the brain. Surely this terrible operation would bring her relief. Yet, after the surgery, she woke up with her pain unchanged. Clearly, any usual medical understanding of pain and its causes was useless in helping Elise.

Cases like that of Elise are not unusual. Even the mildest stimulation can, under some circumstances, set off sensations of pain—even excruciating ones. With all conceivable pathways removed, the pain may persist. In the case of **phantom limb pain,** the offending part of the body may be gone, yet it seems to produce severe pain. None of this makes much sense within the customary biomedical framework.

In a recent issue of the New York Academy of Sciences' magazine, *The Sciences*, Konner (1990) remarked that "The physician's ability to soothe pain has been the mark of the medical profession since time immemorial." Yet, pain continues to challenge the biomedical model perhaps more clearly than any other kind of disorder, and multitudes of chronic pain patients are a somewhat troublesome testimonial to the failures of that model.

A BIOMEDICAL MODEL OF PAIN

The biomedical view of pain matches traditional ideas about the way other sensory systems work. The model generally involves a three-step process. First, find out which organs receive the stimuli; next, locate the pathways that carry the information to the brain; and, finally, map the brain areas that process the incoming information. Thus, we understand sensations by identifying receptors, neural fibers and their pathways, and sensory receiving areas of the brain.

The Search for Pain Receptors

Receptors are cells that respond selectively to the appropriate stimuli. A familiar example is the retina of the eye, which reacts most easily to light. So the researcher's first task is to learn which structures detect painful stimuli.

The fact that pain sensation varies a great deal in different parts of the skin can help us find which structures underlie pain. You can see the variability of pain on your skin for yourself by pinching the back of your upper arm, over the triceps muscle, and comparing the result to what happens when you pinch the back of your hand. The pain is much greater over the triceps. On some spots on the skin pain is very easily and strongly produced, whereas on other spots pain response is pretty much missing.

Regional variations in sensation should make it easy to pinpoint the pain receptors. All we should have to find out is where pain occurs, does not occur, is intense, is mild, and so on. Once the skin is mapped in this way, we can remove layers of it and examine it under a microscope to look for likely candidates for the role of receptor. (Investigators have used this procedure on themselves in the name of science!) The receptors found in skin areas that produce pain, but not found in other areas, should be the pain receptors. Work done in the nineteenth century seemed to show that "free nerve endings" filled the bill, and these have usually been regarded as the mediators of pain from the skin.

Unfortunately, later work has failed to find a clear relationship between pain and these nerve endings. For example, the cornea of the eye gives sensations of touch, cold, warmth, and pain, yet it has *only* free nerve endings (Lele & Weddell, 1956). Pain receptors in parts of the body other than the skin have been no easier to pin down (Melzack & Wall, 1988). Nevertheless, physiology books still list free nerve endings as the receptors for pain. So even at this very first stage, the biomedical understanding of pain is murky.

Nerve Fibers and Pain Pathways

The second step toward a biomedical understanding of pain would be to trace pain pathways from organs to the brain. Naturally, researchers have put a lot of effort into identifying the pertinent neural fibers and tracing the pathways that carry pain signals. Knowing these pathways should give us information that will be likely to lead to pain treatment. Stopping activity in the pain pathways, either with drugs or surgically, should allow us to control pain.

The sensory system, whether it carries signals of vision, touch, or what have you, usually has both specialized receptors and specialized neural paths over which the sensations are carried. For example, the retina of the eye is specialized for the reception of visual stimuli, and the resulting inputs are carried over the optic nerve and tract. Eventually, they reach a part of the brain that is also specialized for handling visual information.

Scientists have tried to identify such pathways for pain. Commonly, the nerves that carry pain signals have to carry other types of information as well. They must also let us know when we are being touched, feeling warmth, having our limbs stretched, and so on. The sensation becomes one of pain when the stimulation is highly intense. So the same nerve that contains fibers for these other sensations must also have fibers that carry pain. This implies that there must be special fibers within the nerve that carry pain sensations.

As it happens, there are indeed distinct subcategories of nerve fiber. We distinguish between three main classes of fiber, which are labeled A-, B-, or C- fibers. In some cases these have been divided further into such categories as A-alpha and A-beta fibers. "A-alpha" indicates the largest of the fibers of class A, and as the suffixes progress through the Greek alphabet (alpha, beta, gamma, delta, and so on), they indicate smaller and smaller fibers within category A. Progression through our familiar Roman alphabet (A, B, C, etc.) indicates even larger transitions toward the small, slow, less myelinated fibers.

The distinctions in fibers are based on several factors. Size, or more specifically, diameter of the fibers is one of the factors. The extent to which they are coated by a fatty sheath of tissue known as myelin is another. Fibers coated with myelin carry faster signals to the brain. The extent to which the fibers are responsive to various drugs is also related to their categorization. C-fibers are more highly responsive to narcotics (Melzack & Wall, 1988), thereby permitting us to block the activity of the fibers that underlie the slow, anguishing pain we are most eager to control.

Studies have indicated that fibers of the category A-delta, which are small, myelinated ones, carry signals of fast, pricking pain. You may have noticed that when you hurt yourself there is a quick pain that is soon followed by a much worse experience of slow pain. The fibers that mediate the slow pain seem to be thin, unmyelinated C-fibers.

A study by Collins, Nulsen, and Shealy (1966) illustrates how we can find out such information. In their unusually direct study of human pain, they exposed nerves of human subjects and stimulated them. Because the larger fibers respond to lower intensities of stimulation, the investigators were able to vary the type of fiber stimulated simply by varying the intensity of an electrical current. When only the fibers larger than the A-delta fibers were firing, no pain sensations occurred. When the stimulus reached the threshold of the A-delta fibers, pricking pain was experienced. They then blocked the conduction of these myelinated fibers and stimulated the thin, unmyelinated C-fibers. Subjects experienced a pain so severe that they refused to have it done to them again.

Studies of this kind seem to support the common biomedical belief that the experience of pain is a simple function of the pathways stimulated. It is not a great leap to come to the conclusion that dealing with pain is a matter of dealing with activity in receptors and pathways. That has been the standard biomedical view, and we will challenge it later. First, however, let's continue to consider the evidence in its favor.

The Receiving Areas of the Brain

We also know of specific pathways that carry pain signals to the brain. For example, a pathway in the spinal cord (the **anterolateral neospinothalamic system**) produces pain in humans. It goes to one of the deeper parts of the brain known as the **thalamus**, which is a relay center for many sensory systems.

Parts of the thalamus are also known to produce pain. From the thalamus, sensory systems usually go to the grey matter that covers the brain, which is called the cortex. However, it has not been easy to find regions of the cortex that give rise to pain. That is why neurosurgeons can stimulate the cortex in humans who are under only local anaesthetic.

ACTIVITY IN PAIN PATHWAYS AND PAIN

Many sources of evidence, then, seem to support the biomedical model. If that model is correct, we should treat pain by interfering with activity in pain pathways. Drugs and surgical modification should be very successful in treating pain, and obviously, they often are. None of this information would particularly encourage us to think that psychosocial factors were relevant.

Yet the example of Elise at the beginning of this chapter gives a very different picture. Removal of the relevant neural tissue had no effect on her pain. But that was just a single case, and we would need more than a single case to get us to reject the traditional view. Indeed, more solid evidence for the influence of psychosocial factors is abundantly available.

Battle Wounds

Pain sensations often fail to correspond to activity in pain pathways. For example, Beecher (1959) found that most American soldiers wounded in a major battle of World War II entirely denied that they felt pain from their extensive wounds or they had so little that they did not want medication to relieve it. Beecher interpreted this phenomenon as being due to the fact that getting wounded permitted them to escape a major threat to their lives. Similarly, Weinstein (1968) told of his own experience of being doused in gasoline and set on fire. Surely, there was massive activity of pain pathways, and yet,

During the entire period of time, which occupied almost half a minute, I was completely aware visually that the flames were engulfing my body, but I had not the slight-

Soldiers wounded in battle often either deny or have so little pain they do not require medication.

est painful or tactile sensation. I was able to put out the flames and did not experience pain at all at the time. I walked a quarter of a mile to the hospital, and during this period I never had any suggestion of pain. Subsequently, I had rather severe pain, was given morphine, and was hospitalized for about a month. (p. 441)

Phantom Limb Pain

At the other extreme are cases in which we have severe pain when there is every reason to suppose that the pain pathways are *not* active. The case of Elise, in which the pain went on after removal of the spinal cord, is a case in point. **Phantom limb pain** gives us another example. People who have lost limbs often have severe pain in the missing limbs. Even seven years after surgery, 60 percent of people who have undergone removal of a limb have phantom pain (Krebs et al., 1984). An even larger percentage of people feel pain for a shorter time.

Often the patient has a phantom image of the limb in a very uncomfortable position. For example, after removal of an arm the person may have an image of an arm with the fingers of the hand squeezed as hard as possible into the palm of the hand. This may not sound very painful, but if you try it, you will find that it is.

Phantom limb pain is not the same as **stump pain**, in which the remaining tissue has not healed properly and neural activity produces pain. Traditional pain medicines usually control stump pain but not phantom limb pain. Furthermore, attempts to control phantom limb pain by surgical means frequently do not work. Everything from removal of the nerves to frontal lobotomy has been tried without producing the desired relief (Sternbach, 1968, p. 130).

Phantom pain is related to the psychological importance of the missing part. It is most likely to occur when the missing body part is especially important to the person's self-image. Elise's case provides a typical example. Obviously, her legs were of the utmost importance to her. Consistent with this psychological influence on phantom pain is the finding that psychotherapy often relieves the phantom pain (Sternbach, 1968).

Sherman (1989) has successfully treated phantom pain within a biopsychosocial framework. In his treatment, he takes into account a wide range of factors that influence the pain, including psychological, physiological, and environmental factors. In particular, he has found that patients with burning pain tend to have impairments of blood flow in the stump, whereas patients with cramping pain tend to have high levels of muscular tension.

Sherman has successfully treated these patients either by teaching them to increase blood flow or through muscular relaxation, depending on the symptoms, through the use of biofeedback. His method also includes stress management and relaxation training, as well as a variety of more strictly biomedical interventions where appropriate (e.g., drugs that dilate blood vessels in the stump). He has even found dietary factors to be important, since physiological malfunction of other bodily organs can show up as pain referred to the phantom limb.

Sherman's program is a very good example of a biopsychosocial approach, in which all the factors that influence symptoms are taken seriously. His approach has proven successful in both the short and the long term. Nonetheless, before we can consider his method to be fully verified, carefully controlled replications by other researchers are needed.

Acute Versus Chronic Pain

Laboratory research is usually done on **acute pain** (see Sheridan, 1971), since we can induce it easily. Researchers have their subjects do such things as plunge their feet or hands in very cold water. This approach will tell us a great deal about short-term, relatively nonthreatening pain, but it may not be generalizable to the chronic pain patient, whose situation is quite different.

Acute pain is normally experienced after such trauma as a broken arm, a sprained ankle, or a cut. It is fairly clearly related to specific tissue damage, though social psychological influences still play a role in it. The recovery period is short. **Chronic pain** is considerably different from acute pain. In the words of Fordyce and Steger (1979):

> . . . while chronic pain typically begins with an acute episode . . . professional advice and prolonged evaluation and treatment strategies have not resulted in significant reduction of pain. In fact, the pain problem can be exacerbated by multiple surgeries or extended narcotic prescriptions, as in the case of low back pain. In these cases, treatment based on a biomedical model has failed to solve the patient's problem and chronicity has begun. (p. 129)

People in acute pain are likely to be anxious, but the anxiety typically goes away once a diagnosis has been made and treatment begun. With chronic pain, the initial anxiety persists after diagnosis. Chronic pain patients are also likely to feel helpless, frustrated, and angry, as treatments fail and professionals treat them as if the pain were not "real." The patient pays the price for the limitations of the biomedical model, which is ill equipped to deal with pain that has no simple relationship to observable tissue damage. Later in this chapter we discuss a model, the "gate control theory," which is much more adequate in dealing with the complications of chronic pain.

According to some estimates, over 50 million Americans are partially or totally disabled by chronic pain at an annual projected cost of between $10 billion and $40 billion each year. These estimates include direct costs of treatment and costs of compensation payments and days out of work (Follick, Ahern, & Aberger, 1987).

Monetary costs are only part of the burden of chronic pain, of course. It has an impact on many other facets of a person's life. It is common for the patient to develop the **chronic pain syndrome,** which may manifest itself in limited ability to function, depression and other emotional distress, chemical dependency, marital and family disruption, and vocational and financial problems (Follick, Aberger, Ahern, & McCartney, 1984).

A major facet of chronic pain is that it teaches a person so affected how to be a chronic pain patient—to cope with distress with drugs, to complain and be inactive, etc. It also teaches people close to the patient a peculiar pattern of behavior that seems suitable for dealing with a chronic pain patient. The patient's entire social system tends to be distorted by the pain syndrome. Chronic pain offers many opportunities for positive reinforcement to follow pain behavior. Chronic pain behaviors are controlled by rewards from the environment and thus may or may not reflect organic pathology.

Cultural and Personal Differences in Pain Response

Major cultural and personal differences are evident in pain response. In a classic study, Hardy, Wolff, and Goodell (1952) found that pain response differed with ethnic background. People from Mediterranean backgrounds (such as Italians and Jews) reported pain in response to radiant heat levels that Northern Europeans regarded only as "warm." In a further analysis of this difference, Sternbach and Tursky (1965) found that the *sensations* of pain did not vary with ethnic background, but *perception* of them did. Perception implies interpretation of the raw sensory experience. Apparently, there are no differences in the information traveling to the brain; different ethnic groups simply interpret the information differently. Nonetheless, interpretation is of pivotal significance, and the *experience* of pain depends on it as much as on the raw sensory information.

Melzack and Wall (1988) discuss the phenomenon of **silent heart attacks** and how they reflect personal differences in pain. It is a common clinical experience for cardiologists to find that patients have had heart attacks without noticing them. Heart attacks without pain occur in as many as 25 percent of cases (Sokolow & Massie, 1989, p.229). Some people have several silent heart attacks before seeking medical treatment. This is a dangerous situation, for heart tissue is lost when heart attacks are not treated properly, and the patient may well die from abnormal electrical activity originating in the damaged tissue.

People who have silent heart attacks tend to respond less strongly to pain in general than other people do. They also respond less than most people to such stimuli as electric shock, heat, or muscle cramps (Droste, Greenlee & Roskamm, 1986). So at least part of the problem of the silent heart attack appears to be due to variations in sensitivity to pain.

Much research has been done on personality differences in relation to pain. For example, Petrie (1967) summarized a body of literature on differences in people who tend to "augment" versus those who tend to "reduce" sensations in general. **Augmenters** amplify pain (and other sensations as well), whereas **reducers** minimize it. Although we could, of course, say much more about differences in pain response, we have said enough to make the point that *psychological* variations are highly important in the experience of pain.

BROADENING OUR CONCEPT OF PAIN

The obvious inadequacy of the biomedical model to explain the experience of pain and find effective treatments for people like Elise has led to the development of theories and approaches to treatment such as those described below.

The Gate Control Theory of Pain

Melzack and Wall (1965) took a major step beyond the usual biomedical concept when they developed their **gate control theory of pain**. This theory concerned nervous system structures, but it replaced the old view that pain depended only on sensory pathways. The gate theory holds that pain pathways are given or denied access to the brain, depending on input from other senses and control messages from higher brain areas. Pain messages are denied or permitted access to the brain, and even the brain itself has considerable say in giving this access. The term "gate control" refers to this process of opening or closing the means of access ("gate") to the brain (see Figure 10.1).

According to this theory, chronic pain is due to the interaction of several systems. Pain depends on neural systems underlying (a) thought and evaluation, (b) emotions and motives, and (c) sensory activity. This model therefore makes room for social and psychological influences. Each set of influential factors (a through c) has a well-known biological basis.[1] It is a biopsychosocial model that lets us explain ordinary pain as well as many pain paradoxes.

The gate control theory acknowledges that certain fibers tend to respond specifically to the highly intense stimuli that we would relate to pain. These are the A-delta and C-fibers mentioned earlier in the context of the more traditional biomedical model. However, signals from these fibers do not necessarily register in the brain as pain. For example, activity in these small fibers may be blocked from the brain by

[1] These are, respectively, (a) dorsolateral neocortex, (b) limbic system and hypothalamus, and (c) sensory nerves.

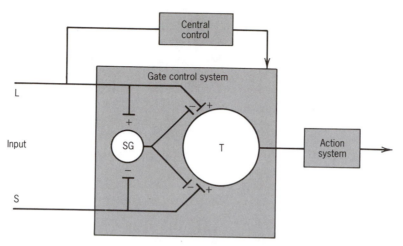

Figure 10.1   Schematic diagram of the gate control theory of pain: L, the large-diameter fibers; S, the small-diameter fibers. The fibers project to the *substantia gelatinosa* (SG) and first central transmission (T) cells. The inhibitory effect exerted by SG on the afferent fiber terminals is increased by activity in L fibers and decreased by activity in S fibers. The central control trigger is represented by a line running from the large fiber system to the central control mechanisms. These mechanisms, in turn, project back to the gate control system. The T-cells project to the action system: + , excitation; − , inhibition. *Source:* From "Pain mechanisms: A new theory," by R. Melzack and P. Wall, *Science*, Figure 4, 150, p. 975. Copyright © 1965 by American Association for the Advancement of Science, Washington, D.C. Reprinted by permission.

activity in larger diameter fibers, which tend to close the gate. In addition, signals coming down from the brain may determine whether to open or close the gate.

Thus, the gate control theory views the familiar, small diameter pain systems (A-delta and C-fibers) as underlying only the first of many stages in the formation of pain sensation. It is in fact true that activity in these sets of fibers corresponds imperfectly to felt pain. For example, the onset of their firing does not correspond well to the onset of pain (Melzack & Wall, 1988, p. 171). This makes little sense within the traditional theory, but it is quite consistent with the gate control concept.

In the second stage of developing pain experience, short neural cells echo the signals from pain-specific fibers. A brief volley of input into the spinal cord results in a relatively prolonged burst of output. Furthermore, repeated "echoing" of pain input tends to make it reverberate even longer. So there is no simple

relationship between the duration of a pain stimulus and the experience of pain.

Direct recordings from cells in the pain-processing areas of the spinal cord reveal a third stage of pain processing. Not only do the pain-specific cells and the facilitating cells influence the message going to the brain, but also some cells that are not specifically responsive to pain help determine that message. These include the cells called wide dynamic range (WDR) cells, which respond to intense stimuli (i.e., "pain"), as well as to such stimuli as light pressure on the skin.

Cells that respond more narrowly to pain and not to touch stimuli are called nociceptive specific (NS) cells. The term "nociceptive" simply means "receiving pain." Recordings also reveal another class of cells that respond exclusively to less intense stimuli of a kind that would encode touch rather than pain. So we have three classes of cells: those that respond selectively to pain stimuli (NS cells); those that respond to both touch and pain stimuli (WDR cells); and those that respond selectively to touch and not to pain stimuli.

From the point of view of the gate control theory, felt pain depends on the *balance* of activity in these systems rather than on the presence or absence of activity of the NS cells. Supporting this view is the finding that severing the pathways underlying the most pain-specific (NS) cells does not cause absence of pain, but rather produces hypersensitivity and increased pain. Apparently, severing the pathways disrupts the normal balance between the three systems, and, in particular, the WDR cells become overactive. The result is pain.

It has also been found that WDR cells can receive input from the heart and abdominal organs, as well as from the skin. These WDR cells can thus regard any painful activity affecting the heart or viscera as equivalent to certain pains from the body's surface. This finding gives us an anatomical basis for understanding referred pain, as when a person having a heart attack feels pain in the left shoulder and arm. It also suggests that stimulation to other parts of the body, such as the skin, may cause variations in pain sensation from the internal organs. This

may be relevant to some of the oriental methods of pain treatment such as acupuncture.

The nervous system's fourth stage of pain processing has to do with inhibition. Neuroscientists have known for a long time that many of the cells of the nervous system are inhibitory. What comes out of the system depends on the balance of excitatory and inhibitory neural activity. The gate control theory assumed from the beginning that inhibitory systems were involved in control of the gate, and this has been amply confirmed. It is through these inhibitory systems that low-level electrical stimulation of the nervous system can block pain.

Some of these inhibitory systems use *endogenous opioids* to inhibit pain. Based on the original finding that the nervous system has receptors specialized for sensing opiates, it was discovered that the body secretes its own version of these narcotics. This is a very lively area of research, and we now know that there is a great variety of these endogenous substances, or *endorphins*. (See Chapter 4 for a discussion of endorphins.)

It is not surprising to find that these substances play a significant role in the regulation of pain. We know, for example, that the kind of

The steady, mild stress produced by jogging causes a relative insensitivity to pain that is associated with increased levels of endorphins.

steady, mild stress produced by such activities as jogging causes a relative insensitivity to pain and that endorphins underlie that change in pain response. One place where opioids are released is in the spinal cord within a system long ago identified as important in mediating pain— the *substantia gelatinosa.*

The fifth stage has to do with control downward from the brain to the sensory input systems. Many years ago it was discovered that the brain is not merely a passive recipient of sensory input. In addition to receiving whatever input comes from the senses, it sends messages out *toward* the sensory systems, helping to determine which information gets through. This ability to regulate input to the brain is a major reason why psychological factors are important determinants of pain.

Signals from certain lower brain areas (the midbrain, hypothalamus, and medulla) influence the pain control centers of the spinal cord and thereby regulate the access of pain inputs to the brain. For example, electrical stimulation of the inner walls of the hypothalamus or midbrain in animals can produce sufficient anesthesia for surgery to be performed on them (Mayer & Liebeskind, 1974). This artificially induced anesthesia is apparently an extreme case of a phenomenon that normally happens in the brain. In fact, a steady inhibitory influence from the lower parts of the brain to the cells controls pain messages to the brain.

Lower brain areas control these inhibitory influences, but higher brain areas can modulate the activity of the lower areas. These higher and lower brain control systems that regulate sensory input have been extensively examined by neurophysiologists and are well established. Thus, the brain can turn up or turn down the pain messages. It is little wonder that psychological state influences the experience of pain.

Operant Control of Pain

The formulation of the gate control theory constituted a first major step toward understanding the role of psychological factors in the experience of pain. A second large step was taken by Fordyce (1976), who showed that, by treating pain as operant behavior, we could control it.

Fordyce views pain as a set of behaviors rather than as a subjective response. Complaining of pain and distress as well as staying in bed and not moving are examples of pain behaviors. Behaviors are under the control of their consequences, and they can be changed through operant conditioning. Thus, nonpain behaviors can be "shaped"; that is, they can be gradually built up by selective reward or "reinforcement." We can get a patient to move around more by at first rewarding small steps, and then gradually requiring more and more movement before giving the rewards. Done with sensitivity to the patient's painful experience, use of this approach can help the patient to deal adaptively with the distress of pain. It may also help the patient handle the subjective experience of pain. This approach is described in more detail in Chapter 5.

The operant analysis of pain helps us see more clearly what happens to the pain patient. For example, traditional treatment reinforces many pain behaviors. Specifically, pain behaviors are reinforced when a person gets drugs for pain when the pain occurs; when pain behaviors get attention and affection for the patient; or when they help the patient stay away from things he or she doesn't like. (Being laid up with pain may keep a person away from work or from disturbing social situations.)

Reinforcement of pain or nonpain behaviors is largely in the hands of other people, especially health care personnel and family members. Thus, social influences are powerful influences on pain. The psychologist has to teach principles of reinforcement and learning to those who care for the patient, and they must learn to apply those principles.

Does operant treatment of pain work? Several studies suggest that it does. Roberts (1981) has pointed out that, one to eight years after discharge, 75 to 80 percent of such patients are leading normal lives without pain-related medication.

Multifaceted and Multimodal Approaches to Pain Treatment

Although the work on operant control of pain was seminal, we usually treat pain with a wide range of techniques. These include operant conditioning as well as use of self-talk, imagery, self-hypnosis, and so on, to control pain. Thus, cognitive therapy has a place in the modern treatment of pain. Medication and surgery often have a role as well. Pain clinics are now widespread and tend to treat pain in many ways. The approaches often seem like a bit of a hodgepodge, the particular techniques used depending on the likes and dislikes of the particular treatment team.

On the other hand, Eimer (1988) has summarized a systematic approach to pain based on the multimodal therapy of A. Lazarus (1981). This treatment is founded on the idea that we can make changes in what Lazarus calls the **BASIC I.D.**—**B**ehavior, **A**ffect, **S**ensations, **I**magery, **C**ognitions, **I**nterpersonal factors, and **D**rugs. The idea is to have a comprehensive treatment program with interventions at all the levels relevant to the patient's pain. For details on how to approach pain from each of these levels, see the paper by Eimer (1988). We will briefly suggest some possibilities here.

The description of operant control of pain shows how we intervene at the first level, that of *behavior*. The view of pain as behavior has taught us a great deal about the nature of pain and about how to treat it. We will let the previous discussion serve to explain this facet of pain treatment.

With respect to *affect*, chronic pain patients are usually depressed and anxious. Both symptoms can be treated with cognitive therapy (e.g., changing self-talk, imagery, and direction of attention; see Chapter 5). Sacco and Beck (1985) have presented a concise summary of this approach to treating depression. Another useful way to treat depression is to increase reinforcements in the person's life. People who are depressed are usually not getting as many reinforcements as they need to maintain positive

affect. They can be taught to change this pattern (see Hoberman & Lewinsohn, 1985 or Rounsaville, Klerman, Weissman, & Chevron, 1985). Cognitive therapy is also useful in treating anxiety (Burns & Beck, 1978). **Relaxation training** (discussed in Chapter 5 and later in this chapter) is usually included when we attempt to reduce anxiety. It has long been known that anxiety aggravates the experience of pain (e.g., Melzack & Wall, 1988, p. 24). The presenting problem with pain patients is at the level of **sensation**. They feel pain. We can often control or at least lessen pain sensations through hypnosis, including self-hypnosis. Figure 10.2 summarizes the experimental work done by Hilgard and his coworkers on the hypnotic control of pain (Hilgard & Hilgard, 1975). It shows that, especially in highly hypnotizable people, the experience of pain can be reduced through hypnosis.

Cognitive therapy can also be used to control pain. Thinking of pain in a new way can change the patient's ability to cope with it. For example, we may teach the patient the **imaginative transformation** of the pain. Turk (1978) describes this method as acknowledging the pain sensations, but viewing them as something other than pain, of seeing them as trivial or unreal. For example, the patient might imagine that Novocaine has been injected into the painful area.

Turk (1978) also describes the use of **imaginative inattention,** a technique in which distracting, goal-directed imagery is used. An example of it would be to picture spending a romantic afternoon with a lover. A third method is the **imaginative transformation of context.** In this approach, the patients are asked to picture a context in which the pain would not bother them so much. For example, they picture themselves as James Bond, having been shot in the arm and driving a stick shift car while being chased by enemy agents. More detailed descriptions of these and other ways of coping with pain sensations may be found in Turk (1978) or Turk, Meichenbaum, and Genest (1983).

Treatment at the level of *imagery* and *cognition* has already been described in several of the

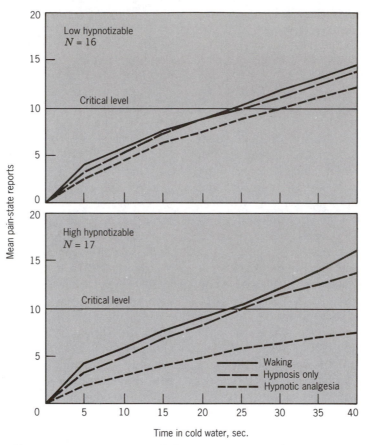

Figure 10.2   Effects of hypnotic suggestion on verbal reports of pain for low and high hypnotizable subjects. *Source*: From "Pain as a Puzzle," by E. Hilgard, *American Psychologist*, 24, Figure 7, p. 109. Copyright 1969 by the American Psychological Association, Arlington, Va. Reprinted by permission.

previous contexts. Some images and cognitions make the pain worse, and they can often be changed to make it better. For example, imagining that the pain may come from a life-threatening source or that it will ruin one's life might make things worse. Imagining oneself getting control over it may help. With respect to cognition, in a situation where we might normally say "I can't stand this!" to ourselves, we can instead say something like "This is a cue to breathe deeply and relax."

Turk (1978) reported that this kind of cognitive therapy almost doubled the length of time people could tolerate a standardized pain stimulus (ischemic pain). He went on to point out

that previous assessments of the impact of morphine on ischemic pain had revealed less effect than that produced by the cognitive therapy.

An obvious step at the *interpersonal* level is to change the tendency of people to reward the pain behaviors of these patients. In this connection, marital therapy is often useful for chronic pain patients. The patient may feel that his or her spouse does not understand or does not do enough, whereas the spouse may feel drained from giving without getting enough in return. The undercurrent of conflict and hostility along with the rewards for pain behavior can greatly exacerbate the pain. In these cases it is important to reopen the lines of communication and to get more reciprocity in the relationship (see Eimer, 1988).

With respect to *drugs*, many pain patients become very dependent on the drugs they are given to ease their pain. In time, the problem of addiction may become greater than the original pain problem. Pain patients often have to be weaned from their dependence on drugs. A common way to do that is to obtain records of the medicines and dosages the patients took while they were taking the drugs on an "as needed" basis. This applies to pain relievers, tranquilizers, and antidepressants, not to essential medications. Next, the patient gets a "pain cocktail" that contains the drugs in the same dosages he or she has been using, but the drugs are now on a *schedule*, and not given on the patient's request. The patient can refuse the cocktail, but he or she cannot get it on demand. The dosage is then lowered by 20 percent each week. This rate of decrease minimizes withdrawal symptoms.

A CASE STUDY OF PAIN TREATMENT

The following case of a boy named Keith is a real case in which health psychologists were able to help a pain patient.

Just for a second or so, imagine the worst pain you have ever had. Unless you have been severely burned, the odds are that it does not come close to what a burn patient has to go through during procedures like "debridement." In this procedure the dead tissue has to be pulled away from the living tissue where the burns took place. It is even worse than procedures like bone marrow aspirations and spinal taps, where the pain is severe but brief. The pain involved in debridement goes on and is so severe that it makes the effects of narcotics barely noticeable. Keith had to go through debridement repeatedly.

Keith was a 17-year-old who lost control of the truck he was driving and ran into an oncoming car. The truck caught fire, and Keith barely managed to dislodge himself. He suffered second and third degree burns over 25 percent of his body.

Keith was lucky to survive, but he found himself in a burn unit in great pain. Narcotics didn't seem to help much, and he screamed and flailed about during debridement and application of antibiotics, making it almost impossible to do the procedure. The nurses were unable to deal with him. A smaller child could be held down during the procedure, but Keith was too strong for that. Eventually he started resisting even painless procedures like taking his temperature.

Keith was in a precarious situation. If he did not cooperate, he would put himself at serious risk. His lower leg was so damaged that he might lose it.

Medical psychotherapists Franklin Hurt and Kenneth Tarnowski were called in to help (Hurt & Tarnowski, 1990). After consulting with everyone involved with Keith's case, including doctors, nurses, and family, the psychologists made their assessment and then asked to meet with staff to explain their recommendations. The psychologists' job was to get a consensus so that Keith, his family, and all the professionals could work as a team.

First, the psychologists observed that Keith had experienced the medical personnel only as sources of pain and that their relationship to him had to change. The doctors, nurses, and physical therapists were prompted to include him as part of the treatment team, to talk to him about what they were doing and to give him accurate and reassuring information. They were also asked to allow Keith to express his anger verbally. Earlier the nurses had rebuked him for showing his anger, but he thought that in so scolding him they were "treating him like a little kid." He was also to be allowed to assist as much as possible with his treatment, including doing as much of the debridement as he could. As the psychologists pointed out, a painful procedure doesn't hurt as much when you can control it yourself.

Second, Keith was taught a cognitive control procedure for dealing with pain. The psychologists taught him deep relaxation and breathing exercises, and how to use imagery and calming self-talk. They also trained him to distract himself during pain. He could count things in the room or focus on sensations from parts of his body that did not hurt. He was also taught to transform the pain by imagining such things as numbness of the painful part.

Keith learned to apply these methods at the different stages of pain. Just before the painful procedure, he could say, "This is going to hurt, but I know how to deal with the pain." During debridement he could say, "Relax, breath deeply, I've made it through other debridement sessions, I'll make it through this one." When he found himself wavering, he could say, "Stay focused, I can switch to another strategy, stay in control." After the procedure was over, he could say, "I made it, each time I get better at using the strategies, I feel more in control." The psychologists coached him during the procedures for several weeks.

Many other changes were made in his treatment. His schedule was kept as predictable as possible and everything was done to give him a sense of control. He was encouraged to involve himself again with his usual activities such as watching movies on a VCR. In addition, he was given counseling to deal with problems surrounding his disfigurement, his loss of function, and other consequences of the accident.

Staff and family were astonished at the change in Keith, who was now much more cooperative and less distressed. Not only did it take only about half as long for the debridement procedure, but also he could now get medically acceptable wound care. At the time Hurt and Tarnowski (1990) wrote their report, he was out of the hospital, and amputation of his limb had been avoided. Even so, they set up an outpatient followup plan for Keith inasmuch as traumatic experiences such as the one he endured can have long-term effects. Treatment does not end when the biomedical procedures are over.

HEADACHE

Headache is one of the most prevalent forms of chronic pain. There are many types of headache, but health psychologists most often deal with three: **migraine headache, tension headache,** and a mixture of the two. In one study over 90 percent of patients with headache got one of these three diagnoses (Lance, 1978). Many people have these types of headache, which respond to behavioral treatment.

Migraine Headache

Migraine headache used to be called "hemicrania" because it usually occurs on one side of the head. It starts quickly and soon builds to a peak. The pain usually throbs, and the headache typically lasts about eight hours, although sometimes they can go on for days without relief. Nausea, vomiting, or diarrhea may accompany them. Aversion to light ("photophobia") is another frequent symptom. Migraines tend to run in families, so a family history of migraine may contribute to one's diagnosis.

The major types of migraine, include classical and common migraine and **cluster headaches. Classical migraine,** unlike the common migraine, is preceded by a clear **prodrome** or set of warning signs that seem to indicate some kind of disturbance of the nervous system. The prodrome may include "scintilla," or flashing lights appearing in the visual field, and "scotoma," which is a blind spot. The patient may look at someone and fail to see that person's head, or look in the mirror and not be able to see some part of his or her own body. Common migraines are like the classical ones except that little or no prodrome precedes them.

About 10 percent of people who suffer migraines have the classical type. The experience of classical migraines differs from that of common migraines, but the distinction between them does not appear to be relevant to choice of treatment. Thus, the same treatment is likely to be used for both.

Cluster headaches are migrainous, but they

occur in bouts that last several weeks and are separated by three or more months. They are shorter than regular migraine headaches (less than two hours). They tend to be associated with tearing and redness of one eye, a drooping eyelid, or congestion or a running of the nose, all on the same side as the headache. Cluster headaches most often occur in middle-aged men.

The Pathophysiology of Migraine

Migraine has, of course, been dealt with primarily within a biomedical framework which requires three major steps in understanding and dealing with a disease: observing the symptoms; identifying the underlying physiological problem (pathophysiology); and designing a treatment to control that underlying pathology.

The traditional view of the pathophysiology of migraine is that, prior to the onset of migraine, blood vessels of the head constrict. This constriction, especially if it is in the internal carotid artery, can cause neurological symptoms. These symptoms are the source of the prodrome of classical migraine. Next, the blood vessels dilate excessively, and the stretching of their walls leads to the pulsating migraine headache itself. Because of this understanding of migraine pathophysiology, migraines are categorized as "vascular" headaches. (The word "vascular" means pertaining to the blood vessels.)

This concept of the cause of migraine is based, among other things, on observations that the drug ergotamine, which makes blood vessels constrict, tends to abort these headaches. Even more obvious evidence supporting this interpretation of the pathology is our ability to feel the dilation of the blood vessels of the head simply by putting a hand on the affected region.

This view of the basis of migraine headache contains more than a little truth. Ergotamine does indeed often stop migraines, and it is easy to see that blood vessels are distended in the head. Newer methods show that blood flow in the vessels of the head varies more in migraineurs (Morley, 1985). It has also been shown

that migraineurs recover more slowly than controls from effects of stress on blood flow to the head (Flor & Turk, 1989).

All these data support the idea that peculiarities of cranial blood flow are involved in migraines. As Flor and Turk (1989) have pointed out, however, given what we know about the complex influences on pain in general, it does not make sense to suppose that the basis of headache pain is so simple. It is now widely acknowledged that the basis of migraine must be more complex than the older notion implies and that its real source is likely to be in the nervous system instead of in the vascular system (see, e.g., Campbell, 1991).

The Biomedical Treatment of Migraine

Patients treated for migraine in a biomedical context are told to avoid situations that tend to trigger migraine and are given drugs that either prevent or abort them. For example, eating certain foods, especially chocolate, peanut butter, aged cheese, and dry red wines, tends to trigger migrainous attacks. These and other foods that are high in tyramine (as these are) should be avoided. Both biomedical and biopsychosocial approaches would agree on the importance of not eating these foods. Table 10.1 summarizes some factors that commonly trigger migraine.

Many different drugs can be used to treat

Table 10.1 Some Common Factors That Trigger Migraine

Stress
Menstruation
Oral contraceptives
Bright lights
Fatigue, lack of sleep
Hunger
Head trauma
Foods and beverages containing nitrite, glutamate, salt, and tyramine
Weather or temperature change

Source: Based on N. H. Raskin & O. Appenzeller (1980). *Headache.* Philadelphia: W. B. Saunders.

migraine. Some of them have been selected on the basis of their relationship to the presumed pathophysiology of migraine. For example, Cafergot is a mixture of caffeine and ergotamine. Together these two drugs have a strong tendency to constrict blood vessels. Cafergot is in wide use as a medication for stopping migraines once they have gotten started.

In contrast, Sansert (generic name *methylsergide*) can prevent migraines from starting, as can *propanolol* which is used mainly to control blood pressure and certain disorders of the heart and was accidentally found to prevent this type of headache. Most people have heard of this drug under its brand name of Inderal.

These drugs have substantial side effects that are frequently disturbing and, less often, may be quite serious. For example, the side effects of ergotamine include allergic reactions, nausea, vomiting, and diarrhea, pain in the chest, arms, or legs, numbness of the extremities, dizziness, confusion, drowsiness, and even headache. In unusual cases, ergotamine can even cause gangrene of the intestine (Long, 1989).

As many as 40 percent of headache patients stop having headaches merely by not taking their medication for two to three weeks (Blanchard & Andrasik, 1985). Many headache medicines, including ergotamine, cause **rebound headaches**.

Statistics on the frequency of side effects are not easy to obtain, since these figures are not commonly listed in pharmacological manuals. However, Diamond and Medina (1981), in their studies of the patient population of the Diamond Headache Clinic in Chicago have reported mild side effects such as nausea and vomiting in about 30 percent of patients and more severe side effects in about 1 in 600 patients.

Of the drugs used in treating migraine, ergotamine is by no means the only one likely to produce side effects. For example, methylsergide, commonly causes weight gain, hair loss, and muscle cramps (Diamond & Medina, 1981) and may produce scar tissue on internal organs

including the valves of the heart (Long, 1989). Further information on the side effects of medications used in treating migraine may be found in Long (1989) or the current issue of *The Physician's Desk Reference*.

Effectiveness of Biomedical Treatment
Given their side effects, a reasonable person might suppose that these drugs are at least highly effective. But we can view effectiveness from two different points of view. On the one hand we can compare the drug to a placebo—an inert substance that the observer, whether health care provider or patient, cannot, on the surface, distinguish from a true drug. Systematic studies indicate little or no superiority of these medicines over placebos (see, e.g., Friedman, 1975, p. 1714). Such psychological influences are usually treated as a mere "nuisance," but they can also be viewed as showing the powerful influence of psychological factors.

On the other hand, we can evaluate a drug by asking how many people get relief from their symptoms when they use it. This process is not as simple as it sounds. Results of such an inquiry depend on how we define "relief." For example, we might say that 50 or 75 percent fewer headaches mean the patient is "much improved." The effectiveness of our treatment will depend on whether we choose the 50 or the 75 percent figure. We might also record reported reductions in the intensity of the headache, but variations in the measure will produce variations in our outcomes here as well. Some investigators have used changes in the amounts and kinds of medications taken in order to get a measure of improvement (see Coyne, Sargent, Segerson, & Obourn, 1976). In each case, our results depend on how we define success.

Since we have no generally agreed upon criteria for successful treatment of headache, our estimates of success are crude. Diamond and Medina (1981), apparently using clinical judgments as measures, reported that methylsergide was effective in about 60 percent of patients. In their work, the effectiveness of ergotamine varied from 50 to 85 percent, depending on the route of administration of the drug (e.g., oral versus injected).

The Psychological Treatment of Migraine

A range of psychological procedures have been used in the treatment of migraine. For example, Kroger and Fezler (1976) and Brown and Fromm (1987) have described the use of hypnosis and a combination of hypnosis and behavioral therapy. Schultz and Luthe (1969) have described the application of autogenic training to migraine. However, since the ground-breaking work of Sargent, Green, and Walters (1973), most work has focused on the use of **biofeedback.** We, too, focus on this technique in this chapter.

Biofeedback-based therapy for migraine was founded on the original methods of Sargent, Green, and Walters (1973). In this method, thermal biofeedback is combined with a modified form of **autogenic training. Thermal biofeedback** simply involves attaching a device for detecting temperature, usually a thermistor, to the body and allowing the patient to see the resulting temperature. These readings are generally taken from one of the fingers or some other place on the hand. Actually, any measure of blood flow in the skin will do, but it is easy to measure from a fingertip and people usually find it fairly easy to control finger temperature.

Patients are usually taught some simple methods of increasing the temperature of the hands including the use of goal-directed imagery (Barber, Spanos, & Chaves, 1974). The kind of imagery they are asked to call up is a set of circumstances in which, if they were really present, the hands would grow warmer. Warming the hands over a campfire or placing them in warm sand on the beach with the sun beaming down on them would be good examples of such imagery. This kind of imagery encourages warming of the hands both directly and by relaxing the person. Relaxation is related to warming of the hands because it is associated with reduced activity in the sympathoadrenal system (see Chapter 4). This system causes the blood vessels of the skin to become smaller. As a result, blood flow is reduced and the hands become cool.

We usually combine-goal-directed imagery with an attitude called **passive volition**. With passive volition, we arrange circumstances so that a desired effect will occur, and then we merely allow to happen whatever happens. In contrast, with active volition we attempt to *make* psychological or physiological changes occur through efforts of will.

Besides learning passive volition and goal-directed imagery, patients are given autogenic training, a method of self-regulation in which they gently turn their attention to (or "meditate on") certain formulas or phrases that have been found to occur in successful hypnotic subjects. These include suggestions of warmth or heaviness of the hands, slowness and calmness of heartbeat and breathing, and warmth of the abdomen.

Sargent, Green, and Walters (1973) devised a series of autogenic phrases based on the formulas of autogenic training and taught the subjects to listen to them while they were in the frame of mind we have described as passive volition. These autogenic phrases are listed in Table 10.2. In current practice a range of clinical tactics are used to enhance the ability of patients to master the skill of warming the hands. (See Sheridan, 1983a, 1983b, and Shellenberger & Green 1986, for further details.)

In the earlier studies, Sargent, Green, and Walters (1973) reported about 81 percent improvement in migraines when this procedure was used. The definition of improvement ranged from "slight," which was defined as reduction in the duration, severity, and frequency of headaches (as assessed by independent observers) to "very good," which meant that the patient was able to abort an oncoming headache and almost completely eliminate the use of medication.

This germinal study stimulated the widespread clinical use of autogenic-biofeedback training for treating migraine; it also stirred a great deal of controversy over whether their findings were in fact valid. The study was not adequately controlled, but later investigations have strongly confirmed that autogenic-biofeedback training is an effective treatment.

Table 10.2 Autogenic Phrases

I feel quite quiet.
I am beginning to feel quite relaxed.
My feet feel heavy and relaxed.
My ankles, my knees, and my hips feel heavy, relaxed, and comfortable.
My abdomen and the whole central portion of my body feel relaxed and quiet.
My hands, my arms, and my shoulders feel heavy, relaxed, and comfortable.
My neck, my jaws, and my forehead feel relaxed. They feel comfortable and smooth.
My whole body feels quiet, heavy, comfortable, and relaxed.
My hands are warm.
(Continue alone for a minute.)
I am quite relaxed.
My arms and hands are heavy and warm.
I feel quite quiet.
My whole body is relaxed and my hands are warm . . . relaxed and warm.
My hands are warm.
(Continue alone for a minute.)
Warmth is flowing into my hands . . . they are warm . . . warm.
I can feel the warmth flowing down my arms into my hands.
My hands are warm . . . relaxed and warm.
My hands are warm.
(Continue alone for a minute.)
My whole body feels quiet, comfortable, and relaxed.
My mind is quiet.
I withdraw my thoughts from the surroundings, and I feel serene and still.
My thoughts are turned inward, and I am at ease.
Deep within my mind I can visualize and experience myself as relaxed, comfortable, and still.
(Continue alone for a minute.)
I am alert, but in an easy, quiet, inward-turned way.
My mind is calm and quiet.
I feel an inward quietness.
My hands are warm.
Continue alone for a minute . . .
The relaxation and reverie are now concluded, and the whole body is re-activated with a deep breath . . . and the following phrases: "I feel life and energy flowing through my legs, hips, abdomen, chest, arms and hands, neck and head. This energy makes me feel light and alive." Now stretch. The exercise is now completed.

Blanchard and Andrasik (1985) summarized their work, as well as major studies done by others, and concluded that thermal biofeedback combined with autogenic phrases is effective in the treatment of migraine. The percentages of improvement tend to be in the vicinity of 60+ where "improved" means that, according to a headache record taken four times daily, severity has been reduced by at least 50 percent. The combination of autogenic phrases and biofeedback is more effective than either alone (Blanchard & Andrasik, 1985).

Despite considerable confirmation of its effectiveness in controlling migraine, thermal biofeedback remains controversial. We do not have the space to go into all the disputes here, but we do want to mention two factors that perpetuate them. First, the large majority of research studies have not used biofeedback in clinically appropriate ways (see Shellenberger & Green, 1986). Second, we really do not understand the underlying mechanisms that produce the headache relief. Suggestion, placebo effects, changes in sympathetic activity, and the like— all are present in clinical treatment protocols. We need to extend our knowledge of the critical influences. But evidence for the effectiveness of this conglomerate treatment is quite good.

Procedures used in research on the effectiveness of biofeedback are not tailored to individuals as are clinical procedures. They also tend to be less complex. Shellenberger and Green (1986) and Sheridan (1983a, 1983b) have discussed these more complex procedures. For example, in the work of Blanchard et al. (1982a), a fixed number of sessions were used rather than training patients until they mastered control of their hand temperature. Several investigators have found that training to mastery is preferable (e.g., Libo & Arnold, 1983). Blanchard and Andrasik themselves (1985, p. 105) report findings in support of this kind of training. Thus, there is reason to suspect that the autogenic-biofeedback technique may be even more effective than research has indicated.

Tension Headache

Tension headache, which is also called muscle contraction headache, is the most prevalent kind of headache. In the United States alone, between 50 and 100 million people suffer from it. This headache is usually described as dull, bandlike, occurring on both sides of the head, and starting at the back of the head and spreading around to the forehead. Frequency and duration are quite variable, and the degree of pain is usually less than that experienced with migraine.

The Pathophysiology of Tension Headache

The tension headache is named after the presumed pathophysiology. Tension in the muscles of the neck and head have long been thought to cause these headaches. Since tense muscles tend to impede blood flow, blood supply may also be impaired. This may add to the pain.

When we use biofeedback, we get direct measurements of head and neck tension. Having taken these measures on large numbers of tension headache patients, we now know that many such patients do not have high levels of muscular tension in the neck and head regions. Rather, we have better evidence that those with tension headaches contract their head muscles when they are under stress (see Flor & Turk, 1989). We do not know whether this action causes the pain.

There is also a question of whether differences in head tension are specific to tension headache sufferers or perhaps are to be found in any headache sufferer or even any tense person. Some researchers argue that tension and migraine are not really different diseases, but are merely on a continuum from less to more severe (Bakal, 1982; Ziegler, Hassanein, & Hassanein, 1972). However, several leading investigators think that the diagnostic distinctions are useful in treating headache patients (see Blanchard & Andrasik, 1985; Sargent, 1982).

Treatment of Tension Headache

Biomedical treatment of pain is designed to relieve both tension and pain. Thus, analgesics and tranquilizers or sedatives are likely to be given. Fiorinal is a common medicine for these headaches; it contains aspirin, codeine, butalbital (a sedative), and caffeine. Interestingly, biofeedback has come to be acknowledged as a medical treatment for tension headache (Schroeder, Krupp, Tierney, & McPhee, 1989).

Budzynski, Stoyva, and Adler (1970) pioneered the development of biofeedback for tension headache. They focused on teaching patients to reduce their muscular tension through both generalized relaxation training and **electromyographic (EMG) biofeedback** from the head muscles.

The relaxation training that these researchers used in their later work was a modification of the **progressive relaxation training** of Jacobson (1929; see Chapter 5). With Jacobson's method, the patient alternately tenses and relaxes muscles in an attempt to learn how to tell the difference between them. Commonly, people will confuse other sensations, such as stretch and pressure, with tension. They have to learn what tension is and what relaxation is, and they also have to learn how to turn off tension. Tension of skeletal muscles is strictly due to commands from the brain. Since skeletal muscles detached from the input of the nervous system will relax completely, the skill to be learned is that of stopping the impulses from brain to muscles. The therapist teaches patients that relaxation is "not doing." Eventually, patients come to sense tension as a blatant signal rather than as a subtle sensation. Jacobson emphasized the importance of learning to tell what tension is and how it differs from relaxation. Accordingly, he had patients study this difference with very small groups of muscles and for long periods of time.

Budzynski et al. (1970), in common with most current teachers of relaxation, used a very abbreviated form of this method, working with larger groups of muscles and covering much of the body in a single session. This approach is probably not as conducive to Jacobson's goal of learning to discriminate tension from relaxation. It is more like "cramming" for a test, but it does seem to work, and it saves time and money.

Budzynski and his co-workers added electromyographic feedback to the relaxation training. In this way, patients got accurate information about tension in at least one part of their body as they learned to relax. The electromyographic biofeedback was obtained from the forehead. Keep in mind that progressive relaxation training entails relaxing all the muscles of the body. Yet, Budzynski's feedback procedure was limited to only a small part of the body. Budzynski maintained that forehead tension is pretty much representative of tension in other muscles. Thus, he argued that forehead EMG feedback gave a good approximation to what one might get with feedback from the entire body.

EMG biofeedback is obtained by placing electrodes in the vicinity of the muscles whose tension is to be measured. These electrodes pick up subtle electrical currents the muscles produce when they contract. To pick up these currents, the electrodes have to be accurately placed, and obstacles to the flow of current from the body must be minimized. Since the electrodes are very good conductors, the major obstacles are factors that impede conduction at the surface of the skin or in between the skin and the electrode.

Contact between the electrodes and the skin can usually be improved by cleansing the skin, sometimes rubbing off a surface layer of dead skin. A highly conductive electrode paste placed between electrode and skin also promotes conduction.

The voltages to be measured, being quite small, must be greatly amplified and then turned into a sound or visual stimulus that reflects the degree of voltage coming from muscles. This voltage, in turn, reflects the degree of tension of the muscles.

Other sources of electrical activity that could be confused with the activity of the muscles must be filtered out. This is done electronically by using filters that reject the frequencies of current other than those characteristic of muscular output. The result is that the patient receives a clear sensory signal indicating when muscles are tense. The machine should be able to detect amounts of tension the patient does not notice. Patients are taught to monitor these indications of tension and to learn how to shut off the tension.

Budzynski et al. (1970), applying a combination of relaxation training and EMG biofeedback, were able to provide relief from tension headaches for patients with a longstanding history of chronic tension headache. Subsequent work seems to have confirmed that this method relieves such headaches. Blanchard and Andrasik (1985) claim that these two methods, whether alone or in combination, provide about 60 percent improvement, whereas placebos yield about 35 percent improvement.

There has been much dispute over whether the EMG biofeedback is superior to mere relaxation training. Some studies say yes; others say no. Both classes of studies usually involve groups of subjects given relaxation training or EMG feedback training, or both. Blanchard et al. (1982a) did an interesting variant of this study in which those who failed to get over their headaches after relaxation training were given EMG feedback training. A substantial proportion of these "failed" cases succeeded when EMG feedback was introduced.

The issue of the relative advantages of EMG biofeedback over relaxation training cannot be considered settled. In fact, Sheridan (1989) has argued that such studies are simply measuring the effects of two different ways to change the body's signal/noise ratios and to make tension signals discriminable. He contends that before these issues about the usefulness of technological biofeedback (i.e., machines) can be settled, the questions will have to be formulated better.

The issue of the superiority of EMG biofeedback (or of any other form of technological feedback, for that matter) should not be confused with the question of whether the overall treatment package works. Evidence supports the view that it does. We should also keep in mind that the medications used in drug treatments have significant side effects. For example, two of the drugs in fiorinal are controlled substances with addictive potential. When such "costs" are taken into account, biofeedback compares quite favorably to traditional treatments.

We have no clear idea of how biofeedback-based treatments work their benefits. In some studies, patients taught to *raise* their muscle tension recovered from tension headaches (Blanchard & Andrasik, 1985). The pathophysiology of tension headache is still relatively unknown. However, like other forms of pain, such head pain is no doubt under the control of a range of biological, psychological, and social variables.

Holroyd and Andrasik (1982) have given a striking demonstration of the importance of psychological factors in tension headache. In their comparison of training in cognitive stress coping strategies to EMG biofeedback or a control condition, the subjects were, of course, tension headache sufferers. The patients given cognitive training learned how to talk to themselves in stress-alleviating ways, to have stress-relieving imagery, and to direct their attention to thoughts that minimized stress response. The cognitive training reduced headaches better than either biofeedback or control conditions. EMG feedback did a better job of teaching them to lower muscular tension, but that did not equate with getting rid of the headaches.

Long ago Meichenbaum (1976) argued that biofeedback sets up conditions for people to change their ways of thinking from those that tend to encourage sickness to those that discourage it. As they go through the process of learning to control their muscles, many of their attitudes shift. For example, they are likely to feel more capable of controlling their experiences. They may also pick up optimistic and health-supporting attitudes and lifestyles from their therapists. Thus, the total impact of biofeedback training may be quite complex. We need a lot more research to pinpoint the critical factors controlling tension headache. As it is now, we have an "empirical" and a fairly successful treatment method.

Mixed Headache

The mixed headache combines symptoms of migraine and tension headache. Although many patients have mixed headache, relatively little research on it has been published. It seems that these patients should be treated either as mi-

graineurs or with a combination of migraine and tension headache treatments (e.g., thermal and EMG feedback). Blanchard et al. (1982b) reported very poor results when using relaxation training alone in such patients (22 percent improvement as opposed to 54 percent when thermal biofeedback was included).

Lake and Pingel (1988) used a combination of thermal biofeedback with EMG feedback, as well as various other forms of stress management training along with relaxation training. The sample size in this study was substantial (102 patients), and it suggests that biofeedback for mixed headache is effective. It also provides some basic information on how to optimize effectiveness.

The focus of their study was on the impact of long relaxation sessions (around 20 minutes) versus brief relaxations incorporated into the patients' daily life. They compared the proportions of patients gaining over 50 percent improvement in their headaches as a function of whether they continued in the use of brief versus extended relaxation after their treatment. They found that continuing brief relaxation gave the best improvement. Sixty-nine percent of patients who continued brief relaxation fell into the "over 50 percent improved" category. Fifty three percent of patients who continued with extended relaxation fell into that category. At more than one year after treatment, patients were much more likely to continue the practice of brief relaxation.

Behavioral methods of treating headache seem to work for many patients. The side effects tend to be positive ones, since the patient learns relaxation, greater self-control, and improved stress management. Some disturbing side effects (e.g., dizziness or bad dreams; see Luthe, 1969–1972 for a detailed account) may occur, but these are usually minor and easily managed. They contrast very favorably to the side effects of medicines, and the positive outcomes of the behavioral procedures are about as well established.

In some special cases, teaching handwarming and other forms of deep relaxation to patients may pose serious risks, especially when the trainer is unsophisticated. For example, diabetics require adjustments of their insulin levels when such procedures are used, and patients on thyroid medication run the risk of destabilizing their reactions to the medication.

Conclusions

We have drawn a sharp contrast between the usual biomedical approach to pain and the biopsychosocial approach. You may wonder why we polarize this into a clearcut opposition of views. Why not just expand the biomedical approach to include the psychological and the social? This is exactly what we would advocate. However, our knowledge of the underlying physiology is so limited that attempts to reduce the psychological and the social to physiology are necessarily crude and are likely to remain so for the foreseeable future. Interventions based on crude models of complex and subtle phenomena are likely to be inadequate and to create unexpected side effects.

The traditional biomedical approach to pain can be modified to encompass psychological and social factors. Those of you who are familiar with the history of science know that old models can usually be patched up to explain new phenomena. For example, the old earth-centered "Ptolemaic" view of the universe was repeatedly modified to account for phenomena that easily fit into the newer sun-centered "Copernican" view. But the best model was the one that spontaneously matched the phenomena. It is not enough for a model to be *able* to account for phenomena; to be a really good model it must

do so in a convenient way that readily improves our ability to deal with what it explains. We would argue that the biopsychosocial model is in this sense better than the biomedical model.

With a biopsychosocial approach, we view pain as determined by many variables—biological, psychological, and social. By making changes in these variables, we change the pain. There is little point in limiting ourselves to one of these three categories of variable, namely, the biological one. If we do so, we fail to understand many cases and we become unable to handle the nuances and complex interactions of the factors that contribute to pain. As a consequence, we fail in our treatment of many cases, and we produce iatrogenic effects in many others. (An iatrogenic effect is a disturbance or side effect resulting from the treatment itself.)

Some psychological approaches, for example, those often used in the treatment of headache, have failed to fully recognize the multiple causes of pain. They could probably be improved by explicitly taking into account the range of factors that influence the pain (Sheridan, 1983a, 1983b). We have reason to suspect that some of the impact of biofeedback for headache is actually due to the use of psychosocial interventions that are not overtly stipulated. For example, people may change their sense of self-control,and this may help relieve the pain (see Meichenbaum, 1976).

The problem of pain clearly reveals the limitations of the biomedical approach in dealing with what at first seems to be a simple biological problem. It also discloses the promise of the biopsychosocial model.

Summary

1. The biomedical model of pain focuses on discovering pain receptors, pain pathways, and pain centers. Although neural structures related to pain have been identified, the experience of pain often fails to show the expected relationship to them.

2. Some important examples of this failure

of "pain structures" to relate in the expected way to pain pathways are as follows: (a) battle wounds produce less pain than comparable surgical wounds, and this difference is thought to be related to the fact that battle wounds get people out of dangerous situations, whereas surgical wounds usually occur when people are taken out of satisfying situations; (b) pain occurs even in body parts that have been surgically removed ("phantom limb pain"); (c) pain varies with the cultural differences of the sufferers; and (d) longer term "chronic" pain differs markedly from short-term "acute" pain in that the chronic pain patient and his or her family members learn behaviors that tend to perpetuate pain.

3. The gate control theory of pain provides a neurological model that accounts for many of the above-mentioned features of pain. It states that the access of pain information to the brain depends on the input from other senses and on control messages from higher brain areas. The term "gate control" refers to this process of opening or closing the means of access ("gate") to the brain.

4. Pain can usefully be seen as a form of operant behavior, that is, behavior under the control of its consequences. When we see pain this way, we attend to "pain behavior" such as complaining, being inactive, and requesting pain-relieving medications. We note and record the stimuli that precede such behavior and the reinforcing consequences that follow it. Families and health care personnel are taught to be alert to inadvertent reinforcement of pain behaviors. They are trained to attend to the patient's needs in ways that do not encourage additional pain behaviors. A very large proportion of patients treated in this way improve markedly.

5. Extending the operant approach to pain, we can include many other variables that influence the pain in a systematic approach known as multimodal therapy. Behavior, affect, sensations, imagery, cognitions, interpersonal factors, and "drugs" (actually any physiological influence) are considered in attempting to bring pain under control. The operant approach com-

monly deals with several of these factors, including behavior, interpersonal factors (i.e., handling of reinforcements), and even such elements as the timing of drug adminstration to avoid reinforcing pain. But the multimodal approach goes on to deal with affect (e.g., anxiety, depression), sensations (i.e., the subjective experience of pain), and the images and cognitions that maintain the pain or even make it worse.

6. Migraine headaches tend to occur on one side of the head, to throb, and to be accompanied by gastrointestinal problems such as nausea. They tend to run in families. Sometimes, in "classical" migraine, odd visual effects such as blind spots and flashing lights warn of the oncoming headache. These warning signs are called the prodrome. Research conducted many years ago seemed to establish that migraines were due to abnormal constrictions of the blood vessels supplying the brain (during the prodrome), followed by unusual dilation of those vessels (during the headache proper). The causes of migraine are more complex than that, but it contains an important kernel of truth.

7. At the center of biomedical treatment for migraine are a variety of medications such as ergotamine, methylsergide and propanolol. These drugs have many side effects ranging from mild to deadly, and they are only modestly effective in dealing with the headaches.

8. A variety of psychological approaches have been devised to treat migraine. Most notable is a method in which patients learn to relax and warm their hands with the aid of biofeedback and autogenic training. Autogenic training involves suggestions such as heaviness and warmth of the hands. Research indicates that the combination of thermal biofeedback and autogenic training is about as effective as the best of the medications and is largely without the negative side effects.

9. Tension headaches tend to feel like a band of constriction around the head; they are usually bilateral. They have long been viewed as stemming from muscular tension in the neck and head, but measurements do not necessarily indicate that tension headache sufferers have greater than average muscular tension. Such sufferers do tend to react to stress with above-average increases in muscular tension.

10. Biomedical treatment for tension headaches centers on pain-relieving medications ranging from aspirin to more powerful drugs such as fiorinal. Even the biomedical framework encourages patients to do something about their stressful lifestyle.

11. A combination of biofeedback and relaxation training are a prevalent behavioral approach to treating tension headache; these techniques are even recognized within the biomedical framework now. Patients are trained to relax by systematically tensing and then relaxing their muscles, and learning to induce the relaxation. In addition, signals of muscular tension, usually from the forehead, are fed back to the patients so that they can clearly tell when they are relaxing. This method seems to be successful in reducing tension headaches, although there is some dispute about whether the biofeedback really needs to be added to the relaxation training.

12. A third highly prevalent type of headache is a mixture of migraine and tension headache. The preferred psychological approach to its treatment is either to use the standard migraine treatment or to use that in combination with tension headache treatment. These methods seem fairly successful. Teaching mixed headache sufferers to use cues to do brief relaxations throughout the day is more effective than having them do longer sessions of relaxation.

13. Behavioral treatments for headache can produce serious side effects. For example, in diabetics, deep relaxation training tends to reduce the need for insulin. To ignore this effect is to set up the conditions for a reaction to excessive insulin. Similarly, some people on thyroid medications are not easily stabilized after relaxation training. Therapists should work with the patients' physicians to manage these side effects. For the most part, however, side effects are positive, with patients learning to deal better with stress and to enjoy greater relaxation.

Key Terms

Acute pain
Anterolateral neospinothalamic system
Augmenters
Autogenic training
BASIC I.D.
Biofeedback
Chronic pain
Chronic pain syndrome
Classical migraine

Cluster headaches
Common migraine
Electromyographic biofeedback
Gate control theory of pain
Imaginative inattention
Imaginative transformation
Imaginative transformation of context
Migraine headache
Passive volition

Phantom limb pain

Prodrome

Progressive relaxation training

Rebound headaches

Relaxation training

Reducers

Sensation

Silent heart attacks

Stump pain

Tension headache

Thalamus

Thermal biofeedback

Discussion Questions

1. Briefly explain the biomedical approach to pain and describe its strengths and limitations.

2. List some major pain phenomena that are not well accounted for within the biomedical model.

3. Show how the distinction between acute and chronic pain is important in evaluat-

ing biomedical versus biopsychosocial approaches to pain.

4. Explain the gate control theory of pain.

5. Show how operant conditioning is relevant to the treatment of pain.

6. Outline a multimodal approach to pain treatment.

7. What are the major types of headache, and what is the biomedical approach to their treatment?

8. What is the traditional concept of the pathophysiology of migraine and tension headache?

9. List some major drugs used in the treatment of migraine and evaluate their use.

10. Explain and evaluate the use of autogenic-biofeedback therapy in the treatment of migraine.

11. Explain and evaluate the use of biofeedback and cognitive therapy in the treatment of tension headache.

12. What is mixed headache, what psychological methods are used to treat it, and how successful have they been?

Chapter 11

Modern Epidemics: Cardiovascular Disease

O n the night of February 23, 1987, celebrity talk show host Larry King had then Surgeon General Edward Koop as a guest on his show. Koop's last words to King that night, off camera, were, "Boy, you ought to stop smoking." Later that same night, King had a heart attack. King had known for a long time he was at high risk for a heart attack. In his own words, he was ". . . a fifty-three year old, twenty pounds overweight, cholesterol-consuming, three-pack-a-day smoker whose father died of heart disease at forty-four." Furthermore, he had already been diagnosed as having coronary artery disease.

Years before, King had suffered chest pains that stopped when he quit exerting himself, a symptom typical when the arteries that nourish the heart are clogged; he was also short of breath. So he went to Georgetown University and had a complete cardiac workup, including a "treadmill test." At the end of the test, the doctor said, "Mr. King, you have a heart problem." This wasn't enough to persuade him to change his habits. It would take a full-fledged heart attack.

King received medical treatment that is pretty typical today. During the actual heart attack he was given a drug that dissolves blood clots. Narrowing of the inner opening of arteries that supply the heart muscle typically precedes a heart attack. Clots of blood tend to form in the abnormal arteries and block the already reduced passageway. By dissolving the clot, the time the heart muscle is deprived of nutrients can be greatly reduced, and the damage to the heart tissue is thereby diminished. Next, he received a **balloon angioplasty**. In this procedure, a deflated "balloon" is threaded into the narrowed opening of a coronary artery and then inflated. It forces the stiffened tissue to yield a wider opening, and, if the patient is lucky, the opening stays wide. Unfortunately, the patient is often not so lucky, and Larry King was one of those unlucky ones.

He got by for a considerable period with the relief obtained from the balloon angioplasty along with various medications designed to maximize the efficiency of his defective heart. He was also instructed to quit smoking, lose weight, exercise, and reduce his cholesterol levels—and maybe even cut down on the stressfulness of his lifestyle. He did remarkably well in adhering to these instructions, except maybe the least-emphasized one—to cut down on stress. But his condition steadily deteriorated until he couldn't even carry his own luggage at the airport. He dreaded going through **coronary bypass surgery,** but eventually he consented to it. With this procedure a leg vein or one of the arteries of the chest is "harvested," and the clogged arteries are bypassed with grafts of the harvested blood vessel.

Once the surgeons had opened his chest, it became clear that King had massive clogging of his coronary arteries. Five of the vessels feeding the heart had to be bypassed. But he came out of it feeling better than he had in years. This is a common result of coronary bypasses; people feel a lot better. They usually believe that they are "as good as new" and that their lifespan has been greatly extended. These beliefs are questionable, and we will consider the impact of coronary bypass surgery later. First, we have to discuss the significance and basis of heart and blood vessel disease in a bit more detail.

Diseases of the heart and blood vessels cripple and kill more people than do diseases of any other type. The range of these diseases is too wide for us to cover them all here. Instead, we focus on two that are massively destructive and that health psychologists have studied extensively—**essential hypertension** and **coronary heart disease.**

ARTERIOSCLEROSIS

A highly significant factor that underlies these diseases and interacts with them is hardening of the arteries or **arteriosclerosis**. With arteriosclerosis the smooth inner layer of the arteries becomes hard and irregular in shape, and the inner layer of muscle overdevelops. The hollow of the artery through which blood must pass grows small, and the arteries themselves lose their elasticity. Anything that makes it harder for blood to pass through the opening can reduce the flow of blood to tissue that requires it for survival. Clot formation, which is encouraged by the abnormalities of the hardened arteries, is especially threatening. Even a single meal high in fat can cause the blood to sludge and impair flow (Friedman & Ulmer, 1984).

Arteriosclerosis is so common in affluent Western societies that it is remarkable, upon autopsy, to find healthy arteries in an elderly man. Women are greatly protected from it until menopause, when, unfortunately, they begin to catch up. This process of catching up tends to complete itself by the time they are 70 years of age.

We know a lot about the underlying influences that produce arteriosclerosis, but no fully coherent interpretation is yet accepted. Factors that are generally recognized as important in determining the extent of our arteriosclerosis are high cholesterol levels, smoking, high blood pressure, amount of exercise, and personality or "behavioral style." Getting these factors under control can be very difficult, but doing so can even *reverse* the disease process (Ornish et al., 1990; Sheldon, 1988).

Although medications can control these influences in some cases, their side effects make them undesirable to use. They are used more or less as a last resort. Behavioral change is therefore a very important key to getting control of the risk factors.

PSYCHOLOGICAL APPROACHES TO ESSENTIAL HYPERTENSION

Hypertension is an elevation of blood pressure in the arteries. It is not the same as an increase of "tension," either of the muscular or psychological variety. It may be related to these, but it is not identical. Hypertension is a major risk factor in diseases of the heart and blood vessels, and very likely it is a contributing cause in the creation of arteriosclerosis. These cardiovascular diseases account for more than half of all deaths in the United States today.

Most industrialized countries have major problems with hypertension (Kaplan, 1986; Lenfant, 1988). In the United States it is the leading reason for physician office visits and for prescribing drugs (Kaplan, 1986). Estimates of the number of hypertensive people run close to 60 million for the United States alone.

Essential Hypertension

Most hypertension falls into the category called **essential hypertension.** The term "essential" implies that the hypertension is a primary disease, that it is not due to some other disease process. Almost all hypertension is essential. A small percentage of cases of high blood pressure are secondary to taking oral contraceptives, kidney malfunction, abnormalities of the adrenal glands, or blockages of arteries (Schroeder, Krupp, Tierney, & McPhee, 1989). These conditions must be treated medically by dealing with their primary cause. Our discussion will be limited to essential hypertension.

Effects of Hypertension

Hypertension is called the *silent* killer because it is such a serious risk factor, yet no consistent pattern of symptoms reveals itself to allow a patient to identify it reliably. Symptoms such as headache, dizziness, shortness of breath, and blurry vision may occur in people with high blood pressure, but the same symptoms present themselves quite frequently in those without elevated blood pressure. Pennebaker (1982) has presented evidence that given individuals may have their own unique cluster of symptoms that go with high blood pressure, but these do not generalize from one person to the other.

High blood pressure is associated with strokes, retinal damage, diseases of the coronary arteries and heart, and kidney disease. Table 11.1 summarizes the health problems of 500 *untreated* hypertensives. Average age at onset was 32, and average survival time was 20 years. Clearly, the results are very serious and life threatening.

The Physiological Basis of Hypertension

Two factors determine how high your blood pressure will be (see Figure 11.1). One is **cardiac output,** or how much blood your heart pumps per unit of time. This output is dictated by variables such as how much blood the chambers of your heart hold and how forcefully and how rapidly your heart beats. The second factor that determines blood pressure is **peripheral resistance.** This is how much back-pressure the heart has to pump against. Back-pressure is increased by the constriction of blood vessels, the sludg-

ing of the blood, and increases in the fluid volume of the body.

In the early stages of hypertension, high cardiac output tends to be the culprit. In the later stages peripheral resistance seems to play a more central role (Kaplan, 1981). Figure 11.2 summarizes this and other aspects of the natural history of essential hypertension.

The activity of the sympathoadrenal "fight or flight" system (see Chapter 4) likely plays a key role in producing essential hypertension in most patients. Activity of the sympathetic nervous system and secretion of epinephrine and norepinephrine can elevate blood pressure in many ways (Kaplan, 1986).

The fight or flight system increases heart rate as well as the strength of its contractions; thus, it increases cardiac output. It also causes the small blood vessels in the periphery of the body to contract. Particularly significant small vessels are the arterioles of the kidney, which regulate the body's fluid volume and therefore the blood pressure. Overall, fight or flight responses lead to increases in peripheral resistance.

The role of the fight or flight system is especially important in hypertensives with high levels of *renin* (Kaplan, 1986; Laragh, 1988). Renin levels are strongly influenced by sympathoadrenal activity. Renin is a hormone that helps keep the blood pressure constant when the body's fluid volume decreases. It does so by encourag-

Table 11.1 Consequences of Untreated Hypertension in 500 Patients

Disorder	Percent of Patients Affected	Mean Years from Onset Until Death
Heart enlargement	59–74[a]	8
Heart failure	50	4
Stroke	12	4
Abnormal protein secretion (kidney)	42	5

[a] Depends on method of measuring heart size.

Source: Based on G. A. Perera. (1955). Hypertensive vascular disease: description and natural history. *Journal of Chronic Disease,* 1, 33.

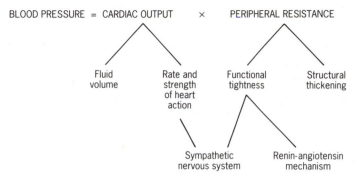

Figure 11.1   Blood pressure depends on the output of the heart and the resistance to the flow of blood through the body, which in turn depend on the elements shown in the schema. The sympathetic nervous system can also activate the renin-angiotensin system. *Source*: From "The control of hypertension," by N. M. Kaplan, *American Journal of Clinical Biofeedback*, 4, Figure 4, p. 143. Copyright © 1981 by Hogrefe & Huber, Toronto, Ontario. Reprinted by permission.

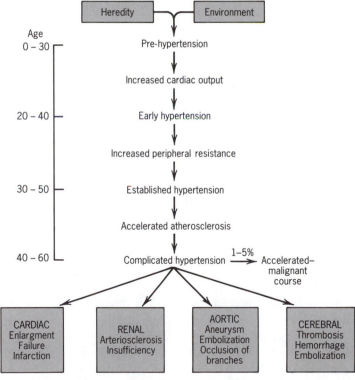

Figure 11.2   The "natural history" of untreated idiopathic hypertension begins with some combination of hereditary and environmental factors. Since hypertension is asymptomatic for the first 10 to 20 years, it is seldom recognized in its early stages. *Source*: From "The control of hypertension," by N. M. Kaplan, *American Journal of Clinical Biofeedback*, 4, Figure 1, p. 139. Copyright © 1981 by Hogrefe & Huber, Toronto, Ontario. Reprinted by permission.

ing the production of another hormone called *angiotensin* II.

Angiotensin II raises blood pressure in several ways. First, it makes small blood vessels constrict, directly increasing pressure. Second, it stimulates the release of *aldosterone*, an adrenal cortical hormone. Aldosterone regulates the degree to which the body throws off sodium and potassium, and the concentrations of these regulate blood pressure. Finally, it stimulates kidney, brain, and sympathetic nervous system in ways that increase blood pressure.

A small percentage of essential hypertensives have been found to be low in renin (20 to 30 percent), but most are high in the hormone. Laragh (1988) indicates that the sympathetic nervous system also plays a key role in low renin hypertension. Since the mechanism is poorly understood, we will not try to describe it here.

Measurement of Blood Pressure

Blood pressure is commonly measured by inflating a cuff against the upper arm until its pressure blocks the blood from flowing through the artery. Then, the cuff pressure is gradually lowered until the first point when the blood begins to spurt past the pressure barrier. We can tell when this is happening by listening for **Korotkoff Sounds,** which are produced by distension of the artery under pressure. We can hear the thumping sound that occurs as blood is forced past the pressure barrier with each contraction of the heart muscle.

The cuff pressure keeps blood from flowing except when the pressure increases during the heart's contraction. Thus, this reading tells us how high the pressure is during the heart's contraction, or *systole*. This is called the **systolic pressure.** We continue to lower the pressure in the cuff until we hear no more of the thumping sounds. The point at which this happens is the point where the cuff pressure matches the baseline pressure of the arteries, which is the pressure when the heart is not contracting, or the **diastolic pressure.**

An average blood pressure reading would be around 120/80 millimeters of mercury (mm

Hg). The standard of measurement is the extent to which the cuff pressure can push up a column of mercury, so the units are in mm Hg. The top number is the systolic pressure, and the bottom number is the diastolic pressure. Measuring blood pressure can be quite intricate, and some important precautions tend to be skipped in ordinary clinical practice.

People should have a period of at least five or ten minutes of rest, and they should urinate prior to the reading. Cuff size should be appropriate. People with large arms require an extra large cuff, or falsely high readings may be obtained. The cuff should be at the level of the heart or above, and the person should be in a relaxed position with the arm supported. One arm should be used consistently because there can be sizable differences between readings obtained on the two arms. The patient should not talk during the reading, since talking, even about rather bland topics, can elevate blood pressure considerably (Lynch, 1985).

The posture of the patient, the time of day, and the setting (home, office, or work) also produce substantial variations in measured blood pressure. More information on the measurement of blood pressure may be found in Schwartz (1987), Blanchard, Martin, and Dubbert (1988), and Llabre et al. (1988).

Although the cutoffs are largely arbitrary, we usually divide blood pressures into normal, borderline, and high. Normal blood pressure is below 140 mm Hg systolic and below 85 mm Hg diastolic. From 140–159 systolic and from 85–89 diastolic is considered borderline, and anything above that is high blood pressure.

Medical Control of Hypertension

Research has shown that lowering high blood pressure with medicines reduces many of the health problems linked to uncontrolled essential hypertension (Kaplan, 1986, pp. 165 ff). However, it is not clear that borderline hypertensives should be treated medically, since the side effects of the medications may outweigh any benefits. There are even some indications that drug therapy may *increase* the risks of coronary heart disease in borderline patients. Keep in mind that treatment of hypertension tends to reduce blood flow. Since heart attacks and strokes involve loss of perfusion of blood to tissue, you can see how treatment could make conditions worse. See Kaplan (1986) for an excellent discussion of the pros and cons of medical intervention in cases of mild hypertension.

There is a well-established medical approach to treatment of essential hypertension. It is called a "stepped care" approach, and it starts with minimal intervention and gradually increases treatment until blood pressure is controlled. The first step is usually to encourage weight loss and reduction of sodium intake. The amount of time that can be allotted to this step depends on how serious the problem is. The seriousness is not estimated solely on the basis of the blood pressure, but also on the presence of other risk factors that reveal themselves upon physical examination. For example, a person with a personal or even a family history of stroke is at much greater risk at any given elevation of blood pressure than a person without such additional risk factors.

In the next step diuretics are added to the step one treatment. Diuretics make the patient excrete fluid, and thereby lower the fluid volume of the body and reduce peripheral resistance. If step two fails to control the pressure, we go to the third step in which we usually add a drug that blocks the effect of the sympathoadrenal system. Since this system speeds the heart and also constricts peripheral blood vessels, its blockage tends to lower blood pressure. If this step fails to achieve control, another drug is added. The step four drug is likely to be a blood vessel dilator. When blood vessels are more wide open, they give less resistance to flow. Finally, in step five a variety of last-ditch drugs are tried.

Research has shown that this stepwise program does a good job of lowering blood pressure. We also know that it lowers the risk of most diseases for which high blood pressure is a risk factor. Remarkably enough, coronary heart disease is a possible exception to this reduction of risk (Blanchard, Martin, & Dubbert, 1988, p. 9). Thus, the kind of damage to the blood vessels of the heart that causes heart attacks and sudden cardiac death may not be counteracted by artificially lowering the blood pressure.

Despite its clear success, the medical treatment of hypertension presents some major problems. The side effects of most of these drugs are quite significant. There are too many to list, but they include such effects as headache, dizziness, drowsiness, anxiety, increases in blood sugar (a special problem for diabetics), induction of gout, rashes and hives, gastrointestinal problems, and inability to function sexually.

Since so many hypertensives do not have symptoms, they have to deal with the fact that they feel much worse when they are on the medication than when they are not. Furthermore, these medications are often costly; the hypertensive may spend as much as $30,000 over a career of hypertension.

Not surprisingly, then, hypertensive patients are notoriously slack in complying with medical instructions. A very substantial proportion of diagnosed hypertensive patients have uncontrolled high blood pressure, largely because of this noncompliance. In some cases it is not easy to bring blood pressure under control even in the cooperative patient. In fact, the 1976–1980 National Health Examination Survey found that only 11 percent of hypertensives had their high blood pressure under control.

Keep in mind also that, for borderline hypertensives, a body of medical opinion holds that the bad effects of the treatment may exceed the benefits of it. Nonetheless, the risks of borderline hypertension are great.

If hypertension is untreated, cardiovascular risks increase steadily with increases in blood pressure from very low values, well below the generally accepted "normal" level of 120/80. There are no abrupt changes in the increase of risk at the clinically accepted definitions of "normal," "borderline," and "hypertensive." In other words, the cutoffs are arbitrary, and the increased risk from 100 to 120 or from 120 to 140 systolic is as great as the increased risk from 140 to 160 (see Figure 11.3). Thus, the best kind of treatment for elevated blood pressure, including the levels we call "borderline," is one that has minimal side effects and is relatively inexpensive.

Role of Health Psychology in the Control of Hypertension

Health psychology should have a role in the management of essential hypertension. We need methods to improve adherence to medical

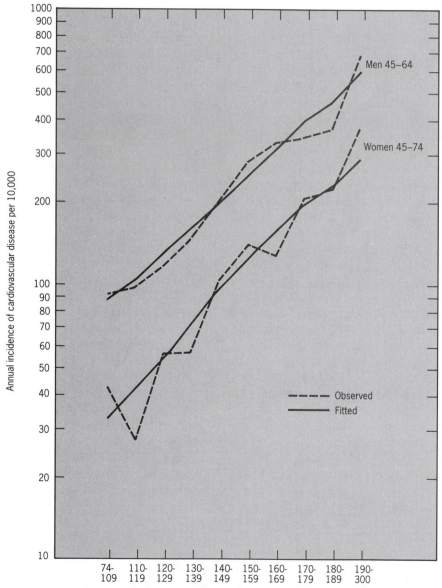

Figure 11.3 The average annual incidence of cardiovascular disease among more than 5000 inhabitants of Framingham, Massachusetts, followed over an 18-year period, rose progressively the higher the level of systolic blood pressure at the outset of the study. Source: From "The control of hypertension," by N. M. Kaplan, American Journal of Clinical Biofeedback, 4, Figure 2, p. 140. Copyright © 1981 by Hogrefe & Huber, Toronto, Ontario. Reprinted by permission.

treatment (see Chapter 6) in hypertensive patients, and we also need nondrug treatments with few or no side effects for those who are mildly hypertensive. In addition, effective nondrug treatments could help medicated patients reduce their need for medication and thereby decrease the side effects and costs of treatment. Finally, nondrug therapies might be useful for hypertensive patients whose pressures do not come down as they should when drug therapies are used. It may seem hard to believe, but clinical experience indicates that some patients with very high, uncontrolled blood pressure may respond to psychological interventions even when medicines fail.

NonDrug Treatments

Nondrug treatments for essential hypertension include relaxation training, hypnosis, biofeedback, breath training, exercise, and dietary change. Often several of these therapies are combined in a single program. Although work on the effects of these kinds of interventions is quite new, we already have respectable evidence of their effectiveness (Stamler et al., 1989).

Blanchard, Martin, and Dubbert (1988) have summarized procedures and outcomes for all nondrug treatments except hypnosis. Hypnosis is treated in Brown and Fromm (1987), and further information can be found in Schneiderman (1988). All these interventions appear to produce statistically and clinically significant reductions in blood pressure. We will now discuss some of them in more detail.

Progressive relaxation (PR) and autogenic training (AT) can reduce blood pressure. (See Chapters 5 and 10 for information on these methods.) Agras and his co-workers did several studies to assess the effectiveness of PR with home practice on blood pressure (Agras, Southam, & Taylor, 1983; Brauer et al., 1979; Southam, Agras, Taylor, & Kramer, 1982; Taylor, Farquhar, Nelson, & Agras, 1977) and found that it produced significant drops in both systolic and diastolic pressure.

On the other hand, Blanchard et al. (1986), failed to reproduce these significant drops in pressure with PR, though they persist in believ-

ing that it is a useful method for treating essential hypertension. This points toward a recurring problem in appraising the effects of procedures as complex and varied as relaxation training, whether in the form of autogenic training, progressive relaxation, or any other similar technique. Small details in the procedure can produce large variations in outcomes. Similar inconsistencies have been found with a modified version of AT, which worked better with Soviet patients than with American patients (Blanchard et al., 1988).

Other methods of relaxation, including mantra meditation, a modified yogic method known as shavasan, and hypnotic relaxation, have also proven useful in reducing hypertension (Brown & Fromm, 1987; Sothers & Anchor, 1989). (For examples of mantra meditation and shavasan, see Box 11.1.) However, the evidence is not quite as extensive for these methods as it is for autogenic training and progressive relaxation.

The Menninger Technique

We will focus on one of the more promising methods—the Menninger Voluntary Controls Project. We single this procedure out not because it is more effective than all others, but because it resembles various techniques used in clinics that use nondrug treatment methods. This method combines autogenic training (AT) with thermal biofeedback to reduce blood pressure (Fahrion et al., 1987; Green, Green, & Norris, 1979). Since the dilation of blood vessels causes increases in skin temperature, it makes sense to use AT and thermal biofeedback, both of which focus on increases in skin temperature. Increased skin temperature implies dilation of blood vessels of the skin.

Before we had medications to control high blood pressure, sympathectomies were sometimes performed in a desperate attempt to lower the pressure. This procedure involves disconnecting the sympathetic nervous system (SNS) from the central nervous system (see Chapter 4). Removal of the influence of the SNS causes the blood vessels of the skin to dilate and thereby should lower peripheral resistance. Other con-

Box 11.1   **Relaxation Techniques Used for Hypertension Treatment**

Mantra Meditation

1. Get in a quiet, comfortable place.
2. Close your eyes.
3. Turn your attention gently to the word "mana."
4. If your mind wanders, that is o.k. It is actually part of the meditation.
5. When you notice your mind is on something other than "mana," gently return to that word.
6. You do not have to *say* the word "mana." You can visualize it, imagine hearing it, or even just be aware of its presence, without regard to whether it is imagined as seen, heard, or anything else.
7. One of the most important things is to take a *passive attitude*, simply observing the various changes that take place in your mind.

8. Do this for 15 or 20 minutes.

Shavasan

1. Take up a relaxed posture (preferably lying on the back, toes pointed outward, legs spread, palms up, arms out).
2. Turn your attention to your breath. On each out-breath, breathe out your tension and think "relax." Gradually extend the word "reeelaaax," thereby extending your exhalation.
3. Attend to one of your lower legs and let it relax during each of two or three exhalations. Tell the leg to "reeelaaax." Then go to the opposite leg and repeat.
4. Continue the same process, working your way up through the rest of the body. Tell each part to "reeelaaax" as you exhale.

---

sequences of sympathectomy should also lower blood pressure. For example, fight or flight reactions tend to result in changes in a system, called the renin-angiotensin system, that determines the fluid volume of the body. Fluid volume has an important influence on peripheral resistance.

The Menninger procedure may have similar effects to those seen upon removal of SNS activity produced by surgery—only it does so in a finely controlled and reversible way. We will now discuss this method to give the reader a sense of the finer details.

The Menninger program is generally done with groups of patients rather than with individuals. In the first session, rapport is built by listening to and discussing patient complaints,

medication status, and similar particulars, as well as seeing to it that patients get acquainted with each other and with the therapist. Drug treatments for hypertension are discussed, and their disadvantages are explained. An account is also given of the development of the psychological approach to treatment of hypertension.

Patients are given a copy of an article that gives a basic explanation of the method they are to learn, as well as of its expected results. This article encourages them to expect a positive outcome. The four key elements of that approach are (1) learning to warm the hands voluntarily, (2) learning to warm the feet, (3) reducing muscular tension, and (4) learning a yogic method of deep, relaxed breathing. An important corollary of this method is that patients practice the methods at home and must take responsibility for regular home monitoring of their blood pressure.

Next, graphed results from previous patients are shown, so that the patients can see that success is possible. The physiological basis for the method is described briefly, and patients are given data sheets and taught how to keep records of their practice and its results.

The patients are carefully trained to measure their own blood pressure, with their accuracy being checked. They are instructed to continue practicing until their blood pressure is in the normal range, and then they can taper off and practice only when they are under particular stress. However, they must *always* monitor their pressure on a regular basis, since it would be dangerous to do otherwise. For the first few days, they are asked to monitor their blood pressure often and in a variety of situations. After that, they must measure it at the same time each day, at a time when they are likely in the future to be able to practice relaxing. The data so obtained provide a baseline for comparison with the results of the training.

In the second session, the patients' data are examined, and they are introduced to a method of learning to warm their hands with the aid of AT and thermal biofeedback. They are given a copy of the autogenic phrases (see Chapter 10), which they can tape if they wish. However, they are encouraged to improvise and develop their own independent form of AT, and not to depend on the prearranged phrases.

The patients are shown how to use a thermal biofeedback machine, and they are asked to practice at home twice a day and record the temperature data at least once daily. Since the sympathetic nervous system constricts blood vessels of the skin, and therefore produces cooling of the hands, learning to warm the hands is related to reducing sympathetic nervous system activity. The sympathetic output acts to increase both cardiac output and peripheral resistance—the two main sources of high blood pressure.

In subsequent sessions, patients are taught **triangular numeric breathing,** so-called be-

cause, when connected to a respiration gauge and recorded on a physiograph, the breathing produces a triangular pattern on the readout chart. It is a method taught by the Swami Rama (see Boyd, 1976), an expert in yoga. It involves continuous deep breathing without stopping at the end of the inhalation or exhalation.

An entire subdiscipline in yoga known as *pranayama* centers on controlling the breath to produce physiological, psychological, and spiritual effects. The importance of breath control to physiological and psychological health has also come to the attention of some Western scientists (see, e.g. Peper & Crane–Gockley, 1990), so there appears to be some consensus on its importance. Patients are also taught to notice when they gasp or hold their breath in stressful situations, and to learn to breathe more freely when this happens.

When a patient's hand temperature reaches 95 degrees F, he or she is asked to begin learning to increase foot temperature. Patients are also given electromyographic biofeedback with forehead placement of the electrodes. The results of their physiological readings are used as a starting point for a stress management program, which takes up a good part of the office sessions.

The central role of the *patient's* efforts to get good results is emphasized. Once the patient is familiar with the whole treatment package, graphs of the results of some successful patients are contrasted with those of unsuccessful patients who failed to practice regularly. Emphasis is placed on the idea that they will fail only if they neglect to practice.

The patient is encouraged to take lower doses of medication as need for it decreases. This reduction is, of course, determined by the primary care physician, who is given suggestions by the psychological trainers. Reductions in medication are suggested whenever the patient succeeds at keeping his or her pressure in the 140/90 range for at least two weeks.

Several studies have shown that this method can be successful (Fahrion et al., 1987; Green, Green, & Norris, 1979), and other investigators have reported good outcomes with similar methods (Aivazyan, Zaitsež, & Yurenev, 1988; Aivazyan et al., 1988; Blanchard, Martin, & Dubbert, 1988; Blanchard et al., 1988). The methods are quite promising, but we still need more and better research before fully valid claims of efficacy can rightly be made.

Despite the successes of many studies, other investigations have produced less impressive results, and we often do not know what factors give rise to the differences. For example, joint work in Soviet and American patients yielded better results in the Soviets (see Blanchard et al., 1988). It is important for us to find an explanation for such variations.

Diet and Exercise

Both diet and exercise appear to have an impact on hypertension (Blanchard, Martin, & Dubbert, 1988; Horan & Rocella, 1988). Exercise has a positive impact on stress responses, provided the exercise is not excessive and is aerobic. It produces a training effect, which reduces the use

Mild aerobic exercise has a positive impact on stress responses and is often prescribed to reduce blood pressure.

of lactate-producing metabolic pathways. Lactate ions are produced as a result of muscular exertion, and untrained muscles produce lactate more readily than trained muscles. Blood lactate levels have long been known to be related to proneness to anxiety. This type of exercise also increases the output of the brain's natural opiates, the endorphins.

Blanchard, Martin, and Dubbert (1988) have summarized the literature which strongly suggests that aerobic exercise reduces blood pressure in hypertensives and that, given the persistence of hypertension, provides a buffer against its physiological effects. They also describe a program that helps patients to develop and adhere to the right kind of exercise program. For example, they note that exercise that comes too close to the patient's aerobic capacity is likely to feel unpleasant, to lead to injuries, and to end in the patient's quitting. Blanchard and his coworkers provide a fairly detailed account of how to assess both the patient and his or her reaction to the exercise. They also give advice on the recruitment of social supports that help maintain the program.

Weight loss can also reduce blood pressure. In fact, researchers indicate that there is about a 1 mm Hg drop in blood pressure with each kilogram (2.2 pounds) of weight lost (Blanchard, Martin, & Dubbert, 1988). Horan and Rocella (1988) point out, however, that there is a "floor" below which further weight loss does not lower blood pressure.

We dealt with psychological approaches to weight loss in Chapter 8. Other facets of diet are also important, however, and we will discuss some of them in brief. Sodium intake is related to hypertension in certain sodium-sensitive individuals but not in everyone. We do not know how to tell beforehand whether or not a person is sodium sensitive, and it is a good idea to try sodium restriction in hypertensive individuals. Langford et al. (1985) found that sodium restriction more than doubled the likelihood that hypertensive patients whose blood pressure had been controlled for at least five years could be withdrawn from medication.

Controlling sodium intake in the modern

American diet is quite difficult because a great deal of dietary sodium does not come from the salt shaker. It is heavily present in processed foods, including some that most people would not suspect (e.g., corn flakes). Servings of fast foods often have several grams of sodium; it is easy to exceed a reasonable daily allotment of sodium by consuming even a single meal of fast food (see Table 11.2).

A second dietary problem relevant to essential hypertension, especially in men, is alcohol consumption. Alcohol raises blood pressure, and even fairly modest levels of daily consumption can cause hypertension. The patient who shows lots of variability in blood pressure from reading to reading and in whom it is hard to find the right levels of medications may be displaying an alcohol-related hypertension. Inquiries about alcohol consumption should be made with hypertensive patients, especially those showing this pattern. Such patients should be encouraged to keep their alcohol consumption to no more than one or two ounces of ethanol per day. Obviously, some patients may be experiencing severe problems regulating alcohol consumption and will have to be referred into appropriate treatment programs.

Table 11.2 Sodium Content of Fast Foods

Fast Food	Milligrams of Sodium
Double burger with sauce	880
Chicken nuggets (6)	700
Fish sandwich with cheese and tartar sauce	676
Cheese pizza (1 slice)	455
Tossed salad with low-calorie dressing	445
Single burger	435
Apple pie	400
Milkshake	190
French fries	120

Source: Based on Massachusetts Medical Society Committee on Nutrition. (1989). Fast-food fare: Consumer Guidelines. *The New England Journal of Medicine*, 321, 752–756.

PSYCHOLOGICAL APPROACHES TO CORONARY HEART DISEASE

As we pointed out earlier, in most industrialized countries no form of illness claims more human lives than cardiovascular disease. Most of these deaths result from **coronary heart disease** (CHD). Currently in the United States, about 300,000 people die annually of sudden cardiac arrest, and about 750,000 are diagnosed as having had a heart attack. Keep in mind that many diseases of the heart (e.g., rheumatic heart disease, congenital heart disease, and congestive heart failure) are not included in these figures. To get a sense of the magnitude of CHD death, compare it to annual deaths due to automobile accidents, which perhaps total 50,000 to 60,000 or to airplane crashes, which take about 1,600 lives per year.

CHD is disease of the arteries that feed the heart. These vessels form a kind of crown over the top of the heart; the Latin word for "crown" is *corona*, hence, the term "coronary." You might think that the heart, which actually provides a source of blood, would never suffer a deficit of it. But just as bankers cannot use the money in the bank according to their whims, the heart cannot use the oxygenated blood it pumps unless that blood goes through the coronary arteries.

The heart actually consists of two pumps joined together. The pump on the right side is a low pressure system designed to send blood that has been depleted of oxygen into the lungs, where fresh oxygen is obtained. The delicate tissue of the lungs could not tolerate the higher pressures produced by the more heavily muscled left pump, which pushes blood through the rest of the body.

The bottom half of each of these pumps consists of a chamber, called an atrium, about half the size of a little finger into which blood is received and from which it is transferred to the upper, main pumping chambers. The right atrium takes in blood from which the oxygen has already been extracted, and it sends that blood to the right ventricle, which pumps the blood to the lungs. The left atrium receives oxygenated blood from the lungs and forwards it to the powerful left ventricle, which in turn distributes it throughout the body.

Just about any part of the heart can be defective, leading to its own particular form of heart disease. The muscle itself can be weak, the valves that keep the blood in the correct chamber may leak, and so on. These are not, however, the most common vulnerabilities of the heart. Much more frequent are obstructions of the coronary arteries; these arteries provide oxygen to the heart muscle itself. Also very common are defects of the very delicate conduction system that times the pumping of the different chambers of the heart. Without fairly accurate timing, the heart cannot effectively pump. Obviously, it does little good for the ventricle to contract efficiently if the blood has not gotten into its chamber.

Since the timing of contraction of heart chambers is so crucial for effective functioning of the pump, conduction of electrical impulses through the heart must be orderly, or pumping may be impaired, or may fail entirely. Failures of the timing system can result in sudden death, which is a major killer. It is in fact the major cause of death in patients after heart attacks.

Ischemia and Angina

When coronary arteries are blocked, the heart muscle fails to get essential oxygen. This condition is called **ischemia.** It can result in intense pain, called **angina,** in the chest and other regions. Angina is a constricting pain in the chest that tends to be produced by effort or emotional stress and that is usually relieved by rest or by chemicals, such as nitrates, that dilate coronary arteries. The pain of angina usually begins behind the sternum (middle of the chest) and commonly spreads to the left chest, shoulder, and arm, and even to the neck.

People with angina often break out in a sweat and are in disabling pain, but it is important not to think that chest pains that are milder or do not follow the exact pattern described here can be safely disregarded. Sometimes pains due to blockage of the coronary arteries fail to follow

the expected pattern. For example, during his heart attack, Larry King had pain in his *right* shoulder and arm. In fact, the arteries can sometimes be heavily blocked without the person noticing any symptoms at all.

Myocardial Infarction

Worse than angina in its impact is the heart attack or **myocardial infarction** (MI). Angina and MI are the two main forms of CHD. MI occurs when the blockage of blood flow causes actual damage to the muscle tissue of the heart. The pain of MI resembles that of angina in its pattern. The patient undergoing an MI may also experience shortness of breath, sweating, weakness, extreme fatigue, vomiting, and severe anxiety.

Closer examination may show that the sufferer has either a very fast or a very slow heart rate and either very high or very low blood pressure. The patient may have a mildly elevated temperature. Peculiar shifts in heart sounds may be detectable with a stethoscope. The electrocardiogram tends to show a well-known pattern of change that can be identified by properly trained health care providers. Laboratory tests may reveal certain changes in the blood, such as increases in white cells.

Oddly enough, some people undergo MI without noticing it. These are called **silent heart attacks.** It is not uncommon for old MIs to be discovered upon cardiac examination. Sometimes people close to the patient will report that they were aware that something serious had happened, so the "silent" heart attack may not always be entirely silent. As noted earlier, there is evidence that those who have silent heart attacks are generally less sensitive to pain than most people (Melzack & Wall, 1988).

Around 30 to 40 percent of people with an MI die from it. Included in this figure are the substantial numbers of people with MI who die before they even reach emergency medical care. As we pointed out above, 300,000 people die annually of sudden cardiac arrest; about 20 percent of these have no warning symptoms at all prior to their sudden death.

Biomedical Treatment of Coronary Heart Disease

The biomedical approach has emphasized dramatic surgical interventions, such as **coronary bypass surgery.** Most of us know someone who has undergone such surgery. It is very expensive, and a substantial portion of the medical effort in this country is taken up doing these operations and managing the patients before and after them, partly in intensive care units.

How effective are such procedures? It is not easy to do ideal experimental studies of such complex procedures. Who would have the power or the right to decide who gets put in an experimental, operated group and who does not? And it is out of the question that such studies should be double-blind, with neither patient nor medical personnel knowing whether or not the patient had surgery. Nor can we ethically have a control group with "sham" surgery, in which the patient is opened up but the actual operation is not done. Strictly speaking, this would be a necessary control condition. Furthermore, we cannot allow patients with clear manifestations of CHD to go entirely untreated. Comparisons of surgical treatment must be made with patients who are being treated with medicines usually paired with lifestyle changes, rather than with untreated patients. Presumably, this makes it more difficult to show a significant effect of the surgery.

Given all these problems, it is remarkable that several studies have been done in which patients have been randomly assigned to medical and some to surgical treatment. The nature of the medical treatment was generally determined by the patient's physician, but we know that it usually involves giving medications such as beta blockers, nitrates, and digitalis. These drugs maximize the flow of blood in coronary arteries and the pumping capacity of the heart. Other medicines are usually given to control risk factors, such as high blood pressure. Furthermore, patients are commonly advised to change various facets of their lifestyle.

Some of these studies have shown coronary bypass surgery to have little positive effect compared to medical treatment (Detre et al., 1985; Killip et al., 1985). In some instances, there have actually been increases in MI rate after the surgery.

Other studies have been somewhat more supportive of the surgical method (e.g., Varnauskas et al., 1985), but even here the results do not consistently favor surgical treatment if we are looking for longer survival and reduction of MIs after treatment. Furthermore, the benefits, when there are such, are probably not as great as most of us might think. Based on these studies, there seems to be little dispute that a patient would be wise to have a coronary bypass if the left main coronary artery were seriously blocked and if there were notable impairment of the pumping capacity of the main pumping chamber of the heart (the left ventricle).

Clinical reports indicate that, despite the limitations of surgery in preventing future MIs and increasing survival, it does a very good job of reducing symptoms and thereby increases the quality of life. Some more systematic evidence for this success shows up in the study by Varnauskas et al. (1985), which found that there was less angina, better exercise performance, and less need for beta blockers and/or nitrates in surgically treated patients. However, surgery did not prevent a gradual increase in retirement from work in the years after treatment was initiated.

Surprisingly, studies done at a time when sham operations were allowed, showed that patients who believed they had received a medical procedure to reduce angina, but whose chests were merely opened without actually doing the surgery, also got relief from angina (Diamond, Kittle, & Crockett, 1960). So we cannot dismiss the possibility that such symptom relief is due to a placebo effect.

The samples of patients used in studies of the effectiveness of coronary bypass surgery are nonrandomly selected, and they may not be representative of the general run of such patients. Perhaps even more important is the nonrandom selection of surgeons and hospitals. One major reason for the modest positive effects of coronary bypass surgery is the procedure's tendency to provoke MIs either at the time of surgery or soon thereafter. If many people die essentially from the operation, the net gain from the surgery will be reduced. Rates of such "peri-operative" MIs differ markedly from surgeon to surgeon and from hospital to hospital. An important consideration is the lack of a regulatory agency to stop incompetent surgeons from continuing to do these operations.

Moore (1989) has pointed out that the best surgeons have about 1 percent fatalities related to the operation, but the worst have 40 to 50 percent fatalities. We would think that surgical units with such a record would immediately shut down and take action to correct their problems, but Moore points out that some have not done that. If *those* surgical units were used to evaluate the effects of bypass surgery, we would be saying that the technique was drastically harmful. As it is, the surgical skill in the reported studies ranges from average (around 5 or 6 percent) to excellent (around 1 percent). The positive results reported here are, of course, for surgical units with excellent skills.

A common objection to the systematic studies of coronary bypass surgery mentioned here is that techniques have changed rapidly, so these long-term outcome studies are evaluations of outmoded methods. For example, a present-day heart attack patient is likely to receive, as Larry King did, a medicine to dissolve blood clots in the coronary arteries even as the MI is taking place. That patient may well also undergo balloon angioplasty at these early stages of the MI. All of these procedures should limit the extent of the damage. In fact, the coronary bypass might be needed only in the more severe cases.

Given the seemingly improved methods of treating these types of heart disease, should we dismiss the cited research? Certainly we must recognize its limitations, but we must also remember that the newer techniques *have not been fully validated scientifically.* To claim that they are obviously superior without adequate scientific

verification would be to regress to a prescientific methodology for medicine. In many instances in the history of human thought, investigators thought it safe to leave out this kind of verification, only to find they were sadly mistaken.

It is clearly not fair to equate the biomedical approach to heart disease with coronary bypass surgery. Modern cardiac care is more varied than that, and includes both medical and preventive approaches. Even in the studies we have cited, comparisons are being made with nonsurgical, medical interventions. Furthermore, the American Heart Association has placed a good deal of emphasis on prevention of heart disease.

Obviously, medical and surgical approaches are limited in their ability to cope with CHD. Considering this limitation, and taking into account that perhaps 25 percent of people suffering an MI have "death as their first symptom," it is best to focus on prevention rather than attempting to compensate for damage already done.

Prevention of Coronary Heart Disease

A number of risk factors set people up for MI. Some of them, such as being older and male, are out of a person's control, but others may be, to varying degrees, manageable. High blood pressure, cigarette smoking, and high levels of cholesterol in the blood serum are good examples. A middle-aged male with all three of these risk factors is six times more likely than a similar person with none of them to have a major MI (Syme, 1984). An important role of the health psychologist is to design and implement programs that help people reduce such risk factors (see Chapters 8 and 9).

Being physically active probably helps lower risk of CHD, but it is hard to demonstrate it because researchers cannot force people to exercise or refrain from exercising according to an experimental plan. Some studies show that those who exert themselves heavily have fewer problems with CHD, but this result could simply mean that those with better heart function are more likely to engage in heavy exertion.

If we take the three risk factors of high blood

pressure, high serum cholesterol, and cigarette smoking as predictors of CHD, an interesting paradox emerges. Even though one's chances of such disease markedly increase with these factors, few people with the risk factors actually develop the disease (Jeffery, 1989). Marmot and Winklestein (1975) found that only 14 percent of men with all three risk factors developed CHD during a ten-year observation period. Only 5 percent of men with one of the factors and 9 percent of those with two factors developed CHD.

This gives us strong reason to believe that there are other, very important risk factors. Even if we expand our list of risk factors to include obesity, lack of exercise, and diabetes mellitus, the most strongly predictive combination of factors will fail to identify most new cases of CHD. Something is missing, and that something may well be various social and psychological factors. We will now discuss some of these in detail.

Psychology's Role in Prevention

Psychology has at least as large a place in prevention as does medicine. Prevention generally involves helping people to learn new habits, to control their motives and drives, and to change their images and cognitions, all of which are psychological changes. We have no foreseeable prospects of finding a medical way to get people to stop smoking, lose weight, exercise, or cope effectively with stress. Where we *do* have medical means of controlling risk factors, as in the case of essential hypertension, psychological approaches are still highly important, as we indicated in the previous section.

Type A Behavior

We deal with the role of psychology in changing lifestyles in several places in this book. Here we will focus on one particular issue, that of a specific pattern of personality or behavior that may be highly relevant to the development of heart disease. This is a pattern called **Type A behavior.**

Interest in the role of Type A behavior in heart disease was stimulated by the work of two cardiologists, Meyer Friedman and Ray Rosen-

man, who summarized and popularized their work in a book called *Type A Behavior and Your Heart* (Friedman & Rosenman, 1974). They noticed that the chairs in their waiting room tended to get worn on the front edges, as if their patients were sitting "on the edge of their seats." This led them to look further into the behavioral characteristics of coronary patients. Eventually, they developed a profile of these features, and categorized them as Type A. Friedman and Ulmer (1984) define Type A behavior as

above all a continuous struggle, an unremitting attempt to accomplish or achieve more and more things or participate in more and more events in less and less time, frequently in the face of opposition—real or imagined—from other persons. The Type A personality is dominated by covert insecurity of status or hyperaggressiveness, or both. (p. 30)

The Type A's struggle fosters a sense of time urgency or what Friedman calls "hurry sickness." They have to speed up their rate of thinking, planning, and carrying out most daily activities. Type A's talk fast and try to get others to talk fast. They try to read, write, walk, eat, and drive as fast as possible while still getting the task done. A typical Type A cannot stand to wait in lines. Type A's engage in "polyphasic activity." They do and think more than one thing at a time. They often think about or do something else while listening to another person.

The aggressiveness and status insecurity result in a kind of diffuse hostility. If the struggle is severe enough, the Type A may sometimes be downright self-destructive. A's Friedman and Ulmer (1984) said:

they would never try to do away with themselves by any conscious act, yet they all felt that sooner or later they would succumb to the stress they were bringing on themselves by living and working at such a killing pace. (p. 41)

A patient of this kind, after having an MI, said, "I'm glad it finally came. I just couldn't seem to find any other way to get out from under all the junky stuff loading me down." Another patient said, "It may seem strange to you, but I knew I was going to get this attack, and I sort of looked forward to it" (Friedman & Ulmer, 1984, p. 41).

Friedman and Ulmer (1984) maintain that Type A's must not only win but also dominate. They do not care about the feelings and rights of competitors, and they may even actively try to damage the competitor's self-esteem. Even highly successful Type A's compare themselves to others who are even more successful.

Friedman and Ulmer (1984) vividly describe Type A's as hostile people who tend to see the source of their hostility as outside themselves. Other people's failings are causing the hostility; things and people are always getting in their way. Thus, they are chronically angry. This is a diffuse anger, and it shows itself even in responses to the most trivial happenings. This hostility is linked to the trouble they experience with personal relationships. It is hard for them to give and take love; they are better at giving loyalty and concern than love.

Measuring Type A Behavior

Our description of Type A behavior is based on that of Freidman and Ulmer (1984). It gives you a sense of what it is like, and it might give you an idea if someone you know is Type A. Be aware, however, that if you try making that kind of judgment about others, or yourself, you will probably soon find that you are not sure how to categorize certain people. If you tried to use plain common sense in putting people into the category, you would likely find yourself disagreeing with someone else who was trying to classify the same people. It would soon be clear that you could not do good research on the topic until some sort of scale had been devised for measuring the behavior.

Accordingly, Rosenman et al. (1964) devised a measuring instrument called the **Structured Interview** (SI). It was a 15-minute interview taped for later rating. An important concept behind the SI was that we would not expect Type A people to have a lot of insight into their own behavior. Thus, the SI contained not only inquiries about how the person behaves, but also provocations to exhibit Type A behaviors. Furthermore, the ratings took into account not just

the content of the responses, but also the *way* the subject responded. In addition, observers were trained to consider nonverbal behaviors, such as gross bodily movements.

The SI met normal standards for a scale of measurement. Different raters could agree on how a person was to be categorized (this is called inter-rater reliability), and they could do so with the kind of consistency we require of a measurement instrument (e.g., see Caffrey, 1969). Ratings also tended to be stable from one time to another (Jenkins, Rosenman, & Friedman, 1968). Unfortunately, the SI was cumbersome to administer and required considerable training under the tutelage of people who knew what to look for. It was not surprising that attempts were soon made to devise a paper-and-pencil test of Type A behavior.

Several such tests of Type A behavior have been constructed, but probably the best known is the **Jenkins Activity Survey** (JAS) (Jenkins, Rosenman, & Zyzanski, 1974). It asks questions that assess speed and impatience, job involvement, and drive. Since it is a self-report scale, it relies on the ability of Type A people to know and report their own characteristics. It gives consistent results, but it is not a good measure of competitiveness, hostility, and impatience (Rosenman, Swan, & Carmelli, 1988). We should not be surprised to learn that it has proven to be a weaker predictor of CHD than the SI.

A Framingham scale of Type A behavior was also devised. It, too, is a questionnaire, and it was derived from a more extensive instrument that inquires about psychosocial factors. It has been shown to correlate with CHD, and it includes items on such characteristics as speed, impatience, and time urgency, but it also assesses drive, fatigue, and work satisfaction. This scale correlates with CHD, but the correlation could be due to the measured dimensions that are not a part of Type A behavior (Rosenman, Swan, & Carmelli, 1988).

Type A Behavior and CHD

Early studies showed a relationship between Type A Behavior and CHD. Most impressive was the Western Collaborative Group Study (WCGS;

Rosenman, Brand, Sholtz & Friedman, 1976) in which 3,454 middle-aged men with no apparent CHD were followed for eight and one-half years. Three techniques were used for predicting future heart attacks: (1) a 15 minute interview to classify them as Type A or B, (2) a measure of the tendency of their blood to clot, and (3) a test of high density lipoproteins. Cholesterol occurs in the blood bound to proteins; the resulting chemical is called a lipoprotein. Low density lipoproteins (LDLs) are primarily responsible for transporting cholesterol to the arteries. "Bad" cholesterol is contained in LDLs. High density lipoproteins (HDLs) contain more protein and less cholesterol, and they are primarily responsible for transporting cholesterol to the liver to be metabolized. HDLs are thought to provide protection against atherosclerosis and CHD—thus, the term "good" cholesterol.

A year after starting the WCGS, it was found that 71 percent of those classified as Type A turned out already to have CHD. There were 257 new MIs in this group of men during the study, and 178 of them occurred in the Type A men. Over the course of the study, Type A men proved to be two to three times more likely to have heart attacks than were Type B men. Not one man classified as a "pure" Type B had an MI. Type A classification was as good at predicting MIs as were serum cholesterol levels, which are the best biomedical predictors.

It would make sense to suppose that the ability of Type A behavior to predict CHD was due to a tendency of that kind of behavior to correlate with well-known biological risk factors such as smoking, high blood pressure, or high cholesterol levels. This would mean that the really effective influences were the well-known biological ones and that the personality variable was just correlated with them. Statistical analyses did not support this notion. Type A behavior predicted CHD quite well, even when the influence of any correlation with these other factors had been removed.

In fact, Friedman and Ulmer (1984) have argued that cholesterol levels are due to high stress and the poor stress coping we find in Type A's. Since the liver metabolizes and manufac-

tures cholesterol, serum cholesterol levels are not as dependent on dietary cholesterol as most people think. In fact, 80 to 90 percent of cholesterol is manufactured in the body. Friedman and Ulmer (1984) point out that changes in the blood supply to the liver occur under stress, and they think that serum cholesterol levels change because of that.

Quite a bit of evidence exists that serum cholesterol levels increase during stress. Friedman, Rosenman, and Carroll (1958) took blood samples from 40 accountants between the months of January and June. During this period the accountants' diet did not change, yet there was a significant increase in serum cholesterol and in the tendency of the blood to clot during the month when, because of tax deadlines, their stress is at a peak. Cholesterol levels dropped sharply after the tax deadline. Similar studies using both animal and human subjects have confirmed the finding that cholesterol levels increase with increased stress. (For more details, see Friedman and Ulmer, 1984 and Suinn, 1980).

Evidence mentioned up to this point seems to show that Type A behavior is as powerful a predictor of CHD as the familiar physical risk factors. Furthermore, this kind of behavior may well be more important than serum cholesterol in that it may set the stage for elevations of the cholesterol levels. In other words, it might have causal priority over the cholesterol. If confirmed, this would place a psychological factor at the top of the list of matters to be dealt with in order to control CHD.

However, several later studies seemed to contradict the notion that Type A behavior was a predictor of CHD. Most of these studies were done on people known to be at high risk for CHD, on the basis of physical risk factors and/or symptoms. For example, several studies related angiographic findings to assessments of Type A behavior.

An angiogram (coronary arteriography) is the definitive diagnostic procedure for coronary artery disease. It is an invasive procedure that permits visualization of blood vessels suspected of being blocked by atherosclerosis. A very small percentage of patients (0.2 percent) die from it, and 1 to 7 percent are physically harmed by it (e.g., have an MI). Obviously, it is done only in patients who require it for good medical reasons, such as those who are being considered for a coronary bypass.

Although some work indicated that Type A behavior predicted angiographically determined CHD (e.g., Blumenthal, Williams, & Kong, 1978), most studies failed to show such a relationship (e.g., Dimsdale, Hackett, & Hutter, 1979; Krantz et al., 1981).

Other studies were done in patients who already had an MI to determine whether being Type A increased the chances of getting another MI later. Several of these studies indicated that Type A categorization did not help in making such predictions. One study, done on original WCGS patients who had an MI, showed that those who had been classified as Type A were *more* rather than less likely to survive an MI!

Probably the greatest blow to the Type A concept came from the Multiple Risk Factor Intervention Trial (MRFIT; Mr. Fit—get it?) (Shekelle et al., 1985). This study was done on 12,866 high risk men from 22 clinics in 18 American cities. It was the most massive study ever done to assess the impact of risk factors and of attempts to modify them. Type A behavior was assessed by both the JAS and the SI. Furthermore, to assure that the SI was done as Friedman and Rosenman would have it done, Rosenman was brought in to verify that those assessing it were doing it correctly. Results showed no relationship between Type A and CHD, whether done by JAS or SI, and regardless of the measure of CHD.

What are we to conclude about the impact of Type A behavior? The efforts of many investigators are being directed toward making sense of the seemingly contradictory findings. Several summaries of their work have been published (see, e.g., Krantz, Contrada, Hill, & Friedler, 1988). We will briefly summarize some of the main ideas here. First, there is the possibility that studies selecting people at high risk for CHD are constricting the range of Type A scores so that this factor becomes a poor predictor.

To illustrate, although IQ is a good predictor of grades, it would probably not be a good predictor in a group of people who were all selected for having IQs over 140. If everyone is smart, other factors become more important in differentiating their performances. Similarly, if everybody in a study is CHD prone, maybe Type A becomes a less useful tool for telling who will and who will not have manifestations of the disease. This is a very familiar characteristic of correlations. Quite a bit of variability must exist or the correlations cannot be very high.

Some problems may reside in limitations of the measuring instruments. The JAS has been widely used as a measure of Type A behavior, and it still is being so used. Yet it is a relatively poor index of Type A behavior. The SI seems to be the best instrument, but it is very difficult to standardize. Despite all the efforts the MRFIT investigators have made to apply it in a standard way, many differences were introduced in the procedure, and there is evidence that these differences have made it a weaker predictor of CHD (Scherwitz, Graham, Grandits, & Billings, 1987).

A standardized instrument for measuring Type A behavior must be devised. Because people tend to be unaware of their Type A behaviors, such an instrument should not be a questionnaire. Chesney, Hecker, and Black (1988) have done serious work to standardize the SI, and this looks like a step in the right direction.

There is a good deal of evidence that the global Type A assessment contains some facets that predict CHD and other facets that do not. One major focus of attention is the dimension of *hostility*. Re-analyses of data, including data in which no relationship between angiographically determined CHD and Type A behavior was found, have shown that the Type A component of hostility *does* predict CHD. This means that hostility predicts CHD even in high risk samples (Krantz, Contrada, Hill, & Friedler, 1988; Williams & Barefoot, 1988).

Chesney, Hecker, and Black (1988) have also obtained evidence that hostility is a strong predictor of CHD. However, they sound an important warning. First, they point out that it is not

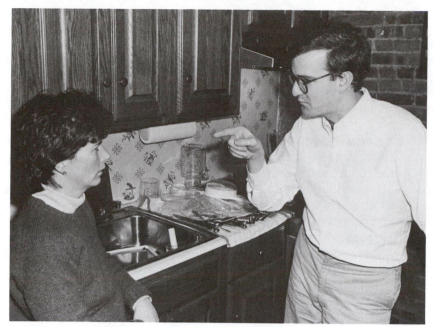

There is evidence that hostility is the component of Type A behavior that predicts coronary heart disease.

the *only* component of Type A behavior that survives when the SI is broken down into basic units. Competitiveness and time urgency also emerge as good predictors. Second, they warn that the concept of hostility might be subject to the same kinds of ambiguities that have plagued the Type A concept. They point out that current measures of hostility do not exactly correspond to those in the WCGS.

Descriptions of "hostility" appear to include moods, behaviors, expressions of feelings, cynicism about others, and perhaps other dimensions. Careful work should be done to get the best possible standardized measures of hostility. It is very important that we not jump to any hasty conclusions about the influence of the hostility factor, because a mistake on this topic might solidify the medical profession's natural skepticism about the possibility of psychological influences on disease.

Modification of Type A Behavior

Given the difficulties delineating Type A behavior and consistently showing its relationship to CHD, it is surprising the there is pretty good evidence that changing it will result in improvements in risk level for CHD. Suinn (1980) argued that Type A behavior could be viewed as a style of managing stress—obviously one with serious limitations. A number of studies show that Type A people react to stress differently than do Type B people (e.g., with greater rises in blood pressure or in norepinephrine; see Houston, 1988).

Suinn (1980) devised a cardiac stress management program for Type A people. He saw that Type A's could not be expected simply to give up their Type A behavior without having something to replace it. Giving it up without knowing how to deal with stress would be expected to increase tension and probably lead to more Type A behavior. Suinn also felt that the intervention program should be brief and show quick results, since Type A's are impatient and have a sense of time urgency. Furthermore, patients need to see that Type B behaviors can be as productive as Type A. (Several people have pointed out that top executives are likely to be Type B; they have Type A's working for them.)

Suinn's program included Anxiety Management Training (AMT) and Visuo-Motor Behavioral Rehearsal (VMBR). In AMT, patients learn relaxation, recognition of early signs that stress is building up, and self-control over stress before it becomes overwhelming. Deep relaxation exercises are used along with gradual exposure to stressful imagery until the patient has learned to recognize stress cues and how to reduce stress reactions. Suinn worked with patients who had an MI three to four weeks before the training, and the AMT lasted for three sessions.

VMBR also includes teaching patients deep relaxation. In addition, it makes use of a technique developed to improve the performance of Olympic athletes. It is a means of allowing people to practice adaptive responses under conditions that are nearly identical with real life ones through the use of imagery. Patients, while relaxed, were trained to visualize interactions prompting Type A behavior and then to substitute alternative behaviors. The VMBR took two sessions.

Both treated and control patients received a rehabilitation program of exercise, cardiac stress testing, dietary assistance, and smoking management. Nearly all the patients in the treatment condition (83 percent) reported reducing daily tensions and improving lifestyle. Measures were also taken of serum cholesterol and triglycerides (which are also correlated with CHD). Trained patients showed significantly greater drops in the levels of these cardiac risk factors than did controls.

Further work showed that Type A behavior as measured by the JAS also decreased. (Be sure to keep in mind the earlier statements about the limitations of the JAS.) A typical statement from a patient was: "I could accomplish as much or more without the previous stress I put on myself." Suinn also showed that blood pressure and cholesterol levels could be decreased independent of changes in diet, exercise, and smoking. So this brief intervention was remarkably successful in creating clinically significant changes.

Even more significant was the Recurrent Coronary Prevention Project (Friedman et al., 1986; Friedman & Ulmer, 1984; Thoresen et al., 1985) in which the impact of a cognitive behavioral program for reducing Type A behavior in MI patients was evaluated. Over 1000 patients participated in the program. They were randomly assigned to one of three groups. The first got the special cognitive behavioral intervention plus cardiology counseling, the second received cardiology counseling alone, and the third got no counseling at all.

In the cardiology counseling group, patients learned how to avoid various activities that might trigger a cardiac catastrophe, such as eating a high-fat meal, going into high altitudes, drinking too much caffeine and alcohol, doing severe physical exercise, or having prolonged exposure to cold. They also received psychological counseling, but treatment of Type A characteristics was avoided.

Besides the cardiac counseling, the cognitive behavioral group received extensive training in changing their thoughts and behaviors with respect to time urgency and free-floating hostility. A readable account of the detailed procedures may be found in Friedman and Ulmer (1984). Controls were merely examined yearly.

Unfortunately, although assignment of patients to the counseled groups was random, assignment to the control condition was not. Patients who volunteered for *some* kind of counseling were assigned randomly either to counseling that included coping with Type A behavior or to counseling that focused on coping with a heart condition, but did not deal with the issue of Type A behavior. Controls appear to have come from the body of patients who did not volunteer for either type of counseling. Thus, we cannot tell whether they had other characteristics that differentiated them from the counseled groups, and differences between controls and counseled groups are difficult to interpret.

Patients in the cognitive behavioral group reduced their Type A behavior more than those in the other groups. Results on MI recurrence after 4.5 years showed significantly less recurrence in the cognitive behavioral intervention group, which had 12.9 percent recurrence compared to 28.2 percent for controls, and 21.2 percent for the group that had only cardiac counseling. Looking at the percentage of fatalities, we find 5.2 percent in the cognitive behavioral group, 7.2 percent in the group that received cardiac counseling alone, and 11.0 percent in the uncounseled control group.

Stress and Coronorary Heart Disease

Although there are problems in clarifying the way Type A behavior relates to CHD, stress reactions undoubtedly play a role in the disease. Animal research, in which tighter control over conditions can be exercised, shows this role rather clearly.

For example, researchers submitted monkeys to a shock avoidance situation in which one monkey could avoid the shock, and the other, a "yoked control" received the same shocks as the monkey that had control, but was unable to do anything about it. Both groups suffered abnormalities of heart functioning. The yoked control monkeys tended to suffer severe slowing of the heart (*bradycardia*) and cessation of pumping of the heart's left ventricle,[1] but had no significant damage to the heart muscle. The animals with control of the shocks developed abnormalities of the electrocardiogram and degeneration of the heart muscle (Corley, Mauck, & Shiel, 1975).

In a related study, Lapin and Cherkovich (1971) removed a dominant male baboon from his social group of females and their young and placed him in a nearby cage. The investigators routinely fed the females and their young before feeding the imprisoned male, and they placed another male with the females and their young. All of this profoundly violated the ways of baboons and diminished the status of the dominant male. He reacted with violent agitation and attempts to escape the cage.

In all, 57 animals were submitted to stress. Forty-one of them developed cardiovascular disease, including hypertension and EKG signs of

coronary insufficiency. Six had MIs. We know that, under normal conditions, cardiac pathology is extremely rare in baboons (see Endicott, 1989 for more information on this and related studies).

Related work has been done with macaque monkeys (e.g., Kaplan, Adams, Clarkson, & Koritnik, 1984; Kaplan et al., 1983). Small groups of monkeys were allowed to form stable social hierarchies, and then several new monkeys were introduced into the established group. This led to fighting as the monkeys tried to establish a new hierarchy.

Control monkeys were left in a stable social situation. High-ranking animals in the unstable social condition developed far more coronary atherosclerosis than did their subordinate counterparts. In the stable social condition, there were no differences in atherosclerosis in dominant versus subordinate monkeys. (Atherosclerosis is a particular form of arteriosclerosis and the most common form. It mainly involves the deposition of cholesterol and lipid in the innermost wall of the arteries. Although there are other forms of arteriosclerosis, atherosclerosis is so common that the two terms are often used interchangeably.)

These results have something in common with findings in humans that relate "status inconsistency" to CHD. People with status inconsistency are those whose place in life is far above or below where most people with their backgrounds would be. For example, a person with a graduate degree who had a minimum wage job would be high in status inconsistency. Epidemiologists have identified status inconsistency as a risk factor in human CHD (see Endicott, 1989).

Conclusions

In this chapter we have dealt with the diseases that do more to kill and impair people than any other. We have only been able to give a partial account of the place of psychology in dealing with these problems. Some other relevant issues are dealt with elsewhere in the book. For exam-

---

[1] The left ventricle of the heart is its major pumping chamber—the one that forces blood through most of the body.

ple, psychological factors are important influences on whether or not hypertensive patients comply with their medical treatment. The issue of compliance is treated in Chapter 6, and lifestyle change in Chapters 8 and 9. There were other topics we could not cover, such as the psychological impact of heart attacks on patient and family (e.g., Croog & Levine, 1982). Had we but space enough and time, we would find an even more extensive use of psychology in preventing and coping with cardiovascular disease. But we believe the case has been well made even with our small selection of major topics.

It seems clear that psychological methods should be put to wider use in the treatment of essential hypertension, especially in the case of borderline hypertension, in which the value of medical intervention has been doubted. Such therapies as relaxation training and biofeedback may also be useful in augmenting the treatment of more severely hypertensive patients, thereby minimizing the side effects of medications.

It also seems clear that the best way to deal with coronary heart disease is to prevent it. Management of stress and changes in eating, drinking, and exercise habits are of critical importance here (see Chapters 8 and 9). Our casual

impression is that cardiologists tend to see psychological factors as of minor significance in heart disease. Friedman and Ulmer (1984) point out that doctors tend to be Type A themselves and are prone to minimize the significance of such behaviors in causing or worsening heart conditions. The difficulties investigators have run into in trying to explicate the role of Type A behavior, or even in measuring it, have made it easy to dismiss this psychological factor. This dismissive attitude tends to spill over onto other psychological influences, such as stress.

The evidence seems strong that somewhere embedded in the complex pattern of Type A behavior are important determinants of heart disease. However, we must be very cautious in drawing conclusions from data on this topic lest we destroy our credibility. Studies such as those on the hostility factor, in which parts of the Type A pattern are dissected out and their effects on heart disease validated, have tended to rely on re-analysis of old data from previous studies of Type A behavior. It is important that these be replicated on new groups of patients and that the methods of measuring the new variables be carefully worked out.

Summary

1. Arteriosclerosis ("hardening of the arteries") is very common in industrialized countries and underlies several of our most significant, killing diseases. Factors generally conceded to encourage it are high cholesterol levels, smoking, high blood pressure, amount of exercise, and personality or "behavioral style." Getting these factors under control can arrest and even reverse the areteriosclerosis.

2. Hypertension is abnormally high blood pressure; over 90 percent of cases are essential hypertension, which means that no organic cause can be identified. Hypertension is "the silent killer" because it has no readily identified symptoms, yet it is a ma-

jor source of strokes, heart attacks, and kidney disease. It also leads to nonlethal disabling disorders such as blindness.

3. Cardiac output and peripheral resistance (back-pressure from bodily tissues) are the sources of blood pressure. Sympathoadrenal, fight or flight reactions tend to increase both cardiac output (e.g., faster, stronger heartbeat) and peripheral resistance (e.g., constriction of small blood vessels).

4. The established, successful medical protocol for treating essential hypertension uses diet and medicines. It is expensive, often produces side effects that for many

patients seem worse than the hypertension, and is not adhered to by a large proportion of patients. Furthermore, it may not be appropriate for milder, borderline cases of hypertension.

5. Nondrug treatments have been devised for hypertension and have produced promising results. They generally involve some form of relaxation training and, often, biofeedback. They have sometimes been found to be effective with very high blood pressure; their clearest use is in cases of borderline hypertension, where the risks of cardiovascular disease are elevated, but medication may do more harm than good.

6. Psychologists can contribute to control of blood pressure by devising ways to help people maintain exercise programs and modify their diets. Exercise is known to lower and protect against the damaging effects of blood pressure. Weight loss and, in some cases, restriction of certain dietary contents, such as sodium and alcohol, can also help control hypertension.

7. Coronary heart disease (CHD) is probably the major single killer in industrialized countries. The heart consists of two pumps that work side by side and must be coordinated to accomplish their task. Many disorders can develop in the heart, including defects of the muscle itself, of the valves, and of the conduction system. The term "heart attack" or "myocardial infarction" refers to the case in which blood supply is cut off to the heart muscle, destroying a piece of it due to lack of oxygen.

8. The heart receives its blood supply from specialized blood vessels known as the coronary arteries. Because of arteriosclerosis, these vessels often become blocked. A variety of biomedical treatments can be employed to improve blood supply despite the blockage. Various medicines to keep the heart from exerting itself too much and to maximize the flow of blood through the arteries may be used. At-

tempts, often only temporarily successful, can be made to mechanically reopen the artery ("balloon angioplasty"). But the centerpiece of biomedical treatment is the coronary bypass operation, in which blood vessels from elsewhere are transplanted to augment blood supply to the heart. Patients seem to feel better after such surgery, but there is little support for the idea that it extends life.

9. It is best to deal with heart disease through prevention. There are many known risk factors, such as smoking, high blood pressure, and high serum cholesterol, and control of these should help to prevent the development of heart disease. Even all three of these factors, however, are quite limited in their ability to predict heart disease, which leads to the suspicion that some major determinants have yet to be discovered. Many believe that behavioral style is one of these determinants.

10. Type A behavior is a pattern of hurrying, usually accompanied by hostility to those who get in your way, and a chronic sense of time urgency. Strong evidence on large samples of subjects indicates that this behavior is related to heart disease. In recent years, however, research has been done in which the Type A pattern failed to predict outcome of heart disease. A good deal of progress has been made in finding out why the newer studies fail to show the expected effect of Type A behavior. One focus has been on the possibility that the hostility component of Type A behavior is the crucial factor. We do not yet have enough evidence to conclude that hostility is the correct predictor.

11. Investigators have attempted to reduce Type A behavior in cardiac patients with considerable success; in at least one of these studies, patients with a cognitive behavioral intervention to reduce Type A behavior had fewer recurrences of heart attacks.

12. Stress has been implicated in heart disease in both humans and animals. In animal research done with baboons and monkeys, fatal coronary disease developed quickly when the animals were stressed by disturbing their social hierarchy.

Key Terms

Angina

Arteriosclerosis

Balloon angioplasty

Cardiac output

Coronary bypass surgery

Coronary heart disease

Diastolic pressure

Essential hypertension

Hypertension

Ischemia

Jenkins Activity Survey

Korotkoff Sounds

Myocardial infarction

Peripheral resistance

Silent heart attacks

Structured Interview

Systolic pressure

Triangular numeric breathing

Type A behavior

Discussion Questions

1. What is arteriosclerosis, what contributes to its development, and why is it important to our health?

2. Define essential hypertension and, in broad terms, explain the bodily processes that produce it.

3. What are the health consequences of essential hypertension?

4. What are the symptoms of essential hypertension, and how is hypertension measured?

5. Describe the physiological mechanisms that provide a link between psychological factors and essential hypertension.

6. Outline a nondrug approach to essential hypertension and give evidence that such approaches are valuable.

7. What is coronary heart disease, and why is it so important to the health status of people in most industrialized countries?

8. What are the strengths and limitations of coronary bypass surgery?

9. What is a proper role for psychology in preventing CHD?

10. What is Type A behavior, and what is our current understanding of its role in CHD?

11. Discuss the problems encountered in measuring Type A behavior. Can you suggest a way to improve its measurement?

12. Explain our current knowledge of the role of hostility in CHD.

13. What has been the impact of programs designed to modify Type A behavior?

14. Give evidence for a relationship between stress and CHD.

Chapter 12

Cancer and AIDS: The Dreaded Diseases

*L*ila was a 78-year-old widow who was convinced she would live to be at least 90 years old as her mother had. She had no chronic illnesses and enjoyed an active life filled with friends and family. One weekend she suddenly began to run an above-normal temperature and had problems breathing. She was diagnosed as having acute myelomonocytic leukemia, a deadly form of blood cancer. Within five weeks of her first symptoms, Lila was dead. The reactions of her family and friends were predictable. They were shocked and they grieved, but her daughter noticed that they also seemed afraid. They seemed to have a need to blame Lila in some way for having leukemia: "Could it be because she smoked cigarettes or drank so much coffee? Maybe it was exposure to all those chemicals she applied so freely to her well-kept lawn." They appeared to be hoping to find a cause for her leukemia that would be unique to Lila in order to reassure themselves that they would escape this dreaded disease.

Cancer and AIDS are diseases that provoke images of a certain death that will be prolonged, painful, and perhaps disfiguring. In addition, persons with AIDS suffer a cruel social stigma. Both diseases have critical psychological and social components that are not addressed by the biomedical model. This chapter will show that effective, humane treatment of these diseases demands a biopsychosocial approach. Furthermore, the information presented here indicates that behavioral and environmental interventions are critically important to the prevention of cancer and AIDS.

CANCER

Cancer has been one of the most feared diseases throughout history. The term "cancer" is commonly used to describe something hidden and evil that spreads destructively. Cancer literally means crab in Latin. The use of the word can be traced to Hippocrates in fifth century B.C. Greece. Hippocrates observed that the distended veins radiating from breast tumors were crablike. The silent, creeping, persistent crab with its voracious appetite became the symbol for a complex group of diseases (Patterson, 1987).

What Is Cancer?

Cancer is not a single disease; it is a term used to describe many different diseases character-ized by the unrestrained growth of abnormal cells. Our bodies contain trillions of cells that are organized into groups to form various tissues and organs. Normally, these cells multiply and divide in a controlled manner to replace cells that are lost or destroyed. A cancer cell is a cell that is "out of control." Cancer is therefore best described as a defect that allows cells to multiply in an uncontrolled manner. These uncontrolled cells breed similar cells that form a mass of tissue called a tumor. Tumors are also referred to as **neoplasms,** which literally means "new growth."

Types of Cancer

Benign tumors do not spread to other sites and are described as growing "in place." They are usually harmless and are unlikely to recur after removal. However, benign tumors can block essential vascular and neurological functions if they grow in enclosed, vital places such as the brain. Tumors that invade normal tissue are called **malignant tumors.** As malignant tumors develop, cancerous cells can break off and travel through the bloodstream or lymphatic system to other parts of the body where they grow into new malignant tumors. This process is called **metastasis.** For example, a tumor in the lung can metastasize to the brain.

Cancers are very complex and are of many types. One way they are classified is by the type of cell from which they originate. The most common type of cancer defined by this criterion is **carcinoma.** Carcinomas originate from the cells of the tissue that cover the internal and external surfaces of the body. Carcinomas account for 85 to 90 percent of all cancers. About 2 percent of all cancers are classified as **sarcomas.** They originate in the connective tissue found in muscles, bones, fat, lymphatic vessels, and nerves (USGAO, 1987). Both types of cancer are malignant.

Not all cancers produce tumors. The leukemias involve the abnormally high production of abnormal white blood cells produced by the bone marrow. The major classifications of leukemias are made by their rate of progression. **Acute leukemias** advance very rapidly and cause death in a matter of months. They can strike people of any age including very young children. **Chronic leukemias** progress very slowly and tend to afflict older people. The leukemias are further defined according to the type of cells showing abnormalities. There are at least eight general kinds of acute leukemia and two types of chronic leukemia (USGAO, 1987).

Cancers are also classified by primary sites, that is, the organ in which the abnormal growth first appears. This type of classification is used primarily for presenting statistics on disease trends. Classifying tumors in this way can be misleading. There is great variation within cancers of the same primary site, and they differ with respect to their cause, treatability, and prognosis (USGAO, 1987).

The Biopsychosocial Precursors of Cancer

Note that in this book we use the term "precursors" rather than "causes" of cancer. Precursor refers to something that precedes, and it indicates the approach of something else. We have to be able to determine the precise time and origin of a cancer to say that a specific factor *caused* it. Such precise determination is difficult because the **initiation** and **promotion** of a cancer may be separated by years. A malignancy requires that both initiation and promotion occur. Initiation is the alteration in the genetic information of a normal cell, whereas promotion involves the abnormal growth of the altered cell.

The distinctions made between biological and psychosocial factors are often blurred as we discuss the etiology of cancer. Even the most rigid proponent of the biomedical model will agree that behavior plays an important role in the development of cancer. Most, if not all, the precursors of cancer have biological and psychosocial dimensions.

Genetic Predisposition

In recent years, the study of **oncogenes** has caused great interest among researchers. Oncogenes are cancer-causing genes that appear to produce uncontrolled growth in cells when they are activated by other genes, viruses, or other **carcinogens** (Patterson, 1987). Carcinogens are cancer-producing agents that may be found in the host or the environment. The discovery of oncogenes does not reduce the importance of psychosocial factors in cancer. Many of the carcinogens that have the potential to trigger oncogenes involve our behaviors and the environments we have created (see Chapters 8 and 9).

Behavioral and Environmental Factors

The National Cancer Institute (Greenwald & Sondik, 1986) estimates that "life-style and environmental factors are related to development of roughly 90% of cancer incidence" (p. 15). It is further estimated that over 30 percent of cancer deaths are related to tobacco use. Another 25 to 35 percent of cancer mortalities may involve dietary factors (see Chapters 8 and 9.)

The environmental factors include all the carcinogens that contaminate our water, air, and soil. Ironically, some of the exposure to carcinogens comes from medical technology (Greenwald & Sondik, 1986). Indeed, most cancer treatments have also been shown to cause cancer, for example, radiation, immunosuppressors, and certain steroid hormones (Rosch, 1984). Many environmental carcinogens are human-made, cancer-causing agents. They are also the by-products of advanced and prosperous societies. Control of these factors, then, involves the values and behaviors of society as a whole and requires broad social action.

Many environmental carcinogens are the by-products of advanced and prosperous societies. Control of these factors requires broad social action.

It is always difficult to separate individual behaviors from the values of the society in which they occur. For example, the incidence of cervical cancer is very low among Jewish, Mormon, and Amish women. It is believed that this low incidence is due to their strict codes of sexual behavior. Women who become sexually active early and have multiple partners are at much higher risk than women who do not engage in those practices (Levy, Ewing, & Lippman, 1988).

Cancer and the Immune System

There seems to be general agreement that the immune system plays an important role in the development of cancer. It is believed that cancer cells are present in most people and are kept in check by an efficient immune system. Therefore, people with decreased immune functioning are more susceptible to cancer. For example, agents to suppress the immune system are given to patients receiving transplants to prevent rejection. These agents may account for the 20 to 30 percent incidence of cancer found in lung transplant patients (Rosch, 1984).

The relationship between the immune system and cancer also has psychosocial dimensions. As we mentioned in Chapter 4, we know that hormones produce changes in the immune system. For example, adrenal-cortical hormones interfere with the body's ability to produce antibodies. There is increasing evidence that the brain, endocrine, and immune systems are linked together in a single network or system (Pert, 1986). Indeed, *psychoneuroimmunology* is now included as a heading in *Medicus Index*. Its inclusion suggests that the limited framework of the biomedical model is being expanded to include psychosocial dimensions.

Stress and the Immune System

Stress may predispose us to cancer by disturbing the competency of our immune systems. We have discussed the link between stress, cancer, and the immune system in Chapter 4. Although we do not clearly understand the controlling variables, there is ample evidence that the two are related (Bartrop et al., 1977; Locke & Hornig-Rohan, 1983; Rosch, 1984). There are special problems in identifying the mechanisms that link stress and cancer—namely, the problems of defining and quantifying stress. And, as we mentioned earlier, we are hard pressed to identify the exact moment of the origin of the cancer (Rosch, 1984).

Animal studies have shown that stress affects the promotion of tumors rather than their initiation. Experimental stressors have included electric shock, crowding, and restraint. These studies indicate that stress can increase or inhibit tumor growth depending on a number of factors. Two of the most important factors are the type of tumor and its stage of development. Another critical factor appears to be the animal's ability to control the stressor (Redd & Jacobsen, 1988).

Several researchers have suggested that the

increased cancer rate is related to societal disorder and lack of control (e.g., the high crime and breakdown of traditional family structures). This lack of a sense of control increases the levels of stress experienced by members of society. Researchers note that cancer is rarely found in more primitive cultures, and many have concluded that cancer is truly a "disease of civilization." For example, Albert Schweitzer, the famed physician and humanitarian, saw little or no cancer when he first arrived in Africa in 1913. As the natives began to adopt the white culture, the incidence of cancer rose (Rosch, 1984).

Stressful Life Events

Several studies have found a relationship between stress due to negative life events and cancer (Cooper, 1984; LeShan, 1966). For example, one study (Jacobs & Charles, 1980) found some striking differences between the families of children with cancer and a group of matched controls. Seventy-two percent of the cancer group had changed residences compared to only 24 percent of the control group. Sixty percent of the children in the cancer group had experienced a change in the health or behavior of a family member compared to 24 percent of the control group. Marital separations and arguments between spouses were also much more common in the families of the cancer group. A case history from this research follows:

> The parents of a twelve-year-old boy had been having marital difficulty for some years. About a year before he became ill, however, the mother insisted on a separation. The father resisted this, but finally, was forced to agree. The boy was extremely unhappy about this situation, became visibly depressed, and felt torn between his parents and their conflicting wishes. Shortly before his father actually moved out of the home, he developed fever and lymphodenopathy and was diagnosed as having Hodgkin's disease. (p. 18)

The evidence from the study we just described seems quite compelling, but there are several admitted flaws in this research. The measures relied primarily on parents' memories. Such measures do not reflect what these life events actually meant to the child. There are other possible confounding variables in this study as well. For example, there was a higher incidence of cancer among family members of the cancer group compared to the control group. These criticisms are made not to disprove the relationship between stress and cancer, but to remind us that correlation does not "prove" causation.

Appraisals. Individual appraisals of stressors and available resources may have greater impact than the actual stressor. Readers will recall our discussion of primary and secondary appraisals from Chapter 7. Preliminary research has found relationships between cancer and death of spouse, academic examinations, and social isolation. However, a direct causal connection between psychosocial stress and human cancer has not been established yet (Redd & Jacobsen, 1988).

Coping. Researchers have found that one of the most fruitful ways to study the links between cancer and stress is through the coping process. As a risk factor for cancer, exposure to stressors may not be as critical as the ability to cope with them. One of the most direct links between stress and cancer are maladaptive coping responses to stress. These maladaptive responses often involve risk factors, for example, cigarette smoking, increased alcohol intake, and overeating (Cox, 1984).

Personality Traits

It is difficult to determine whether personality traits or psychological states are risk factors or symptoms of cancer. It may take years before clinical symptoms appear after a normal cell has been transformed into a cancer cell. Therefore, it is hard to know whether the measures reflect the state before or after the initiation of the disease. The distinction is especially hard to make with psychological variables. Some cancers result in hormonal imbalances that can affect mental function and mood (Redd & Jacobsen, 1988).

Depression As a Risk Factor. Woody Allen has been quoted as saying: "I don't get depressed, I grow a tumor instead." His remark reflects the widespread notion that depression is a risk factor for cancer. However, the results of research into this area are conflicting (Kaplan & Reynolds, 1988; Persky, Kempthorne–Rawson, & Shekelle, 1987). The methods used for measuring depression may account for some of the inconsistency. Bieliauskas (1984) suggests that chronic mild distress is a risk factor for cancer rather than clinical depression. Other researchers found a measure of "pure" depression more strongly associated with cancer mortality than with cancer incidence.[1] These findings suggest that depression may not *initiate* cancer, but it may play a role in its promotion (Persky, Kempthorne–Rawson, & Shekelle, 1987). Again, it may be that depression is an early symptom of some cancers.

The Cancer-Prone Personality.   In spite of inconsistent findings, the idea of a cancer-prone personality persists (Linn, 1988). Sometimes referred to as the Type C personality, this collection of traits seems to be the polar opposite of the Type A behavior pattern mentioned in the previous chapter. Type C individuals are described as nice, industrious, conventional, and sociable. Such people have a tendency to give rather than fight (Hughes, 1987; Temoshok & Fox, 1984). On the other hand, survival of breast cancer patients has been linked to a "fighting spirit," expression of emotions, and social contacts and support (Stolbach & Brandt, 1988).

Eysenck (1988) concludes that the cancer-prone personality has two major traits: (1) reaction to stress with helplessness or hopelessness, and (2) repressed emotional reaction to emotion-provoking life events. In a study of medical students over a 30-year period, "loners" were 16 times more likely to develop cancer than those students described as emotionally expressive (Shaffer, Graves, Swank, & Pearson, 1987).

Many other psychological traits are said to be related to the incidence or progression of cancer, for example, impaired self-awareness,

self-sacrificing, and self-blaming. Social factors related to cancer are intervals between sibling births, closeness to parents, and adverse childhood and adult events. There is also some suggestion that schizophrenics are in some way protected from cancer progression (Fox, 1983).

The investigation of the relationship between psychosocial factors and cancer is still in its "discovery" phase (see Chapter 3). Eysenck (1988) has reported that personality variables are much more predictive of cancer mortality than smoking. Others have failed to find any relationship between psychosocial variables and cancer (Cassileth et al., 1985).

The Psychosocial Effects of Cancer and Its Treatment

Cancer can have a devastating psychological impact on patients and their families. To many people, a diagnosis of cancer is an irreversible death sentence. Fear of disfigurement, prolonged disability, and the cost of treatment threaten the psychological well-being of patients and the long-term economic stability of their families (Slaby, 1988).

The treatment of cancer is sometimes dreaded more than the disease. Unfortunately, the chemicals and radiation used to kill the cancer cells also cause damage to healthy tissue. Most of the therapies produce adverse side effects that can be quite severe. Some treatment agents have the potential to cause irreparable loss of function. Nausea, vomiting, and hair loss are among the most common and distressing side effects for patients (Burish, Carey, Krozely, & Greco, 1987). Cancer treatments are also associated with pain, anxiety, sexual dysfunction, and long hospital stays (Redd & Jacobsen, 1988).

It is difficult to separate the symptoms of the disease from the side effects of cancer therapy. For example, anorexia and the resulting weight loss can be caused by the nausea and vomiting secondary to chemotherapy or by the cancer itself. The disease can interfere with the patient's ability to utilize the nutrients through changes in metabolism or obstructions. Ano-

---

[1] "Pure" depression is considered presented when the D score is greater than the scores for the other scales contained in the MMPI.

rexia is also associated with anxiety and depression (Spirito, Hewett, & Stark, 1988).

Depression and Cancer

Clinical observations suggest that cancer patients are generally depressed, although some researchers have questioned whether cancer patients are any more depressed than other equally ill patients (Kaplan & Reynolds, 1988). It is estimated that about 20 percent of patients with advanced cancer suffer from moderately severe depression (Goldberg & Tull, 1983). Cancer and depression share many of the same symptoms, for example, anorexia, fatigue, weight loss, insomnia, and the inability to experience pleasure. It has been suggested that the diagnosis of depression should focus on psychological symptoms, including dysphoric mood, loss of self-esteem, feelings of helplessness, guilt, concentration problems, and suicidal thoughts (Massie & Holland, 1988).

Physicians and staff often mistake the early symptoms of delirium and dementia for depression; these symptoms can involve withdrawal, apathy, and mood swings. Poorly controlled pain can also cause depression and is often linked with despair, acute anxiety, and the inability to sleep. Many barbiturates, tranquilizers, and hormones can produce symptoms of depression. Only a few chemotherapies produce depressive symptoms, but when they do occur they are severe (Massive & Holland, 1988).

Organic Mental Disorders

Cancer often involves complex medical problems that can lead to organically induced mental disorders. Some of the psychological problems experienced by cancer patients may be due to damage to the central nervous system. For example, **delirium** can result from generalized metabolic impairment. Symptoms of delirium include attentional and memory deficits, disorientation, perceptual distortion, psychomotor disturbances, and insomnia or daytime drowsiness. It has been documented that many patients diagnosed with psychiatric disorders actually have medical illnesses that have directly caused or worsened their symptoms (Goldberg & Tull, 1983).

Cancers of the lung, breast, and testicles and malignant melanoma may metastasize to the central nervous system (Silberfarb & Oxman, 1988). Personality change is often one of the early symptoms of brain tumor. A 52-year-old woman began to have personality changes about a year after "successful" treatment for breast cancer. Her family and friends assumed her symptoms were psychological. Later, it was discovered that a brain tumor had metastasized from the original breast tumor (Goldberg & Tull, 1983).

A number of other conditions can produce psychiatric symptoms, including elevated calcium levels and low levels of sodium, potassium, or magnesium. Hypercalcemia is the most common feature of a malignant disease. Liver failure sometimes leads to confusion, restlessness, and mood swings. Hypothyroidism can result in a depression in which patients feel worthless and excessively guilty about past events (Goldberg & Tull, 1983).

Steroid treatments and general anesthesia can also produce psychological changes, including inappropriate social behavior (Goldberg & Tull, 1983). The effects of cancer therapy can have an impact on the central nervous system ranging from mild to severe **dementia.** Dementia is the impairment of intellectual functioning due to organic factors. Many chemotherapies can produce symptoms that vary from anxiety and hallucinations (delirium) to drowsiness and sluggishness (lethargy).

Radiation treatments often have direct and indirect psychological consequences for patients. The short-term effects are well known and include loss of appetite, nausea, vomiting, and diarrhea. The debilitating nature of these side effects may result in depression for some patients. The delayed effects involve damage to the central nervous system. Symptoms from radiation injury may not show up for months or years after treatment (Goldberg & Tull, 1983; Silberfarb & Oxman, 1988).

Cancer patients are vulnerable to infections

of the central nervous system for several reasons. Cancer treatments compromise the immune system, making the brain more vulnerable to bacteria, fungi, parasites, or viruses. The hospital environment and the tumor itself may predispose the patient to infection. Delirium or other behavioral disorders are often the first subtle symptoms of these infections (Goldberg & Tull, 1983; Silberfarb & Oxman, 1988).

State of the art treatments have increased the survival rates for many cancer patients, especially children. Unfortunately, these treatments are often accompanied by short- and long-term complications. The short-term effects include pain, nausea, and vomiting; the delayed effects include damage to the reproductive and central nervous systems. Learning and school problems are common among survivors of childhood leukemia (Silberfarb & Oxman, 1988).

Hair loss is one of the most difficult side effects for many patients to handle because it results in a major disruption to their self-image. The loss of hair in children is also very upsetting to parents. Parents can help themselves and their children by reassuring them that the hair will grow back and that they have not really changed (Goldberg & Tull, 1983).

The Psychological Side Effects of Drugs

Many of the psychological problems experienced by patients are due to the unrecognized effects of drugs that affect the central nervous system. For example, anticonvulsant drugs are often required to control seizures associated with brain tumors. These medications require careful management to avoid psychiatric side effects. Similarly, drugs to reduce blood pressure have been associated with depression, fatigue, confusion, and impotence. High levels of caffeine can produce psychiatric symptoms including anxiety and depression. Not only is caffeine present in many popular beverages, it is found in a number of over-the-counter and prescription drugs that may be used by cancer patients (Goldberg & Tull, 1983).

Other drugs prescribed to cancer patients that may have aversive side effects are anti-depressants, tranquilizers, and sleeping pills. A survey of five major cancer treatment centers found that sleeping pills accounted for 44 percent of all psychotropic drugs prescribed (Spirito, Hewett, & Stark, 1988). Sleep-inducing medication can result in physical dependency, daytime sedation, confusion, memory loss, and poor coordination. These side effects are more likely to occur in older adults and when taken in combination with other depressants, for example, alcohol and tranquilizers (Wolfe, Fugate, Hulstrand, & Kamimoto, 1988).

Because many oncologists are unfamiliar with antidepressants, they tend to prescribe tranquilizers to treat depression. Unfortunately, tranquilizers can worsen depression (Goldberg & Tull, 1983). Other mental side effects of tranquilizers are confusion, delirium, memory problems, and impaired attention. Antidepressants share the side effects we just mentioned and, in addition, have the potential for some serious cardiovascular effects. Older patients and those with cardiac conditions are particularly at risk (Wolfe, Fugate, Hulstrand & Kamimoto, 1988).

The Effects of Cancer on Family

Cancer patients whose diseases are in remission often live in a constant state of alert for signs that the disease has returned. Many family members also share this kind of emotional readiness (Leventhal, Leventhal, & Nguyen, 1985). Family members of cancer patients who do not get well have to cope with the physical and personality changes that may result from the cancer or its treatment. Some family members tend to withdraw from the patient to protect themselves at the very time when patients are becoming increasingly concerned about having their needs met (Slaby, 1988).

Caring for a terminal cancer patient can become an overwhelming task even for the most dedicated loved ones. Many people simply do not have the knowledge or the physical or emotional strength to cope with the round-the-clock care required for these patients. For this reason, cancer patients and their families become very dependent on professional caregivers. Relationships between professionals and family members often become strained as both groups become frustrated with the capricious nature of the disease (Slaby, 1988).

What is more, cancer and its treatment threaten the economic stability of many families: treatment can easily run into thousands of dollars (Slaby, 1988). In addition to the high cost of treatment, employees with cancer may lose their jobs or find themselves unemployable. Employers are often reluctant to hire or keep people who have cancer, even if they have been successfully treated. One reason is that the cost of treating cancer increases the employer's health insurance premiums. Sometimes the reason has more to do with the dreaded nature of cancer. For example, Patterson (1987) quotes a 42-year-old bookkeeper who had a colostomy:

> I received a death sentence twice: Once when my doctor told me that I have cancer, then when my boss asked me to quit because the cancer would upset my fellow workers. Except for my wife, that job was my whole world. (p. 271)

Research (Bordieri, Drehmer, & Taricone, 1990) supports the observation that job applicants with cancer may suffer from personnel selection bias. Using a simulated personnel selection exercise, the researchers found that participants made lower hiring recommendations for applicants with certain kinds of cancer compared to an applicant who had suffered pneumonia.

Psychosocial Interventions for Cancer Patients

Adequate treatment of cancer patients is beyond the biomedical model. Research indicates that psychological interventions have helped reduce negative emotions, increase levels of activity, and lower distress (Redd & Jacobsen, 1988). Hoffman (1988) and Goldberg and Tull (1983) present excellent descriptions of multidisciplinary cancer treatment teams that include psychosocial interventions.

Social Support Interventions

Crisis intervention involving brief supportive therapy is most often used with cancer patients. These interventions are designed to improve coping skills and to decrease distress while increasing self-esteem and morale. Several studies have found that support groups can be effective in helping cancer patients reduce emotional distress. Linn (1988) described a support group that stressed feelings of control and meaningful activity, and that sought to reduce denial and increase hope. One technique to increase self-esteem and life satisfaction involved listening to patients' "life reviews." This helped the patients to review their successes and find a sense of meaning to their lives.

The right kind of social support can be very helpful in dealing with the denial that often accompanies the news that one has cancer. Patients often use denial to cope with the threat and loss connected with cancer. Those with strong stress resistance resources may use it for a short time to avoid being overwhelmed. This period of denial gives them time to gather their resources and adjust to the idea of having a life-threatening disease. Those who lack these resources may be more extreme in their denial and use it longer, leading them to ignore symptoms or to refuse medical care (Wool, 1988).

Social support, either from family members or groups, can help restore some of the loss of control that cancer patients so commonly feel. Thus, they need to be provided with as many opportunities as possible to increase their sense of control. Toward this end, patients should be given some form of control over their therapies and environments. Information and knowledge increase a sense of control through intellectual mastery. Patients should be urged to remain involved in family and financial matters (Goldberg & Tull, 1983).

Patients often experience profound grief when they lose parts of their bodies to cancer or its treatment. The psychological trauma that results from an amputation can be more severe than the physical consequences of the disease itself. These patients should be given the opportunity to express their grief and sense of loss. It is also very helpful if they can meet other people who have completed the rehabilitation process after a similar amputation (Goldberg & Tull, 1983). The American Cancer Society has a very successful program for women undergoing mastectomies.

Treating Depression

Many medical professionals consider depression or distress as a natural part of cancer. Concerns about depression by family members are often dismissed with the statement, "You'd be depressed too if you had cancer."

Patients may be more vulnerable to depression at certain points in the progression of their disease: (1) the time of diagnosis, (2) during relapse or worsening of the condition, (3) beginning new treatments, and (4) learning that a treatment is not effective. A history of depression or alcoholism also places a patient at higher risk for depression (Massie & Holland, 1988). A patient's reaction to cancer is greatly influenced by his or her family's history with the disease. Patients will feel less optimism if family members have died or suffered severe side effects from cancer therapies (Leventhal, Leventhal, & Nguyen, 1985).

Treating Nausea and Vomiting

Several studies have found various cognitive behavioral methods to be effective in treating nausea and vomiting, particularly in the case of **conditioned nausea and vomiting**. Conditioned nausea and vomiting is a conditioned response to the aversive stimuli associated with chemotherapy. In other words, this type of nausea and vomiting results from classical conditioning. Remember how Pavlov's dogs learned to salivate at the sound of a bell? In this case, neutral stimuli (e.g., waiting or treatment rooms) become paired with the toxic effects of the chemotherapy (Burish, Carey, Krozely, & Greco, 1987).

It is estimated that 25 to 33 percent of all patients experience conditioned nausea and

vomiting and 60 percent experience anticipatory anxiety. Conditioned nausea and vomiting can occur before, after, or during treatment and is very resistant to drugs that are supposed to prevent or treat nausea. Studies indicate that relaxation training and guided imagery can reduce, and perhaps prevent, the problem (Burish, Carely, Krozely, & Greco, 1987). Other studies have found systematic desensitization training and relaxation training (see Chapter 5) to be effective in reducing anticipatory nausea and vomiting (Campbell, Dixon, Sanderford, & Denicola, 1984; Morrow & Morrell, 1982).

The studies mentioned above were experimental designs with subjects randomly assigned to experimental and control groups. However, all the studies had fewer than 25 subjects, and the last study contained other admitted flaws. (As we noted in Chapter 3, studies with small sample sizes may not have enough power to detect the true effect of the independent variable.) The researchers do give some reasonable explanations for their results. Morrow and Morrell (1982) suggest that systematic desensitization gives patients a measure of control and reduces their feeling of helplessness.

Burish and colleagues (1987) suggest that three mechanisms are involved in the success of relaxation training: (1) it serves as a diversion, (2) it reduces vomiting contractions in the gastrointestinal tract, and (3) it reduces the anxiety that may serve as a conditioned stimulus for CNV. Burish notes that the early introduction of these kinds of methods may be advantageous in reducing chemotherapy distress. In practice, however, we find that they are commonly used as a "last-ditch" treatment.

Pain and Its Management

Pain may be one of the most dreaded effects associated with cancer and its treatment. It is estimated that 40 percent of adult patients experience moderate-to-severe disease-related pain in the intermediate stages of disease (Jay, Elliott, & Varni, 1986). Sixty to 90 percent of adult cancer patients experience pain in the advanced stages (Dalton & Feuerstein, 1988). Disease-related pain results from a tumor's invasion of bone, nerve, or other organ systems. The degree of severity depends on the type of malignancy and its location and progression. Treatment-related pain is associated with surgery, radiation, chemotherapy, and invasive testing procedures such as spinal taps.

The control of pain remains a serious problem for many patients and their families in spite of advances in this area. Studies indicate that 25 percent of cancer patients do not find relief from pain (Dalton & Feuerstein, 1988). There seems to be some agreement that physicians are not well trained in cancer pain management (Goldberg and Tull, 1983; Jay, Elliot, & Varni, 1986). The biomedical approach taken by most medical schools is simply not adequate for understanding and treating cancer pain. (Pain is treated in more detail in Chapter 10.)

Biomedical Management. Biomedical pain management techniques involve two approaches: (1) eliminating the cancer with such treatments as surgery, radiation therapy, or chemotherapy, and (2) providing symptomatic relief of pain without affecting the cancer. The second approach includes the use of systemic drugs, nerve blocks, or neurosurgical operations (Jay, Elliot, & Varni, 1986). Of course, the treatments to eliminate the cancer also result in at least some temporary pain and the other effects mentioned earlier.

The biochemical relief of symptoms is also associated with some unwanted side effects. According to Silberfarb and Oxman (1988), virtually all of these medications can result in cognitive impairment. Respiratory depression, nausea, immune suppression, and sedation are associated with morphine. Constipation is a less serious, but still unpleasant, side effect that accompanies the use of all narcotics.

It is not unusual for people to have moral biases against pain medication; many view their use as a sign of weakness. Many patients receiving Demerol will begin to complain about pain about 3 1/2 hours after an injection. Health care providers and family members often interpret such complaints as reflecting the patients' preoccupation with their pain control. Actually, patients' complaints accurately reflect Demerol's duration of effective action, which is about three hours (Goldberg & Tull, 1983).

Psychological Approaches. Hypnosis has been shown to be an effective therapy for acute pain that results from aversive medical procedures (Spirito, Hewett, & Stark, 1988). This technique has been used as a psychological approach to cancer pain management for a long time. Its effectiveness depends on the skill of the therapist and the patient's responsiveness to being hypnotized. Although individuals differ greatly in hypnotizability, it is a stable trait that can be measured (Jay, Elliot, & Varni, 1986). Hypnosis and cognitive behavioral therapy share some techniques, including relaxation training, imagery, and motivation enhancement and reinforcement by the therapist.

A cognitive behavioral program was found to be effective in reducing distress, pain, and physiological arousal in children undergoing painful cancer testing (Jay, Elliott, Katz & Siegel, 1987). There were five components to the program: (1) filmed modeling, (2) breathing training, (3) imagery and distraction, (4) behavioral rehearsal, and (5) positive reinforcement. In a three-year controlled outcome study, this program was compared to a Valium sedation condition and an attention control group. The cognitive behavioral program was found to be significantly more effective than the other two groups.

In Summary

Several studies indicate that psychosocial interventions can be very effective. Patients who receive interventions are more likely to return to work, to be more active, and to have fewer mood disturbances. There is a great need to design low-cost, broad-based programs that can be implemented in a variety of cancer care settings. The success of these programs will not depend entirely on the training of mental health professionals. The psychological and social needs of patients will not be met unless oncologists and their staffs recognize that these problems should not be dismissed as "normal" and that they often require professional care (Goldberg & Tull, 1983).

The interventions described above deal primarily with the psychological symptoms of cancer. As we mentioned in Chapter 4, there is increasing interest in using psychological therapies to enhance the medical treatments themselves. This approach began to receive some credibility with the work of the Simontons (Matthews–Simonton, Simonton, & Creighton, 1978). Their success has encouraged others to develop psychological methods to unleash "mind power" to conquer cancer (Achterberg, 1985; Borysenko, 1987; Norris & Porter, 1987; Siegel, 1986).

Many people are beginning to seek treatment outside of the biomedical establishment. Until recently, it was commonly believed that these people were of lower socioeconomic status and in the final stage of their diseases. This belief appears to be incorrect. Cassileth and her colleagues found that the patients using unorthodox therapy, either alone or with traditional therapies, were more likely to be better educated than those using traditional therapies alone. The global approach of unorthodox treatment and its mind-body emphasis appear to be logical and appealing to these patients (Cassileth, Lusk, Strouse, & Bodenheimer, 1984).

The assumption that unorthodox practitioners are quacks and charlatans also appears to be unfounded. The Cassileth study found many of these practitioners to be well trained and to believe sincerely in the efficacy of their treatments. Few of them charged high fees, and about 60 percent held degrees in medicine. The researchers suggest that the move toward unorthodox care may be related to the poor quality of the relationship between traditional physicians and their patients. The emphasis on self-responsibility also allows patients to gain some sense of self-control.

ACQUIRED IMMUNE DEFICIENCY SYNDROME

Three brothers, Ricky, Robert, and Randy Ray, contracted AIDS through transfusions to treat hemophillia. Local school officials banned them from attending classes at their elementary school. The parents moved to another state, but the boys were forced from the new school when their condition was discovered. The Rays returned to their hometown and waged a battle to return their children to school. A U.S. District Judge ordered the school system to admit the boys. Local parents boycotted the school, held rallies against the enrollment of the Ray brothers, and the principal urged teachers to focus on personal hygiene for all students. The town mayor removed his child from the school. The Ray family received death threats and a bomb threat forced the evacuation of the school. Finally, the Rays fled town when their home and all their possessions were destroyed by fire. Arson was suspected.

These three little boys were treated as though they had contracted the black plague because, unlike the other modern epidemics, AIDS is an infectious disease. In spite of its being an infectious disease, the biomedical model is clearly inadequate for solving the AIDS crisis. The AIDS virus is not transmitted through the water supply, nor is it airborne. The transmission of AIDS is behaviorally based. An effective vaccine is unlikely because of the rapidly changing nature of the virus. Moreover, the impact of AIDS goes far beyond the physical effects of the disease. It has had devastating psychological and social consequences for its victims and society.

The American Psychological Association was one of the first national professional organizations to respond to the AIDS epidemic (Matarazzo, Bailey, Kraut, & Jones, 1988). Psychologists have addressed many facets of the AIDS immune system. Helper T-cells identify the "enemy" and stimulate the production of other cells to fight infections (see Chapter 4). The ability of the HIV virus to invade and kill these cells disables the entire immune response (Hall, 1988). The AIDS patient is then open to attack from opportunistic infections. In other words, AIDS is not the direct cause of death. It weakens the immune system, which allows other diseases to do their harm.

The leading cause of death in AIDS patients is *pneumocystis carinii* pneumonia (PCP). Before AIDS, this disease was rarely seen except in patients with suppressed immunological responses caused by therapies used to combat cancer or to prevent transplant rejection. *Kaposi's sarcoma* (KS) is the second leading cause of death in AIDS patients. It is a rare malignant skin tumor and is also seen in cancer and transplant patients (Gong & Shindler, 1987).

The HIV virus first infects the monocytes and macrophages of the immune system. The virus does not destroy these cells and is dormant at this stage of the disease. At this stage there may be no warning signs or symptoms of the disease. (See Table 12.1 for a description of symptoms.) Exposed individuals who begin to experience serious, but not life-threatening, in-

The Ray brothers contracted AIDS through transfusions for hemophilia. They were prevented from attending school, received death and bomb threats, and were forced to leave their home when all of their possessions were destroyed by suspected arson.

crisis, including (1) prevention and treatment programs, (2) program evaluations, and (3) interventions to reduce stigma, and to relieve stress and burnout (Backer, Batchelor, Jones, & Mays, 1988).

The HIV Virus and Its Effects

AIDS is an acronym for **acquired immune deficiency syndrome.** "Acquired" means that people are not born with it. AIDS is apparently contracted from a virus which is generally referred to as the **human immunodeficiency virus** (HIV). The HIV virus attacks the Helper T-cells of the

Table 12.1 Signs and Symptoms of AIDS

Persistent fevers or night sweats
Severe fatigue
Weight loss
Swollen glands
Oral thrush (persistent white patches on tongue, throat, and esophagus)
Persistent diarrhea
Coughing or shortness of breath
Skin rashes and spots
Bruising or bleeding
Neurological problems

Source: Based on V. Gong. Signs and symptoms of AIDS. In V. Gong & N. Rudnick (eds.), *Aids: Facts and Issues.* Copyright 1987 by Rutgers University Press, New Brunswick, N.J., pp. 49–53.

fections have **AIDS-related complex** (ARC). Studies indicate that persons with ARC suffer from at least as much emotional distress as those with AIDS. This may be because they have to live with the constant uncertainty about developing AIDS (Tross & Hirsch, 1988).

The virus directly infects and damages nerve tissue, resulting in dementia and peripheral nerve damage (Johnson & Vieira, 1987). The early symptoms are difficult to distinguish from common mental disorders such as depression. Symptoms range from apathy and difficulty in performing normal activities to severe dementia and motor disturbances (Hall, 1988). Neuropsychological impairment due to direct HIV brain impairment is referred to as **AIDS dementia complex** (ADC).

The Transmission of AIDS

HIV virus is found in most body fluids, including blood, semen, saliva, urine, tears, breast milk, and vaginal/cervical secretions. Nevertheless, AIDS is not an easy disease to contract. The amount of HIV virus found in clear bodily fluids is very small. It is estimated that direct injection into the bloodstream of about one quart of infected clear fluids would be required for infection to occur (Batchelor, 1988).

The virus is also fragile outside the human body and can easily be killed with soap, alcohol, peroxide or household bleach. Blood and semen appear to be the most effective vehicles to transmit the HIV virus. Casual contact with intact skin is not considered to be an effective means of transmission. Transmission is much more likely for individuals with a depressed immune system and for those who have been repeatedly exposed to a high level of the virus (Sensakovic & Greer, 1987).

Populations at Risk

AIDS is associated primarily with the high risk sexual and drug-taking behaviors of homosexual/bisexual males and intravenous drug users. However, we want to focus attention on the behaviors rather than the groups. As Ross (1989) points out, a sizable minority of homosexual

men do not engage in high risk sexual behaviors, nor do all intravenous drug users share needles. A small percentage of the population is exposed through blood transfusions and births to infected mothers (Rubinstein, 1987).

High Risk Behaviors

Sexual Activities.   Before the HIV virus was identified, it was clear that certain behaviors placed individuals at high risk for contracting the disease. The first AIDS cases in the United States began to appear in male homosexuals. Early studies showed that male homosexuals who got AIDS tended to be more promiscuous than their healthy counterparts. In one study, AIDS patients averaged 60 partners per year compared to 25 per year for controls (Choi, 1987).

The practice of anal intercourse appears to be the most likely behavior for the transmission of the HIV virus. Receptive anal intercourse results in tearing of rectal tissue, allowing semen to be absorbed into the bloodstream. Other sexual behaviors that are considered unsafe are oral intercourse, oral-anal contact, and manual-anal intercourse (Sensakovic & Greer, 1987). According to the Center for Disease Control (1989), any activity that *directly* exposes a person to the blood, semen, or vaginal fluid of an HIV-infected person should be considered unsafe.

Intravenous Drug Use.   AIDS also appears in heterosexual men and women who are intravenous drug users. The HIV virus is transmitted in this population through the sharing of needles. The incidence of AIDS among intravenous drug users is increasing and is expected to continue to increase in the future. Intravenous drug users account for approximately 20 percent of the AIDS population (Rubinstein, 1987). The high incidence of AIDS among intravenous drug users may account for the growing problem of AIDS in prison systems (Guerrero & Koenigsfest, 1987).

High Risk Groups

Hemophiliacs.   By 1982 AIDS symptoms were reported in hemophiliacs. Hemophiliacs suffer from a blood disorder that requires them to receive injections of a blood-clotting protein. These injections are derived from donor blood, which expose hemophiliacs to the blood of thousands of people each year (Mason, Olson, & Parish, 1988). However, the transmission of HIV through blood products has been virtually eliminated through the use of blood screening programs and inactivation processes (Glasner & Kaslow, 1990).

Women at Risk. Women who share unsterilized needles for intravenous drugs are at risk for contracting AIDS. Women who are sexual partners of IV-drug users, hemophiliacs, or bisexual, homosexual, or promiscuous males are also at risk. Women who have undergone artificial insemination are theoretically at risk if the donors' sperm has not been screened for antibodies to the AIDS virus. There have been reports of a few women contracting AIDS this way (Gong & Shindler, 1987). Although the number of women infected with AIDS has increased, they account for only 10.6 percent of all reported cases (USBC, 1990).

Children at Risk. Although the percentage of women with AIDS is relatively small, it is a matter of serious concern. The number of AIDS cases reported in children under the age of 13 rose from 13 in 1981 to 360 in 1989 (USBC, 1990). The majority of these children acquired AIDS from their mothers before they were born. The HIV virus may be transmitted to the fetus through (1) the placenta, (2) exposure to infected maternal blood during labor and delivery of the infant, or (3) through breast milk. (Brooks-Gunn, Boyer, & Hein, 1988).

Health Care Workers. There have been few reports of health care workers contracting AIDS from their patients. The few cases that have occurred have involved unprotected contact with the blood and body secretions of AIDS patients. The majority of cases seem to have resulted from workers not observing recommended precautions (Shulman & Mantell, 1988). The small number of health care workers who have become infected with AIDS through their work supports the notion of the fragility of the HIV virus. This support is especially strong when we consider that significant precautionary measures were not implemented until late 1982 (Rubinstein, 1987).

Haitians. The prevalence of the HIV antibody among Haitians in the United States is about five times that in the general population. At first, the incidence of AIDS among Haitians was puzzling because of their cultural taboos against homosexuality and drug use. However, it is now believed that the majority of Haitians get AIDS through sexual activity involving male and female prostitution. Transmission of AIDS between males and females is more common among Haitians. It may be that being the receptor of anal intercourse puts Haitian women at high risk; this practice is a common means of contraception in Haiti and Africa (Vieira, 1987).

The Psychosocial Impact of AIDS

AIDS patients have very high mortality rates. The average length of survival from time of diagnosis is between 18 and 24 months. Patients may need to be hospitalized several times, and extensive and expensive care may be required to stabilize them during acute illness episodes. The AIDS epidemic has placed a heavy economic burden on health care resources (Shulman & Mantell, 1988). Between 1984 and 1989, Public Health Service expenditures for AIDS were well over $3 billion (USBC, 1990). In addition, physical disability, job discrimination, and medical expenses force many AIDS patients to apply for public aid (Tross & Hirsch, 1988).

The AIDS epidemic has had a profound impact on the gay community. Gay men without AIDS symptoms have developed acute psychological reactions that include panic attacks and generalized anxiety. Some have developed somatic reactions that mimic AIDS symptoms such as fatigue and night sweats. In some cases, severe anxiety reactions have impaired social and occupational functioning (Morin, Charles, & Malyon, 1984).

Acute Fear Regarding AIDS (AFRAIDS)

The specter of the AIDS epidemic is so terrifying that some suggest it has given rise to a related epidemic—AFRAIDS. AFRAIDS is an acronym for

Acute Fear Regarding Aids (Doubleday, 1987). Although AIDS is a difficult disease to contract, AFRAIDS is easily transmitted through gossip, media sensationalism, and well-meaning, but perhaps ill-informed, people. Doubleday charges conservative television and radio evangelists with spreading AFRAIDS; that is no doubt true. However, we suspect that AFRAIDS was also unintentionally transmitted by those who wanted to erase the public image that AIDS was strictly a problem of the gay community.

The Stigma of AIDS

AIDS patients must endure the stigma of their disease as well as the physical suffering. Like the lepers of biblical times, AIDS victims wear a badge of shame. There are many reasons for the stigma associated with AIDS. The most important being the disease's association with homosexuality and drug abuse, behaviors that violate the norms of large numbers of people. Moreover, it is a terminal disease that is transmittable to other people. Patients often suffer from wasting and disfigurement, and the lesions from Kaposi's sarcoma are very visible.

Many people hold the view that AIDS is a punishment for sinful behaviors. *Los Angeles Times* polls found that approximately 25 percent of their respondents agreed that "AIDS is a punishment God has given homosexuals for the way they live" (Herek & Glunt, 1988). Some clergy share this attitude. For example, a chaplain in a New York City hospital was reported to begin his visits with AIDS patients by saying, "You are very sick because God is punishing you. If you repent, you might get better. Otherwise, you are going to die a miserable death" (Doubleday, 1987, p. 281).

The stigma of AIDS has greatly added to the burden of patients dealing with a life-threatening illness. Several restrictions have been proposed to control the spread of AIDS. Among the most drastic are tabooing and quarantining those who test positive for the HIV virus. Hogan (1989) has found that, as the perceived threat of AIDS increases, people are more willing to impose social restrictions. AIDS patients may face the loss of their employment and housing because of the stigma associated with the disease. They may also be denied services ranging from health care to burial services (Tross & Hirsh, 1988).

Misconceptions about AIDS

Many of the unfounded fears and misconceptions about AIDS have created serious problems. For example, blood banks report fewer donors since the AIDS crisis because many people are afraid they will get AIDS by donating blood. Blood collection facilities have enforced strict hygiene measures for a long time—and long before the AIDS crisis—to protect donors and staff. These measures have obviously been successful because not one case of AIDS has been reported among the nursing staff at these facilities (Hirsch, 1988).

The fear of contracting AIDS from infected persons has led to a great deal of hysteria among the general public. For example, policemen in Washington, D.C., were issued yellow latex gloves to deal with gay protesters, and children afflicted with AIDS have been prevented from attending school by well-meaning, but ill-informed, school officials. The fear may be understandable, but apparently there is no reason for this kind of panic. A study published in the *New England Journal of Medicine* (Friedland et al., 1986) has concluded that the risk of contracting AIDS through casual contact is "minimal to nonexistent." This is true even in intimate household settings. Family members shared eating utensils, toothbrushes, combs, razors, hugs and kisses without infection.

The Psychosocial Treatment of AIDS

Psychological interventions should begin before people are tested for the HIV virus. Counseling should be provided to reduce anxiety that might result from misunderstanding the significance of the test. Assessment should be made to identify potential problems such as depression and suicidal ideation. Denial or a desire for revenge may actually increase high risk behaviors in some people with positive HIV tests. Information should also be provided regarding the prevention of the spread of disease. In addition, individuals should be notified in person of positive results, and followup counseling should be provided. Encouraging emotional discharge or challenging the patient's denial should not be attempted without providing psychological support (Ross, 1989).

Social Support Programs

Social support is a critical issue to AIDS patients. Because of the stigma attached to the disease, patients often feel a sense of isolation. In addition, those who decide to discontinue sexual activity to avoid infecting their partners may lose an important part of their social support system. Some studies indicate that coping abilities are more important than social support in predicting mental and physical health. However, there is some evidence that "good" copers are able to develop better support systems than "poor copers" (Namir, Wolcott, & Fawzy, 1989). Again, we have a case where the poor get poorer and the rich get richer.

Namir and her colleagues (1989) found that *who* provides *what* kind of support is important. Emotional support is best received from those who are closest to the patients rather than strangers. However, informational support is more valued and helpful when it comes from an expert rather than family members. Namir also found that support groups may not always benefit AIDS patients. For example, less structured and emotionally focused groups may actually create anxiety. It appears that patients prefer highly structured groups. Group interventions that focus on relaxation training, education, stress management, and problem-solving skills were found to be the most helpful.

Prevention Programs

Successful Programs. One study has indicated that psychological interventions to prevent AIDS have potential (Kelly, St. Lawrence, Hood, & Brasfield, 1989). In this study, over 100 subjects were randomly assigned to an experimental or a waiting-list control group. The experimental intervention consisted of 12 weekly group ses-

sions led by two psychologists and their assistants. The intervention involved AIDS risk education, behavioral self-management, assertion training, relationship skills, and social support development. Participants in the experimental group increased their AIDS risk knowledge and reduced the frequency of high risk sexual behaviors, including unprotected anal intercourse.

Psychologists were also involved in the design of an extensive prevention campaign in the San Francisco area that has enjoyed some measure of success. Studies show that the campaign, which included media efforts, town meetings, workshops, and phone referral services, reduced high risk behaviors and the incidence of HIV infections among gay and bisexual men in that city. This intervention is serving as a model for other cities (Morin, 1988).

Changing Community Norms. Providing information about high risk behaviors is an important part of prevention programs, but it is not sufficient. Attention must be given to changing behaviors and community interventions to change group norms. The San Francisco model placed a heavy emphasis on shifting community norms to accept low risk behaviors. Members of the gay community were included in the program planning to ensure the likely success of the program (Morin, 1988).

People in high risk groups are more likely to change their sexual practices if they have close friends who are making similar changes. Those without close friends and who feel isolated tend to increase their high risk behaviors. People with AIDS or at risk for the disease need informational, instrumental and emotional support (Namir, Wolcott, & Fawzy, 1989).

Public norms, as well as the norms of high risk communities, need to be changed to prevent AIDS. A possible solution to preventing the spread among intravenous drug users is to provide sterile needles to intravenous drug users. Such programs are strongly resisted because, first, they violate public norms about drug use and, second, it is feared that they will increase the number of drug users. If the experience of other countries is any criterion, this fear may be groundless. Amsterdam has developed a needle exchange program that is distributing 750,000 sterile needles and syringes per year. Since the inception of this program, the number of IV drug users has remained stable (Des Jarlais & Friedman, 1988).

Reaching Minority Groups. The focus of AIDS prevention has been primarily on white homosexual and bisexual males; however, ethnic minorities account for over 40 percent of deaths due to AIDS (USBC, 1990). Heterosexual intravenous drug users are responsible for most of the AIDS cases among black and Hispanic women and children. AIDS information directed at white homosexual males does not reach minorities. It is recommended that minority interventions employ street outreach campaigns using men from the target culture and appropriate language for this culture (Peterson & Marin, 1988).

Sexual abstinence or the use of condoms is often advised as the best way to avoid contact with the AIDS virus. Some people may not readily accept these recommendations. For example abstinence may not be a realistic option for many low-income women. For many of these women, sex is seen as the source of economic, social, and emotional support. Advising women to take the initiative in using condoms is not always a viable option either. Some women are actually abused by their partners for making such a suggestion. Furthermore, such "bold" behavior by women may violate social norms for some ethnic groups (Mays & Cochran, 1988).

Controversy and Contradiction

Since the first case was reported in 1981, AIDS has been surrounded by political, social, political, and economic controversy, primarily because it is associated in the public mind with two groups that are strongly censured by the society, homosexuals and drug abusers. Ross (1989) charges that the stigma associated with homosexuality prevented an adequate response to the AIDS epidemic during the Reagan years. The AIDS epidemic also added to the spiraling costs of a health care system that was already in economic crisis. The controversy surrounding AIDS has made it difficult to sort fact from fiction and science from politics.

For example, AIDS is often referred to as the "number one health problem in America" (Pelosi, 1988). Such statements must be questioned when we look at the data from the U.S. Census Bureau (1990). For example, the total number of reported AIDS cases from 1981 to 1989 was 99,939 and the total number of estimated new cases of cancer was 1,010,000 for 1989 alone. Those numbers suggest that cancer is a more pressing health problem.

Of course, AIDS has the potential to disrupt society massively if it spreads to populations who do not engage in the high risk behaviors associated with the transmission of the HIV virus. The increase of AIDS among heterosexuals is often pointed to as evidence that this may be happening. AIDS transmission among heterosexuals has been primarily from male intravenous drug abusers to their female sexual partners. In spite of a high infection rate, there is no clear evidence that female prostitutes transmit AIDS to their clients (Khabbaz et al., 1990). Like many sexually transmitted diseases, female-to-male transmission of HIV virus appears to be less efficient.

In contrast, the vast majority of AIDS cases in Africa appear to be connected with promiscuous heterosexual activity (Vieira, 1987). There are many plausible explanations for the differences in expression of AIDS between the United States and Africa. For example, public health clinics in Africa commonly reuse needles. Lack of sanitation, epidemics of venereal disease, and malnutrition may also affect African susceptibility (Gong & Shindler, 1987). A higher rate of genital ulcer disease may also contribute to heterosexual transmission of AIDS in Africa (Glasner & Kaslow, 1990).

Conclusions

The prevention of cancer and AIDS demands the expansion of the biomedical model to include psychological and social factors. Given the complex nature of both disorders, it is not likely that a successful vaccine will be developed to prevent either in the near future. However, both can be prevented to a large degree through lifestyle and environmental interventions.

We are not suggesting that these kinds of interventions involving behavioral changes are easy to accomplish. We have much to learn about motivating people to change behaviors and to maintain them once the decision to change has been made. This kind of knowledge requires rigorous research and has received relatively little economic support. It is estimated that only 4.3 percent of the National Institutes of Health budget is devoted to funding health behavioral research (Raub, 1990).

The treatment of cancer and AIDS also demands a biopsychosocial approach. Rather than abandoning medical technology, the biopsychosocial approach encourages the medical profession to consider the patient as a human being instead of a medical statistic. Dissatisfaction with the biomedical approach to treating cancer and AIDS has contributed greatly to the health care crisis in America today. Students in our health psychology classes increasingly want to share their stories of the insensitive nature of the biomedical approach. The following is a vivid example of these stories:

My father had lung cancer and had been told that he had only five to six months to live. As some sort of denial mechanism, I suppose, Dad "heard" the physician say five to six *years* instead of months. He became obsessed about living that long and being a burden to his family. I was with him one day when he expressed this concern to the oncologist. The physician replied, "Ed, I said five or six *months*, not years." My father opened his mouth to speak, but could only mumble incoherent sounds. He seemed to be struck "dumb" by those insensitive words. The physician responded to Dad's condition by saying the cancer must have metastasized to his brain. Extensive tests did not reveal that to be the case; he apparently suffered a stroke. Dad died six *weeks* later without regaining his speech.

The biopsychosocial approach is important not only to avoid the kind of insensitive treatment of patients we have just described, but it also holds great promise to augment the medical treatment of these dreaded diseases (see Box 12.1). The acceptance of the work of people like Bernie Siegel, Norman Cousins, the Simontons, and others suggests that the zeitgeist is ready.

Summary

1. Cancer is many different diseases characterized by the unrestrained growth of abnormal cells. Uncontrolled cells result in benign or malignant tumors. Benign tumors are usually harmless, but malignant tumors invade normal tissue and can metastasize to other areas of the body. Leukemias involve high production of abnormal white blood cells. Acute leukemias advance very rapidly, whereas chronic leukemias progress slowly.

2. The causes of cancer are hard to identify because of the length of time between the initiation and promotion of the disease. Most of the precursors of cancer have biological and psychosocial dimensions. It is estimated that lifestyle and environmental factors are related to the development of about 90 percent of cancer incidence.

3. Cancer cells are thought to be present in most people and are kept in check by efficient immune systems. Stress may predispose us to cancer by disturbing the competency of our immune systems. Correlational studies have found a relationship between negative life events and cancer, and appraisal and coping may be critical components in the relationship.

4. Research suggests that depression does not initiate cancer, but it may play a role in its promotion. It may also be an early symptom of cancer. Although it is in the

Box 12.1   Fighting Cancer with the Mind

Garrett was diagnosed as having an inoperable brain tumor when he was nine years old. In spite of being given the maximum medically safe amount of radiation, Garrett's symptoms worsened. To some extent, they involved the entire left side of his body. Garrett lived in Topeka, Kansas, where the famed Menninger's Clinic is located. Because of his worsening condition, his family took him to Menninger's Biofeedback and Psychophysiology Center. It was there that he began to work with Dr. Pat Norris.

Together they developed a visualization to "battle" his tumor. At the time, Garrett was quite taken with *Star Trek* and space exploration, so his visualization revolved around the idea of a space battle. His brain was the solar system, his tumor was an invading planetoid, and he was the leader of his squadron of fighter planes. The fighter planes were armed with his white cells and other immune defenses. Pat was Ground Control. He also used an organic visualization in which his tumor looked like a "dumb" chunk of raw hamburger, very disorganized and powerless. In this visualization, he saw millions of his white cells eating and destroying the tumor. In addition to the visualizations, Garrett's therapy included a comprehensive program that included biofeedback, deep relaxation, nutrition, and exercise.

For several months, his symptoms worsened. CAT scans revealed that his tumor was growing. Further treatment was not indicated and it was believed that Garrett had less than a year to live. It became difficult for Garrett to walk, and he began to have vision problems that interfered with his school work. In spite of all this, he continued his work with Pat and established his own hotline for kids with life-threatening illnesses.

About a year after his tumor was first diagnosed, Garrett began to show some improvement. One night when doing his visualizations, he was unable to "see" his tumor. All he could see was a "funny little white spot" where the tumor had been. Garrett was so convinced that the tumor was really gone, he and Pat switched their imagery to patrolling every corner of his body for unwanted invaders. He continued to improve physically and was able to go from a leg brace to tennis shoes. He kept at his daily visualizations of his white cells doing a surveillance job.

Because Garrett was not undergoing medical treatment, it was decided that there was no reason to subject him to further CAT scans. However, after a series of mysterious falls, a CAT scan was ordered. The physician who performed the scan asked if Garrett had had surgery. The tumor was gone. All that was left was a tiny fragment of calcification—"the funny little white spot." Everyone was amazed, except Garrett.

''discovery stage,'' a Type C or cancer personality has been described. It involves reacting with helplessness and hopelessness and repressed emotional reaction.

5. Cancer has a powerful psychosocial impact on patients and their families. The treatment is sometimes more dreaded than the disease because of its adverse side effects. Nausea, vomiting, and hair loss are among the most common. Cancer and depression share many of the same symptoms. Poorly controlled pain and medication can result in depression.

6. Cancer often involves complex medical problems that can lead to organically induced mental disorders. Elevated calcium levels and low levels of sodium, potassium, or magnesium can produce psychiatric symptoms. Steroid treatments, general anesthesia, and other cancer therapies can produce psychological changes. Many of the adverse side effects of treatment do not show themselves until months or years later—for example, damage to the reproductive and central nervous systems.

7. Many of the psychological problems experienced by patients are due to the unrecognized side effects of drugs that affect the central nervous system. Some of the drugs that are commonly prescribed for cancer patients are anticonvulsants, hypertensive medications, antidepressants, tranquilizers, and sleeping pills.

8. Families of cancer patients in remission tend to live in a constant state of alert for signs of recurrence. Families of patients who do not get well have to cope with the physical and personality changes in the patient. Many family members withdraw from the patient to protect themselves, and relationships between health care providers and family members often become strained. Cancer and its treatment threaten the economic stability of many families.

9. Psychological interventions for cancer patients result in a reduction of negative emotions, higher levels of activity, and lower distress. Social support interventions can be helpful in dealing with denial, strengthening self-esteem and life satisfaction, and restoring a sense of control. Patients who have lost parts of their bodies benefit from meeting other people who have been rehabilitated after similar amputations.

10. Patients are more vulnerable to depression at certain points in the progression of their disease. A history of depression or alcoholism and family history with cancer influences a patient's reaction to cancer. Conditioned nausea and vomiting is a conditioned response to the negative side effects associated with cancer treatment. Relaxation training, guided imagery, and systematic desensitization have been effective in reducing this condition.

11. Studies indicate that 25 percent of cancer patients do not find relief from pain. Biochemical pain treatment is associated with some aversive side effects, for example, cognitive impairment, respiratory depression, and nausea. Research indicates that psychological interventions can be effective. They include hypnosis, cognitive behavioral therapy, relaxation training, and imagery.

12. Psychosocial interventions for cancer patients can be effective. Such patients are more likely to return to work, be more active, and have fewer mood disturbances. There is an increasing interest in using psychological therapies to enhance medical treatments.

13. Many people seek treatment outside of the biomedical establishment. Research suggests that these patients tend to be more educated than those who rely on traditional medicine alone. Unorthodox practitioners are not necessarily frauds. Many are well trained and sincere in their beliefs.

14. AIDS is an infectious disease that is apparently contracted through the HIV virus which attacks the immune system, making the patient vulnerable to opportunistic infections. Patients with serious, but not life-threatening, infections have AIDS-related complex. Neuropsychological impairment due to direct HIV brain impairment is referred to as AIDS dementia complex.

15. The HIV virus can be found in most body fluids, but the highest concentrations are in blood and semen. It is a fragile virus outside the human body and is easily killed with soap or disinfectant. It is most often transmitted through specific sexual activities and the use of contaminated needles.

16. Hemophiliacs have contracted AIDS through transfusions. However, this threat has been greatly reduced through the use of blood screening. Women who are sexual partners of IV drug users, bisexual, homosexual, or promiscuous men are at risk. Mothers with AIDS can transmit the HIV virus to their children during pregnancy or breast feeding.

17. Many people have developed an irrational fear of contracting AIDS. As a result, AIDS patients must endure the stigma of their disease as well as the physical suffering. They may face losing their jobs and housing and being denied all kinds of social services. Children with AIDS have been prevented from attending school.

18. The psychosocial treatment of AIDS includes counseling to reduce anxiety about HIV testing, support groups for patients and their families, and prevention programs. Prevention programs should focus on education and changing individual behaviors and community norms. Individuals are more likely to change high risk behaviors if close friends are also making the changes.

19. Critics charge that the government has provided an inadequate response to AIDS because of the stigma attached to homosexual behaviors and drug abusers. Many consider AIDS to be the number one health problem in United States, yet the total number of reported AIDS is a fraction of the new cancer cases reported yearly.

20. The biopsychosocial model would facilitate prevention of cancer and AIDS because both diseases are greatly affected by environmental and lifestyle factors. This model would also promote more sensitive treatment for patients and their families.

Key Terms

Acquired immune deficiency syndrome
Acute leukemias
AIDS dementia complex
AIDS-related complex
Benign tumors
Cancer
Carcinogens
Carcinoma
Chronic leukemias
Conditioned nausea and vomiting
Delirium
Dementia
Human immunodeficiency virus
Initiation
Malignant tumors
Metastasis
Neoplasms
Oncogenes
Promotion
Sarcomas

Discussion Questions

1. What are the major categories of cancer?
2. List and briefly explain the major bio-psychosocial factors that influence the development of cancer.
3. What is the association between stress and cancer?
4. What is the relationship between depression and cancer?
5. Describe the psychological approaches used to augment medical treatments of cancer.
6. Which kinds of cancer are most likely to spread to the brain, and what kinds of behavioral changes usually signal such metastases?
7. Discuss organic factors other than metastasis that can produce psychological changes in cancer patients.
8. Discuss the psychological impact of drugs commonly given to cancer patients.
9. Discuss the impact of cancer and its treatment on the families of cancer patients.
10. Describe the nature of the HIV virus.
11. What are the risk behaviors that are associated with the transmission of the HIV virus?
12. What is AFRAIDS and how is it transmitted?
13. Describe the various types of psychosocial programs that have been developed to prevent and treat AIDS.
14. Describe the controversies that surround AIDS.
15. Why would prevention of cancer and AIDS be facilitated by the acceptance of the biopsychosocial model?

Chapter 13

The Widening Scope of Health Psychology

*L*aura had an underbite and a wide bottom jaw. Braces were not enough to correct her problem, so she was referred to an oral surgeon. Her experience with this surgery follows in her own words: "I visited the oral surgeon for an exam. He didn't tell me much about the surgery, but what he did manage to say was a lot of big words that I didn't understand anyway. The surgery took about an hour and a half, and I woke up to find myself vomiting blood. My stomach was the thing that hurt the worst, until I got hold of a mirror. The surgeon said that I would have a *space* between my two front teeth, not a 6-lane highway! I was crushed, but this wasn't the end! Every day I had to insert a key into this device in my mouth and turn it. This was to widen my top jaw even more. It was self-torture. I eventually had to go back to work. I was very hurt. It was different with everyone looking at your mouth instead of into your eyes. A second surgery was required and, like clockwork, I awoke vomiting blood. But this time my entire head, except for my eyes, nose, and mouth, was mummified. My mouth was not wired shut, but I could not open it. I was fed baby food by a syringe for about a week and a half. It got so terrible that I began to gag on it. After two weeks, the surgeon took the stitches out from both sides of my face where the screws were. Everytime I looked into a mirror, I wanted to cry. It wasn't me, and I wanted me back (crooked teeth and all). I never really told anybody how I felt. They never gave me a chance."

Can you see how important psychological knowledge could be in a case like this? "Jaw surgery" and "psychology" are not concepts we normally put together, but think how much difference it might have made if Laura had been psychologically prepared for what she was to go through and had gotten to talk through her feelings about this terrible experience with someone who knew how to help her process it. Her sense of lost identity is quite familiar to psychologists who work with such patients, and she could have been helped through it. And what if she had been psychologically disturbed in the first place and the surgeons had failed to notice? For example, she might have gone into severe panic during the period in which she could not move her jaw. In such a situation, and there are many instances of them, a health psychologist can be of great help to both doctor and patient.

We said at the start of this book that health psychology is a new field in the process of defining itself. One role of a book like this one is to survey the developing field of health psychology, and another is to help define the field. What we have written so far has shown the diversity and importance of health psychology, but we have, naturally, emphasized the most central topics. The real breadth of health psychology is easy to miss if we focus exclusively on the themes that have stimulated the most research and received the most attention.

Many areas of research and treatment in health psychology are not as widely known as the work of psychologists on cancer, AIDS, high blood pressure, or coronary heart disease. The inroads psychologists have made in these major areas are so well known that even a person who has never had a course in health psychology is likely to have heard about them. This work has shown the broad value of health psychology and the need for a shift to a biopsychosocial model. But psychologists have made many other important, though less well-known, contributions to the study of health and disease. In this chapter we will describe several of these less familiar topics.

HEALTH PSYCHOLOGY AND TEMPOROMANDIBULAR JOINT SYNDROME

Not many years ago it would have been hard to imagine a less likely candidate for psychological intervention than **temporomandibular joint syndrome** (TMJ). This disorder manifests itself with facial pain, often accompanied by headaches and ringing in the ears. A popping sound tends to occur when the mouth is opened wide. Because such opening can be painful, the person cannot open the mouth as widely as one normally could. The temporomandibular joint, which is the joint where the jawbone is connected to the skull, is commonly sore to the touch, as are the facial muscles around it.

TMJ is linked to the disorder called **bruxism,** in which affected individuals clench their teeth and grind them. Bruxism leads to tooth damage, with enamel being worn away and the teeth often being cracked or chipped.

History of Temporomandibular Joint Syndrome

TMJ was not likely to be dealt with psychologically because Costen (1934), the person who gave the first detailed description of it, presented convincing arguments that it was due to abnormalities in the structure of the temporomandibular joint. The disorder has been called Costen's syndrome because of his early contribution to describing it and explaining its purported causes. For Costen, TMJ was a mechanical problem of the joint, related to abnormalities in the way the teeth fit together, their "occlusion."

Costen's theory of TMJ was accepted for over 20 years, though it was never verified in research and was actually based on some erroneous ideas about the anatomy of the joint. People treated in accordance with this model tended to get better, and patients with the disorder often were found to have the expected abnormalities of the mouth and jaw. The history of Costen's view of TMJ is a nice example of the importance of doing controlled outcome research even with theories that seem to be too obviously correct to require testing.

Costen's views evolved in the 1950s and early 1960s to emphasize the role of dental reflexes that produce strained movements of the jaw muscles if the teeth do not occlude properly. Treatments within this framework tend to focus on "equilibration" of the teeth. The dentist makes a cast of the patient's teeth, observes points where the teeth fail to mesh properly, and then grinds the teeth to make a better fit. Again, most patients will get better with such treatment.

It was quite a surprise when controlled outcome studies with such placebos as sham equilibrations (the dentist does not really equilibrate the teeth but seems to) started showing that the placebo was about as good as the real treatment. Apparently, psychological factors were important enough to match the effectiveness of the mechanical manipulations.

Response Specificity

Eventually, this kind of work led to the development of a psychological view of TMJ. Actually, the new view was biopsychosocial, so it included physiological as well as mechanical factors, while giving an important place to psychological influences. A major approach emphasized **response specificity,** a term meaning that individuals tend to react to stimuli in unique ways. One person may respond to a stressor with jaw tension, while another may respond with an increased heartbeat or elevated blood pressure.

There is room within the response specificity view for the possibility that whole classes of people may tend to give a certain kind of bodily response when stressed. That is, although certain *unique* responses are as individual as a fingerprint, there might also be responses that characterize a certain *class* of patients, such as hypertensives, migraineurs, or those with TMJ.

Incidentally, once the newer interpretations of this disorder no longer gave such a central position to the temporomandibular joint in producing the symptoms, researchers started changing its name to reflect the changed concept. Many names have been given to it, but a very common current one is **myofascial pain dysfunction syndrome** (MPD).

The response specificity hypothesis implies that patients with this diagnosis tend to give stronger reactions in facial and, especially, jaw muscles than do people who do not have the problem. A recent paper gives strong support to this interpretation (Kapel, Glaros, & McGlynn, 1990). MPD patients were compared to nonpatients during exposure to horrific scenes from the movie *Dawn of the Dead* and to idyllic scenes from the movie *Jonathan Livingston Seagull*. During these viewings, measures were taken of heart rate, electrical conductance of the skin (a measure used in "lie detectors" to detect emotional responses), and electrical response of several muscles of the face, including jaw muscles. Forearm tension was also measured. Not only did TMJ patients have higher baseline muscular tension in several facial sites, but also they showed higher forehead tension under stress than did nonpatient participants. Furthermore, the MPD patients showed a distinctive pattern of heightened forehead tension and *decreased* heart rate and skin conductance. Thus, this class of patients seems to show a very specific physiological pattern of response to stress.

Further research is required before we can know why this particular and unexpected pattern of response was specific to MPD patients. One possibility suggested by the authors is that the pattern of responses is specific to a given type of stressor. The next step should be to study the effects of different stressors.

McGlynn et al. (1989) also tried to do an experimental test of whether mechanical and psychological factors interact to produce jaw tension. A multifactorial view is often put forth as the correct one. From that view, several factors interact with each other to produce the disorder. This notion makes sense and is widely believed, but there is little research on it. What McGlynn and his colleagues did was to create an artificial abnormality of the contact between the teeth with a device that prevented normal contact on one side of the mouth. They also had a control device that was designed to fit over the teeth but not produce occlusal interference. Then they had the subjects watch movies presumed to be stressful versus some that were not.

The multifactorial notion would lead to the expectation that there would be some interaction between occlusal interference and psychologically stressful stimulation. For example, we might expect people with occlusal interference to show greater tensing of the muscles than those without occlusal interference when psychic stress was present. This kind of interaction did not take place.

On the surface, we could conclude that the factors used in this study did not interact. However, the authors felt that more work should be done on this topic before rejecting the multifactorial view. The apparatus designed to produce occlusal interference caused elevated muscular tension in the side opposite the device. This suggests it produced an expected effect. However, the control device also produced such an effect.

Biofeedback Treatment

Another line of research that supports the idea that psychological factors are important in MFD is the use of biofeedback in treating it. The attitude taken by many students of biofeedback, especially with regard to a disorder so poorly understood as MFD, has been that it is best to focus on what makes it better rather than on eliminating the perhaps unknown cause of the symptoms (Rugh & Solberg, 1976).

Many investigators have done studies, more or less well controlled, on the effects of EMG biofeedback on MFD. Mealiea and McGlynn (1987) have summarized this research and are critical of it. They conclude that, although biofeedback shows great promise and is probably as well founded a treatment as any other, it has not really been adequately evaluated yet. Obviously, much more work remains to be done in this area, but it is notable that a psychological procedure can do so well in treating a disorder that seems so clearly mechanistic in its origins.

HEALTH PSYCHOLOGY AND PLASTIC SURGERY

The significance of psychological intervention in plastic surgery is brought into clear focus by a statement from Edgerton and Langman (1982): "the only legitimate indication for purely aesthetic surgery is to improve the emotional health of the patient." At least in the case of cosmetic surgery, the ultimate goal of the operation is psychological change. Furthermore, psychological factors are important at every stage of treatment from the initial interview through long-term adjustments to the changes of appearance.

The appropriateness of the patient's decision to seek surgery, the degree to which the patient can cope with and recover from the operation, and the patient's satisfaction or dissatisfaction with the result all depend on psychological factors. Failure to take these factors into account can result in harm being done to the patient as well as the kind of chagrin over the surgery that results in malpractice suits.

Pruzinsky (1988) has outlined the functions of the psychologist at each of these stages. The first stage is that of the patient's decision to seek help from the plastic surgeon. Patients have usually been self-conscious and low in self-esteem prior to making this decision. Their social life has been impaired because of their distress about some aspect of their appearance. They are often embarrassed to ask for this kind

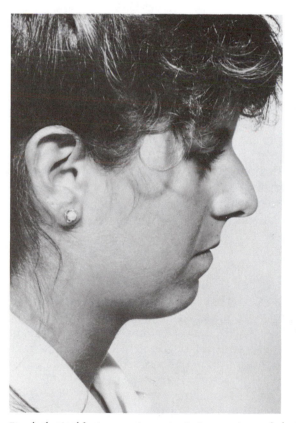

Psychological factors are important at every stage of plastic surgery, from the initial interview to the adjustments to changes in appearance.

of help and feel guilty over their "vanity" for wanting to make such changes.

The older literature tends to emphasize that patients seeking cosmetic surgery are neurotic. In contrast, contemporary psychological research on this topic is based more on actual observation of the patients (Goin & Goin, 1986). This work suggests that each patient is influenced by multiple factors in deciding to seek cosmetic surgery, and this decision need not have its basis in neurosis.

Pruzinsky's second stage is that of the initial consultation. The patient is usually quite anxious, regardless of whether the "deformity" to be changed is large or small. There seems to be little relationship between the objective degree of deformity and the patient's reaction to it. That the patient is distressed over what appears to the outsider as a small defect is not necessarily an indication of psychopathology. During the initial consultation several psychological factors must be assessed. What is the source of the patient's motivation? It is best if the patient is motivated by internal factors, such as the wish to feel better about himself or herself. Wishes to please others are more problematic. How stressful is the patient's life? If the patient is highly stressed, it may be best to delay surgery. Pruzinsky maintains that the surgeon should take seriously his intuition about how well he or she will work with this particular patient.

At this stage the health psychologist must assess the patient's psychological distress and note any evidence of mental disorder or other psychological factors that might set up problems with various stages of the medical intervention. Keep in mind that some patients who seek this kind of surgery are mentally disturbed. The psychologist must watch for such signs as significant depression and various psychiatric disorders that involve major distortions of body image. For example, there is a disorder called **body dysmorphic disorder** in which the patient has a grossly exaggerated impression of deformity, which is either nonexistent or only slightly evident. About 2 percent of patients seeking elective cosmetic surgery have this disorder.

Psychotic patients sometimes have delusions about parts of their bodies and may seek plastic surgery as a solution.

Plastic surgeons usually reject such patients. The patients often respond with animosity and proceed to go from surgeon to surgeon seeking satisfaction. Not all such patients must be rejected. Sometimes a course of psychotherapy can help resolve whether surgery is appropriate.

In Pruzinsky's third phase, patients are prepared for surgery and go through the actual operation. Presurgically, patients tend to be anxious, and the therapist can provide relaxation training as well as various cognitive behavioral interventions to help them cope (see Chapter 5). Because highly anxious patients tend to have longer recovery periods, attention to this phase can be quite valuable.

Patients frequently experience psychological trauma during surgery, although surgeons are often unaware of it. Burgoyne, Goin, and Goin (1977) reported significant psychological trauma during surgery in about 10 percent of patients. They pointed out that this condition would have gone undetected in the absence of skilled interviews on the part of mental health professionals. Many of these traumatic reactions stemmed from conversations the anaesthetized patients overheard and sometimes distorted.

The fourth stage is the postoperative period. Patients often experience depression and anxiety as a result of the general stress of surgery, doubt as to outcome, and various bodily reactions they are not in a position to interpret. The psychologist who has already established rapport with the patient can help the patient by offering reassurance and empathy at this stage.

Finally, the patient and the treatment team must cope with long-term recovery from surgery. A major step in this recovery must actually take place prior to the surgery. Patients must be prepared for adjustment to both good and less than ideal outcomes. The treatment team must see to it that they are so prepared.

Strangely, patients may have problems even

when the surgery goes well, and so they must also be prepared to adjust to a good outcome. Some patients suffer a loss of identity after plastic surgery, especially when they have an operation that brings about a basic change in their appearance, for example, a rhinoplasty or "nose job." This identity loss is not so common in patients whose features were restored to a previous state.

A few patients prove to be insatiable for further surgery, wanting to be operated on over and over again to "get it right." Some even have psychotic reactions after surgery. Obviously, these problems must be dealt with psychologically, and not by further surgery.

Psychologists have studied the outcome of elective plastic surgery, and the results are mostly positive. Patients tend to be satisfied, less depressed, and less self-conscious, and to have higher self-esteem. Reductions in social anxiety have also been documented (Marcus, 1984).

THE ROLE OF THE PSYCHOLOGIST IN ORAL SURGERY

There are clear similarities between the role of the psychologist in dealing with problems of oral surgery and the role just described for plastic surgery. Buffone (1989) has described how a psychologist can contribute to oral surgery, in particular **orthognathic surgery,** which is surgery to correct abnormalities of the jaw. It has been estimated that as many as 10 million Americans suffer from such defects. Besides the cosmetic problems, patients may suffer from jaw and head pain, difficulty in talking, trouble in chewing and swallowing, and so on.

As Laura's story at the beginning of the chapter indicates, undergoing jaw surgery is not easy. It is done under general anaesthetic, involves a hospital stay of four to seven days, and requires mechanical restraint of the jaw during a healing period of several weeks. The emotional trauma of jaw deformities has been documented (Heldt, Haffke, & Davis, 1982), and it is not surprising that the large majority of patients

(around 70 percent) experience a positive personality change after the surgery. They usually are less self-conscious and shy, and they have more confidence in themselves.

But there are many unstable patients who experience psychological complications as a result of this kind of surgery. Buffone (1989) points out that, despite successful surgery, some of these patients are very upset and act out in various ways against medical personnel, including filing suits against them. Patients should be screened prior to this surgery to determine their suitability for it and to find out if psychological interventions can improve that suitability.

Table 13.1 summarizes the major predictors of successful outcome for othognathic surgery. The psychologist must provide interviews, tests, or other forms of assessment to learn where the prospective patient stands with regard to these factors. It is best that the patient have accurate information about the procedure and realistic expectations about results. Discrepancies between expectations and outcomes lead to discontentment. For example, patients who have more pain than they expected fare worse than those who anticipated the correct amount of pain.

Positive attitudes toward professional staff and rapport with them are helpful. So is good social support, especially from the family. Patients with a lot to gain from the surgery are better prospects. Thus, those with more serious deformities and those who have had a long, difficult disturbance are likely to do better, as are those who have a history of good results from some previous surgical intervention.

It is best if the problem is a clearly definable one that is likely to be highly responsive to surgery. Patients who have a history of handling life stresses well and who feel they are in control of the decision to have the surgery are more likely to do well. A good overall body image is another positive indicator.

The psychologist must give attention to many other problems in dealing with this kind of surgery. For example, the patient's jaw must be wired shut for several days and then immobi-

Table 13.1   Summary of Predictive Variables for Orthognatic Surgery

Positive	Negative
Accurate information, giving patient clear understanding of surgical process. Positive correlation between time spent in orientation and outcome.	Inadequate orientation or information on surgical process.
Good rapport, trust, and respect for treating surgeon. Attitude and demeanor of surgeon and staff are important in this regard. Positive reputation enhances outcome.	Poor relationship with surgeon or professional staff, sometimes related to poor fit or patient personality characteristics.
Good quality of social support via professional staff, family, friends, or support group.	Poor social support available from family due to their attitudes or resistance to surgery, lack of availability, or disturbed relationships. This is especially a problem with adolescent patients.
Realistic expectations as to surgical result, particularly cosmetic changes.	Unrealistic or unclear expectations as to the surgical outcome.
Female	Prior history of unsuccessful surgical or treatment outcomes or complications.
Prior history of positive surgical outcomes/hospital experience.	
Patient control of	Male

Table 13.1   Summary of Predictive Variables for Orthognatic Surgery   (Continued)

Positive	Negative
decision; decision made due to internal motivation.	Marked ambivalence or a "do or die" attitude whereby patient's whole life seems to hinge on surgical outcome.
Patient with more obvious deformity more favorable candidate than one with minor deformity.	Substance abuse.
Patient more likely to accept results if problem course longer and more severe.	Depression, anxiety, phobias, or other psychopathology.
Ego strength or ability to handle life stresses.	Complete lack of significant anxiety or fear associated with procedure itself.
Good overall body image.	Symptoms related to other than purely structural causes (e.g., muscle tension, stress).
Clear, discretely defined condition for which surgery appropriate (orthognatic versus TMJ).	Significant stresses impacting on patient or family (e.g., divorce, death).
	Compliance problems in this or other treatment regimens.

Source: "Consultations with oral surgeons: New roles for medical psychotherapists." by G. Buffone, *Medical Psychotherapy: An International Journal*, 2, p. 38, copyright © 1989 by Hogrefe & Huber Publishers, Toronto. Reprinted by permission.

lized with screws for several weeks. Some patients experience feelings of panic and fear of suffocation due to this immobilization. They can usually be helped through this period by giving them reassurance and by providing them with wire cutters in case the anxiety becomes unbearable and they must free their jaws.

Patients are restricted to a liquid diet. Prior to surgery, then, it is especially important to detect any patients with eating disorders that may be compounded by immobilization of the jaw. In particular, patients with a history of mental illness must be screened. Even without this kind of history, many patients—about 30 percent—will experience a reactive depression as a result of the medical procedure. It helps if they know ahead of time that they can expect such reactions. This kind of depression usually lifts on its own, but the treatment team must be alert to any prolongation of it or to any suicidal ideation.

Buffone (1989) has advocated using the MMPI as a predictor of certain difficulties with the surgery. For example, patients who receive MMPI scores indicating that they have a borderline pathology or paranoid tendencies are likely to have trouble forming a relationship of trust and rapport with the treatment team. Earlier we noted that a positive relationship with the professional team is a predictor of positive outcome. There is also a subscale, called the McAndrew Scale, that predicts the tendency toward substance abuse. Since the patients are given pain medication, this may be a point of concern. Buffone (1989) also describes other problems predicted by the MMPI.

On the basis of interview and test results, patients are categorized according to the promise they show for surgical success. In the first category are the majority of patients, who are cleared for the surgery but usually with suggestions for interventions to improve their results. The cleared patients may require minor interventions centering around their rapport with staff, mild depression, presurgical anxiety, and the like.

A second category of patient has greater psychological or social deficits. These people may still be able to go through the surgery but not until therapeutic interventions have been completed. In a third category are the patients who either are told that they are not good candidates for the surgery or that an indefinite postponement is necessary. These are usually either patients who want surgery for the wrong reasons or who have serious physical or psychological problems.

The psychologist's role is to see to it that the patient receives the best possible care, to communicate any recommendations both to patient and surgeon, and to help in needed psychological interventions. The interventions may include brief, behaviorally focused counseling or family counseling to help the patient deal with stress, anxiety, fear, or situational depression. Sometimes psychological treatments may be offered as an alternative for patients who are not suitable for surgery. For example, EMG biofeedback may be given to help relieve facial pain.

HEALTH PSYCHOLOGY AND SKIN DISORDERS

There have been many anecdotal reports of people who, given hypnotic suggestions that they were being burned, winced and later developed blisters. (See Box 13.1 for another kind of example.) Attempts to verify the development of blisters experimentally have been successful, but the blistering cannot be produced in most individuals. For example, in one study only one of 40 subjects produced blisters in response to hypnotic suggestions of burning (Johnson & Barber, 1976). The successful subject reported having had a severe burn in the past that happened to correspond closely to the suggested one.

Barber (1984) has summarized studies designed to verify the production of blisters through hypnosis and has reported many successful cases. It seems clear that the personality characteristics and background experiences of subjects are important determinants of success. Chertok (1981) has indicated that three features must be present for such suggestions to produce blisters:

1. There must be a strong transferential relationship with the hypnotist. A transferential relationship is one in which the subject or patient, usually unconsciously, regards the experimenter or helping professional as like his or her father or mother and responds accordingly. Freud introduced us to this idea and maintained that memories patients have repressed, and thus cannot recall to talk about, are revealed in actions displayed in the therapy. This display of the past through action is called acting out. Transference is a form of acting out in which the special relationship to a parent is displayed in a present situation.

2. There must be an exceptional degree of skin reactivity, as occurs in a person with a history of conversion reactions. A conversion reaction is one in which psychological content is manifest as bodily symptoms that mimic organic disease.

3. There must be a previous, significant experience of having been burned.

Interestingly, this tendency to conversion reactions does not seem to relate to a high degree of hypnotic talent or susceptibility. Even with highly responsive hypnotic subjects who displayed the ability to hallucinate, very few developed blisters (Barber, 1984).

The research study on blisters verifies that, under the right circumstances, mental events

Box 13.1 Stigmata Induced by Hypnosis

The photographs on the opposite page illustrate a remarkable phenomenon known as **stigmata.** These are marks on the body similar to the wounds Jesus received at His crucifixion. Many cases of stigmata have been recorded, beginning with their manifestation in the renowned Saint Francis of Assisi. They have long been viewed solely from a religious point of view, but since a substantial number of contemporary people have displayed them, they have come under some degree of scientific scrutiny. The stigmata illustrated in the photographs on the opposite page were brought on with the aid of hypnosis, although they occurred in a context of religious fervor.

The stigmatic woman pictured here probably provides us with the best controlled case ever recorded. There is al-

ways the possibility that the stigmatic wounds may be self-inflicted, either consciously or unconsciously. Elizabeth K., who is pictured in these photographs was observed very closely during the production of her wounds and as they started to bleed. The observers reported that she could not possibly have made the wounds herself in some mechanical way. It appears likely that she, and probably many other stigmatics, have great mental control over their skin.

This is not to imply that just anyone would be able to produce such profound changes in the skin and other bodily tissues through mental processes. Wilson (1989), who gathered data on a large number of recorded stigmatics, has argued that they often have strong tendencies to hysteria and multiple personality.

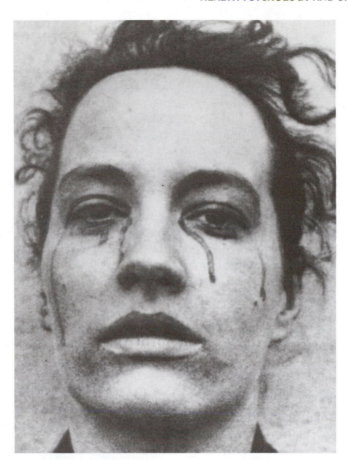

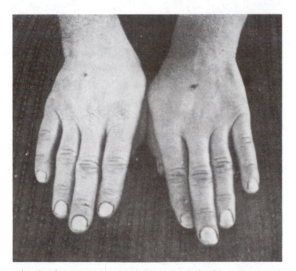
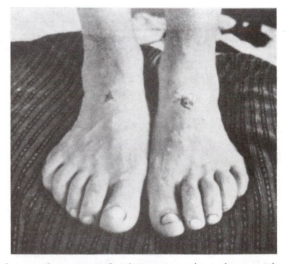

Elizabeth K.'s wounds (stigmata), which correspond to the crucifixion wounds of Jesus, were brought on with the aid of hypnosis, although they occurred in a context of religious fervor.

can produce palpable modifications of the skin. Other work has been even more successful in demonstrating this phenomenon. For example, Ikemi and Nakagawa (1962) have shown that a contact dermatitis can be created or inhibited by suggestion and imagination. These investigators worked with boys whose skin was highly sensitive to a leaf found in Japan that produces effects very similar to those of poison ivy. Some boys underwent a hypnotic induction, while others received authoritative suggestions without a formal hypnotic induction ritual. Authoritative suggestions constitute a hypnotic induction in their own right, despite its informal nature. The boys were told they were being touched by the allergenic leaf when it was actually a leaf from a harmless tree. Both modes of suggestion produced skin inflammation to some degree, and in some cases it was quite severe.

In a second stage of the study, the boys were actually touched by the allergenic leaf but were given suggestions that it was merely a leaf of another, harmless variety. In almost all cases, whether formal hypnosis or the suggestion procedure was used, the boys developed no skin inflammation.

Psychological Factors in Skin Disorders

Given the mental control we seem to have over our skin, what role does it play in skin disease? There are several ways we can get a sense of this role. One approach is that of Griesemer (1978), who interviewed patients with skin diseases, asking them about the occurrence of any emotional upsets just prior to the onset of the disease. He found large variations from disease to disease. Table 13.2 gives a simple summary of them. From his point of view, skin diseases ranged from those disorders such as hyperhidrosis (profuse sweating) that always seemed to be emotionally triggered to those such as basal cell cancer that did not seem to be emotionally triggered at all.

Grossbart and Sherman (1986) have pointed out that Griesemer did not probe for psychologi-

cal factors to any great depth. For example, he avoided discussion of sexual conflicts. Furthermore, his interview method could only detect emotional distress of which the patient was aware. A major theory of how psychological factors come to be expressed as diseases is that unconscious processes find a roundabout way to express themselves in the disease (e.g., Alexander, 1950; Boss, 1979; Grossbart & Sherman, 1986; Lynch, 1985). All of these considerations lead to the obvious conclusion that Griesemer's approach underestimates the contribution of psychological influences (Grossbart & Sherman, 1986, p. 82). Yet his estimates suggest a very large role for psychological distress in producing most skin diseases.

A related approach is that of Lester, Wittkower, Kalz, and Azima (1962) who studied the effects of tranquilizing and antidepressant drugs on a number of patients with various skin diseases. The study was double-blind (i.e., neither patient nor experimenter knew what kind of treatment a given person was getting) and otherwise well designed. The effectiveness of the drugs in relieving skin symptoms depended on the degree to which the patient had psychological symptoms.

In particular, tense patients with high anxiety tended to get relief from symptoms involving skin when they were given tranquilizers. Similarly, depressed patients got relief from bodily symptoms when they were given antidepressants. Patients with few indications of psychological distress showed little relief from skin disease after receiving medication. In general, degree of relief from emotional distress and degree of relief from skin symptoms went hand in hand.

These results clearly link psychological influences to skin disease, but they are open to interpretation. One might be that stress increases both psychological and somatic symptoms. On this hypothesis, medications might be providing a buffer against the stress reactions and thereby relieving both kinds of symptoms in tandem.

Table 13.2 The Griesemer Index: How Often Emotions Trigger Skin Problems

Diagnosis	Percentage of Diagnoses Emotionally Triggered	Biological Incubation Interval Between Stress and Start of Problem
Profuse sweating	100	Seconds
Severe scratching	98	Seconds
Focused itching	98	Days to 2 weeks
Specific hair loss	96	2 weeks
Warts, multiple spreading	95	Days
Rosacea	94	2 days
Itching	86	Seconds
Lichen planus	82	Days to 2 weeks
Hand eczema (dyshidrosis)	76	2 days for vesicles
Atopic eczema	70	Seconds for itching
Self-inflicted wounds	69	Seconds
Hives	68	Minutes
Psoriasis	62	Days to 2 weeks
Traumatic eczema	56	Seconds
All eczema except contact	56	Days
Acne	55	2 days for tender red papules
Diffuse hair loss	55	2–3 weeks
Nummular eczema	52	Days
Seborrheic eczema	41	Days to 2 weeks
Herpes: oral, genital, zoster	36	Days
Vitiligo	33	2–3 weeks
Nail dystrophy	29	2–3 weeks
Pyoderma	29	Days
Bacterial infections	29	Days
Cysts	27	2–3 days
Contact eczema	15	2 days
Fungus infections	9	Days to 2 weeks
Keratoses	0	—
Basal cell cancer	0	—
Nevi	0	—

Source: *Skin Deep*, copyright 1986 by Ted A. Grossbart & C. Sherman, reprinted with permission of William Morrow & Co., Inc.

Psychological Treatments of Skin Disorders

The literature contains some striking examples of relief from skin diseases through use of psychological interventions. Most interesting are the findings, summarized by Barber (1984), on the relief of "fish-skin disease" (congenital ichthyosiform erythrodermia) through suggestion. The first reported case of this kind of treatment was one in which a 16-year-old boy's skin had, since birth, been transformed by the disease into a thick, black crust covered with small, nipple-shaped elevations. The skin was about as hard as fingernails and numb to a depth of several millimeters. Instead of bending, it would break and ooze blood-stained serum. It provided a haven for bacteria, and infections resulted in a putrid odor that made normal social interactions, including attendance at school, impossible.

This disease is not susceptible to medical treatment, and attempts at such treatment had failed for this boy. He sought out the help of a hypnotherapist who did a hypnotic induction and suggested that the boy could feel the skin of his left arm becoming normal. Within five days, the hard, horny layer of skin softened and fell off.

At first, the new skin was reddish, but within ten days it appeared normal. The hypnotist proceeded to give similar suggestions about additional segments of the body, and the disease was almost entirely eliminated. There were a few spots that did not respond. Four years later the improvements had been retained, and further improvements were accomplished.

Barber (1984) describes several similar case reports. He goes on to describe studies of the impact of suggestion on removal of warts. He concludes that, provided the suggestions are believed in and have an impact on the feelings, thoughts, imaginings, and emotions of the patient, warts can be removed by these means. Such results are most likely to occur in people who are hypnotically talented.

Not all cases are as fascinating or as dramatic as the ones we have described, but psy-chology clearly has an important role to play in treating skin diseases. Brown and Fromm (1987) have reviewed treatment methods for a range of these diseases, including acne, pruritus, psoriasis, eczema, neurodermatitis, and virus-mediated diseases such as warts and herpes. Psychological interventions have proven useful in each of these types of disorder, though there have been few systematically controlled investigations of effectiveness. Most of the supportive data come from case studies or from small studies with less than a full array of controls. This would appear to be a promising area for the kind of verification that comes from well-controlled, large-scale studies.

The treatments described by Brown and Fromm (1987) and by Grossbart and Sherman (1986) are varied, including direct suggestions with or without hypnotic induction. For example, a patient with pruritus may be given the suggestion that the skin irritation will go away and the skin will return to normal. In many cases this kind of simple procedure will work. It is noteworthy that the hypnotic induction may not be necessary; mere suggestions will often work quite well.

Posthypnotic suggestions may also be included. For example, the person might be given the suggestion that the skin disease will gradually diminish and disappear over a period of time or that the desire to scratch will be diminished upon awakening. In addition to such suggestions the person may be taught to use healing imagery. Typically, the person will be taught to imagine circumstances in which the symptom would go away. This is called goal-directed imagery, and it tends to work with or without training in self-hypnosis. As an example, Grossbart and Sherman (1986) advocate imagining a "cellular battle" in which the patient imagines his or her healing forces attacking and overwhelming the source of the skin disease.

In addition to procedures that involve direct mental attacks on the offending agent, it is common to use methods that help patients meet any needs that may be satisfied by the disease. We refer here to the familiar concept of "secondary gain," in which a disease results in positive benefits to the patient. For example, a person who has anxiety over dating may be distressed over severe acne but may also gain relief from the threat entailed in dating.

It is useful to teach patients better ways of coping with their problems than through having a disease. This sometimes involves learning to attend better to their own needs. Grossbart and Sherman (1986) describe a technique in which patients imagine an environment in which their skin gets what it really needs. Patients are given the following instructions:

> In this exercise you'll imagine yourself in the environment most likely to make your skin comfortable and healthy. To begin, take some time and write down everything that makes your skin feel better and worse. Emphasize concrete things like heat, cold, sunlight, coolness, dryness, friction or a smooth surface. Think of creams, ice, warm compresses. Times, places—extend your list to psychological factors, if you wish. Your guide is your own experience: what has made your skin feel better? What has soothed it, relieved itching, eased burning and pain? (p. 143)

Behavioral or cognitive behavioral interventions may also be used so that the patient can be more effective in the real world. For example, Schoenberg and Carr (1963) helped patients with neurodermatitis learn how to express their hostility in healthy ways. Brown and Fromm (1987) maintain that successful treatment in these patients is linked to their learning to express their hostility.

In Chapter 5, we mentioned the view that symptoms stem from conflicts that are outside of the patient's awareness. Many psychologists reject this view, but others would advocate taking this perspective in treating at least some patients. In these cases, treatment is directed at helping patients become aware of and deal with unconscious conflicts. Patients who do not respond to the more direct techniques are seen as needing to do some work to uncover and deal with such conflicts.

Brown and Fromm (1987) exemplify those researchers who advocate dealing with unconscious conflicts in some patients. They propose the use of hypnoanalysis for such purposes. With hypnotherapy, various suggestions are given to foster recovery from the disease. With hypnoanalysis, hypnosis is used to reveal forgotten feelings, thoughts, and experiences that impair the patient's ability to respond to direct suggestions, and to bring any conflicts to a healthy resolution.

These and many other techniques are used in the psychological approach to diseases of the skin. It seems very clear that cognitions, emotions, motives, and behaviors have an impact on these diseases. Treatment programs are highly varied and often appear to be successful. Larger scale systematic studies are needed in this promising area of health psychology.

HEALTH PSYCHOLOGY AND ASTHMA

Asthma is a disease in which the patient has episodic attacks of wheezing, tightness of the chest, difficulty in breathing, and cough. Its causes are not well understood, although it seems clear there are several varieties of it. One major distinction is between extrinsic and intrinsic asthma. **Extrinsic asthma** is precipitated by allergens, whereas **intrinsic asthma** appears to occur spontaneously.

Asthma has long been considered a psychosomatic disease. Alexander (1950), in his classic work on psychosomatics, attributed asthma attacks to conflicts over dependence. Some argued that an asthma attack was a suppressed cry for the mother. This view, though widely influential, was never well supported by systematic research. However, many investigators have maintained that there is a subgroup, and a rather large one, of asthmatics whose attacks are emotionally triggered (see Graham, 1972 for review).

Somewhat consistent with the notion that asthma has an emotional basis in some patients was the finding that some asthmatic children recover quickly from their attacks when removed from their parents. At first, this quick recovery was thought to be due to removal of the children from allergens in the home. However, Purcell et al. (1969) arranged for the parents to be removed from the home while the children were taken care of by another adult. These children also showed significant reductions in their symptoms, though the reductions were small. Based on such findings, it has even been suggested that "parentectomy" (removal of the parents) might be an appropriate treatment for childhood asthma.

More recent work tends to place less emphasis on emotional disturbance as a source of asthma, but psychological factors play an important role in coping with asthma, if not in its origin. Psychological influences may reveal themselves in "the emotional exacerbation of the already available symptom" (Minuchin, Rosman, & Baker, 1978, p. 29) or in reducing the effectiveness of coping with the disease (Fix, Daughton, & Kass, 1981).

Fix, Daughton, and Kass (1981) have emphasized the importance of the status of the asthmatic patient with respect to a dimension known as "panic-fear." Kinsman and co-workers derived a measure of this panic-fear dimension from the MMPI. Patients low on panic-fear tend to ignore or deny symptoms, whereas those high on this dimension react with powerful anxiety. Those low in panic-fear may tend to neglect treatment, whereas those high on this dimension tend to amplify the symptoms by such reactions as hyperventilating with rapid, shallow breathing. Those high in panic-fear also tend to take more medicine and have to be hospitalized more often (Kinsman, Spector, Schucard, & Luparello, 1974).

The asthma of those high on panic-fear is no worse than that of those low on the dimension. Direct measures of pulmonary function reveal no differences, but their subjective ratings of the symptoms are higher, and they end up taking more and stronger medicines. As Fix and colleagues (1981) put it:

> There is no clear evidence that emotions can cause, or even make people susceptible to asthma. But once a person has asthma, his or her capacity for dealing with it may be critical to the course of the disease. (p. 268)

Complexities of Asthma and Its Treatment

Shellenberger and Green (1986) and Sheridan (1983a, 1983b) have described many of the nuances of biofeedback-based treatment for various disorders. Research studies tend to evaluate a very crude version of the methods used by clinicians. We need better outcome assessments for procedures that are like those actually used by clinicians, lest we find ourselves with all art and no science. The dangers of using methods that have not gone through the process of verification have been described earlier in this book (Chapter 3). On the other hand, it is pretentious to evaluate crude methods and to consider the evaluation as a serious assessment of something far more complex and subtle.

In the case of asthma, the complexity is especially great because the disorder is not well understood, its subtleties are difficult to measure, and its ramifications in patient and family are wide. Furthermore, there seem to be many subtypes of asthmatic. The distinction between patients with intrinsic versus extrinsic asthma has already been mentioned. Many other distinctions may be important.

Take the role of the panic-fear dimension. Some asthmatics are high on this dimension and exacerbate their symptoms with reactions like overbreathing in a fast, shallow pattern. On the other hand, other asthmatics are low on this dimension and have a tendency to ignore or deny their symptoms, and perhaps to neglect medical care. These two subgroups are likely to have very different reactions to relaxation and EMG biofeedback. We can well imagine that such procedures would be harmful for patients very low on panic-fear (Fix, Daughton, & Kass, 1981).

Despite the fairly general dismissal of earlier psychodynamic ideas about asthma (e.g., that asthma attacks are "cries for the mother"), there is some evidence that in a subset of patients the attacks are triggered by emotional distress. It is difficult to study such patients with standardized procedures, since the emotional triggers may be unique to the individual. In several studies it has been possible to show that discussion of a patient's unpleasant memories can induce wheezing and bronchospasm (see Brown & Fromm, 1986). For example, Dekker and Groen (1956) found that stressful stimuli from a patient's personal history could induce asthma attacks.

Another problem in relating asthma to emotions stems from the problem of identifying emotions that are outside of awareness. The psychodynamic concept always held that *unconscious* conflict was at the bottom of asthmatic episodes. Others have argued that psychosomatic diseases quite generally tend to be related to emotions that the patient cannot articulate verbally (e.g., Lynch, 1985).

This notion has been put in a nutshell by Sifneos (1974) who refers to such patients as **alexithymic.** Alexithymia is a condition in which a person is unable to articulate emotions and gives bodily reactions in their stead. We have methods of uncovering unconscious feelings and ideas, but it has been very difficult to bring them to the level of measurement we need for good scientific research.

The identification of asthmatic triggers is complicated all the more by the likely presence of conditioned triggers. Very elegant animal research has been published showing that neutral stimuli paired with allergens can produce asthma (Justesen, Braun, Garrison, & Pendleton, 1970). The similarity of the asthmatic responses of the animals used in this study to those of humans has been called into question on somewhat nebulous grounds (King, 1980).

King (1980) also points out the difficulties encountered in attempts to condition asthma in humans. For example, he points out that attempts to condition asthma attacks in about 100 human asthma patients, using an apparatus employed in allergy investigation as the conditioned stimulus, were successful in only two people (Dekker & Groen, 1956).

Even this small success, however, indicates that such conditioning *can* occur. We have

learned a lot since that study was done about how to get neutral stimuli to become conditioned stimuli. Sometimes the right kind of neutral stimulus must be found. For example, smells and tastes pair most readily with "gut" responses (see Garcia & Ervin, 1968). We should be cautious about dismissing the phenomenon of conditioned asthma. It is, after all, an instance of accepting the null hypothesis (see Chapter 3).

In any case, it seems quite likely that conditioned fear responses occur in patients who have had severe and even life-threatening asthma attacks. These can have an important effect on the ability to cope with the attacks.

The impact of asthma varies with the time of life when it began. Asthma has devastating effects on the developing child and his or her family. Alexander (1977) has done an excellent job of describing the many ramifications of childhood asthma on the child's social development, academic performance, self-concept, relationships to family, and so on. There can be serious and often pathological disturbances in all these spheres.

Perhaps the most important contribution the psychologist could make to the asthmatic would be to help prevent or correct these distortions. Related problems are faced by the late-onset asthmatic who has to change fixed life patterns to adjust to the disease. Both groups may face very frightening attacks of the disease, serious side effects of medications such as epinephrine-like drugs and steroids, and large financial burdens.

Psychological Interventions

The psychological management of asthma is complex and impinges on many aspects of the lives of patients and their families. The individual and family must become skilled at coping with asthma attacks and the fearful anticipation of them. Families must learn to live full lives in the context of the disease and to avoid encouraging more symptoms. Patients must thread their way between the extremes of neglecting and exacerbating the disease.

We will discuss some of the psychologist's

basic tools in helping people to deal with this disease. A very helpful one is relaxation training. Many patients will find relaxation training, with or without biofeedback, useful. Some will not, but relaxation training is easy to do, and it costs little.

Relaxation Training and Biofeedback

Important problems are involved in assessing the effects of procedures like relaxation and biofeedback on asthma. The fine-grained details of asthma are not easy to see. Accordingly, a number of measures have been devised, one of which is peak expiratory flow rate (PEFR). In this measure the patient is asked to blow very hard, and the greatest flow rate of the breath in the first tenth of a second is recorded in liters per second. With a total respiratory resistance (TRR) measure, pressure is briefly increased in the air passages, and the respiratory resistance to air is measured. Both measures indicate how well the person can breathe by telling how forcefully the patient can blow out. Asthma impairs this ability.

Numerous studies have shown that relaxation training produces improvement in these measures. For example, Alexander, Miklich, and Hershkoff (1972) showed that such training increased PEFR in asthmatic children. As Alexander (1977) has pointed out, these effects are modest but real.

Other investigators have used biofeedback to diminish asthmatic symptoms. Several researchers have found that EMG biofeedback of the forehead muscles can teach patients to increase PEFR (Kotses, et al., 1976). These studies were well controlled for such factors as placebo effects.

Overall, the research on biofeedback and relaxation shows that asthma patients may improve to some degree with such training. This training might help them to cope with the disease and permit them to use less medication. It is a useful supplement to medical treatment, but certainly it is not a substitute.

According to Alexander (1977), who has extensive experience with asthma patients, relaxation training is a very useful procedure for helping many patients control mild or moderate attacks and to make medications more effective. The bottom line is that use of medications can be reduced through such training.

Systematic Desensitization

A second widely useful intervention is systematic desensitization. (See Chapter 5 for a description of this method.) This technique is used to control intense anxiety reactions that commonly occur during attacks, or even at the slightest sign that an attack might be starting.

Obviously, not all the varied psychological problems related to asthma can be handled with these two simple procedures. Alexander (1977) describes the use of behavioral management procedures to deal with many of these problems. For example, a child with asthma may learn to avoid school or social stress by intensifying his or her reactions to asthma. Parents and medical personnel may have to use behavioral control procedures, such as extinction, to prevent the child from getting reinforced for sicker and sicker behavior. A case study reported by Neisworth and Moore (1972) illustrates the use of extinction. The patient was a seven-year-old boy who had more severe coughing episodes than his physician regarded as consistent with the severity of his disease. Upon analysis of what happened as a result of the coughing episodes, it seemed that parental attention was probably reinforcing the coughing. Neisworth and Moore trained the parents to avoid giving their attention to the coughing episodes. Subsequently, the number of such episodes decreased substantially. It would be even more valuable to teach parents to reinforce healthy reactions.

Cognitive Behavioral Therapy Combined with Biofeedback

One interesting approach to coping with asthma involves having patients use a simple device, called a mini-Wright peak flow meter, to monitor pulmonary function on a regular basis. It can act as a feedback device that tells the patient how well the airways are functioning under various circumstances (Brown & Fromm, 1987). Use of the device can be pivotal in a cognitive behavioral program to teach the patient the best ways to cope with the disorder. It helps the patient notice situations that help or hinder breathing. It also gives feedback that helps develop the subtle skills needed to optimize breathing. A more detailed account of these and various other types of psychological intervention in asthma may be found in Brown and Fromm (1987).

PSYCHOLOGICAL APPROACHES TO DIABETES

As in the case of asthma, diabetes is a chronic disease that commonly occurs in children as well as adults, is difficult to manage, and has psychological and social effects. Diabetes is a widespread problem, with about 7 million cases in the United States (USBC, 1989). It has very serious consequences, including blindness, kidney damage, and strokes as well as sexual dysfunction, circulatory disturbances including gangrene, and loss of normal sensation owing to neural damage.

There are two main types of diabetes. **Type I diabetes** is called insulin-dependent diabetes and usually begins in childhood. Without artificial insulin, it is associated with ketosis, an abnormal chemical state that can result in coma and death if untreated. With this type of diabetes, circulating insulin is virtually absent, and pancreatic cells that would normally produce insulin fail to respond to the triggers that are supposed to set off its production. In addition, plasma glucagon levels are high. Glucagon usually works to raise blood sugar levels when they get too low.

Type II diabetes is called noninsulin-dependent diabetes. It includes a varied grouping of disorders of sugar metabolism and usually occurs in adults. Natural production of **insulin** is too low for real health but enough to prevent **ketosis.**

Diabetes has long been seen as a genetic disease, but recently it has come to be viewed as an autoimmune disorder (e.g., Karam, 1989).

This class of disorders is often under strong psychological control. There is surprising evidence of psychological control of diabetes. Some of the evidence is not extensive and at this time must be viewed in the framework of the discovery mode. It has not yet been submitted to the full rigors of scientific verification. Still, we have some very promising leads.

Psychosocial Factors in Diabetes

Diabetes is difficult to manage in many cases, particularly those of Type I. Insulin alone does not really bring the person's physiology to normal, and fairly meticulous restriction of diet along with other lifestyle management, including a program of exercise, is needed in order to get really good control. Given the behavioral requirements entailed in management of diabetes, it goes without saying that the health psychologist has a role to play in it. In fact, several fascinating findings make the case of diabetes of even more interest to the psychologist than we would imagine.

Psychological Interventions

Apparently, little work has been done on the impact of hypnosis on diabetes. However, Rossi and Cheek (1988) report an interesting case of a diabetic woman who had a history of difficulty regulating her diabetes and had experienced diabetic coma on two occasions while pregnant. She also had to have insulin injections every 15 minutes following the trauma of her brother's death and had remained in critical condition for several days. She came into hypnotic treatment at a time when she had to undergo a medically necessary abortion and a hysterectomy.

The hypnosis was done in an attempt to forestall any severe diabetic reaction to the stress of the surgery. She was hypnotized to mentally anesthetize her abdomen and succeeded in developing a complete anesthesia. The surgery itself was done under a spinal anesthetic, so the purpose of this hypnotic control was to enable her to regulate postsurgical pain and thus minimize the stress of the recovery.

Not only did this patient have no trouble

maintaining control of her blood glucose, but it also was found to be at levels that indicated she did not require insulin. In fact, during the subsequent 11 months she used insulin only occasionally during periods of emotional stress.

The idea that diabetic control is related to stress is confirmed by another finding, this one having to do with the use of biofeedback to teach people to warm their hands. As we pointed out in Chapter 5, temperature feedback is commonly combined with a form of autogenic training. Many investigators working with this kind of feedback training soon found that patients required adjustments of their insulin dosages as a result of that training. A description of this kind of result is given in the classic work on autogenic training by Schultz and Luthe (1969). It involves autogenic training alone, but the description is typical of that found in many biofeedback clinics.

> A young diabetic who required relatively high quantities of insulin and who mastered the standard exercises was asked to continue autogenic training by emphasizing the development of warmth in the upper abdomen. After effective exercises had been practiced frequently, the patient began to suffer from hypoglycemic shocks because he continued injecting the same amount of insulin as he had taken before. After taking 20 units less, the patient felt well though he was none too careful about dietary indiscretions. (Schultz & Luthe, 1969, p. 116)

Notice that the patient had to use *less* insulin. That is typical of people who learn to warm their bodies through autogenic training or thermal biofeedback. Their body's regulatory system is somehow functioning better. Little seems to have been published on this clinically well-known phenomenon, although there have been at least a few written accounts. For example, Fowler, Budzynski, and Vandenbergh (1976) published a case study of a diabetic woman who was subject to frequent episodes of ketoacidosis. They gave her relaxation training with the aid of EMG biofeedback. Her insulin requirements were substantially reduced, so much so that she had several hypoglycemic attacks. Once again, the insulin levels she was used to administering were too high after relaxation training.

Guthrie, Moeller, and Guthrie (1983) also published a paper showing that a combination of EMG biofeedback, thermal biofeedback, and progressive relaxation produced this kind of improvement in a majority of a small sample of patients they studied.

Stress and Diabetes

How can relaxation training reduce the need for insulin in a person whose body does not produce this hormone? The answer seems to lie in the tendency of various stress-related hormones (e.g., ACTH, catecholamines), even in normal individuals, to raise blood sugar levels, decrease insulin production, and raise the levels of free fatty acids. Free fatty acids (FFA) are the materials from which the body builds ketones, and these lead to ketoacidosis. In the nondiabetic person these physiological changes are soon reversed by the body's natural insulin. In the diabetic, the ability to neutralize these effects of stress is impaired or even absent (Johnson, 1980).

Several laboratory studies have been done in diabetics using induced stress accompanied by measurements of various physiological reactions such as the production of FFA. They confirm the picture we described in the previous paragraph. A summary of them may be found in Johnson (1980). The influence of stress on the control of diabetes has been confirmed in more recent work (Gonder-Frederick, Carter, Cox & Clarke, 1990; Halford, Cuddihy & Mortimer, 1990).

One of the most striking bodies of research done on stress and the control of diabetes is work that eventually focused on the role of the family in destabilizing the state of diabetic children. Most children, with the help of their families, readily learn to control their diabetes. Some children, however, have repeated episodes of ketosis that require hospitalization and yet easily come under control when in the hospital. Minuchin, Rosman, and Baker (1978) cite the case of a girl whose insulin requirement was 30 units, but who received 500 units over an 18-hour period at home and still had to be hospitalized for ketosis. The insulin that was being administered at home was checked for its biological potency and was found to be fine.

First, Minuchin and his co-workers tried to deal with this problem as one of individual stress coping. It was not hard to find deficits in stress management in these patients, but attempts to treat the patients through psychotherapy were unsuccessful. The therapy focused on modifying personality characteristics and teaching the patients to reduce stress. Families were told to be very gentle with the patients. None of this treatment worked.

Minuchin and his colleagues did metabolic studies in which they showed that, during a stressful interview designed to arouse anger but inhibit its expression, these patients had a dramatic rise in FFA—one that would quickly have produced ketosis if allowed to go on. Next, they assessed the effect of a chemical blockade designed to prevent production of FFA. Drugs called beta blockers are able to do this. The investigators found that the drugs successfully blocked FFA production in these children but in the long run the physiological blockade was overcome, just as the effects of insulin had been.

Minuchin and his co-workers then focused on the role of family interactions in producing these reactions. They gave families tasks to perform that tended to produce conflict in the family. They found that FFA levels climbed steadily in the diabetic children during these conflicts. This pattern did not occur in children used as normal controls or with diabetic children who controlled their diabetes, but who were referred for psychiatric care due to behavioral problems (see Figure 13.1).

Measures of FFA levels were also taken in the parents. Levels climbed in the parents during conflict if the diabetic child was not present, but *parent FFA levels dropped when the child was introduced into the conflictual situation.* The child's FFA levels, of course, rose as the parents' levels dropped.

Psychosomatic Families

All of this information fits a family systems theory model that says families maintain a

Researchers found that during family conflicts, levels of free fatty acids (precursors of ketoacidosis) rose steadily in children with uncontrolled diabetes.

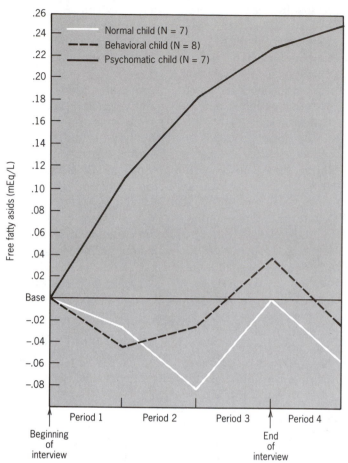

Figure 13.1 Changes in the free fatty acid (FFA) levels of diabetic children during family interview. *Source:* Reprinted by permission of the publishers from *Psychosomatic Families: Anorexia Nervosa in Context* by Salvador Minuchin, Bernice L. Rosman, and Leslie Baker, Cambridge, Mass.: Harvard University Press. Copyright © 1978 by the President and Fellows of Harvard College.

balanced state by shifting conflict to certain members, often called the identified patient. In this case the identified patient is the child. The Minuchin group went on to identify a set of characteristics of **psychosomatic families.** The Minuchin group uses the term "psychosomatic" to mean that failures to cope with the disease are brought on by failures to deal with psychological problems.

Psychosomatic families tend to be enmeshed; that is, the family interactions tend to be extremely close and intense. Two-person interactions are quickly diffused by the entrance of

other family members. Typical boundaries tend to be crossed within family subsystems. For example, a child may be "parentified," or one parent may form an alliance with a child to deal with the other parent. The individual is less differentiated than normal from other members of the family. For example, family members intrude on each other's thoughts and feelings.

Psychosomatic families are also overprotective. Family members are exquisitely sensitive to signs of distress in other family members. This is not just a matter of overprotecting the sick child. It runs throughout the family, extending also to the diabetic child protecting other family members. It is likely that one of the secondary gains from diabetic crises is their ability to draw family members away from their emotional distress.

A third feature of psychosomatic families is rigidity. This means that the family tries to avoid basic changes in the system. They have great difficulties with the natural experiences of change and growth. The child's transitions from one developmental stage to another are resisted by the rigid family structure. Changes in outside events can place unusual stress on such a family system.

A fourth feature is lack of conflict resolution. The other three features make their reactiveness to conflict very great, and yet they try very hard to avoid conflict. They commonly have a family ideology that provides a rationale for avoiding conflict, which they do in many different ways. They may simply stay away from each other when conflict is possible, or they may rapidly change the subject, using distractions and position shifts to obscure disagreements. As a result, conflicts do not get resolved and are left to fester.

Minuchin and his co-workers found that the psychosomatic diabetic children were heavily involved in the conflict between their parents. This was regarded as a fifth characteristic of the psychosomatic family. It could just as well be viewed as a specific fulfillment of enmeshment and overprotectiveness.

The study also identifies three patterns of child involvement in parental conflict. First, parents sometimes triangulate the child, which means that the child is trapped into siding with one parent against the other. The parents in effect force the child into a choice that requires him or her to take sides. Second is the formation of a parent–child coalition in which the child is more or less permanently aligned with one par-

ent against the other. The third pattern is called detouring wherein the parents manifestly submerge their conflicts and instead protect or blame the child. The parental childrearing roles become so dominant that marital discord is put aside or ignored. These patterns occur in normal families as well. It is the inflexibility with which they are used, and the failure sometimes to deal openly with conflict that distinguishes the psychosomatic family.

The key to reducing the ketosis-inducing conflicts seems to be primarily to get the parents to deal with their conflicts more directly without utilizing the child as a means of diffusing them. Minuchin et al. (1975) have reported that such an approach yields good results.

Conclusions

This chapter demonstrates the breadth of applications of psychology to problems of health. Psychology's role is not limited to helping people overcome habits that put their health at risk and to providing alternatives and supplements to usual biomedical treatment. As we learned in an earlier chapter, psychologists work to help health care providers and their patients to develop the skills needed to deal most effectively with disease. In this chapter we have shown that psychologists can and should (1) contribute to the treatment of a wide range of physical disorders, (2) help screen patients to establish their suitability for a given treatment, (3) devise and implement psychological interventions tailored to help given patients to cope best with treatments and to recover with maximum efficiency, (4) help patients with psychological reactions to medical treatments, and (5) come to grips with the broader social and psychological context that may create obstacles that impair the effectiveness of medical treatment.

Summary

1. The symptoms of temporomandibular joint syndrome are facial pain, headaches, ringing in the ears, a popping sound when the mouth is opened wide, and restricted ability to open the mouth. In addition, the temporomandibular joint and the muscles

around it are sore to the touch. It has been regarded as being due to mechanical abnormalities of the joint, which develop as a result of such defects as poor meshing (occlusion) of the teeth. Given this interpretation of the symptoms, it makes sense that the primary focus of treatment has been on mechanical modification of the teeth. However, studies evaluating such treatment have shown that it is not superior to the effect of a placebo.

2. A more psychological interpretation is the specificity hypothesis. This hypothesis states that people tend to respond to stress with a specific bodily reaction—in this case jaw tension. It has been confirmed that TMJ patients give a peculiar response to stress and that it includes high facial tension.

3. The "multifactorial" hypothesis holds that such factors as stress and abnormal occlusion interact to produce the jaw symptoms. For example, a person might not react strongly to abnormal occlusion unless they are stressed. This interpretation has not yet been confirmed, and there has been some evidence against it, but it remains a possibility.

4. EMG biofeedback has been used to treat TMJ with some success. This form of treatment shows great promise and is probably as well founded a treatment as any other, but more research needs to be done on this topic.

5. Some of the problems psychologists can deal with in a plastic surgery practice are: (a) to identify psychological disturbances that make the surgery inappropriate or excessively risky; (b) to deal with depression and anxiety, which can lead to severe postsurgical reactions; (c) to identify psychological trauma that took place during and around the time of the surgery; and (d) to treat psychological reactions such as loss of identity that often occur after surgery.

6. The applications of psychology to jaw surgery are very similar to those in plastic surgery. Many people have jaw abnormalities, and, despite successful surgery, some of these patients get very upset and act out in various ways against medical personnel, including filing suits against them. Patients must be screened prior to this surgery to determine their suitability for it and to find out if psychological interventions can make them more suitable.

7. Various factors are known to influence patients' reaction. The psychologist's role is to assess these factors in order to select patients who would be likely to profit from the surgery, and to carry out interventions to maximize the patients' ability to profit from the medical intervention.

8. Psychological research clearly shows that such skin eruptions as blisters and rashes can be induced psychologically. There is also evidence that psychological factors contribute to naturally occurring diseases of the skin. Many skin diseases tend to occur immediately after an emotional upset. Patients with skin disease who also show psychological symptoms such as anxiety and depression tend to show improvement of their skin when given medications appropriate for the psychological problem.

9. Psychological interventions to treat skin diseases, perhaps most strikingly "fish-skin disease," have been quite successful. Hypnosis has been used a lot, but dealing with complex factors such as the reinforcing payoffs for having the disease is also important. Most of the literature in support of this kind of intervention is in the form of case studies that lack important controls. However, there is enough evidence to encourage our taking the role of psychology in skin diseases very seriously.

10. Some psychologists attempt to uncover unconscious conflicts, which they think are responsible for the skin disease. There are

many encouraging case studies on this topic, but systematic research should be done.

11. Asthma is a disease in which a person has episodic attacks of wheezing, tightness of the chest, difficulty in breathing, and cough. Extrinsic asthma is precipitated by allergens, whereas intrinsic asthma appears to occur spontaneously. Asthma is widely viewed as a disease with a strong psychological component. Some research has identified family conflicts as having an important role in asthma.

12. A dimension known as panic-fear is an important determinant of patients' reaction to asthma, though probably not to the asthma itself. Some have argued that the reaction to asthma is the only aspect of it under psychological control.

13. Asthma's complexity makes it hard to evaluate psychological treatment methods since the different forms of the disease may respond differentially to a given intervention. We need research that takes this complexity into account. Patients vary in how strongly they react to attacks, in their tendency to have attacks in response to emotional triggers, and in their awareness of the emotions that give rise to attacks. If asthma is indeed psychosomatic, we might expect these patients to have special problems talking about their feelings. This limited ability to express emotions has been called alexithymia.

14. Classical and operant conditioning may also influence asthma attacks. Conditioned attacks have been demonstrated in animals, although early work led to the rejection of this possibility in humans, somewhat prematurely in our opinion.

15. Relaxation training and systematic desensitization can help diminish asthma attacks, as can biofeedback, either of muscular tension or of various indices of full breathing capacity.

16. Cognitive behavior therapy has been used in combination with measures of breathing capacity in teaching asthma patients the best strategies for controlling their attacks. Evaluation of this technique is still largely at the level of clinical observation; systematic research should be done on it.

17. There are two main types of diabetes. Type I, "childhood diabetes," is called insulin-dependent diabetes. Without artificial insulin, it can result in coma and death. Type II diabetes, called noninsulin-dependent diabetes, is a varied grouping of disorders of sugar metabolism that usually occur in adults.

18. Diabetes is to some degree influenced by psychological factors, but the evidence remains in the "discovery mode" and needs firmer verification. Reports have indicated that hypnosis, autogenic training, and biofeedback can be helpful in diabetic control.

19. There is evidence that poor handling of family conflicts can worsen diabetic reactions. In fact, a family structure typical of "psychosomatic families" has been identified, and this applies to at least some families with children who have trouble controlling their diabetes.

Key Terms

Alexithymia
Asthma
Body dysmorphic disorder
Bruxism
Diabetes
Extrinsic asthma
Insulin
Intrinsic asthma

Ketosis

Myofascial pain dysfunction syndrome

Orthognathic surgery

Psychosomatic families

Response specificity

Stigmata

Temporomandibular joint syndrome

Type I diabetes

Type II diabetes

Discussion Questions

1. What is temporomandibular joint syndrome, and what is the role of psychologists in understanding and treating it?

2. Make the best case you can to persuade a plastic surgeon that he or she should work in collaboration with a psychologist.

3. Outline the various stages at which psychological interventions are needed for people undergoing jaw surgery, and briefly explain what the psychologist does at each of these stages.

4. Describe the major factors that predict successful outcome of jaw surgery.

5. Give evidence that psychological factors and interventions influence skin disease.

6. Describe the major types of psychological interventions used in treating diseases of the skin.

7. What are the major types of asthma, and what evidence is there that asthma is under a degree of social-psychological control?

8. Explain the contributions psychologists can make to the treatment of asthma.

9. What are the main types of diabetes, and what role do social and psychological factors play in it? Present evidence for what you say.

10. Describe the characteristics of Minuchin's "psychosomatic families."

Glossary

Acquired immune deficiency syndrome (AIDS) AIDS is an infectious disease that is apparently caused by a virus that attacks the immune system, making the host vulnerable to a variety of diseases that would readily be controlled by a healthy immune system ("opportunistic diseases").

Acquired immunity Acquired immunity, in contrast to innate immunity, is a type of immunity in which the body recognizes pathogens and takes action to destroy them.

Acute illness Acute illnesses have a sudden onset and last a relatively short period of time or become chronic.

Acute leukemias Acute leukemias involve the abnormally high production of abnormal white blood cells produced by the bone marrow. Acute leukemia advances very rapidly and can cause death in a matter of months.

Acute pain Acute pain is usually related to specific tissue damage and lasts a relatively short period of time.

Adrenal cortex The adrenal cortex is the outer portion of the adrenal gland located above the kidneys. It secretes many hormones, including cortisol, aldosterone, and corticosterone.

Adrenal medulla The adrenal medulla is the center portion of the adrenal gland located above the kidneys. It secretes epinephrine (adrenalin) and norepinephrine (noradrenalin).

Adrenocorticotrophic hormone (ACTH) ACTH is a hormone secreted from the pituitary gland which stimulates the adrenal cortex.

Aerobic exercise Aerobic exercise is any exercise that stimulates heart and lung activity for a time period long enough to produce beneficial changes in the body.

AIDS dementia complex (ADC) ADC is neuropsychological impairment due to direct HIV brain impairment.

AIDS-related complex (ARC) ARC occurs in individuals who have been exposed to the HIV virus and are experiencing serious, but not life-threatening, symptoms.

Alcohol abuse Alcohol abuse is a chronic pattern of maladaptive drinking behavior that continues despite an awareness that it causes persistent problems.

Alcohol dependence Alcohol dependence is the impaired control of alcohol use that continues over a period of time in spite of its adverse consequences and involves tolerance and withdrawal.

Alexithymia Alexithymia describes a condition in which a person is unable to articulate emotions and gives bodily reactions in their stead.

Anabolic steroids Anabolic steroids are androgenic hormones, such as testosterone, or drugs that imitate these hormones.

Angina Angina is a constricting pain in the chest that tends to be produced by effort or emotional stress. It is associated with arteriosclerosis.

Anorexia nervosa Anorexia nervosa is an eating disorder marked by a distorted body image and self-starvation.

Anterolateral neospinothalamic system The anterolateral neospinothalamic system is a pain pathway in the spinal cord that is connected to the thalamus.

Antibodies Antibodies are protein molecules that travel to an infection site either to neutralize the pathogen or to identify it so that other cells or chemicals will attack it.

Antigens Antigens are foreign substances that stimulate an immune response.

Arteriosclerosis Arteriosclerosis (hardening of the arteries) is a disease of the arteries resulting in the thickening and loss of elasticity of the arterial walls.

Asthma Asthma is a disease in which a person has episodic attacks of wheezing, tightness of the chest, difficulty in breathing, and coughing.

Attentional strategies Attentional strategies are coping strategies in which the person focuses on the disease in order to take action to control either the disease or the emotional reactions to it.

Augmenters Augmenters are people who tend to amplify pain and other sensations.

Autogenic training Autogenic training is a self-regulation method in which trainees gently turn their attention to certain phrases that create the physical sensations of warmth and heaviness which are associated with increased blood flow and muscle relaxation.

Autoimmune diseases Autoimmune diseases are a group of diseases characterized by tissue injury caused by the immune system attacking the person's own tissue.

Autonomic nervous system The autonomic nervous system is a division of the peripheral nervous system that regulates the "involuntary" actions of the internal organs and glands. It includes the sympathetic and parasympathetic nervous systems.

Availability heuristic The availability heuristic involves judging the probability of something happening based on how readily it can be imagined or recalled.

Avoidant strategy An avoidant strategy is a way of coping with a stressor in which attention is turned away from aspects of the disease.

B-cells B-cells are cells of the immune system that produce antibodies.

Background stressors Background stressors are the small, but persistent, problems that irritate and distress people.

Balloon angioplasty Balloon angioplasty is a procedure in which a "balloon" is inflated into a coronary artery to force stiffened tissue to yield a wider opening.

Base-rate fallacy A base-rate fallacy occurs when probability judgments are made without taking into account how often something occurs in the overall population.

BASIC I.D. BASIC I.D. refers to Behavior, Affect, Sensations, Imagery, Cognitions, Interpersonal factors, and Drugs, which are all the levels of intervention relevant to a multimodal treatment program for pain.

Behavioral approach The behavioral approach applies learning theories to understanding and modifying health-related behaviors.

Behavioral health Behavioral health is a subarea of behavioral medicine concerned with illness prevention and health enhancement.

Behavioral medicine   Behavioral medicine is the application of behavioral science to the diagnosis and treatment of illness.

Behavioral rehearsal   Behavioral rehearsal involves "role playing" a new coping skill in a therapeutic setting.

Benign tumors   A benign tumor is a mass of tissue produced by uncontrolled cells that does not spread to other sites and is growing "in place."

Binge eating   Binge eating is episodic, rapid eating of large amounts of food.

Biofeedback   Biofeedback is a "tool" to train people to gain voluntary self-regulation of their psychophysiological processes by augmenting the sensory feedback from bodily processes.

Biomedical model   The biomedical model is the dominant paradigm of medical science in the twentieth century. Only the biochemical influences on illness are considered within the framework of this model.

Biopsychosocial model   The biopsychosocial model is an expansion of the biomedical model to include the psychological and social factors of health and illness.

Body dysmorphic disorder   Body dysmorphic disorder is a psychiatric disorder in which the patient has a grossly exaggerated impression of deformity that is either not present at all or is only slightly evident.

Bruxism   Bruxism is a condition in which individuals clench and grind their teeth.

Buffering model   The buffering model focuses on aspects of social support that act as a "buffer" to protect people against the negative effects of stress.

Bulimia nervosa   Bulimia nervosa is an eating disorder marked by recurrent episodes of binge eating, followed by self-induced vomiting, heavy use of laxatives, or both.

Cancer   Cancer is a term used to describe many different diseases characterized by the unrestrained growth of abnormal cells.

Carcinogens   Carcinogens are cancer-producing agents that may be found in the host or the environment.

Carcinoma   Carcinoma is a type of cancer that originates from the cells of the tissue that cover the internal and external surfaces of the body.

Cardiac output   Cardiac output is the amount of blood your heart pumps per unit of time.

Cartesian dualism   Cartesian dualism is a philosophical position that defines mind and body as separate elements. The biomedical model has been strongly influenced by this view.

Cataclysmic stressors   Cataclysmic stressors refer to those negative events that happen to several people or whole communities at the same time, for example, hurricanes, wars, and massive layoffs.

Cellular system of immunity   The cellular system of immunity is a type of immunity in which cells called T-lymphocytes initiate reactions to foreign bodies and command other T-Cells and macrophages to attack them.

Central nervous system   The central nervous system consists of the brain and spinal cord.

Central route   The central route of communication involves careful and thoughtful consideration of an issue.

Channel capacity   Channel capacity is the inherent limit on the amount of information we can process at any one time.

Chronic illness   Chronic illnesses progress slowly and persist over long periods of time.

Chronic leukemias   Chronic leukemias involve the abnormally high production of abnormal white blood cells produced by the bone marrow and progress very slowly, tending to afflict older people.

Chronic pain   Chronic pain typically begins with an acute episode but persists over a long period of time.

Chronic pain syndrome   Chronic pain syndrome is a collection of symptoms associated with chronic pain that includes limited functioning, depression, chemical dependency, family disruption, and financial problems.

Classical conditioning   Classical conditioning involves forming a connection between a "neutral" stimulus and a stimulus that elicits an unlearned response.

Classical migraine   Classical migraine is a recurrent, intense headache, generally severe, unilateral, pulsing, and accompanied by gastrointestinal symptoms. It is preceded by a set of cues (prodrome) that indicate the headache is coming.

Clinical neuropsychology   Clinical neuropsychology is the subarea of psychology that specializes in diagnosing and treating injuries of the nervous system.

Clinical psychological approach   The clinical psychology approach focuses on evaluation and treatment of psychological health-related problems.

Cluster headaches   Cluster headaches are migrainous, but they occur in short-lived bouts that last several weeks and are separated by three or more months.

Cognitive appraisal   Cognitive appraisals are the ways in which individuals appraise their stressors and the resources they have to meet the demands of stressors.

Cognitive behavioral approach   A cognitive behavioral approach to therapy that emphasizes the modification of thoughts and images to obtain psychological and behavioral changes.

Communication model   The communication model is a variant of the psychodynamic model that views symptoms of illness as an attempt to express something to other people.

Community psychology approach   The community psychology approach places strong emphasis on disease prevention and health enhancement through environmental interventions.

Conditioned nausea and vomiting (CNV)   CNV is the conditioned response to the aversive stimuli associated with chemotherapy.

Contingencies of reinforcement   Contingencies of reinforcement are the consequences of behaviors that come to control those behaviors.

Controlling variables   Controlling variables are the factors that must be identified in scientific research that actually control whether something happens or not.

Coping   Coping is the effort that is expended to manage stressors.

Coronary bypass surgery   Coronary bypass surgery involves "bypassing" diseased arteries of the heart with sections of arteries from other parts of the patient's body, for example, the leg or chest.

Coronary heart disease   Coronary heart disease is disease of the arteries that supply the heart with blood.

Corrective emotional experiences   Corrective emotional experiences are a form of supportive psychotherapy in which the therapist responds more supportively than the parents did and allow the person to mature in ways that original parenting did not permit.

Correlation   A correlation means that two or more things are associated with one another or vary together.

Corticotrophin-releasing factor (CRF)   CRF is a chemical released by the hypothalamus that stimulates secretion of adrenocorticotrophic hormone (ACTH), which in turn controls activity of the adrenal cortex.

Cortisol   Cortisol is a hormone of the adrenal cortex that is secreted under stress.

Counterconditioning   Counterconditioning involves replacing a disturbing response to a given stimulus with a more positive one.

Defense mechanisms   Defense mechanisms are unconscious or sometimes conscious mental processes used to defend against anxiety and unconscious impulses.

Delirium   Delirium is a mental disorder that is characterized by attentional and memory deficits, disorientation, perceptual distortion, psychomotor disturbances, and sleep disorders.

Delirium tremens Delirium tremens is a set of symptoms that often follows alcohol withdrawal and is marked by sweating, tremor, anxiety, and visual and auditory hallucinations.

Dementia Dementia is the impairment of intellectual functioning due to organic factors.

Dependent variable The dependent variable is the variable that is measured to determine how it was influenced by the independent variable.

Diagnostic-related groups (DRGs) DRGs are Medicare price controls based on the average cost of treating patients with a specific diagnosis.

Diastolic pressure Diastolic pressure is the measure of blood pressure at which muscles of the heart chambers are not contracting. It is the lower reading of blood pressure measurement.

Dispositional analyses Dispositional analyses emphasize the impact of abiding traits of the person coping with illness.

Distress Distress is the negative effect that results from exposure to a stressor.

Drug addiction Drug addiction is the compulsive use of a psychoactive substance to produce pleasure or to avoid physical or emotional discomfort.

Electromyographic biofeedback Electromyographic biofeedback records muscle tension in the form of electrical impulses generated by muscles and feeds back information to the patient.

Emotion-focused coping Emotion-focused coping is directed at controlling the emotional response associated with a stressor.

Endorphins Endorphins are a group of peptides found in the nervous system that are capable of producing effects similar to those of opiates.

Epinephrine Epinephrine is a hormone secreted by the core of the adrenal gland which acts in concert with the sympathetic nervous system. It is also known as adrenaline.

Essential hypertension Essential hypertension is high arterial blood pressure that does not appear to be due to some other disease process.

Esteem support Esteem support is a form of social support that provides individuals with the sense that they are valued and held in esteem.

Eustress Eustress is the term used to describe the positive outcomes that may result from exposure to a stressor.

Existential-phenomenological approach This approach is based in phenomenology and suggests that illness may be a way of self-fulfillment or self-expression when normal outlets have been blocked.

Experimental method The experimental method is an investigation that directly manipulates one variable while measuring the effects on another in order to pinpoint variables that control an outcome.

Experiential testing Experiential testing is a thought countering approach used in cognitive behavioral therapy that involves objectively examining the experience that produces disturbing thoughts and developing more constructive cognitions based on the trial experience.

Expressive therapies Expressive therapies are those that emphasize finding healthy ways to express unconscious conflicts or problems.

Extinction Extinction is a method of reducing behaviors by withholding reinforcement for a response that was previously reinforced.

Extrinsic asthma Extrinsic asthma is a disorder with episodic attacks of wheezing, tightness of the chest, difficulty in breathing, and coughing that is precipitated by allergens.

False alarms A false alarm occurs when a medical test result is positive, yet the person does not have the disease in question.

Family systems approach The family systems approach views illness as an attempt to adapt to the family system.

Farsightedness Farsightedness is the ability to anticipate the consequences of various coping strategies.

Fetal alcohol syndrome Fetal alcohol syndrome is a collection of symptoms found in a percentage of the offspring of mothers who abuse alcohol during pregnancy.

Flexibility Flexibility refers to the availability of a variety of coping strategies to overcome a stressor and the willingness to consider them.

Frequency Frequency is one of the basic components of exercise and refers to the number of exercise sessions per week.

Gambler's fallacy The gambler's fallacy is committed when a person thinks that something is less likely to occur if it has happened recently. This is not true when events occur independently of previous ones.

Gamma globulins Gamma globulins is another commonly used name for antibodies or immunoglobulins. Because not all antibodies are gamma globulins, the term immunoglobulins is preferred.

Gate control theory of pain This theory states that the experience of pain depends on neural systems underlying (1) thought and evaluation, (2) emotions and motives, and (3) sensory activity.

General Adaptation Syndrome The General Adaptation Syndrome is an orderly, three-stage pattern of response to physical and psychological stressors. The three stages are the stage of alarm, the stage of resistance, and the stage of exhaustion.

General systems theory General systems theory assumes that systems exist within systems which forces researchers and practitioners to take a global view of their work.

General systems theory approach This approach takes a global view of health and emphasizes the fact that an intervention at one level of a system affects other levels of the system.

Glucocorticoids Glucocorticoids are a major class of hormones that are considered the "stress hormones" of the adrenal cortex.

Glucostatic theory The glucostatic theory suggests that hunger and satiety depend on the rate at which our bodies use glucose.

Hardiness Hardiness is a set of personality traits that may make a person resistant to stress. It includes a high degree of commitment to one's activities, feeling in control, and seeing stressors as a challenge.

Health belief model The health belief model suggests that health-related motivations are predicted by perceived threat and severity of illness or injury and the perceived benefits and barriers to specified preventive behaviors.

Health maintenance organizations (HMOs) HMOs are prepaid health care plans that provide stated services for a flat fee.

Health psychology Health psychology is the systematic application of psychology to the relevant areas of health, disease, and the health care system.

Heroic medicine Heroic medicine is the use of invasive, painful, and sometimes harmful interventions. The patient has to be "heroic" to submit to these treatments.

Heuristics Heuristics are rules for deriving subjective probabilities.

Histocompatibility antigens Histocompatibility antigens are a key factor in permitting the immune system to distinguish between materials that are part of the body and those that are foreign.

Holistic approach The holistic approach sees physical illnesses as having mental and spiritual causes as well as those stressed by traditional methods.

Hospice Hospice is a program or facility that provides for the psychological, social, and physical needs of terminally ill patients and their families.

Human immunodeficiency virus (HIV) HIV is the term generally used to refer to the virus that is believed to cause AIDS by attacking the immune system.

Hypertension Hypertension is a pathological elevation of blood pressure in the arteries.

Humoral system of immunity The humoral system of immunity is an advanced system of immunity based on the buildup of antibodies that undermines the activities of destructive foreign agents in the body (see also B-Cells, immunoglobulins, gamma globulins).

Hypothalamic-pituitary-adrenal cortical system   This system is an important regulatory system that is involved in the release of major hormones and plays a key role in the General Adaptation Syndrome.

Hypothalamus   The hypothalamus is located at the base of the brain and regulates basic biological functions, for example, hunger, thirst, sexual arousal, internal temperature, and hormonal functioning.

Iatrogenic   Iatrogenic means "caused by the treatment." It is the term used to describe illness caused by physicians or medical treatments.

Illness behavior   Illness behavior is the interpretation of certain signs and sensations as symptoms and the initiation of action to learn their meaning and get treatment for them.

Imaginary rehearsal   Imaginary rehearsal involves imagining the use of a new coping skill in specific situations.

Imaginative inattention   Imaginative inattention is a cognitive method used to control pain by using goal-directed imagery that distracts the patient's attention from the pain.

Imaginative transformation   Imaginative transformation is a cognitive method used to control pain by viewing pain sensations as something other than pain.

Imaginative transformation of context   This is a cognitive method to control pain in which patients imagine situations in which the pain would not bother them as much.

Immune system   The immune system allows the body to neutralize, eliminate, or control the factors that produce disease.

Immunoglobulins   Immunoglobulins is commonly used as an equivalent term for "antibody"; a protein with antibody activity.

Impersonal impact hypothesis   The impersonal impact hypothesis states that media reports may have an impact on beliefs about the seriousness of a problem as it affects the society, but they do not influence beliefs about how a risk factor affects an individual personally.

Independent variable   An independent variable is the variable that is manipulated by the researcher to determine what effect it has on some other variable.

Informational support   Informational support involves giving information, advice, or feedback to individuals about how they are doing.

Initiation   Initiation is the term used to refer to the phase of cancer in which the genetic information of a normal cell is altered.

Innate system of immunity   The innate system of immunity is a primitive system in which, without specifically recognizing the invading agent, the body takes actions that undermine the functioning of that agent; e.g. sneezing or raising body temperature to eject or impair pathogens.

Instrumental support   Instrumental support is one of the types of social support we use in dealing with stress. It involves direct aid to an individual in the form of loans, gifts, or services.

Insulin   Insulin is a hormone involved in the regulation of carbohydrate metabolism through the control of glucose levels in the blood.

Intensity   Intensity is one of the three basic components of exercise and is expressed as the percentage of the individual's maximal capacity such as maximum heart rate.

Intimacy   Intimacy is the sense that one is appreciated and held in affection and that important thoughts and feelings can be shared with another.

Intrinsic asthma   Intrinsic asthma is a disorder with episodic attacks of wheezing, tightness of the chest, difficulty in breathing, and coughing that appear to occur spontaneously.

Invisible drugs   Invisible drugs are those that are so much a part of our lifestyles that we do not perceive them to be significant drugs, but they are nonetheless.

Ischemia Ischemia is impairment of blood supply to tissue. For example, it occurs when the coronary arteries become blocked and the heart muscles fail to get essential nutrients, especially oxygen, that are carried in the blood.

Jenkins Activity Survey The Jenkins Activity Survey is a widely used paper-and-pencil test of Type A behavior.

Ketosis Ketosis is an abnormal chemical state that occurs in diabetics who fail to regulate their insulin correctly. It can result in coma and death if untreated.

Killer cells Killer cells are a type of immune cell that is not a lymphocyte but is very similar to one. It attacks pathogens without their first being coated with antibodies. It probably is an important component of the system that attacks cancer cells.

Korotkoff sounds Korotkoff sounds are produced by distension of the artery under pressure and are an important part of measuring blood pressure.

Life expectancy Life expectancy is the average number of years a person of a certain age can expect to live.

Life span Life span is the *maximum* age that any individual can expect to reach.

Lifestyle Lifestyle refers to the health-related decisions and behaviors that are, to an extent, controlled by individuals.

Limbic system The limbic system is an interconnected series of brain structures that govern emotional, hormonal output, and other physiological reactions relevant to health.

Lymphocytes Lymphocytes are white blood cells which are an important part of immune system functioning.

Lymphokines Lymphokines are chemical messengers, secreted by lymphocytes, that permit communication between cells of the immune system to regulate their activity.

Main effect model The main effect model involves large social networks that have positive effects on well-being unrelated to stress.

Mainstream smoke Mainstream smoke is the smoke that is pulled through the mouthpiece into the smoker's mouth.

Malignant tumors Malignant tumors are masses of tissue formed by uncontrolled growth of cells that invade normal tissue and can metastasize to other sites.

Managed-care health care plans Managed-care health care plans are cost-containment efforts to reduce health care costs by limiting the employee's choice of physicians, hospitals, and treatments.

Mastery Mastery is the sense that we are responsible for what happens to us and that our actions can lead to a favorable outcome.

Metastasis Metastasis is the process in which cancerous cells break off from malignant tumors and travel to other parts of the body to form new malignant tumors.

Medical imperialism Medical imperialism is the insistence that anything that is remotely connected with health or illness belongs under the supervision of the medical profession.

Medical psychotherapy Medical psychotherapy is a newly defined field that applies psychology to medical treatment.

Migraine headache Migraine headaches are recurrent intense headaches with throbbing pain that are often accompanied by nausea, vomiting, and aversion to light.

Mineralocorticoids Mineralocorticoids are a major class of hormones secreted by the adrenal cortex that regulate the balance of materials dissolved in the fluids that surround cells of the body.

Modeling Modeling involves having the therapist role play different methods of coping with situations that are difficult for the patient.

Monocytes Monocytes are a type of circulating phagocyte and are considered an immature form of macrophage.

Morbid obesity Obesity is considered morbid when it threatens health or restricts activities.

Myocardial infarction Myocardial infarction occurs when a blockage of blood flow causes damage to the muscle tissue of the heart. It is the technical term for a heart attack.

Myofascial pain dysfunction syndrome This is one of the most common labels currently given to a disorder involving symptoms resulting from excessive jaw tension, formerly known as temporomandibular joint syndrome.

Natural killer cells Natural killer cells play an important role in killing some types of tumor cells and also can kill cells infected with viruses or bacteria. They are distinct from monocytes, B-Cells, and T-Cells.

Neoplasms Neoplasm is another term for tumor and literally means "new growth."

Neuropeptides Neuropeptides are chemicals, many of which have long been familiar as hormones, but that are now known to carry information in the nervous system ("neurotransmitter substances"). Neuropeptides have receptors throughout the body, so brain and body regulation seem to be carried out by the same substances.

Neutral effects Neutral effects are the outcome of exposure to stressful events that do not have any notable influence on the individual.

Nominal scaling Nominal scaling involves identifying and labeling variables without quantification.

Norepinephrine Norepinephrine is a hormone and neural messenger that communicates between the sympathetic nervous system and various organs of the body. It is produced and stored by the inner core of the adrenal gland. (It is also known as noradrenaline.)

Null hypothesis The null hypothesis states that there is no relationship between variables other than that produced by chance influences.

Obesity Obesity is an excessive accumulation of fat in the subcutaneous tissues located immediately beneath the skin.

Object relations model The object relations model emphasizes the role of very early parenting from which individuals learn how to regard and treat themselves.

Oncogenes Oncogenes are cancer-causing genes that appear to produce uncontrolled growth in cells when activated by outside factors.

Operant conditioning Operant conditioning occurs when voluntary behavior is influenced by its consequences.

Opioids Opioids are natural or synthetic morphine-like compounds.

Orthognathic surgery Orthognathic surgery is surgery that is used to correct abnormalities of the jaw.

Osteoporosis Osteoporosis is a crippling disease that involves bone loss and occurs most frequently in postmenopausal women.

Palliative care Palliative care is treatment that provides temporary relief but does not effect a cure.

Paradigm A paradigm is a model or framework of how science is to be conducted. It identifies the questions that can be studied and determines the research methods that may be used.

Parasympathetic nervous system The parasympathetic nervous system is a subdivision of the autonomic nervous system that conserves energy and returns the body to a "resting" state.

Passive smoking Passive smoking is the involuntary exposure of nonsmokers to the effects of tobacco smoke.

Passive volition Passive volition is an attitude that involves arranging circumstances so that a desired effect will occur and then allowing whatever happens to happen.

Pathogens Pathogens are destructive microorganisms or substances.

Peripheral nervous system The peripheral nervous system consists of the sensory and motor nerves that provide messages to and from the central nervous system and the autonomic nervous system.

Peripheral resistance   Peripheral resistance is the amount of back-pressure the heart has to pump against and is one of two factors that determines blood pressure levels.

Peripheral route   Peripheral route communication is most effective with a weak argument and avoids careful or deliberate thinking about an issue.

Personal stressors   Personal stressors are those that affect individual people, for example, death of a spouse.

Phagocytes   Phagocytes are ''scavenger'' immune cells that destroy antigens.

Phantom limb pain   Phantom limb pain occurs in people who have lost limbs and who experience severe pain in the missing limb despite adequate healing of the stump.

Physical dependence   Physical dependence is the alteration of bodily processes to the extent that continued use of the substance is necessary to prevent withdrawal symptoms.

Pituitary gland   The pituitary gland is regulated by the hypothalamus and produces and secretes a variety of hormones that affect other glands of the body. It is considered the ''master gland.''

Preferred provider organization (PPO)   A PPO is a managed-care health plan in which employers or union have a contract with a group of hospitals and health care providers to provide services to their members at a reduced rate.

Primary appraisal   Primary appraisal refers to the evaluation of a stressor.

Primary prevention   Primary prevention attempts to reduce the risks of illness for an entire population.

Primitive defenses   Primitive defenses are the immature defense mechanisms typically used by children.

Problem-focused coping   Problem-focused coping is directed at controlling a stressor to reduce or eliminate its effects.

Process analyses   Process analyses emphasize the fit between various situational demands and coping responses.

Process of discovery   The process of discovery involves approaching a problem with a sensitivity to subtle cues that lays aside criticism and emphasis on error avoidance.

Process of verification   The process of verification involves careful measurement and controlled experimental research.

Prodrome   A prodrome is a set of warning signs that precedes classical migraine headaches, for example, visual disturbances.

Progressive relaxation training   Progressive relaxation training involves developing a clear sense of the difference between tension and relaxation through gently tensing groups of muscles and then abruptly relaxing them while attending to the resulting sensations of tenseness and relaxation.

Projective identification   A primitive defense mechanism that involves projecting ''bad'' parts of ourselves to a proxy with whom we can identify.

Promotion   Promotion is a phase of cancer progression which involves the abnormal growth of an altered cell.

Psychodynamic model   The psychodynamic model of therapy stems from Freudian theory which suggests that physical symptoms are the result of unconscious conflicts or impulses.

Psychoneuroimmunology   Psychoneuroimmunology is an interdisciplinary investigation of the relationship between the nervous system and the immune system.

Psychophysiological approach   The psychophysiological approach emphasizes the relationship between psychological events and health-related physical reactions.

Psychophysiological disorders   Psychophysiological disorders refer to physical symptoms with tissue damage that have psychological origins. These disorders were formerly known as psychosomatic.

Psychophysiology   Psychophysiology is the subfield of psychology that studies influences on physiological psychological processes.

Psychosomatic families   Psychosomatic families is a term used to describe families in which failure to cope with illness is brought on by failure to deal with psychological problems in the family system.

Psychosomatic medicine Psychosomatic medicine is the study of the interaction of the psychosocial and biological factors of health and illness.

Public health psychology Public health psychology focuses on community interventions and emphasizes prevention over cure.

Punishment Punishment involves suppressing a behavior by presenting a noxious stimulus after the behavior.

Rational disputation Rational disputation involves the examination of the meaning, premises, and logical coherence of the client's thoughts in order to demonstrate fallacies.

Rationality Rationality is an accurate, objective assessment of a situation or stressor.

Reasoned action theory Reasoned action theory states that intention is the best predictor of behavior and is influenced by our attitudes, including the belief that a behavior will result in a certain outcome, the evaluation of the outcome, and what we believe other people think about these actions.

Rebound headaches Rebound headaches are those caused by headache medication that at first alleviates the headache.

Reducers Reducers are people who respond to pain and other stimuli less than most people.

Relaxation training Relaxation training covers a range of techniques to reduce physical and emotional arousal.

Reliability Reliability refers to the degree to which measures are stable and repeatable.

Representativeness heuristic The representativeness heuristic involves making judgments on the basis of resemblance to typical cases.

Response specificity Response specificity is the tendency of individuals to respond to stressors in unique ways, for example, jaw tension and increased blood pressure.

Restrained eating theory The restrained eating theory proposes that many obese people constantly restrain their eating to weigh less than their biological set-point and that negative emotions and other factors disinhibit the restraint.

Sarcomas Sarcomas are tumors that originate in the connective tissue found in muscles, bones, fat, lymphatic vessels, and nerves.

Secondary appraisal Secondary appraisal involves the evaluation of one's ability to overcome a stressor.

Secondary prevention Secondary prevention involves reducing risk factors in groups at high risk for a given disease.

Selective reinforcement Selective reinforcement involves the reinforcement of desirable responses while withholding reinforcement for undesirable responses.

Self-efficacy theory Self-efficacy theory states that our beliefs about our capabilities of meeting some particular challenge determine our choice of activities and the amount of effort we will expend when faced with obstacles.

Sensations Sensations are subjective experiences, such as pain that may or may not be interpreted as illness symptoms.

Sense of coherence Sense of coherence is the central characteristic that leads to resistance to stress. It is a sense that one's internal and external environments are fairly predictable and that things will work out as well as can reasonably be expected.

Set Set refers to the individual's personality and expectations that are brought to the use of a psychoactive substance.

Set-point theory According to the set-point theory, our bodies are programmed to contain a certain amount of fat and eating behavior is increased or decreased when fat levels exceed or fall below the set-point.

Setting Setting is the physical and social environment in which a psychoactive drug is used.

Short-term reaction Short-term reaction is

the temporary response to the demands of the stressor.

Sick role The sick role is that assigned to an ailing person after diagnosis by a health care professional. It gives patients certain rights and reduced responsibilities.

Sidestream smoke Sidestream smoke comes from the burning end of the cigarette, cigar, or pipe.

Signs Signs are health-related events that are observable by other people and may be interpreted as symptoms of illness.

Silent heart attacks Silent heart attacks are those attacks that are not noticed or acknowledged by the patient.

Social support Social support comprises the resources provided to individuals through their interactions with other people.

Splitting Splitting is a primitive defense mechanism that involves isolating the good and bad features of significant others as if they were totally separate entities. This mechanism creates extreme and often distorted views of people.

Spontaneous recovery Spontaneous recovery is a term used in learning theory to describe the reappearance of a conditioned response after it has been extinguished.

Stage of alarm Stage of alarm is the first stage of the General Adaptation Syndrome in which the body reacts strongly to a foreign entity.

Stage of exhaustion Stage of exhaustion is the final stage of the General Adaptation Syndrome in which increased levels of cortisol produce effects that may lead to death.

Stage of resistance Stage of resistance is the second stage of the General Adaptation Syndrome in which bodily reactions appear to have returned to normal, however, the body may not be able to react effectively to a new stressor.

Stigmata Stigmata are marks or wounds similar to those received by Jesus during His crucifixion. They appear on the body spontaneously in the absence of external physical injury.

Stimulus control Stimulus control occurs when the likelihood of a response varies systematically with the presence or absence of a cue.

Stress resistance resources Stress resistance resources are all of the material, physical, social, cultural, and psychological resources available to a person to manage short-term reactions stressors.

Stressor A stressor is anything that makes a demand on an individual.

Structured interview The structured interview is a 15-minute videotaped interview that is used as a measuring instrument for Type A behavior.

Stump pain Stump pain is the pain experienced in the remaining tissue of an amputated limb that has not healed properly.

Subjective probabilities Subjective probabilities are intuitive estimates of the likelihood that something will occur.

Sympathetic nervous system The sympathetic nervous system is a subdivision of the autonomic nervous system that, combined with the adrenal medulla, prepares the body for "fight or flight."

Sympathoadrenal system The sympathoadrenal system consists of the sympathetic nervous system and the adrenal medulla and prepares the body for "fight or flight."

Symptoms Symptoms are signs and sensations that are interpreted as an indication of illness.

Systematic desensitization Systematic desensitization involves combining deep relaxation with graded imagining of stressful or anxiety-producing situations.

Systolic pressure Systolic pressure is the measure of blood pressure at which muscles of the heart chambers are contracting. It is the upper reading of blood pressure measurement.

T-cells T-cells are lymphocytes that mature in the thymus and are responsible for cell-mediated immunity and the regulation of other immunologically competent cells, such as B-cells and phagocytes.

GLOSSARY

Technological imperative The technological imperative is the desire of physicians to do everything they have been trained to do and use all of the modern technologies that are available whether or not they are appropriate.

Temporomandibular joint syndrome (TMJ) TMJ is the term that was formerly in common usage to describe a collection of symptoms resulting from excessive jaw tension. Currently, it is more commonly known as myofascial pain dysfunction syndrome.

Tension headache The tension headache involves dull, bandlike pain that is associated with muscle contractions.

Tertiary prevention Tertiary prevention seeks to reduce the duration or intensity of the illness in those who are already inflicted.

Thalamus The thalamus is a structure located deep in the brain and is a relay center for many sensory systems.

Theory perseverance Theory perseverance is the tendency to hold onto an idea in spite of evidence to the contrary.

Thermal biofeedback Thermal biofeedback involves detecting changes in peripheral skin temperature.

Thought countering Thought countering is a technique for eliminating or modifying thoughts that produce symptoms or undesirable behaviors; it is done by challenging, disputing, or testing the validity of those thoughts.

Thought stopping Thought stopping is a method of self-punishment for undesirable thoughts, usually by *inwardly* shouting "STOP!" when the thoughts occur.

Thymus The thymus is a glandlike structure that lies right above the heart and is critically important to the development of the immune system's T-cells.

Tolerance Tolerance occurs when a psychoactive substance becomes less effective with repeated use and more frequent and larger doses are required to achieve the same effect.

Triangular numeric breathing Triangular numeric breathing is a behavioral method used to treat hypertension that involves continuous deep breathing without stopping at the end of the inhalation or exhalation.

Type A behavior Type A behavior is a specific pattern of behavior that may be relevant to the development of heart disease.

Type I diabetes Type I diabetes, or insulin-dependent diabetes, usually begins in childhood and is associated with the failure of the pancreas to produce insulin normally.

Type II diabetes Type II diabetes, or non-insulin-dependent diabetes, is a varied group of disorders of sugar metabolism and usually occurs in adults.

Unconscious conflict model The unconscious conflict model is a psychodynamic model that attributes symptoms to unconscious conflicts and that treats the symptoms by making these conflicts conscious.

Validity Validity refers to the extent to which something measures what it is intended to measure.

Withdrawal symptoms Withdrawal symptoms are unpleasant effects caused by abstaining from a drug, for example, tremors, nausea, and headache.

Zeitgeist The zeitgeist is the general economic, political, and cultural climate of a particular era—the "spirit of the times."

Bibliography

Achterberg, J. (1985). *Imagery in healing: Shamanism and modern medicine*. Boston: New Science Library.

Ackerman, S. J. (1988, Fall). Tobacco and politics: Smoke-filled rooms. *Philip Morris Magazine*, p. 19.

Adam, G. (1967). Interoception and behavior: An experimental study. Akademiai Kaido (Hungarian Academy of Sciences), Budapest, Hungary.

Ader, R. (1980). Psychosomatic and psychoimmunologic research. *Psychosomatic Medicine*, 42, 307–321.

Ader, R. (1981). An historical account of conditioned immunobiologic responses. In R. Ader (ed.), *Psychoneuroimmunology*. New York: Academic Press.

Ader, R. (1989). Psychoneuroimmunology. Presented at Annual Meeting of the American Psychological Association, New Orleans.

Ader, R., & Cohen, N. (1975). Behaviorally conditioned immunosuppression. *Psychosomatic Medicine*, 37, 333–340.

Ader, R., & Cohen, N. (1984). Behavior and the immune system. In W. D. Gentry (ed.), *Handbook of behavioral medicine*. New York: Guilford Press.

Agras, W. S., Southam, M., & Taylor, C. (1983). Relaxation training in essential hypertension: A failure of retraining in relaxation procedures. *Behavior Therapy*, 15, 191–196.

Aivazyan, T., Zaitsev, V., Salenko, B., Yurenev, A., & Patrusheva, I. (1988). Efficacy of relaxation techniques in essential hypertension. *Health Pschology*, 7, 193–200.

Aivazyan, T., Zaitsev, V., and Yurenev, A. (1988). Autogenic training in the treatment and secondary prevention of essential hypertension: Five year follow-up. *Health Psychology*, 7, 201–208.

Ajzen, I., & Fishbein, M. (eds.). (1980). *Understanding attitudes and predicting social behavior*. Englewood Cliffs, NJ: Prentice-Hall.

Alexander, A. B. (1977). Chronic asthma. In R. W. Williams & W.D. Gentry (eds.), *Behavioral approaches to medical treatment* (pp. 7–23). Cambridge, Mass.: Ballinger.

Albert, R. K., & Condie, F. (1981). Handwashing patterns in medical intensive-care units. *New England Journal of Medicine*, 304, 1465–1466.

Alexander, A. B. (1977). Chronic asthma. In R. W. Williams & W. D. Gentry (eds.), *Behavioral approaches to medical treatment* (pp. 7–23). Cambridge, MA: Ballinger.

Alexander, A. B., Miklich, D. R., & Hershkoff, H. (1972). The immediate effects of systematic relaxation training on peak expiratory flow rates in ashtmatic children. *Psychosomatic Medicine*, 34, 388–394.

Alexander, A. B., & Solanch, L. S. (1981). Psychological aspects in the understanding and treatment of bronchial asthma. In J. M. Ferguson & C. B. Taylor (eds.), *The comprehensive handbook of behavioral medicine* (Vol. 2) (pp. 3–40). New York: SP Medical & Scientific Books.

Alexander, F. (1950). *Psychosomatic medicine: Its principles and applications*. New York: W. W. Norton.

Alpert, B., Field, T., Goldstein, S., & Perry, S. (1990). Aerobics enhances cardiovascular fitness and agility in preschoolers. *Health Psychology*, 9, 48–56.

Altman, D. G., & Cahn, J. (1987). Employment options for health psychologists. In G. C. Stone, S. M. Weiss, J. D. Matarazzo, N. Miller, J. Rodin, C. D. Belar, M. J. Follick, & J. E. Singer (eds.), *Health psychology: A discipline and a profession* (pp. 231–244). Chicago: University of Chicago Press.

American College of Sports Medicine. (1978). The recommended quantity and quality of exercise for developing and maintaining fitness in healthy adults. *Medicine and Science in Sports*, 10, vii–x.

American Psychiatric Association. (1987). *Diagnostic and statistical manual of mental disorders* (3rd ed. rev.). Washington, D.C.: American Psychiatric Association.

Antoni, M. H. (1987). Neuroendocrine influences in psychoimmunology and neoplasia: A review. *Psychology and Health*, 1, 3–24.

Antonovsky, A. (1979). *Health, stress, and coping*. San Francisco: Jossey–Bass.

Antonovsky, A. (1987). *Unraveling the mystery of health: How people manage stress and stay well*. San Francisco: Jossey–Bass.

ASHA (American School Health Association). (1989). *The national adolescent student health survey: A report on the health of America's youth*. Oakland, Calif.: Third Party Publishing.

Asterita, M. F. (1985). *The physiology of stress with special reference to the neuroendocrine system*. New York: Human Sciences Press.

Backer, T. E., Batchelor, W. F., Jones, J. M., & Mays, V. M. (eds.). (1988). *Psychology and AIDS* (special issue). *American Psychologist*, 43(11).

Bakal, D. A. (1982). *The psychobiology of chronic headache*. New York: Springer.

Balint, M. (1968). *The basic fault*. London: Tavistock.

Bandura, A. (1977). Self-efficacy: Toward a unifying theory of behavioral change. *Psychological Review*, 84, 191–215.

Bandura, A. (1982). Self-efficacy mechanism in human agency. *American Psychologist*, 37, 122–147.

Banks, J. K., & Gannon, L. R. (1988). The influence of hardiness on the relationship between stressors and psychosomatic symptomatology. *American Journal of Community Psychology*, 16, 25–37.

Barber, J. G., Bradshaw, R., & Walsh, C. (1989). Reducing alcohol consumption through television advertising. *Journal of Consulting and Clinical Psychology*, 57, 613–618.

Barber, T. X. (1978). "Hypnosis" suggestions and psychosomatic phenomena: A new look from the standpoint of recent studies. In J. L. Fosshage & P. Olsen (eds.), *Healing: Implications for psychotherapy* (pp. 269–297). New York: Human Sciences Press.

Barber, T. X. (1984). Changing "unchangeable" bodily processes by (hypnotic) suggestions: A new look at hypnosis, cognitions, imagining, and the mind-body problem. In A. A. Sheikh (ed.), *Imagination and healing*. New York: Baywood.

Barber, T. X., Spanos, N. P., & Chaves, J. F. (1974). *Hypnotism, imagination and human potentialities*. New York: Pergamon Press.

Bardos, P., Degenne, D., Lebranchu, Y., Biziere, K., & Renoux, G. (1981). Neocortical lateralization of NK activity in mice. *Scandinavian Journal of Immunology* 13, 609–611.

Bartrop, R. W., Lazarus, L., Luckhurst, E., Kiloh, L. G., & Penny, R. (1977). Depressed lymphocyte function after bereavement. *The Lancet*, 1, 834–836.

Batchelor, W. F. (1988). AIDS 1988: The science and the limits of science. *American Psychologist*, 43, 853–858.

Batistella, P. A., Rufilli, R., & Zacchello, F. (1989). Pupillary adrenergic sensitivity and idiopathic headache in pediatric patients. *Headache*, 29, 163–166.

Beck, A., Rush, A. J., Shaw, B., & Emery, G. (1979). *Cognitive therapy of depression*. New York: Guilford Press.

Becker, M. H. (ed.). (1974). The health belief model and personal health behavior. *Health Education Monographs*, 2, 409–419.

Becker, M. H., Drachman, R. H., & Kirscht, J. P. (1972). Predicting mothers' compliance with pediatric medical regimens. *Journal of Pediatrics*, 81, 843–854.

Becker, M. H., & Rosenstock, I. M. (1984). Compliance with medical advice. In A. Steptoe & A. Mathews (eds.), *Health care and human behavior*. London: Academic Press.

Beecher, H. K. (1959). *Measurement of subjective responses: Quantitative effects of drugs*. New York: Oxford University Press.

Belar, C. D., Deardorff, W. W., & Kelly, K. E. (1987). *The practice of clinical health psychology*. New York: Pergamon Press.

Belisle, M., Roskies, E., & Leveseque, J. (1987). Improving adherence to physical activity. *Health Psychology*, 6, 159–172.

Beller, A. S. (1977). *Fat and thin: a natural history of obesity*. New York: Farrar, Straus, and Giroux.

Belloc, N. D., & Breslow, L. (1972). Relationship of physical health status and family practices. *Preventive Medicine*, 1, 409–421.

Bender, E. V. (1988). The self-care revolution: How it saves lives, builds health. In R. Yarian (eds.), *Annual editions: Health* (9th ed.) (pp. 11–18). Guilford, Conn.: Dushkin.

Benson, H. (1975). *The relaxation response*. New York: William Morrow.

Benson, H. (1977). Systemic hypertension and the relaxation response, *New England Journal of Medicine*, 296, 1152–1156.

Benson, H. (1984). *Beyond the relaxation response*. New York: Times Books.

Bergland, R. (1985). *The fabric of mind*. New York: Viking Press.

Berkman, L. F. (1984). Assessing the physical health effects of social networks and social support. *Annual Review of Public Health*, 5, 413–432.

Berkman, L. F., & Syme, S. L. (1979). Social networks, host resistance and mortality: A nine-year follow-up study of Alameda County residents. *American Journal of Epidemiology*, 109, 186–204.

Besodovsky, H. O., Sorkin, E., Felix, D., & Haas, H. (1977). Hypothalamic changes during the immune response. *European Journal of Immunology*, 7, 323–325.

Bettelheim, B. (1947). Individual and mass behavior in exreme situations. In T. M. Newcomb & E. L. Hartley (eds.), *Readings in social psychology*. New York: Henry Holt.

Bieber, I. (1974). The concept of irrational belief systems as primary elements of psychopathology. *Journal of the American Academy of Psychoanalysis*, 2, 91–100.

Bieliauskas, L. A. (1984). Depression, stress, and cancer. In C. L. Cooper (ed.), *Psychosocial stress and cancer* (pp. 37–48). Chichester: John Wiley & Sons.

Billings, A. G., & Moos, R. H. (1982). Social support and functioning among community and clinical groups: A panel model. *Journal of Behavioral Medicine*, 5, 295–312.

Bjorntorp, P. (1986). Fat cells and obesity. In K. D. Brownell & J. P. Foreyt (eds.), *Handbook of eating disorders* (pp. 88–98). New York: Basic Books.

Blair, S. N., Kohl, H. W., Paffenbarger, R. S., Jr., Clark, D. G., Cooper, K. H., & Gibbons, L. W. (1989). Physical fitness and all-cause mortality: A prospective study of healthy men and women. *Journal of the American Medical Association*, 262, 2395–2401.

Blanchard, E. B., & Andrasik, F. (1985). *Management of chronic headaches*. New York: Pergamon Press.

Blanchard, E. B., Andrasik, F., Neff, D. F., Teders, S. J., Pallmeyer, T. P., Arena, J. G., Jurish, S. E., Saunders, N. L., & Rodichok, L. D. (1982a). Sequential comparisons of relaxation training and biiofeedback in the treatment of three kinds of chronic headache or, the machines may be necessary some of the time. *Behaviour Research and Therapy*, 20, 469–481.

Blanchard, E. B., Andrasik, F., Neff, D. F., Arena, J. G., Ahles, T. A., Jurish, S. E., Pallmeyer, T. P., Saunders, N. L., Teders, S. J., Barron, K. D., & Rodichok, L. D. (1982b). Biofeedback and relaxation training with three kinds of headache: Treatment effects and their prediction. *Journal of Consulting and Clinical Psychology*, 50, 562–575.

Blanchard, E., Khramelasvilii, V., McCoy, G., Aivazyan, T., McAffrey, R., Salenko, B., Musso, A., Wittrock, D., Berger, M., Gerardi, M., & Pangburn, L. (1988). The USA–USSR collaborative cross-cultural comparison of autogenic training and thermal biofeedback in the treatment of mild hypertension. *Health Psychology*, 7, 175–192.

Blanchard, E., Martin, J., & Dubbert, P. (1988). *Nondrug treatments for essential hypertension*. New York: Pergamon Press.

Blanchard, E. B., McCoy, G. C., Musso, A., Gerardi, M. A., Pallmeyer, T. P., Gerardi, R. J.,

Cotch, P. A., Siracusa, K., & Andrasik, F. (1986). A controlled comparison of thermal biofeedback and relaxation training in the treatment of essential hypertension: I. Short-term and long-term outcome. *Behavior Therapy*, 17, 563–579.

Bloch, G. J. (1985). *Body and self: Elements of human biology, behavior, and health*. Los Altos, Calif.: William Kaufmann.

Bloch, R., & Bloch, A. (1981). *Cancer: There's hope*. Kansas City, Mo.: R. A. Bloch Cancer Foundation.

Bloom, F. E. (1987). Endorphins. In G. Adelman (ed.), *Encyclopedia of neuroscience* (Vol. 1) (pp. 393–395). Boston: Birkhauser.

Blum, K., Noble, E. P., Sheridan, P. J., Montgomery, A., Ritchie, T., Jagadeeswaran, P., Nogami, H., Briggs, A. H., & Cohn, J. B. (1990). Allelic association of human dopamine D_2 receptor gene in alcoholism. *Journal of the American Medical Association*, 263, 2055–2060.

Blumenthal, J. A., Emery, C. F., Madden, D. J., George, L. K., Coleman, R. E., Riddle, M. W., McKee, D. C., Reasoner, J., & Williams, R. S. (1989). Cardiovascular and behavioral effects of aerobic exercise training in healthy older men and women. *Journal of Gerontology*, 44, M147–M157.

Blumenthal, J. A., Williams, R. B., & Kong, Y. (1978). Type A behavior pattern and coronary atherosclerosis. *Circulation*, 58, 634–639.

Blundell, J. E., Hill, A. J., & Lawton, C. L. (1989). Neurochemical factors involved in normal and abnormal eating in humans. In R. Shepherd (ed.), *Handbook of psychophysiology of human eating* (pp. 85–114). Chichester: John Wiley & Sons.

Bongar, B., Forcier, L. A., & Peterson, L. (in press). The difficult and dreaded patient. *Medical Psychotherapy: An International Journal*, 4.

Bordieri, J. E., Drehmer, D. E., & Taricone, P. F. (1990). Personnel selection bias for job applicants with cancer. *Journal of Applied Social Psychology*, 20, 244–253.

Borland, R., Chapman, S., Owen, N., & Hill, D.

(1990). Effects of workplace smoking bans on cigarette consumption. *American Journal of Public Health*, 80, 178–180.

Borysenko, J. (1984). Psychoneuroimmunology: Behavioral factors and the immune response. *ReVision*, 7, 56–65.

Borysenko, M. (1987). The immune system: An overview. *Annals of Behavioral Medicine*, 9, 3–10.

Boss, M. (1979). *Existential foundations of medicine and psychology*. New York: Jason Aronson.

Botvin, G. J., Baker, E., Tortu, S., Dusenbury, L., & Gessula, J. (1989). Smokeless tobacco use among adolescents: Correlates and concurrent predictors. *Developmental and Behavioral Pediatrics*, 10 (4), 181–186.

Bourne, L. E., Dominowski, R. L., Loftus, E. F., & Healy, A. F. (1986). *Cognitive processes* (2nd. ed.) Englewood Cliffs, N.J.: Prentice–Hall.

Boyd, D. (1976). *Swami*. New York: Random House.

Boyd, G. M., & Glover, E. D. (1989). Smokeless tobacco use by youth in the U.S. *Journal of School Health*, 59 (5), 189–194.

Boyd, J., Covington, T., Stanaszck, W., & Coussons, R. (1974). Drug defaulting—Part I: Determinants of compliance. *American Journal of Hospital Pharmacy*, 31, 362–364.

Brauer, A., Horlick, L., Nelson, E., Farquhar, J., and Agras, W.S. (1979). Relaxation therapy for essential hypertension: A Veterans Administration outpatient study. *Journal of Behavioral Medicine*, 2, 21–29.

Bray, G. A. (1986). Effects of obesity on health and happiness. In K. D. Brownell & J. P. Foreyt (eds.), *Handbook of eating disorders* (pp. 3–44). New York: Basic Books.

Breuer, J., & Freud, S. (1895). *Studien uber hysterie*. Vienna: Franz Deuticke.

Brody, J. E. (1982). *Jane Brody's the New York Times guide to personal health*. New York: Times Books.

Brooks, W. H., Cross, R. J., Roszman, T. L., & Markesbery, W. R. (1982). Neuroimmunomodulation: Neuroanatomical basis for impairment and facilitation. *Annals of Neurology*, 12, 56–61.

Brooks–Gunn, J., Boyer, C. B., & Hein, K. (1988). Preventing HIV infection and AIDS in children and adolescents: Behavioral research and intervention strategies. *American Psychologist*, 43, 958–964.

Brown, D. P., & Fromm, E. (1987). *Hypnosis and behavioral medicine*. Hillsdale, N.J.: Lawrence Erlbaum.

Brown, J. D., & Siegel, J. M. (1988). Exercise as a buffer of life stress: A prospective study of adolescent health. *Health Psychology*, 7, 341–353.

Brown, S. (1988). *Treating adult children of alcoholics: A developmental perspective*. New York: John Wiley & Sons.

Brownell, K. D., Marlatt, G. A., Lichtenstein, E., & Wilson, G. T. (1986). Understanding and preventing relapse. *American Psychologist*, 41, 765–782.

Brownell, K. D., Rubin, C. J., & Smoller, J. W. (1988). Exercise and regulation of body weight. In M. Shangold & G. Mirkin (eds.), *Women and exercise: Physiology and sports medicine* (pp. 40–54). Philadelphia: F. A. Davis Co.

Brownell, K. D., & Wadden, T. A. (1986). The very-low-calorie diet: A weight-reduction technique. In K. D. Brownell & J. P. Foreyt (eds.), *Handbook of eating disorders: Physiology, psychology, and treatment of obesity, anorexia, and bulimia*. New York: Basic Books.

Budzynski, T. H., Stoyva, J., & Adler, C. S. (1970). Feedback-induced muscle relaxation: Application to tension headache. *Journal of Behavior Therapy and Experimental Psychiatry*, 1, 205–211.

Buffone, G. (1989). Consultations with oral surgeons: New roles for medical psychotherapists, *Medical Psychotherapy: An International Journal*, 2, 33–48.

Bulloch, K. (1981). Neuroendocrine-immune circuitry: Pathways involved with the induction and persistence of humoral immunity. *Dissertation Abstracts International*, 41, 4447–B.

Burgoyne, R. W., Goin, M. K., & Goin, J. M. (1977). Intraoperative psychological reactions in face-lift patients under local anesthesia. *Plastic and Reconstructive Surgery,* 60, 270–280.

Burish, T. G., Carey, M. P., Krozely, M. G., & Greco, F. A. (1987). Conditioned side effects induced by cancer chemotherapy: Prevention through behavioral treatment. *Journal of Consulting and Clinical Psychology,* 55, 42–48.

Burnham, J. C. (1989). American physicians and tobacco use: Two surgeons general, 1929 and 1964. *Bulletin of the History of Medicine,* 63, 1–31.

Burns, D. D., & Beck, A. T. (1978). Cognitive behavior modification of mood disorders. In J. P. Foreyt & D. P. Rathjen (eds.), *Cognitive behavior therapy.* New York: Plenum Publishing Corp.

Caffrey, B. (1969). Behavior patterns and personality characteristics related to prevalence rates of coronary heart disease. *Journal of Chronic Diseases,* 22, 93–103.

Califano, J. A., Jr. (1979). *Healthy people: The surgeon general's report on health promotion and disease prevention.* Washington, D.C.: U.S. Government Printing Office.

Califano, J. A., Jr. (1988). American health care: who lives? who dies? who pays? In R. Yarian (ed.), *Annual editions: Health* (9th ed.) (pp. 13–18). Guilford, Conn.: Dushkin.

Campbell, D. F., Dixon, J. K., Sanderford, L. D., & Denicola, M. A. (1984). Relaxation: Its effect on the nutritional status and performance status of clients with cancer. *Journal of the American Dietetic Association,* 84, 201–204.

Campbell, J. K. (1991). Pathophysiology, genetics, and epidemiology of headache. In R. M. Gallagher (ed.), *Drug therapy for headache* (pp. 15–28). New York: Marcel Dekker.

Casement, P. (1985). *On learning from the patient.* London: Tavistock.

Cassileth, B. R., Lusk, E. J., Miller, D. S., Brown, L. L., & Miller, C. (1985). Pyschosocial correlates of survival in advanced malignant disease? *New England Journal of Medicine,* 312, 1551–1555.

Cassileth, B. R., Lusk, E. J., Strouse, T. B., & Bodenheimer, B. J. (1984). Contemporary unorthodox treatments in cancer medicine. *Annals of Internal Medicine,* 101, 105–112.

Castro, F. G., Newcomb, M. D., McCreary, C., & Baezconde–Garbanati, L. (1989). Cigarette smokers do more than just smoke cigarettes. *Health Psychology,* 8, 1007–129.

Chapman, P. L. H., & Huygens, I. (1988). An evaluation of three treatment programmes for alcoholism: An experimental study with 6- and 18-month follow-ups. *British Journal of Addiction,* 83, 67–81.

Charness, M. E., Simon, R. P., & Greenberg, D. A. (1989). Medical progress: Ethanol and the nervous system. *New England Journal of Medicine,* 321, 442–451.

Chertok, L. (1981). *Sense and nonsense in psychotherapy: The challenge of hypnosis.* New York: Pergamon Press.

Chesney, M. A., Hecker, M. H. L., & Black, G. W. (1988). Coronary-prone components of Type A behavior in the WCGS: A new methodology. In B. K. Houston, & C. R. Snyder (eds.), *Type A behavior: Research, theory, and intervention.* New York: John Wiley & Sons.

Choi, K. (1987). Assembling the AIDS puzzle: Epidemiology. In V. Gong & N. Rudnick (eds.), *AIDS: Facts and issues* (pp. 15–24). New Brunswick, N.J.: Rutgers University Press.

Cobb, S. (1979). Social support as a moderator of life stress. *Psychosomatic Medicine,* 38, 300–314.

Cohen, F. (1984). Coping. In J. Matarazzo, S. Weiss, J. Herd, N. Miller, & S. M. Weiss (eds.), *Behavioral health: A handbook of health enhancement and disease prevention* (pp. 261–274). New York: John Wiley & Sons.

Cohen, F., & Lazarus, R. S. (1979). Coping with the stresses of illness. In G. C. Stone, F. Cohen, & N. E. Adler (eds.), *Health psychology: A handbook* (pp. 217–254). San Francisco: Jossey–Bass.

Cohen, S., Evans, G. W., Stokols, D., & Krantz, D. S. (1986). *Behavior, health, and environmen-*

tal stress. New York: Plenum Publishing Corp.

Cohen, S., Lichtenstein, E., Prochaska, J. O., Rossi, J. S., Gritz, E. R., Carr, C. R, Orleans, C. T., Schoenbach, V. J., Biener, L., Abrams, D., DiClemente, C., Curry, S., Marlatt, G. A., Cummings, K. M., Emont, S. L., Giovino, G., & Ossip-Klein, D. (1989). Debunking myths about self-quitting: Evidence from 10 prospective studies of persons who attempt to quit smoking by themselves. *American Psychologist*, 44, 1355–1366.

Cohen, S., & Wills, T. A. (1985). Stress, social support, and the buffering hypothesis. *Psychological Bulletin*, 98, 310–357.

Collins, W. F., Nulsen, F. E., & Shealy, C. N. (1966). Electrophysiological studies of peripheral and central pathways conducting pain. In R. S. Knighton & P. R. Bumke, (eds.), *Pain*. Boston: Little, Brown.

Committee on Diet, Nutrition, and Cancer, National Research Council. (1983). *Diet, nutrition, and cancer*. Washington, D.C.: National Academic Press.

Cooper, C. L. (1984). The social psychological precursors to cancer. In C. L. Cooper (ed.), *Psychosocial stress and cancer* (pp. 21–36). Chichester: John Wiley & Sons.

Cooper, K. H. (1970). *The new aerobics*. New York: M. Evans & Co.

Cooper, W. H., & Kohn, P. M. (1989). The social image of the young female smoker. *British Journal of Addiction*, 84, 935–941.

Copeland, D. (1989). Hypnosis, medicine, and miracles. Presidential Address: Division 30, Annual Meeting of the American Psychological Association, New Orleans.

Corley, K. C., Mauck, H. P., & Shiel, F. O. (1975). Cardiac responses associated with "yoked-chair" shock avoidance in squirrel monkeys. *Psychophysiology*, 12, 439–444.

Costen, J. B. (1934). A syndrome of ear and sinus symptoms dependent upon disturbed function of the temporomandibular joint. *Annals of Otology, Rhinology, and Laryngology*, 43, 1–15.

Council on Scientific Affairs. (1990). Home care in the 1990s. *Journal of the American Medical Association*, 263(9), 1241–1244.

Cousins, N. (1979). *Anatomy of an illness*. New York: W. W. Norton.

Cousins, N. (1985). Anatomy of an illness (as perceived by the patient). In A. Monat & R. S. Lazarus (eds.), *Stress and coping: An anthology* (2nd ed.). New York: Columbia University Press.

Cousins, N. (1989). *Head first: The biology of hope*. New York: E. P. Dutton.

Cox, T. (1984). Stress: A psychophysiological approach to cancer. In C. L. Cooper (ed.), *Psychsocial stress and cancer* (pp. 149–172). Chichester: John Wiley & Sons.

Cox, T., & MacKay, C. (1982). Psychosoical factors and psychophysiological mechanisms in the aetiology and development of cancer. *Social Science and Medicine*, 381–396.

Cox, W. M., & Klinger, E. (1988). A motivational model of alcohol use. *Journal of Abnormal Psychology*, 97(2), 168–180.

Coyne, L., Sargent, J., Segerson, J., & Obourn, R. (1976). Relative potency scale for analgesic drugs: Use of psychophysical procedures with clinical judgments. *Headache*, 16, 70–71.

Critchlow, B. (1986). The powers of John Barleycorn: Beliefs about the effects of alcohol on social behavior. *American Psychologist*, 41, 751–764.

Croog, S. H., & Levine, S. (1982). *Life after a heart attack*. New York: Human Sciences Press.

Cullen, J. W. (1989). The National Cancer Institute's smoking, tobacco, and cancer program. *Chest*, 96 (Suppl.), 9S–13S.

Cummings, C. M., Becker, M. H., & Maile, M. C. (1980). Bringing the models together: An empirical approach to combining variables used to explain health actions. *Journal of Behavioral Medicine*, 3, 123–145.

Cummings, R., Hansen, B., Richard, R. J., Stein, J., & Coates, T. J. (1988). Internists and nicotine gum. *Journal of the American Medical Association*, 260, 1565–1569.

Dahl, J. (1990, April 23). Smokers go out of their way to beat restrictions on lighting up in flight. *The Wall Street Journal*, pp. B1, B7.

Dalton, J. A., & Feuerstein, M. (1988). Biobehavioral factors in cancer pain. *Pain*, 33(2), 137–147.

Davies, N. E., & Felder, L. H. (1990). Applying brakes to the runaway American health care system. *Journal of the American Medical Association*, 263, 73–76.

Davis, M. S. (1966). Variations in patients' compliance with doctors' analysis of congruence between survey responses and results of empirical observations. *Journal of Medical Education*, 41, 1037–1048.

Dawson, B. L., Jeffrey, D. B., & Walsh, J. A. (1988). Television food commercials' effect on children's resistance to temptation. *Journal of Applied Social Psychology*, 18, 1353–1360.

Dekker, E., & Groen, J. (1956). Reproducible psychogenic attacks of asthma. *Journal of Psychosomatic Research*, 1, 58–67.

DeLeon, P. H., & Pallack, M. S. (1982). Public health and psychology: An important, expanding interaction. *American Psychologist*, 37, 934–936.

Des Jarlais, D. C., & Friedman, S. R. (1989). The psychology of preventing AIDS among intravenous drug users. *American Psychologist*, 43, 865–870.

Detre, K. M., Takaro, T., Hultgren, H., Peduzzi, P., & the Study Participants. (1985). Long-term mortality and morbidity results of the Veterans Administration randomized trial of coronary artery bypass surgery. *Circulation*, 72, 84–89.

DeVries, H. A. (1977). Physiology of physical conditioning for the elderly. In R. Harris & L. J. Frankel (eds.), *Guide to fitness over fifty*. New York: Plenum Publishing Corp.

DeVries, H. A., & Adams, G. M. (1972). Electromyographic comparison of single doses of exercise and meprobamate as to effects on muscular relaxation. *American Journal of Physical Medicine*, 51, 130–141.

Diamond, E. G., Kittle, C. F., & Crockett, J. F. (1960). Comparison of internal mammary artery ligation and sham operation for angina pectoris. *American Journal of Cardiology*, 5, 483–486.

Diamond, S., & Medina, J. L. (1981). Pharmacological treatment of migraine. In R. J. Mathew (ed.), *Treatment of migraine* (pp. 27–36). New York: SP Medical & Scientific Books.

Dilley, J. W., & Goldblum, P. B. (1987). AIDS and mental health. In V. Gong & N. Rudnick (eds.), *AIDS: Facts and issues* (pp. 264–277). New Brunswick, N.J.: Rutgers University Press.

Dilman, V. M. & Ostroumova, M. N. (1984). Hypothalamic and immune mechanisms of the influence of stress on the tumor process. In B. H. Fox & B. H. Newberry (eds.), *Impact of psychoendocrine systems in cancer and immunity*. Lewiston, N.Y.: C. J. Hogrefe.

DiMatteo, M. R., & DiNicola, D. D. (1982). *Achieving patient compliance: The psychology of the medical practitioner's role*. New York: Pergamon Press.

Dimsdale, J. E., Hackett, T. P., & Hutter, A. M. (1979). Type A behavior and angiographic findings. *Journal of Psychosomatic Research*, 23, 273–276.

Dohrenwend, B. S. (1978). Social stress and community psychology. *American Journal of Community Psychology*, 6, 1–14.

Dohrenwend, B. S., & Dowhrenwend, B. P. (eds.). (1974). *Stressful life events: Their nature and effects*. New York: John Wiley & Sons.

Dohrenwend, B. S., Dohrenwend, B. P., Dodson, M., & Shrout, P. E. (1984). Symptoms, hassles, social support, and life events: Problems of confounded measures. *Journal of Abnormal Psychology*, 93, 222–230.

Donelson, A. C. (1988). The alcohol-crash problem. In M. Laurence, J. Snortum, & F. Zimring (eds.), *Social control of the drinking driver* (pp. 3–42). Chicago: University of Chicago Press.

Dossey, L. (1984) *Beyond Illness: Discovering the Experience of Health*. Boulder & London: Shambala.

Doubleday, W. A. (1987). Spiritual and religious issues of AIDS. In V. Gong & N. Rudnick (eds.), *AIDS: Facts and issues* (pp. 278–290). New Brunswick, N.J.: Rutgers University Press.

Dougherty, C. J. (1988). *American health care: Realities, rights, and reforms*. New York: Oxford University Press.

Dox, I., Melloni, B. J., & Eisner, G. M. (1985). *Melloni's Illustrated Medical Dictionary* (2nd ed.). Baltimore: Williams & Wilkins.

Dreyfus, J. K. (1990). Cognitive behavioral interventions in psychiatric liaison nursing practice. *Medical Psychotherapy: An International Journal*, 3, 157–170.

Droste, C., Greenlee, M. W., & Roskamm, H. (1986). A defective angina pectoris pain warning system: Experimental findings of ischemic and electrical pain test. *Pain*, 26, 199–209.

Druker, B. J., Mamon, H. J., & Roberts, T. M. (1989). Oncogenes, growth factors, and signal transduction. *New England Journal of Medicine*, 321, 1383–1391.

Dubos, R. (1959). *The mirage of health*. New York: Harper & Row.

Dubos, R. (1965). *Man adapting*. New Haven, Conn.: Yale University Press.

Dunbar, J., & Agras, S. (1980). Compliance with medical instructions. In J. Ferguson & C. B. Taylor (eds.), *The comprehensive handbook of behavioral medicine* (Vol. 3) (pp. 115–145). New York: SP Medical & Scientific Books.

Dunlop, M. (1987). *Body defenses*. Toronto: Irwin.

Dwyer, J. M. (1988). *The body at war*. New York: New American Library.

Easterbrook, G. (1987, January 26). The revolution. *Newsweek*, pp. 40–74.

Eddy, D. M. (1982). Probablistic reasoning in clinical medicine: Problems and opportunities. In D. Kahneman, P. Slovic, & A. Tversky (eds.), *Judgment under uncertainty: Heuristics and biases*. Cambridge, Mass.: Cambridge University Press.

Edgerton, M. T., & Langman, M. W. (1982). Psychiatric considerations. In E. H. Courtiss (ed.), *Male aesthetic surgery*. St. Louis, Mo.: C. V. Mosby.

Eimer, B. (1988). The chronic pain patient: Multimodal assessment and psychotherapy. *Medical Psychotherapy: An International Journal*, 1, 23–40.

Eisenberg, C. (1989). Medicine is no longer a man's profession. *New England Journal of Medicine*, 321, 1542–1544.

Ellwood, P. M. (1987). Alternative delivery systems: Health care on the move. In N. Goldfield & S. B. Goldsmith (eds.), *Alternative delivery systems* (pp. 1—4). Rockville, Md.: Aspen.

Elstein, A. S., & Bordage, G. (1979). Psychology of clinical reasoning. In G. C. Stone, F. Cohen, & N. E. Adler (eds.) *Health Psychology* (pp. 333–368). San Francisco: Jossey–Bass.

Endicott, N. A. (1989). Psychosocial and behavioral factors in myocardial infarction and sudden cardiac death. In S. Cheren (ed.), *Psychosomatic medicine: Theory, physiology, and practice* (Vol. 2), (pp. 611–659). Madison, Conn.: International Universities Press.

Engel, B. T. (1986). Psychosomatic medicine, behavioral medicine, just plain medicine. *Psychosomatic Medicine*, 48(7), 466.

Engel, G. L. (1977). The need for a new medical model: A challenge for biomedicine. *Science*, 196, 129–135.

Engel, G. L. (1980). The clinical application of the biopsychosocial model. *American Journal of Psychiatry*, 137, 535–544.

Erikson, E. H. (1963). *Childhood and society* (2nd ed.). New York: W. W. Norton.

Ermann, D. (1987). Health maintenance organizations: The future of the for-profit plan. In N. Goldfield & S. B. Goldsmith (eds.), *Alternative delivery systems* (pp. 171–183). Rockville, Md.: Aspen.

Evans, H. E. (1968). Tonsillectomy and adenoidectomy: Review of published evidence for and against the T and A. *Clinical Pediatrics*, 7, 71–75.

Everly, G. S., Jr., & Sobelman, S. A. (1987). *Assessment of the human stress response*. New York: AMS Press.

Eysenck, H. J. (1988). Personality, stress and cancer: Prediction and prophylaxis. *British Journal of Medical Psychology*, 61, 57–75.

Fahrion, S., Norris, P., Green, A., Green, E., & Snarr, C. (1987). Biobehavioral treatment of essential hypertension: A group outcome study. *Biofeedback and Self-Regulation*, 12, 142–143.

Fairburn, C. G., & Beglin, S. J. (1990). Studies of the epidemiology of bulimia nervosa. *The American Journal of Psychiatry*, 147, 401–408.

Fanshel, S. (1972). A meaningful measure of health for epidemiology. *International Journal of Epidemiology*, 1, 319–337.

Fenichel, O. (1954). Brief psychotherapy. In H. Fenichel and D. Rapoport (eds.), *The collected papers of Otto Fenichel* (2nd Series) (pp. 243–259). New York: W. W. Norton.

Ferguson, T. (1980). A conversation with John-Henry Pfifferling. *Medical Self Care*, 10, 4–9.

Field, T., Alpert, B., Vega-Lahr, N. Goldstein, S., & Perry, S. (1988). Hospitalization stress in children: Sensitizer and repressor coping styles. *Health Psychology*, 75, 433–445.

Finn, C. E. (1988, January). U.S. campuses are bursting at the quads. *The Wall Street Journal*, p. 18.

Fishbein, M., & Ajzen, I. (1975). *Belief, attitude, intention, and behavior: An introduction to theory and research*. Reading, Mass.: Addison–Wesley.

Fix, J. A., Daughton, D., & Kass, I. (1981). Behavioral sciences in pulmonary rehabilitation. In C. J. Golden, S. S. Acaparras, F. D. Strider, & B. Graber (eds.), *Applied techniques in behavioral medicine* (pp. 263–294). New York: Grune & Stratton.

Fleming, I., Baum, A., Davidson, L. M., Rectanus, E., & McArdle, S. (1987). Chronic stress as a factor in psychologic reactivity to challenge. *Health Psychology*, 6, 239–253.

Flor, H., & Turk, D. C. (1989). Psychophysiology of chronic pain: Do chronic pain patients exhibit symptom-specific psychophysioligical responses? *Psychological Bulletin*, 105, 215–259.

Folkins, C. H., & Sime, W. E. (1981). Physical fitness training and health. *American Psychologist*, 36, 373–389.

Folkman, S., & Lazarus, R. S. (1980). An analysis of coping in a middle-aged community sample. *Journal of Health and Social Behavior*, 21, 219–239.

Folkman, S., & Lazarus, R. S. (1988). The relationship between coping and emotion: Implications for theory and research. *Social Science and Medicine*, 26, 309–317.

Follick, M. J., Aberger, E. W., Ahern, D. K., & McCartney, J. R. (1984). The chronic low back pain syndrome: Identification and management. *Rhode Island Medical Journal*, 67, 219–224.

Follick, M. J., Abrams, D. B., Pinto, R. P., & Fowler, J. L. (1987). Health psychology at the worksite. In G. Stone, S. Weiss, J. Matarazzo, N., Miller, J., Rodin, C., Belar, M., Follick, & J., Singer (eds.), *Health psychology: A discipline and a profession* (pp. 137–150). Chicago: University of Chicago Press.

Follick, M. J., Ahern, D. K., & Aberger, E. W. (1987). Behavioral treatment of chronic pain. In J. A. Blumenthal & D. McKee (eds.), *Applications in behavioral medicine and health psychology: A clinician's source book* (pp. 237–270). Sarasota, Fla.: Professional Resource Exchange.

Fordyce, W. E. (1976). *Behavioral methods for chronic pain and illness*. St. Louis, Mo.: C. V. Mosby.

Fordyce, W. E., & Steger, J. C. (1979). Chronic pain. In O. F. Pomerleau, & J. P. Brady (eds.), *Behavioral medicine: Theory and practice* (pp. 125–153). Baltimore: Williams & Wilkins.

Foreyt, J., & Rahtjen, D. (1978). *Cognitive behavior therapy*. New York: Plenum Publishing Corp.

Fortmann, S. P., Killen, J. D., Telch, M. J., & Newman, B. (1988). Placebo controlled trial of nicotine polacrilex with self-directed relapse prevention: Initial results of the Stanford stop smoking project. *Journal of the American Medical Association,* 260, 1575–1580.

Fowler, J. E., Budzynski, T. H., & Vandenbergh, D. I. (1976). Effects of EMG biofeedback relaxation program on the control of diabetes. *Biofeedback and Self-Regulation,* 1, 105–112.

Fox, B. H. (1983). Current theory of psychogenic effects on cancer incidence and prognosis. *Journal of Psychosocial Oncology,* 1, 17–31.

Frankenhaeuser, M. (1980). Psychoneuroendocrine approaches to the study of stressful person–environment transactions. In H. Selye (ed.), *Selye's guide to stress research* (Vol. 1) (pp. 46–70). New York: Van Nostrand Reinhold.

Frankenhaeuser, M. (1986). A psychobiological framework for research and human stress and coping. In M. H. Appley & R. Trumbull (eds.), *Dynamics of stress: Physiological, psychological, and social perspectives* (pp. 101–116). New York: Plenum Publishing Corp.

Freeman, A. M. (1990, December 18). Deadly diet. *Wall Street Journal,* p. A8.

Freedman, A. M. (1990, December 18). Deadly diet. *Wall Street Journal,* pp. 1, B1.

Freeman, L. (1972). *The story of Anna O.* New York: Frank R. Walker.

Freud, A. (1966). *The ego and the mechanisms of defense.* New York: International Universities Press.

Freud, S. (1959). Further recommendations in the technique of psychoanalysis. Recollection, repetition, and working through. In E. Jones (ed.), *Sigmund Freud collected papers* (Vol. 2). New York: Basic Books.

Friedland, G. H., Saltzman, B. R., Rogers, M. F., Kahl, P. A., Lesser, M. L., Mayers, M. M., & Kelin, R. S. (1986). Lack of transmission of HTLV–III/LAV infection to household contacts of patients with AIDS or AIDS-related complex with oral candidiasis. *New England Journal of Medicine,* 314, 344–349.

Friedman, A. P. (1975). Headaches. In A. M. Freedman, H. I. Kaplan, & B. J. Sadock (eds.), *Comprehensive handbook of psychiatry*/II. Baltimore: Williams & Wilkins.

Friedman, H., & Taub, H. (1977). The use of hypnosis and biofeedback procedures for essential hypertension. *The International Journal of Clinical and Experimental Hypnosis,* 25, 184–188.

Friedman, H., & Taub, H. (1978). A six-month follow-up of the use of hypnosis and biofeedback procedures. *The American Journal of Clinical Hypnosis,* 20, 184–188.

Friedman, M., & Rosenman, R. H. (1974). *Type A behavior and your heart* New York: Alfred A. Knopf.

Friedman, M., Rosenman, R. H., & Carroll, V. (1958). Changes in the serum cholesterol and blood-clotting time in men subjected to cyclic variation of occupational stress. *Circulation,* 17, 852–861.

Friedman, M., Thoresen, C. E., Gill, J. J., Ulmer, D., Powell, L. H., Price, V. A., Brown, B., Thompson, L., Rabin, D. D., Breall, W. S., Bourg, E., Levy, R., & Dixon, T. (1986). Alteration of Type A behavior and its effect on cardiac recurrences in post myocardial infarction patients: Summary results of the Recurrent Coronary Prevention Project. *American Heart Journal,* 112, 653–665.

Friedman, M., & Ulmer, D. (1984). *Treating type A behavior and your heart.* New York: Alfred A. Knopf.

Friedman, R., & Dahl, L. K. (1975). The effect of chronic conflict on the blood pressure of rats with a genetic susceptibility to experimental hypertension. *Psychosomatic Medicine,* 37, 402–416.

From the CDC. (1990). Apparent per capita ethanol consumption—United States, 1977–1986. *Journal of the American Medical Association,* 263, 354–360.

Fryback, D. G. (1974). Use of radiologists' subjective probability estimates in a medical decision making problem. Michigan Mathematical Psychology Program (Report No. 74–14). Ann Arbor: University of Michigan.

Fuchs, V.R. (1974). *Who shall live?* New York: Basic Books.

Ganster, D. C., & Victor, B. (1988). The impact of social support on mental and physical health. *British Journal of Medical Psychology*, 61, 17–36.

Garcia, J., and Ervin, F. (1968). Gustatory-visceral and telereceptor-cutaneous conditioning-adaptation in internal milieus. *Communications in Behavioral Biology*, Part A, 1, 389–415.

Garland, S. B. (1989, November 20). Ouch! The squeeze on your health benefits. *BusinessWeek*, pp. 110–116.

Garrison, R.H., Jr., & Somer, E. (1985). *The nutrition desk reference.* New Canaan, Conn.: Keats Publishing.

Geschwind, N. (1965). Disconnection syndromes in animals and man, I. *Brain*, 88, 237–294.

Geschwind, N., & Behan, P. (1982). Left handedness: Association with immune disease, migraine and developmental disorder. *Proceedings of the National Academy of Sciences*, 79, 5097–5100.

Glantz, S. A., & Parmley, W. W. (in press). Passive smoking and heart disease: Epidemiology, physiology, and biochemistry. *Circulation*.

Glasner, P. D., & Kaslow, R. A. (1990). The epidemiology of human immunodeficiency virus infection. *Journal of Consulting and Clinical Psychology*, 58, 13–21.

Glover, E. D., Schroeder, K. L., Henningfield, J. E., Severson, H. H., & Christen, A. G. (1989). An interpretative review of smokeless tobacco research in the United States: Part II. *Journal of Drug Education*, 19(1), 1–19.

Goin, M. K., & Goin, J. M. (1986). Psychological effects of aesthetic facial surgery. *Advances in Psychosomatic Medicine*, 15, 84–108.

Goldberg, J. (1988). *Anatomy of a scientific discovery.* New York: Bantam Books.

Goldberg, R. J., & Tull, R. M. (1983). *The psychosocial dimensions of cancer.* New York: Free Press.

Goldsmith, M. F. (1990). Forgotten (almost) but not gone, tuberculosis suddenly looms large on domestic scene. *JAMA*, 264,(2), 165–166.

Gonder-Frederick, L. A., Carter, W. R., Cox, D. J., & Clarke, W. L. (1990). Environmental stress and blood glucose change in insulin-dependent diabetes mellitus. *Health Psychology*, 9, 503–515.

Goodwin, D. W. (1988). *Is alcoholism hereditary?* (2nd ed.). New York: Ballantine Books.

Goodwin, D. W., Schulsinger, F., Hermansen, L., Guze, S. B., & Winokur, G. (1973). Alcohol problems in adoptees raised apart from alcoholic biological parents. *Archives of General Psychiatry*, 28, 238–243.

Goodwin, D. W., Schulsinger, F., Moller, N., Hermansen, L., Winokur, G., & Guze, S. B. (1974). Drinking problems in adopted and non-adopted sons of alcoholics. *Archives of General Psychiatry*, 31, 164–169.

Goodyear, B. (1989). Unresolved questions about alcoholism: The debate (war?) goes on—Is a resolution possible? *Alcoholism Treatment Quarterly*, 6, 1–27.

Gong, V., & Shindler, D. (1987). Questions and answers about AIDS. In V. Gong & N. Rudnick (eds.), AIDS: *Facts and issues* (pp. 305–322). New Brunswick, N.J.: Rutgers University Press.

Gordis, E., Tabakoff, B., Goldman, D., & Berg, K. (1990). Finding the gene(s) for alcoholism. *Journal of the American Medical Association*, 263, 2094–2095.

Gordon, D. J., & Rifkind, B. M. (1989). High-density lipoprotein—The clinical implications of recent studies. *New England Journal of Medicine*, 321, 1311–1316.

Gordon, J. S., & Fadiman, J. (1984). Toward an integral medicine. In J. S. Gordon, D. T. Jaffe, & D. E. Bresler (eds.), *Mind, body, and health* (pp. 3–18). New York: Human Sciences.

Graham, D. T. (1972). Psychosomatic medicine. In N. S. Greenfield & R. A. Sternbach, *Handbook of Psychophysiology* (pp. 839–924). New York: Holt, Rinehart, & Winston.

Green, E., & Green, A. (1977). *Beyond biofeedback.* Ft. Wayne, Ind.: Knoll Publishing Co.

Green, E., Green, A., & Norris, P. (1979). Preliminary report on a new non-drug method for the control of hypertension. *Journal of the South Carolina Medical Association*, 75, 575–582.

Greenberg, P. D. (1987). Tumor immunology. In D. P. Stites, J. D. Stobo, & J. V. Wells (eds.), *Basic and clinical immunology* (6th ed.). Norwalk, Conn.: Appleton & Lange.

Greenwald, P., & Sondik, E. J. (eds.). (1986). *Cancer control objectives for the nation: 1985—2000.* Bethesda, Md.: National Cancer Institute.

Griesemer, R. D. (1978). Emotionally triggered disease in a dermatological practice. *Psychiatric Annals*, 8, 49–56.

Grilo, C. M., Shiffman, S., & Wing, R. R. (1989). Relapse crises and coping among dieters. *Journal of Consulting and Clinical Psychology*, 57, 488–495.

Groddeck, G. (1950). *The book of the it.* (Trans. M. E. Collins.) London: Vision Press.

Gross, J., Stitzer, M. L., & Maldonado, J. (1989). Nicotine replacement: Effects of postcessation weight gain. *Journal of Consulting and Clinical Psychology*, 57, 87–92.

Grossbart, T., & Sherman, C. (1986). *Skin deep: A mind/body program for healthy skin.* New York: William Morrow.

Guerrero, I. C., & Koenigsfest, A. C. (1987). AIDS in prisons. In V. Gong & N. Rudnick (eds.), *AIDS: Facts and issues* (pp. 124–138). New Brunswick, N.J.: Rutgers University Press.

Guthrie, D., Moeller, T., & Guthrie, R. (1983). Biofeedback and its application to the stabilization and control of diabetes mellitus. *American Journal of Clinical Biofeedback*, 6, 82–87.

Gutmann, M., & Benson, H. (1971). Interaction of environmental factors and systemic arterial blood pressure: A review. *Medicine*, 50, 543–553.

Hagberg, J. M., Montain, S. J., Martin, W. H., & Ehsani, A. A. (1989). Effect of exercise training in 60- to 69-year-old persons with essential hypertension. *American Journal of Cardiology*, 64, 348–353.

Haier, R. J., Quaid, K., Vice, S., et al. (1980). Naloxone alters pain perception after jogging. Paper presented at American Psychological Association Annual Convention, Montreal.

Halford, W. K., Cuddihy, S., & Mortimer, R. H. (1990). Psychological stress and blood glucose regulation in Type I diabetic patients. *Health Psychology*, 9, 516–528.

Hall, N. R. S. (1988). The virology of AIDS. *American Psychologist*, 43, 907–913.

Hamburg, D. A., Elliot, G., & Parron, D. (1982). *Health and behavior.* Washington, D.C.: National Academy Press.

Hamilton, E. M. N., Whitney, E. N., & Sizer, F. S. (1982). *Nutrition: Concepts and controversies* (3rd ed.). St. Paul, Minn.: West Publishing Co.

Haney, C. A. (1984). Psychosocial factors in the management of patients with cancer. In C. L. Cooper (ed.), *Psychosocial stress and cancer* (pp. 201–230). Chichester: John Wiley & Sons.

Hank, H. (1979, April). But will they still be running in 1989? *Family Health*, p. 28.

Hardy, J. D., Wolff, B. B., & Goodell, H. (1951). *Pain sensations and reactions.* Baltimore: Williams & Wilkins.

Harwood, A. (1981). Mainland Puerto Ricans. In A. Harwood (ed.), *Ethnicity and medical care* (pp. 397–481). Cambridge, Mass.: Harvard University Press.

Haskell, W. L. (1984). Overview: Health benefits of exercise. In J. D. Matarazzo, S. M. Weiss, J. A. Herd, N. E. Miller, & S. M. Weiss (eds.), *Behavioral health: A handbook of health enhancement and disease prevention* (pp. 409–423). New York: John Wiley & Sons.

Haugen, G., Dixon, H. & Dickel, H. (1958). *A therapy for anxiety-tension reactions.* New York: Macmillan.

Hayashida, M., Alterman, A. I., McLellan, A. T., O'Brien, C. P., Purtill, J. J., Volpicelli, J. R., Raphelson, A. H., & Hall, C. P. (1989). Comparative effectiveness and costs of inpatient and outpatient detoxification of patients with mild-to-moderate alcohol withdrawal syndrome. *New England Journal of Medicine, 320,* 358–365.

Haynes, S. G., & Feinleib, M. (1980). Women, work, and coronary heart disease: Prospective findings from the Framingham Heart Study. *American Journal of Public Health, 70,* 133–141.

Heather, N. (1986). Change without therapists: The use of self-help manuals by problem drinkers. In W. Miller & N. Heather (eds.), *Treating addictive behaviors: Processes of change* (pp. 331–359). New York: Plenum Publishing Corp.

Hefferman, J. A., & Albee, G. W. (1985). Prevention perspectives: From Vermont to Washington. *American Psychologist, 40,* 202–205.

Heldt, L., Haffke, E. A., & Davis, L. F. (1982). The psychological and social aspects of orthognathic treatment. *American Journal of Orthodontics, 82,* 318–328.

Henderson, J. B., Hall, S. M., & Lipton, H. L. (1979). Changing self-destructive behaviors. In G. C. Stone, F. Cohen, & N. E. Adler (eds.), *Health psychology: A handbook* (pp. 141–160). San Francisco: Jossey-Bass.

Herek, G. M., & Glunt, E. K. (1988). An epidemic of stigma: Public reactions to AIDS. *American Psychologist, 43,* 886–891.

Herman, C. P., & Mack, D. (1975). Restrained and unrestrained eating. *Journal of Personality, 43,* 647–660.

Hilgard, E. R., & Hilgard, J. R. (1975). *Hypnosis in the relief of pain.* Los Altos, CA: William Kaufman.

Hillman, A. L., Pauly, M. V., & Kerstein, J. J. (1989). How do financial incentives affect physicians' clinical decisions and the financial performance of health maintenance organizations? *New England Journal of Medicine, 321*(2), 86–92.

Hirsch, J. (1988). Medicine and the psychosomatic society. *Psychosomatic Medicine, 50*(3), 3–7.

Hoberman, H. M., & Lewinsohn, P. M. (1985). The behavioral treatment of depression. In E. E. Beckham & W. R. Leber (eds.), *Handbook of depression: Treatment, assessment, and research.* Homewood, IL: Dorsey Press.

Hobfoll, S. E. (1988). *The ecology of stress* (The series in health psychology and behavioral medicine). New York: Hemisphere Publishing.

Hobfoll, S. E. (1989). Conservation of resources: A new attempt at conceptualizing stress. *American Psychologist, 44*(3), 513–524.

Hobfoll, S. E., & Leiberman, J. R. (1987). Personality and social resources in immediate and continued stress resistance among women. *Journal of Personality and Social Psychology, 52,* 18–26.

Hobfoll, S. E., & Lerman, M. (1988). Personal relationships, personal attributes and stress resistance: Mothers' reactions to their child's illness. *American Journal of Community Psychology, 16,* 565–589.

Hobfoll, S. E., London, P., & Orr, E. (1988). Mastery, intimacy, and stress resistance during war. *Journal of Community Psychology, 16,* 317–331.

Hoffman, R. S. (1988). The psycho-oncologist in a multidisciplinary breast treatment center. In C. L. Cooper (ed.), *Stress and breast cancer* (pp. 171–196). Chichester: John Wiley & Sons.

Hogan, T. (1989). Psychophysical relation between perceived threat of AIDS and willingness to impose social restrictions. *Health Psychology, 8,* 255–266.

Holmes, J. A., & Stevenson, C. A. Z. (1990). Differential effects of avoidant and attentional coping strategies on adaptation to chronic and recent-onset pain. *Health Psychology, 5,* 577–584.

Holmes, T. H., & Rahe, R. H. (1967). The social readjustment rating scale. *Journal of Psychosomatic Research, 11,* 213–218.

Holroyd, K. A., & Andrasik, F. (1978). Coping and the self-control of chronic tension headache. *Journal of Consulting and Clinical Psychology, 5,* 1036–1045.

Holroyd, K. A., & Andrasik, F. (1982). A cognitive behavioral approach to recurrent tension and migraine headache. In P. E. Kendall (ed.), *Advances in cognitive-behavioral research and therapy* (Vol. 1). New York: Academic Press.

Holroyd, K. A., Andrasik, F., & Westbrook, T. (1977). Cognitive control of tension headache. *Cognitive Therapy and Research*, 1, 121–133.

Horan, M., & Rocella, E. (1988). Nonpharmacologic treatment of hypertension in the United States. *Health Psychology*, 7, 267–282.

Houston, B. K. (1988). Cardiovascular and neuroendocrine reactivity, global Type A, and components of Type A behavior. In B. K. Houston & C. R. Snyder (eds.), *Type A behavior: Research, theory, and intervention*. New York: John Wiley & Sons.

Hudgens, R. W. (1974). Personal catastrophe and depression: A consideration of the subject with respect to medically ill adolescents, and a requiem for life-event studies. In B. S. Dohrenwend & B. P. Dohrenwend, (eds.), *Stressful life events: Their nature and effects*. New York: John Wiley & Sons.

Hughes, J. (1987). *Cancer and emotion: Psychological preludes and reactions to cancer*. Chichester: John Wiley & Sons.

Hull, J. G., Young, R. D., & Jouriles, E. (1986). Applications of the self-awareness model of alcohol consumption: Predicting patterns of use and abuse. *Journal of Personality and Social Psychology*, 51, 790–796.

Hulley, S. B., Rosenman, R. H., Bawol, R. D., & Brand, R. J. (1980). Epidemiology as a guide to clinical decisions. The association between triglyceride and coronary heart disease. *New England Journal of Medicine*, 302, 1383–1418.

Hurt, F., & Tarnowski, K. (1990). Behavioral consultation in the management of pediatric burns. *Medical Psychotherapy: An International Journal*, 3, 117–123.

Ikemi, Y., & Nakagawa, S. (1962). A psychosomatic study of contagious dermatitis. *Kyushu Journal of Medical Science*, 13, 335–350.

Illich, I. (1976). *Medical nemesis: The expropriation of health*. New York: Pantheon Books.

Iscoe, I. (1982). Toward a viable community health psychology: Caveats from the experiences of the community mental health movement. *American Psychologist*, 37, 961–965.

Ivancevich, J. M., & Matteson, M. T. (1989). Promoting the individual's health and well-being. In C. L. Cooper & R. Payne (eds.), *Causes, coping and consequences of stress at work* (pp. 267–301). Chichester: John Wiley & Sons.

Jackson, J. J. (1981). Urban black Americans. In A. Harwood (ed.), *Ethnicity and medical care* (pp. 37–129). Cambridge, Mass.: Harvard University Press.

Jaco, E. G. (ed.). (1979). *Patients, physicians, and illness: A sourcebook in behavioral science and health*. New York: Free Press.

Jacobs, G. A., Neufeld, V. A., Sayers, S., Spielberger, C. D., & Weinberg, H. (1988). Personality and smokeless tobacco use. *Addictive Behaviors*, 132(4), 311–318.

Jacobs, T. J., & Charles, E. (1980). Life events and the occurrence of cancer in children. *Psychosomatic Medicine*, 42, 11–24.

Jacobson, E. (1929). *Progressive relaxation*. Chicago: University of Chicago Press.

Janerich, D. T., Thompson, W. D., Varela, L. R., Greenwald, P., Chorost, S., Tucci, C., Zaman, M. B., Melamed, M. R., Kiely, M., & McKneally, M. F. (1990). Lung cancer and exposure to tobacco smoke in the household. *New England Journal of Medicine*, 323, 632–636.

Jaret, P. (1986). Our immune system: The wars within. *National Geographic*, 169, 702–735.

Jarvik, M. E., & Hatsukami, D. K. (1989). Tobacco dependence. In T. Ney & A. Gale (eds.), *Smoking and human behavior* (pp. 577–68). Chichester: John Wiley & Sons.

Jasnoski, M. L., & Schwartz, G. E. (1985). A synchronous systems model for health. *American Behavioral Scientist*, 28(4), 468–485.

Jay, S. M., Elliott, C. H., Katz, E., & Siegel, S. E. (1987). Cognitive-behavioral and pharmacologic interventions for children's distress during painful medical procedures. *Journal of Consulting and Clinical Psychology*, 55, 860–865.

Jay, S. M., Elliott, C., & Varni, J. W. (1986). Acute and chronic pain in adults and children with cancer. *Journal of Consulting and Clinical Psychology*, 54, 601–607.

Jeffery, R. W. (1989). Risk behaviors and health: Contrasting individual and population perspectives. *American Psychologist,* 44, 1194–1202.

Jenkins, C. D., Rosenman, R. H., & Friedman, M. (1968). Replicability of rating the coronary-prone behavior pattern. *British Journal of Preventive Social Medicine.* 22, 16–22.

Jenkins, C. D., Rosenman, R. H., & Zyzanski, J. S. (1974). Prediction of clinical coronary heart disease by a test for the coronary-prone behavior pattern. *New England Journal of Medicine,* 290, 1271–1275.

Jobe, J., Sampson, J., Roberts, D., & Kelly, J. (1986). Comparison of behavioral treatments for Raynaud's disease. *Journal of Behavioral Medicine,* 9, 89–96.

Johnson, E. S., & Vieira, J. (1987). Cause of AIDS: Etiology. In V. Gong & N. Rudnick (eds.), *AIDS: Facts and issues* (pp. 25–36). New Brunswick, NJ: Rutgers University Press.

Johnson, J. (1990, May 21). Bringing sanity to the diet craze. *Time,* p. 74.

Johnson, M., Radmacher, S., & Terry, J. (1986). The effects of aerobic exercise on self-esteem. *Anali: dell' ISEF,* 5, 17–24.

Johnson, R., & Barber, T. X. (1978). Hypnosis, suggestion, and warts: An experimental investigation implicating the importance of "believed-in efficacy." *American Journal of Clinical Hypnosis,* 20, 165–174.

Johnson, S. B. (1980). Psychosocial factors in juvenile diabetes: A review. *Journal of Behavioral Medicine,* 3, 95–116.

Jones, M. (1989). Multimodal treatment of irritable bowel syndrome: A preview and proposal. *Medical Psychotherapy: An International Journal,* 2, 11–20.

Jones, M. C. (1924). A laboratory study of fear: The case of Peter. *Journal of Genetic Psychology,* 31, 308–315.

Joyce, C., Capla, G., Mason, M., Reynolds, E., & Matthews, J. (1969). Quantitative study of doctor-patient communication. *Quarterly Journal of Medicine,* 38, 183–194.

Justesen, D. R., Braun, E. W., Garrison, R. G., & Pendleton, R. B. (1970). Pharmacological differentiation of allergic and classically conditioned asthma in guinea pigs. *Science,* 170, 864–866.

Kahneman, D., & Tversky, A. (1982). On the study of statistical intuitions. *Cognition,* 11, 123–142.

Kanner, A. D., Coyne, J. C., Schaefer, C., & Lazarus, R. S. (1981). Comparison of two modes of stress measurement: Daily hassles and uplifts versus major life events. *Journal of Behavioral Medicine,* 4, 1–39.

Kapel, L., Glaros, A. G., & McGlynn, F. D. (1989). Psychophysiological responses to stress in patients with myofascial pain-dysfunction syndrome. *Behavioral Medicine,* 12, 397–406.

Kaplan, G. A., & Reynolds, P. (1988). Depression and cancer mortality and morbidity: Prospective evidence from the Alameda County study. *Journal of Behavioral Medicine,* 11, 1–13.

Kaplan, J. R., Adams, M. R., Clarkson, T. B., & Koritnik, D. R. (1984). Psychosocial influence on "protection" in female cynomolgus macaques. *Atherosclerosis,* 53, 283–295.

Kaplan, J. R., Manuck, S. B., Clarkson, T. B., Lusso, F. M., Taub, D. B., & Miller, E. W. (1983). Social stress and atherosclerosis in normocholestorlemic monkeys. *Science,* 220, 733–735.

Kaplan, N. M. (1981). The control of hypertension. *American Journal of Clinical Biofeedback,* 4, 138–145.

Kaplan, N. M. (1986). *Clinical hypertension* (4th ed.). Baltimore: Williams & Wilkins.

Kaplan, R. M. (1984). The connection between clinical health promotion and health status. *American Psychologist* 39, 755–765.

Karam, J. H. (1989). Diabetes mellitus, hypoglycemia, and lipoprotein disorders. In S. A. Schroeder, M. A. Krupp, L. M. Tierney, & S. J. McPhee (eds.), *Current Medical Diagnosis & Treatment.* East Norwalk, CT: Appleton & Lange.

Kaufman, E., & Micha, V. G. (1987). A model for psychotherapy with the good-prognosis cancer patient. *Psychosomatics,* 28, 540–546.

Kawachi, I., Pearce, N. E., & Jackson, R. T. (1989). Deaths from lung cancer and ischaemic heart disease due to passive smoking in New Zealand. *New Zealand Medical Journal*, 102, 337–340.

Keesey, R. E. (1986). A set-point theory of obesity. In K. D. Brownell & J. P. Foreyt (eds.), *Handbook of eating disorders* (pp. 63–87). New York: Basic Books.

Keller, S. E., Shapiro, R., Schliefer, S. J., & Stein, M. (1982). Hypothalamic influences on anaphylaxis. (Abstract). *Psychosomatic Medicine*, 44, 302.

Kelly, J. A., St. Lawrence, J. S., Hood, H. V., & Brasfield, T. L. (1989). Behavioral intervention to reduce AIDS risk activities. *Journal of Consulting and Clinical Psychology*, 57, 60–67.

Kennedy, S., Kiecolt–Glaser, J. K., & Glaser, R. (1988). Immunological consequences of acute and chronic stressors: Mediating role of interpersonal relationships. *British Journal of Medical Psychology*, 61, 77–85.

Khabbaz, R. F., Darrow, W. W., Hartley, T. M., Witte, J., Cohen, J. B., French, J. Gill, P. S., Potterat, J., Sikes, R. K., Reich, R., Kaplan, J. E., & Laimore, M. D. (1990). Seroprevalence and risk factors for HTLV-I/II infection among female prostitutes in the United States. *Journal of the American Medical Association*, 263, 60–64.

Kidder, D. (1988a). Hospice services and cost savings in the last weeks of life. In V. Mor, D. S. Greer, & R. Kastenbaum (eds.), *The hospice experiment* (pp. 69–87). Baltimore: Johns Hopkins University Press.

Kidder, D. (1988b). The impact of hospices on the health-care costs of terminal cancer patients. In V. Mor, D. S. Greer, & R. Kastenbaum (eds.), *The hospice experiment* (pp. 48–68). Baltimore: Johns Hopkins University Press.

Kiecolt–Glaser, J. K., Garner, W., Speicher, C., Hilliday, H., & Glaser, R. (1984). Effects of stress on two components of the cellular immune response. *Advances*, 1, 73.

Kiecolt–Glaser J. K., & Glaser, R. (1987). Psychosocial moderators of immune function. *Annals of Behavioral Medicine*, 9, 16–20.

Kiecolt–Glaser, J. K., Glaser, R., & Strain, E. C., et al. (1986). Modulation of cellular immunity in medical students. *Journal of Behavioral Medicine*, 9, 311–320.

Kiecolt–Glaser, J. K., Glaser, R., Williger, D., et al. (1985). Psychosocial enhancement of immunocompetence in a geriatric population. *Health Psychology*, 4, 25–41.

Killen, J. D., Fortmann, S. P., Newman, B., & Varady, A. (1990). Evaluation of a treatment approach combining nicotine gum with self-guided behavioral treatments for smoking relapse prevention. *Journal of Consulting and Clinical Psychology*, 58, 85–92.

Killip, T., Passamani, E., Davis, K., & the CASS Principal Investigators and Their Associates. (1985). Coronary artery surgery study (CASS): A randomized trial of coronary bypass surgery: Eight years follow-up and survival in patients with reduced ejection fraction. *Circulation*, 72, 102–109.

King, A. C., Taylor, C. B., Haskell, W. L., & DeBusk, R. F. (1989). Influence of regular aerobic exercise on psychological health: A randomized, controlled trial of healthy middle-aged adults. *Health Psychology*, 8, 305–324.

King, N. J. (1980). The behavioral management of asthma and asthma-related problems in children: A critical review of the literature. *Journal of Behavioral Medicine*, 3, 169–189.

Kinsman, R. A., Spector, S., Schucard, D. W., & Luparello, T. J. (1974). Observations on patterns of subjective symptomatology of acute asthma. *Psychosomatic Medicine*, 36, 129–143.

Kirby, P. (1980). Why nurses quit. *Medical Self Care*, 10, 10–12.

Kirkley, B. G. and Fisher, E. B. (1988). Relapse as a model of nonadherence to dietary treatment of diabetes. *Health Psychology*, 7, 221–230.

Kirscht, J. P., & Rosenstock, I. M. (1979). Patients' problems in following recommendations of health experts. In G. C. Stone, F. Cohen, & N. E. Adler (eds.), *Health psychology: A handbook* (pp. 189–216). San Francisco: Jossey–Bass.

Kobasa, S. C. (1979). Stressful life events, personality, and health: An inquiry into hardiness. *Journal of Personality and Social Psychology,* 37(1), 1–11.

Kobasa, S. C. (1982a). The hardy personality: Toward a social psychology of stress and health. In G. S. Sanders & J. Suls (eds.), *Social psychology of health and illness* (pp. 3–32). Hillsdale, N.J.: Lawrence Erlbaum.

Kobasa, S. C. (1982b). Commitment and coping in stress resistance among lawyers. *Journal of Personality and Social Psychology,* 42, 707–717.

Konner, M. (1990, January/February). Minding the pain. *The Sciences,* 6–9.

Koop, C. E. (1983). Perspectives on future health care. *Health Psychology,* 2, 303–312.

Koplan, J. P., Caspersen, C. J., & Powell, K. E. (1989). Physical activity, physical fitness, and health: Time to act. *Journal of American Medical Association,* 262, 2437.

Kosslyn, S. (1987). Mental imagery. In Adelman, G. (ed.) *Encyclopedia of Neuroscience,* Vol. I (pp. 521–522). Boston: Birkhauser.

Kotses, H., Glaus, K. D., Crawford, P. L., Edwards, J. E., & Scherr, M. S. (1976). Operant reduction of fronatlis EMG activity in the treatment of asthma in children. *Journal of Psychosomatic Research,* 20, 453–459

Krantz, D. S. Contrada, R. J., Hill, D. R., & Friedler, E. (1988). Environmental stress and biobehavioral antecedents of coronary heart disease. *Journal of Consulting and Clinical Psychology,* 56, 333–341.

Krantz, D. S., Schaeffler, M. A., Davia, J. E., Dembroski, T. M., MacDougall, J. M., & Schaffer, R. T. (1981). Extent of coronary atherosclerosis, Type A behavior, and cardiovascular response to social interaction. *Psychophysiology,* 18, 654–664.

Krebs, B., Jensen, T. S., Kroner, K., Nielsen, J., & Jorgensen, H. S. (1984). Phantom limb phenomena in amputees 7 years after limb amputation. *Pain Supplements,* 2, S85.

Kroger, W. S., & Fezler, W. D. (1976). *Hypnosis and behavior modification: Imagery conditioning.* Philadelphia: J. B. Lippincott.

Kuhn, T. S. (1962). *The structure of scientific revolutions.* Chicago: University of Chicago Press.

Kulik, J. A., & Mahler, H. I. M. (1989). Social support and recovery from surgery. *Health Psychology,* 8, 221–238.

Kunitz, S. J., & Levy, J. E. (1981). Navajos. In A. Harwood (ed.), *Ethnicity and medical care* (pp. 337–396). Cambridge, Mass.: Harvard University Press.

Laguerre, M. S. (1981). Haitian Americans. In A. Harwood (ed.), *Ethnicity and medical care* (pp. 173–210). Cambridge, Mass.: Harvard University Press.

Lake, A. E., & Pingel, J. D. (1988). Brief versus extended relaxation: Relationship to improvement at follow-up in mixed headache patients. *Medical Psychotherapy: an International Journal,* 1, 119–129.

Lalonde, M. (1975). *A new perspective on the health of Canadians.* Ottawa: Government of Canada.

Lance, J. W. (1978). *Mechanisms and management of headache,* (3rd ed.). Boston: Butterworth.

Landers, S. (1990, February). The bleach battle. *APA Monitor,* p. 28.

Landy, D., & Aronson, E. (1969). The influence of the character of the criminal and his victim on the decisions of simulated jurors. *Journal of Experimental Social Psychology,* 5, 141–152.

Langford, H. G., Blaufox, D., Oberman, A., Hawkins, M., Curb, J. D., Cutter, G. R., Wassertheil–Smoller, S., Pressel, S., Babcock, C., Abernathy, J. D., Hotchkiss, J., & Tyler, M. (1985). Dietary therapy slows the return of hypertension after stopping prolonged medication. *Journal of the American Medical Association,* 253, 657–664.

Langs, R. (1978). *The listening process.* New York: Jason Aronson.

Langs, R. (1982). *The psychotherapeutic conspiracy.* New York: Jason Aronson.

Langs, R. (1985). *Workbooks for psychotherapists* (Vols. 1–3). Emerson, N.J.: New Concept Press.

Lapin, B. A., & Cherkovich, G. M. (1971). Environmental change causing the development of neuroses and corticovisceral pathology in monkeys. In L. Levi (ed.), *Society, stress and disease* (vol. 1), *The psychosocial environment and psychosomatic diseases* (pp. 226–280). London: Oxford University Press.

Laragh, J. H. (1988). Pathophysiology of diastolic hypertension. *Health Psychology*, 7 (Suppl.), 15–31.

Laszlo, J. (1987). *Understanding cancer.* New York: Harper & Row.

Lau, R. R., & Hartman, K. A. (1983). Commonsense representations of common illnesses. *Health Psychology*, 8, 226–227.

Laudenslager, M. L., Ryan, S. M., Drugan, R. C., Hyson, R. L., & Maier, S. F. (1983). Coping and immunosuppression: Inescapable but not escapable shock suppresses lymphocyte proliferation. *Science*, 221, 568–570.

Lazarus, A. A. (1981). *The practice of multimodal therapy: Systematic, comprehensive, and effective therapy.* New York: McGraw–Hill.

Lazarus, R. S. (1983). The costs and benefits of denial. In S. Breznitz (ed.), *The denial of stress* (pp. 1–30). New York: International Universities Press.

Lazarus, R. S. (1984). The trivialization of distress. In B. L. Hammonds & C. J. Scheirer (eds.), *Psychology and health* (the Master lecture series; Vol. 3) (pp. 121–144). Washington, D.C.: American Psychological Association.

Lazarus, R. S., & Cohen, J. B. (1977). Environmental stress. In L. Altman & J. F. Wohlwill (eds.), *Human behavior and the environment: Current theory and research* (Vol. 2). New York: Plenum Publishing Corp.

Lazarus, R. S. & Folkman, S. (1984). *Stress, appraisal, and coping.* New York: Springer.

Lele, P. P., & Weddell, G. (1956). The relationship between neurohistology and corneal sensibility. *Brain*, 79, 119–154.

Lenfant, C. (1988). Randomized control trial of yoga and biofeedback in the management of hypertension. *Lancet*, 2, 93–95.

Leo, J. (1985, December 2). Battling over masochism. *Time*, p. 76.

LeShan, L. (1966). An emotional life-history pattern associated with neoplastic disease. *Annals of New York Academy of Science*, 125, 780–793.

Lester, E. P., Wittkower, E. D., Kalz, F., & Azima, H. (1962). Phenotropic drugs in psychosomatic disorders (skin). *American Journal of Psychiatry*, 119, 136–143.

Leventhal, H., Baker, T., Brandon, T., & Fleming, R. (1989). Intervening, and preventing cigarette smoking. In T. Ney & A. Gale (eds.), *Smoking and human behavior* (pp. 313–336). Chichester: John Wiley & Sons.

Leventhal, H., Leventhal, E. A., & Nguyen, T. V. (1985). Reactions of families to illness: Theoretical models and perspectives. In D. C. Turk & R. D. Kerns (eds.), *Health, illness, and families: A life-span perspective* (pp. 108–145). New York: John Wiley & Sons.

Leventhal, H., Zimmerman, R., & Gutmann, M. (1984). Compliance: A self-regulation perspective. In W. Doyle Gentry (ed.), *Handbook of behavioral medicine* (pp. 3695–436). New York: Guilford Press.

Levy, R. L. (1987). Compliance and clinical practice. In Blumenthal, J. A. and McKee, D. C. (Eds.) *Applications in behavioral medicine and health psychology: a clinician's source book.* Professional Resource Exchange, Inc., Sarasota, Florida, 567–587.

Levy, S. M. (1985a). *Behavior and cancer: Life-style and psychosocial factors in the initiation and progression of cancer.* San Francisco: Jossey–Bass.

Levy, S. M. (1985b). Emotional response to disease and its treatment. In J. C. Rosen & L. J. Solomon (eds.), *Prevention in health psychology* (pp. 299–310). Hanover, N.H.: University Press of New England.

Levy, S. M., Ewing, L. J., & Lippman, M. (1988). Gynecological cancers. In E. A. Blechman & K. D. Brownell (eds.), *Handbook of behavioral med-*

icine for women (pp. 126–140). New York: Pergamon Press.

Levy, S., Herberman, R., Maluish, A., Schlien, B., & Lippman, M. (1985). Prognostic risk assessment in primary breast cancer by behavioral and immunological parameters. *Health Psychology*, 4, 99–113.

Libo, L., & Arnold, G. (1983). Does training to criterion influence improvement? A follow up study of EMG and thermal biofeedback. *Journal of Behavioral Medicine*, 6, 217–227.

Libow, L. S., & Starer, P. (1989). Care of the nursing home patient. *New England Journal of Medicine*, 321(2), 93–96.

Lichstein, K. L. (1988). *Clinical relaxation strategies.* New York: John Wiley & Sons.

Linn, M. W. (1988). Psychotherapy with cancer patients. In R. J. Goldberg (ed.), *Psychiatric aspects of cancer: Advances in psychosomatic medicine*, Vol. 18 (pp. 54–65). Basel, Switzerland: Karger.

Lipowski, Z. J. (1986). Psychosomatic medicine: Past and present. Part I. Historical background. *Canadian Journal of Psychiatry*, 31, 2–7.

Lippmann, W. (1965). *Public opinion.* Toronto, Ontario: First Free Press Paperback Edition. (Original work published in 1922.)

Llabre, M, Ironson, G., Spitzer, S., Gellman, M, Weidler, D., & Schneiderman, N. (1988). Blood pressure of normotensives and mild hypertensives in different settings. *Health Psychology*, 7, 127–137.

Locke, S. E. (1982). Stress, adaptation, and immunity: Studies in humans. *General Hospital Psychiary*, 4, 49–58.

Locke, S. E., & Hornig–Rohan, M. (1983). *Mind and immunity: Behavioral immunology.* New York: Institute for the Advancement of Health.

Locke, S. E., Kraus, L., Leserman, J., Hurst, M. W., Heisel, J. S., & Williams, R. M. (in press). Life change stress, psychiatric symptoms and natural killer cell activity. *Psychosomatic Medicine*, 46 (4).

Loken, B., & Howard–Pitney, B. (1988). Effectiveness of cigarette advertisements on women:

An experimental study. *Journal of Applied Psychology*, 73, 378–382.

Long, J. W. (1989). *The essential guide to prescription drugs.* New York: Harper & Row.

Luthe, W. (1965). *Autogenic training: Correlationes Psychosomaticae.* New York: Grune & Stratton.

Luthe, W. (1969–1972). *Autogenic therapy* (Vols. 1–6). New York: Grune & Stratton.

Lynch, J. E. (1977). *The broken heart: The medical consequences of loneliness.* New York: Basic Books.

Lynch, J. E. (1985). *The language of the heart.* New York: Basic Books.

Maclure, M., Katz, B., Bryant, M. S., Skipper, P. L., & Tannenbaum, S. R. (1989). Elevated blood levels of carcinogens in passive smokers. *American Journal of Public Health*, 79, 1381–13l84.

Macrae, N. (1984, April). Health care international: A survey. *The Economist*, pp. 17–35.

Mahler, M., Pine, F., & Bergman, A. (1975). *The psychological birth of the human infant.* New York: Basic Books.

Malan, D. (1979). *Individual psychotherapy and the science of psychodynamics.* London: Butterworths.

Marcus, P. (1984). Psychological aspects of cosmetic rhinoplasty. *British Journal of Plastic Surgery*, 37, 313–318.

Marlatt, G. A., & Gordon, J. R. (eds.). (1985). *Relapse prevention: Maintenance strategies in the treatment of addictive behaviors.* New York: Guilford Press.

Marmot, M. G., & Winklestein, W. (1975). Epidemiological observations on intervention trials for prevention of coronary heart disease. *American Journal of Epidemiology*, 101, 177–181.

Maslow, A. H. (1971). *The farther reaches of human nature.* New York: Viking Press.

Mason, P. J., Olson, R. A., & Parish, K. L. (1988). AIDS, hemophilia, and prevention efforts within a comprehensive care program. *American Psychologist*, 43, 971–976.

Massachusetts Medical Society Committee on Nutrition. (1989). Fast-food fare: Consumer guidelines. *New England Journal of Medicine*, 321, 752–756.

Massie, M. J., & Holland, J. C. (1988). Assessment and management of the cancer patient with depression. In R. J. Goldberg (ed.), *Psychiatric aspects of cancer: Advances in psychosomatic medicine,* Vol. 18 (pp. 1–12). Basel, Switzerland: Karger.

Masterson, J. F. (1981). *The narcissistic and borderline disorders: An integrated developmental approach.* New York: Brunner/Mazel.

Masterson, J. F. (1988). *The search for the real self: Unmasking the personality disorders of our age.* New York: Free Press.

Matarazzo, J. D. (1980). Behavioral health and behavioral medicine: Frontiers for a new health psychology. *American Psychologist,* 35, 807–817.

Matarazzo, J. D. (1982). Behavioral health's challenge to academic, scientific, and professional psychology. *American Psychologist,* 37, 1–14.

Matarazzo, J. D., Bailey, W. A., Kraut, A. G., & Jones, J. M. (1988). APA and AIDS: The evolution of a scientific and professional initiative in the public interest. *American Psychologist,* 43, 978–982.

Matarazzo, J. D., Weiss, S. M., Herd, J. A., Miller, N. E., & Weiss, S. M. (1984). *Behavioral health: A handbook of health enhancement and disease prevention.* New York: John Wiley & Sons.

Matheny, K. B., Aycock, D. W., Pugh, J. L., Curlette, W. L., & Cannella, K. A. S. (1986). Stress coping: A qualitative and quantitative synthesis with implications for treatment. *The Counseling Psychologist,* 14, 499–549.

Matthews, K. A., & Avis, N. E. (1982). Psychologists in schools of public health: Current status, future prospects, and implication for other health settings. *American Psychologist,* 37, 949–542.

Matthews, K. A., Cottington, E. M., Talbott, E., Kuller, L. H., & Siegel, J. M. (1987). Stressful work conditions and diastolic blood pressure among blue collar factory workers. *American Journal of Epidemiology,* 126, 280–291.

Matthews–Simonton, S., Simonton, O. C., & Creighton, J. L. (1978). *Getting well again.* Toronto: Bantam Books.

Mattson, M. E., Boyd, G., Byar, D., Brown, C., Callahan, J. F., Corte, D., Cullen, J. W., Greenblatt, J., Haley, N., Hammond, S. K., Lewtas, J., & Reeves, W. (1989). Passive smoking on commercial airline flights. *Journal of the American Medical Association,* 261, 867–873.

Mayer, D. J., & Liebeskind, J. C. (1974). Pain reduction by focal electrical stimulation of the brain: An anatomical and behavioral analysis. *Brain Research,* 68, 79–93.

Mayer, J. (1968). *Overweight: Causes, cost, and control.* Englewood Cliffs, N.J.: Prentice–Hall.

Mays, V. M., & Cochran, S. D. (1988). Issues in the perception of AIDS risk and risk reduction activities by black and Hispanic/Latina women. *American Psychologist,* 43, 949–957.

McCarthy, M. J. (1990, February 26). Antismoking groups grow more sophisticated in tactics used to put heat on tobacco firms. *The Wall Street Journal,* pp. B1, B3.

McClelland, D. C. (1985). The social mandate of health psychology. *American Behavioral Science,* 28, 451–467.

McCollam, J. B., Burish, T. G., Maisto, S. A., & Sobell, M. B. (1980). Alcohol's effects of physiological and self-reported affect and sensations. *Journal of Abnormal Psychology* 89, 224–233.

McGlynn, F. D., Bichajian, C., Tira, D. E., Lundeen, H. C., Mahan, P. E., & Nicholas, B. V. (1989). The effect of experimental stress and experimental occlusal interference on masseteric EMG activity. *Journal of Craniomandibular Disorders: Facial and Oral Pain,* 3, 87–92.

McKenney, J. M., Slining, J. M., Henderson, H. R., Devins, D., & Barr, M. (1973). The effects of clinical pharmacy service on patients with essential hypertension. *Circulation,* 48, 1104–1111.

McKeown, T. (1979). *The role of medicine.* Princeton, N.J.: Princeton University Press.

McKinnon, W., Weisse, C. S., Reynolds, C. P., Bowles, C. A. & Baum, A. (1989). Chronic stress, leukocyte subpopulations, and humoral response to latent viruses. *Health Psychology*, 8, 389–402.

McMullin, R. (1986). *Handbook of cognitive therapy techniques*. New York: W. W. Norton.

Mealiea, W. L., & McGlynn, F. D. (1987). Temporomandibular disorders and bruxism. In J. Hatch, J. G. Fisher, & J. D. Rugh (eds.), *Biofeedback: Studies in clinical efficacy*. (pp. 123–151). New York: Plenum Publishing Corp.

Mechanic, D. (1985). Some modes of adaptation: Defense. In A. Monat & R. S. Lazarus (eds.), *Stress and coping: An anthology* (2nd ed.) (pp. 208–219). New York: Columbia University Press.

Meichenbaum, D. (1976). Cognitive factors in biofeedback therapy. *Biofeedback and Self-regulation*, 1, 201–216.

Meichenbaum, D. (1985). *Stress inoculation training*. New York: Pergamon Press.

Melamed, B. G. (1984). Health intervention: Collaboration for health and science. In B. L. Hammonds & C. J. Scheirer (eds.), *Psychology and health* (The Master lecture series; Vol. 3) (pp. 45–120). Washington, D.C.: American Psychological Association.

Melzack, R. (1979). *The puzzle of pain*. New York: Basic Books.

Melzack, R., & Wall, P. D. (1965). Pain mechanisms: A new theory. *Science*, 150, 971–979.

Melzack, R., & Wall, P. D. (1988). *The challenge of pain* (2nd ed.). New York: Basic Books.

Mikamo, K., Takeshima, T., & Takahashi, K. (1989). Cardiovascular sympathetic hypofunction in muscle contraction headache and migraine. *Headache*, 29, 86–89.

Millar, W. J. (1989). The use of chewing tobacco and snuff in Canada, 1986. *Canadian Journal of Public Health*, 80, 131–135.

Miller, G. (1956). The magical number seven plus or minus two. *Psychological Review*, 63, 81–97.

Miller, H. L., Fowler, R. D., & Bridgers, W. F. (1982). The public health psychologist: An ounce of prevention is not enough. *American Psychologist*, 37, 945–948.

Miller, N. E. (1987). Education for a lifetime of learning. In G. C. Stone, S. M. Weiss, J. D. Matarazzo, N. E. Miller, J. Rodin, C. D. Belar, M. J. Follick, & J. E. Singer (eds.), *Health psychology: A discipline and a profession* (pp. 3–15). Chicago: University of Chicago Press.

Miller, W. R., & Hester, R. K. (1986a). The effectiveness of alcoholism treatment: What research reveals. In W. Miller & N. Healther (eds.), *Treating addictive behaviors: Processes of change*. New York: Plenum Publishing Corp.

Miller, W. R., & Hester, R. K. (1986b). Inpatient alcoholism treatment: Who benefits? *American Psychologist*, 41, 794–805.

Millon, T. (1982). On the nature of clinical health psychology. In T. Millon, C. Green, & R. Meagher (eds.), *Handbook of Clinical Health Psychology* (pp. 1–27). New York: Plenum Publishing Corp.

Minuchin, S., Baker, L., Rosman, B., Liebman, R., Milman, L., & Todd, T. (1975). A conceptual model of psychosomatic illness in children: Family organization and family therapy. *Archives of General Psychiatry*, 32, 1031–1038.

Minuchin, S., Rosman, B., & Baker, L. (1978). *Psychosomatic families: Anorexia nervosa in context*. Cambridge, Mass.: Harvard University Press.

Moffatt, R. J. (1988). Strength and flexibility considerations for exercise prescription. In S. Blair, P. Painter, R. Pate, L. Smith, & C. Taylor (eds.), *Resource manual for guidelines for exercise testing and prescription/American College of Sports Medicine* (pp. 263–270). Philadelphia: Lea & Febiger.

Monjan, A. A. (1981). Stress and immunologic competence: Studies in animals. In R. Ader (ed.), *Psychoneuroimmunology* (pp. 185–228). New York, Academic Press.

Mooney, A. J., III. (1982). Alcohol use. In R. Taylor, J. Ureda, & J. Denham (eds.), *Health promotion: Principles and clinical applications* (pp. 233–258). Norwalk, Conn.: Appleton–Century–Crofts.

Moore, T. J. (1989, September). The cholesterol myth. *The Atlantic Monthly*, pp. 37–70.

Moore, T. J. (1989). *Heart Failure*. New York: Random House.

Moos, R. (ed.). (1977). *Coping with physical illness*. New York: Plenum Publishing Corp.

Moos, R., & Tsu, V. (1977). The crisis of physical illness: An overview. In R. Moos (ed.), *Coping with physical illness*. New York: Plenum Publishing Corp.

Mor, V., Greer, D. S., & Kastenbaum, R. (eds.). (1988a). *The hospice experiment*. Baltimore: Johns Hopkins University Press.

Mor, V., Greer, D. S., & Kastenbaum, R. (1988b). The hospice experiment: An alternative in terminal care. In V. Mor, D. S. Greer, & R. Kastenbaum (eds.), *The hospice experiment* (pp. 1–15). Baltimore: Johns Hopkins University Press.

Morin, S. F. (1988). AIDS: The challenge to psychology. *American Psychologist*, 43, 838–842.

Morin, S. F., Charles, K. A., & Malyon, A. K. (1984). The psychological impact of AIDS on gay men. *American Psychologist*, 39, 1288–1293.

Morley, S. (1985). An experimental investigation of some assumptions underpinning psychological treatments of migraine. *Behavior research and therapy*, 23, 65–74.

Morrow, G. R., & Morrell, C. (1982). Behavioral treatment for anticipatory nausea and vomiting induced by cancer chemotherapy. *New England Journal of Medicine*, 307, 1476–1480.

Mortimer, E. A. (1978). Immunization against infectious diseases. *Science*, 200, 902–907.

Mosnaim, A. D., Diamond, S., Wolf, M. E., Puente, J., & Freitag, F. G. (1989). Endogenous opioid-like peptides in headache. An overview. *Headache*, 29, 368–372.

Moss, R. W. (1982). *The cancer syndrome*. New York: Grove Press.

Mostofsky, D. I., & Piedmont, R. L. (1985). *Therapeutic practice in behavioral medicine*. San Francisco: Jossey–Bass.

Multiple Risk Factor Intervention Trial Group. (1982). Multiple risk factor intervention trial. *Journal of the American Medical Association*, 248, 1465–1477.

Najman, J. M. (1980). Theories of disease causation and the concept of a general susceptibility. *Social Science & Medicine*, 14A, 231–237.

Namir, S., Wolcott, D. L., & Fawzy, F. I. (1989). Social support and HIV spectrum disease: Clinical and research perspectives. *Psychiatric Medicine*, 7, 97–105.

Nathan, P. E. (1985). Prevention of alcoholism: A history of failure. In J. C. Rosen & L. J. Solomon (eds.), *Prevention in health psychology* (pp. 34–71). Hanover, N.H.: University Press of New England.

Nazario, S. L. (1990, April 11). California ads attack cigarettes. *The Wall Street Journal*, pp. B1, B8.

NCHS (National Center for Health Statistics). (1989, March). *Health, United States, 1988*. DHHS Pub No. (PHS)89–1232. Public Health Service. Washington, D.C.: U.S. Government Printing Office.

Negri, E., & Vecchia, C. L. (1989). Determinants of stopping smoking: Italian national health survey [Letter to the editor]. *American Journal of Public Health*, 79, 1307.

Neisworth, J. T., & Moore, F. (1972). Operant treatment of asthmatic responding with the patient as therapist. *Behavior Therapy*, 3, 95–101.

Niaura, R. S., Rohsenow, D. J., Binkoff, J. A., Monti, P. M., Pedraza, M., & Abrams, D. B. (1988). Relevance of cue reactivity to understanding alcohol and smoking relapse. *Journal of Abnormal Psychology*, 97(2), 133–152.

Nisbett, R. E. (1972). Hunger, obesity, and the ventromedial hypothalamus. *Psychological Review*, 79, 433–453.

Norman, J. R. (1989, January 1). Can insurers nurse their HMOs back to health? *Business Week*, pp. 80–82.

Norris, P. A., & Porter, G. (1987). *I choose life: The dynamics of visualization and biofeedback*. Walpole, Conn.: Stillpoint Publishing.

Not enough for all. (1990, May 14). *Newsweek*, p. 53.

Orman, M. (1989). Physician stress: is it inevitable? *Missouri Medicine, 86,* 21–25.

Ornish, D., Brown, S. E., Scherwitz, L. W., Billings, J. H., Armstrong, W. T., Ports, T. A., McLanahan, S. M., Kirkeeide, R. L., Brand, R. J., & Gould, K. L. (1990). Can lifestyle changes reverse coronary heart disease? *Lancet, 336,* 129–133.

Oskamp, S. (1965). Overconfidence in case study judgments. *Journal of Consulting and Clinical Psychology, 29,* 261–265.

Ostlund, R. E., Jr., Staten, M., Kohrt, W. M., Schultz, J., & Malley, M. (1990). The ratio of waist-to-hip circumference, plasma insulin level, and glucose intolerance as independent predictors of the HDL2 cholesterol level in older adults. *New England Journal of Medicine, 322,* 229–234.

Palmer, R. L. (1987). Bulimia: The nature of the syndrome, its epidemiology and its treatment. In R. Boakes, D. Popplewell, & M. Burton (eds.), *Eating habits: Food, physiology and learned behavior* (pp. 1–24). Chichester: John Wiley & Sons.

Papez, J. W. (1937). A proposed mechanism of emotion. *Archives of Neurology and Psychiatry, 38,* 725–743.

Patel, C. H. (1973). Yoga and biofeedback in the management of hypertension. *Lancet, 2,* 1053–1055.

Patel, C. H. (1975). Biofeedback-aided relaxation and meditation in the management of hypertension. *Biofeedback and Self-Regulation, 2,* 1–42.

Patterson, J. T. (1987). *The dread disease: Cancer and modern American culture.* Cambridge, Mass.: Harvard University Press.

Peele, S. (1988). Can alcoholism and other drug addiction problems be treated away or is the current treatment binge doing more harm than good? *Journal of Psychoactive Drugs, 20,* 375–383.

Peele, S. (1989). *Diseasing of America: Addiction treatment out of control.* Lexington, Mass.: Lexington Books.

Pelosi, N. (1988). AIDS and public policy: A legislative view. *American Psychologist, 43,* 843–845.

Penick, S. B., & Fisher, S. (1965). Drug-set interaction: Psychological and physiological effects of epiniphrine under differential expectations. *Psychosomatic Medicine, 27,* 177–182.

Peniston, E. G., & Kulkosky, P. J. (1989). Brainwave training and B-endorphin levels in alcoholics. *Alcoholism: Clinical and Experimental Research, 13,* 271–279.

Pennebaker, J. W. (1982). *The psychology of physical symptoms.* New York: Springer.

Pennebaker, J. W. (1990). *Opening up: The healing power in confiding in others.* New York: William Morrow.

Pentz, M. A., MacKinnon, D. P., Flay, B. R., Hansen, W. B., Johnson, C. A., & Dwyer, J. H. (1989). Primary prevention of chronic diseases in adolescence: Effects of the Midwestern prevention project on tobacco use. *American Journal of Epidemiology, 130,* 713–724.

Peper, E., & Crane-Gockley, V. (1990). Towards effortless breathing. *Medical Psychotherapy: An International Journal. 3,* 135–140.

Perera, G. A. (1955). Hypertensive vascular disease: Description and natural history. *Journal of Chronic Disease, 1,* 33.

Perkins, K. A., Epstein, L. H., & Pastor, S. (1990). Changes in energy balance following smoking cessation and resumption of smoking in women. *Journal of Consulting and Clinical Psychology, 58,* 121–125.

Persky, V. W., Kempthorne-Rawson, J., & Shekelle, R. B. (1987). Personality and risk of cancer: 20-year follow-up of the Western Electric study. *Psychosomatic Medicine, 49,* 435–449.

Pert, C. B. (1986). The wisdom of the receptors: neuropeptides, the emotions, and bodymind. *Advances, 3* (3), 8–16.

Pervin, L. A. (1989). *Personality: Theory and research* (5th ed.). New York: John Wiley & Sons.

Peterson, J. L., & Marin, G. (1988). Issues in the prevention of AIDS among black and Hispanic men. *American Psychologist, 39,* 871–877.

Petrie, A. (1967). *Individuality in pain and suffering.* Chicago: University of Chicago Press.

Plante, M. C. (1987). Caring for the AIDS patient. In V. Gong & N. Rudnick (eds.), AIDS: *Facts and issues* (pp. 217–233). New Brunswick, N.J.: Rutgers University Press.

Plaut, S. M., & Friedman, S. B. (1982). Stress, coping behavior, and resistance to disease. *Psychotherapy, Psychosomatics, 38,* 274–283.

Plotnikoff, N. P., Faith, R. E., Murgo, A. J., & Good, R. A. (1986). *Enkephalins and endorphins: Stress and the immune system.* New York: Plenum Publishing Corp.

Polivy, J., & Herman, C. P. (1985). Dieting and binging: A causal analysis. *American Psychologist, 40,* 193–201.

Poppen, R. (1988). *Behavioral relaxation training and assessment.* New York: Pergamon Press.

Pratt, L., Seligman, A., and Reader, G. (1957). Physicians' views on the level of medical information among patients. *American Journal of Public Health, 47,* 1277–1283.

Pritikin, N. (1979). *The Pritikin program for diet and exercise.* New York: Grosset & Dunlap.

Prochaska, J. O., & DiClemente, C. C. (1986). Toward a comprehensive model of change. In W. Miller & N. Heather (eds.), *Treating addictive behaviors: Process of change* (pp. 3–27). New York: Plenum Publishing Corp.

Pruzinsky, T. (1988). Collaboration of plastic surgeon and medical psychotherapist. *Medical Psychotherapy: An International Journal, 1,* 1–13.

Purcell, K., Brady, K., Chai, H., Muser, J., Molk, L, Gordon, N., & Means, J. (1969). The effects on asthma in children of experimental separation from family. *Psychosomatic Medicine, 31,* 144–164.

Purcell, K. P., & Weiss, J. H. (1970). Asthma. In C. G. Costello (ed.), *Symptoms of psychopathology* (pp. 597–623). New York: John Wiley & Sons.

Purtillo, R. (1984). *Health professional/patient interaction,* (3rd ed.) Philadelphia: W. B. Saunders.

Rachman, S. J. (1990). *Fear and courage.* New York: W. H. Freeman.

Radmacher, S. (1987). The relationship between threatened unemployment and stress among airline employees. *International Journal of Psychosomatics, 34,* 31–34.

Radmacher, S. A., & Sheridan, C. L. (1989). The global inventory of stress: A comprehensive approach to stress assessment. *Medical Psychotherapy: An International Journal, 2,* 183–185.

Raglin, J. S., & Morgan, W. P. (1987). Influence of exercise and quiet rest on state anxiety and blood pressure. *Medicine and Science in Sports and Exercise, 19,* 456–463.

Ramadan, N. M., Halvorson, H., Vande–Linde, A., Levine, S. R., Helpern, J. A., & Welch, K. M. A. (1989). Low brain magnesium in migraine. *Headache, 29,* 416–419.

Ramstrom, L. M. (1985). Passive smoking in aircraft—A current WHO project. *Tokai Journal of Experimental Clinical Medicine, 10,* 451–455.

Rappaport, J. (1977). *Community psychology: Values, research, and action.* New York: Holt, Rinehart & Winston.

Raskin, N. H., & Appenzeller, O. (1980). *Headache.* Philadelphia: W. B. Saunders.

Raub, W. F. (1989). High fiber diet may inhibit large-bowel neoplasia. *Journal of the American Medical Association, 262,* 2359.

Raub, W. F. (1990, February). *Health and behavior research initiatives by the* NIH. Bethesda, Md.: Department of Health & Human Services.

Redd, W. H. (1982). Treatment of excessive crying in a terminal cancer patient: A time-series analysis. *Journal of Behavioral Medicine, 5,* 225–235.

Redd, W. H., & Jacobsen, P. B. (1988). Emotions and cancer: New perspectives on an old question. *Cancer, 62,* 1871–1879.

Redfield, J., & Stone, A. (1979). Individual viewpoints of stressful life events. *Journal of Consulting and Clinical Psychology, 21,* 339–349.

Regan, T. J. (1990). Alcohol and the cardiovascular system. *Journal of the American Medical Association, 264,* 377–381.

Register, C. (1987). *Living with chronic illness.* New York: Free Press.

Relman, A. S. (1989). The changing demography

of the medical profession. *New England Journal of Medicine*, 321, 1540–1542.

Reynolds, R. A., Rizzo, J. A., & Gonzalez, M. L. (1987). The cost of medical professional liability. *Journal of the American Medical Association*, 257, 2776–2781.

Richard, A., & Reiter, J. (1990). *Epilepsy: A new approach*. New York: Prentice–Hall.

Richardson, J. L., Marks, G., Johnson, C. A., Graham, J. W., Chan, K. K., Selser, J. N., Kishbaugh, C., Barranday, Y., & Levine, A. M. (1987). Path model of multidimensional compliance with cancer therapy. *Health Psychology*, 6, 183–207.

Riley, D., & Eckenrode, J. (1986). Social ties: Subgroup differences in costs and benefits. *Journal of Personality and Social Psychology*, 51, 770–778.

Rinzler, C. A. (1987). *The complete book of food: A nutritional, medical, and culinary guide*. New York: World Almanac.

Roberts, A. H. (1981). The behavioral treatment of pain. In J. M. Ferguson & C. B. Taylor (eds.). *The comprehensive handbook of behavioral medicine* (Vol. 2). Jamaica, N.Y.: SP Scientific & Medical Publications.

Rook, K. S. (1984). The negative side of social interaction: Impact on psychological well-being. *Journal of Personality and Social Psychology*, 46(5), 1097–1108.

Roosa, M., Gensheimer, L., Ayers, T., & Short, J. (1990). Development of a school-based prevention program for children in alcoholic families. *Journal of Primary Prevention* (Vol. 11) 119–141.

Rosch, P. J. (1984). Stress and cancer. In C. L. Cooper (ed.), *Psychsocial stress and cancer* (pp. 3–20). Chichester: John Wiley & Sons.

Rosen, L. A., Bender, M. E., Sorrell, S., Booth, S. R., McGrath, M. L., & Drabman, R. S. (1988). Effects of sugar (sucrose) on children's behavior. *Journal of Consulting and Clinical Psychology*, 56, 583–589.

Rosen, R. H. (1984). Worksite health promotion: Factor or fantasy. *Corporate Commentary*, 1, 1–8.

Rosenman, R. H., Brand R. J., Sholtz, R. I., & Friedman, M. (1976). Multivariate prediction of coronary heart disease during 8.5 year follow-up in the Western Collaborative Group Study. *American Journal of Cardiology*, 37, 903–910.

Rosenman, R. H., Friedman, M., Straus, R., Wurm, M, Kositchek, R., Hahn, W., & Werthessen, N. T. (1964). A predictive study of coronary heart disease: The Western Collaborative Group Study. *Journal of the American Medical Association*, 189, 15–22.

Rosenman, R. H., Swan, G. E., & Carmelli, D. (1988). Definition, assessment, and evolution of the Type A behavior pattern. In B. K. Houston and C. R. Snyder (eds.), *Type A behavior: Research, theory, and intervention*. New York: John Wiley & Sons.

Ross, M. W. (1989). Psychosocial ethical aspects of AIDS. *Journal of Medical Ethics*, 15, 74–81.

Rossi, E. L. & Cheek, D. B. (1988). *Mind-body therapy: Methods of ideodynamic healing in Hypnosis*. New York: Norton.

Rossi, S. R., Rossi, J. S., & Prochaska, J. O. (1990). Temptation for high fat foods: A measurement model. Paper presented at the 98th annual convention of the American Psychological Association, Boston.

Roth, S., & Cohen, L. J. (1986). Approach, avoidance, and coping with stress. *American Psychologist*, 41, 813–819.

Rounsaville, B. J., Klerman, G. I., Weissman, M. M., & Chevron, E. S. (1985). Short-term interpersonal psychotherapy (IPT) for depression. In E. E. Beckham & W. R. Leber (eds.), *Handbook of depression: Treatment, assessment, and research*. Homewood, Ill.: Dorsey Press.

Rozanski, A., Bairey, C. N., Krantz, D. S., et al. (1988). Mental stress and the induction of silent myocardial ischemia in patients with coronary artery disease. *New England Journal of Medicine*, 318, 1005–1012.

Rubinstein, A. (1987). Children with AIDS and the public risk. In V. Gong & N. Rudnick (eds.), *AIDS: Facts and issues* (pp. 93–103). New Brunswick, N.J.: Rutgers University Press.

Rudy, D. R. (1986). *Becoming alcoholic: Alcoholics*

Anonymous and the reality of alcoholism. Carbondale, Ill.: Southern Illinois University Press.

Rugh, J. D., & Solberg, W. K. (1976). Psychological implications in temporomandibular pain and dysfunction. *Oral Science Review, 7,* 3–30.

Sacco, W. P., & Beck, A. T. (1985). Cognitive therapy of depression. In E. E. Beckham & W. R. Leber (eds.), *Handbook of depression: treatment, assessment, and research.* Homewood, Ill.: Dorsey Press.

Sackett, D. L. (1976). The magnitude of compliance and noncompliance. In D. L. Sackett & R. B. Haynes (eds.), *Compliance with therapeutic regimens.* Baltimore: Johns Hopkins University Press.

St. Clair, M. (1986). *Object relations and self-psychology: An introduction.* Monterey, Calif.: Brooks/Cole.

Samora, J., Saunders, L., & Larson, R. F. (1961). Medical vocabulary knowledge among hospital patients. *Journal of Health and Human Behavior, 2,* 83–89.

Sanders. R. (1988). Somatic communications: Interpersonal theory and therapy of psychosomatic disorders. *Medical Psychotherapy: An International Journal, 1,* 95–111.

Sarason, S. B. (1981). An asocial psychology and a misdirected clinical psychology. *American Psychologist, 36,* 827–836.

Sargent, J. D. (1982). Stress and headaches. In L. Goldberger & S. Breznitz (eds.), *Handbook of stress* (pp. 599–610). New York: Free Press.

Sargent, J. D., Green, E. E., & Walters, E. D. (1973). Preliminary report on the use of autogenic feedback training in the treatment of migraine and tension headaches. *Psychosomatic Medicine, 35,* 129–135.

Sargent, J., Solbach, P. Coyne, L., Spohn, H., & Segerson, J. (1986). Results of a controlled, experimental, outcome study of nondrug treatments for the control of migraine headaches. *Journal of Behavioral Medicine, 9,* 291–323.

Savitz, S. A., & Roberts, P. R. (1987). Some notes on the development of an IPA model HMO. In N. Goldfield & S. B. Goldsmith (eds.), *Alternative delivery systems* (pp. 131–151). Rockville, Md.: Aspen.

Schachter, S. (1982). Recidivism and self-cure of smoking and obesity. *American Psychologist, 37,* 436–444.

Schachter, S., & Singer, J. (1962). Cognitive, social, and physiological determinants of emotional state. *Psychological Review, 69,* 379–399.

Schatzman, M. (1982). *The story of Ruth.* New York: Kensington.

Scherwitz, L. (1988). Interviewer behaviors in the Western Collaborative Group Study and the Multiple risk Factor Intervention trial structured interviews. In B. K. Houston & C. R. Snyder (eds.), *Type A behavior: Research, theory, and intervention.* New York: John Wiley & Sons.

Scherwitz, L., Graham, L. E., Grandits, G., & Billings, J. (1987). Speech characteristics and behavior type assessment in the MRFIT Structured Interviews. *Journal of Behavioral Medicine, 10,* 173–195.

Schiffman, J. R. (1990, May 11). Practice makes better. *The Wall Street Journal,* p. R24.

Schneider, N. G., Jarvik, M. E., Forsythe, A. B., Read, L. L., Elliott, M. L., & Schweight, A. (1983). Nicotine gum in smoking cessation: A placebo-controlled, double-blind trial. *Addictive Behaviors, 8,* 253–261.

Schneiderman, N. (ed.). (1988). Arterial hypertension: Proceedings of the fifth joint USA–USSR symposium on hypertension research. *Health Psychology, 7,* (Entire volume).

Schoenberg, B., & Carr, A. C. (1963). An investigation of criteria for brief psychotherapy of neurodermatitis. *Psychosomatic Medicine, 25,* 253–263.

Schroeder, S. A., Krupp, M. A., Tierney, L. M., & McPhee, S. J. (1989). *Current medical diagnosis and treatment.* East Norwalk, Conn.: Appleton & Lange.

Schuckit, M. A. (1985). Genetics and the risk for alcoholism. *Journal of the American Medical Association, 254,,* 2614–1617.

Schultz, J., & Luthe, W. (1959). *Autogenic training: A psychophysiological approach in psychotherapy.* New York: Grune & Stratton.

Schultz, J., and Luthe, W. (1969). *Autogenic Therapy,* (Vol. 1: *Autogenic Methods*). New York, Grune & Stratton.

Schunk, D. H., & Carbonari, J. P. (1984). Self-efficacy models. In J. Matarazzo, S. Weiss, J. Herd, N. Miller, & S. M. Weiss (eds.), *Behavioral health: A handbook of health enhancement and disease prevention* (pp. 261–274). New York: John Wiley & Sons.

Schutz, H. G., & Diaz-Knauf, K. V. (1989). The role of the mass media in influencing eating. In R. Shepherd (ed.), *Handbook of the psychophysiology of human eating* (pp. 141–157). Chichester: John Wiley & Sons.

Schwartz, M. (1987). *Biofeedback: A practitioner's guide.* New York: Guilford Press.

Scripture, E. W. (1899). *The new psychology.* New York: Charles Scribner's Sons.

Searles, J. S. (1988). The role of genetics in the pathogenesis of alcoholism. *Journal of Abnormal Psychology,* 97(2), 153–167.

Seeman, J. (1989). Toward a model of positive health. *American Psychologist,* 44(8), 1099–1109.

Segall, A., & Roberts, L. W. (1980). A comparative analysis of physician estimates and levels of medical knowledge among patients. *Sociology of health and illness,* 2, 317–334.

Seltzer, W. J. (1985a). Conversion disorder in childhood and adolescence. Part I: A familial-cultural approach. *Family Systems Medicine,* 3(3), 261–280.

Seltzer, W. J. (1985b). Conversion disorder in childhood and adolescence. Part II: Therapeutic issues. *Family Systems Medicine,* 3(4), 397–416.

Selye, H. (1936). A syndrome developed by diverse nocuous agents. *Nature,* 138, 32.

Selye, H. (1956). *The stress of life.* New York: McGraw–Hill.

Selye, H. (1964). *From dream to discovery: On being a scientist.* New York: McGraw–Hill.

Selye, H. (1978). *The stress of life* (rev. ed.). New York: McGraw–Hill.

Sensakovic, J. W., & Greer, B. (1987). Preventing AIDS. In V. Gong & N. Rudnick (eds.), *AIDS: Facts and issues* (pp. 234–245). New Brunswick, N.J.: Rutgers University Press.

Shaffer, J. W., Graves, P. L., Swank, R. T., & Pearson, T. A. (1987). Clustering of personality traits in youth and the subsequent development of cancer among physicians. *Journal of Behavioral Medicine,* 10, 441–447.

Shaughnessy, P. W., & Kramer, A. M. (1990). The increased needs of patients in nursing homes and patients receiving home health care. *New England Journal of Medicine,* 322(1), 21–27.

Shavit, Y., & Martin, F. C. (1987). Opiates, stress, and immunity: Animal studies. *Annals of Behavioral Medicine,* 9, 11–15.

Shekelle, R., Hulley, S., Neaton, J., Billings, J. H., Borhani, N. O., Gerace, T. A., Jacobs, D. R., Lasser, N. L., Mittlemark, M. B., & Stamler, J. (1985). The MRFIT behavior pattern study: II. Type A behavior and incidence of coronary heart disease. *American Journal of Epidemiology,* 122, 559–570.

Shekelle, R., Raynor, W., Jr., Ostfield, A., et al. (1981). Psychological depression and 17-year risk of death from cancer. *Psychosomatic Medicine,* 43, 117–125.

Sheldon, H. (1988). *Boyd's introduction to the study of disease* (10th ed.). Philadelphia: Lea & Febiger.

Shellenberger, R., & Green, J. A. (1986). *From the ghost in the box to successful biofeedback training.* Greeley, Colo.: Health Psychology Publications.

Shephard, R. J. (1989a). Nutritional benefits of exercise. *Journal of Sports Medicine and Physical Fitness,* 29, 83–90.

Shephard, R. J. (1989b). Passive smoking: Attitudes, health and performance. In T. Ney & A. Gale (eds.), *Smoking and human behavior* (pp. 263–288). Chichester: John Wiley & Sons.

Sheridan, C. L. (1971). *Fundamentals of experimental psychology.* New York: Holt, Rinehart, & Winston.

Sheridan, C. L. (1976). *Fundamentals of experimental psychology* (2nd ed.). New York: Holt, Rinehart, & Winston.

Sheridan, C. L. (1979). *Methods in experimental psychology.* New York: Holt, Rinehart, & Winston.

Sheridan, C. L. (1983a). A multidimensional approach to the clinical application of biofeedback. I: Environments, sensations, and cognitive apprisals. *American Journal of Clinical Biofeedback,* 6, 46–64.

Sheridan, C. L. (1983b). A multidimensional approach to the clinical application of biofeedback. II: Chemical substrates and brain programs. *American Journal of Clinical Biofeedback,* 6, 118–130.

Sheridan, C. L. (1986). The role of muscular tension in the control of psychophysiological discharge phenomena. *Clinical Biofeedback and Health,* 9, 48–55.

Sheridan, C. L. (1989). Are biofeedback machines necessary? A theoretical analysis in the light of the theory of signal detection. *Medical Psychotherapy: An International Journal,* 2, 93–102.

Sheridan, C. L., Boehm, M., Ward, L., & Justesen, D. (1976). Autogenic–biofeedback, autogenic phrases, and biofeedback compared. *Proceedings of the Biofeedback Research Society Seventh Annual Meeting,* 68.

Sherman, R. A. (1989). Stump and phantom limb pain. In R. K. Portenoy (ed.), *Neurologic clinics: Pain: mechanisms and syndromes* (pp. 249–264). Philadelphia: W. B. Saunders.

Shulman, L. C., & Mantell, J. E. (1988). The AIDS crisis: A United States health care perspective. *Social Science and Medicine,* 26, 979–988.

Siegel, B. S. (1986). *Love, medicine, and miracles.* New York: Harper & Row.

Siegel, B. S. (1989). *Peace, love, and healing.* New York: Harper & Row.

Sifneos, P. E. (1974). A reconsideration of psychodynamic mechanisms in symptom formation in view of recent clinical observations. *Psychotherapeutics and Psychosomatics,* 24, 151–155.

Silberfarb, P. M., & Oxman, T. E. (1988). The effects of cancer therapies on the central nervous system. In R. J. Goldberg (ed.), *Psychiatric aspects of cancer: Advances in psychosomatic medicine* (Vol. 18) (pp. 13–25). Basel, Switzerland: Karger.

Sime, W. E. (1984). Psychological benefits of exercise training in the healthy individual. In J. Matarazzo, S. Weiss, J. Herd, N. Miller, & S. M. Weiss (eds.), *Behavioral health: A handbook of health enhancement and disease prevention* (pp. 488–508). New York: John Wiley & Sons.

Singer, J. A., Neale, M. S., Schwartz, G. E., & Schwartz, J. (1986). Conflicting perspectives on stress reduction in occupational settings: A systems approach to their resolution. In M. F. Cataldo & T. J. Coates (eds.), *Health and industry: A behavioral medicine perspective* (pp. 162–192). New York: John Wiley & Sons.

Slaby, A. (1988). Cancer's impact on caregivers. In R. J. Goldberg (ed.), *Psychiatric aspects of cancer: Advances in psychosomatic medicine* (Vol. 18) (pp. 135–153). Basel, Switzerland: Karger.

Smith, E. L. (1988). Bone concerns. In M. Shangold & G. Mirkin (eds.), *Women and exercise: Physiology and sports medicine* (pp. 79–87). Philadelphia: F. A. Davis Co.

Smith, S. F., & Smith, C. M. (1990). *Personal health choices.* Boston: Jones & Bartlett Publishers.

Sokolow, M., & Massie, B. D. (1989). Heart and great vessels. In S. A. Schroeder, M. A. Krupp, L. M. Tierney, & S. J. McPhee (eds.), *Current medical diagnosis and treatment.* East Norwalk, CT: Appleton & Lange.

Solomon, G. F., & Amkraut, A. A. (1981). Psychoneuroendocrinological effects on the immune response. *Annual Review of Microbiology,* 35, 155–184

Solomon, Z., Mikulincer, M., & Hobfoll, S. E. (1987). Objective versus subjective measurement of stress and social support: Combat-related reactions. *Journal of Consulting and Clinical Psychology,* 55, 577–583.

Sosa, R., Kennell, J., Klaus, M., Robertson, S., & Urrutia, J. (1980). The effect of a supportive

companion on perinatal problems, length of labor, and mother-infant interaction. *New England Journal of Medicine*, 303, 597–600.

Sothers, K., & Anchor, K. (1989). Prevention and treament of essential hypertension with meditation–relaxation methods. *Medical Psychotherapy: An International Journal*, 2, 137–156.

Southam, M., Agras, W. S., Taylor, C., & Kramer, H. (1982). Relaxation training: Blood pressure lowering during the working day. *Archives of General Psychiatry*, 39, 715–717.

Spector, N. H., & Korneva, E. A. (1981). Neurophysiology, immunophysiology, and immunomodulation. In R. Ader (ed.). *Psychoneuroimmunology* (pp. 449–473). New York: Academic Press.

Spirito, A., Hewett, K., & Stark, L. J. (1988). The application of behavior therapy in oncology. In R. J. Goldberg (ed.), *Psychiatric aspects of cancer: Advances in psychosomatic medicine* (Vol. 18) (pp. 66–81). Basel, Switzerland: Karger.

Spring, B., & Alexander, B. L. (1989). Sugar and hyperactivity: Another look. In R. Shepherd (ed.), *Handbook of psychophysiology of human eating* (pp. 231–250). Chichester: John Wiley & Sons.

Stachnik, T. J. (1980). Priorities for psychology in medical education and health care delivery. *American Psychologist*, 35, 8–15.

Stall, R. D., Coates, T. J., & Hoff, C. (1988). Behavioral risk reduction for HIV infection among gay and bisexual men. *American Psychologist*, 43, 878–885.

Stamler, R., Stamler, J., Gosch, F.C., Civinelli, J., Fishman, J., McKeever, P., McDonald, A., & Dyer, A. R. (1989). Primary prevention of hypertension by nutritional-hygienic means: Final report of a randomized, controlled trial. *Journal of the Americal Medical Association*, 262, 1801–107.

Stanton, A. (1987). Determinants of adherence to medical regimens by hypertensive patients. *Journal of Behavioral Medicine*, 10, 377–394.

Starr, P. (1982). *The social transformation of American medicine*. New York: Basic Books.

Stefanek, M. E., Derogatis, L. P., & Shaw, A. (1987). Psychological distress among oncology outpatients. *Psychosomatics*, 28, 530–539.

Sternbach, R. A. (1968). *Pain*. New York: Academic Press.

Sternbach, R. A. (ed.). (1978). *The psychology of pain*. New York: Raven Press.

Sternbach, R. A., & Tursky, B. (1965). Ethnic differences among housewives in psychophysical and skin potential responses to electric shock. *Psychophysiology*, 1, 241–246.

Stolbach, L. L., & Brandt, U. C. (1988). Psychosocial factors in the development and progression of breast cancer. In C. L. Cooper (ed.), *Stress and breast cancer* (pp. 3–26). Chichester: John Wiley & Sons.

Stone, G. C. (1979). Health and the health system: A historical overview and conceptual framework. In G. C. Stone, F. Cohen, & N. E. Adler (eds.), *Health psychology—A handbook* (pp. 1—17). San Francisco: Jossey–Bass.

Stone, G. C. (1987). The scope of health psychology. In G. C. Stone, S. M. Weiss, J. D. Matarazzo, N. E. Miller, J. Rodin, C. D. Belar, M. J. Follick, & J. E. Singer (eds.), *Health psychology: A discipline and a profession*. Chicago: University of Chicago Press.

Stoyva, J., & Kamiya, J. (1968). Electrophysiological studies of dreaming as the prototype of a new strategy for the study of consciousness. *Psychological Review*, 75, 192–205.

Strachan, D. P., Jarvis, M. J., & Feyerabend, C. (1989). Passive smoking, salivary continine concentrations, and middle ear effusion in 7 year old children. *British Medical Journal*, 298, 1549–1552.

Strauss, A., & Corbin, J. M. (1988). *Shaping a new health care system: The explosion of chronic illness as a catalyst for change*. San Francisco: Jossey–Bass.

Stress on the job. (1988, April). *Newsweek*, pp. 40–45.

Striegel–Moore, R., & Rodin, J. (1986). The influence of psychological variables in obesity. In K. D. Brownell & J. P. Foreyt (eds.), *Handbook*

of eating disorders (pp. 3–44). New York: Basic Books.

Stroebel, C. F. (1982). QR: *The quieting reflex.* New York: G. P. Putnam's Sons.

Stroebel, C. F. (1983). *Quieting reflex training for adults.* New York: BMA Audio Cassette Publications.

Stuart, R. B. (1980). Weight loss and beyond: Are they taking it off and keeping it off? In P. Davidson & S. Davidson (eds.), *Behavioral medicine: Changing health lifestyles.* New York: Brunner/Mazel.

Stunkard, A. J. (1986). The control of obesity: Social and community perspectives. In K. D. Brownell & J. P. Foreyt (eds.), *Handbook of eating disorders* (pp. 213–230). New York: Basic Books.

Stunkard, A. J., & Mendelson, M. (1967). Obesity and the body image: I. Characteristics of disturbances in the body image of some obese people. *American Journal of Psychiatry,* 123, 1296–1300.

Stunkard, A. J., Sorensen, T. I. A., Hanis, C., Teasdale, T. W., Chakraborty, R., Schull, W. J., & Schulsinger, F. (1986). An adoption study of human obesity. *New England Journal of Medicine,* 314, 193–198.

Subcommittee on Oversight and Investigations, U.S. House of Representatives. (1976). *Cost and quality of health care: Unnecessary surgery* (subcommittee print 64–695). 94th Congress, 2nd Session. Washington, D.C.: U.S. Government Printing Office.

Suinn, R. M. (1980). Pattern A behaviors and heart disease: Intervention (eds.) approaches. In J. M. Ferguson & C. B. Taylor, *The comprehensive handbook of behavioral medicine,* Vol. 1: *Systems intervention* (pp. 5–27). New York: SP Medical & Scientific Books.

Suls, J., & Fletcher, E. (1985). The relative efficacy of avoidant and nonavoidant coping strategies: A meta-analysis. *Health Psychology,* 4, 249–288.

Svarstad, B. (1976). Physician-patient communication and patient conformity with medical advice. In D. Mechanic (ed.), *The growth of bureaucratic medicine.* New York: John Wiley & Sons.

Swain, J. F., Rouse, I. L., Currley, C. B., & Sacks, F. M. (1990). Comparison of the effects of oat bran and low-fiber wheat on serum lipoprotein levels and blood pressure. *New England Journal of Medicine,* 322(3), 147–152.

Syme, S. L. (1984). Sociocultural factors and disease etiology. In W. D. Gentry (ed.), *Handbook of behavioral medicine* (pp. 13–37). New York: Guilford Press.

Syme, S. L. (1989). Control and health: A personal perspective. In A. Steptoe & A. Appels (eds.), *Stress, personal control and health* (pp. 3–18). Chichester: John Wiley & Sons.

Szmukler, G. I. (1987). Anorexia nervosa: A clinical view. In R. A. Boakes, D. A. Popplewell, & M. J. Burton (eds.), *Eating habits: Food, physiology and learned behavior* (pp. 25–44). Chichester: John Wiley & Sons.

Szmukler, G. I. (1989). The psychopathology of eating disorders. In R. Shepherd (ed.), *Handbook of the psychophysiology of human eating* (pp. 273–300). Chichester: John Wiley & Sons.

Tache, J., & Selye, H. (1986). On stress and coping mechanisms. In C. D. Spielberger & I. G. Sarason (eds.), *Stress and anxiety: A sourcebook of theory and research* (Vol. 10.) (pp. 3–24). Washington, D.C.: Hemisphere Publishing.

Tanabe, G. (1982). The potential for public health psychology. *American Psychologist,* 37, 942–944.

Taras, H. L., Sallis, J. F., Patterson, T. L., Nader, P. R., & Nelson, J. A. (1989). Television's influence on children's diet and physical activity. *Developmental and Behavioral Pediatrics,* 10, 176–180.

Taylor, C., Farquhar, J., Nelson, E., & Agras, W. S. (1977). Relaxation therapy and high blood pressure. *Archives of General Psychiatry,* 34, 339–343.

Taylor, P., Abrams, D., & Hewstone, M. (1988). Cancer, stress and personality: A correlational investigation of life-events, repression-sensitization and locus of control. *British Journal of Medical Psychology*, 61, 179–183.

Taylor, R. B., Denham, J. W., & Ureda, J. R. (1982). Health promotion: A perspective. In R. Taylor, J. Ureda, & J. Denham (eds.), *Health promotion: Principles and clinical applications* (pp. 1–18). Norwalk, Conn.: Appleton–Century–Crofts.

Taylor, S. E. (1987). The progress and prospects of health psychology: Tasks of a maturing discipline. *Health Psychology*, 6(1), 73–87.

Temoshok, L., & Fox, B. H. (1984). Coping styles and other psychosocial factors related to medical status and to prognosis in patients with cutaneous malignant melanoma. In B. H. Fox & B. H. Newberry (eds.), *Impact of psychoendocrine systems in cancer and immunity* (pp. 258–287). Lewiston, N.Y.: C. J. Hogrefe.

Thibodeau, G. & Anthony, K. (1988). *Structure and function of the body*. St. Louis: Times Mirror/Mosby College Publishing.

Thoresen, C. E., Friedman, M., Powell, L. H., Gill, J. J., & Ulmer, D. K. (1985). Altering the Type A behavior pattern in postinfarction patients. *Journal of Cardiopulmonary Rehabilitation*, 5, 258–266.

Trauner, J. B. (1987). The second generation of selective contracting: Another look at PPOs. In N. Goldfield & S. B. Goldsmith (eds.), *Alternative delivery systems* (pp. 109–117). Rockville, Md.: Aspen.

Traynor v Turnage (108 S.Ct.). (1988). *Supreme Court Reporter* (interim ed.). St Paul, Minn.: West Publishing Co.

Treating our ailing health care system. (1989, November 20). *BusinessWeek*, p. 156.

Tross, S., & Hirsch, D. A. (1988). Psychological distress and neuropsychological complications of HIV infections and AIDS. *American Psychologist*, 43, 929–934.

Tucker, L. A. (1989). Use of smokeless tobacco, cigarette smoking, and hypercholesterolemia. *American Journal of Public Health*, 79(8), 1048–1051.

Tulkin, S. R. (1987). Health care services. In G. C. Stone, S. M. Weiss, J. D. Matarazzo, N. E. Miller, J. Rodin, C. D. Belar, M. J. Follick, & J. E. Singer (eds.), *Health psychology: A discipline and a profession* (pp. 121–136). Chicago: University of Chicago Press.

Turk, D. C. (1978). Cognitive behavioral techniques in the management of pain. In J. P. Foreyt & D. P. Rathjen (eds.), *Cognitive behavior therapy*. New York: Plenum Publishing Corp.

Turk, D. C., Meichenbaum, D., & Genest, M. (1983). *Pain and behavioral medicine: A cognitive behavioral perspective*. New York: Guilford Press.

Tyler, T. R., & Cook, F. L. (1984). The mass media and judgments of risk: Distinguishing impact of personal and societal level judgments. *Journal of Personality and Social Psychology*, 47, 693–708.

Urbano–Marques, A., Estruch, R., Navarro–Lopez, F., Grau, J. M., Mont, L., & Rubin, E. (1989). The effects of alcoholism on skeletal and cardiac muscle. *New England Journal of Medicine*, 320, (409–415).

USBC (U.S. Bureau of the Census). (1953). *Statistical abstract of the United States* (63th ed.). Washington, D.C.: U.S. Government Printing Office.

USBC (U.S. Bureau of the Census). (1989). *Statistical abstract of the United States* (109th ed.). Washington, D.C.: U.S. Government Printing Office.

USBC (U.S. Bureau of the Census). (1990). *Statistical abstract of the United States* (110th ed.). Washington, D.C.: U.S. Government Printing Office.

USDHEW (U.S. Department of Health, Education, and Welfare). (1979). *Smoking and health: A report of the Surgeon General* (DHEW Publication No. PHS 79–50066). Washington, D.C.: Author.

USDHHS (U.S. Department of Health and Human Services). (1982). *The health consequences of smoking—cancer: A report of the Surgeon General*. (DHHS Publication No. 82–50179). Washington, D.C.: U.S. Government Printing Office.

USDHHS (U.S. Department of Health and Human Services). (1984). *The health consequences of smoking: Chronic obstructive lung disease: A report of the Surgeon General.* (DHHS Publication No. 84–50205). Washington, D.C.: U.S. Government Printing Office.

USDHHS (U.S. Department of Health and Human Services). (1986a). *The health consequences of involuntary smoking: A report of the Surgeon General.* (DHHS Publication No. CDC 87–8398). Washington, D.C.: U.S. Government Printing Office.

USDHHS (U.S. Department of Health and Human Services). (1986b). *The health consequences of using smokeless tobacco: A report of the advisory committee to the Surgeon General.* (DHHS Publication No. 86–2874). Washington, D.C.: U.S. Government Printing Office.

USDHHS (U.S. Department of Health and Human Services). (1988a). *The health consequences of smoking: Nicotine addiction: A report of the Surgeon General.* (DHHS Publication No. CDC 88–8406). Washington, D.C.: U.S. Government Printing Office.

USDHHS (U.S. Department of Health and Human Services). (1988b). *The Surgeon General's report on nutrition and health.* (DHHS Publication No. 88–50210). Washington, D.C.: U.S. Government Printing Office.

USDHHS (U.S. Department of Health and Human Services). (1989). *Reducing the Health Consequences of Smoking: 25 years of progress. A report of the Surgeon General.* (DHHS Publication No. CDC 89–8411). Rockville, Md.: USDHHS.

USGAO (U.S. General Accounting Office). (1987). *Cancer patient survival: What progress has been made?* (T–PEMD–87–6). Washington, D.C.: U.S. Government Printing Office.

Vaillant, G. E. (1977). *Adaptation to life.* Boston: Little, Brown.

Vaillant, G. E. (1983). *The natural history of alcoholism.* Cambridge, Mass.: Harvard University Press.

VanDyke, C., Zegans, L., & Temoshok, L. (1983). *Emotions in health and illness.* Orlando, Fla.: Grune & Stratton.

Van Toller, C. (1979). *The nervous body.* New York: John Wiley & Sons.

Varnauskas, E., and the European Coronary Surgery Study Group (1985). Survival, myocardial infarction, and employment status in a prospective randomized study of coronary bypass surgery. *Circulation, 72,* 90–101.

Vernikos-Danellis, J., & Heybach, J. P. (1980). Psychophysiologic mechanisms regulating the hypothalamic-pituitary-adrenal response to stress. In H. Selye (ed.), *Selye's guide to stress research,* Vol. 1 (pp. 46–70). New York: Van Nostrand Reinhold.

Vieira, J. (1987). The Haitian link. In V. Gong & N. Rudnick (eds.), AIDS: *Facts and issues* (pp. 117–124). New Brunswick, N.J.: Rutgers University Press.

Vinsonhaler, J., Wagner, C., & Elstein, A. S. (1977). The inquiry theory: An information-processing approach to clinical problem solving. In D. B. Shires & H. K. Wolf (eds.), MEDINFO, 1977: *Proceedings of the Second World Congress on Medical Informatics.* Amsterdam: North–Holland.

Visintainer, M. A., Volpicelli, J. R., & Seligman, M. E. P. (1982). Tumor rejection in rats after inescapable or escapable shock. *Science, 216,* 437–438.

Wachtel, P. (1977). *Psychoanalysis and behavior therapy.* New York: Basic Books.

Wadden. T. A., Van Itallie, T. B., & Blackburn, G. L. (1990). Responsible and irresponsible use of very-low-calorie diets in the treatment of obesity. *Journal of the American Medical Association, 263,* 83–85.

Wallace, J. (1989). Can Stanton Peele's opinions be taken seriously? A reply to Peele. *Journal of Psychoactive Drugs, 21,* 259–271.

Wallerstein, R. (1986). *Forty-two lives in treatment: A study of psychoanalysis and psychotherapy.* New York: Guilford Press.

Wallis, C. (1983, June 6). Stress: Can we cope? *Time,* pp. 48–54.

Walster, E., Aronson, V., Abrahams, D., & Rottmann, L. (1966). Importance of physical attractiveness in dating behavior. *Journal of Personality and Social Psychology*, 4, 508–516.

Warner, K. (1986). *Selling smoke: Cigarette advertising and public health.* Washington, D.C.: American Public Health Association.

Waitzkin, H., and Stoeckle, J. B. (1976). Information control and the micropolitics of health care. *Social Science and Medicine*, 10, 263–276.

Weil, A. (1980). *The marriage of sun and moon: A quest for unity in consciousness.* Boston: Houghton Mifflin.

Weil, A. (1983). *Health and healing: Understanding conventional and alternative medicine.* Boston: Houghton Mifflin.

Weiner, H. (1981). Brain, behavior, and bodily disease: A summary. In H. Weiner, M. A. Hofer, & A. J. Stunkard (eds.), *Brain, behavior, and bodily diseases* (pp. 335–361). New York: Raven Press.

Weiner, H. (1982). Psychobiological factors in bodily disease. In T. Millon, C. Green, & R. Meagher (eds.), *Handbook of clinical health psychology* (pp. 31–52). New York: Plenum Publishing Corp.

Weinstein, S. (1968). Intensive and extensive aspects of tactile sensitivity as a function of body part, sex, and laterality. In D. R. Kenshalo (ed.), *The skin senses* (pp. 195–222). Springfield, Ill.: Charles C. Thomas.

Weisbrod, B. A. (1988). America's health-care dilemma. In R. Yarian (ed.) *Annual editions: Health* (9th ed.) (pp. 25–29). Guilford, Conn.: Dushkin.

Weiss, S. (1989). Behavioral medicine and health psychology: History and issues. Presented at the Annual Meeting of the American Psychological Association, New Orleans.

Welch, K. M. A. (1987). Migraine, a biobehavioral disorder. *Archives of Neurology*, 44, 323–327.

Wells, A. J. (1988). An estimate of adult mortality in the United States from passive smoking. *Environment International*, 14, 249–265.

Weltman, A. (1984). Exercise and diet to optimize body composition. In J. Matarazzo, S. Weiss, J. Herd, N. Miller, & S. M. Weiss (eds.), *Behavioral health: A handbook of health enhancement and disease prevention* (pp. 509–524). New York: John Wiley & Sons.

Whelan, E. M. (1988). The truth about Americans' health. In R. Yarian (ed.), *Annual editions: Health* (9th ed.) (pp. 25–29). Guilford, Conn.: Dushkin.

Wiebe, D. J., & McCallum, D. M. (1986). Health practices and hardiness as mediators in the stress-illness relationship. *Health Psychology*, 5, 425–438.

Wiley, J. A., & Camacho, T. C. (1980). Life-style and future health: Evidence from the Alameda County study. *Preventive Medicine*, 9, 1–21.

Williams, N. J., Arreola, M., Covington, J. S., Arheart, K., & Mills, K. (1989). Adolescent smokeless tobacco use: Relationship between epidemiologic and cognitive factors. *Advances in Cancer Control: Innovation and Research*, 293, 211–220.

Williams, R. B. (1989). *The trusting heart: Great news about Type A behavior.* New York: Timesbooks.

Williams, R. B., & Barefoot, J. C. (1988). Coronary-prone behavior: The emerging role of the hostility complex. In B. K. Houston & C. R. Snyder (eds.), *Type A behavior: Research, theory, and intervention.* New York: John Wiley & Sons.

Wilson, G. T. (1984). Weight control treatments. In J. Matarazzo, S. Weiss, J. Herd, N. Miller, & S. M. Weiss (eds.), *Behavioral health: A handbook of health enhancement and disease prevention* (pp. 657–670). New York: John Wiley & Sons.

Wilson, I. (1989). *Stigmata.* New York: Harper & Row.

Winawer, S. J., Flehinger, B. J., Buchalter, J., Herbert, E., & Shike, M. (1990). Declining serum cholesterol levels prior to diagnosis of colon cancer. *Journal of the American Medical Association (JAMA)*, 263, 2083–2085.

Winslow, R. (1989, August 29). Hospitals rush to transplant organs. *The Wall Street Journal*, p. B1.

Winslow, R. (1990, March 22). AMA, Rand go after modern ill: Unneeded procedures. *The Wall Street Journal*, pp. B1, B5.

Winslow, R. (1990, May 30). Focused psychotherapy shrinks medical bills. *The Wall Street Journal*, p. B1.

Wise, R. A. (1988). The neurobiology of craving: Implications for the understanding and treatment of addiction. *Journal of Abnormal Psychology* 97(2), 118–132.

Wolfe, S. M., Fugate, L., Hulstrand, E. P., & Kamimoto, L. E. (1988). *Worst pills, best pills: The older adult's guide to avoiding drug-induced death or illness.* Washington, D.C.: Public Citizen Health Research Group.

Woody, R. H. (1988). *Fifty ways to avoid malpractice.* Sarasota, Fla.: Professional Resource Exchange.

Wool, M. S. (1988). Understanding denial in cancer patients. In R. J. Goldberg (ed.), *Psychiatric aspects of cancer: Advances in psychosomatic medicine* (Vol. 18) (pp. 37–53). Basel, Switzerland: Karger.

Wright, L. (1988). The Type A behavior pattern and coronary artery disease: Quest for the active ingredients and the elusive mechanism. *American Psychologist*, 43, 2–14.

Wysocki, T., Green, L., & Huxtable, K. (1988). Behavioral application of reflectance meters with memory in juvenile diabetics. *Diabetes*, 37 (Suppl. 1, 18A.

Yerkes, R. M., & Dodson, J. D. (1908). The relation of strength of stimulus to rapidity of habit-formation. *Journal of Comparative Neurological Psychology*, 18, 459–482.

Zaslow, J. (1986, February 11). Fourth-grade girls these days ponder weighty matters. *Wall Street Journal*, pp. 1, 29.

Ziegler, D. K., Hassanein, R., & Hassanein, K. (1972). Headache syndromes suggested by factor analysis of symptom variables in headache prone population. *Journal of Chronic Diseases*, 25, 353–363.

Zinn, L. (1989, November 20). What you need to know about "enhanced benefits." *Business Week*, pp. 18–20.

Zolbrod, A. (1988). The emotional distress of the artificial insemination patient. *Medical Psychotherapy: An International Journal*, 1, 161–172.

Photo Credits

Chapter 1
Page 7 (*Top*): Robert Goldstein/Photo Researchers; *Page* 7 (*Bottom*): Beringer/Dratch/The Image Works; *Page* 11: Tim Davis/Photo Researchers.

Chapter 2
Page 35: Bob Daemmrich/The Image Works.

Chapter 3
Page 45: Courtesy American Cancer Society; *Page* 47: Courtesy The Menninger Clinic.

Chapter 4
Page 70: Annie Hunter/The Image Works; *Page* 78: Dr. A. Liepins/Science Photo Library/Photo Researchers.

Chapter 5
Page 98: Dion Ogust/The Image Works; *Page* 105: Alexander Lowry/Photo Researchers; *Page* 111: Michael Weisbrot/Stock, Boston.

Chapter 6
Page 121: Tim Davis/Photo Researchers; *Page* 128: Tom Sayler/UPI/Bettmann Newsphotos; *Page* 134: Mary Harrison/Jeroboam.

Chapter 7
Page 153: Courtesy British Information Services; *Page* 155: Frank Siteman/The Picture Cube; *Page* 162: Courtesy Hewlett-Packard.

Chapter 8
Page 181: AP/Wide World Photos; *Page* 187: Eric Neurath/Stock, Boston.

Chapter 9
Page 204: Annie Hunter/The Image Works; *Page* 206: Courtesy American Cancer Society; *Page* 216: Courtesy MADD.

Chapter 10
Page 225: UPI/Bettmann Newsphotos; *Page* 229: Lionel Delevingne/Stock, Boston.

Chapter 11
Page 258: Jon Feingersh/Camerique; *Page* 267: Michael Kagan/Monkmeyer Press.

Chapter 12
Page 276: Fairchild Aerial Surveys; *Page* 285: Carol Guzy/The Miami Herald.

Chapter 13
Page 301: Dr. Simons/Courtesy American Academy of Facial Plastic and Reconstructive Surgery; *Page* 307: Dr. Alfred Lechter/Courtesy Dr. Theodore Stockle/Collection of Ian Wilson; *Page* 317: Randy Matusow/Monkmeyer Press.

Author Index

Subject Index